THE ROYAL PALACE
Goong

vol. 12

Park SoHee

Yen
Press

Words from the Creator

Volume 15

Strangely enough, Volume 15 was easy to write and draw. I do better with the material when the main characters are in pain than I do when they're happy. I'm an awful person! I would like to thank the people who helped bring Volume 15 to publication: the readers who enjoy my book, my editor, Ji-Eun Yoon, and the other editors at *Wink*, my friends, and my dear assistants, Yoon-Joo and Jae-Hyun.

SoHee Park

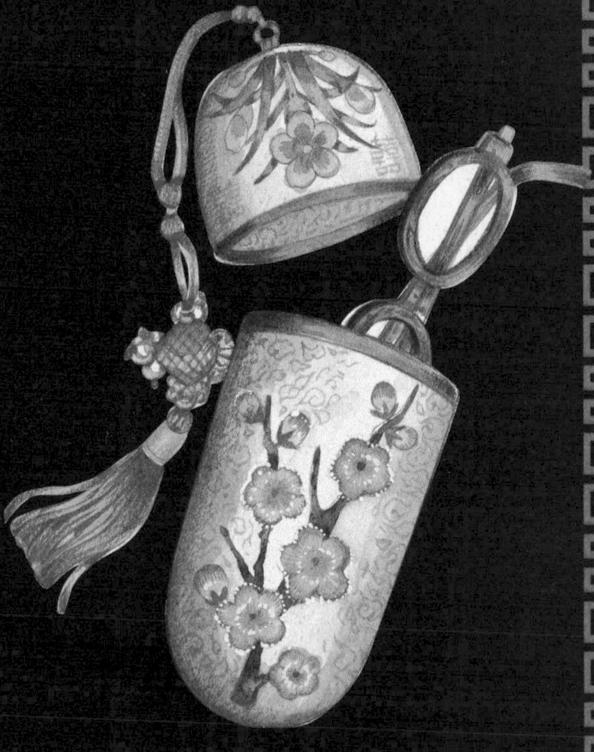

Words from the Creator

Volume 16

It sounds pathetic, but I cried a few times while working on this volume. It wasn't because I felt like I was one of the characters, but because of my selfishness as a creator. I teared up whenever I thought, "Oh, this might be the last time I draw them doing this," "I can't draw this scene anymore," or "I love to draw this kind of situation, but this'll be the last time it's possible." We face great difficulties in our lives, and the characters of this book have it especially rough, even though they're young. Please keep reading the book to see what will happen to them and how their lives will develop once they've made their way through these crises. Will there be hope or despair?

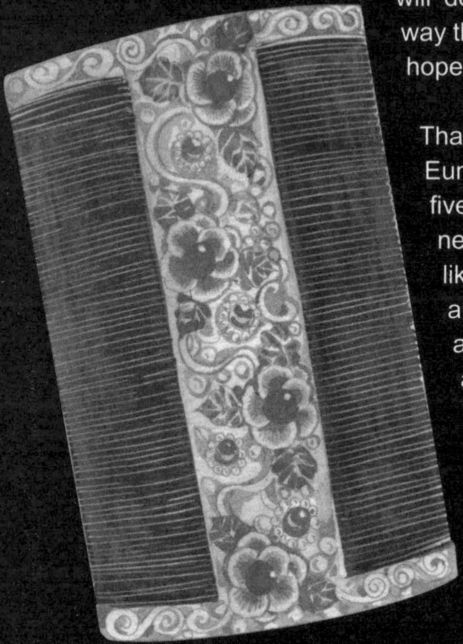

Thank you so much to my editor, Ji-Eun Yoon, who worked with me for five years. Please go easy on my new editor, Kyung-Eun Oh. I would like to thank all of you who continually give love to this comic. I would also like to thank my cutie-pie assistants, Yoon-Joo and Jae-Hyun.

SoHee Park

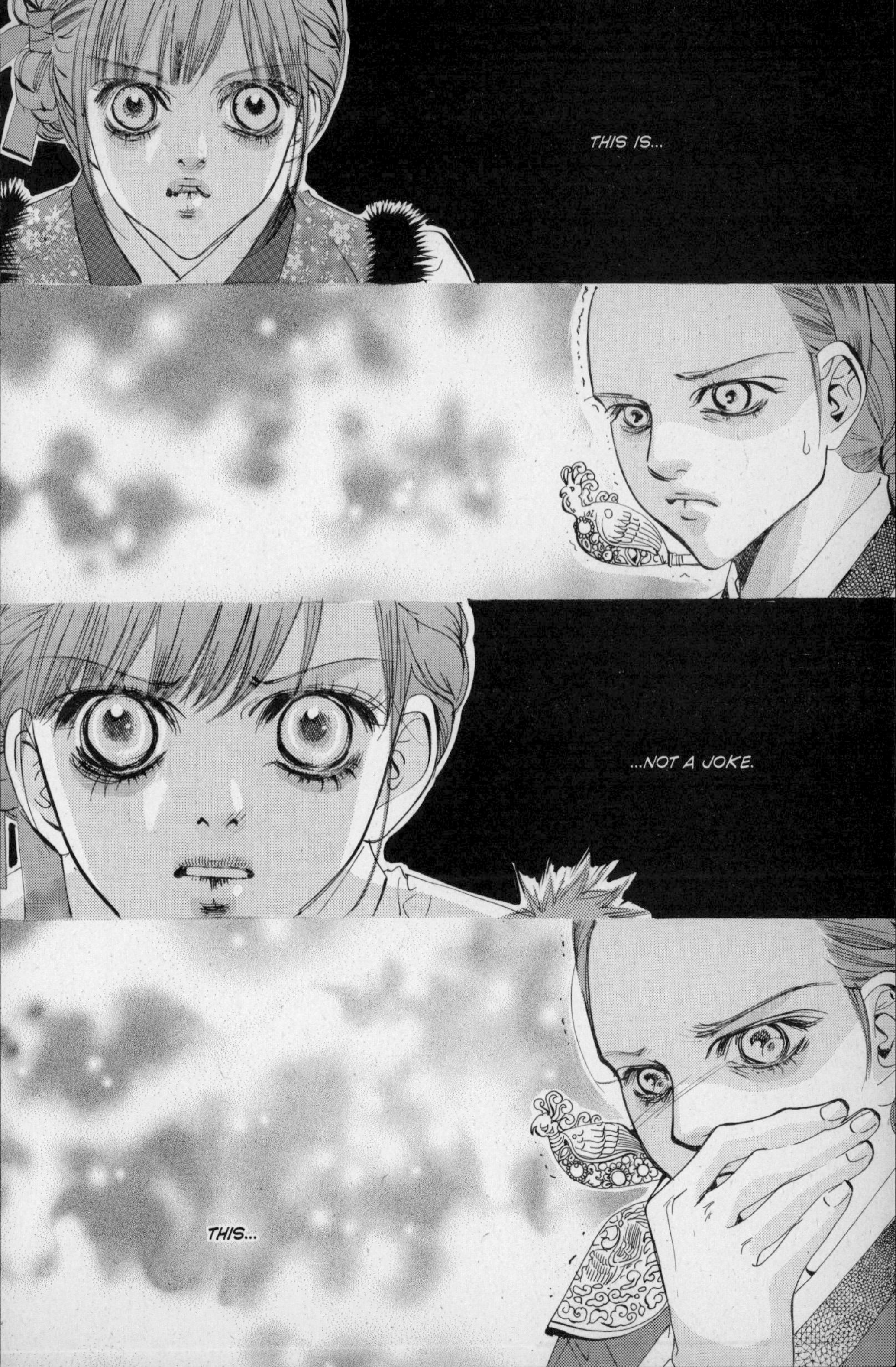
THIS IS...
...NOT A JOKE.
THIS...

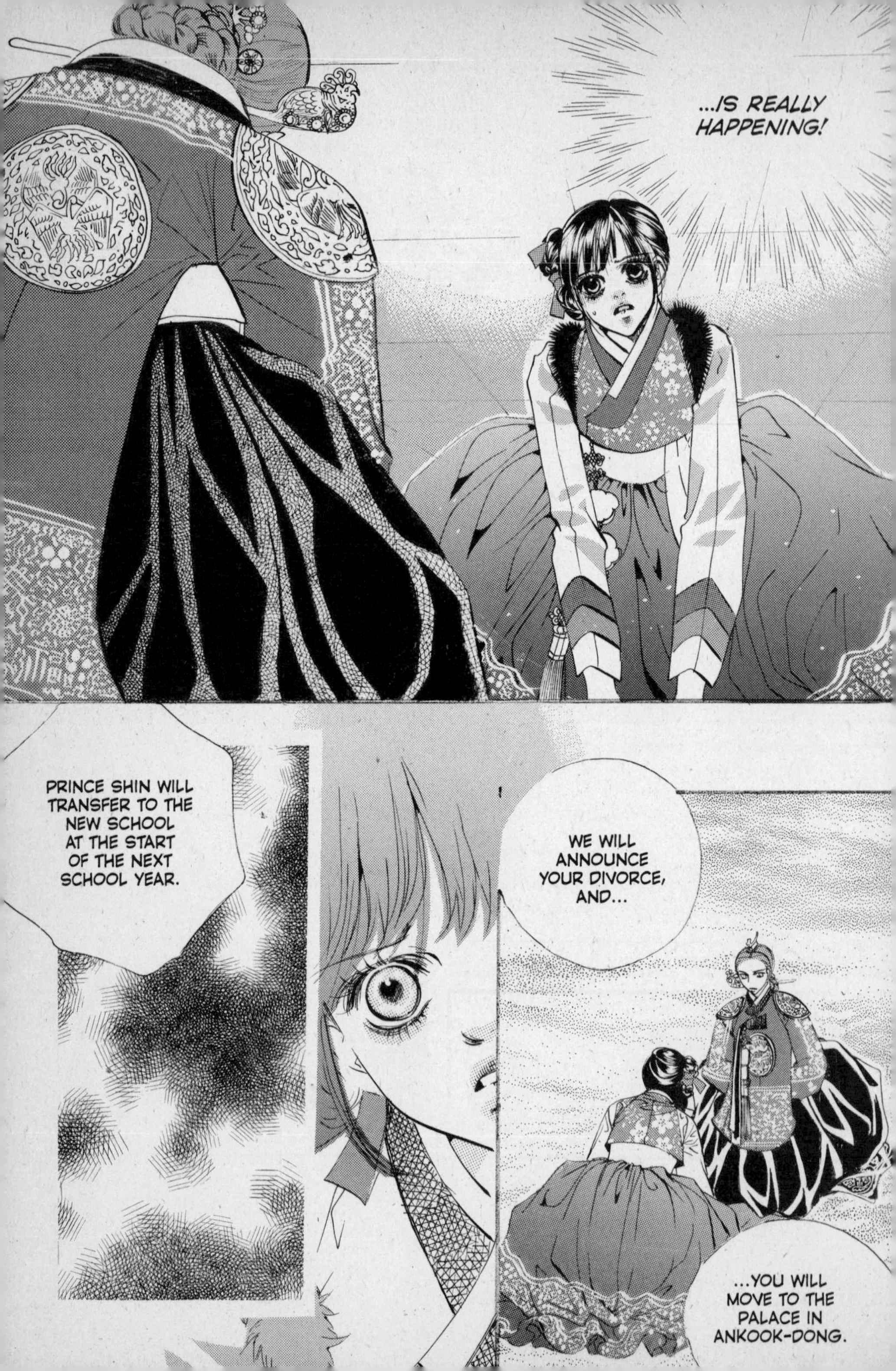
...IS REALLY HAPPENING!
PRINCE SHIN WILL TRANSFER TO THE NEW SCHOOL AT THE START OF THE NEXT SCHOOL YEAR.
WE WILL ANNOUNCE YOUR DIVORCE, AND...
...YOU WILL MOVE TO THE PALACE IN ANKOOK-DONG.

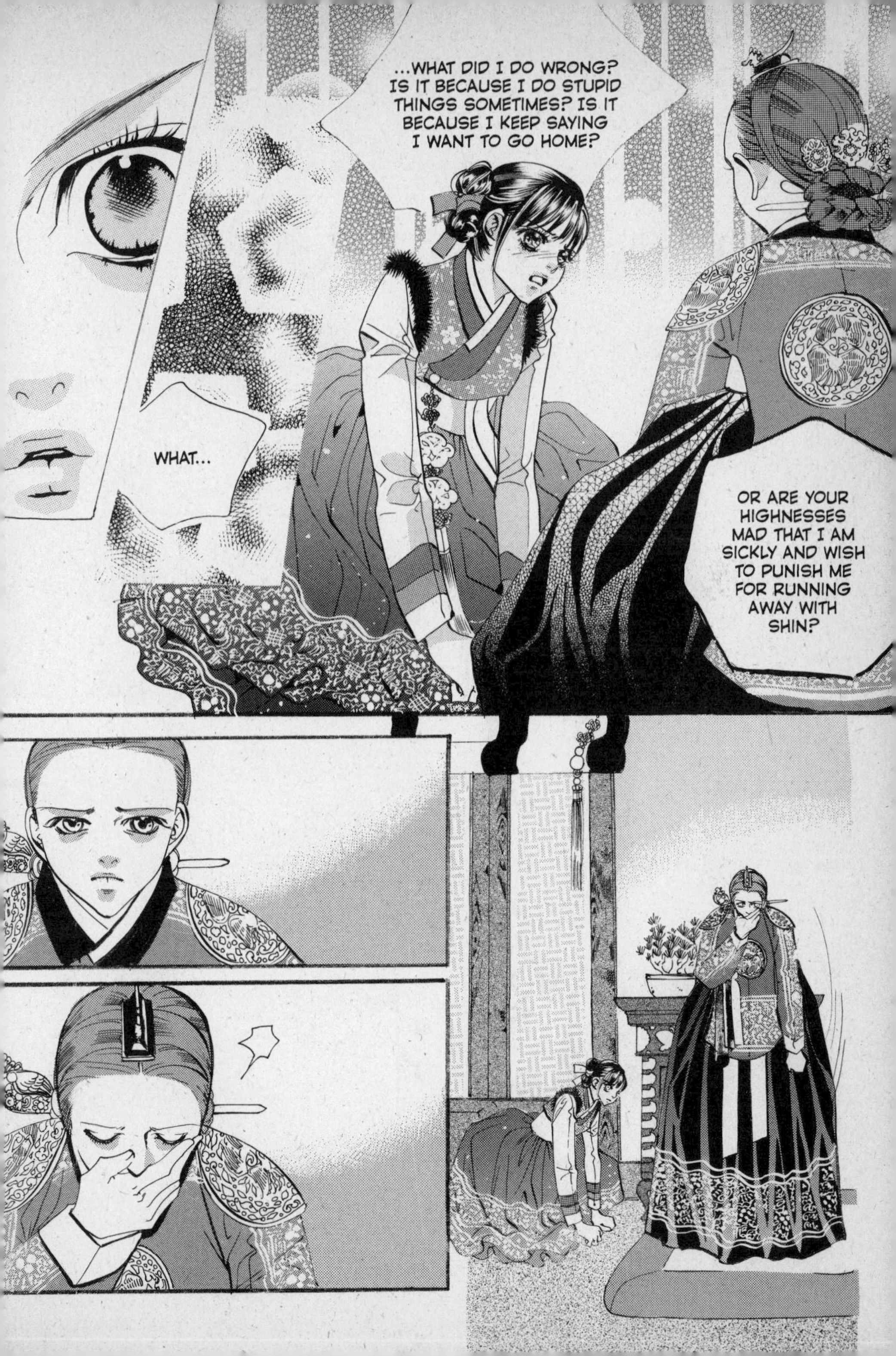
...WHAT DID I DO WRONG? IS IT BECAUSE I DO STUPID THINGS SOMETIMES? IS IT BECAUSE I KEEP SAYING I WANT TO GO HOME?
WHAT...
OR ARE YOUR HIGHNESSES MAD THAT I AM SICKLY AND WISH TO PUNISH ME FOR RUNNING AWAY WITH SHIN?

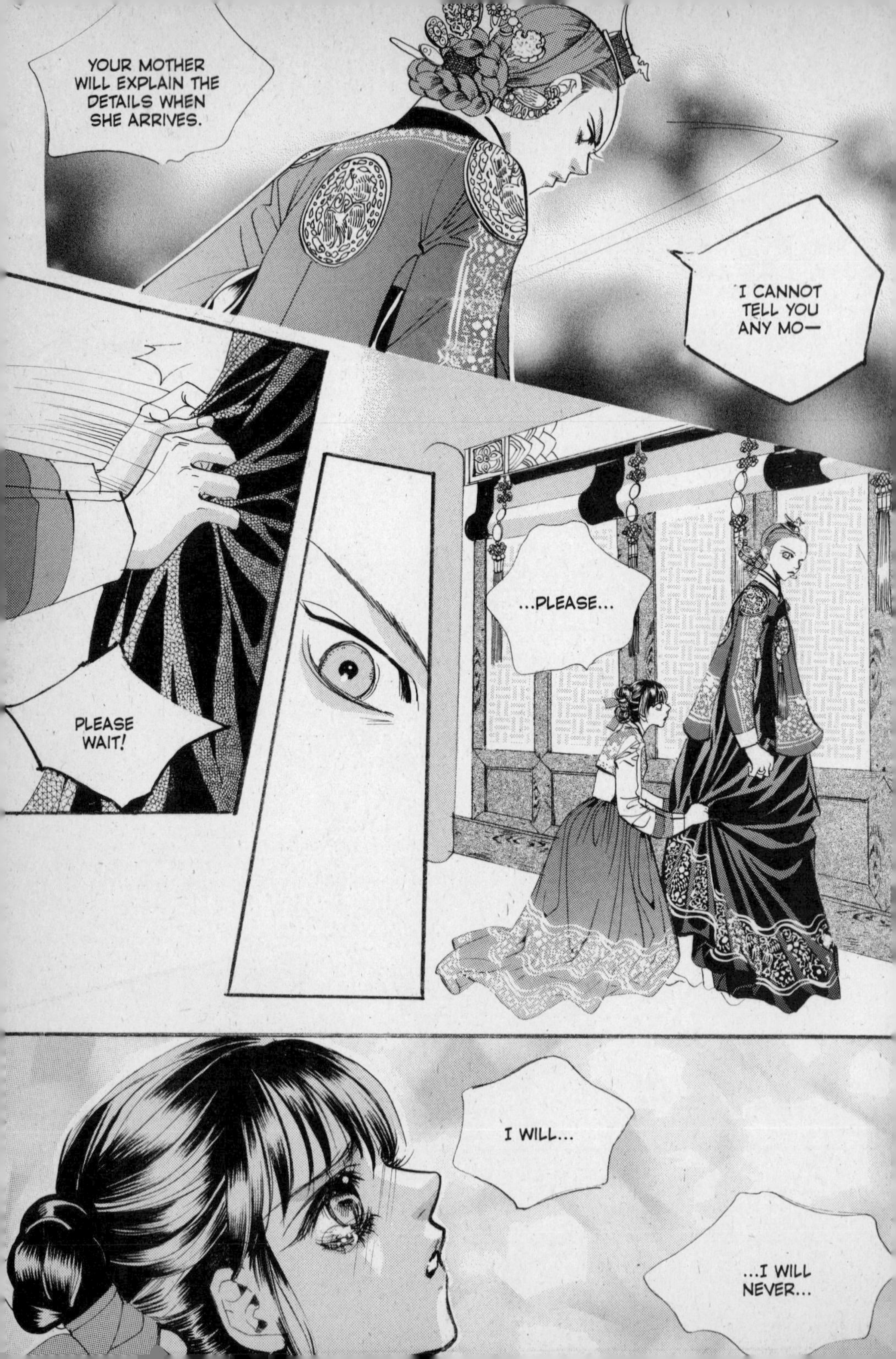
YOUR MOTHER WILL EXPLAIN THE DETAILS WHEN SHE ARRIVES.
I CANNOT TELL YOU ANY MO—
PLEASE WAIT!
...PLEASE...
I WILL...
...I WILL NEVER...

...ASK YOU TO SEND ME HOME AGAIN...I WILL TAKE MY MEDICINE AS I AM TOLD AND LEARN ALL THE PALACE ETIQUETTE BY HEART.
I WILL STUDY HARD AND GET MY GRADES UP. AND I WILL STOP HOLDING A GRUDGE OVER MY GRANDFATHER'S DEATH.
SO PLEASE...

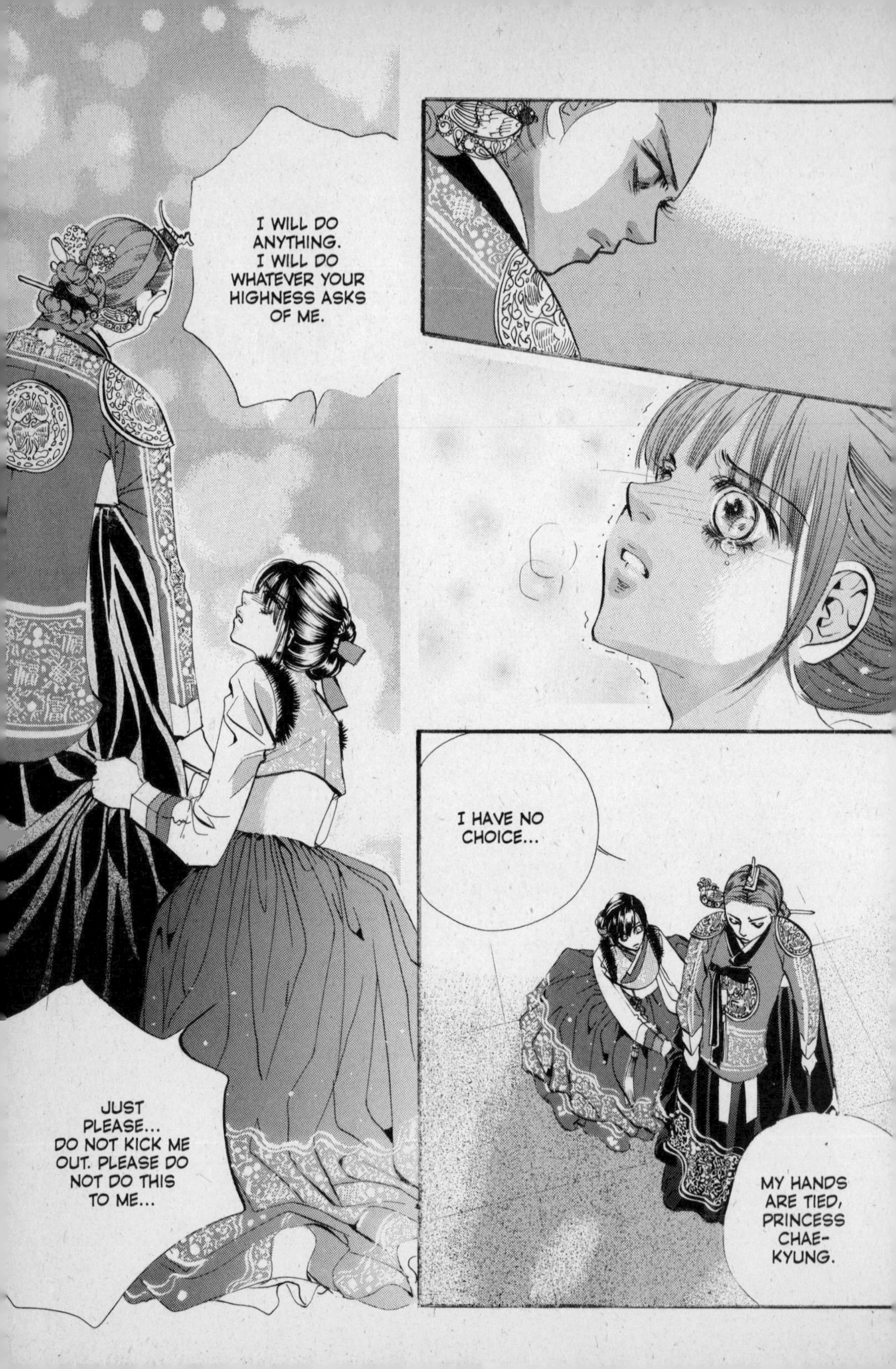
I WILL DO ANYTHING. I WILL DO WHATEVER YOUR HIGHNESS ASKS OF ME.
JUST PLEASE... DO NOT KICK ME OUT. PLEASE DO NOT DO THIS TO ME...
I HAVE NO CHOICE...
MY HANDS ARE TIED, PRINCESS CHAE-KYUNG.

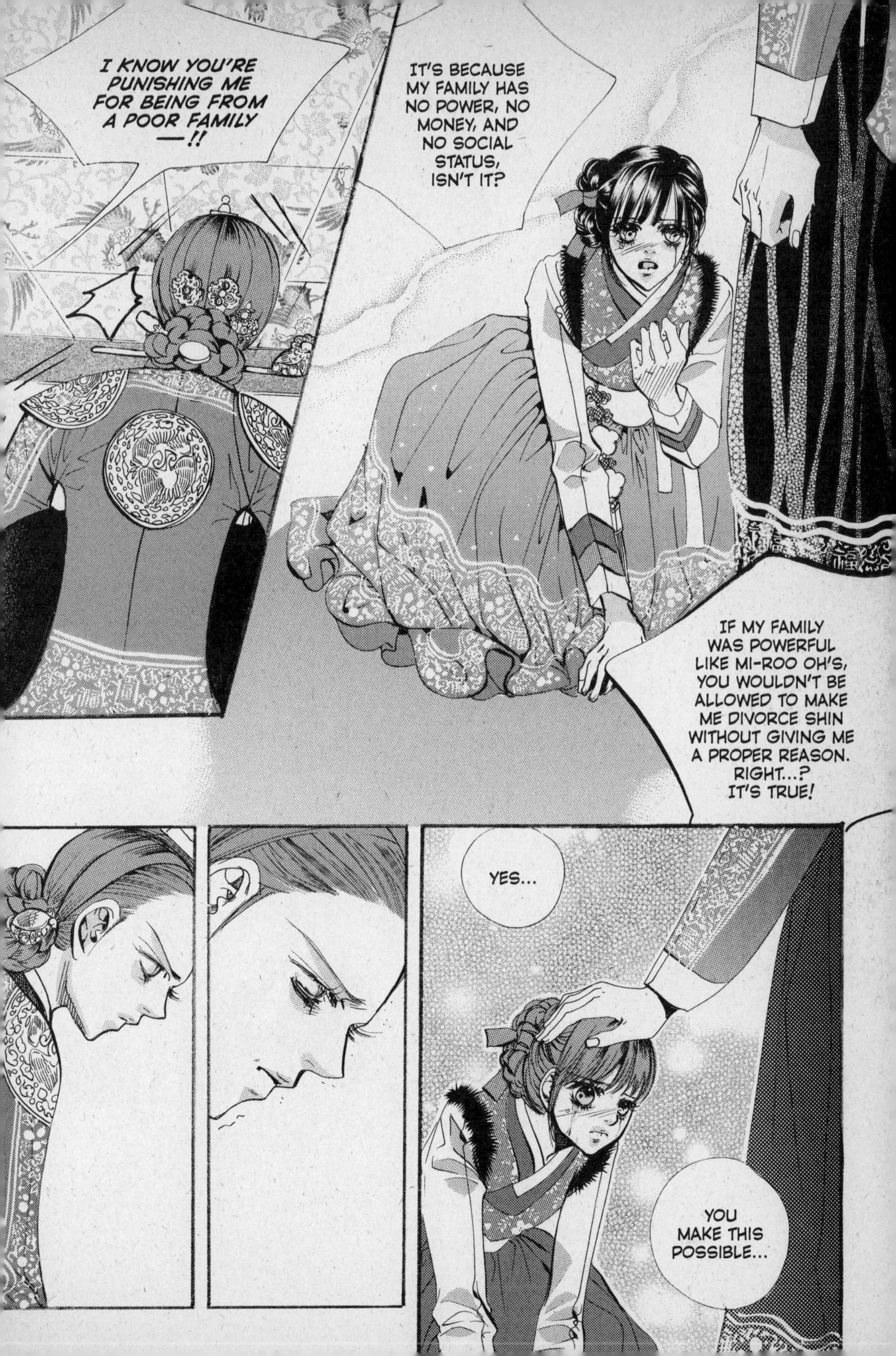
I KNOW YOU'RE PUNISHING ME FOR BEING FROM A POOR FAMILY —!!
IT'S BECAUSE MY FAMILY HAS NO POWER, NO MONEY, AND NO SOCIAL STATUS, ISN'T IT?
IF MY FAMILY WAS POWERFUL LIKE MI-ROO OH'S, YOU WOULDN'T BE ALLOWED TO MAKE ME DIVORCE SHIN WITHOUT GIVING ME A PROPER REASON. RIGHT...? IT'S TRUE!
YES...
YOU MAKE THIS POSSIBLE...

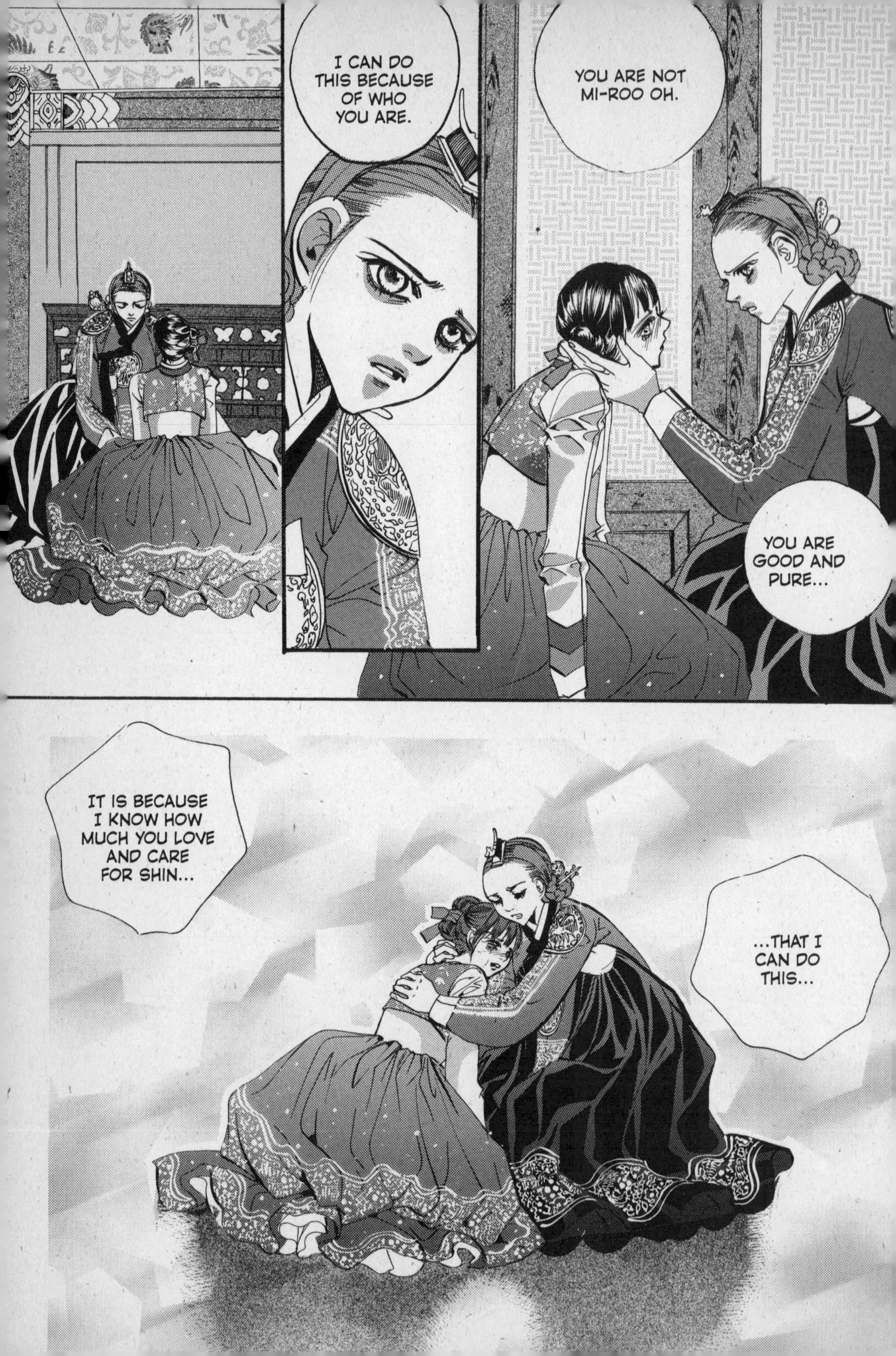
I CAN DO THIS BECAUSE OF WHO YOU ARE.
YOU ARE NOT MI-ROO OH.
YOU ARE GOOD AND PURE...
IT IS BECAUSE I KNOW HOW MUCH YOU LOVE AND CARE FOR SHIN...
...THAT I CAN DO THIS...

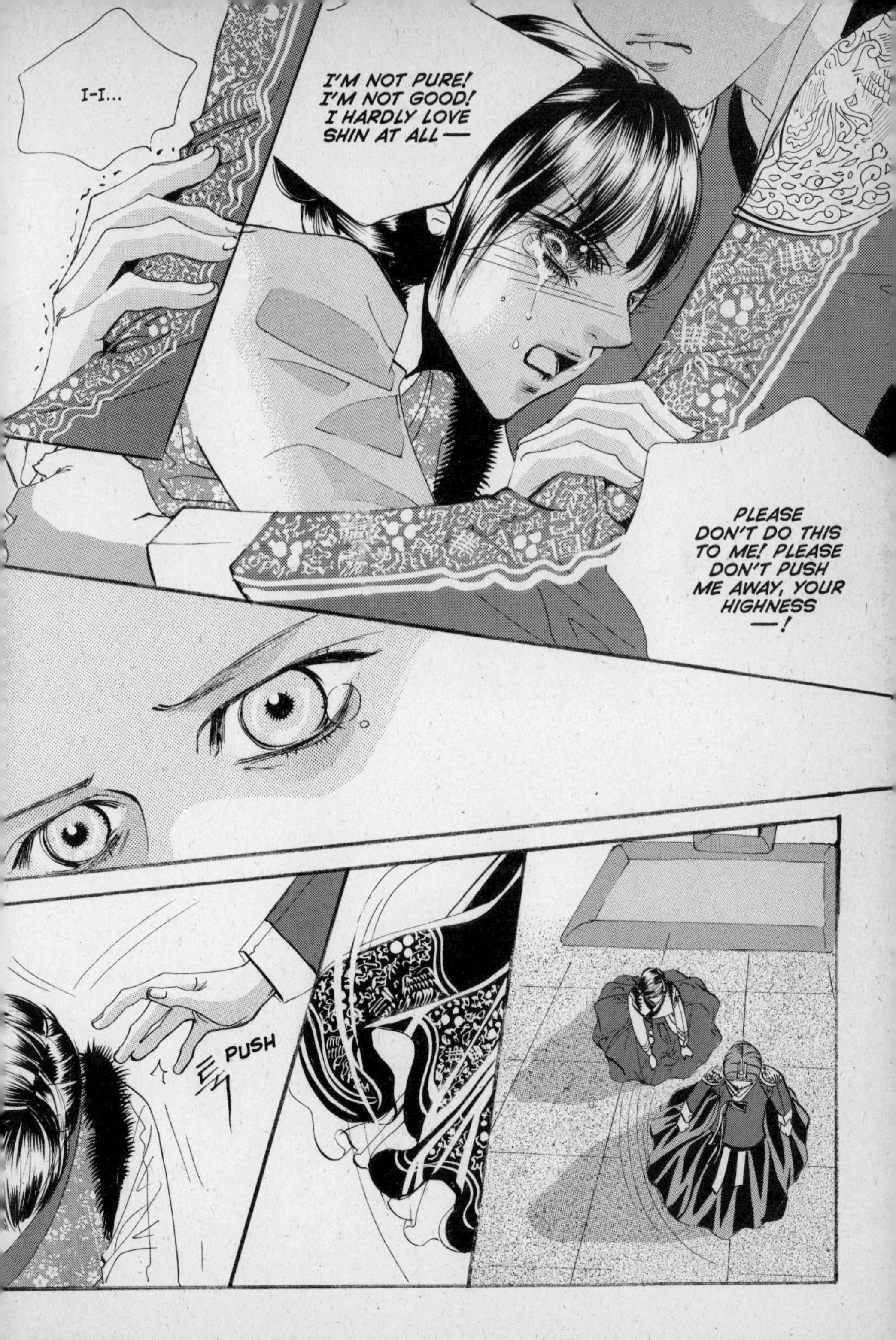
I-I...
I'M NOT PURE! I'M NOT GOOD! I HARDLY LOVE SHIN AT ALL—
PLEASE DON'T DO THIS TO ME! PLEASE DON'T PUSH ME AWAY, YOUR HIGHNESS—!
PUSH

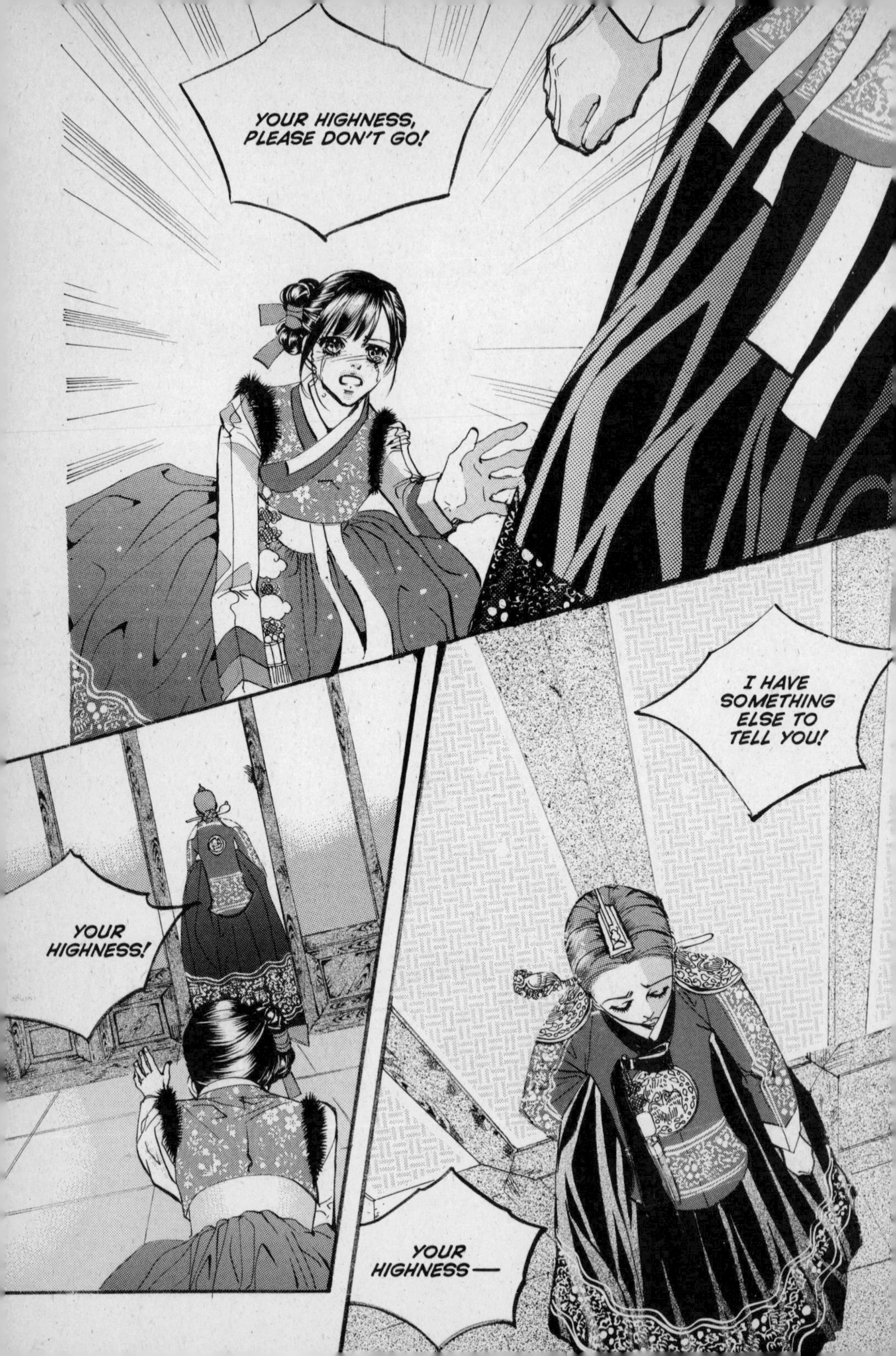
YOUR HIGHNESS, PLEASE DON'T GO!
YOUR HIGHNESS!
I HAVE SOMETHING ELSE TO TELL YOU!
YOUR HIGHNESS—

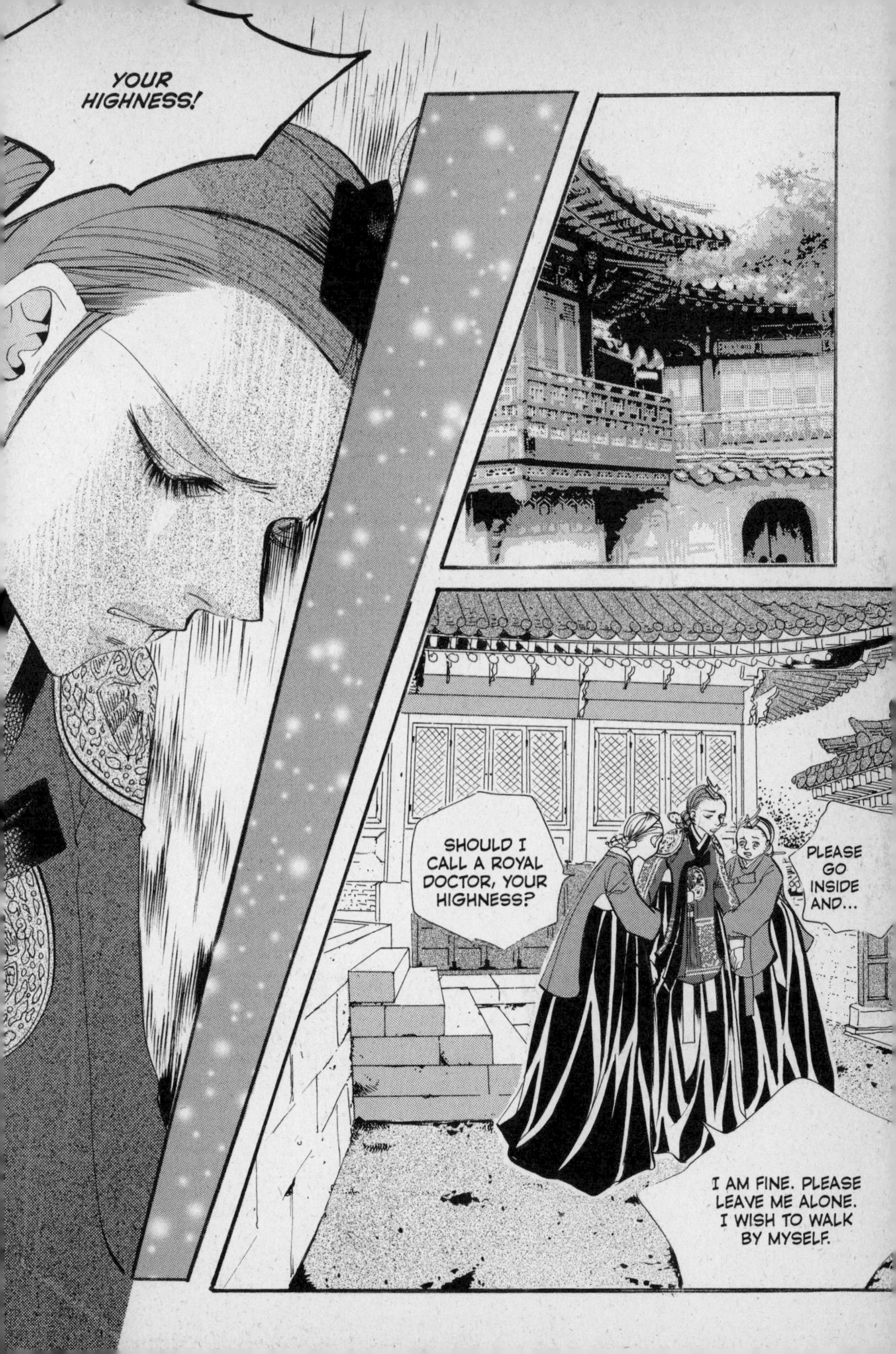
YOUR HIGHNESS!
SHOULD I CALL A ROYAL DOCTOR, YOUR HIGHNESS?
PLEASE GO INSIDE AND...
I AM FINE. PLEASE LEAVE ME ALONE. I WISH TO WALK BY MYSELF.

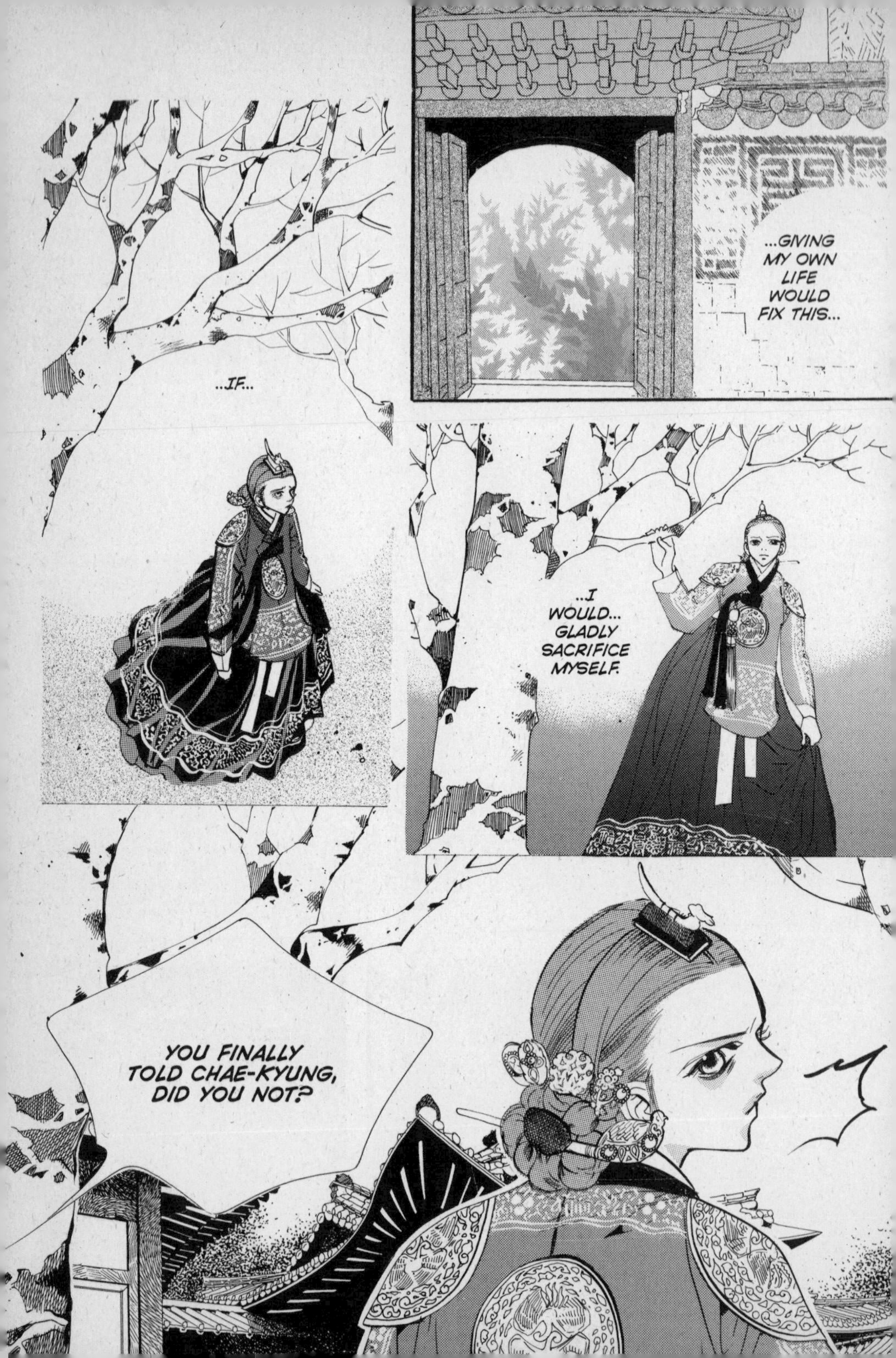
...IF...
...GIVING MY OWN LIFE WOULD FIX THIS...
...I WOULD... GLADLY SACRIFICE MYSELF.
YOU FINALLY TOLD CHAE-KYUNG, DID YOU NOT?

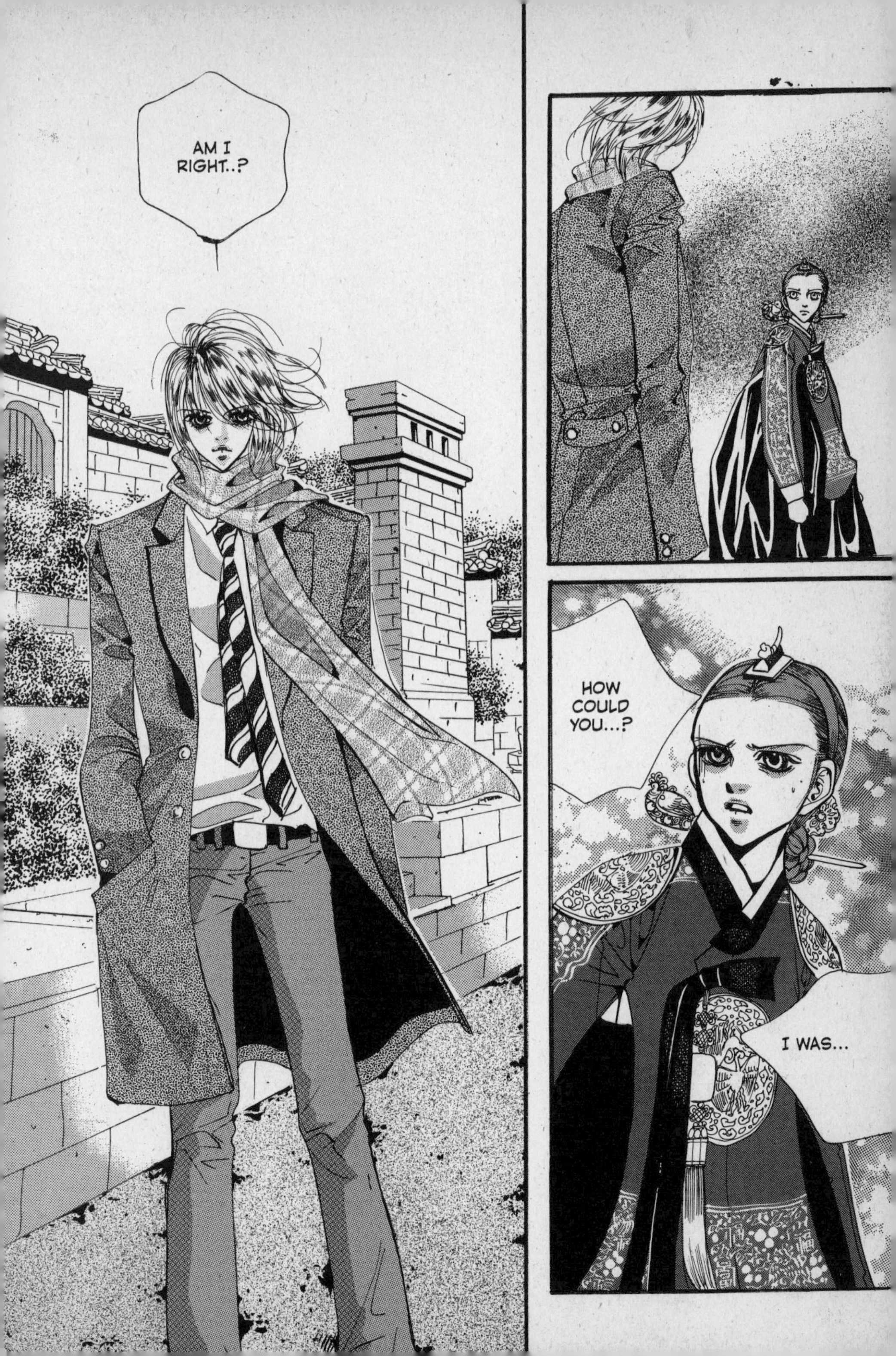
AM I RIGHT..?
HOW COULD YOU...?
I WAS...

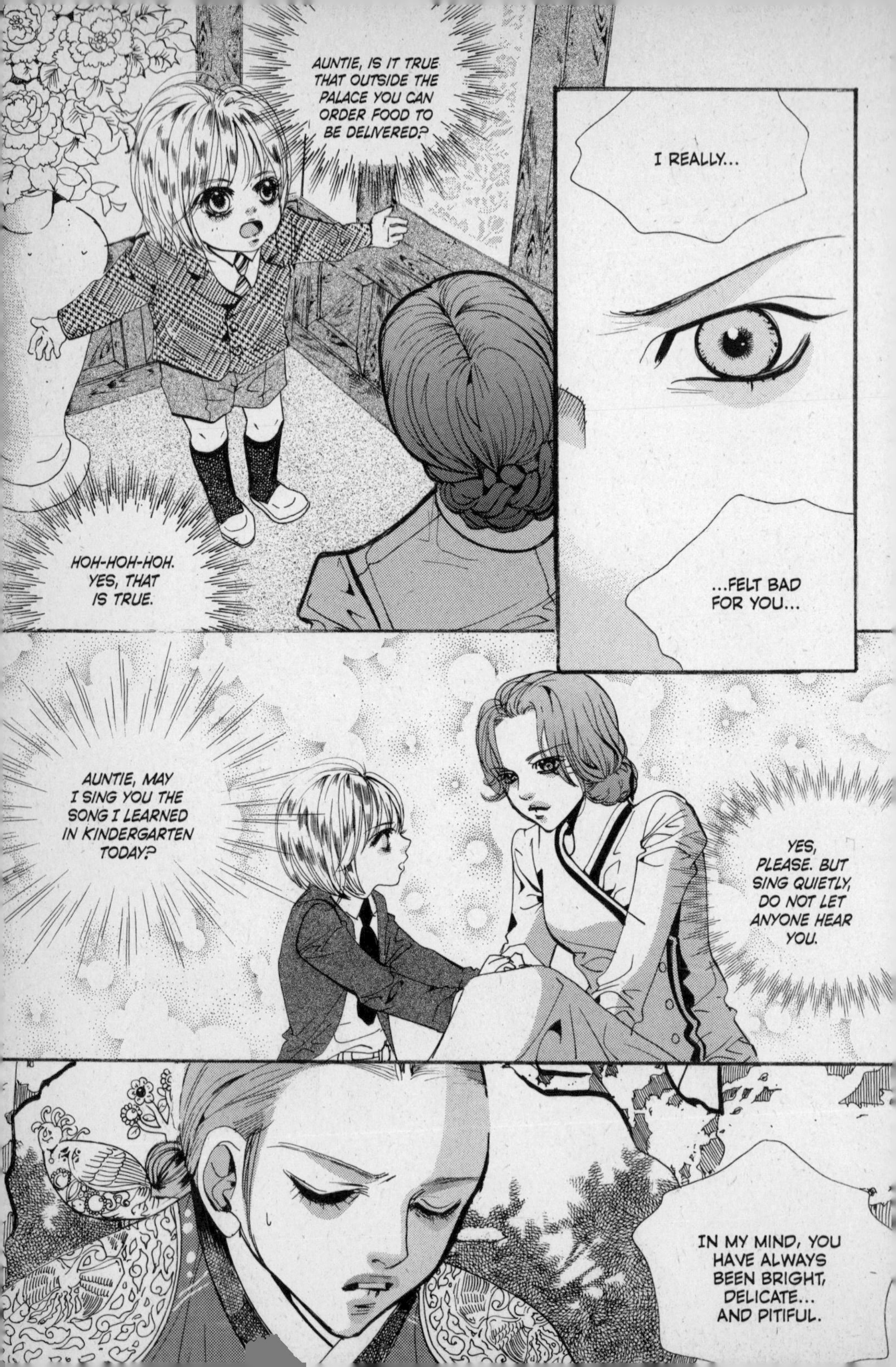
I REALLY...
...FELT BAD FOR YOU...
AUNTIE, IS IT TRUE THAT OUTSIDE THE PALACE YOU CAN ORDER FOOD TO BE DELIVERED?
HOH-HOH-HOH. YES, THAT IS TRUE.
AUNTIE, MAY I SING YOU THE SONG I LEARNED IN KINDERGARTEN TODAY?
YES, PLEASE. BUT SING QUIETLY, DO NOT LET ANYONE HEAR YOU.
IN MY MIND, YOU HAVE ALWAYS BEEN BRIGHT, DELICATE... AND PITIFUL.

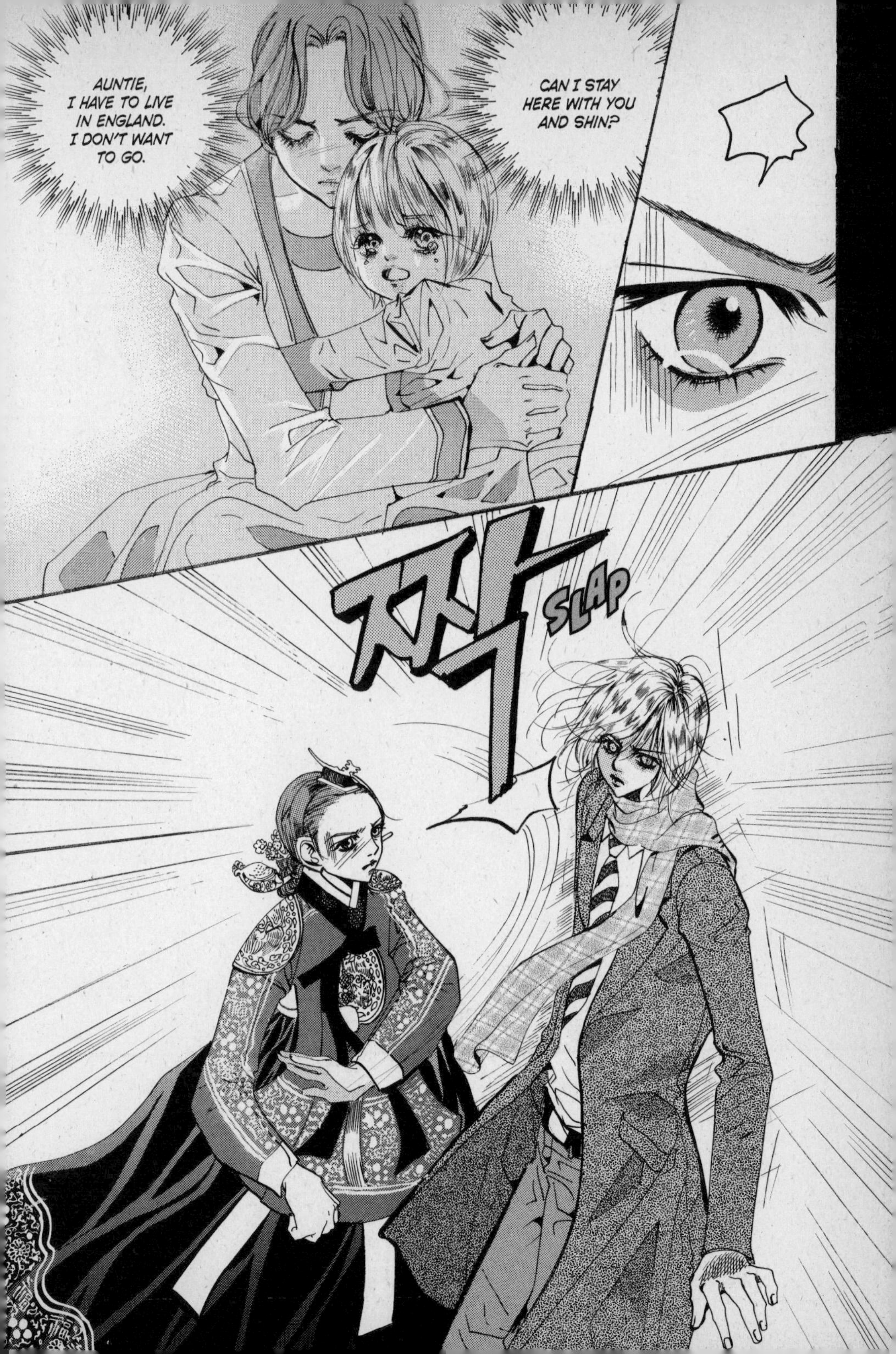
AUNTIE, I HAVE TO LIVE IN ENGLAND. I DON'T WANT TO GO.
CAN I STAY HERE WITH YOU AND SHIN?
짝
SLAP

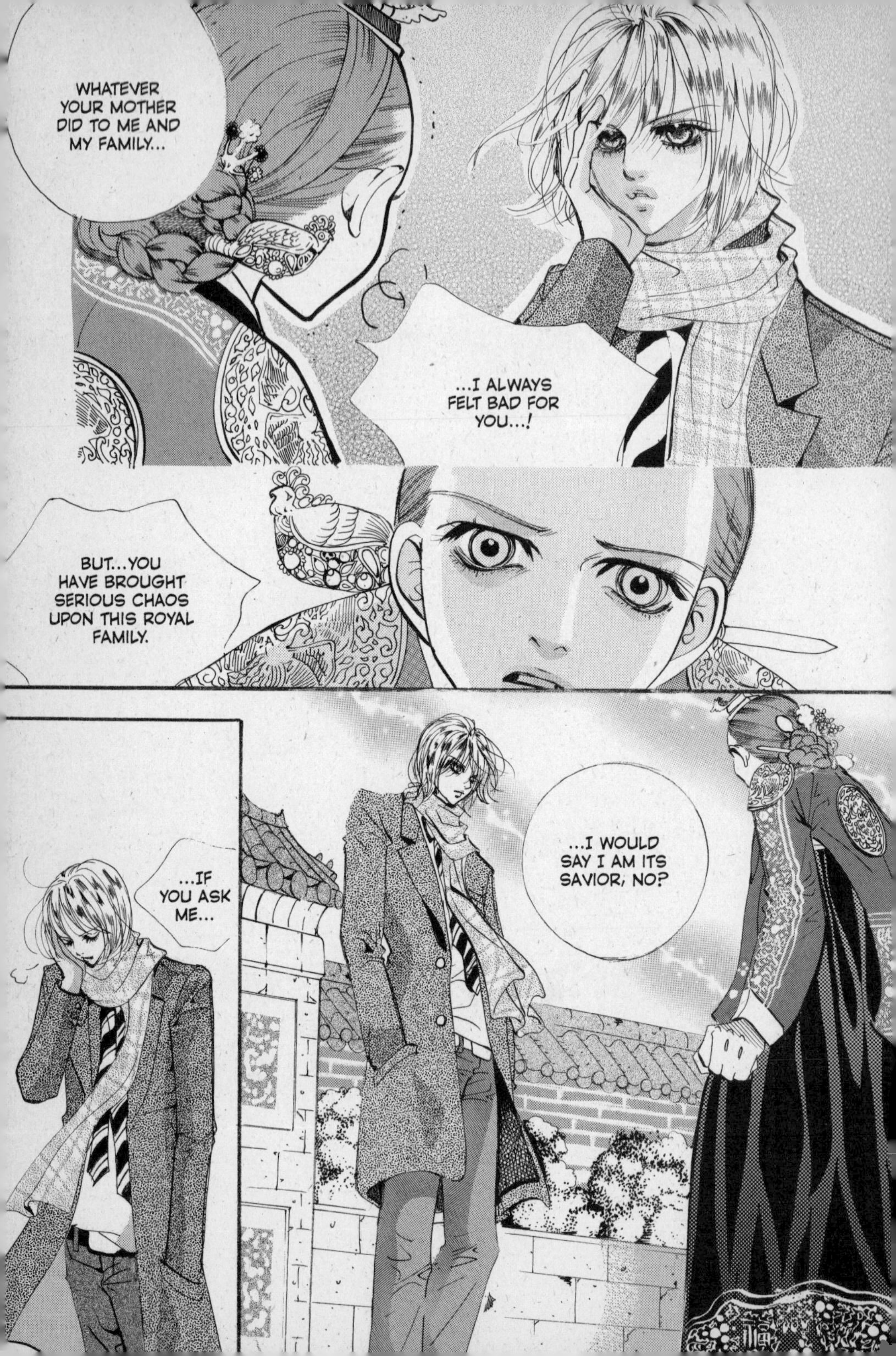
WHATEVER YOUR MOTHER DID TO ME AND MY FAMILY...
...I ALWAYS FELT BAD FOR YOU...!
BUT...YOU HAVE BROUGHT SERIOUS CHAOS UPON THIS ROYAL FAMILY.
...IF YOU ASK ME...
...I WOULD SAY I AM ITS SAVIOR, NO?

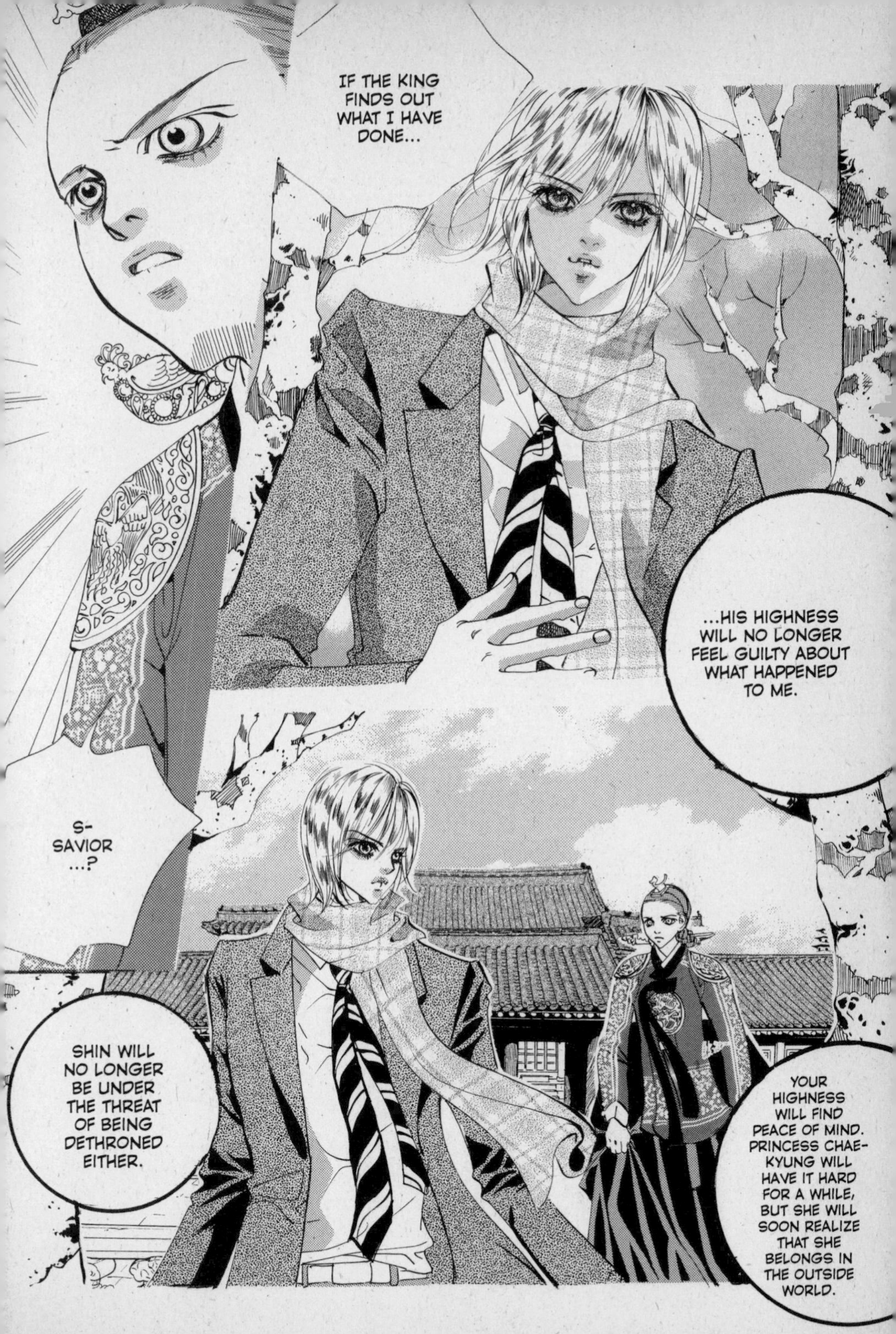
IF THE KING FINDS OUT WHAT I HAVE DONE...
...HIS HIGHNESS WILL NO LONGER FEEL GUILTY ABOUT WHAT HAPPENED TO ME.
S-SAVIOR ...?
YOUR HIGHNESS WILL FIND PEACE OF MIND. PRINCESS CHAE-KYUNG WILL HAVE IT HARD FOR A WHILE, BUT SHE WILL SOON REALIZE THAT SHE BELONGS IN THE OUTSIDE WORLD.
SHIN WILL NO LONGER BE UNDER THE THREAT OF BEING DETHRONED EITHER.

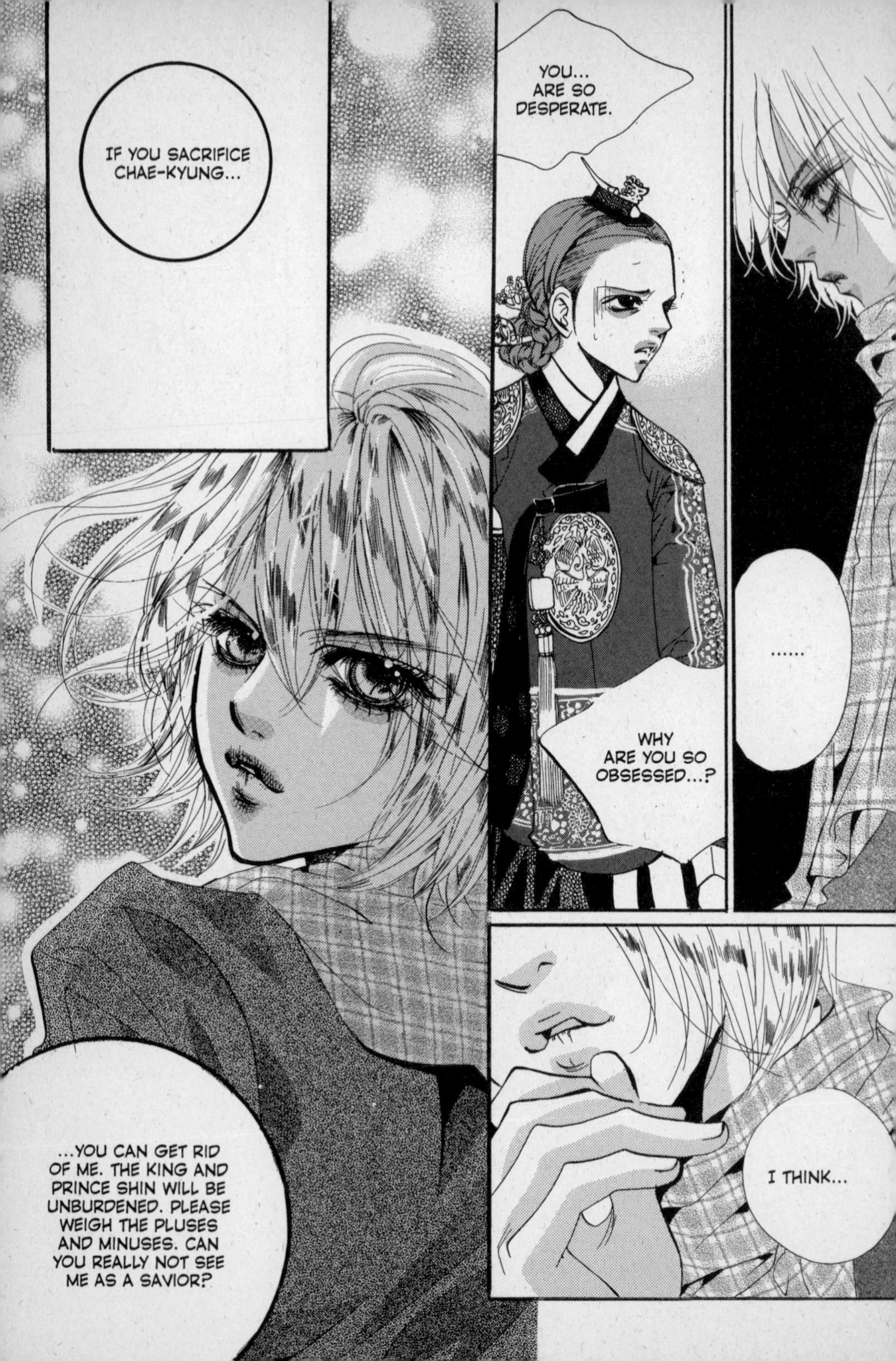
IF YOU SACRIFICE CHAE-KYUNG...
...YOU CAN GET RID OF ME. THE KING AND PRINCE SHIN WILL BE UNBURDENED. PLEASE WEIGH THE PLUSES AND MINUSES. CAN YOU REALLY NOT SEE ME AS A SAVIOR?
YOU... ARE SO DESPERATE.
WHY ARE YOU SO OBSESSED...?
......
I THINK...

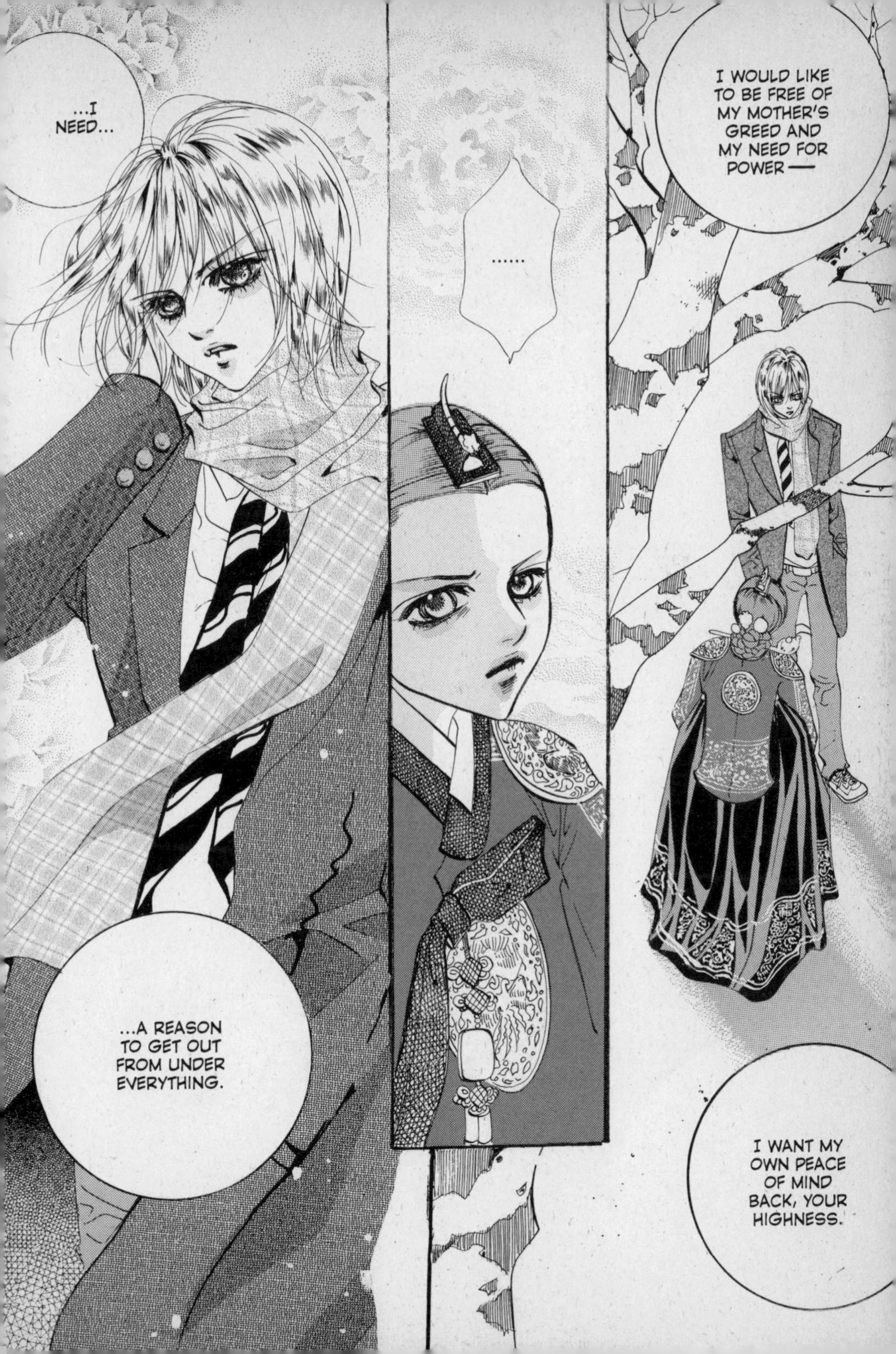
I WOULD LIKE TO BE FREE OF MY MOTHER'S GREED AND MY NEED FOR POWER—
......
...I NEED...
...A REASON TO GET OUT FROM UNDER EVERYTHING.
I WANT MY OWN PEACE OF MIND BACK, YOUR HIGHNESS.

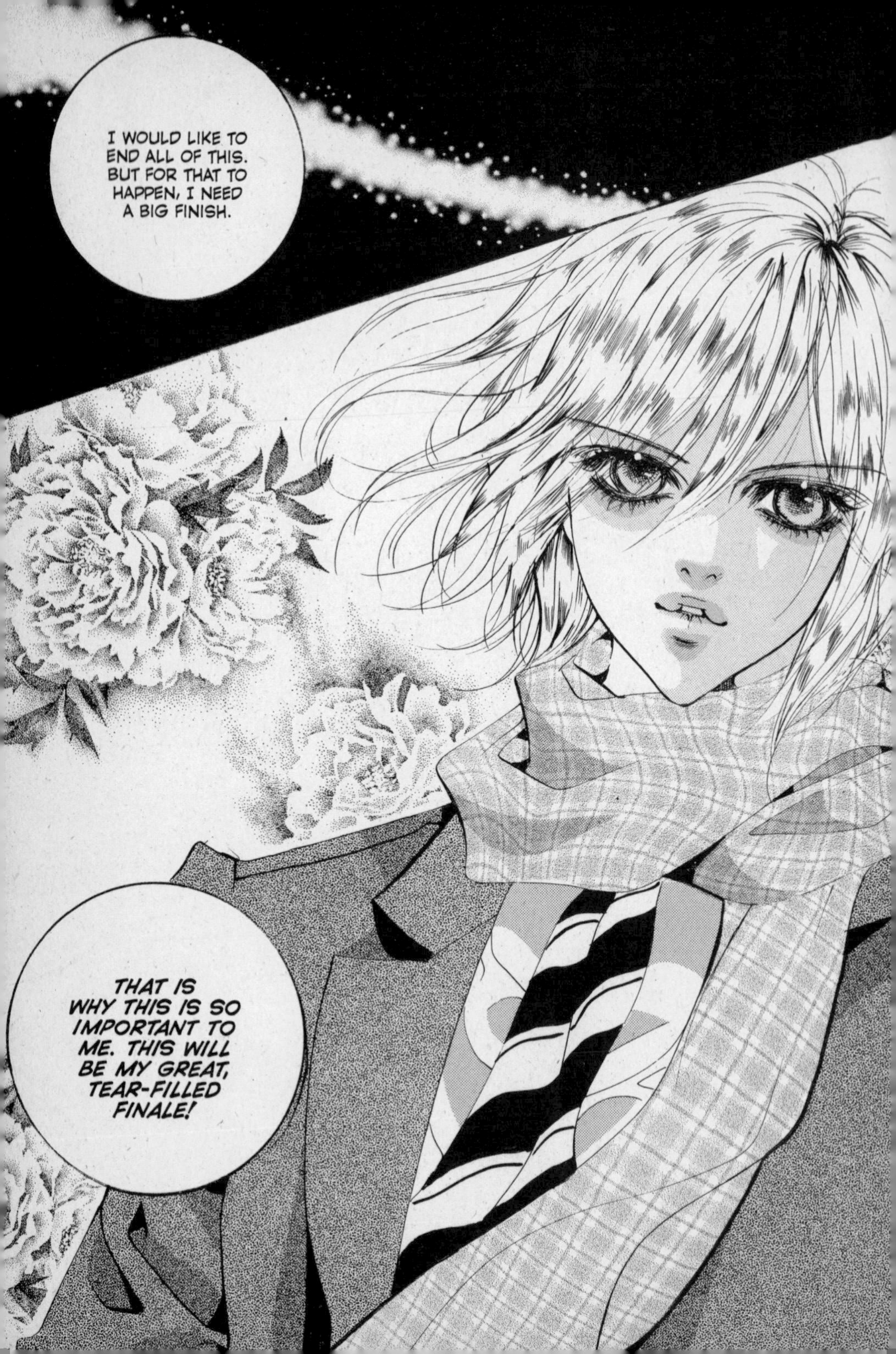
I WOULD LIKE TO END ALL OF THIS. BUT FOR THAT TO HAPPEN, I NEED A BIG FINISH.
THAT IS WHY THIS IS SO IMPORTANT TO ME. THIS WILL BE MY GREAT, TEAR-FILLED FINALE!

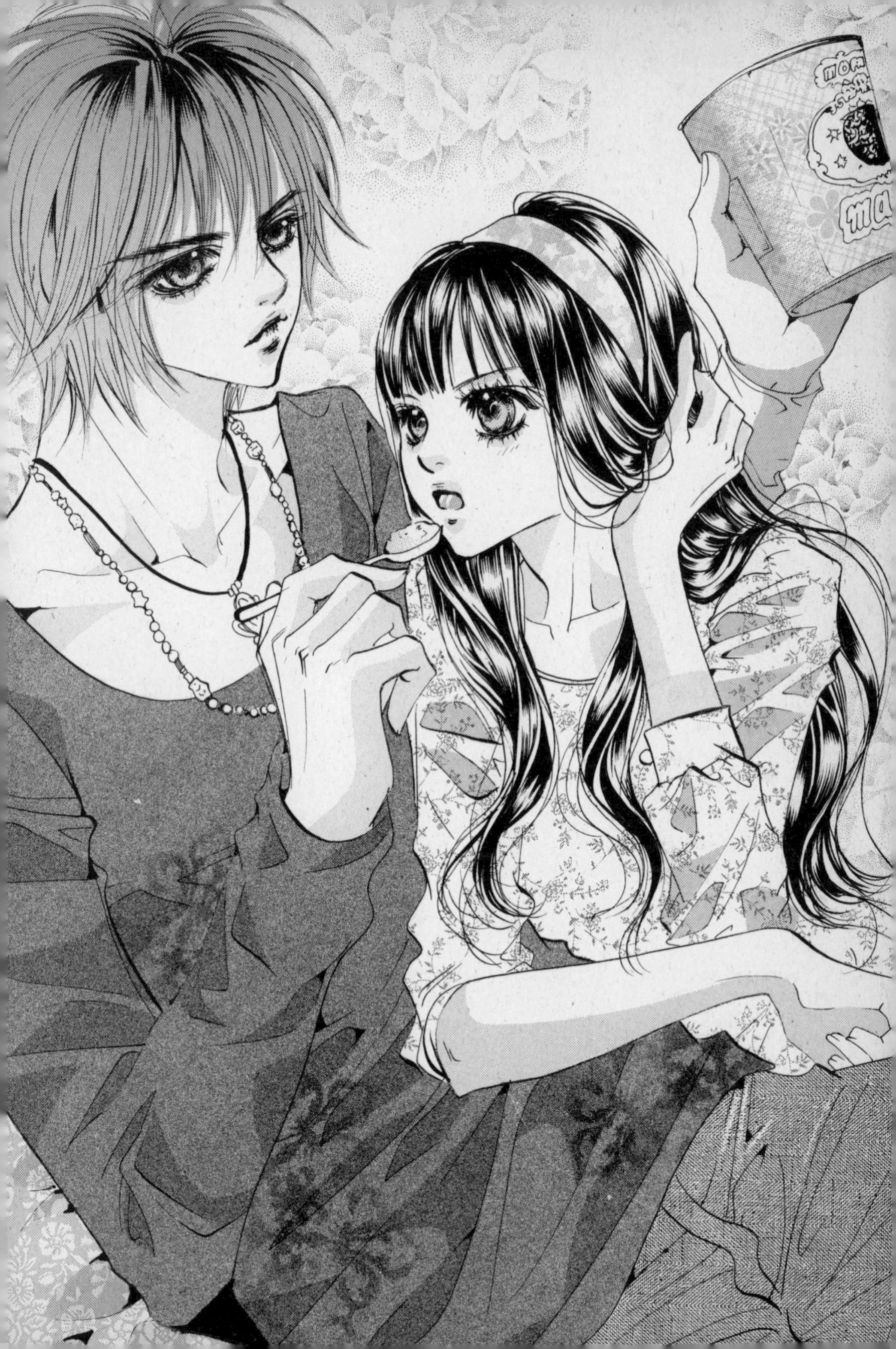

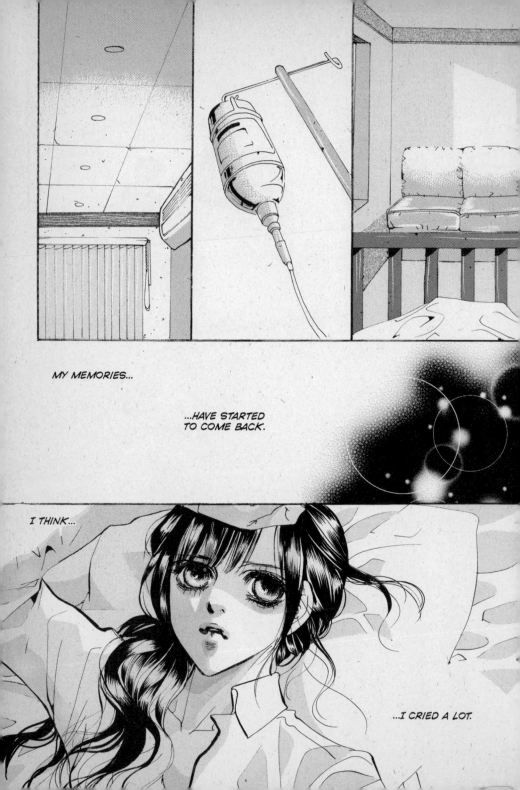

MY MEMORIES...

...HAVE STARTED
TO COME BACK.

I THINK...

...I CRIED A LOT.

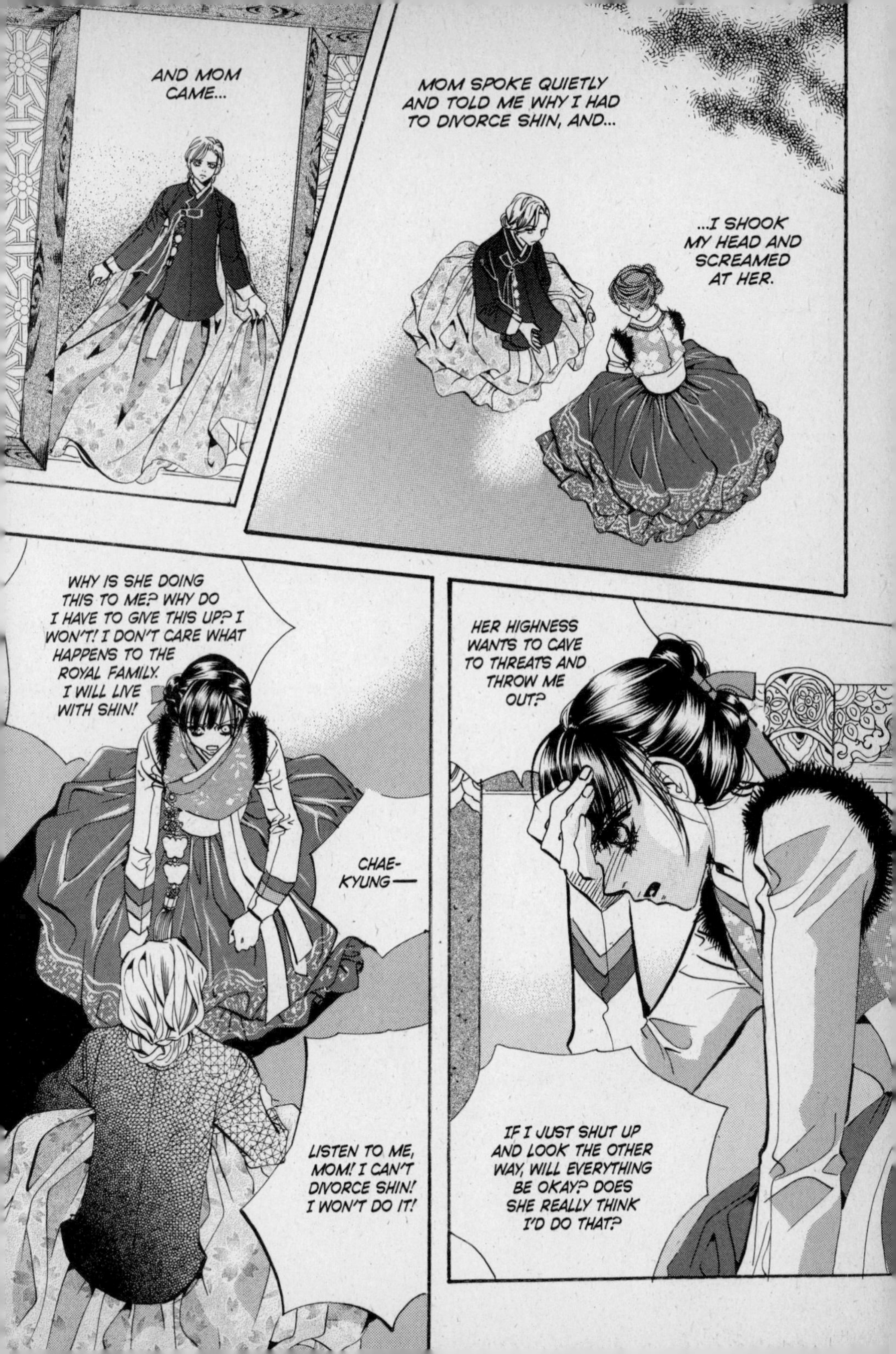
AND MOM CAME...
MOM SPOKE QUIETLY AND TOLD ME WHY I HAD TO DIVORCE SHIN, AND...
...I SHOOK MY HEAD AND SCREAMED AT HER.
WHY IS SHE DOING THIS TO ME? WHY DO I HAVE TO GIVE THIS UP? I WON'T! I DON'T CARE WHAT HAPPENS TO THE ROYAL FAMILY. I WILL LIVE WITH SHIN!
CHAE-KYUNG—
LISTEN TO ME, MOM! I CAN'T DIVORCE SHIN! I WON'T DO IT!
HER HIGHNESS WANTS TO CAVE TO THREATS AND THROW ME OUT?
IF I JUST SHUT UP AND LOOK THE OTHER WAY, WILL EVERYTHING BE OKAY? DOES SHE REALLY THINK I'D DO THAT?

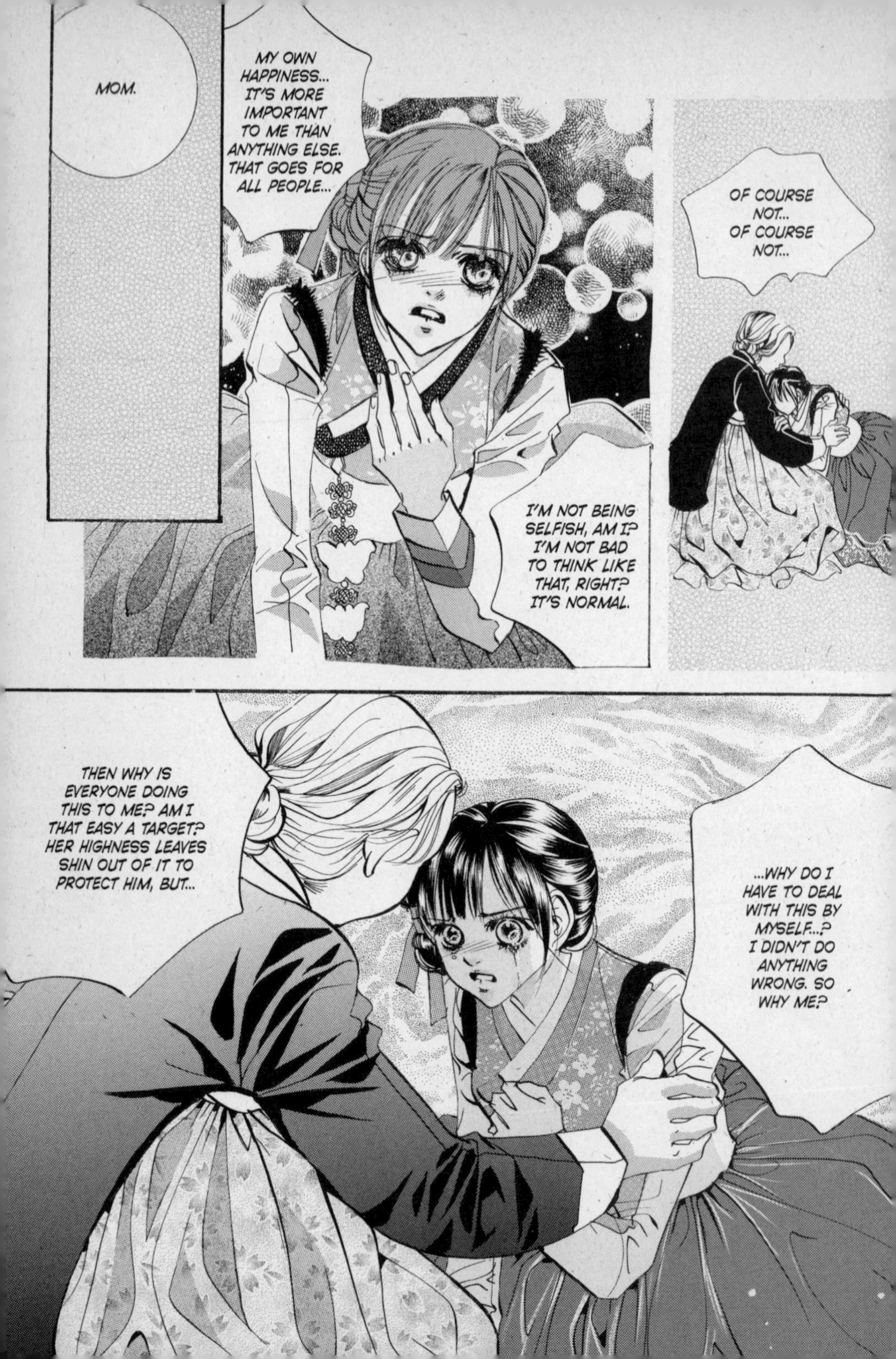
MOM.
MY OWN HAPPINESS... IT'S MORE IMPORTANT TO ME THAN ANYTHING ELSE. THAT GOES FOR ALL PEOPLE...
I'M NOT BEING SELFISH, AM I? I'M NOT BAD TO THINK LIKE THAT, RIGHT? IT'S NORMAL.
OF COURSE NOT... OF COURSE NOT...
THEN WHY IS EVERYONE DOING THIS TO ME? AM I THAT EASY A TARGET? HER HIGHNESS LEAVES SHIN OUT OF IT TO PROTECT HIM, BUT...
...WHY DO I HAVE TO DEAL WITH THIS BY MYSELF...? I DIDN'T DO ANYTHING WRONG. SO WHY ME?

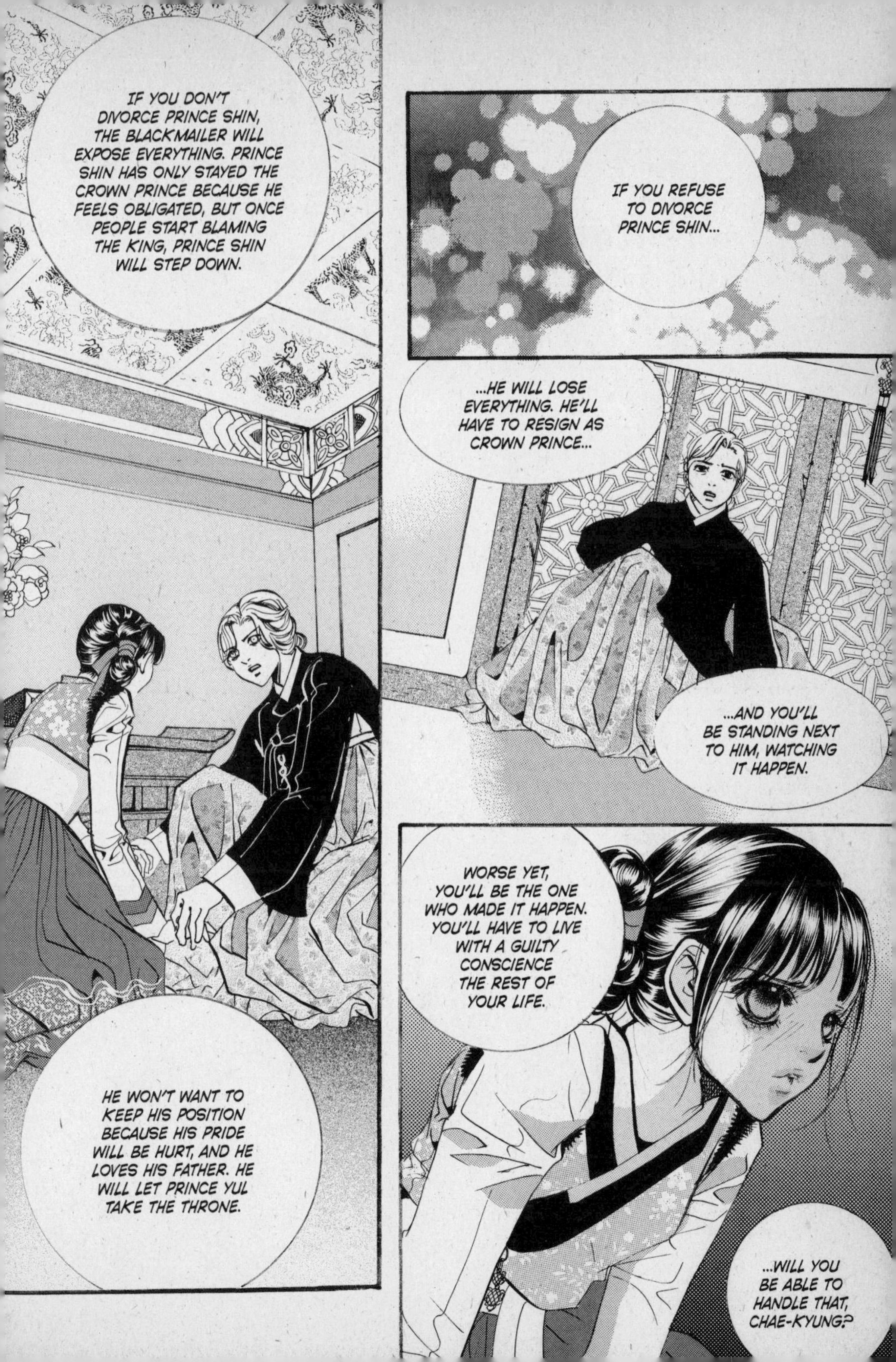
IF YOU DON'T DIVORCE PRINCE SHIN, THE BLACKMAILER WILL EXPOSE EVERYTHING. PRINCE SHIN HAS ONLY STAYED THE CROWN PRINCE BECAUSE HE FEELS OBLIGATED, BUT ONCE PEOPLE START BLAMING THE KING, PRINCE SHIN WILL STEP DOWN.
HE WON'T WANT TO KEEP HIS POSITION BECAUSE HIS PRIDE WILL BE HURT, AND HE LOVES HIS FATHER. HE WILL LET PRINCE YUL TAKE THE THRONE.
IF YOU REFUSE TO DIVORCE PRINCE SHIN...
...HE WILL LOSE EVERYTHING. HE'LL HAVE TO RESIGN AS CROWN PRINCE...
...AND YOU'LL BE STANDING NEXT TO HIM, WATCHING IT HAPPEN.
WORSE YET, YOU'LL BE THE ONE WHO MADE IT HAPPEN. YOU'LL HAVE TO LIVE WITH A GUILTY CONSCIENCE THE REST OF YOUR LIFE.
...WILL YOU BE ABLE TO HANDLE THAT, CHAE-KYUNG?

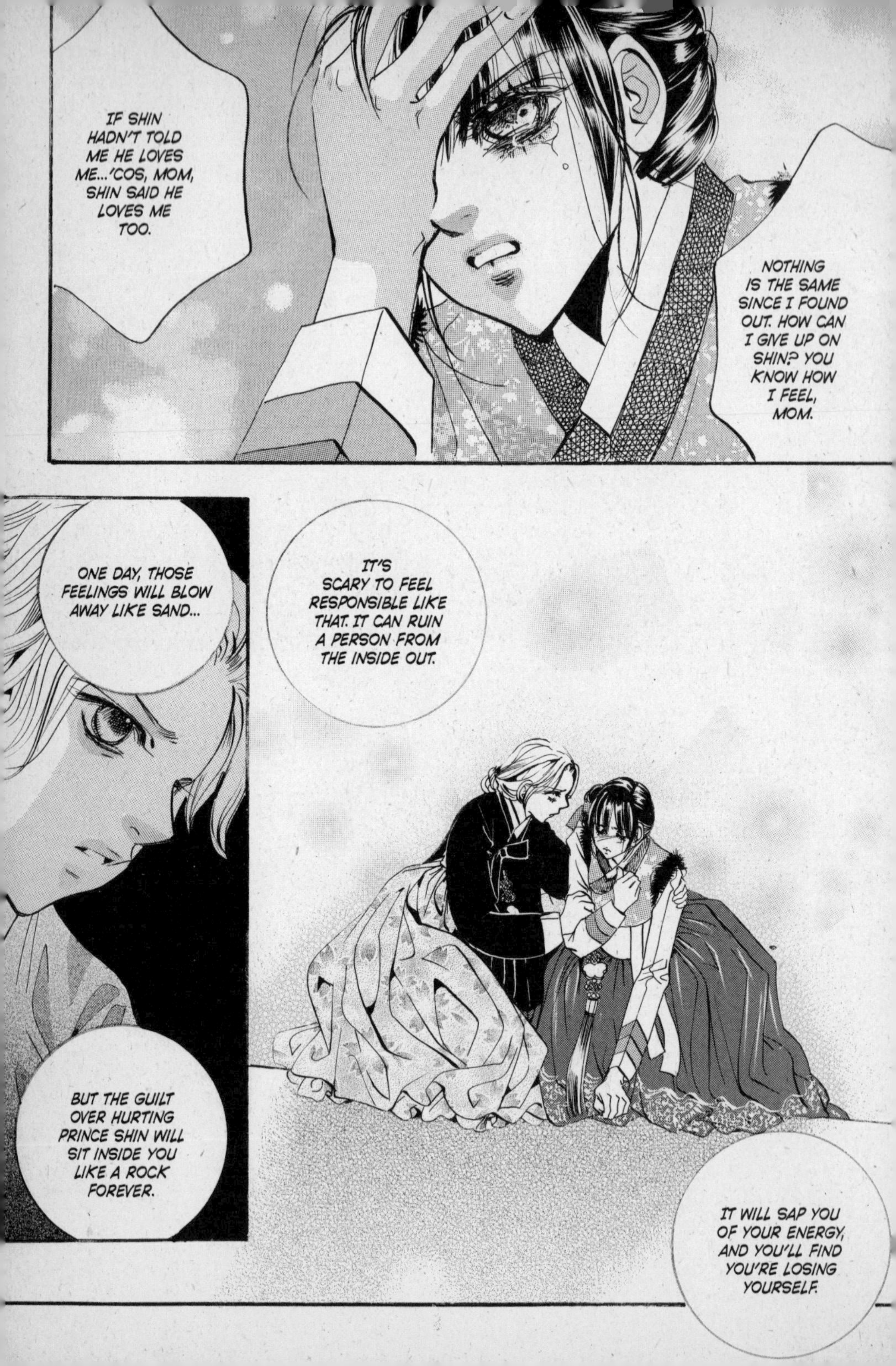
IF SHIN HADN'T TOLD ME HE LOVES ME...'COS, MOM, SHIN SAID HE LOVES ME TOO.
NOTHING IS THE SAME SINCE I FOUND OUT. HOW CAN I GIVE UP ON SHIN? YOU KNOW HOW I FEEL, MOM.
IT'S SCARY TO FEEL RESPONSIBLE LIKE THAT. IT CAN RUIN A PERSON FROM THE INSIDE OUT.
ONE DAY, THOSE FEELINGS WILL BLOW AWAY LIKE SAND...
BUT THE GUILT OVER HURTING PRINCE SHIN WILL SIT INSIDE YOU LIKE A ROCK FOREVER.
IT WILL SAP YOU OF YOUR ENERGY, AND YOU'LL FIND YOU'RE LOSING YOURSELF.

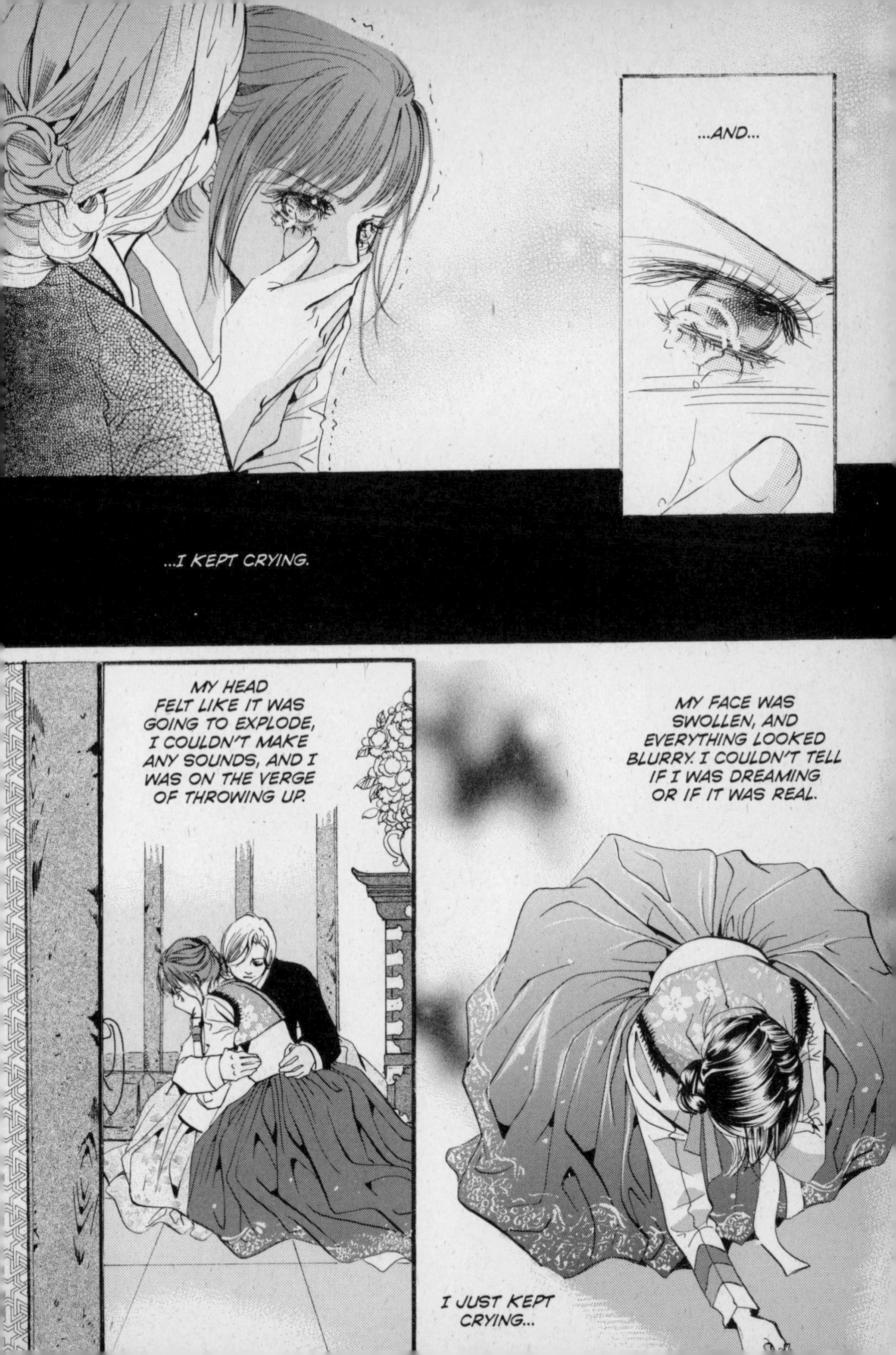
...AND...
...I KEPT CRYING.
MY HEAD FELT LIKE IT WAS GOING TO EXPLODE, I COULDN'T MAKE ANY SOUNDS, AND I WAS ON THE VERGE OF THROWING UP.
MY FACE WAS SWOLLEN, AND EVERYTHING LOOKED BLURRY. I COULDN'T TELL IF I WAS DREAMING OR IF IT WAS REAL.
I JUST KEPT CRYING...

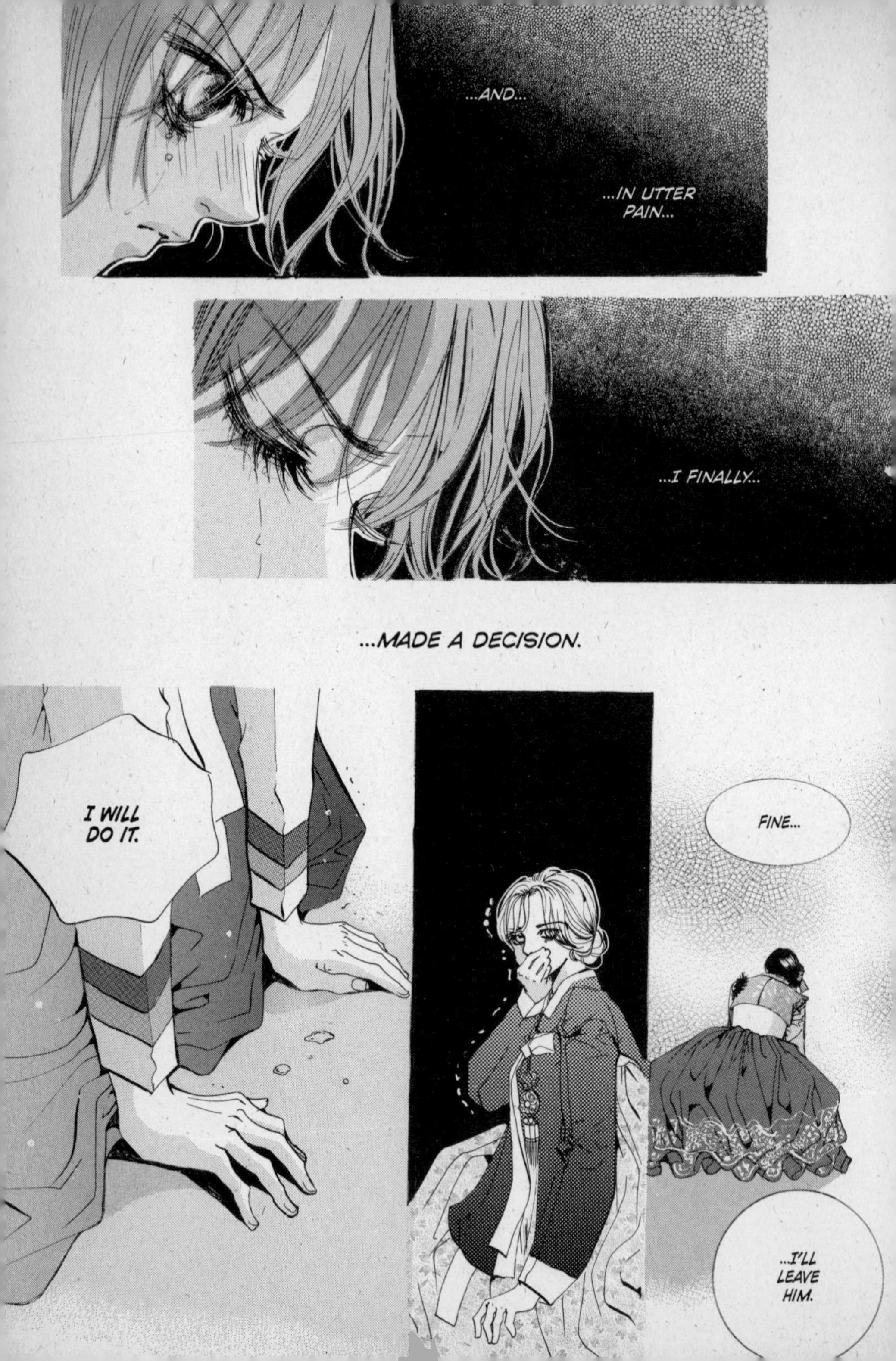
...AND...
...IN UTTER PAIN...
...I FINALLY...
...MADE A DECISION.
FINE...
...I'LL LEAVE HIM.
I WILL DO IT.

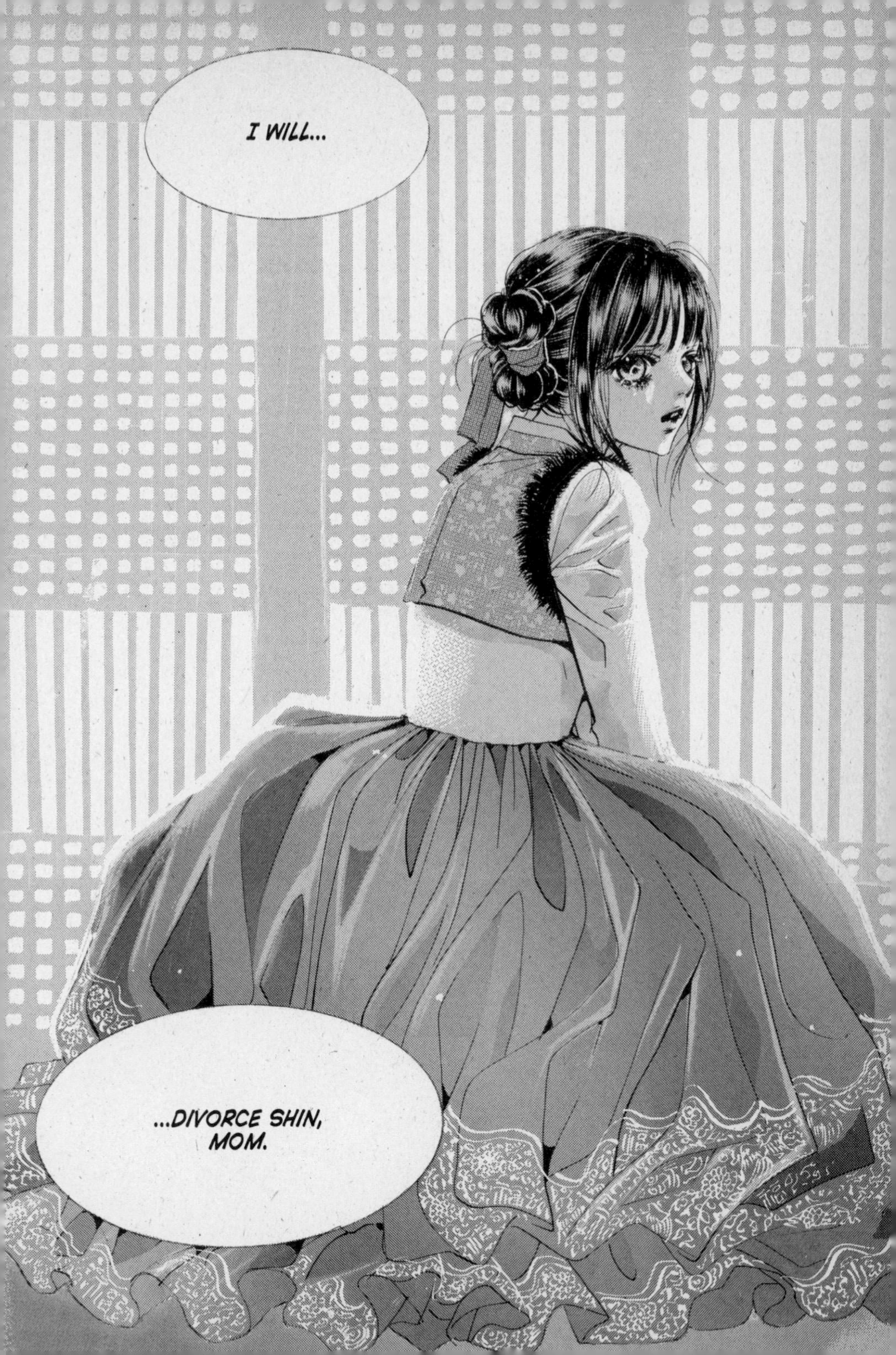
I WILL...
...DIVORCE SHIN, MOM.

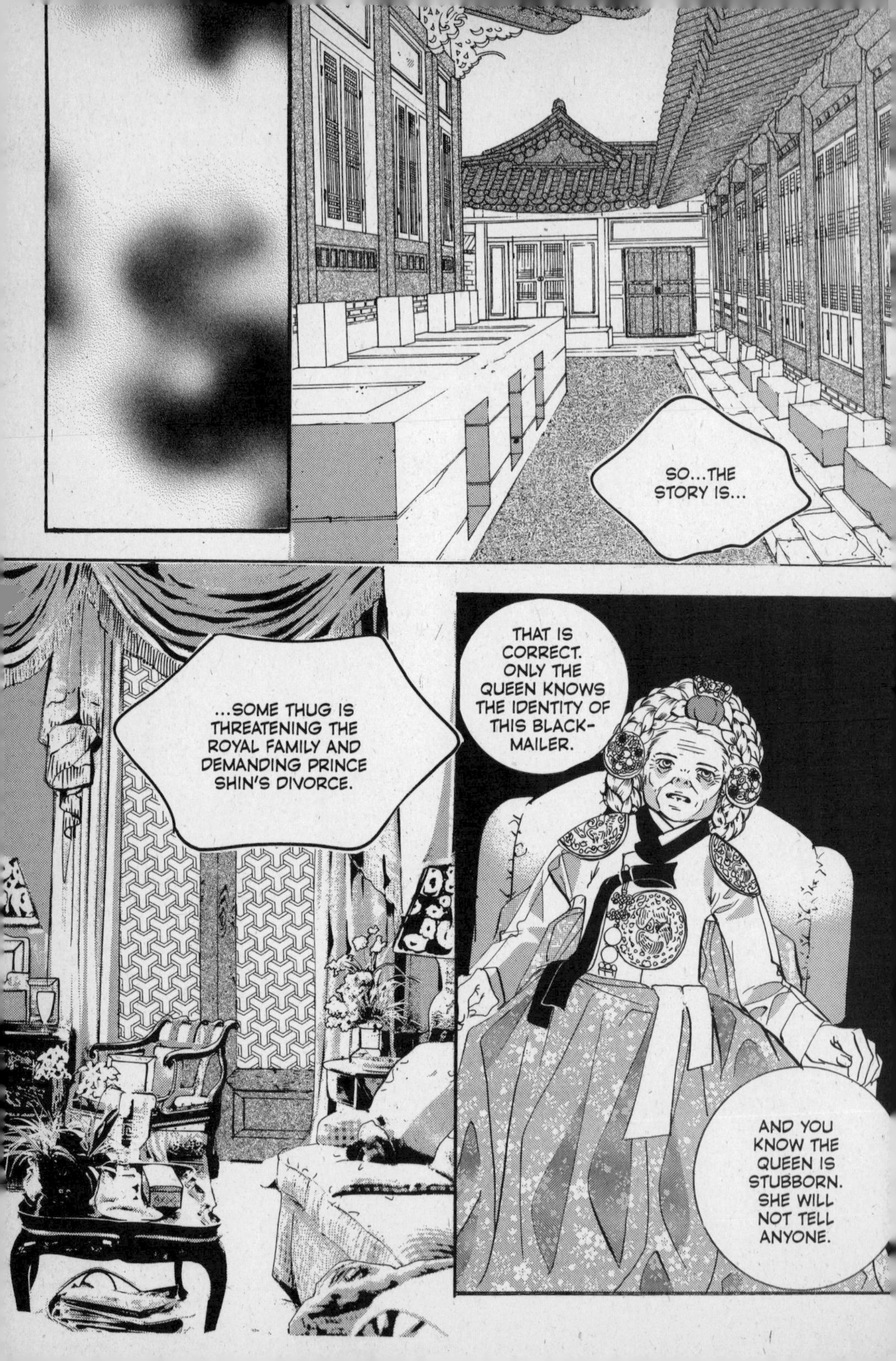
SO...THE STORY IS...
...SOME THUG IS THREATENING THE ROYAL FAMILY AND DEMANDING PRINCE SHIN'S DIVORCE.
THAT IS CORRECT. ONLY THE QUEEN KNOWS THE IDENTITY OF THIS BLACK-MAILER.
AND YOU KNOW THE QUEEN IS STUBBORN. SHE WILL NOT TELL ANYONE.

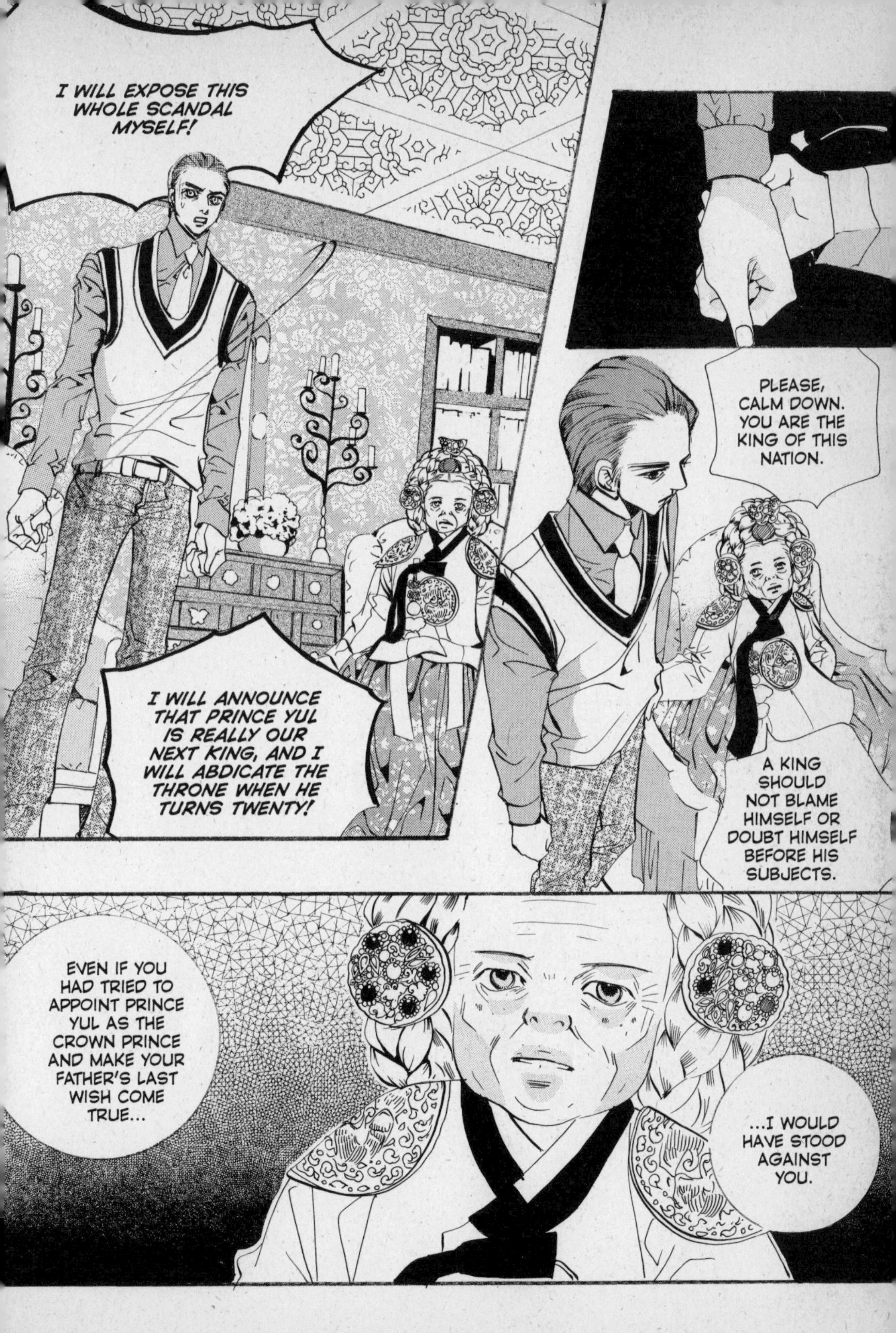

I WILL EXPOSE THIS WHOLE SCANDAL MYSELF!
I WILL ANNOUNCE THAT PRINCE YUL IS REALLY OUR NEXT KING, AND I WILL ABDICATE THE THRONE WHEN HE TURNS TWENTY!
PLEASE, CALM DOWN. YOU ARE THE KING OF THIS NATION.
A KING SHOULD NOT BLAME HIMSELF OR DOUBT HIMSELF BEFORE HIS SUBJECTS.
EVEN IF YOU HAD TRIED TO APPOINT PRINCE YUL AS THE CROWN PRINCE AND MAKE YOUR FATHER'S LAST WISH COME TRUE...
...I WOULD HAVE STOOD AGAINST YOU.

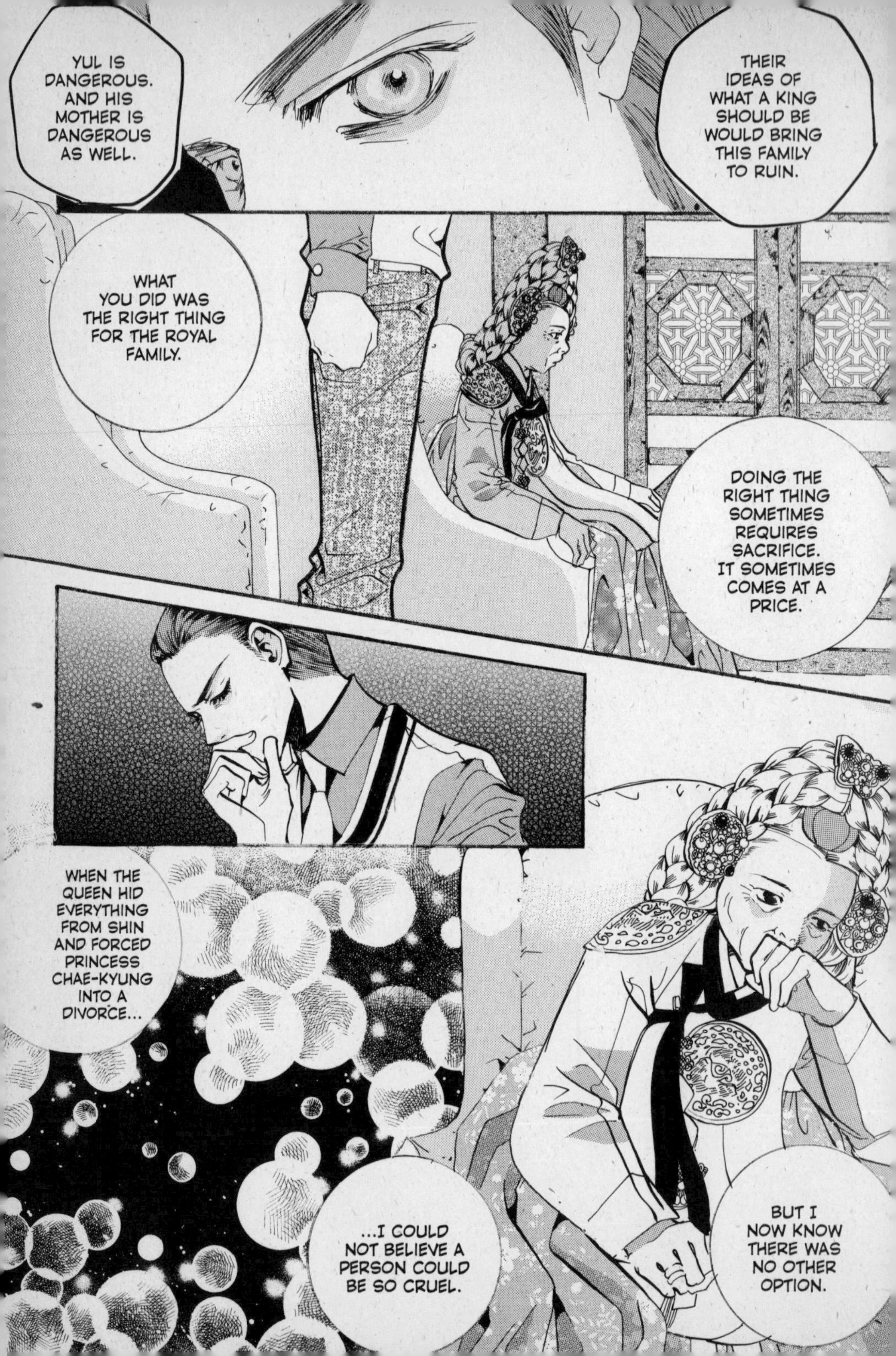
YUL IS DANGEROUS. AND HIS MOTHER IS DANGEROUS AS WELL.
THEIR IDEAS OF WHAT A KING SHOULD BE WOULD BRING THIS FAMILY TO RUIN.
WHAT YOU DID WAS THE RIGHT THING FOR THE ROYAL FAMILY.
DOING THE RIGHT THING SOMETIMES REQUIRES SACRIFICE. IT SOMETIMES COMES AT A PRICE.
WHEN THE QUEEN HID EVERYTHING FROM SHIN AND FORCED PRINCESS CHAE-KYUNG INTO A DIVORCE...
...I COULD NOT BELIEVE A PERSON COULD BE SO CRUEL.
BUT I NOW KNOW THERE WAS NO OTHER OPTION.

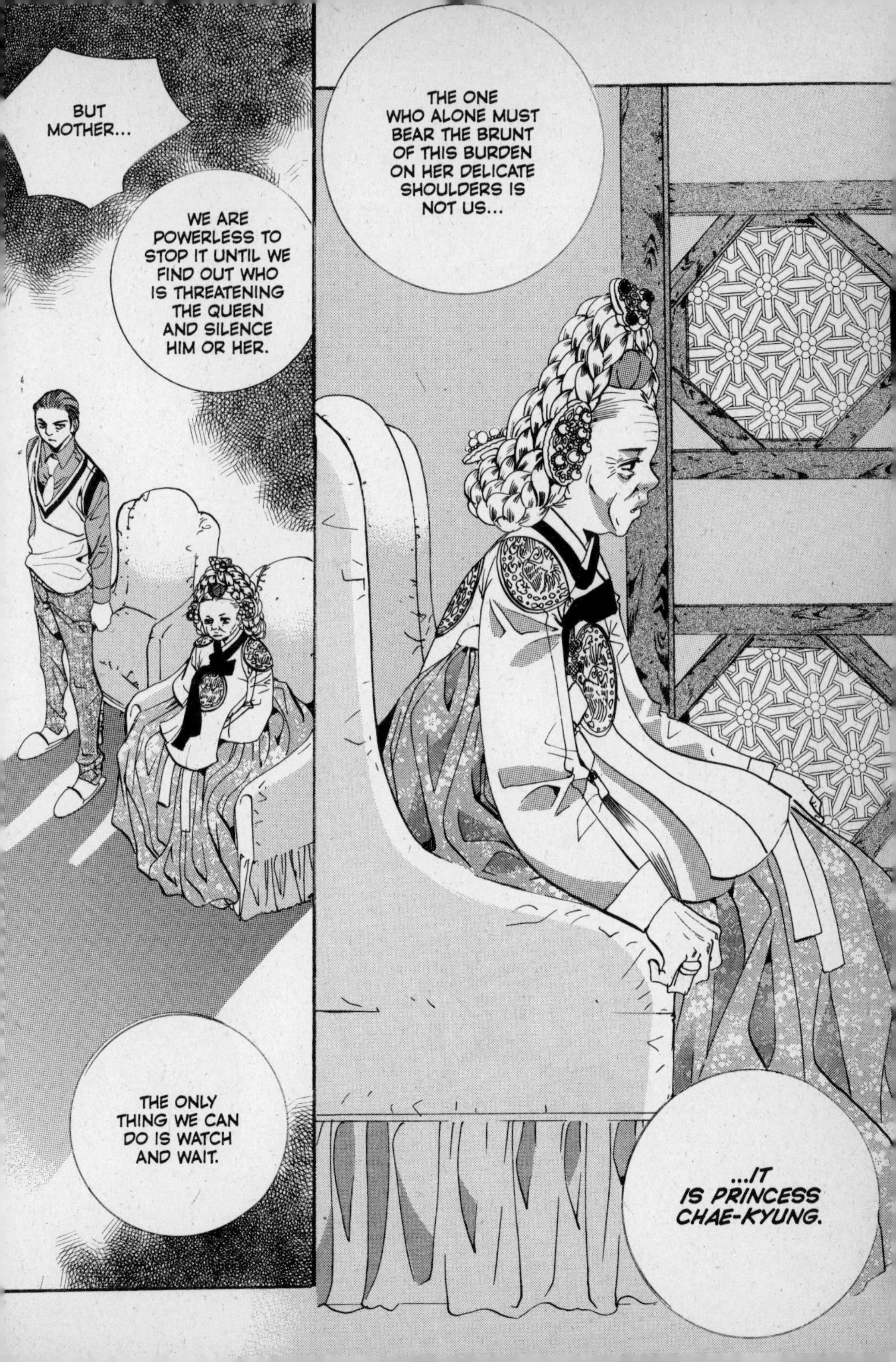
BUT MOTHER...
WE ARE POWERLESS TO STOP IT UNTIL WE FIND OUT WHO IS THREATENING THE QUEEN AND SILENCE HIM OR HER.
THE ONLY THING WE CAN DO IS WATCH AND WAIT.
THE ONE WHO ALONE MUST BEAR THE BRUNT OF THIS BURDEN ON HER DELICATE SHOULDERS IS NOT US...
...IT IS PRINCESS CHAE-KYUNG.

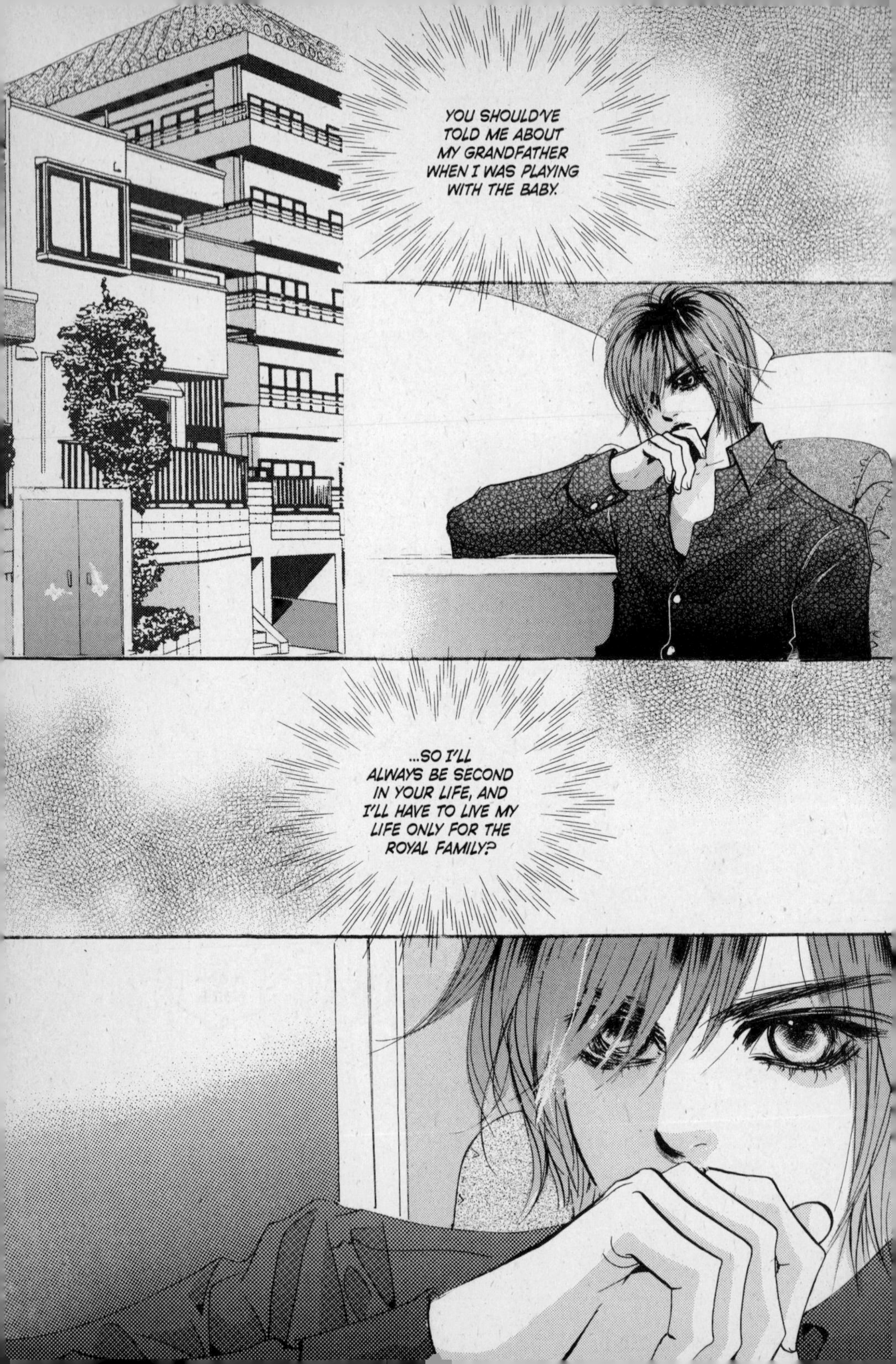
YOU SHOULD'VE TOLD ME ABOUT MY GRANDFATHER WHEN I WAS PLAYING WITH THE BABY.
...SO I'LL ALWAYS BE SECOND IN YOUR LIFE, AND I'LL HAVE TO LIVE MY LIFE ONLY FOR THE ROYAL FAMILY?

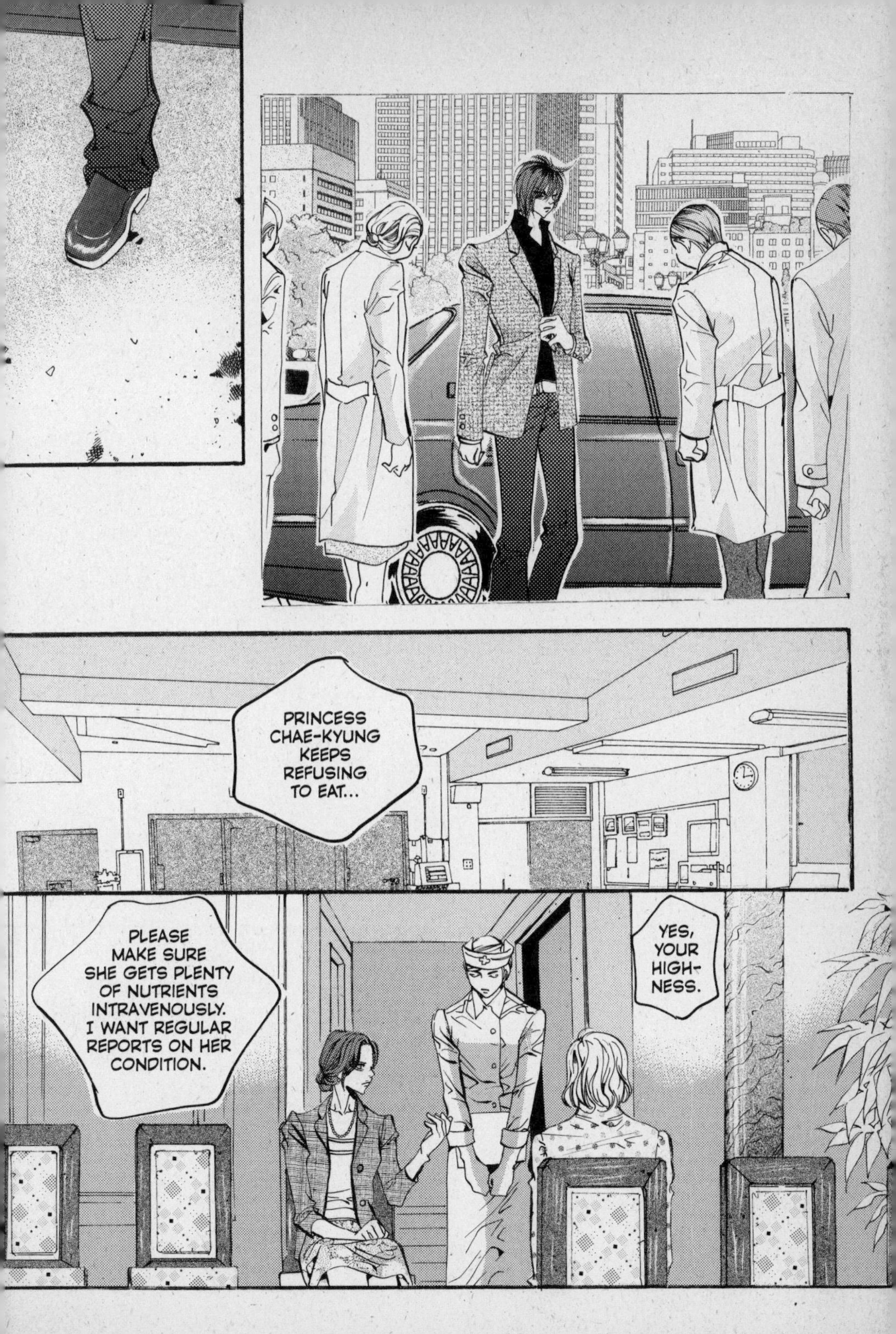
PRINCESS CHAE-KYUNG KEEPS REFUSING TO EAT...
YES, YOUR HIGH-NESS.
PLEASE MAKE SURE SHE GETS PLENTY OF NUTRIENTS INTRAVENOUSLY. I WANT REGULAR REPORTS ON HER CONDITION.

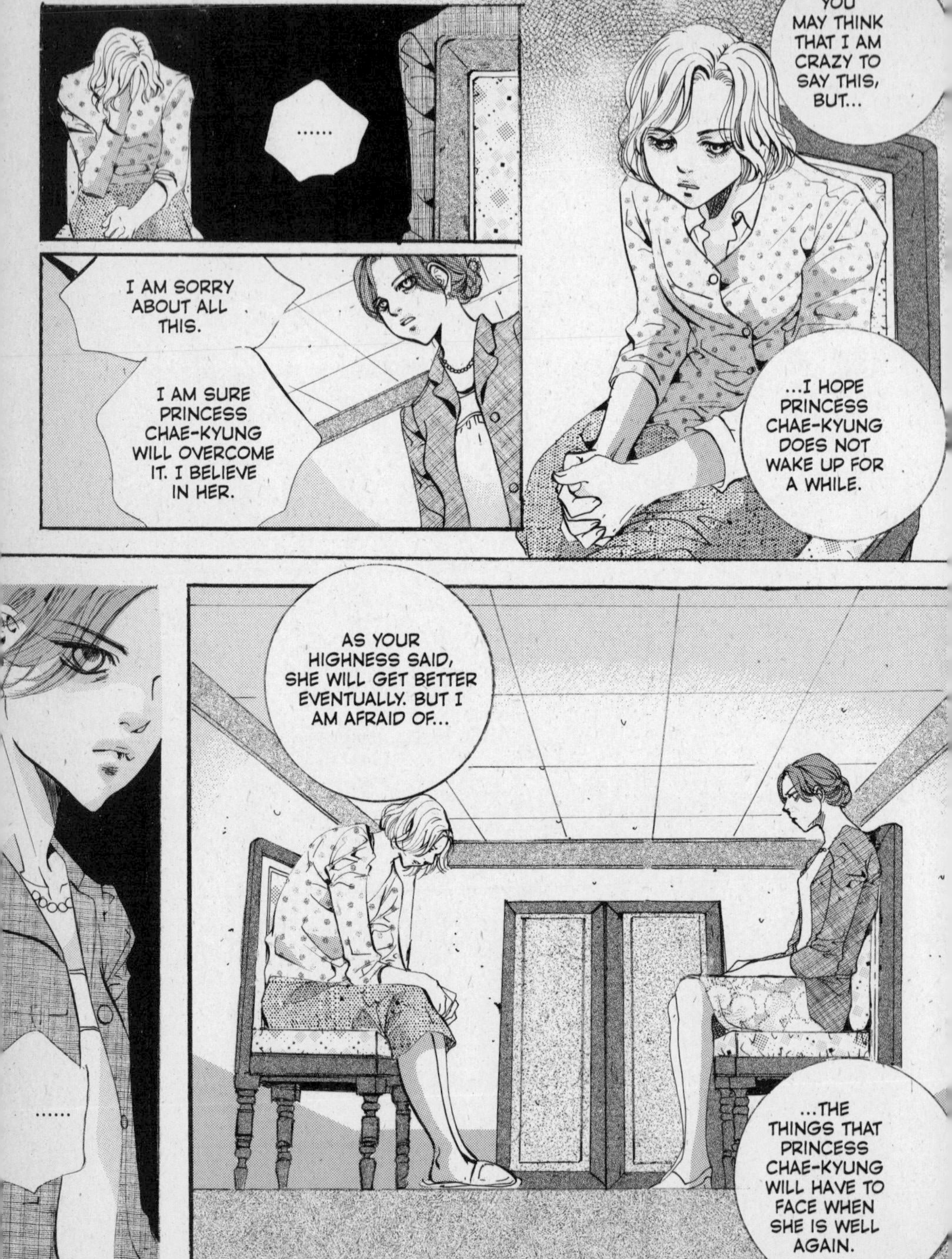
......
YOU MAY THINK THAT I AM CRAZY TO SAY THIS, BUT...
I AM SORRY ABOUT ALL THIS.
I AM SURE PRINCESS CHAE-KYUNG WILL OVERCOME IT. I BELIEVE IN HER.
...I HOPE PRINCESS CHAE-KYUNG DOES NOT WAKE UP FOR A WHILE.
AS YOUR HIGHNESS SAID, SHE WILL GET BETTER EVENTUALLY. BUT I AM AFRAID OF...
......
...THE THINGS THAT PRINCESS CHAE-KYUNG WILL HAVE TO FACE WHEN SHE IS WELL AGAIN.

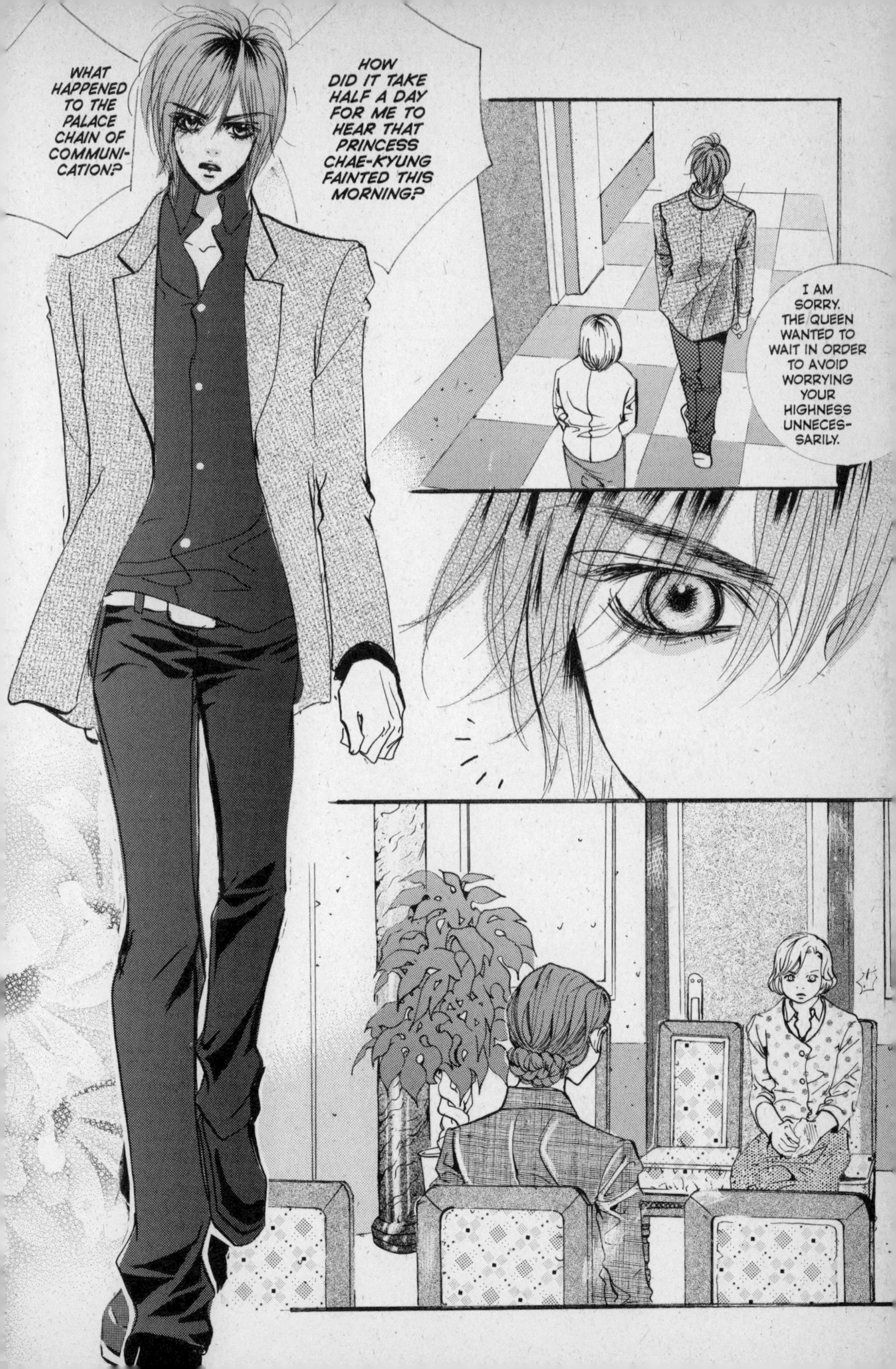
WHAT HAPPENED TO THE PALACE CHAIN OF COMMUNI-CATION?
HOW DID IT TAKE HALF A DAY FOR ME TO HEAR THAT PRINCESS CHAE-KYUNG FAINTED THIS MORNING?
I AM SORRY. THE QUEEN WANTED TO WAIT IN ORDER TO AVOID WORRYING YOUR HIGHNESS UNNECES-SARILY.

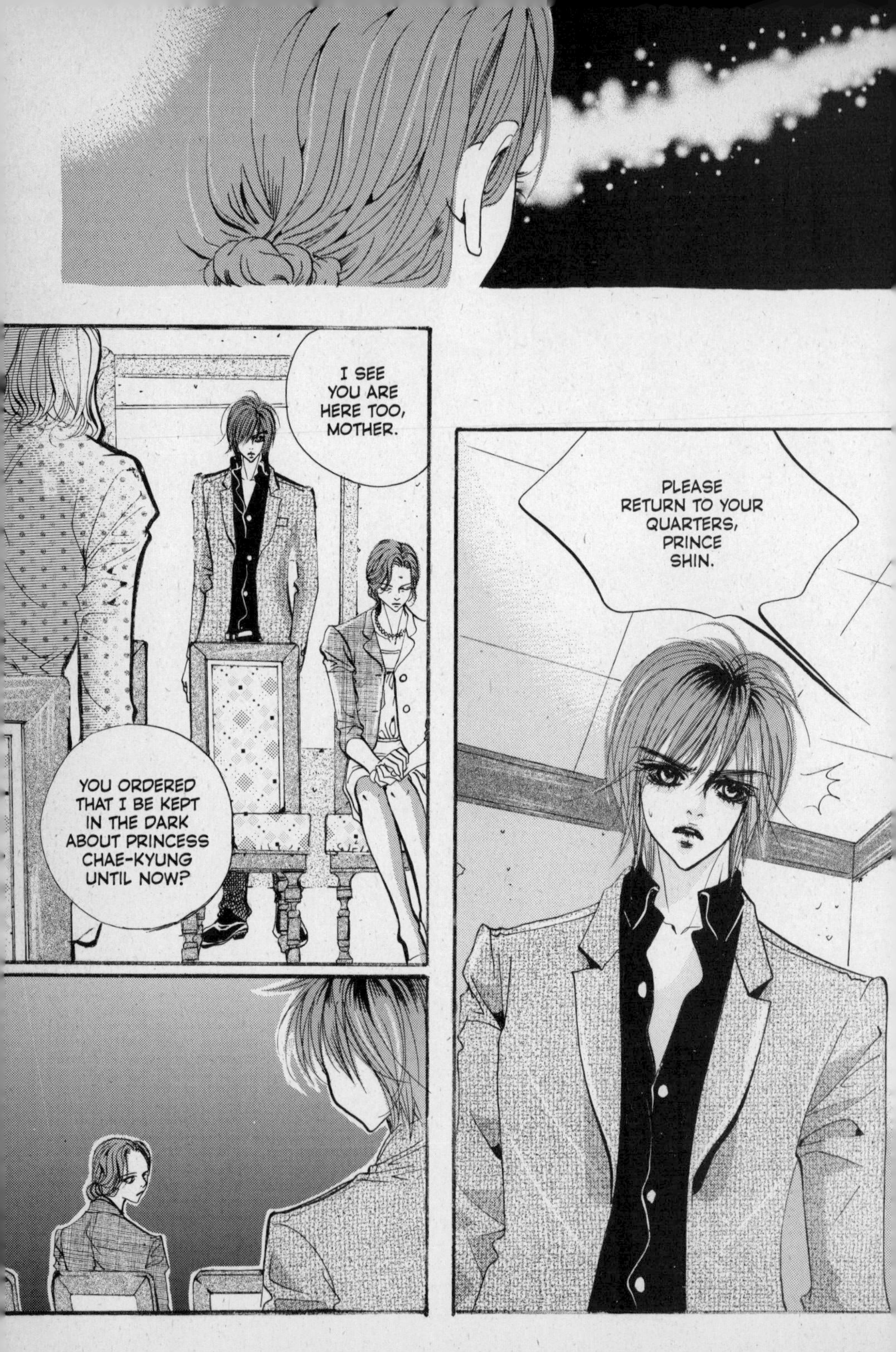

I SEE YOU ARE HERE TOO, MOTHER.
YOU ORDERED THAT I BE KEPT IN THE DARK ABOUT PRINCESS CHAE-KYUNG UNTIL NOW?
PLEASE RETURN TO YOUR QUARTERS, PRINCE SHIN.

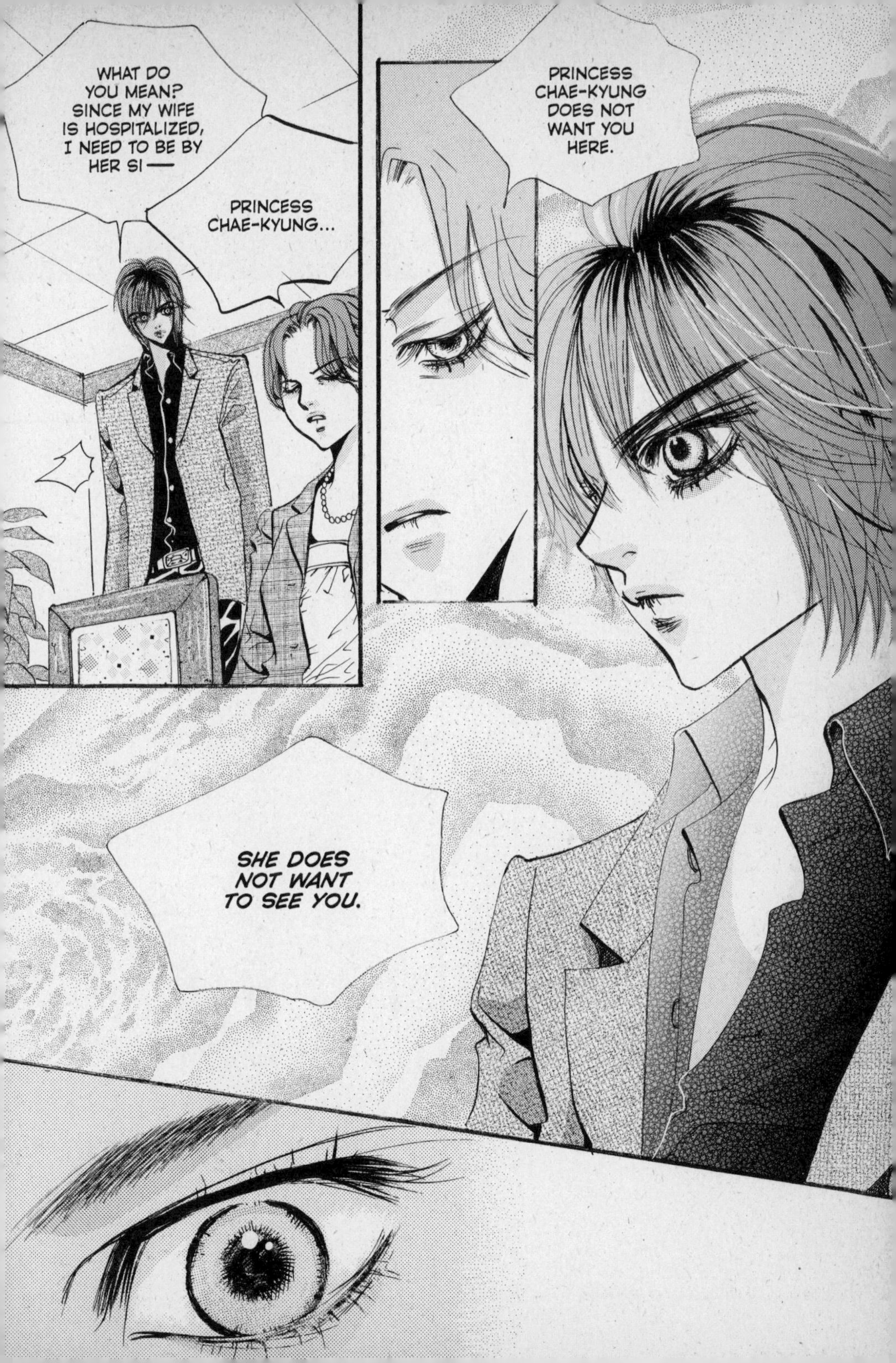
WHAT DO YOU MEAN? SINCE MY WIFE IS HOSPITALIZED, I NEED TO BE BY HER SI—
PRINCESS CHAE-KYUNG...
PRINCESS CHAE-KYUNG DOES NOT WANT YOU HERE.
SHE DOES NOT WANT TO SEE YOU.

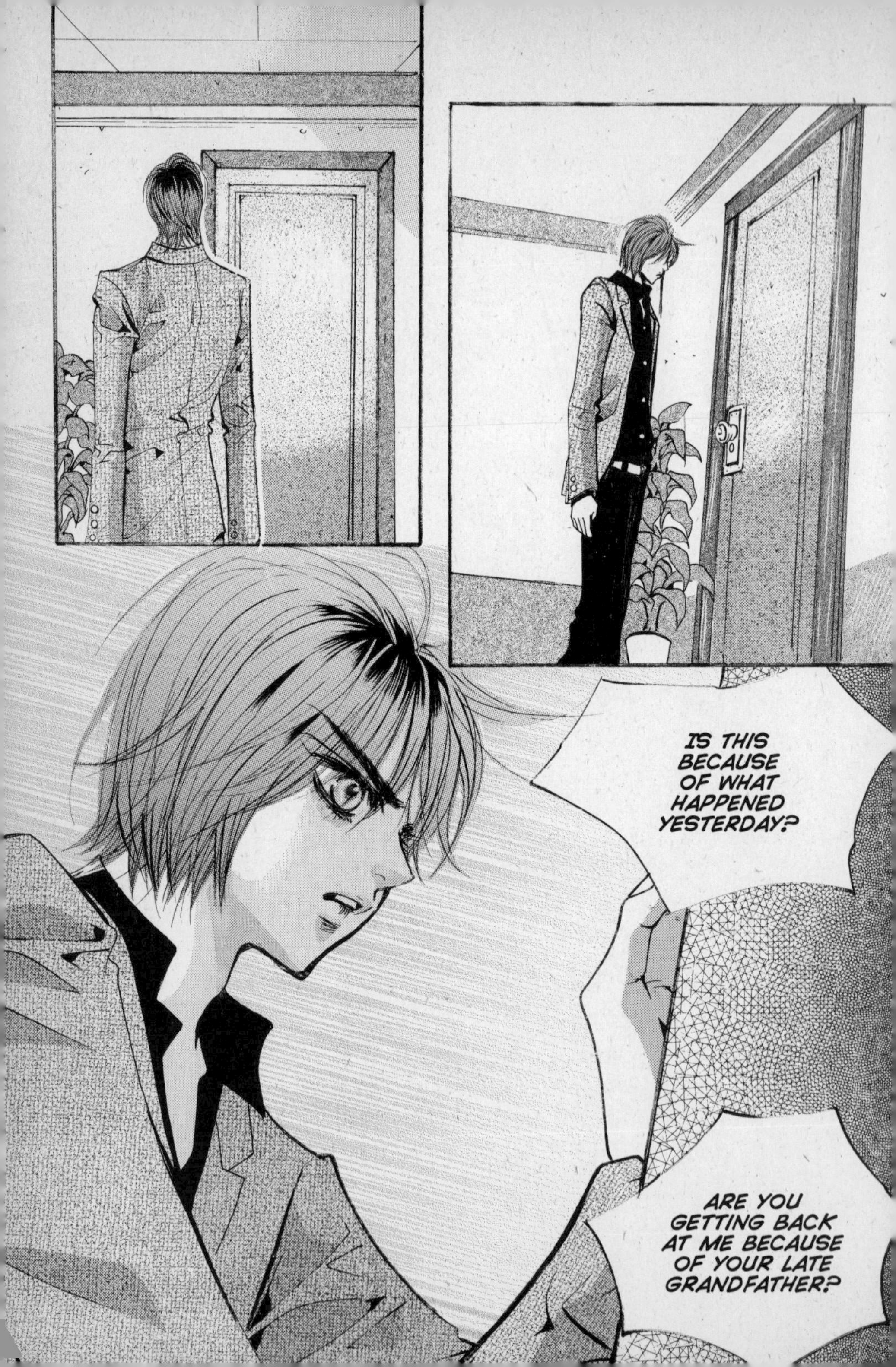
IS THIS BECAUSE OF WHAT HAPPENED YESTERDAY?
ARE YOU GETTING BACK AT ME BECAUSE OF YOUR LATE GRANDFATHER?

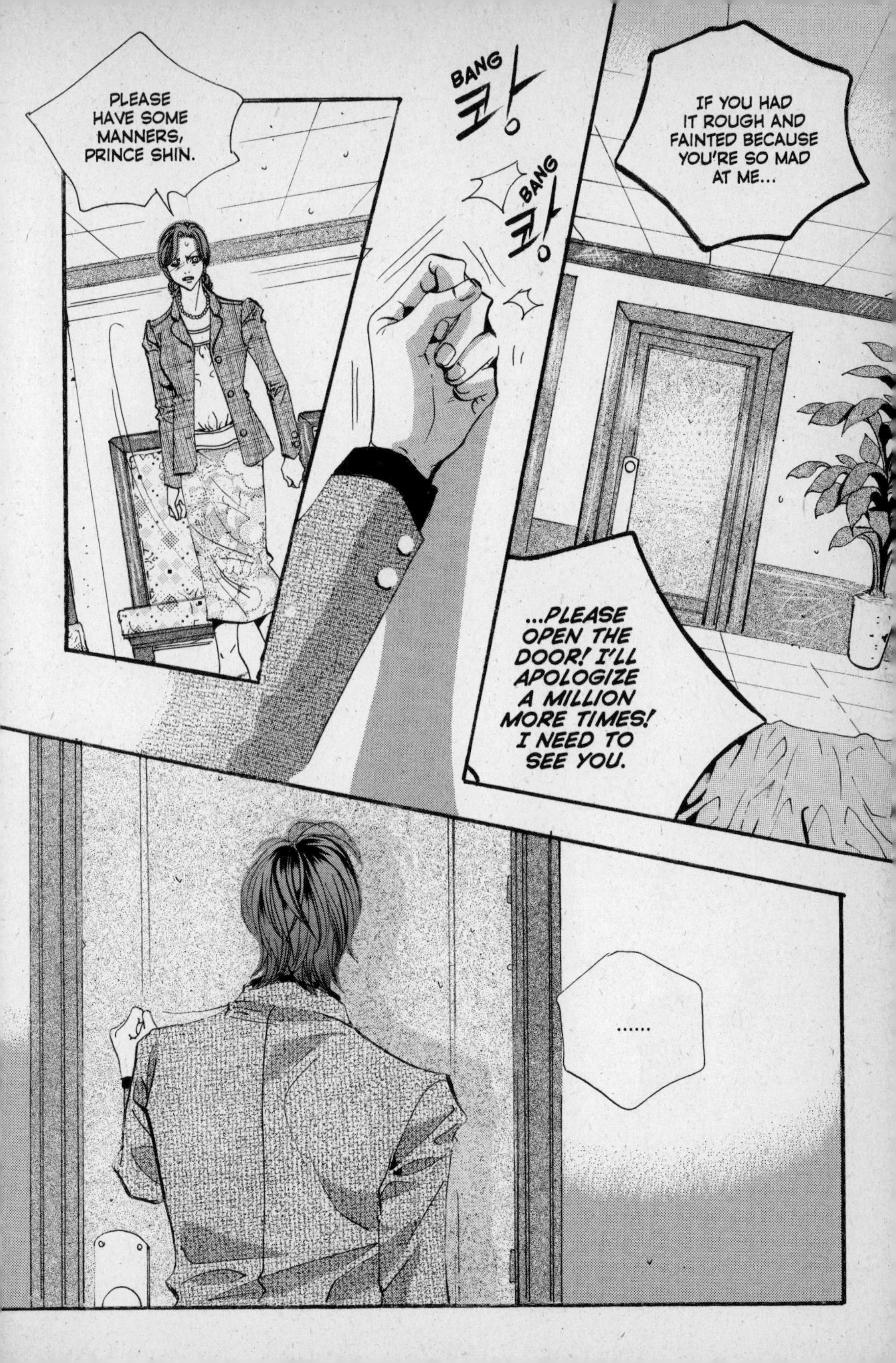
PLEASE HAVE SOME MANNERS, PRINCE SHIN.
BANG
쾅
BANG
쾅
IF YOU HAD IT ROUGH AND FAINTED BECAUSE YOU'RE SO MAD AT ME...
...PLEASE OPEN THE DOOR! I'LL APOLOGIZE A MILLION MORE TIMES! I NEED TO SEE YOU.
......

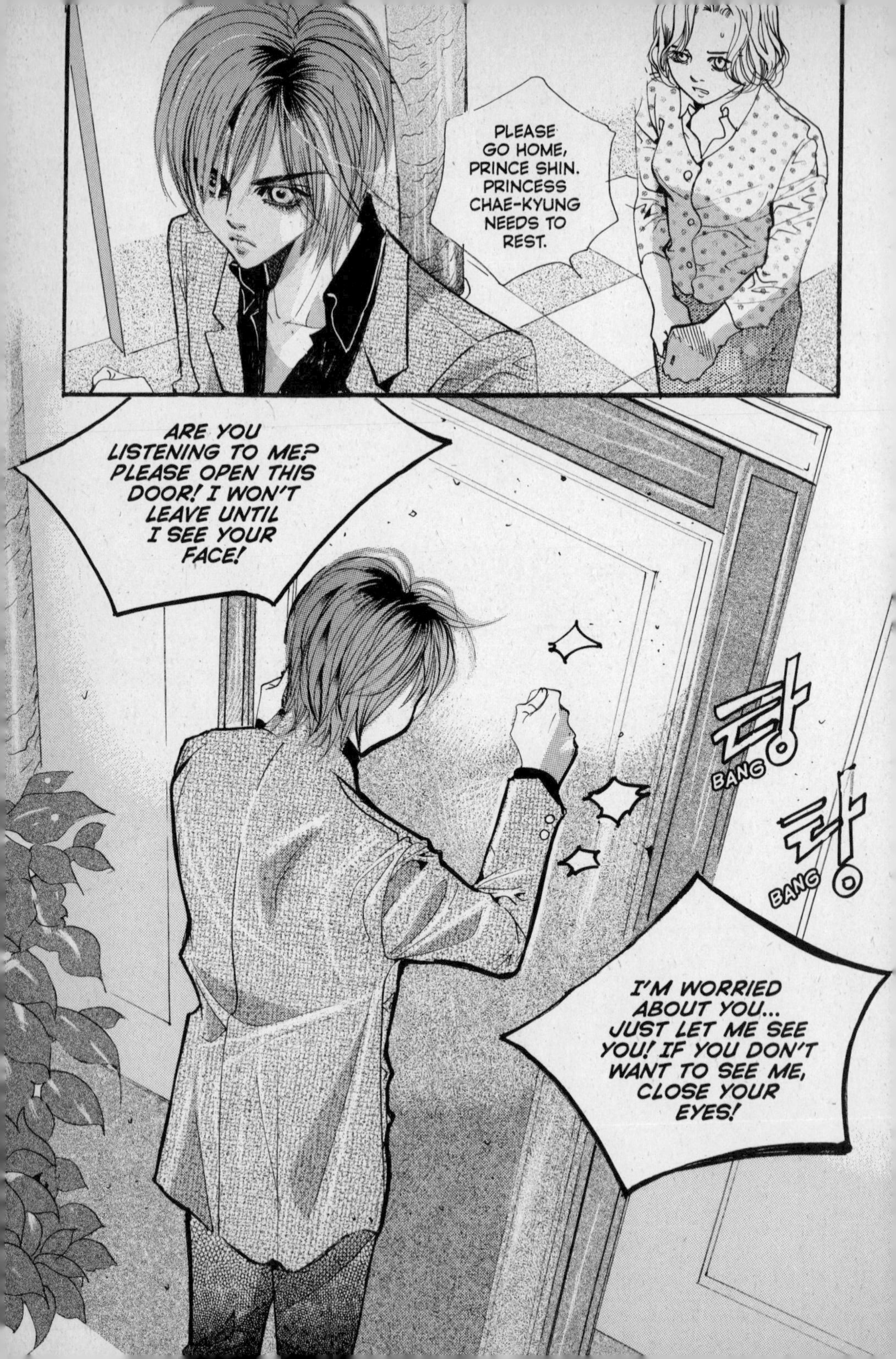
PLEASE GO HOME, PRINCE SHIN. PRINCESS CHAE-KYUNG NEEDS TO REST.
ARE YOU LISTENING TO ME? PLEASE OPEN THIS DOOR! I WON'T LEAVE UNTIL I SEE YOUR FACE!
쾅 BANG
쾅 BANG
I'M WORRIED ABOUT YOU... JUST LET ME SEE YOU! IF YOU DON'T WANT TO SEE ME, CLOSE YOUR EYES!

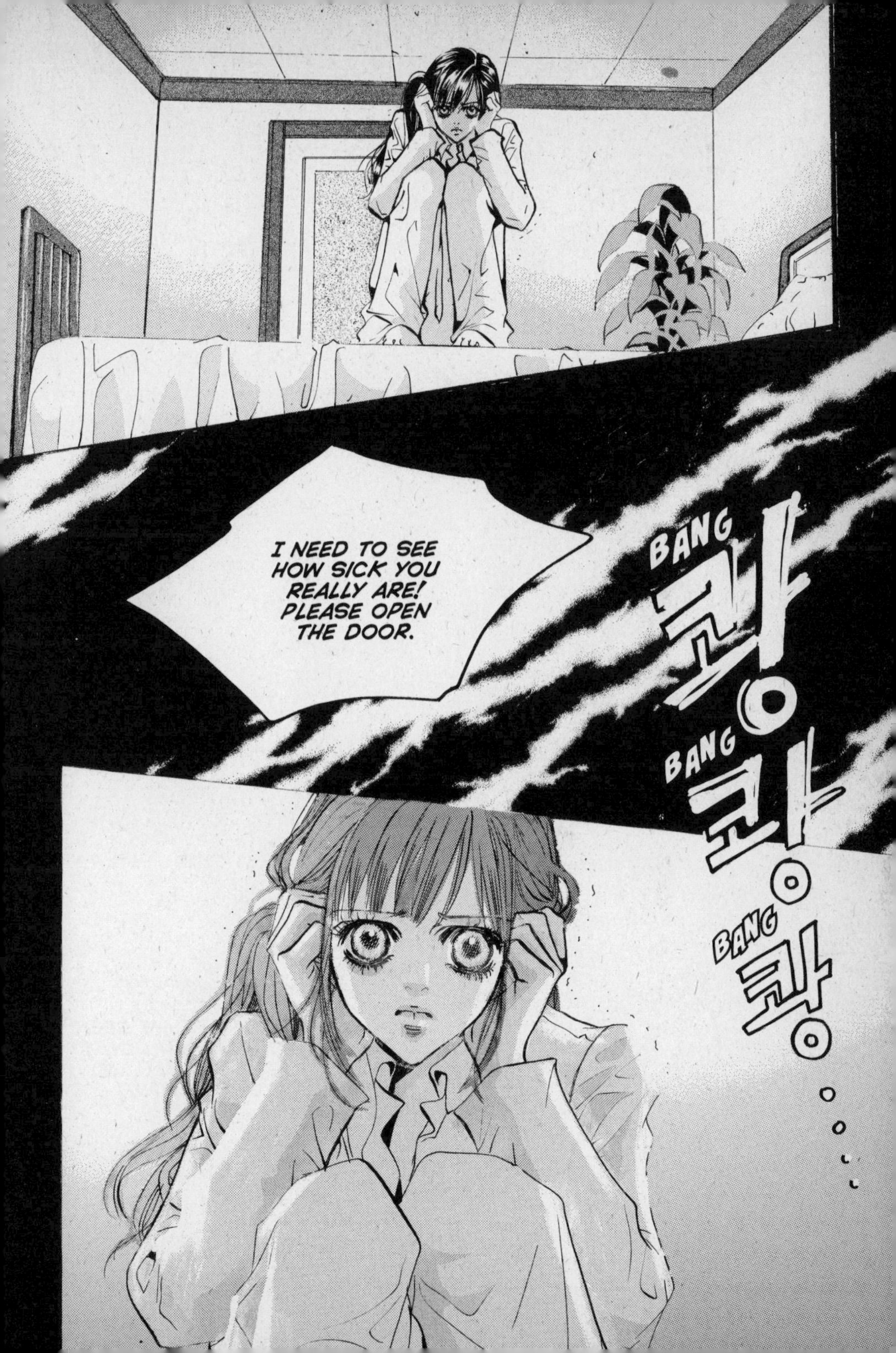
I NEED TO SEE HOW SICK YOU REALLY ARE! PLEASE OPEN THE DOOR.
BANG
쾅
BANG
쾅
BANG
쾅

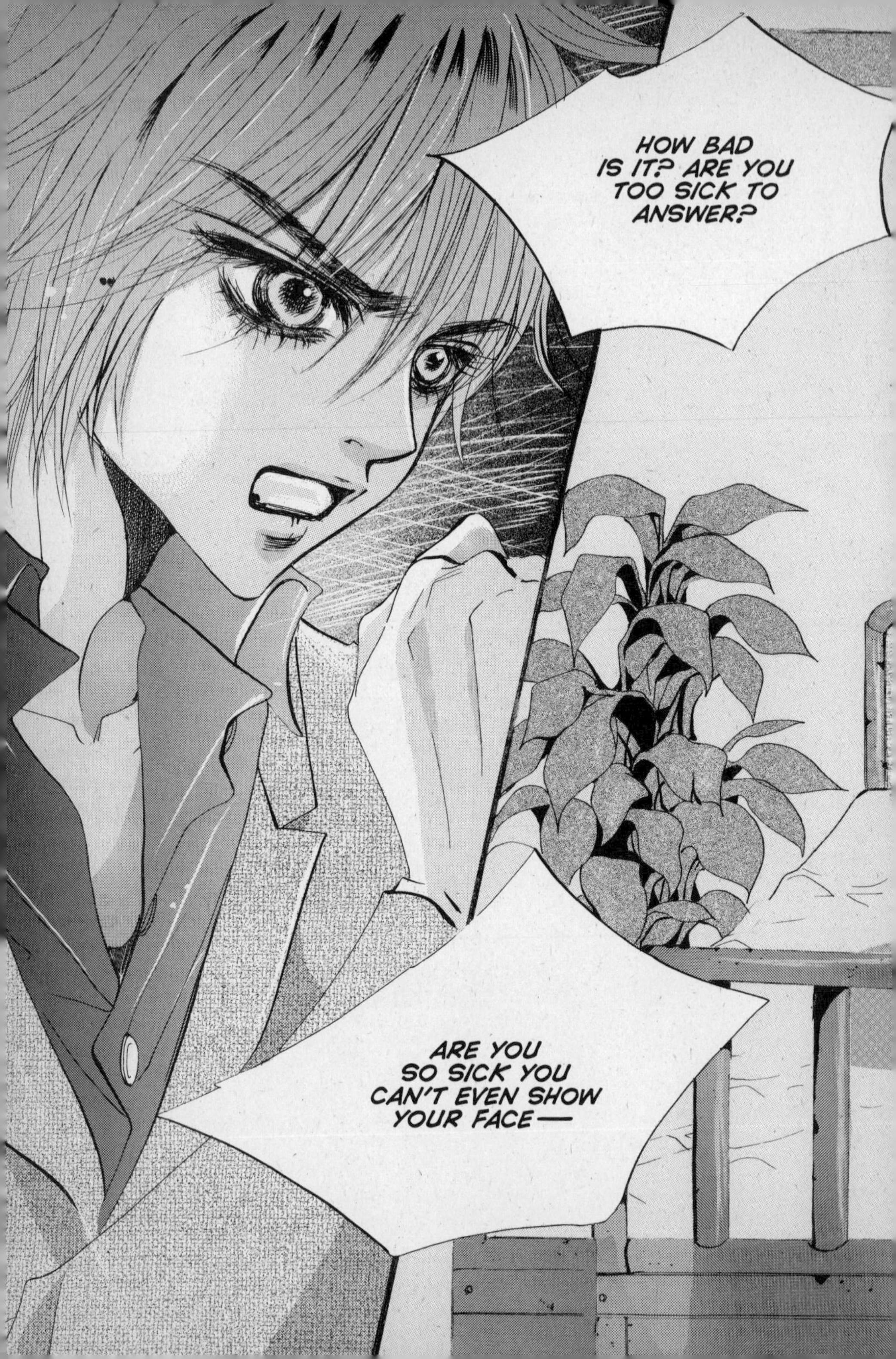
HOW BAD IS IT? ARE YOU TOO SICK TO ANSWER?
ARE YOU SO SICK YOU CAN'T EVEN SHOW YOUR FACE—

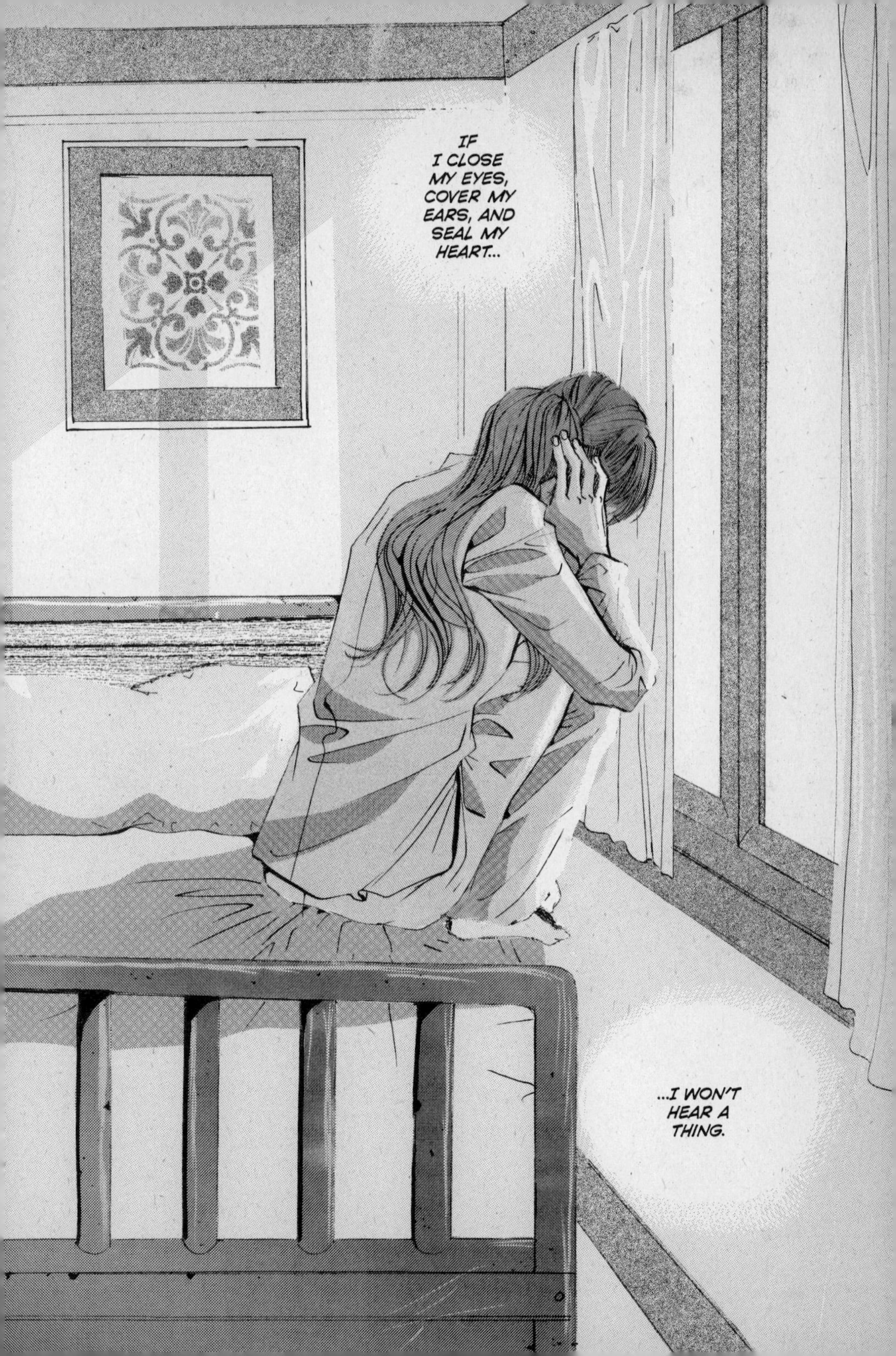
IF I CLOSE MY EYES, COVER MY EARS, AND SEAL MY HEART...
...I WON'T HEAR A THING.

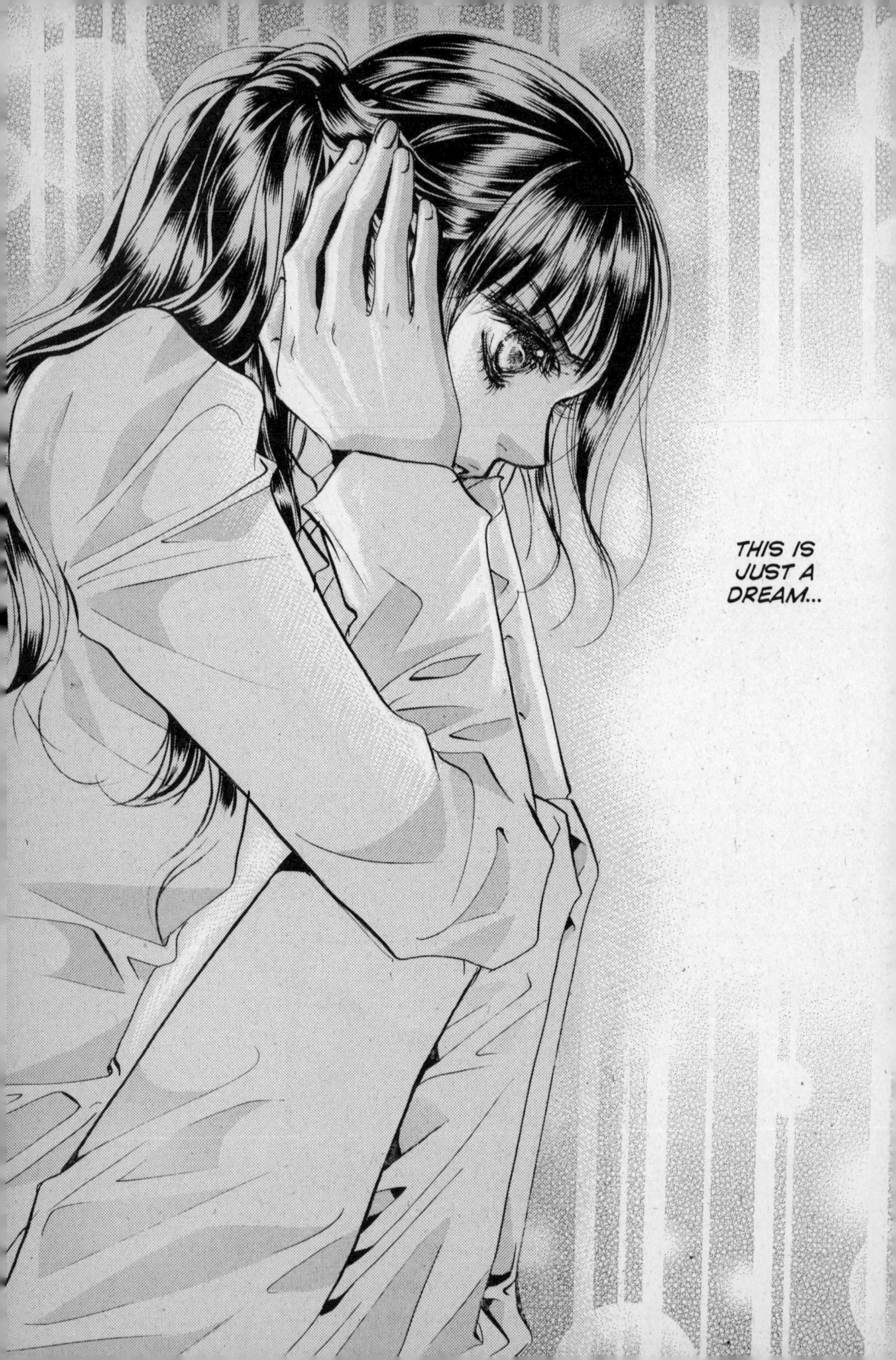
THIS IS JUST A DREAM...

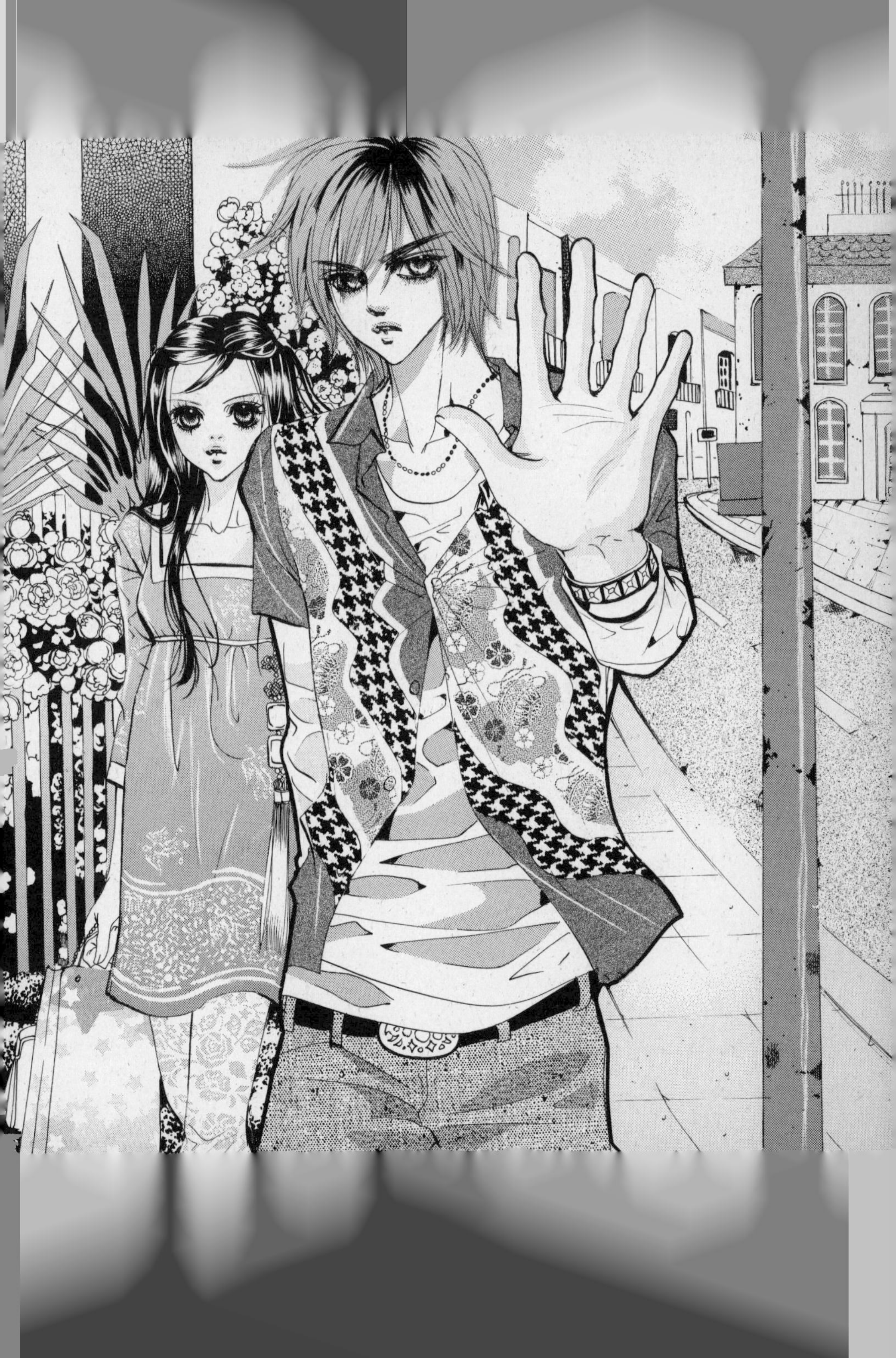

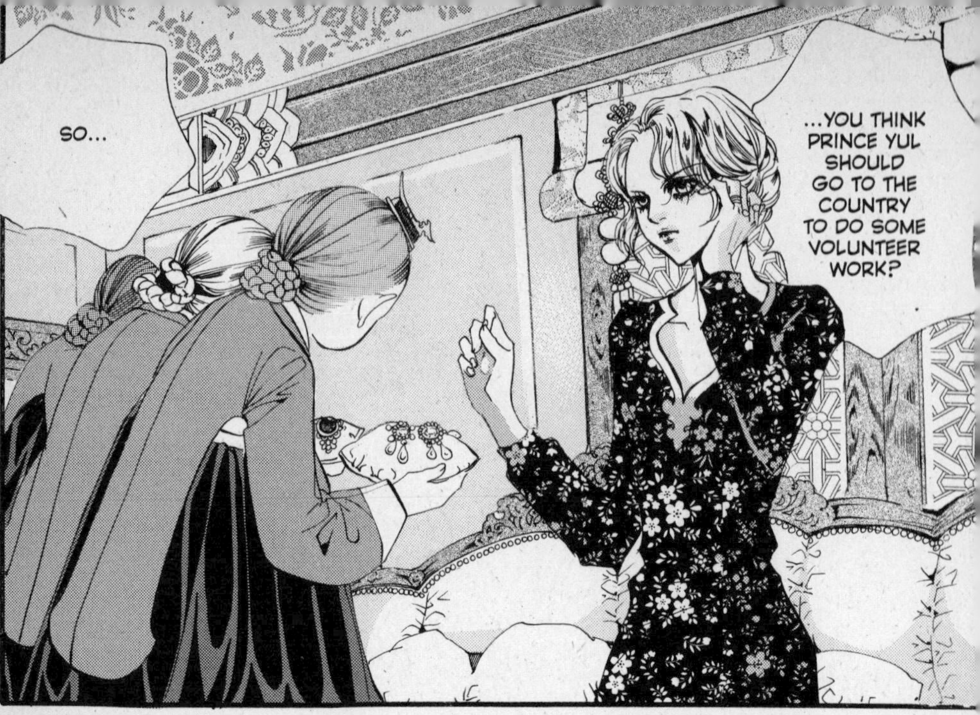
SO...
...YOU THINK PRINCE YUL SHOULD GO TO THE COUNTRY TO DO SOME VOLUNTEER WORK?

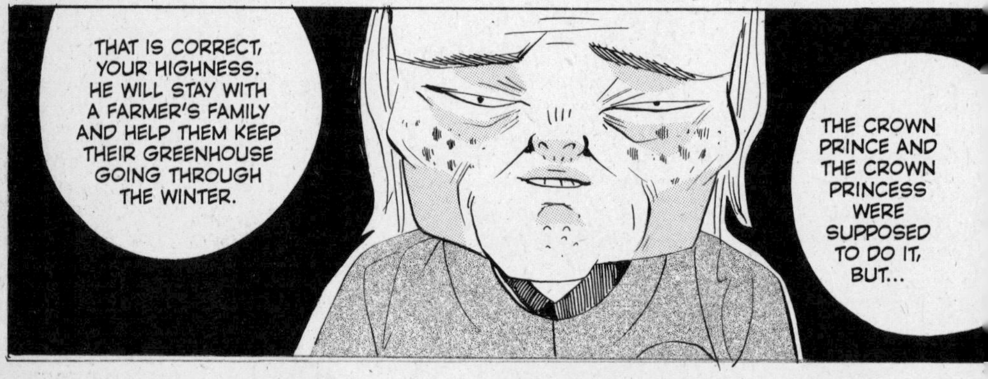
THAT IS CORRECT, YOUR HIGHNESS. HE WILL STAY WITH A FARMER'S FAMILY AND HELP THEM KEEP THEIR GREENHOUSE GOING THROUGH THE WINTER.
THE CROWN PRINCE AND THE CROWN PRINCESS WERE SUPPOSED TO DO IT, BUT...

VOLUNTEER WORK FOR THE ROYAL FAMILY

VOLUNTEER WORK IS A DUTY OF EVERY MEMBER OF THE ROYAL FAMILY AS SOON AS THEY ARE BORN. MANY ROYAL FAMILIES SERVE AS PUBLIC REPRESENTATIVES OF CHARITY ORGANIZATIONS. THEY SPEARHEAD VOLUNTEER PROJECTS AND CHARITIES. THE LATE PRINCESS DIANA WAS PARTICULARLY WELL-KNOWN FOR HER CHARITY WORK. SHE DEVOTED HER LIFE TO AIDS RESEARCH AND EDUCATION. THE KOREAN ROYAL FAMILY DOES MANY GOOD THINGS FOR ITS PEOPLE AS WELL, SUCH AS HELPING OUT IN RURAL COMMUNITIES, ORPHANAGES, AND NURSING HOMES. THEY ALSO RAISE MONEY THROUGH CHARITY AUCTIONS.

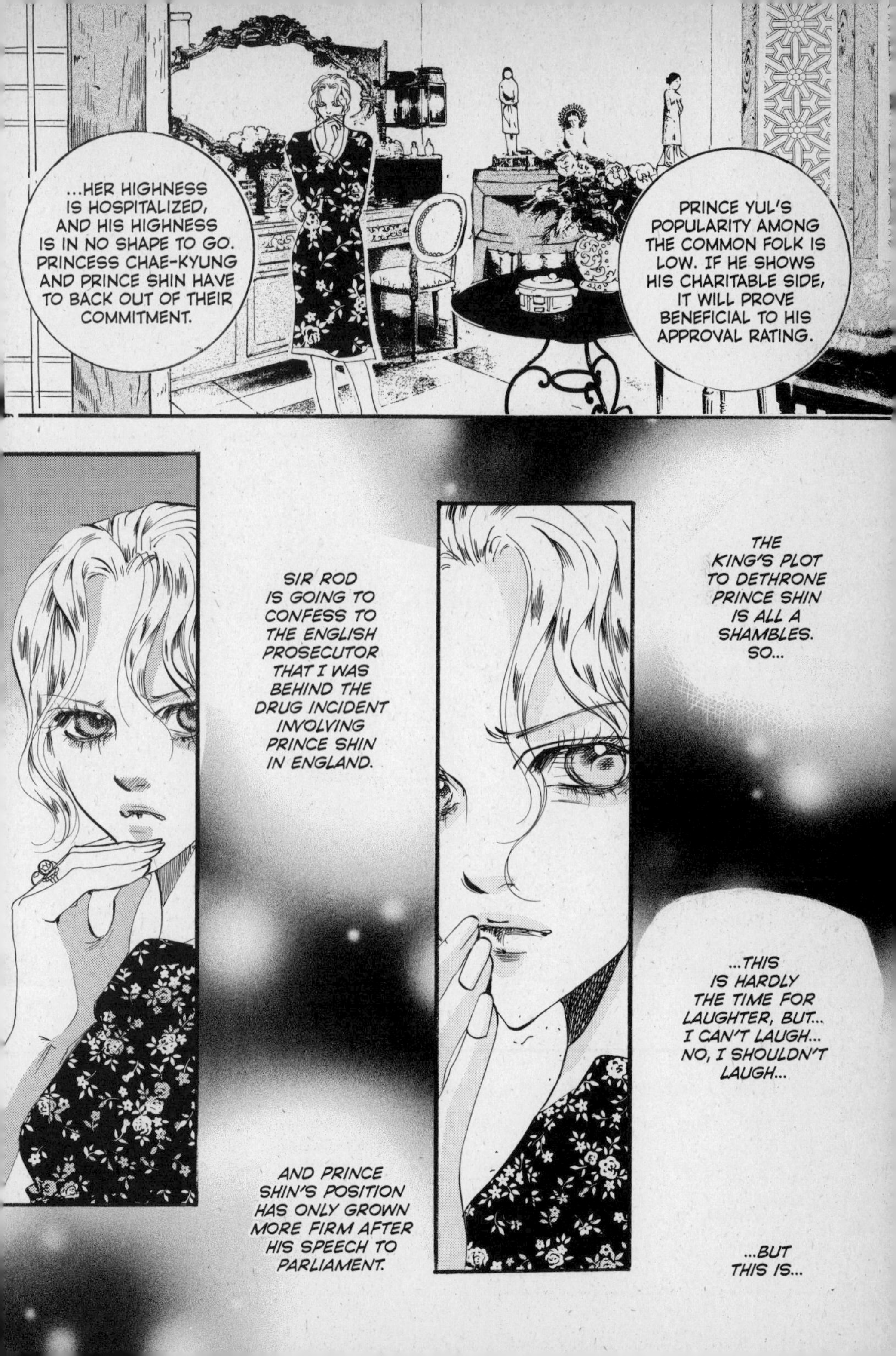
...HER HIGHNESS IS HOSPITALIZED, AND HIS HIGHNESS IS IN NO SHAPE TO GO. PRINCESS CHAE-KYUNG AND PRINCE SHIN HAVE TO BACK OUT OF THEIR COMMITMENT.
PRINCE YUL'S POPULARITY AMONG THE COMMON FOLK IS LOW. IF HE SHOWS HIS CHARITABLE SIDE, IT WILL PROVE BENEFICIAL TO HIS APPROVAL RATING.
THE KING'S PLOT TO DETHRONE PRINCE SHIN IS ALL A SHAMBLES. SO...
SIR ROD IS GOING TO CONFESS TO THE ENGLISH PROSECUTOR THAT I WAS BEHIND THE DRUG INCIDENT INVOLVING PRINCE SHIN IN ENGLAND.
AND PRINCE SHIN'S POSITION HAS ONLY GROWN MORE FIRM AFTER HIS SPEECH TO PARLIAMENT.
...THIS IS HARDLY THE TIME FOR LAUGHTER, BUT... I CAN'T LAUGH... NO, I SHOULDN'T LAUGH...
...BUT THIS IS...

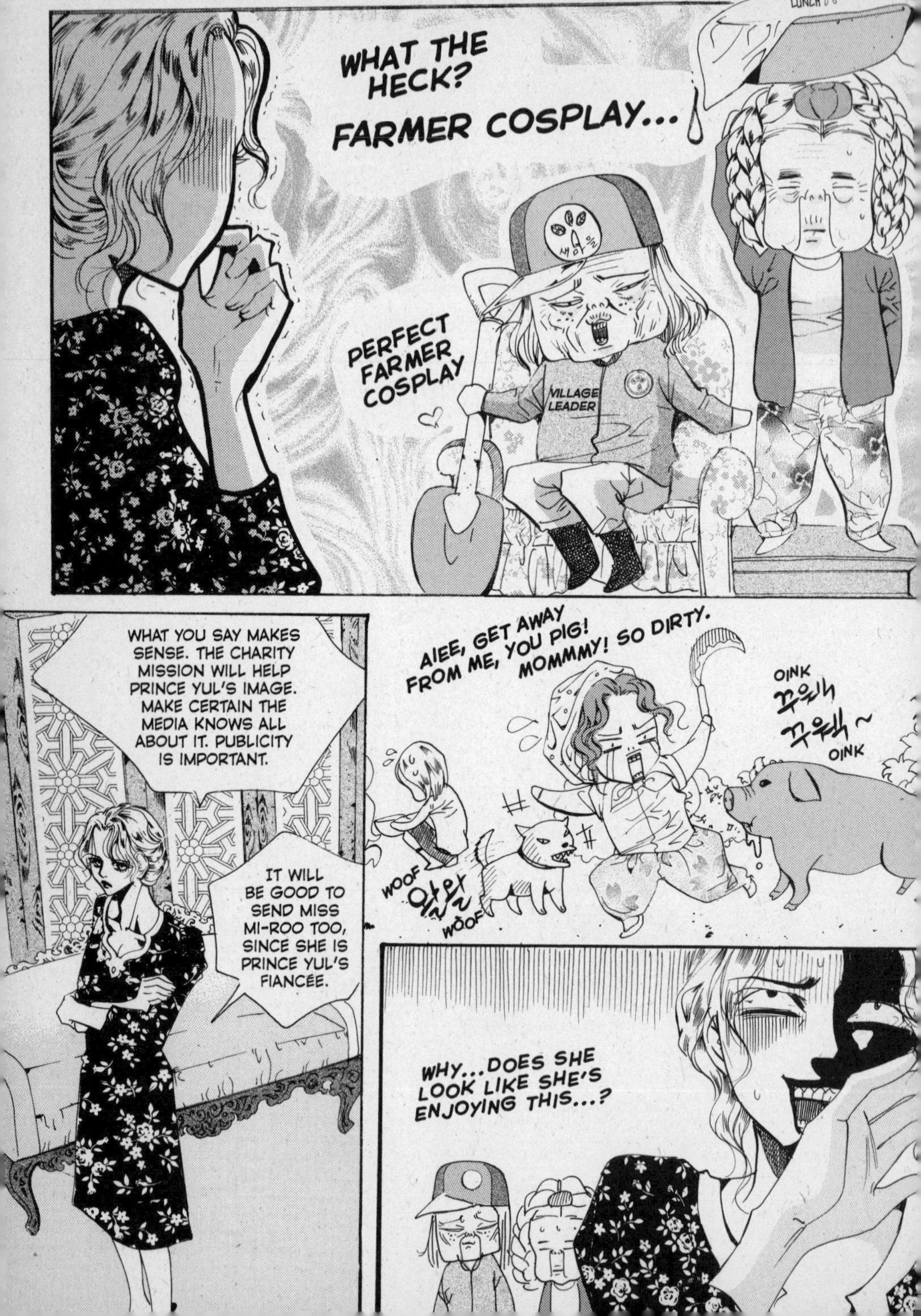

WHAT THE HECK?
FARMER COSPLAY...
LUNCH
PERFECT FARMER COSPLAY
VILLAGE LEADER
WHAT YOU SAY MAKES SENSE. THE CHARITY MISSION WILL HELP PRINCE YUL'S IMAGE. MAKE CERTAIN THE MEDIA KNOWS ALL ABOUT IT. PUBLICITY IS IMPORTANT.
IT WILL BE GOOD TO SEND MISS MI-ROO TOO, SINCE SHE IS PRINCE YUL'S FIANCÉE.
AIEE, GET AWAY FROM ME, YOU PIG! MOMMMY! SO DIRTY.
OINK
OINK
WOOF
WOOF
WHY...DOES SHE LOOK LIKE SHE'S ENJOYING THIS...?

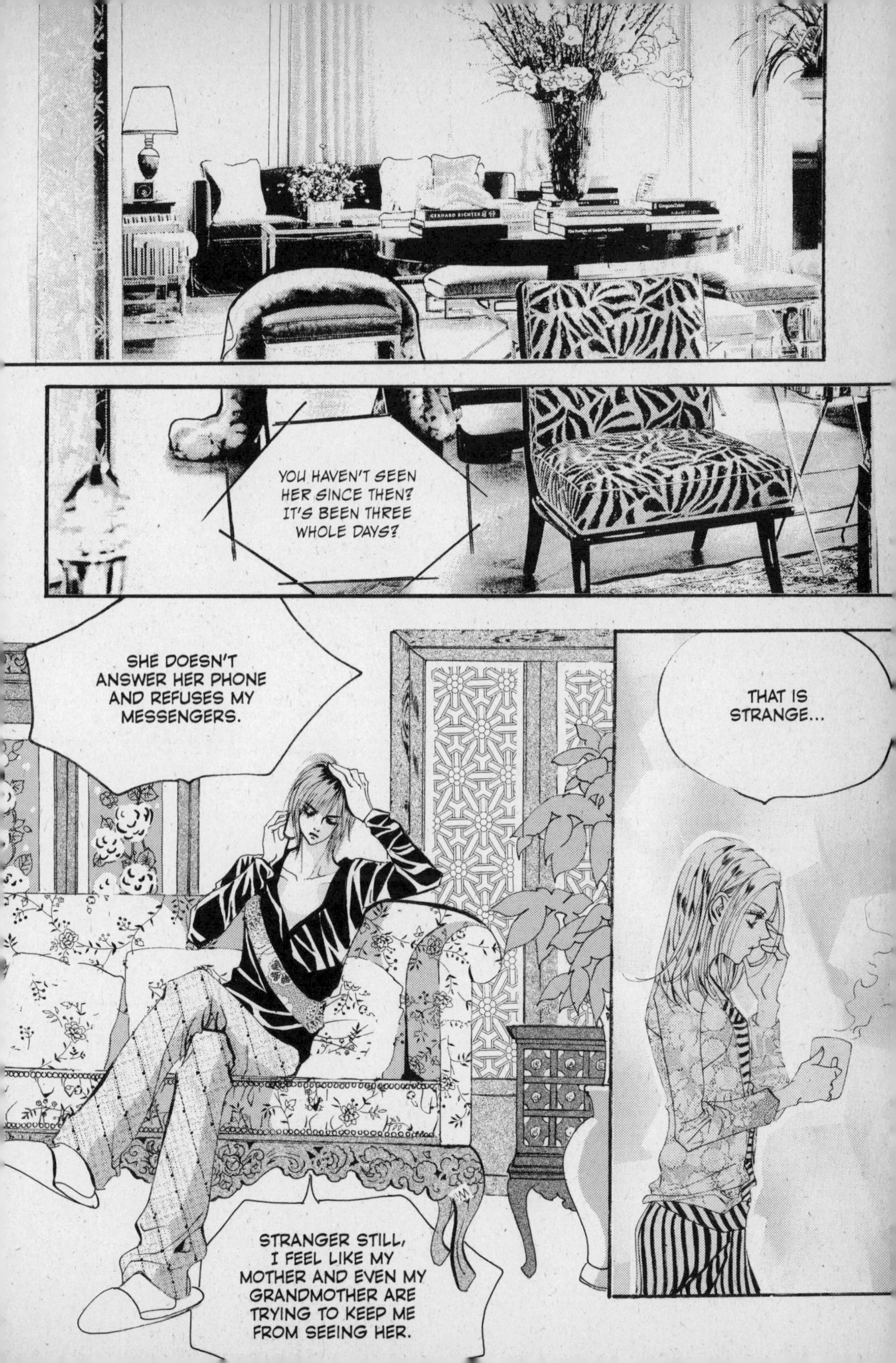

YOU HAVEN'T SEEN HER SINCE THEN? IT'S BEEN THREE WHOLE DAYS?
THAT IS STRANGE...
SHE DOESN'T ANSWER HER PHONE AND REFUSES MY MESSENGERS.
STRANGER STILL, I FEEL LIKE MY MOTHER AND EVEN MY GRANDMOTHER ARE TRYING TO KEEP ME FROM SEEING HER.

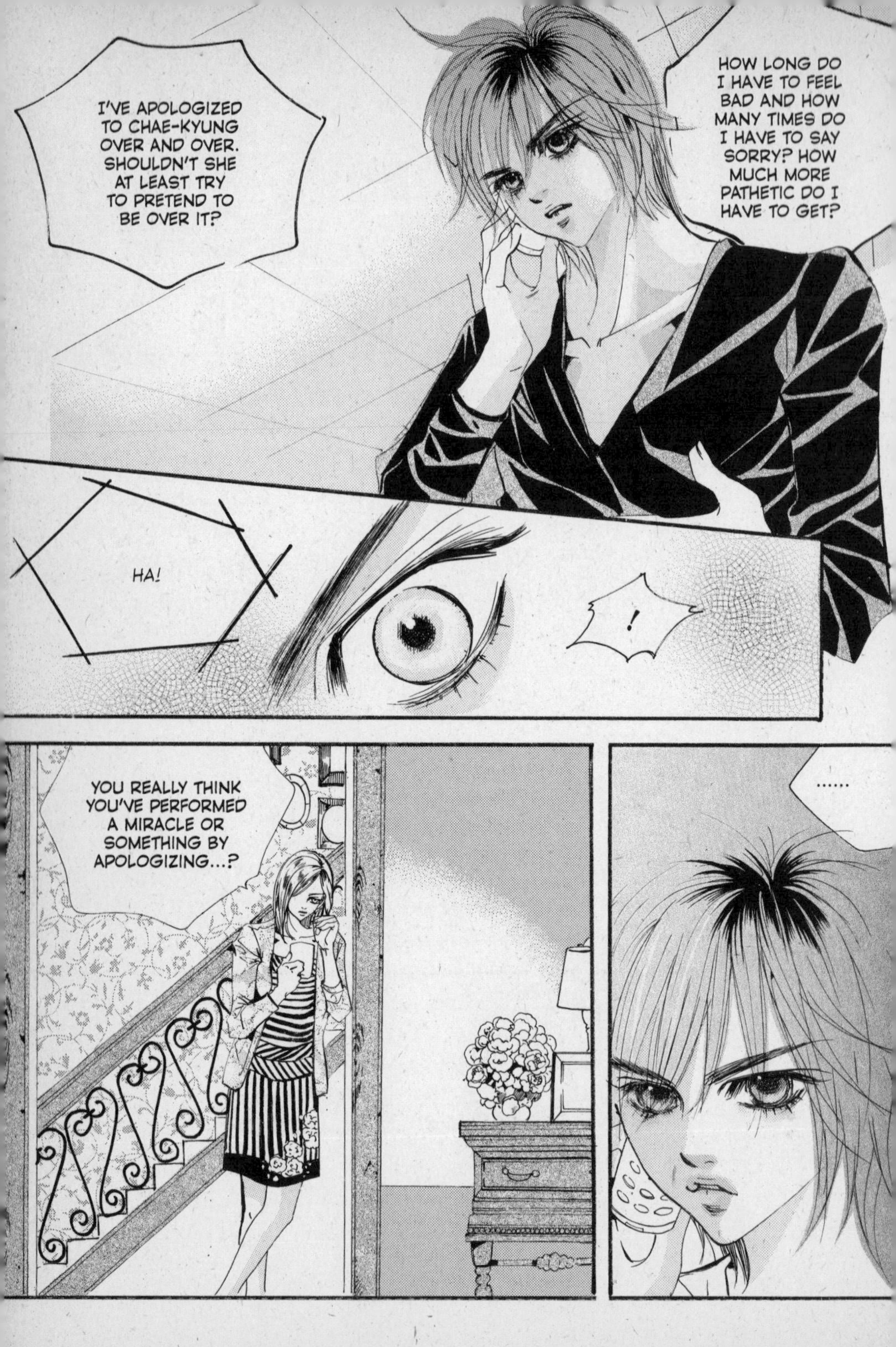
HOW LONG DO I HAVE TO FEEL BAD AND HOW MANY TIMES DO I HAVE TO SAY SORRY? HOW MUCH MORE PATHETIC DO I HAVE TO GET?
I'VE APOLOGIZED TO CHAE-KYUNG OVER AND OVER. SHOULDN'T SHE AT LEAST TRY TO PRETEND TO BE OVER IT?
!
HA!
......
YOU REALLY THINK YOU'VE PERFORMED A MIRACLE OR SOMETHING BY APOLOGIZING...?

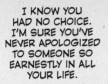

I KNOW YOU HAD NO CHOICE. I'M SURE YOU'VE NEVER APOLOGIZED TO SOMEONE SO EARNESTLY IN ALL YOUR LIFE.

BUT BE IT A HUNDRED MORE TIMES OR A THOUSAND, KEEP SAYING YOU'RE SORRY...

YOU'VE PROBABLY NEVER WRONGED ANYONE THIS BADLY. AND EVEN IF YOU DID, IT WASN'T SOMEONE WHOSE FORGIVENESS YOU WERE SO DESPERATE FOR.

YOU HAVE ONLY YOURSELF TO BLAME FOR WHAT HAPPENED. CHAE-KYUNG CAN'T FORGIVE YOU JUST BECAUSE YOU'RE THE ONE SHE LOVED AND TRUSTED MOST.

DON'T THINK IT'LL ALL GO AWAY JUST BECAUSE CHAE-KYUNG LOVES YOU.

THE OPPOSITE IS TRUE. IT'S GOING TO TAKE LONGER BECAUSE OF THAT.

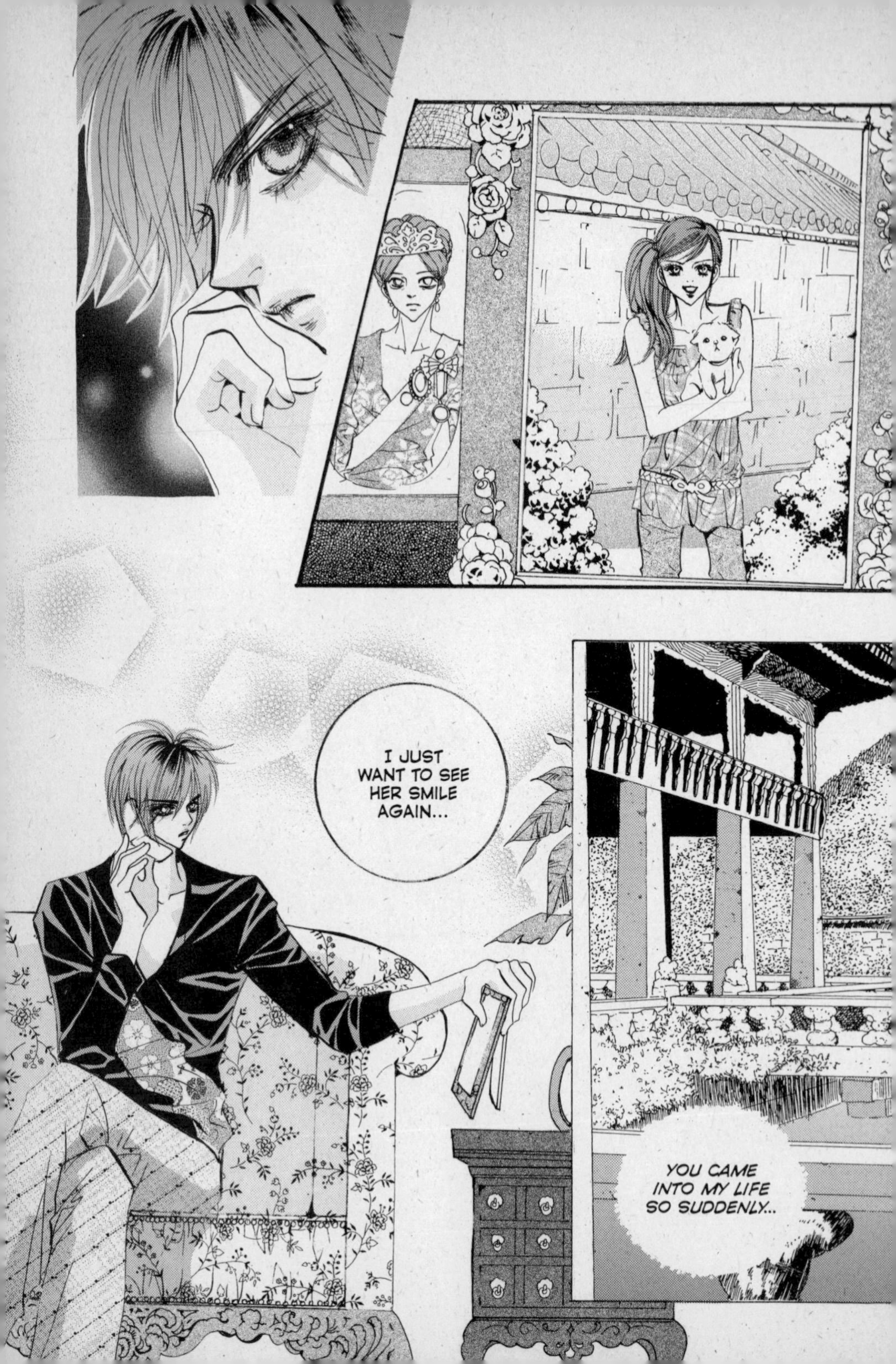
I JUST WANT TO SEE HER SMILE AGAIN...
YOU CAME INTO MY LIFE SO SUDDENLY...

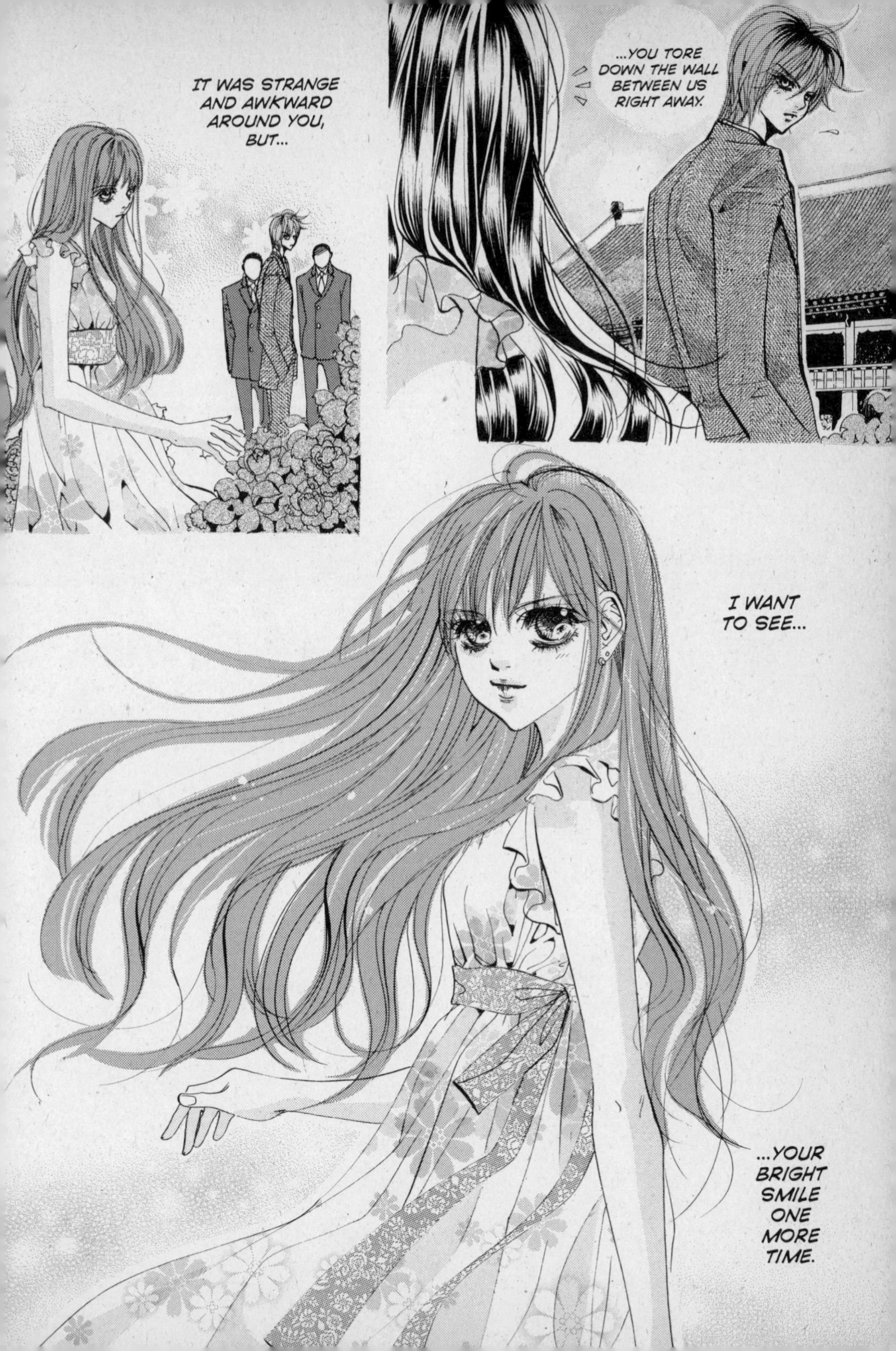
...YOU TORE DOWN THE WALL BETWEEN US RIGHT AWAY.
IT WAS STRANGE AND AWKWARD AROUND YOU, BUT...
I WANT TO SEE...
...YOUR BRIGHT SMILE ONE MORE TIME.

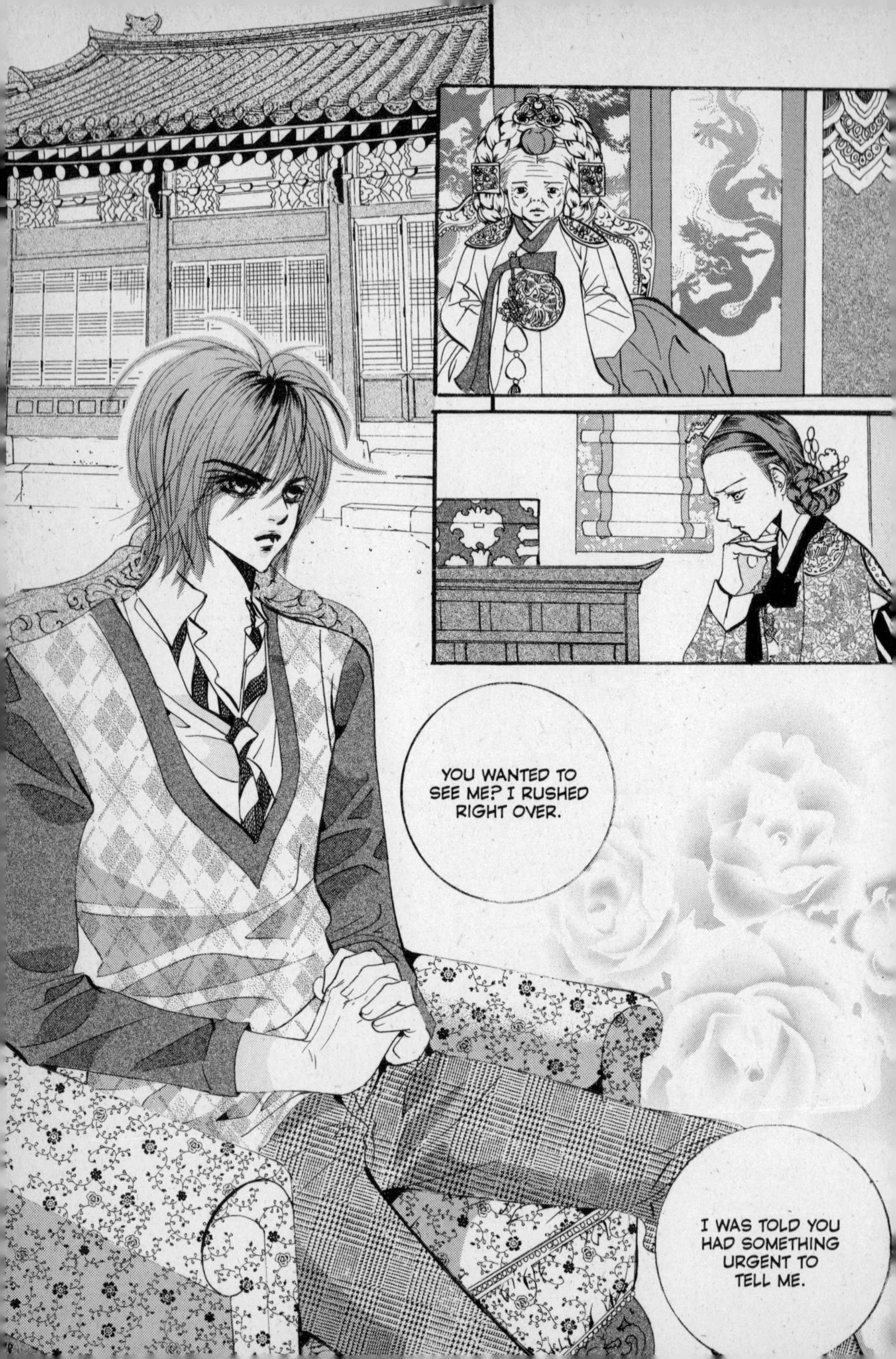
YOU WANTED TO SEE ME? I RUSHED RIGHT OVER.
I WAS TOLD YOU HAD SOMETHING URGENT TO TELL ME.

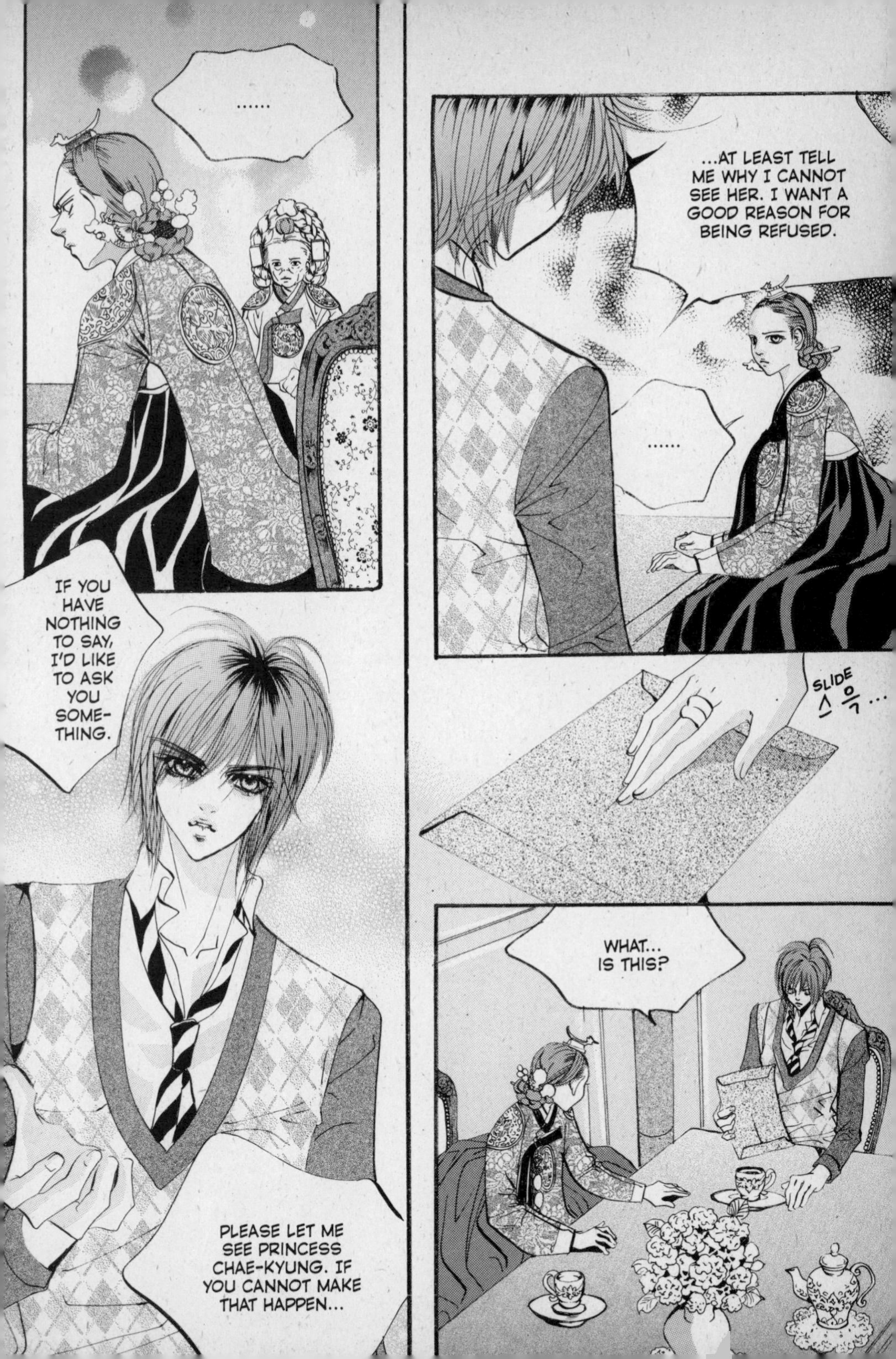
......
IF YOU HAVE NOTHING TO SAY, I'D LIKE TO ASK YOU SOMETHING.
PLEASE LET ME SEE PRINCESS CHAE-KYUNG. IF YOU CANNOT MAKE THAT HAPPEN...
...AT LEAST TELL ME WHY I CANNOT SEE HER. I WANT A GOOD REASON FOR BEING REFUSED.
......
SLIDE
WHAT... IS THIS?

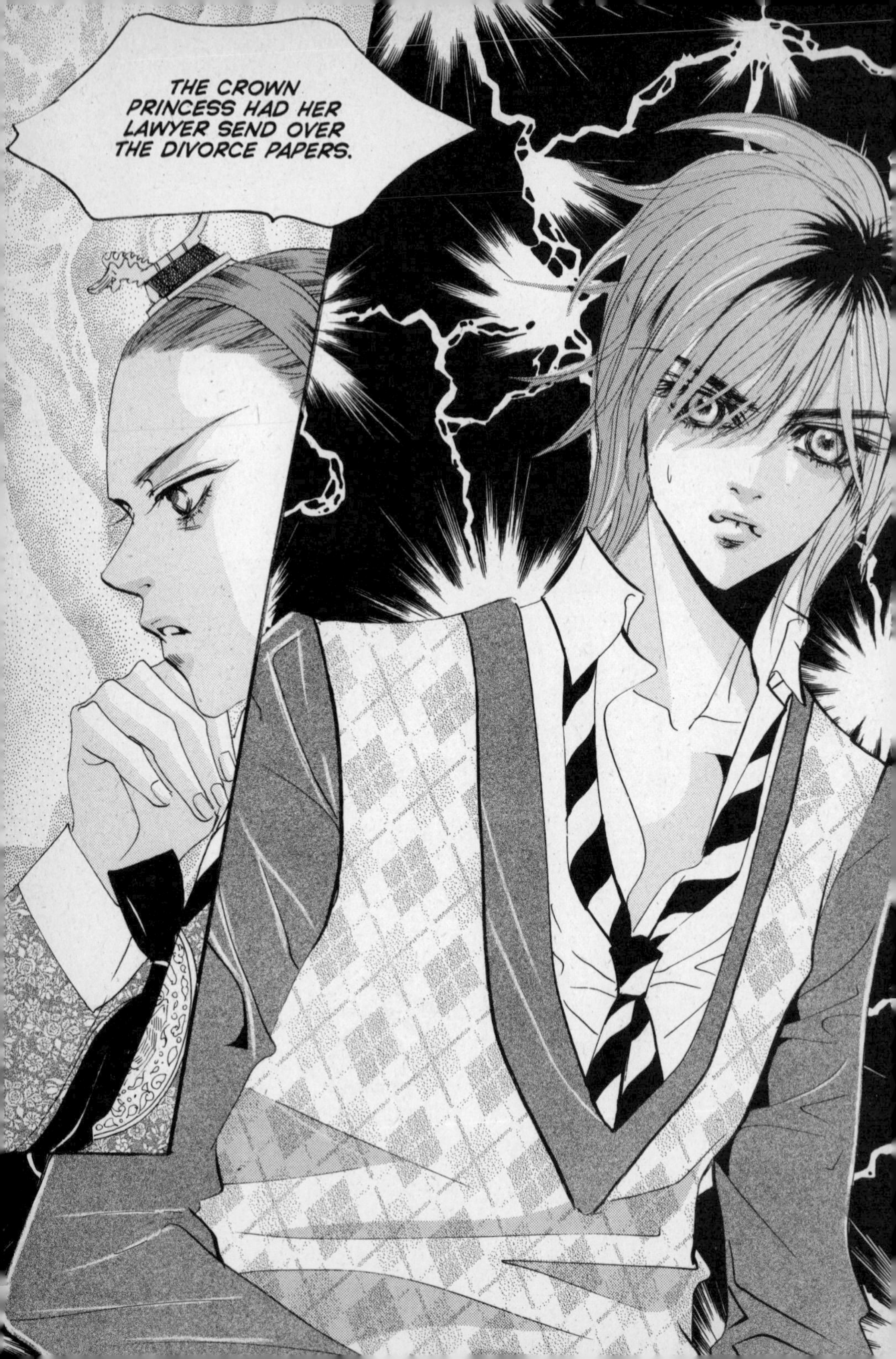
THE CROWN PRINCESS HAD HER LAWYER SEND OVER THE DIVORCE PAPERS.

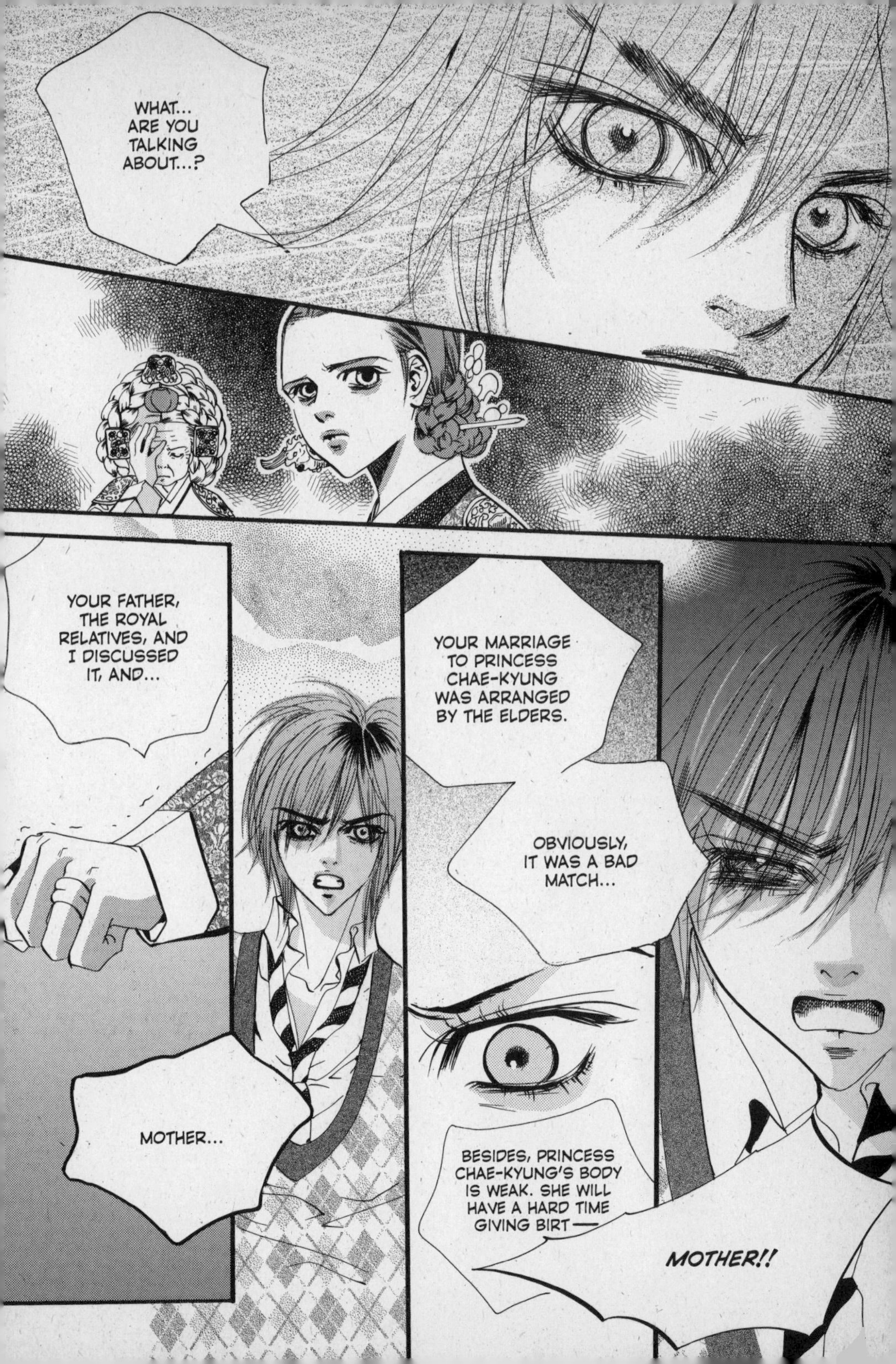
WHAT... ARE YOU TALKING ABOUT...?
YOUR FATHER, THE ROYAL RELATIVES, AND I DISCUSSED IT, AND...
YOUR MARRIAGE TO PRINCESS CHAE-KYUNG WAS ARRANGED BY THE ELDERS.
OBVIOUSLY, IT WAS A BAD MATCH...
MOTHER...
BESIDES, PRINCESS CHAE-KYUNG'S BODY IS WEAK. SHE WILL HAVE A HARD TIME GIVING BIRT—
MOTHER!!

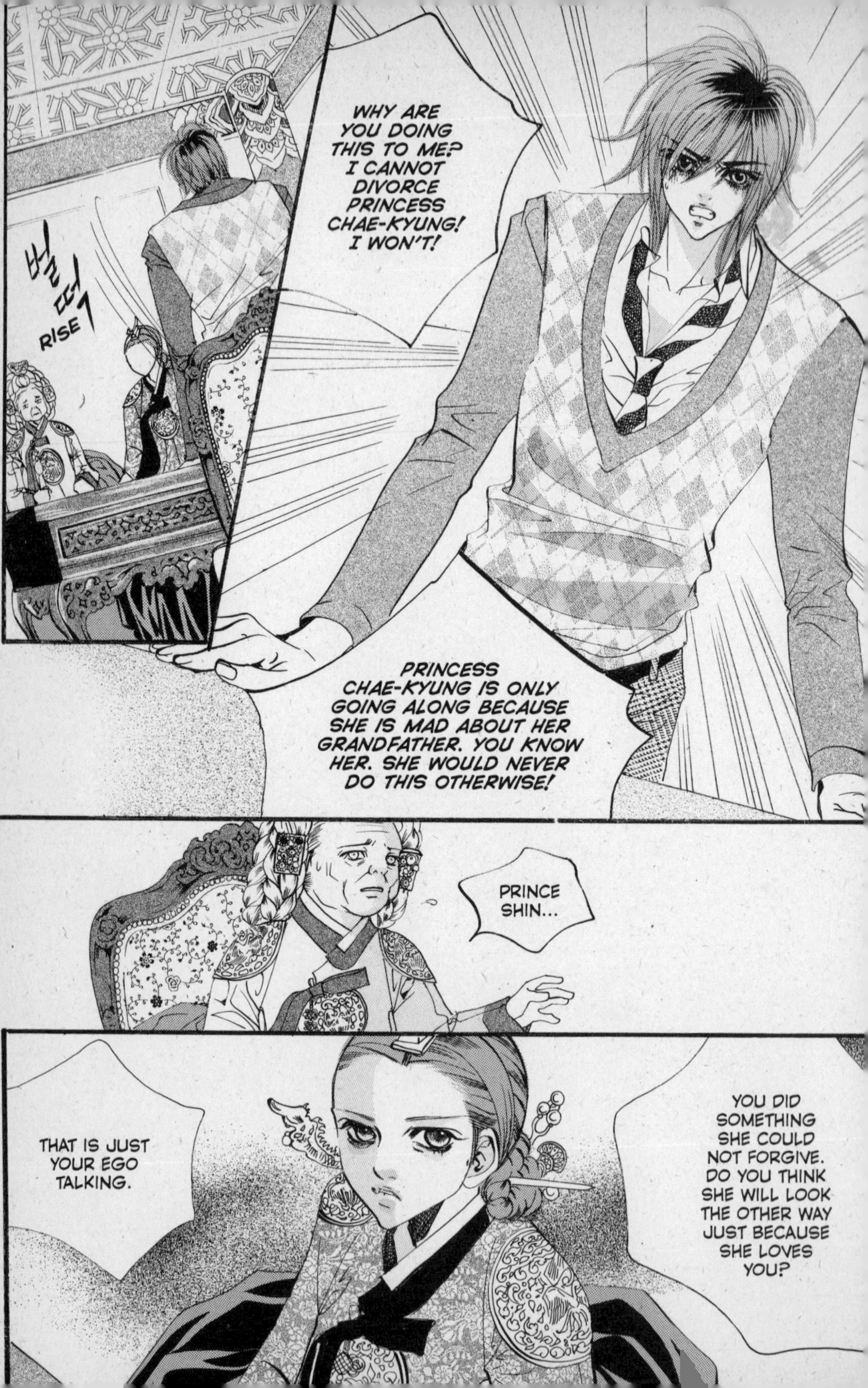
벌떡
RISE
WHY ARE YOU DOING THIS TO ME? I CANNOT DIVORCE PRINCESS CHAE-KYUNG! I WON'T!
PRINCESS CHAE-KYUNG IS ONLY GOING ALONG BECAUSE SHE IS MAD ABOUT HER GRANDFATHER. YOU KNOW HER. SHE WOULD NEVER DO THIS OTHERWISE!
PRINCE SHIN...
THAT IS JUST YOUR EGO TALKING.
YOU DID SOMETHING SHE COULD NOT FORGIVE. DO YOU THINK SHE WILL LOOK THE OTHER WAY JUST BECAUSE SHE LOVES YOU?

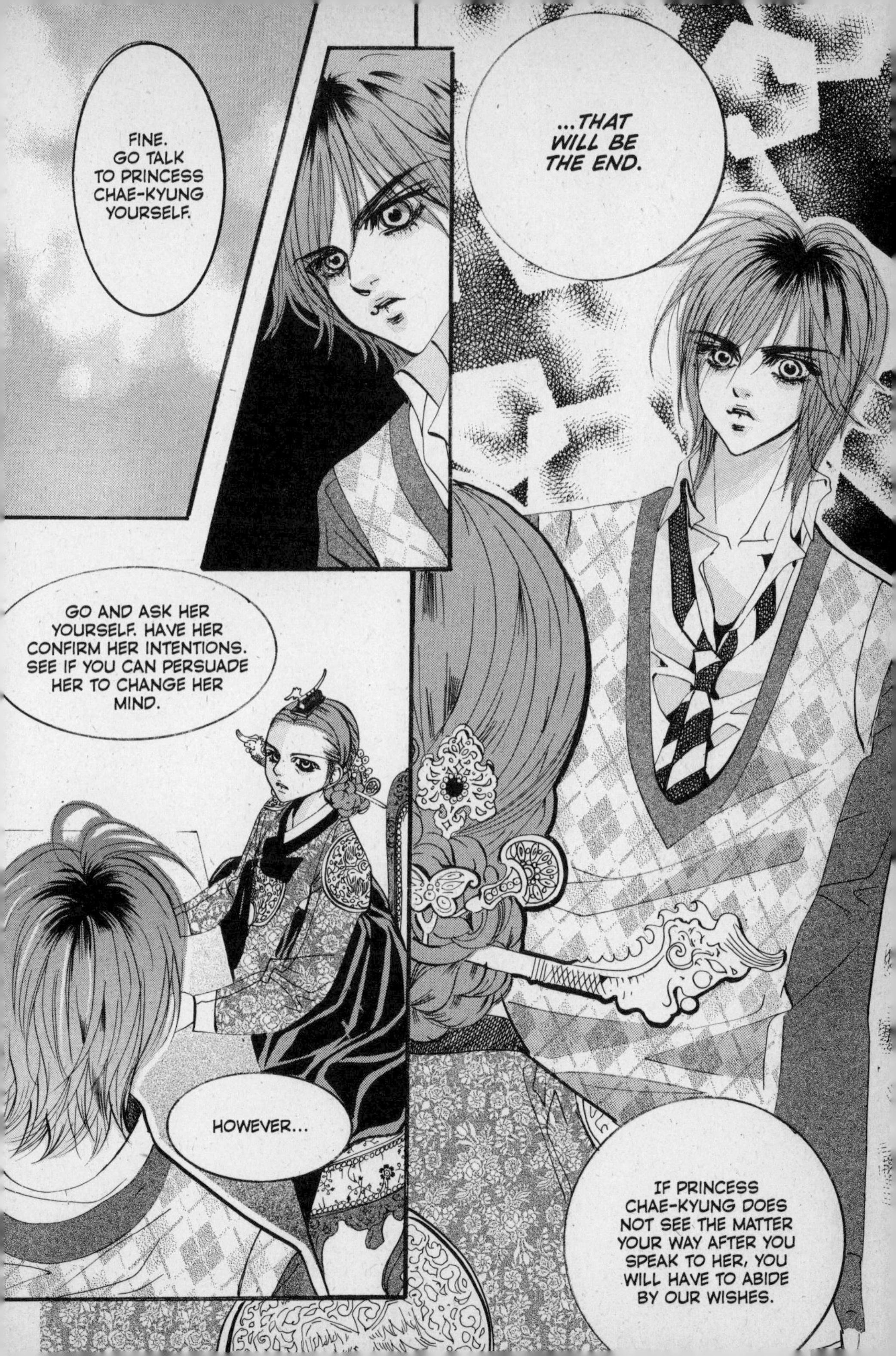
...THAT WILL BE THE END.
FINE. GO TALK TO PRINCESS CHAE-KYUNG YOURSELF.
GO AND ASK HER YOURSELF. HAVE HER CONFIRM HER INTENTIONS. SEE IF YOU CAN PERSUADE HER TO CHANGE HER MIND.
IF PRINCESS CHAE-KYUNG DOES NOT SEE THE MATTER YOUR WAY AFTER YOU SPEAK TO HER, YOU WILL HAVE TO ABIDE BY OUR WISHES.
HOWEVER...

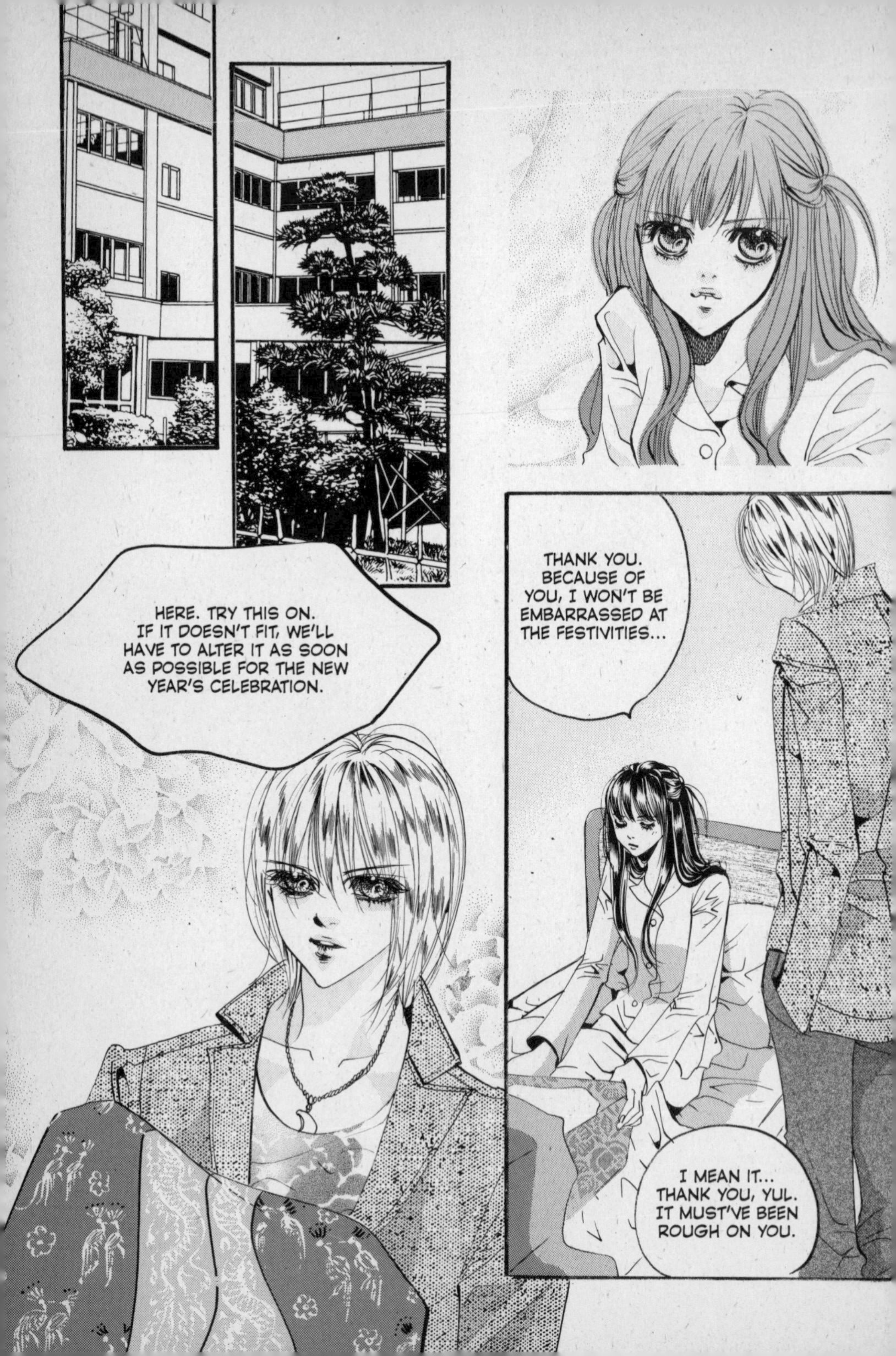
HERE. TRY THIS ON. IF IT DOESN'T FIT, WE'LL HAVE TO ALTER IT AS SOON AS POSSIBLE FOR THE NEW YEAR'S CELEBRATION.
THANK YOU. BECAUSE OF YOU, I WON'T BE EMBARRASSED AT THE FESTIVITIES...
I MEAN IT... THANK YOU, YUL. IT MUST'VE BEEN ROUGH ON YOU.

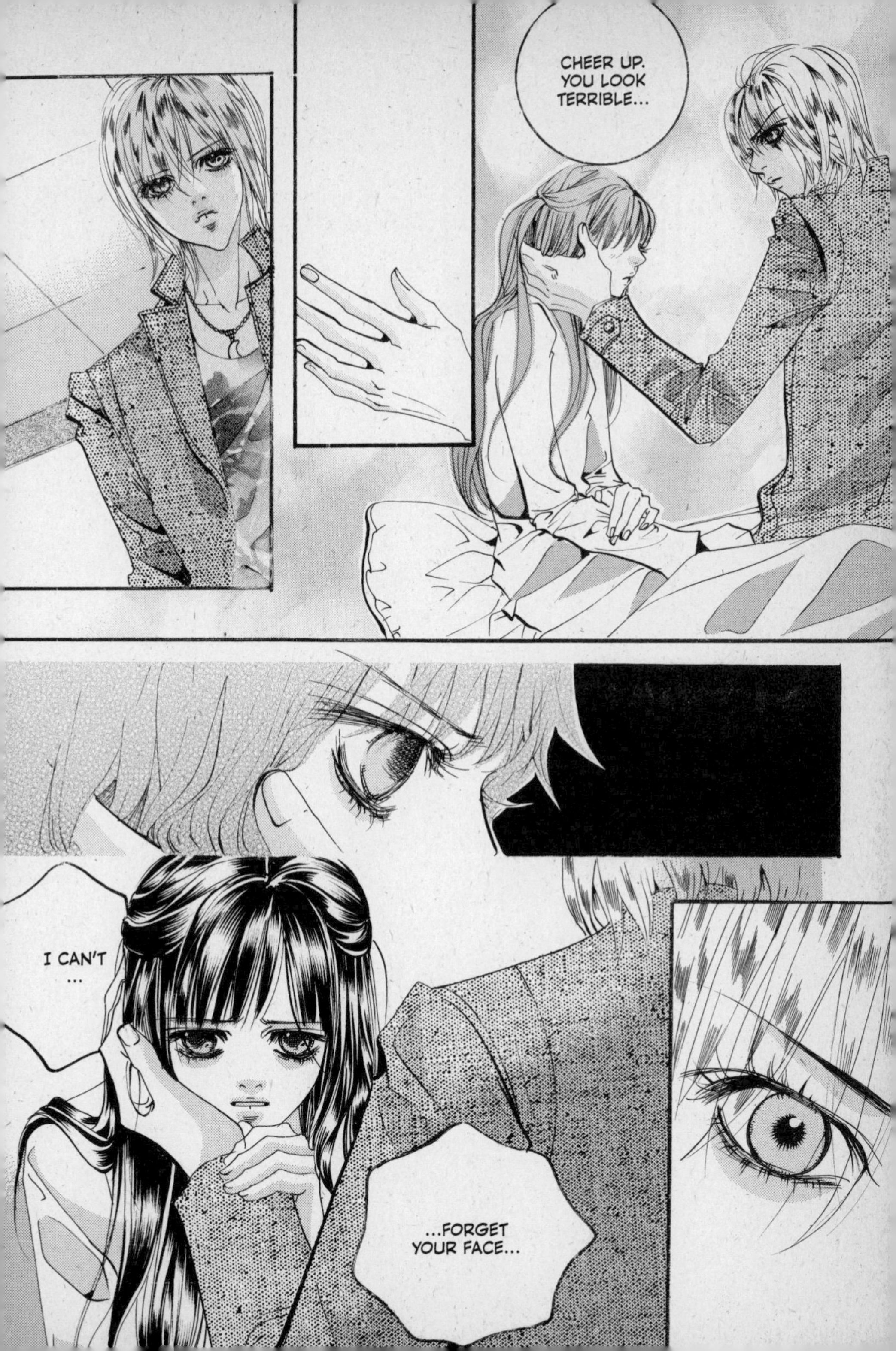
CHEER UP. YOU LOOK TERRIBLE...
I CAN'T ...
...FORGET YOUR FACE...

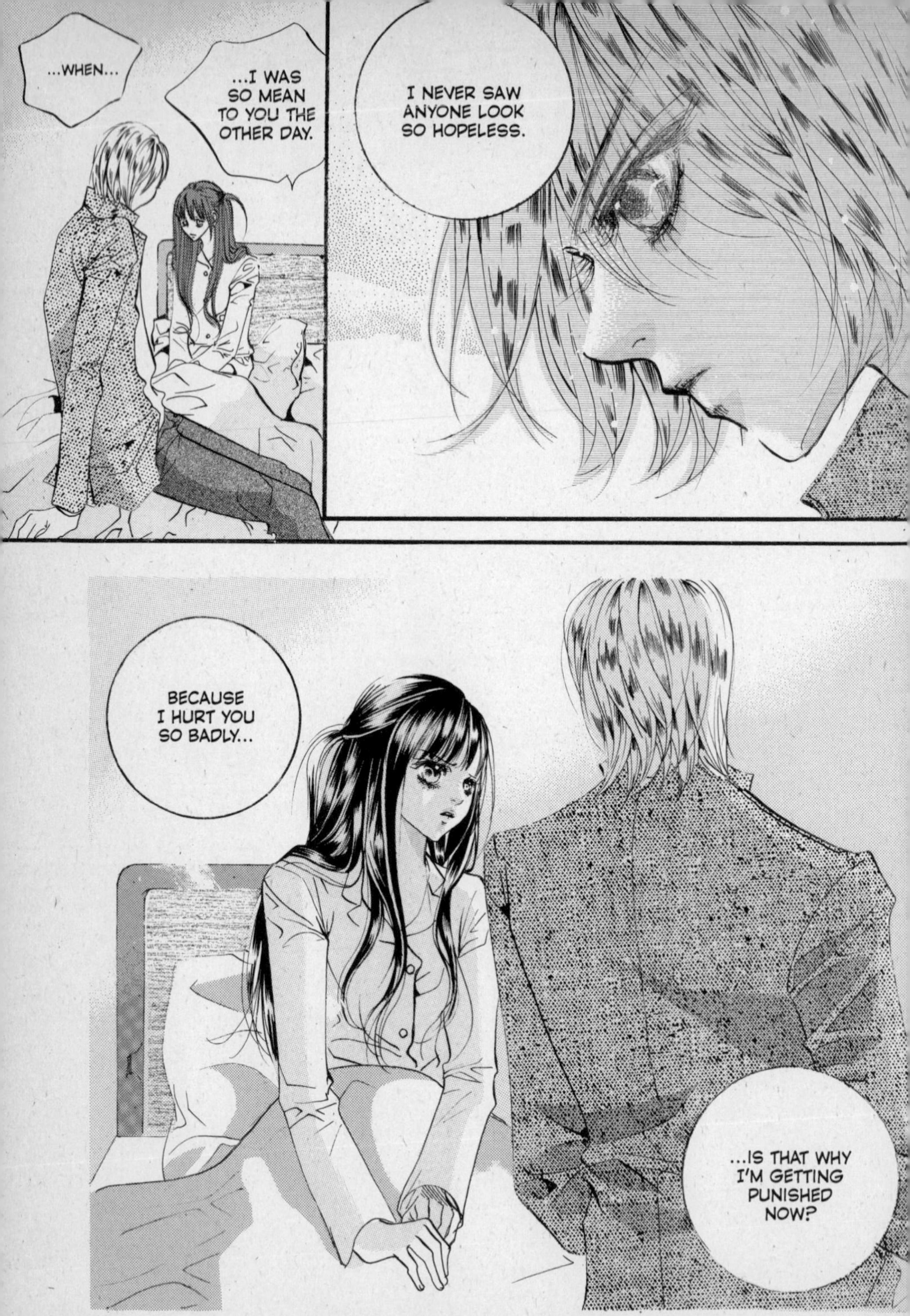
...WHEN...
...I WAS SO MEAN TO YOU THE OTHER DAY.
I NEVER SAW ANYONE LOOK SO HOPELESS.
BECAUSE I HURT YOU SO BADLY...
...IS THAT WHY I'M GETTING PUNISHED NOW?

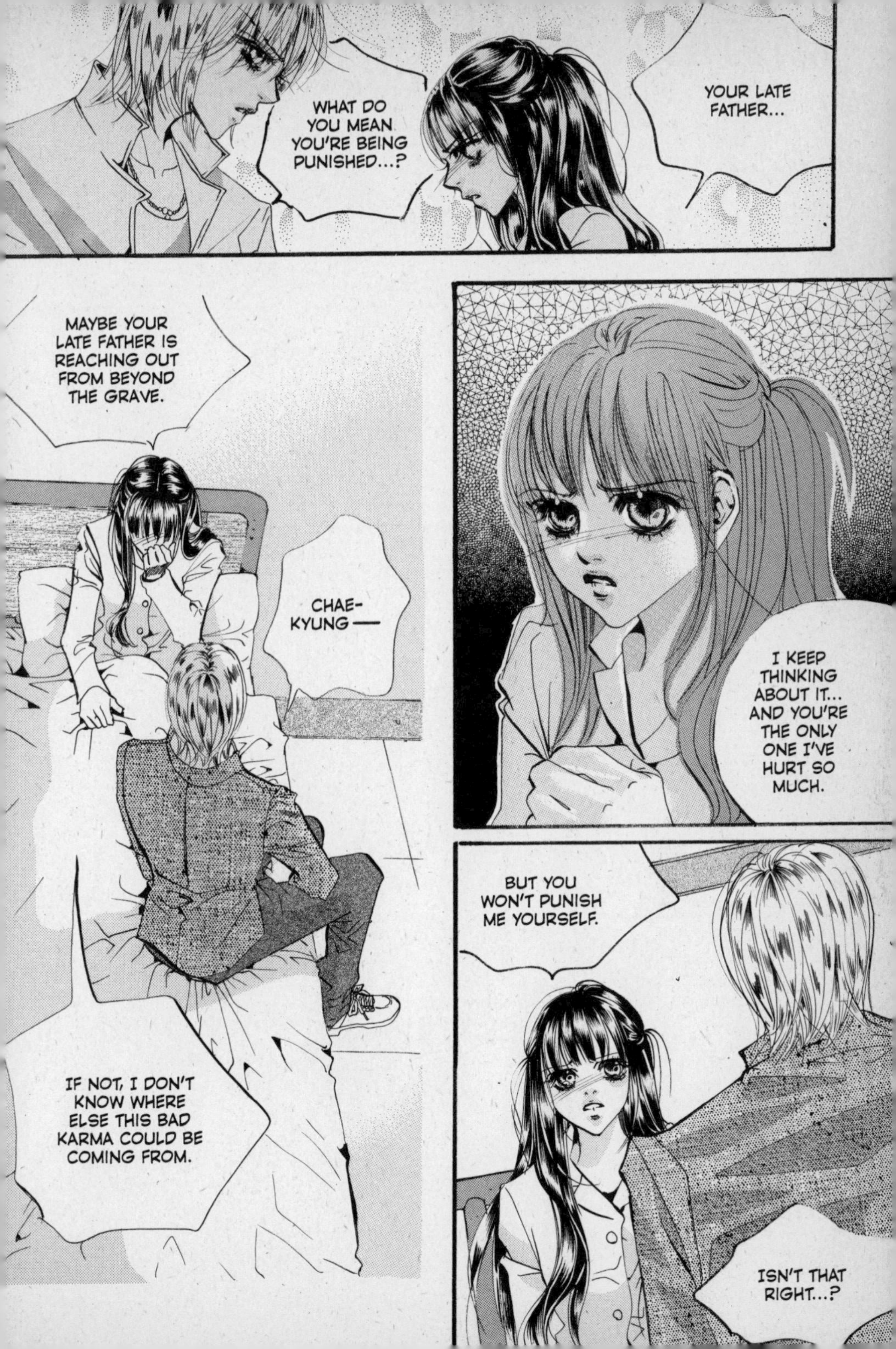
WHAT DO YOU MEAN YOU'RE BEING PUNISHED...?
YOUR LATE FATHER...
MAYBE YOUR LATE FATHER IS REACHING OUT FROM BEYOND THE GRAVE.
CHAE-KYUNG—
IF NOT, I DON'T KNOW WHERE ELSE THIS BAD KARMA COULD BE COMING FROM.
I KEEP THINKING ABOUT IT... AND YOU'RE THE ONLY ONE I'VE HURT SO MUCH.
BUT YOU WON'T PUNISH ME YOURSELF.
ISN'T THAT RIGHT...?

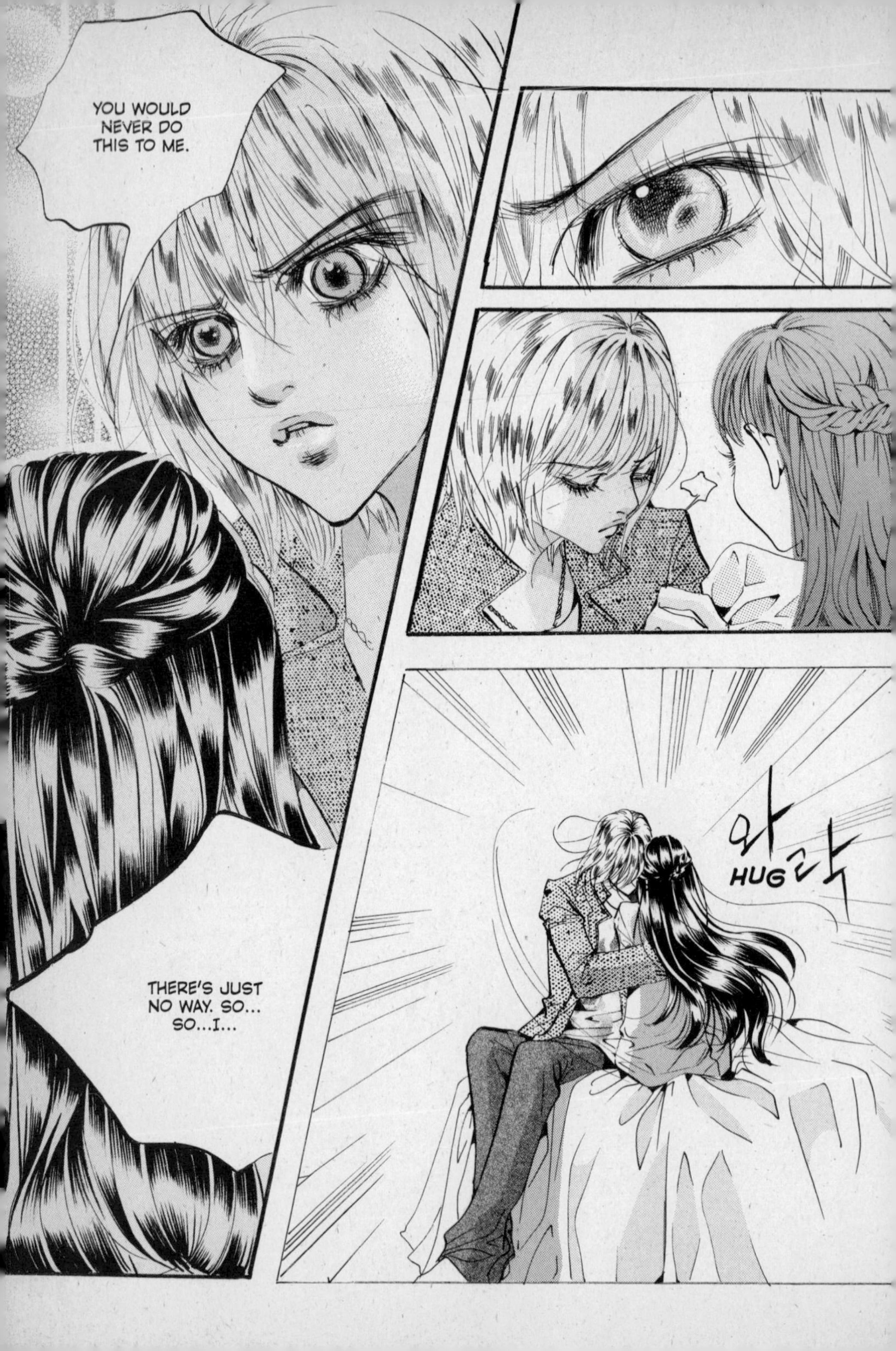
YOU WOULD NEVER DO THIS TO ME.
THERE'S JUST NO WAY. SO... SO...I...
HUG

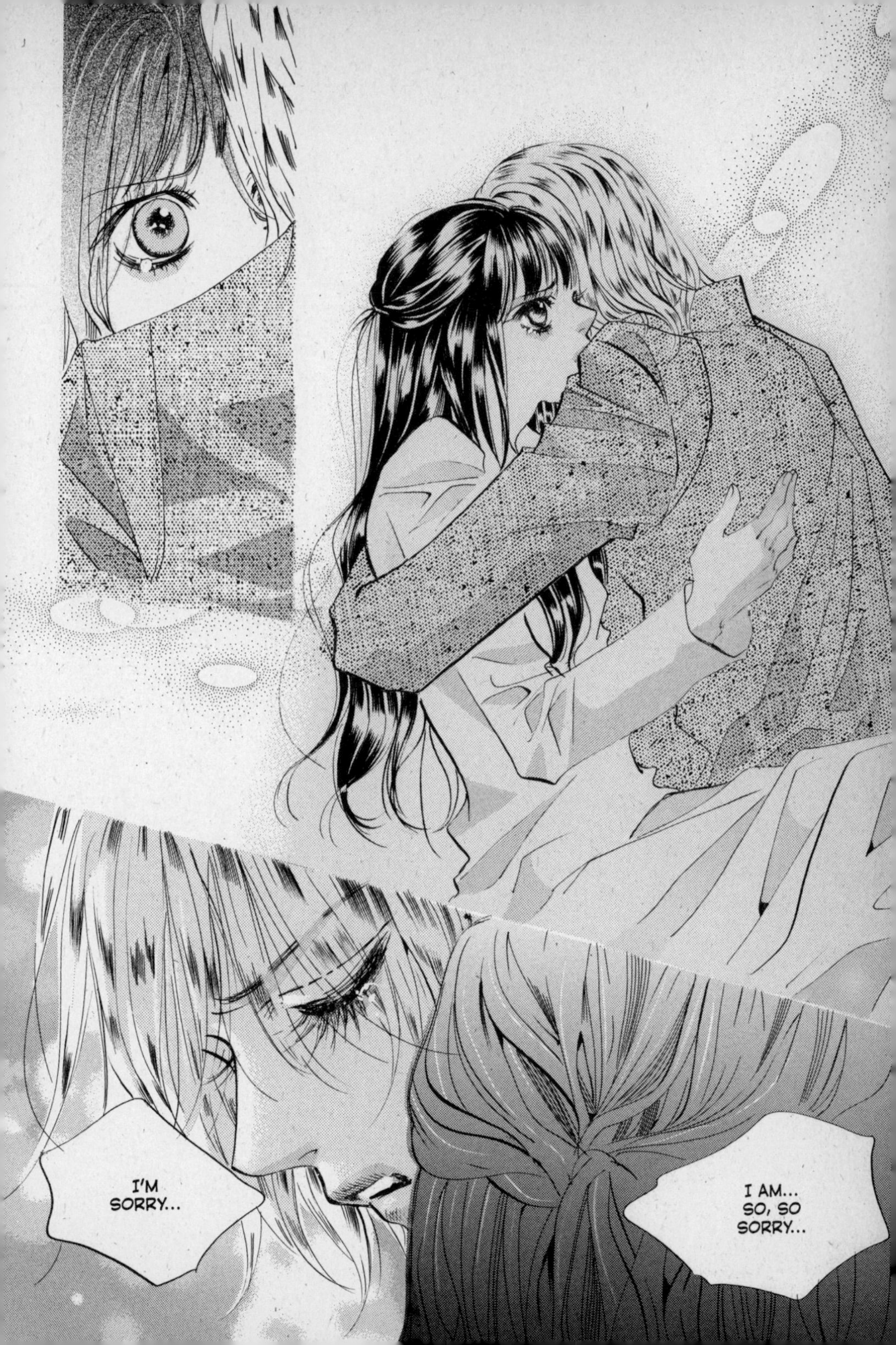
I AM... SO, SO SORRY...
I'M SORRY...

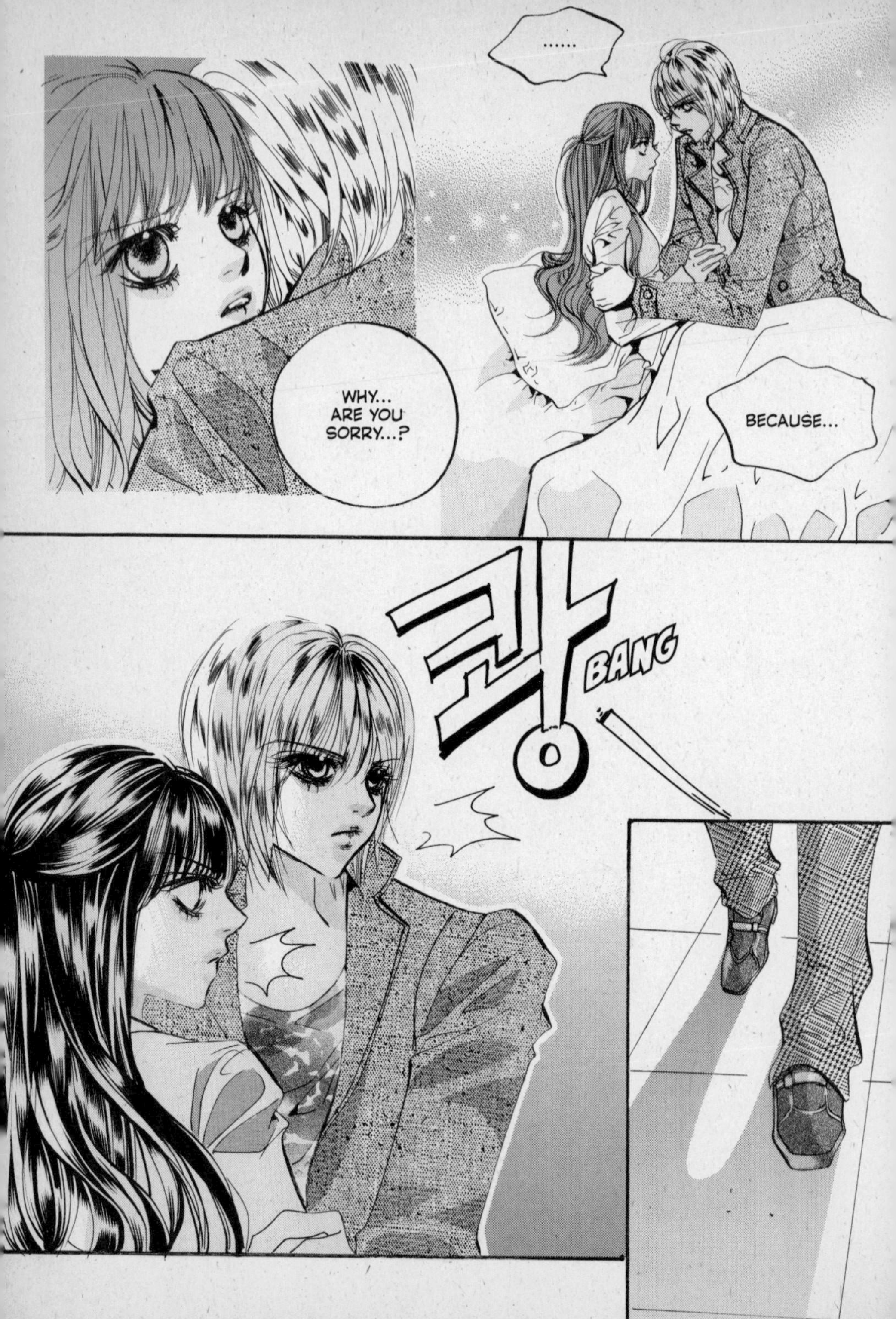

......
WHY... ARE YOU SORRY...?
BECAUSE...
쾅
BANG

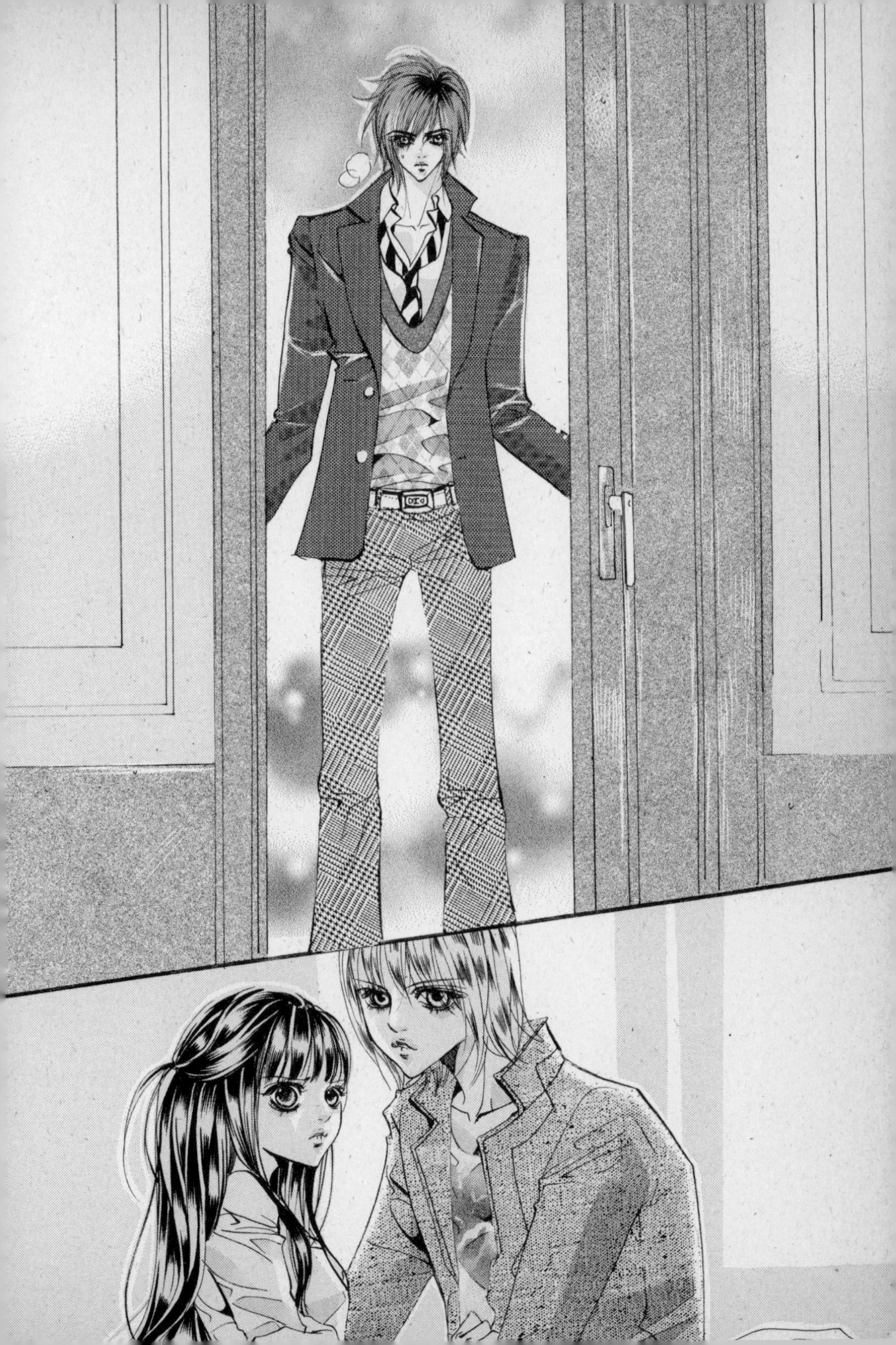

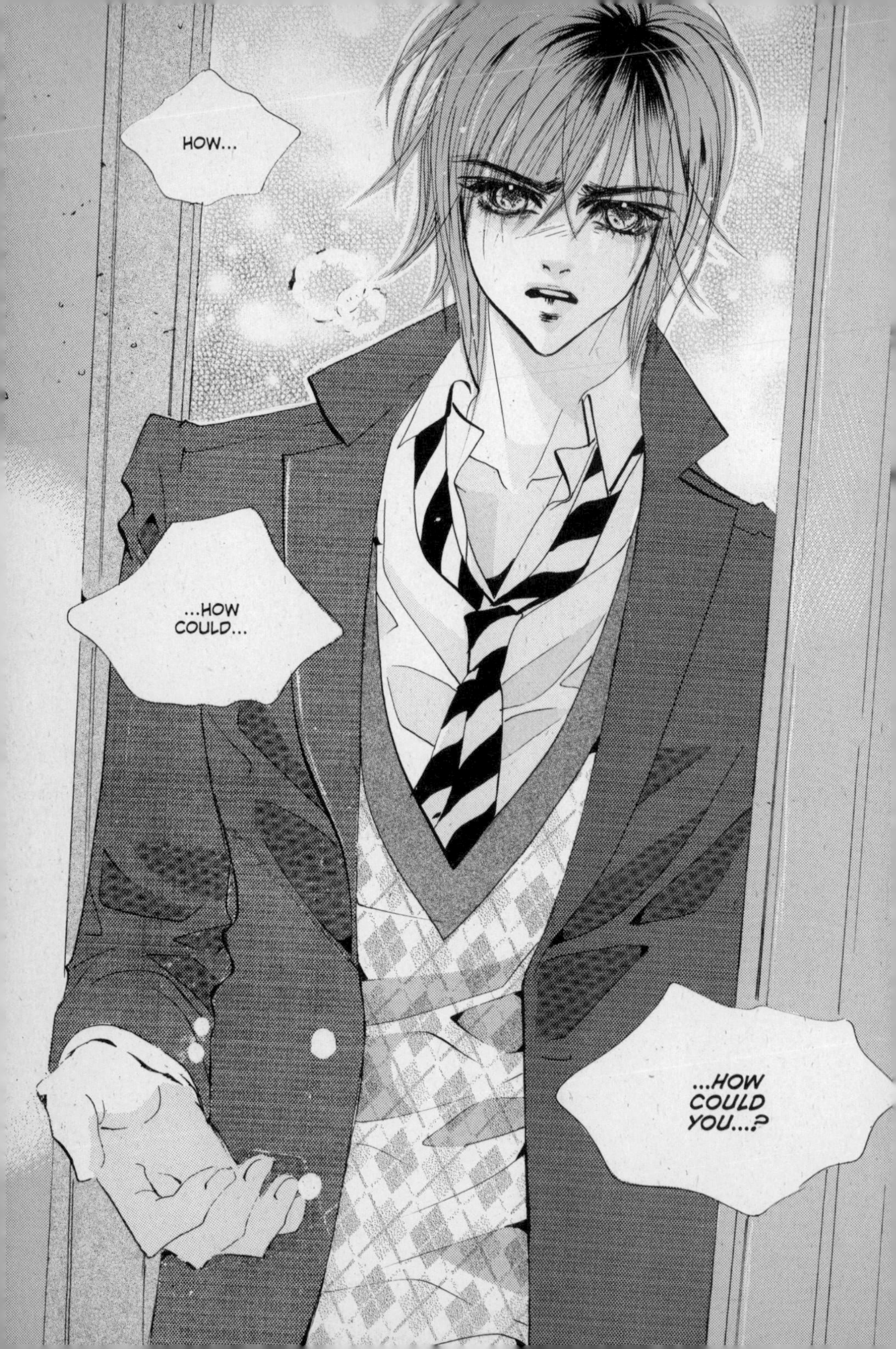
HOW...
...HOW COULD...
...HOW COULD YOU...?

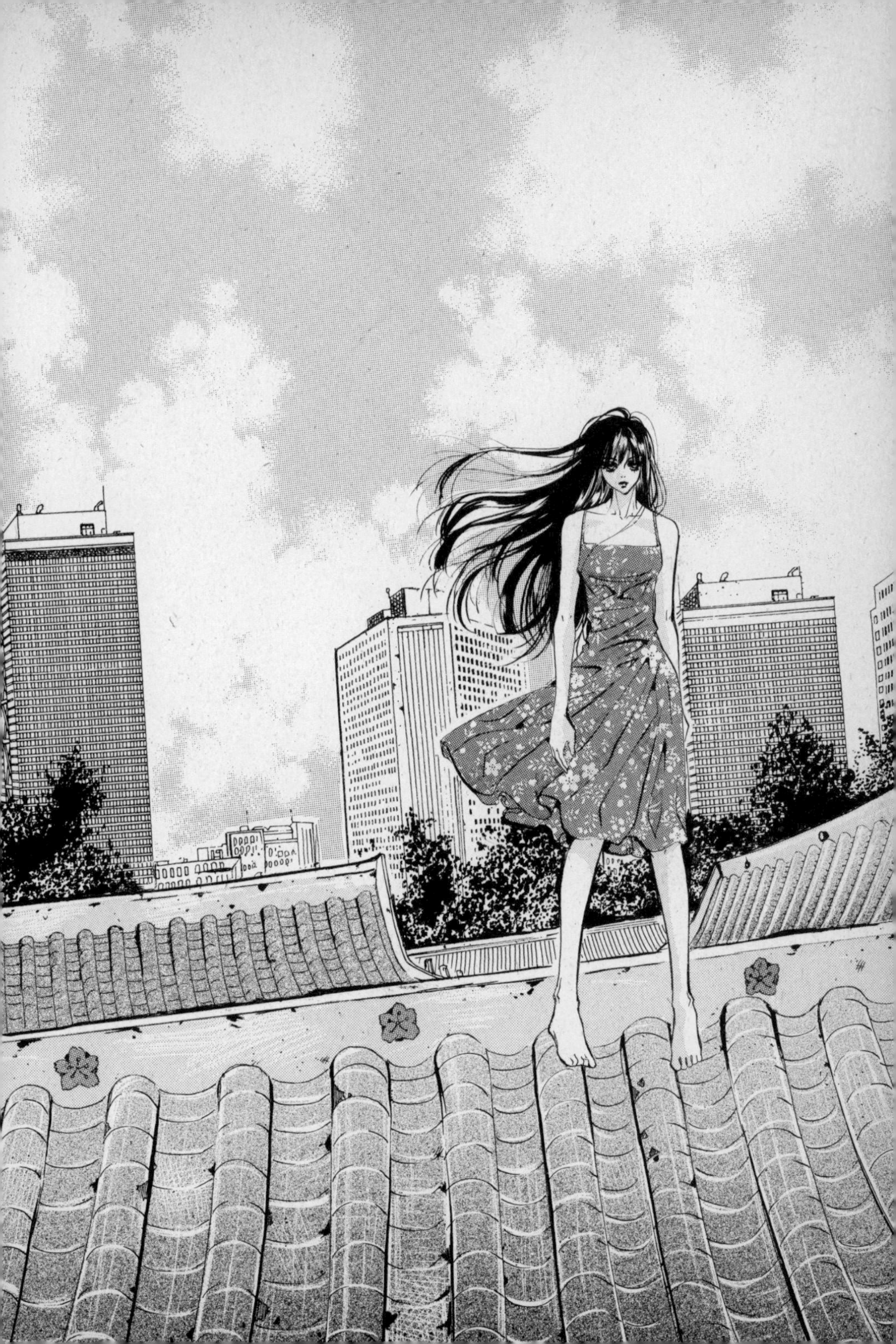

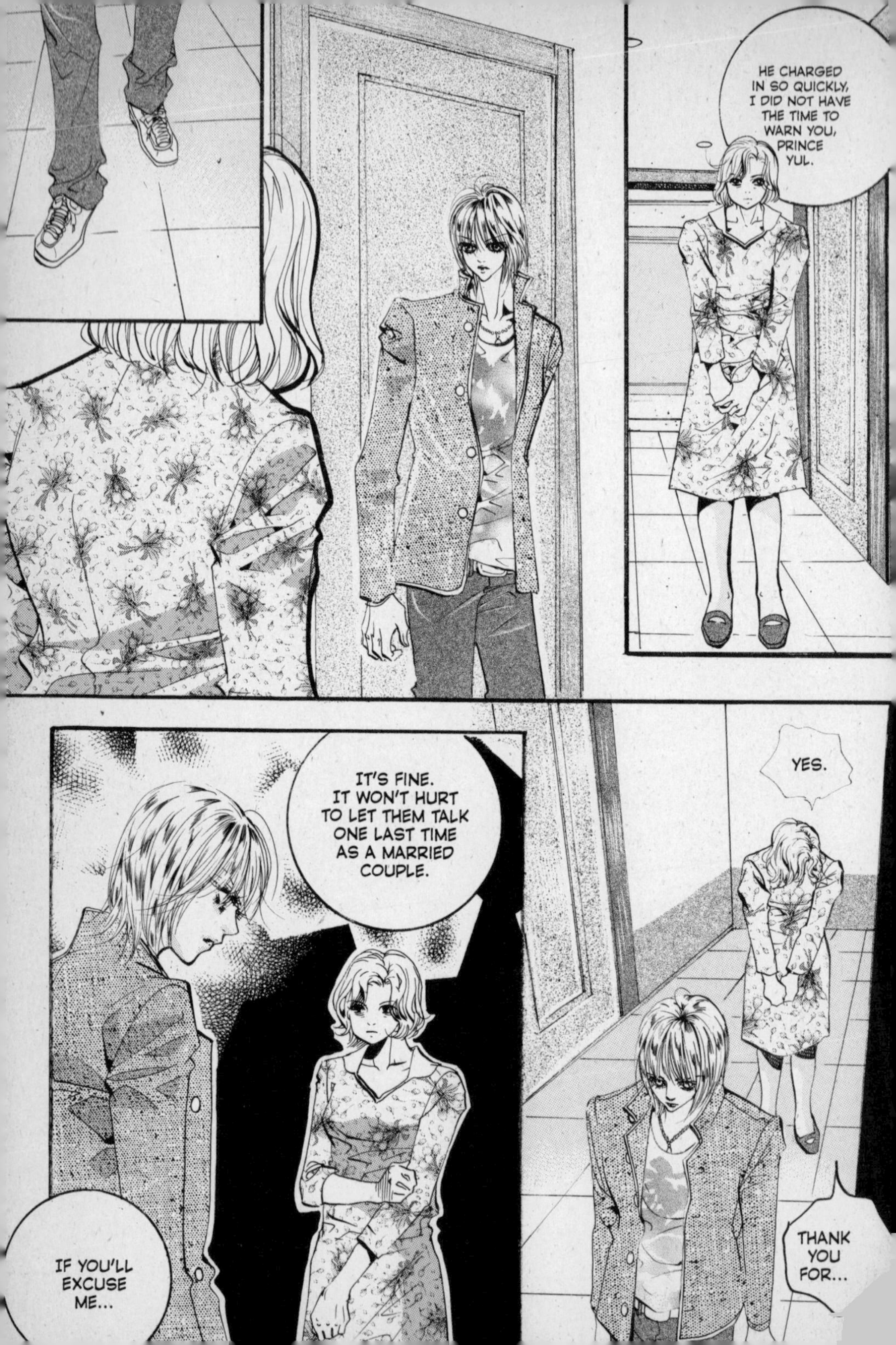
HE CHARGED IN SO QUICKLY, I DID NOT HAVE THE TIME TO WARN YOU, PRINCE YUL.
YES.
IT'S FINE. IT WON'T HURT TO LET THEM TALK ONE LAST TIME AS A MARRIED COUPLE.
THANK YOU FOR...
IF YOU'LL EXCUSE ME...

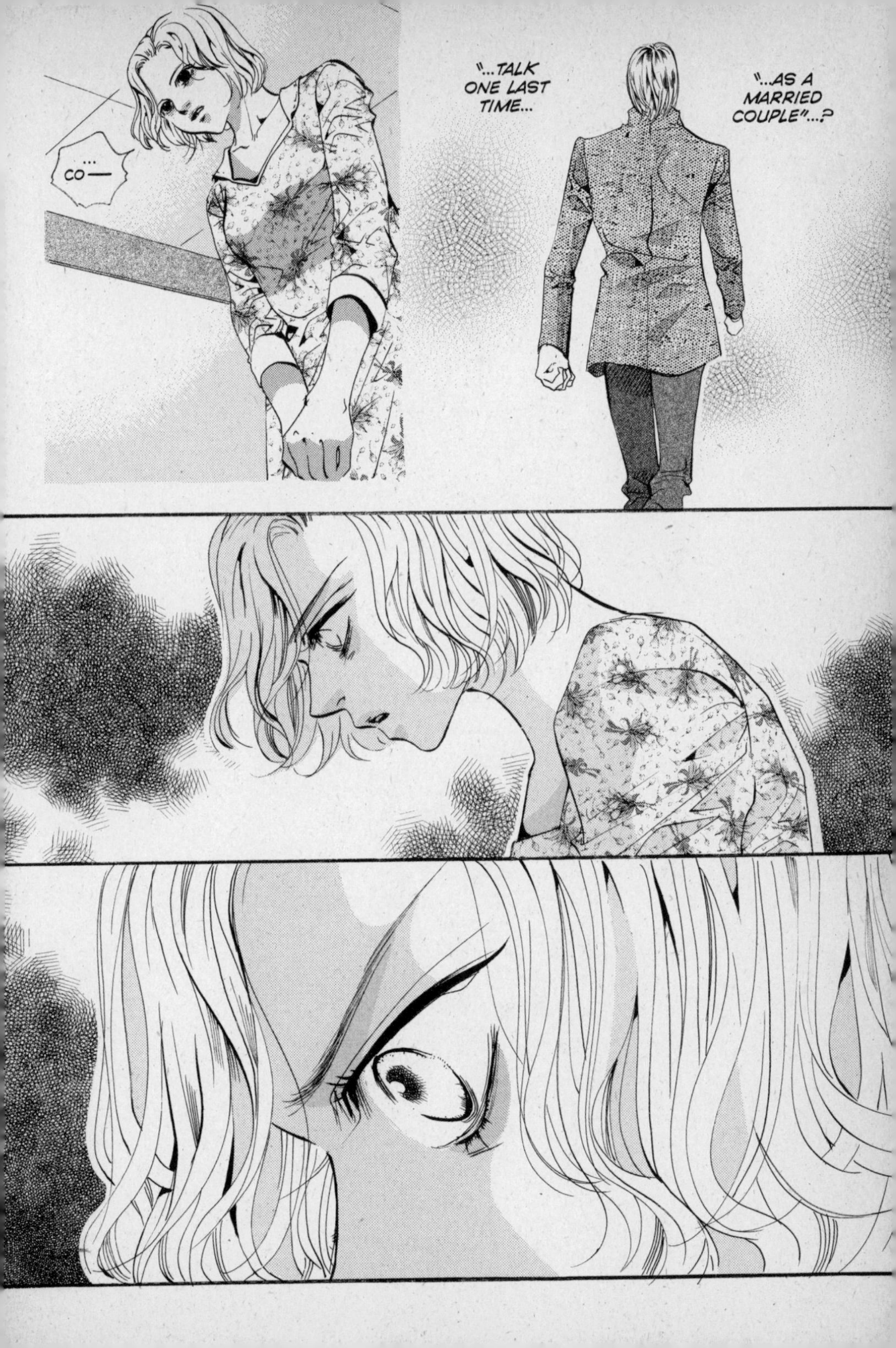
"...AS A MARRIED COUPLE"...?
"...TALK ONE LAST TIME...
... CO—

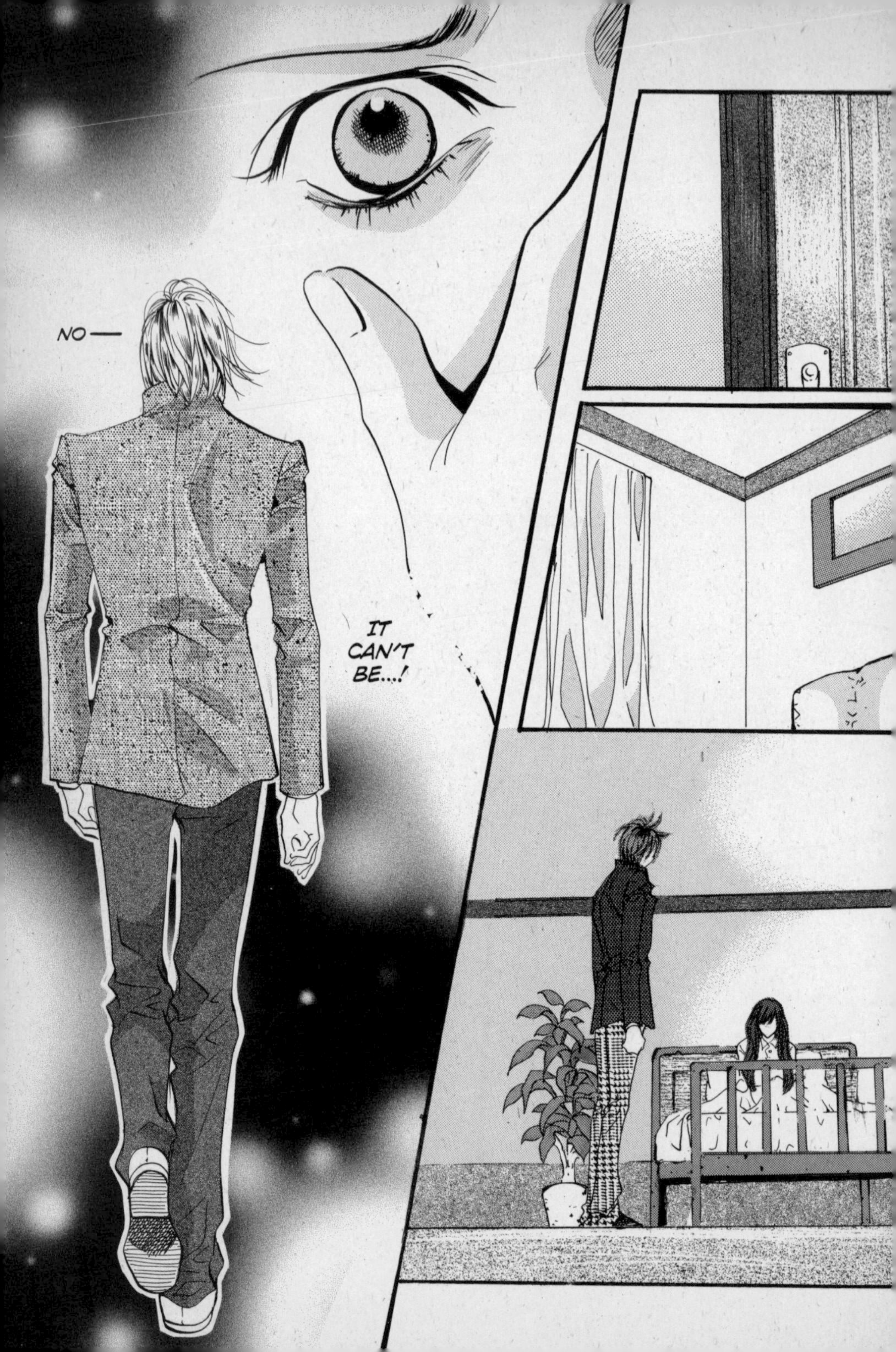
NO—
IT CAN'T BE...!

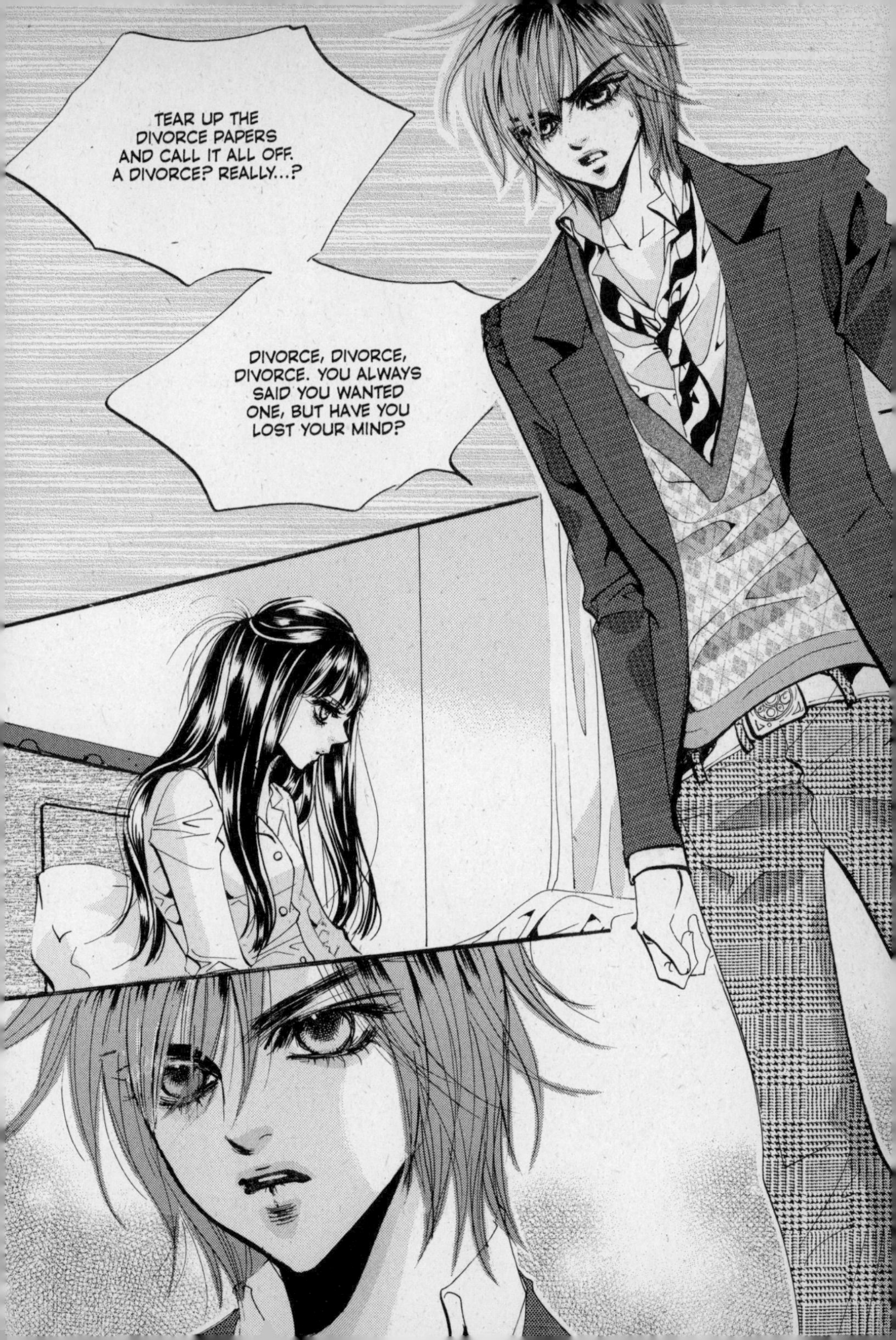
TEAR UP THE DIVORCE PAPERS AND CALL IT ALL OFF. A DIVORCE? REALLY...?
DIVORCE, DIVORCE, DIVORCE. YOU ALWAYS SAID YOU WANTED ONE, BUT HAVE YOU LOST YOUR MIND?

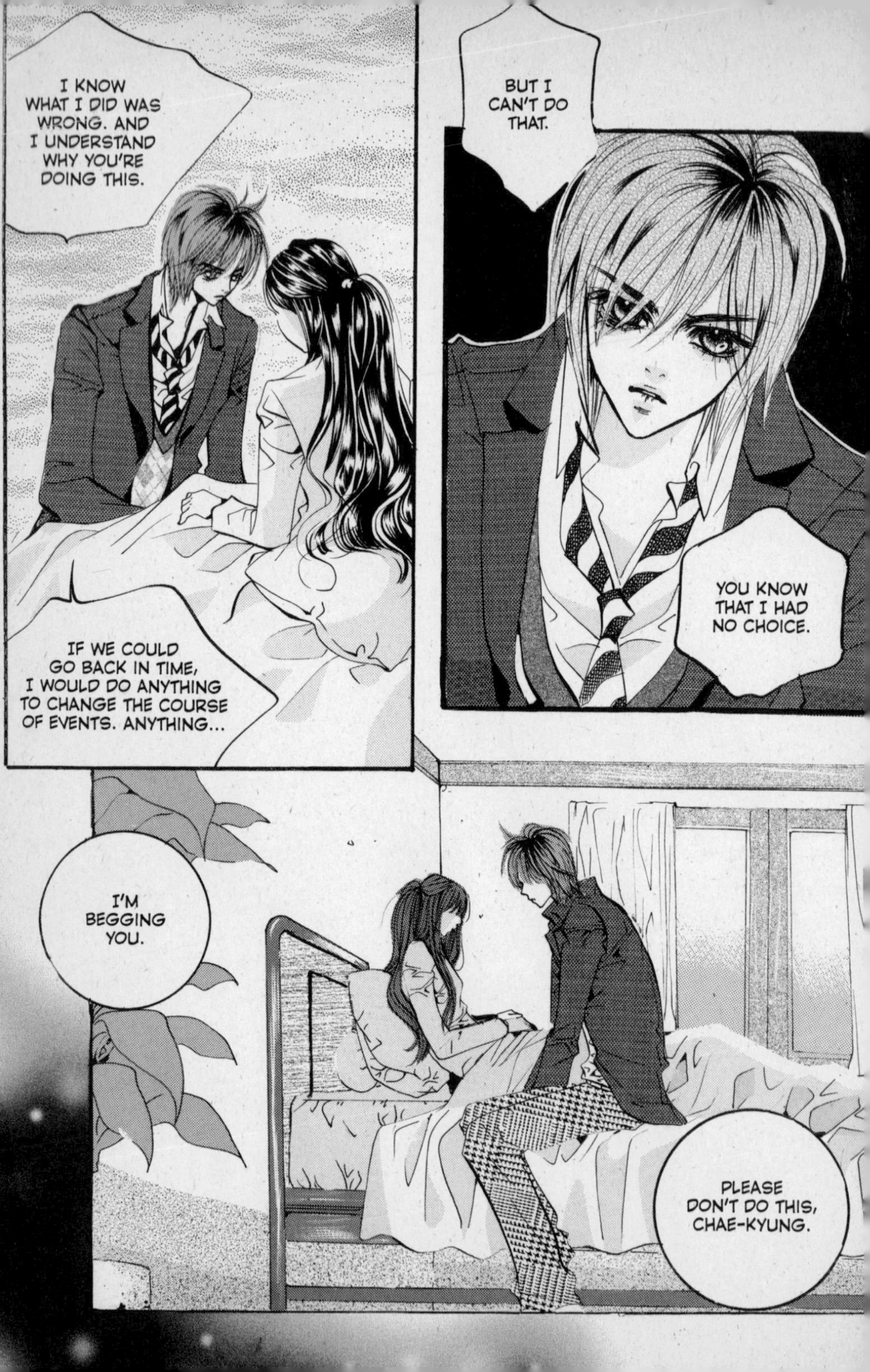
I KNOW WHAT I DID WAS WRONG. AND I UNDERSTAND WHY YOU'RE DOING THIS.
IF WE COULD GO BACK IN TIME, I WOULD DO ANYTHING TO CHANGE THE COURSE OF EVENTS. ANYTHING...
BUT I CAN'T DO THAT.
YOU KNOW THAT I HAD NO CHOICE.
I'M BEGGING YOU.
PLEASE DON'T DO THIS, CHAE-KYUNG.

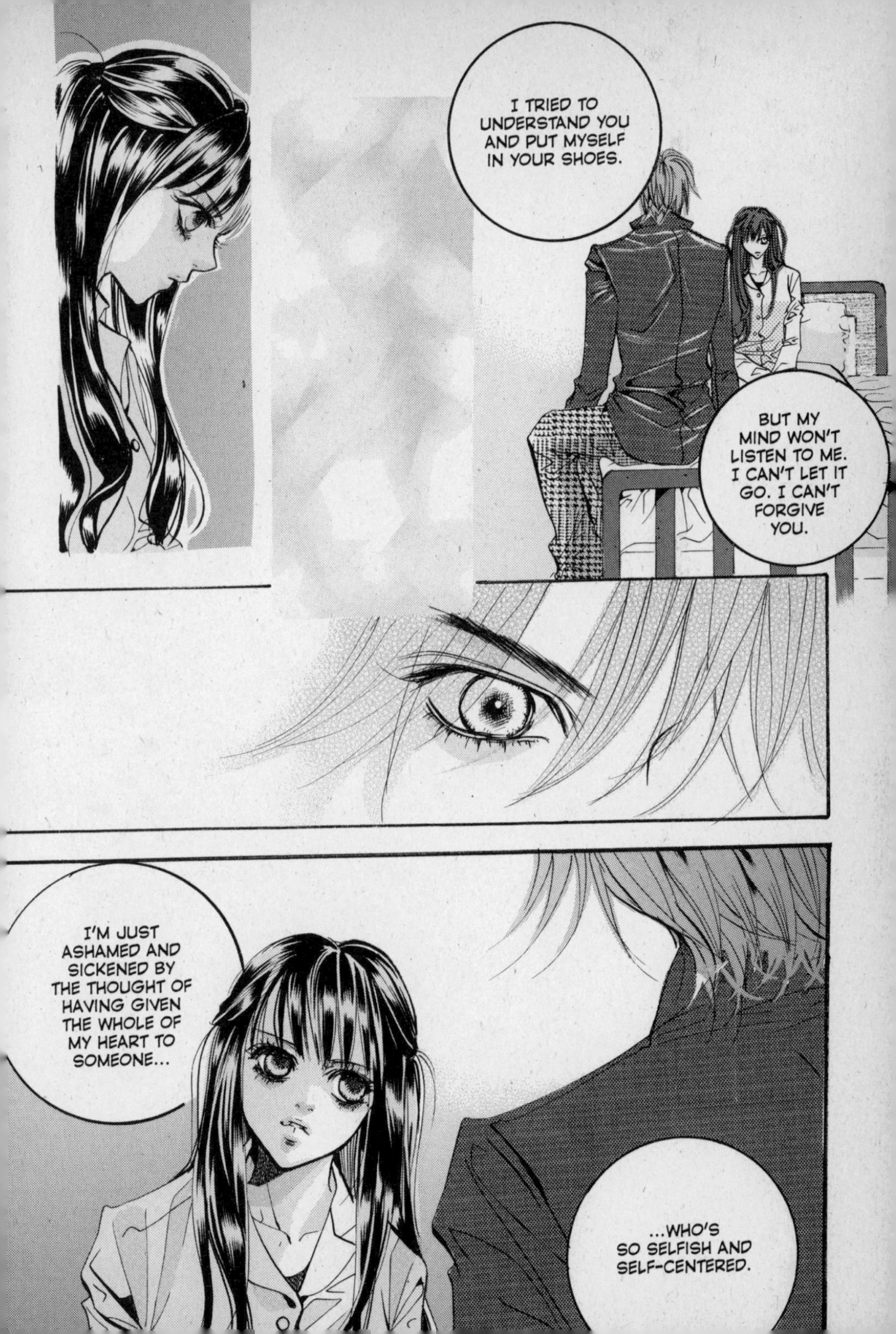
I TRIED TO UNDERSTAND YOU AND PUT MYSELF IN YOUR SHOES.
BUT MY MIND WON'T LISTEN TO ME. I CAN'T LET IT GO. I CAN'T FORGIVE YOU.
I'M JUST ASHAMED AND SICKENED BY THE THOUGHT OF HAVING GIVEN THE WHOLE OF MY HEART TO SOMEONE...
...WHO'S SO SELFISH AND SELF-CENTERED.

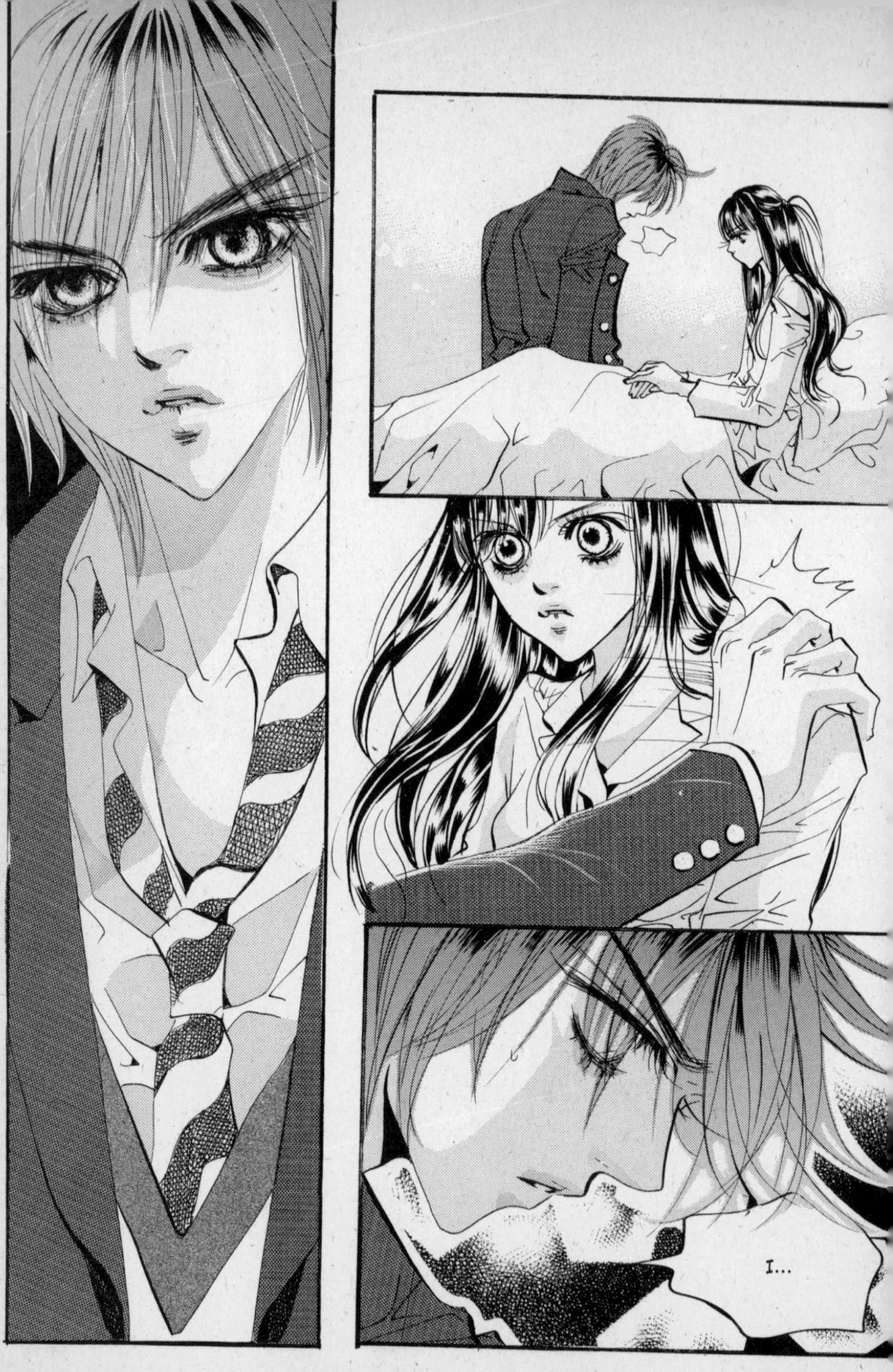
I...

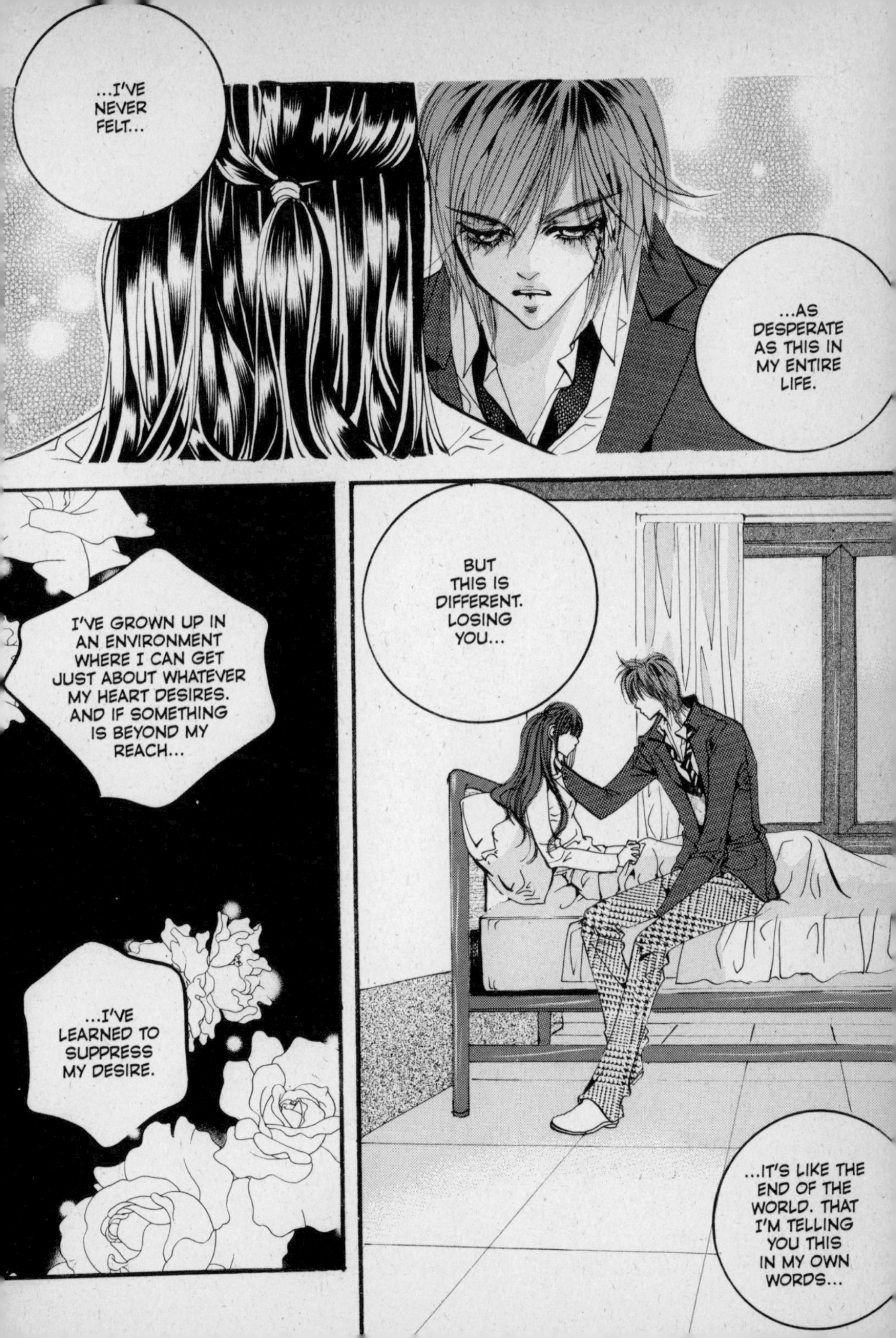
...I'VE NEVER FELT...
...AS DESPERATE AS THIS IN MY ENTIRE LIFE.
I'VE GROWN UP IN AN ENVIRONMENT WHERE I CAN GET JUST ABOUT WHATEVER MY HEART DESIRES. AND IF SOMETHING IS BEYOND MY REACH...
...I'VE LEARNED TO SUPPRESS MY DESIRE.
BUT THIS IS DIFFERENT. LOSING YOU...
...IT'S LIKE THE END OF THE WORLD. THAT I'M TELLING YOU THIS IN MY OWN WORDS...

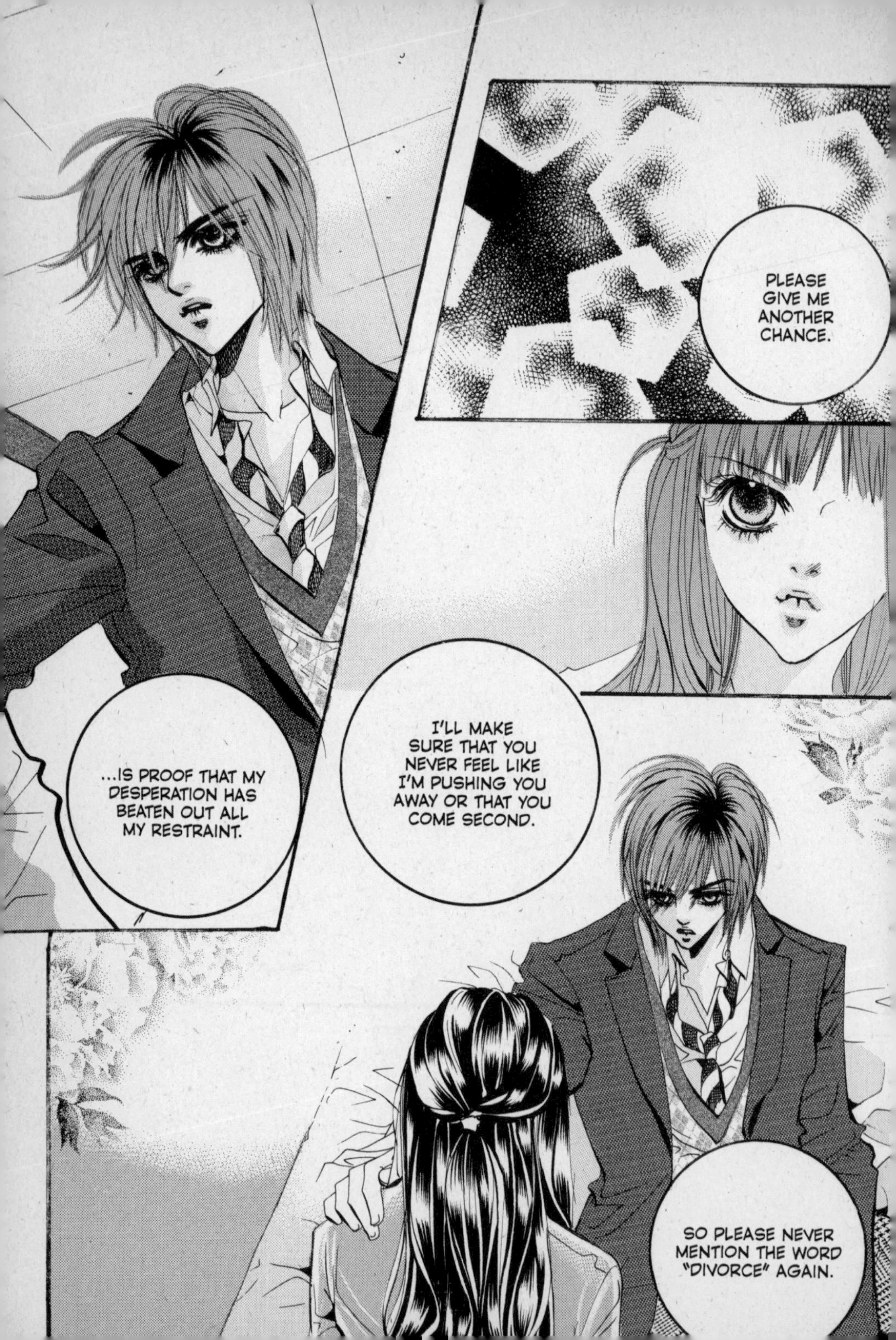
...IS PROOF THAT MY DESPERATION HAS BEATEN OUT ALL MY RESTRAINT.
PLEASE GIVE ME ANOTHER CHANCE.
I'LL MAKE SURE THAT YOU NEVER FEEL LIKE I'M PUSHING YOU AWAY OR THAT YOU COME SECOND.
SO PLEASE NEVER MENTION THE WORD "DIVORCE" AGAIN.

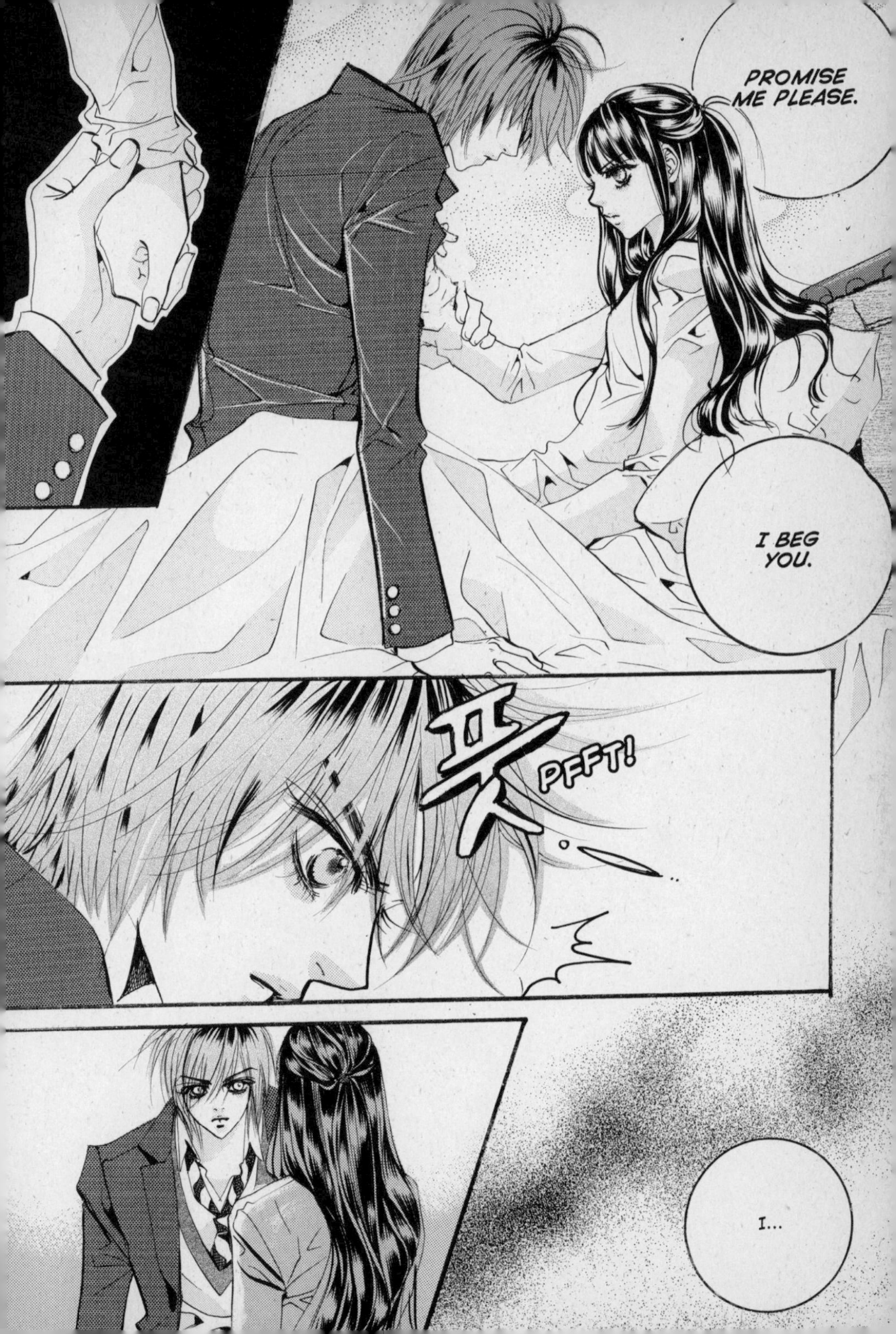
PROMISE ME PLEASE.
I BEG YOU.
PFFT!
I...

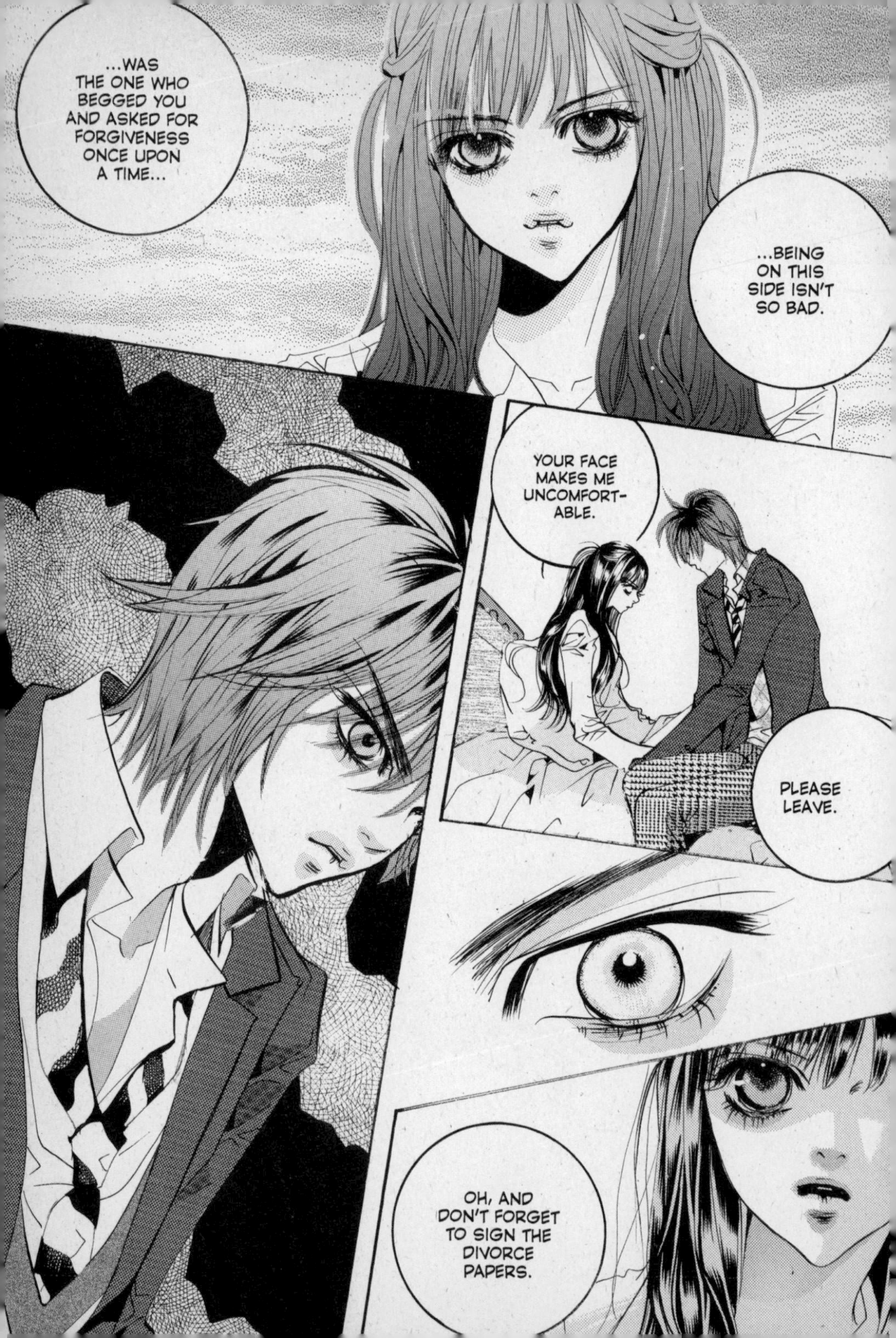
...WAS THE ONE WHO BEGGED YOU AND ASKED FOR FORGIVENESS ONCE UPON A TIME...
...BEING ON THIS SIDE ISN'T SO BAD.
YOUR FACE MAKES ME UNCOMFORT-ABLE.
PLEASE LEAVE.
OH, AND DON'T FORGET TO SIGN THE DIVORCE PAPERS.

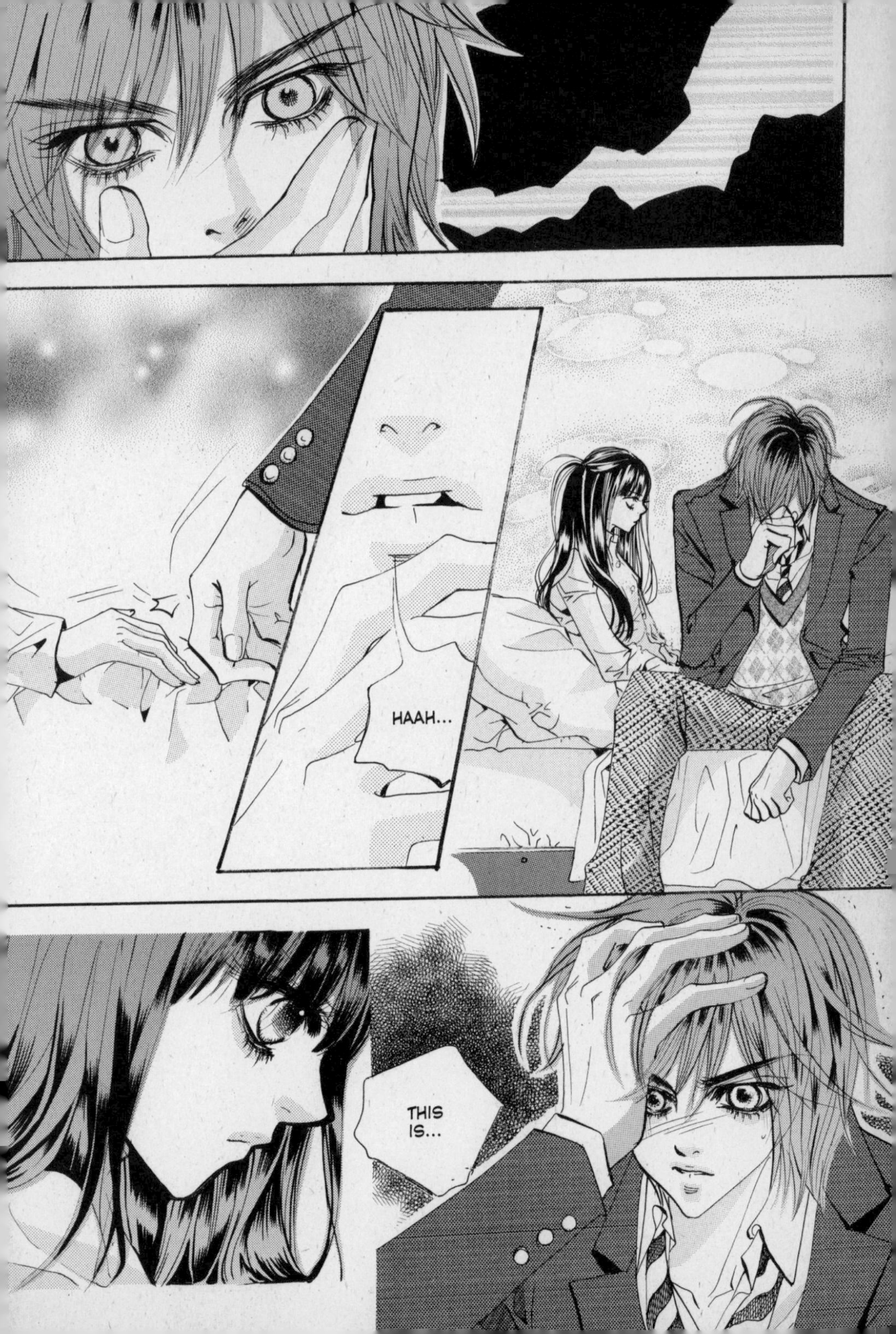
HAAH...
THIS IS...

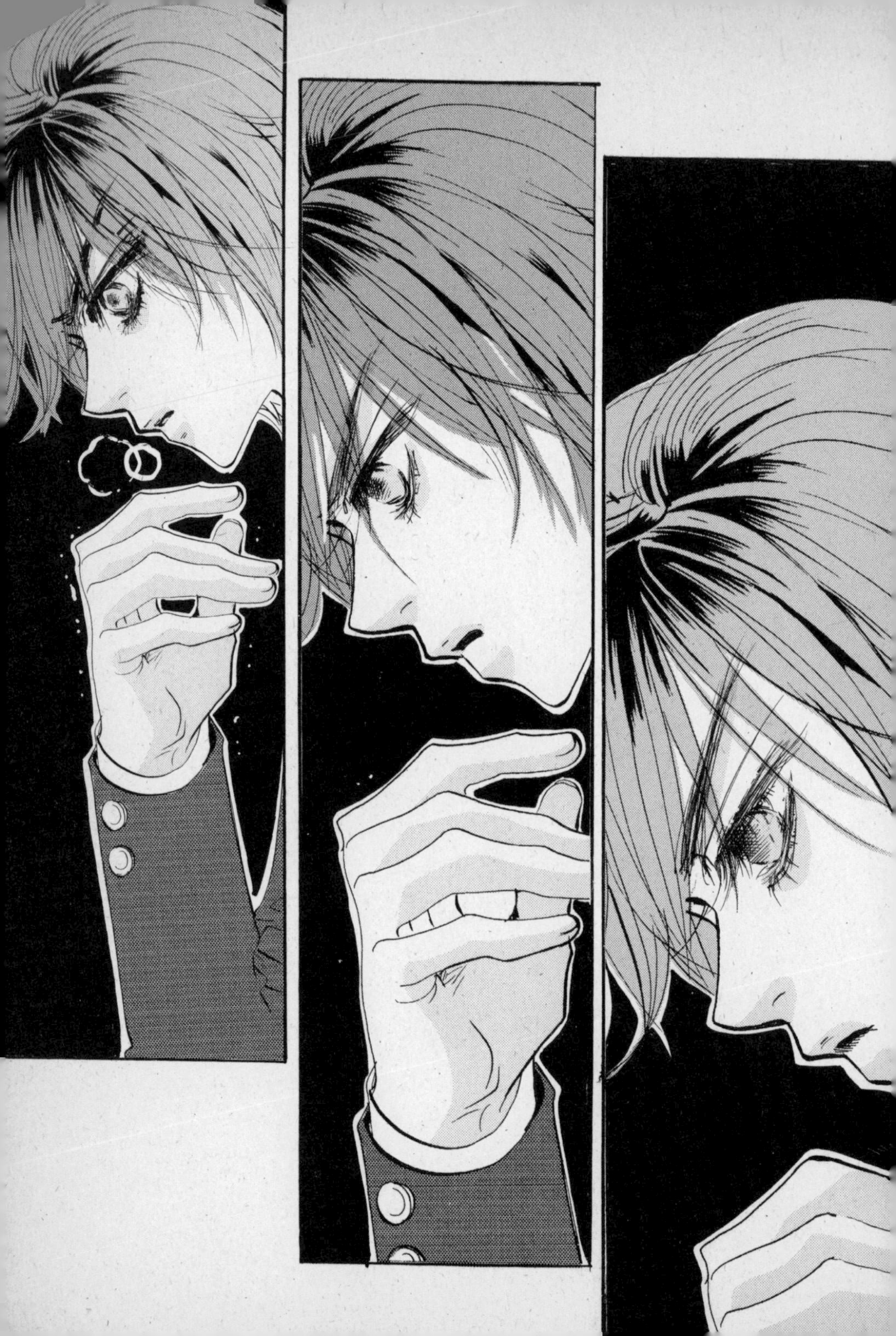

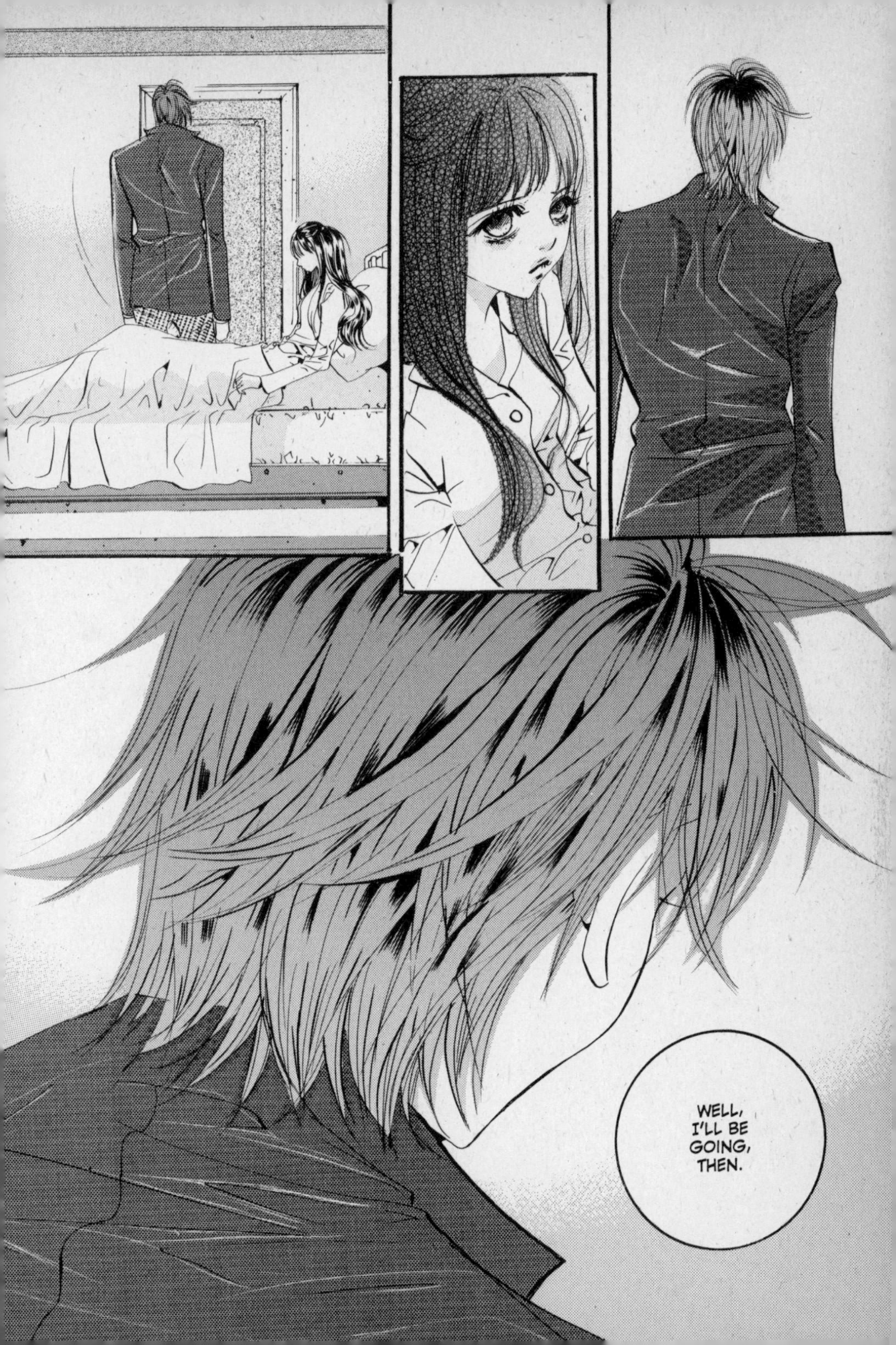
WELL, I'LL BE GOING, THEN.

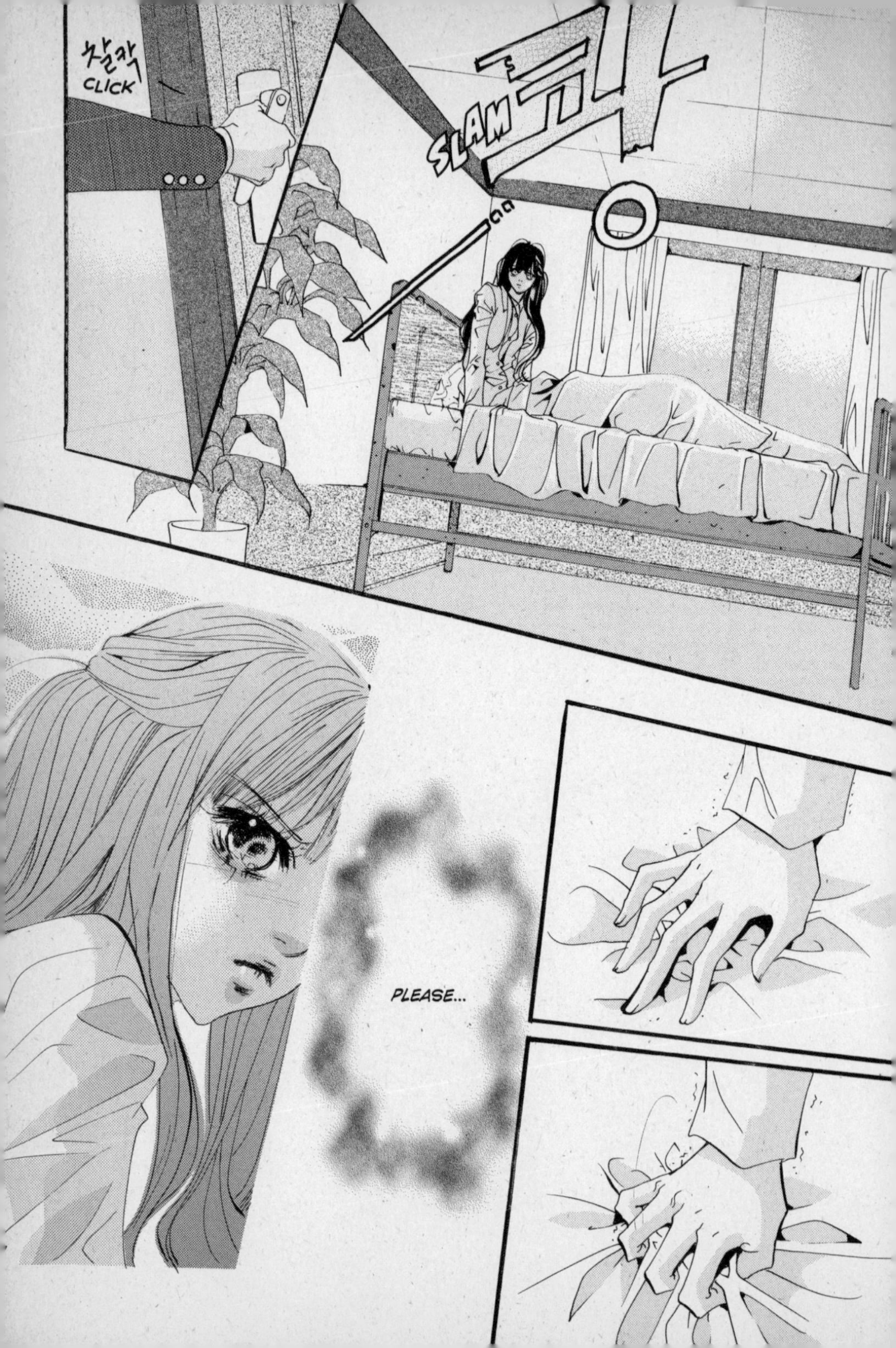
찰칵
CLICK
SLAM
PLEASE...

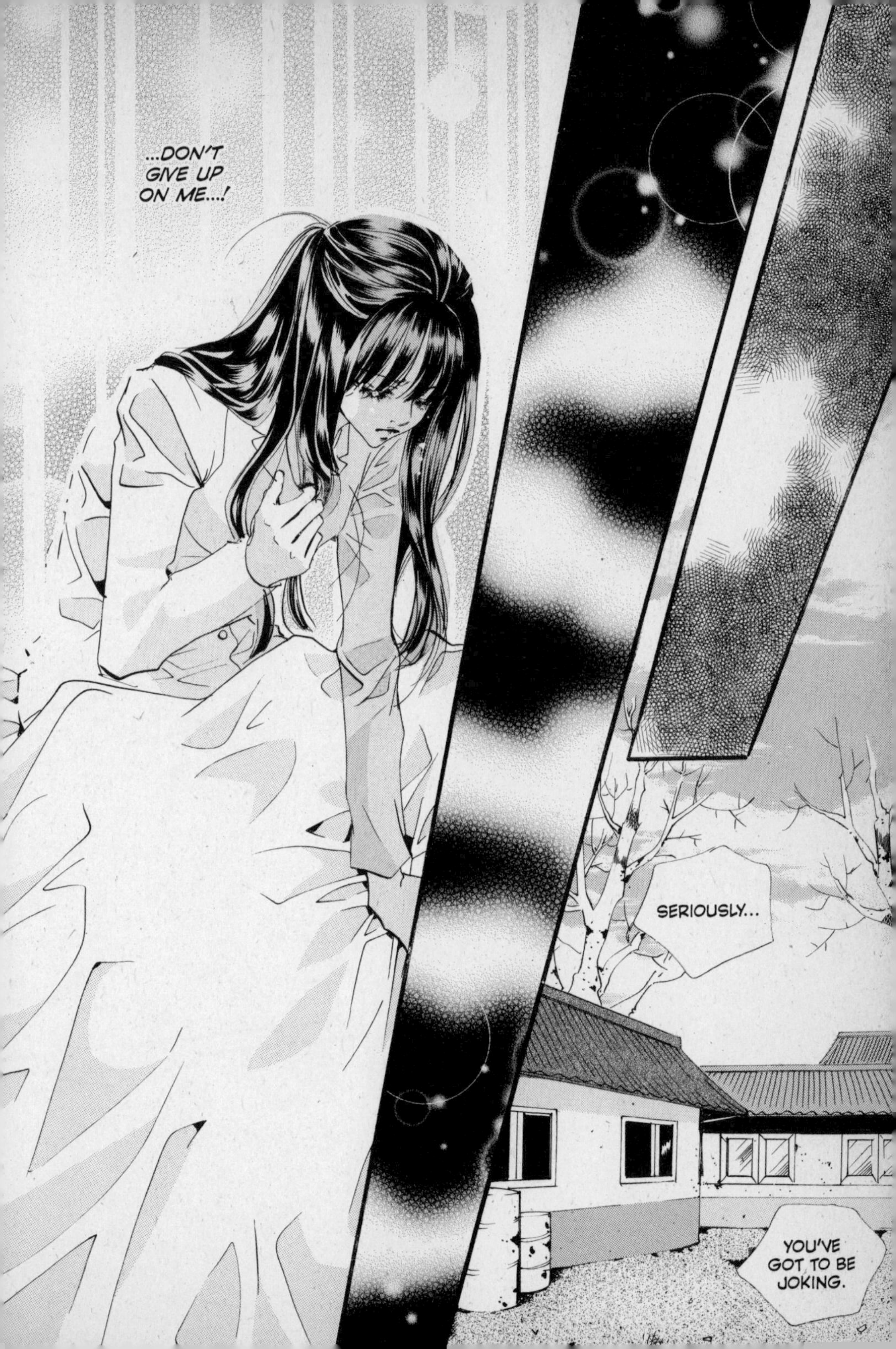
SERIOUSLY...
YOU'VE GOT TO BE JOKING.
...DON'T GIVE UP ON ME...!

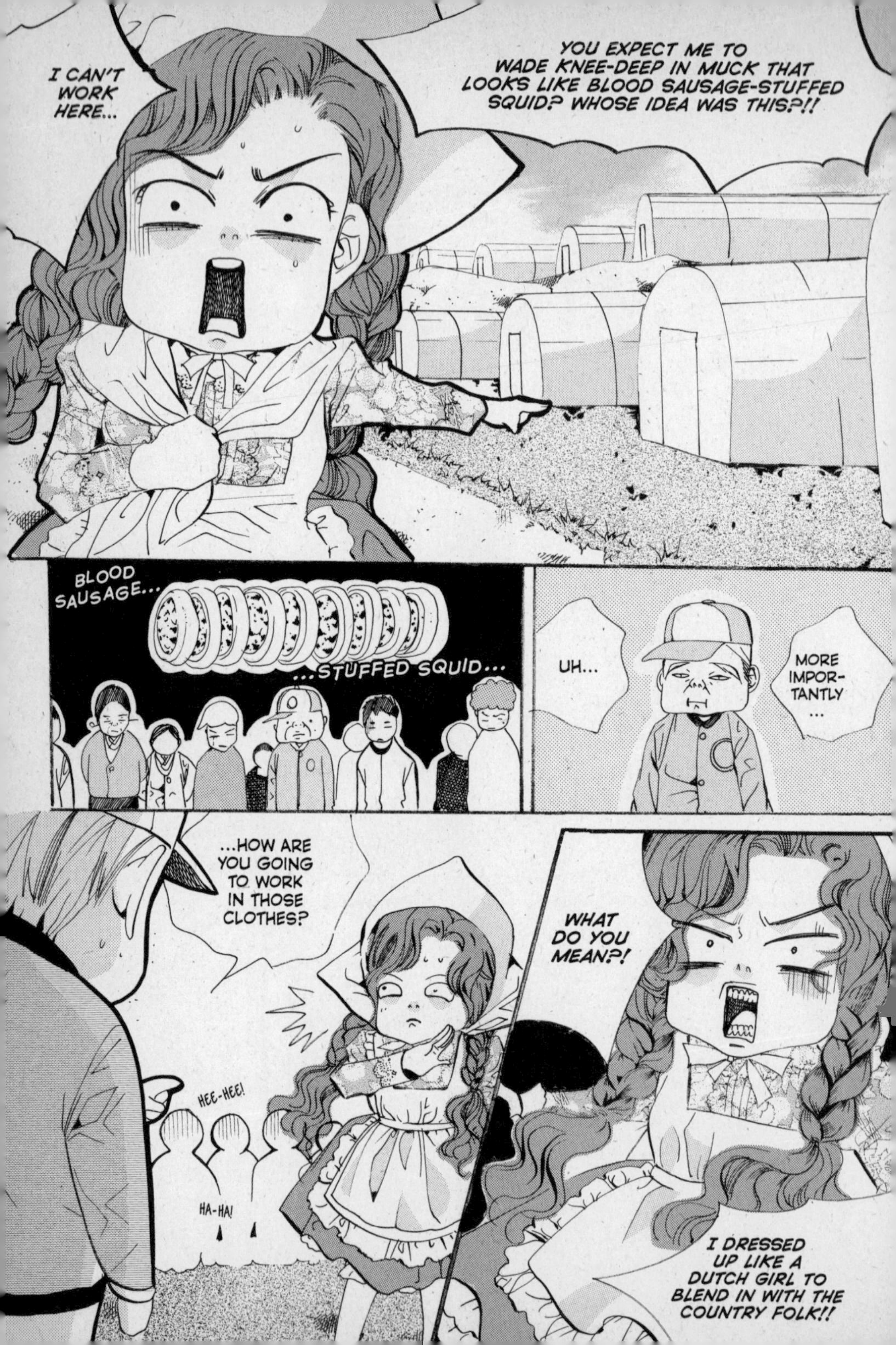
YOU EXPECT ME TO WADE KNEE-DEEP IN MUCK THAT LOOKS LIKE BLOOD SAUSAGE-STUFFED SQUID? WHOSE IDEA WAS THIS?!!
I CAN'T WORK HERE...
BLOOD SAUSAGE...
...STUFFED SQUID...
MORE IMPORTANTLY...
UH...
...HOW ARE YOU GOING TO WORK IN THOSE CLOTHES?
WHAT DO YOU MEAN?!
I DRESSED UP LIKE A DUTCH GIRL TO BLEND IN WITH THE COUNTRY FOLK!!
HEE-HEE!
HA-HA!

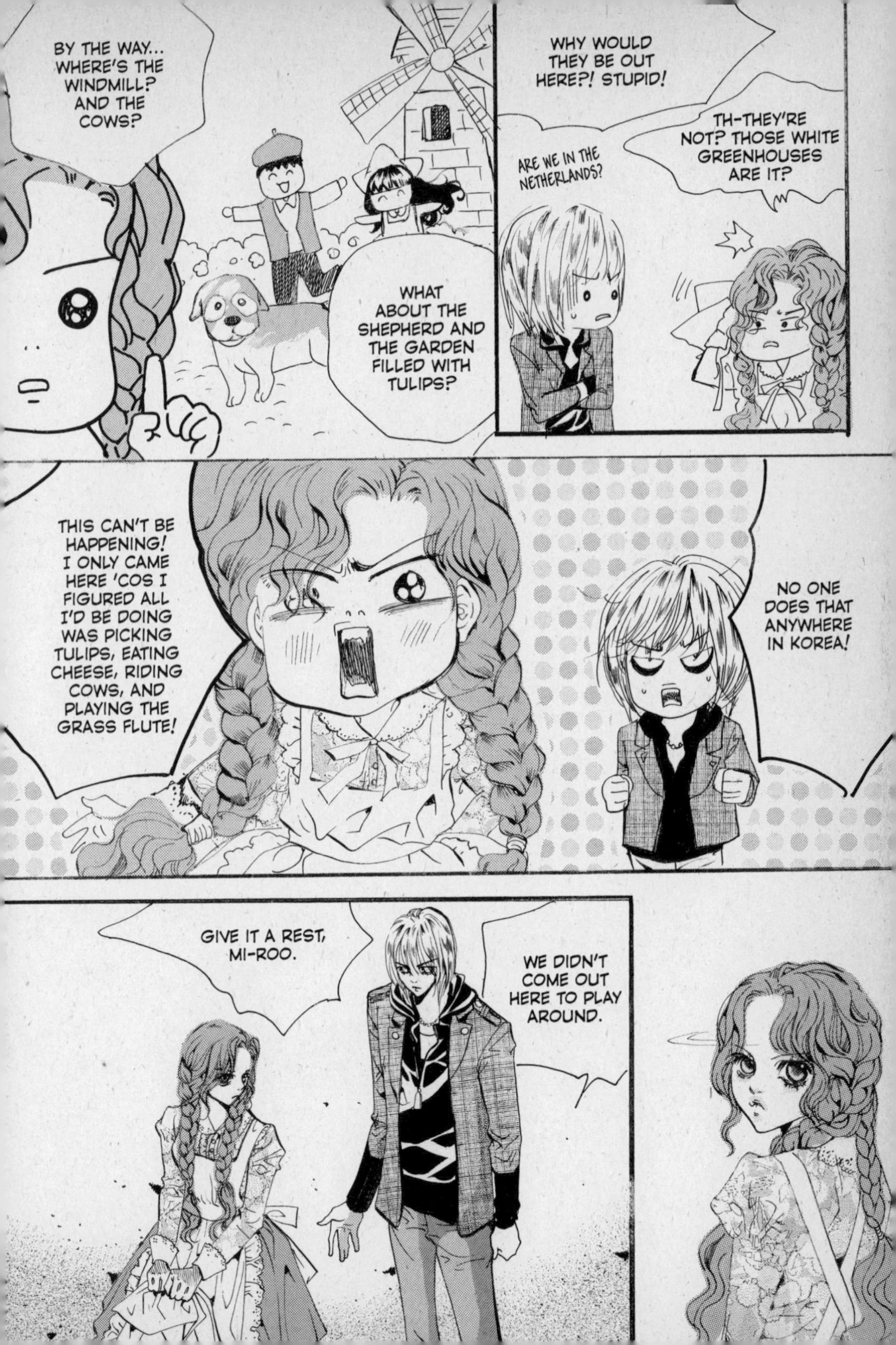
BY THE WAY... WHERE'S THE WINDMILL? AND THE COWS?
WHAT ABOUT THE SHEPHERD AND THE GARDEN FILLED WITH TULIPS?
WHY WOULD THEY BE OUT HERE?! STUPID!
ARE WE IN THE NETHERLANDS?
TH-THEY'RE NOT? THOSE WHITE GREENHOUSES ARE IT?
THIS CAN'T BE HAPPENING! I ONLY CAME HERE 'COS I FIGURED ALL I'D BE DOING WAS PICKING TULIPS, EATING CHEESE, RIDING COWS, AND PLAYING THE GRASS FLUTE!
NO ONE DOES THAT ANYWHERE IN KOREA!
GIVE IT A REST, MI-ROO.
WE DIDN'T COME OUT HERE TO PLAY AROUND.

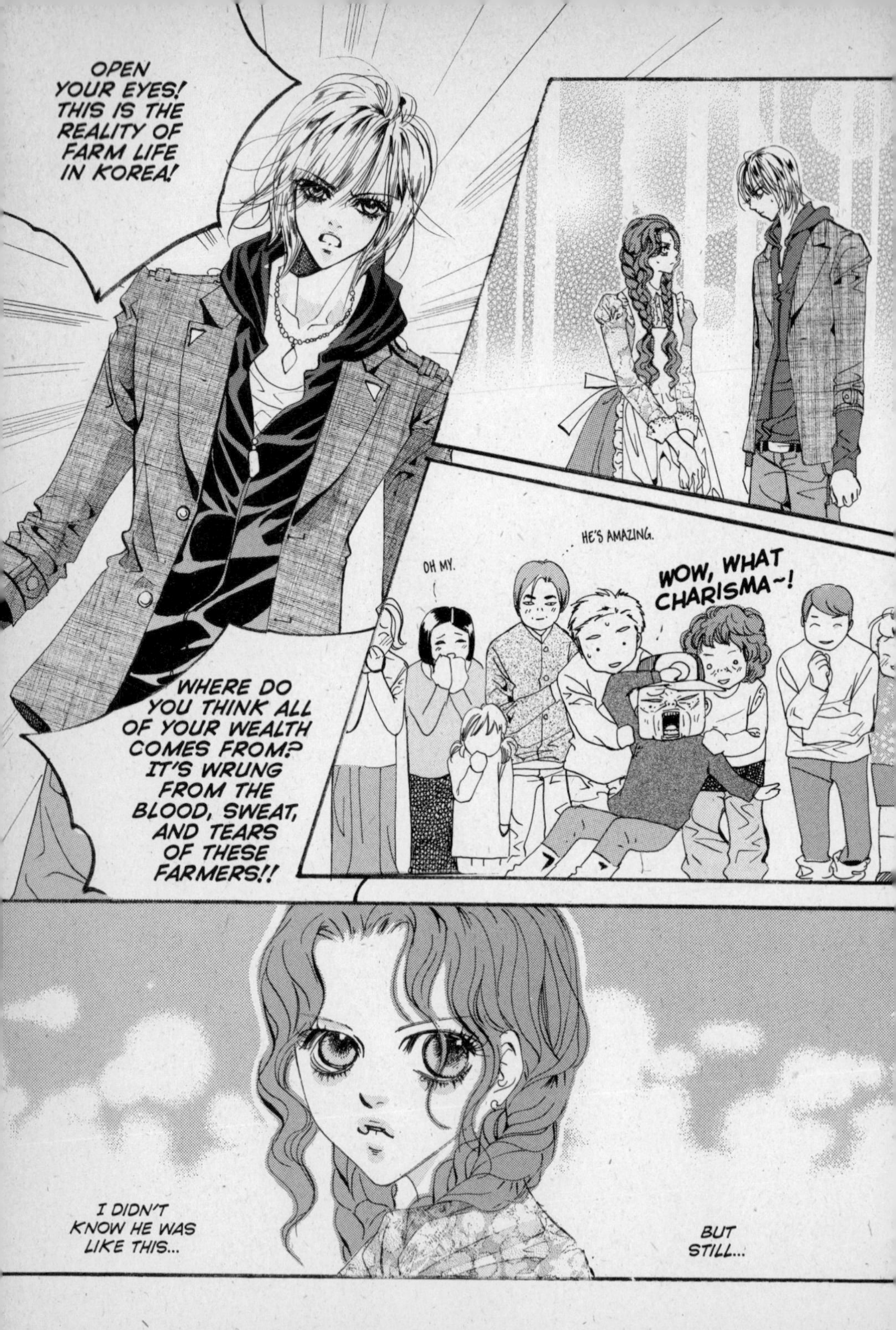
OPEN YOUR EYES! THIS IS THE REALITY OF FARM LIFE IN KOREA!
WHERE DO YOU THINK ALL OF YOUR WEALTH COMES FROM? IT'S WRUNG FROM THE BLOOD, SWEAT, AND TEARS OF THESE FARMERS!!
OH MY.
...HE'S AMAZING.
WOW, WHAT CHARISMA~!
I DIDN'T KNOW HE WAS LIKE THIS...
BUT STILL...

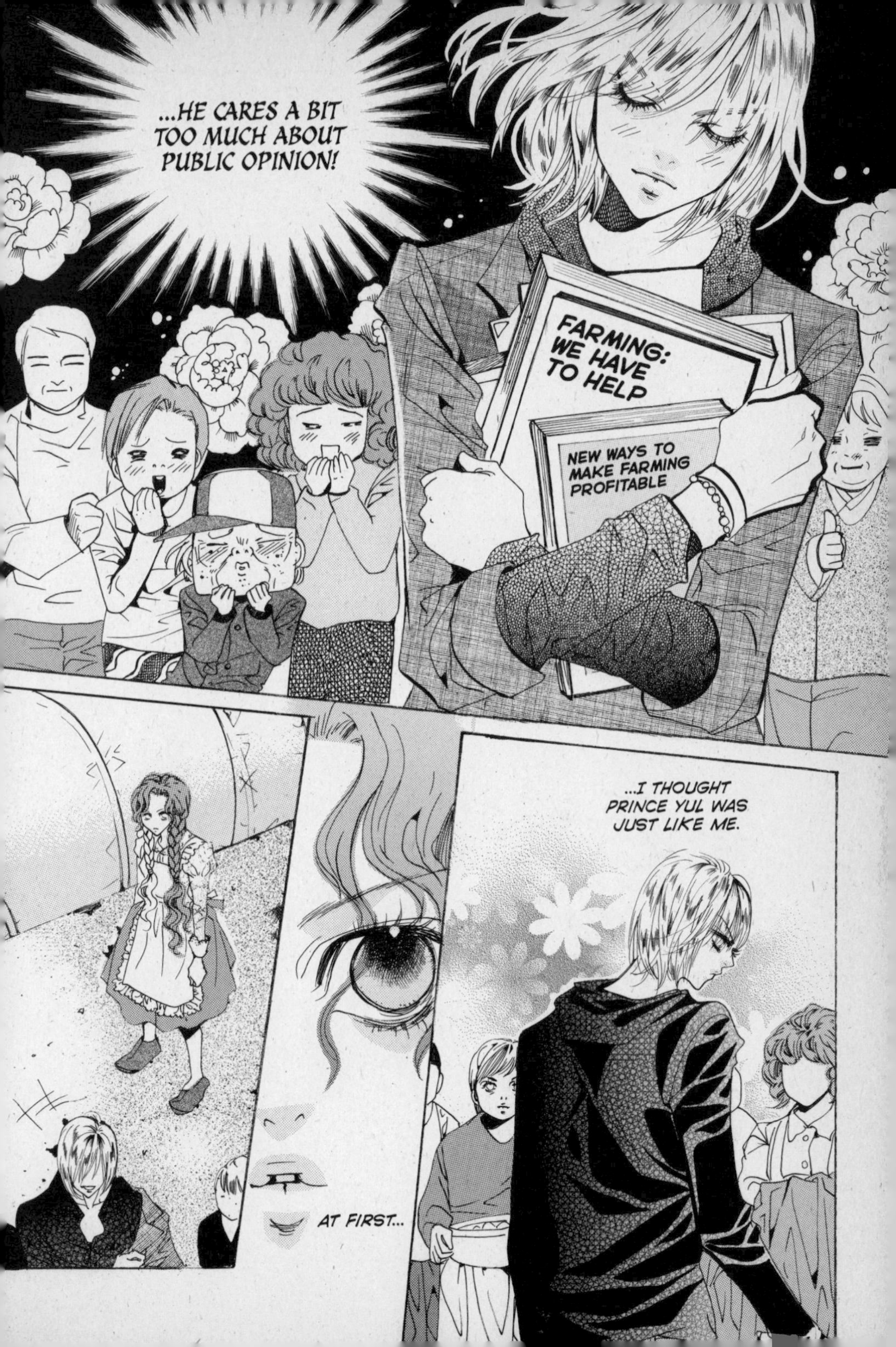
...HE CARES A BIT TOO MUCH ABOUT PUBLIC OPINION!
FARMING: WE HAVE TO HELP
NEW WAYS TO MAKE FARMING PROFITABLE
...I THOUGHT PRINCE YUL WAS JUST LIKE ME.
AT FIRST...

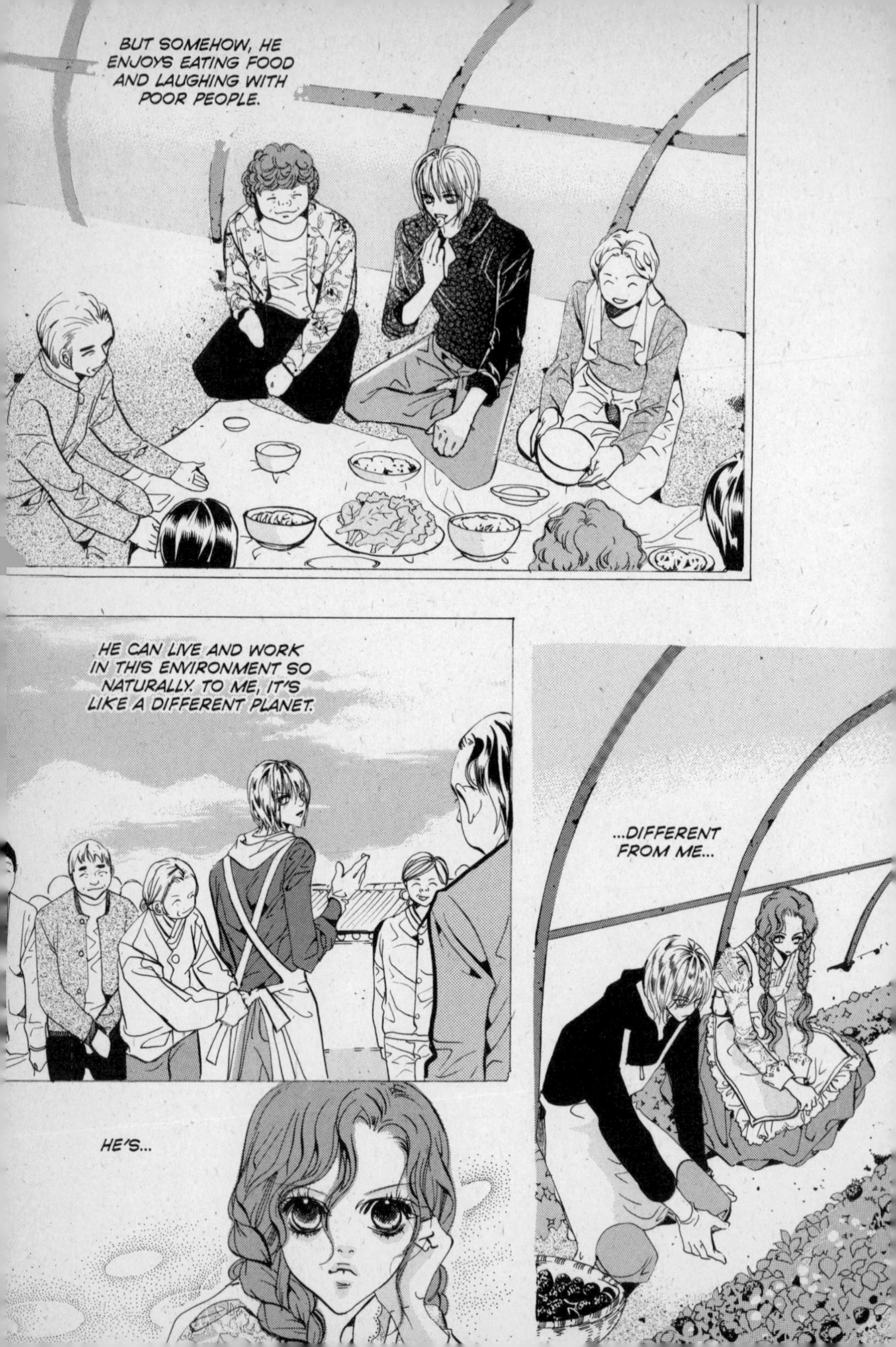
BUT SOMEHOW, HE ENJOYS EATING FOOD AND LAUGHING WITH POOR PEOPLE.
HE CAN LIVE AND WORK IN THIS ENVIRONMENT SO NATURALLY. TO ME, IT'S LIKE A DIFFERENT PLANET.
...DIFFERENT FROM ME...
HE'S...

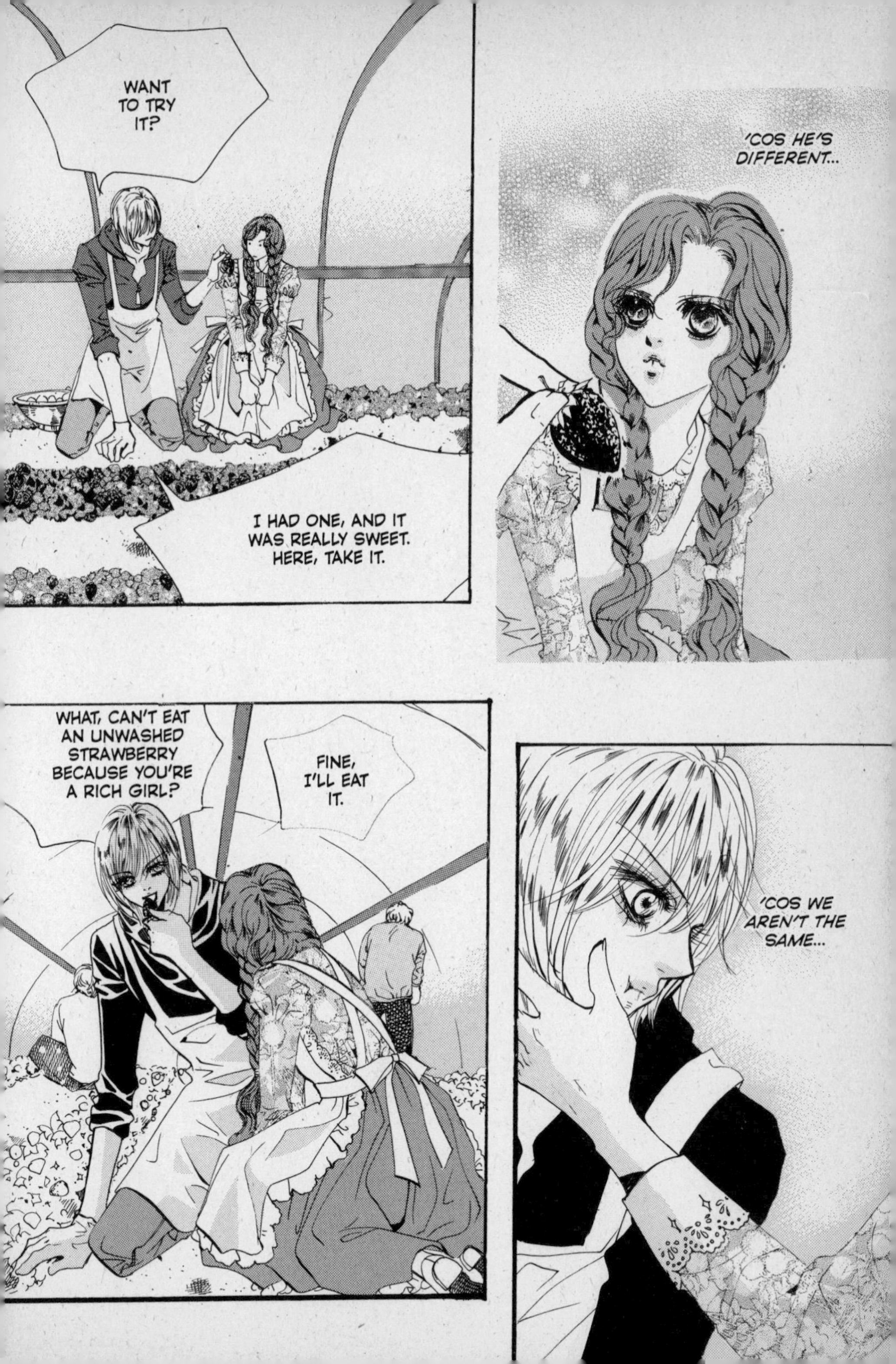
WANT TO TRY IT?
I HAD ONE, AND IT WAS REALLY SWEET. HERE, TAKE IT.
'COS HE'S DIFFERENT...
WHAT, CAN'T EAT AN UNWASHED STRAWBERRY BECAUSE YOU'RE A RICH GIRL?
FINE, I'LL EAT IT.
'COS WE AREN'T THE SAME...

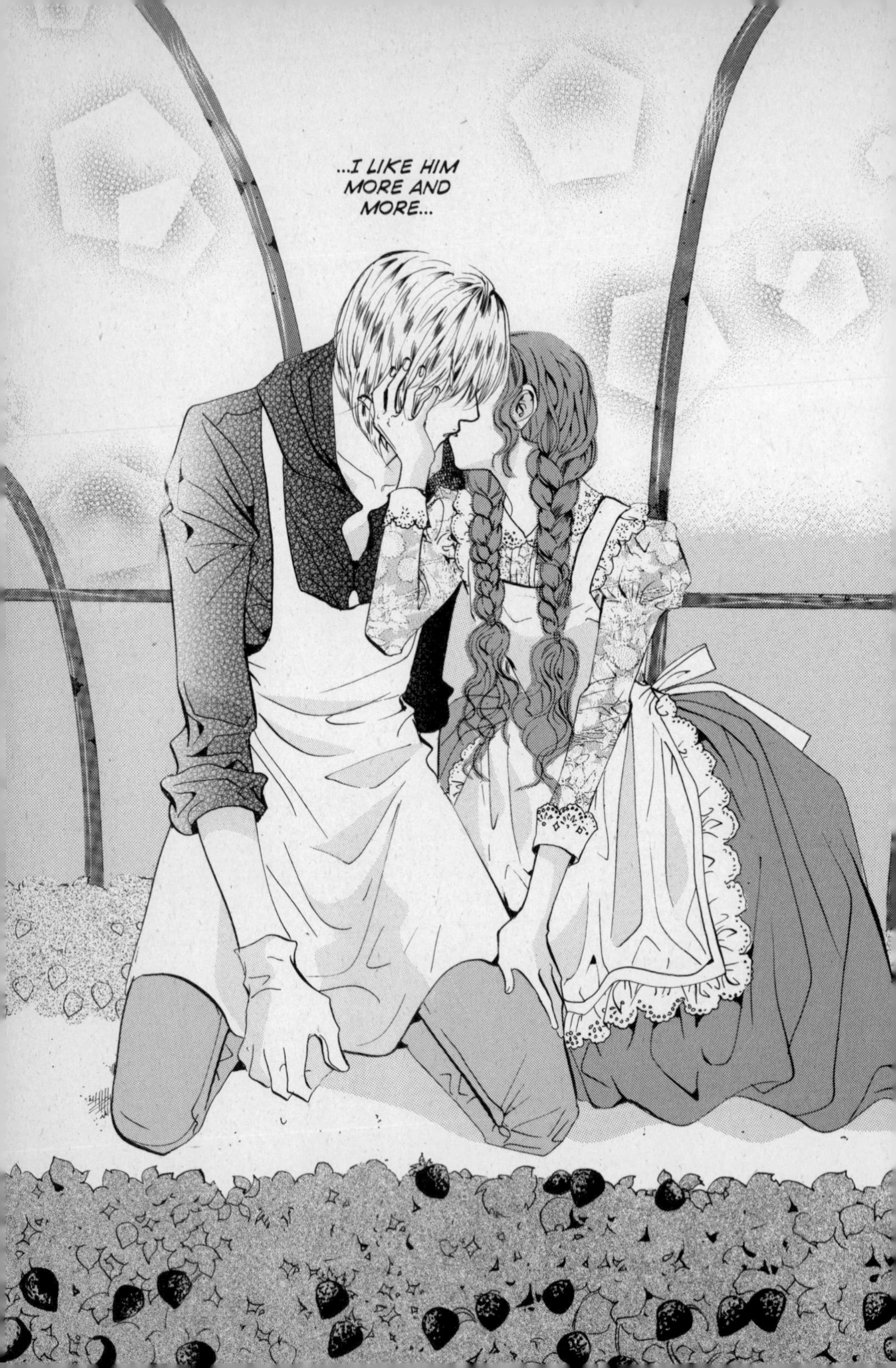
...I LIKE HIM MORE AND MORE...

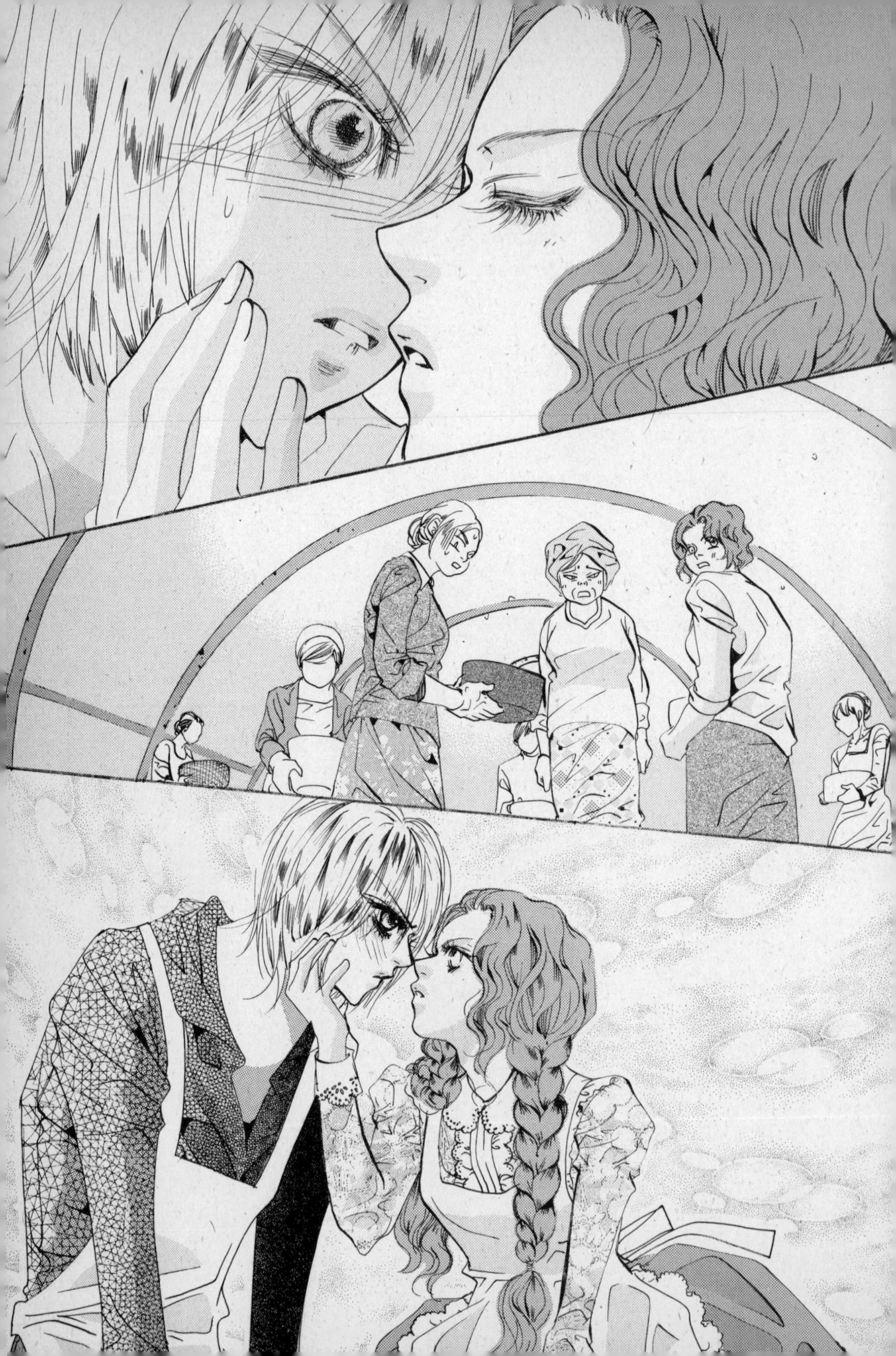

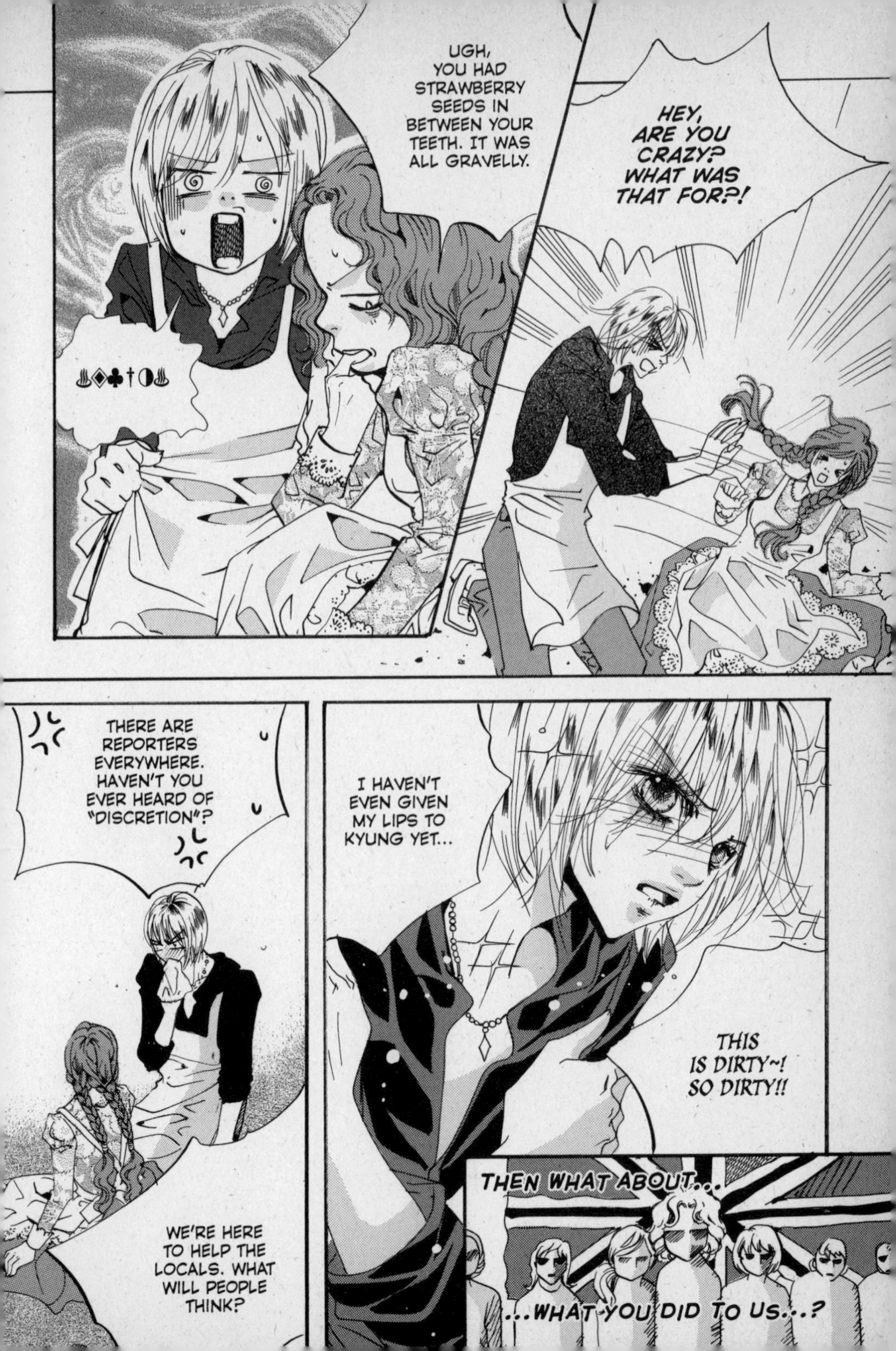
UGH, YOU HAD STRAWBERRY SEEDS IN BETWEEN YOUR TEETH. IT WAS ALL GRAVELLY.
HEY, ARE YOU CRAZY? WHAT WAS THAT FOR?!
THERE ARE REPORTERS EVERYWHERE. HAVEN'T YOU EVER HEARD OF "DISCRETION"?
WE'RE HERE TO HELP THE LOCALS. WHAT WILL PEOPLE THINK?
I HAVEN'T EVEN GIVEN MY LIPS TO KYUNG YET...
THIS IS DIRTY~! SO DIRTY!!
THEN WHAT ABOUT...
...WHAT YOU DID TO US...?

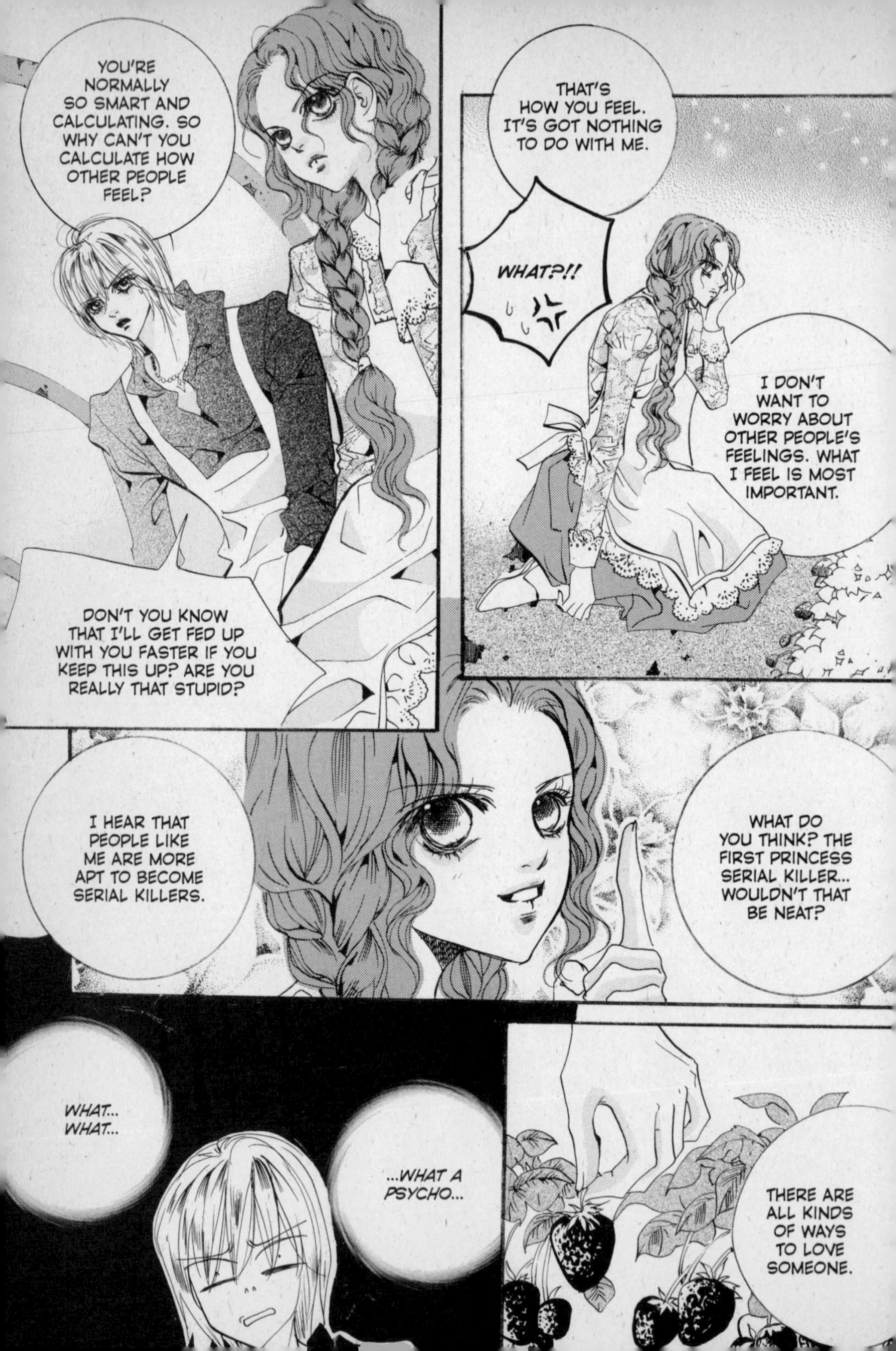
YOU'RE NORMALLY SO SMART AND CALCULATING. SO WHY CAN'T YOU CALCULATE HOW OTHER PEOPLE FEEL?
DON'T YOU KNOW THAT I'LL GET FED UP WITH YOU FASTER IF YOU KEEP THIS UP? ARE YOU REALLY THAT STUPID?
THAT'S HOW YOU FEEL. IT'S GOT NOTHING TO DO WITH ME.
WHAT?!!
I DON'T WANT TO WORRY ABOUT OTHER PEOPLE'S FEELINGS. WHAT I FEEL IS MOST IMPORTANT.
I HEAR THAT PEOPLE LIKE ME ARE MORE APT TO BECOME SERIAL KILLERS.
WHAT DO YOU THINK? THE FIRST PRINCESS SERIAL KILLER... WOULDN'T THAT BE NEAT?
WHAT... WHAT...
...WHAT A PSYCHO...
THERE ARE ALL KINDS OF WAYS TO LOVE SOMEONE.

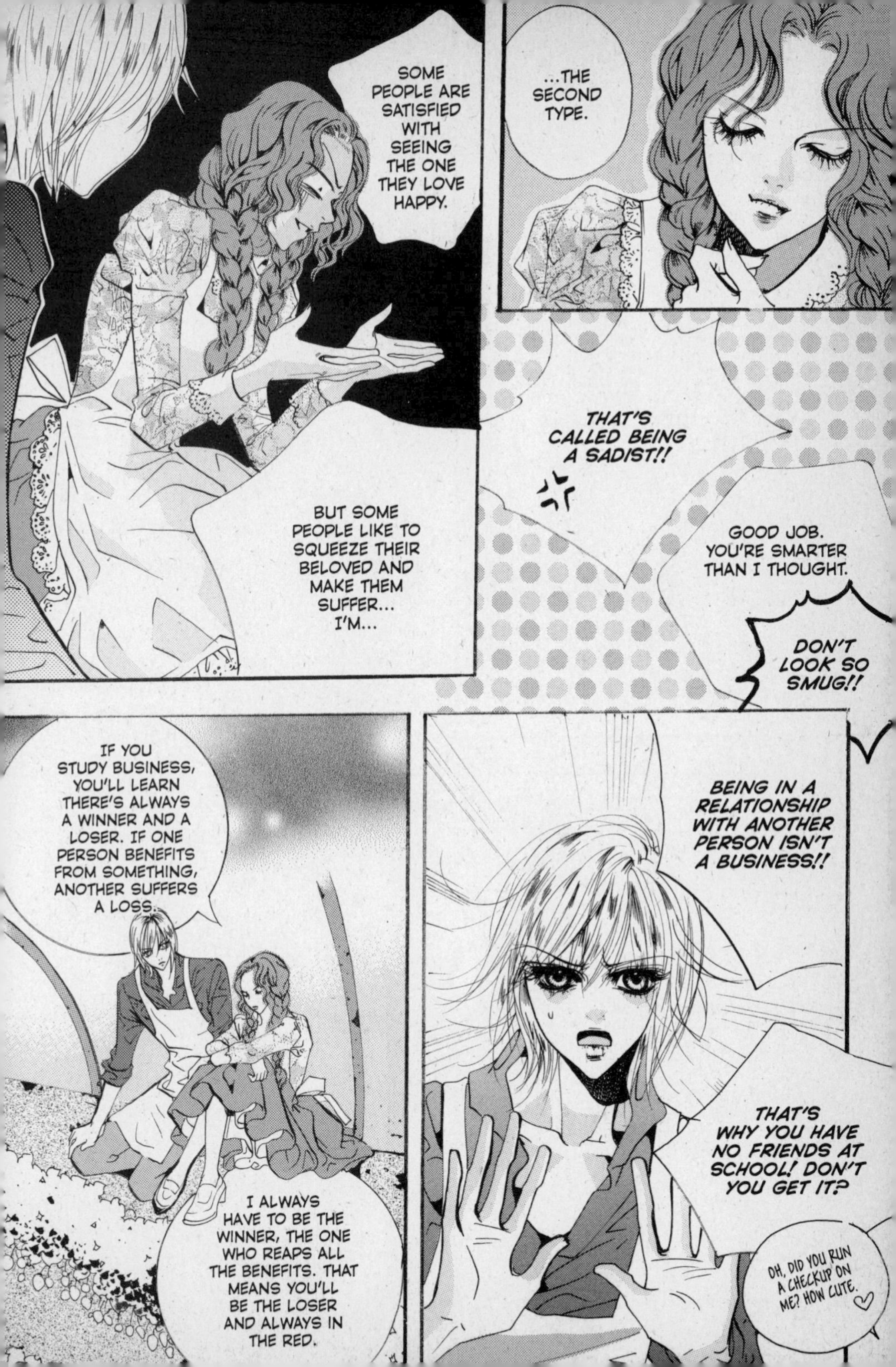
SOME PEOPLE ARE SATISFIED WITH SEEING THE ONE THEY LOVE HAPPY.
BUT SOME PEOPLE LIKE TO SQUEEZE THEIR BELOVED AND MAKE THEM SUFFER... I'M...
...THE SECOND TYPE.
THAT'S CALLED BEING A SADIST!!
GOOD JOB. YOU'RE SMARTER THAN I THOUGHT.
DON'T LOOK SO SMUG!!
IF YOU STUDY BUSINESS, YOU'LL LEARN THERE'S ALWAYS A WINNER AND A LOSER. IF ONE PERSON BENEFITS FROM SOMETHING, ANOTHER SUFFERS A LOSS.
I ALWAYS HAVE TO BE THE WINNER, THE ONE WHO REAPS ALL THE BENEFITS. THAT MEANS YOU'LL BE THE LOSER AND ALWAYS IN THE RED.
BEING IN A RELATIONSHIP WITH ANOTHER PERSON ISN'T A BUSINESS!!
THAT'S WHY YOU HAVE NO FRIENDS AT SCHOOL! DON'T YOU GET IT?
OH, DID YOU RUN A CHECKUP ON ME? HOW CUTE.

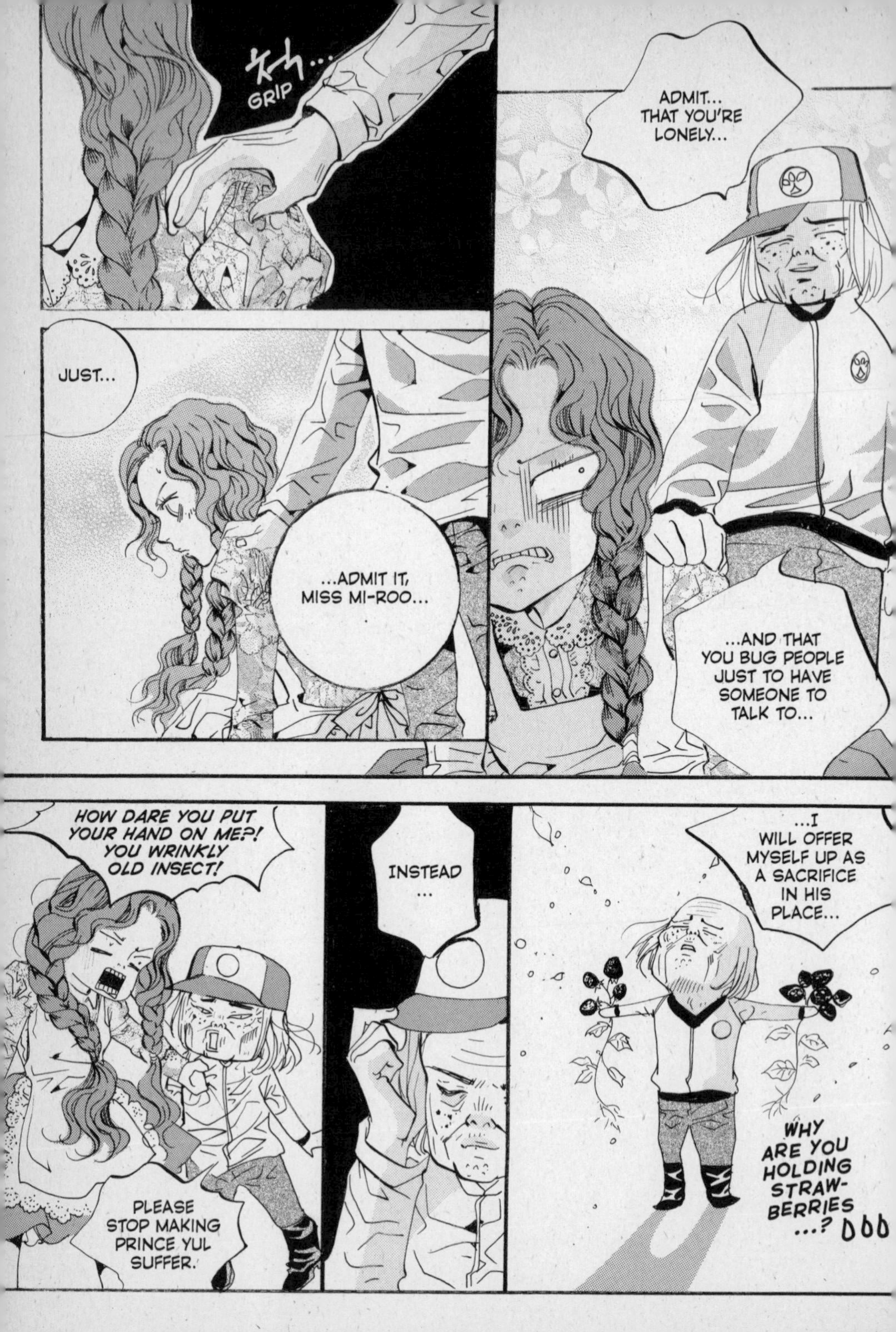
GRIP
ADMIT... THAT YOU'RE LONELY...
JUST...
...ADMIT IT, MISS MI-ROO...
...AND THAT YOU BUG PEOPLE JUST TO HAVE SOMEONE TO TALK TO...
HOW DARE YOU PUT YOUR HAND ON ME?! YOU WRINKLY OLD INSECT!
PLEASE STOP MAKING PRINCE YUL SUFFER.
INSTEAD ...
...I WILL OFFER MYSELF UP AS A SACRIFICE IN HIS PLACE...
WHY ARE YOU HOLDING STRAW-BERRIES ...?

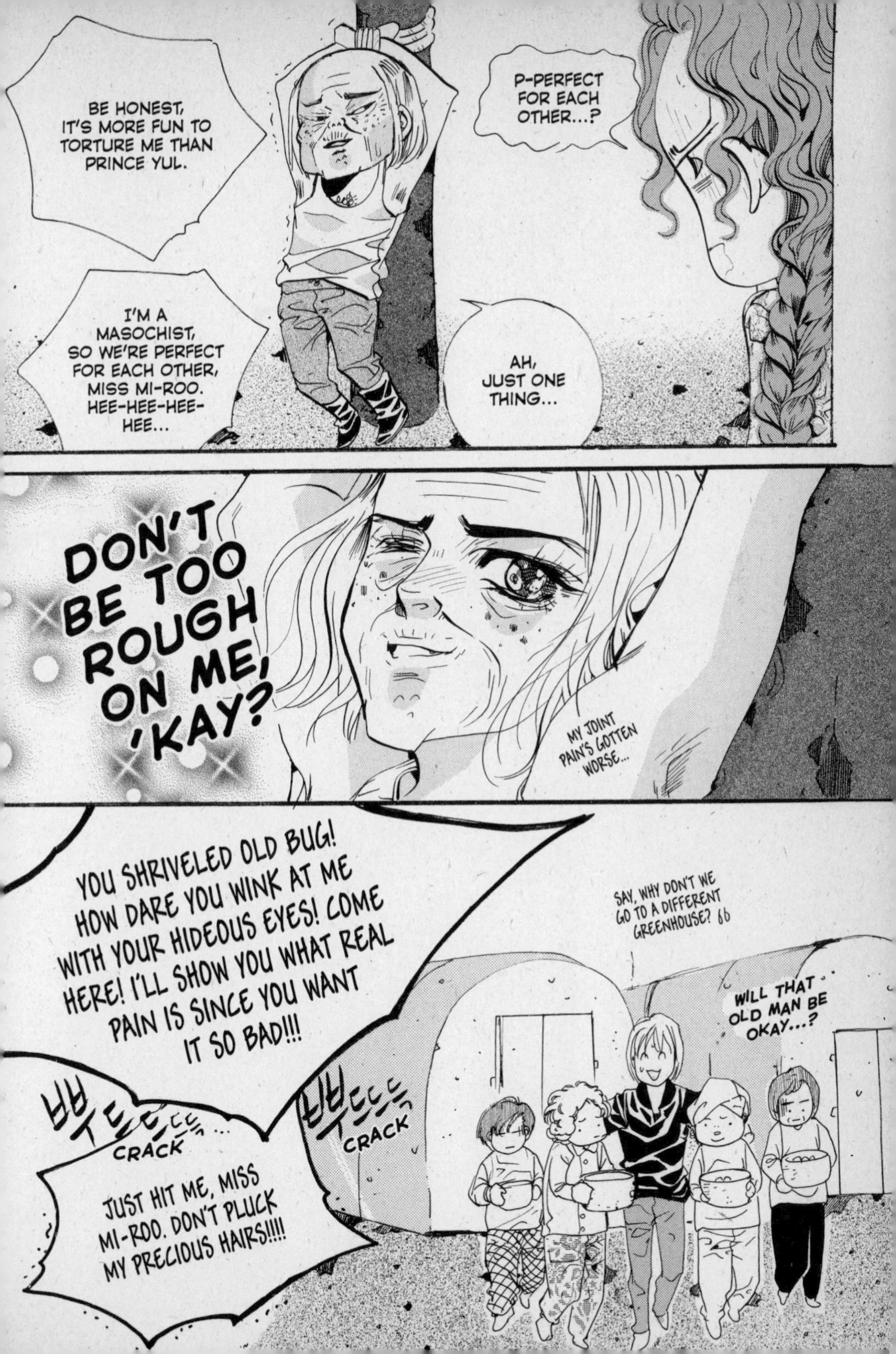
BE HONEST, IT'S MORE FUN TO TORTURE ME THAN PRINCE YUL.
I'M A MASOCHIST, SO WE'RE PERFECT FOR EACH OTHER, MISS MI-ROO. HEE-HEE-HEE-HEE...
P-PERFECT FOR EACH OTHER...?
AH, JUST ONE THING...
DON'T BE TOO ROUGH ON ME, 'KAY?
MY JOINT PAIN'S GOTTEN WORSE...
YOU SHRIVELED OLD BUG! HOW DARE YOU WINK AT ME WITH YOUR HIDEOUS EYES! COME HERE! I'LL SHOW YOU WHAT REAL PAIN IS SINCE YOU WANT IT SO BAD!!!
SAY, WHY DON'T WE GO TO A DIFFERENT GREENHOUSE?
WILL THAT OLD MAN BE OKAY...?
CRACK
CRACK
JUST HIT ME, MISS MI-ROO. DON'T PLUCK MY PRECIOUS HAIRS!!!!

CONFIRMATION OF DIVORCE AGREEMENT

성 명 :
주민등록번호
본 적
주 소

여 성 명 :
주민등록번호
본 적 상 주( )
주 소

정리 위기
저 양자의 사이에는 진의에 따라 서로 이혼하기로 합의하였다.
위와 같이 이혼의사가 확인되었다.
라는 확인을 구함.

첨부서류

1.   3.   1)
2.   )
3.   (   )
4.   190 0 0

위 신청인 부( )

(위중

DIVORCE APPLICATION

특수택합번호는 해당변호에 "○"으로 표시하여 주시기 바랍니다.

구	본 남				처	
본 적		호 주 일 관계 의			처	호 주 일 관계
주 소		세 대 주 일 관계 의				세 대 주 일 관계
한글	서영(인) 전 화		한글		서영(인)	전
한자			한자			본
민 등 록 번 호			주민등록번호			
	본 적			본 적		
	성 명			성 명		
	여			여		
	석			석		
본적			본적			
	성 명			성 명		
						호주
가장방장소			일가장일원인			
년			월		일 법원명	
지전일자						

IT'S BIZARRE, FATHER AND THE ROYAL RELATIVES ACCEPTING MY DIVORCE.

IT'S EVEN STRANGER ABOUT GRAND-MOTHER AND MOTHER.

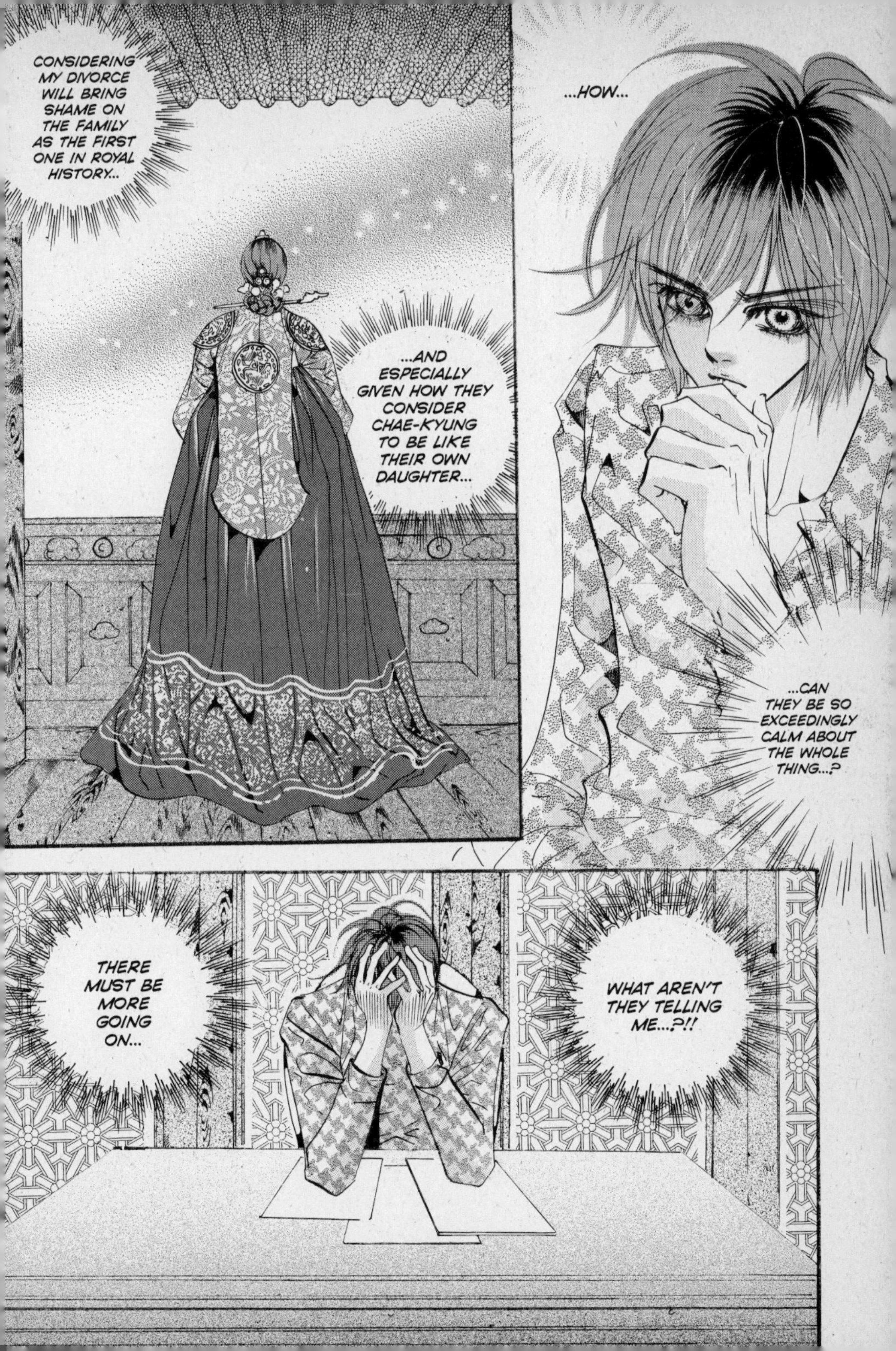
CONSIDERING MY DIVORCE WILL BRING SHAME ON THE FAMILY AS THE FIRST ONE IN ROYAL HISTORY...
...AND ESPECIALLY GIVEN HOW THEY CONSIDER CHAE-KYUNG TO BE LIKE THEIR OWN DAUGHTER...
...HOW...
...CAN THEY BE SO EXCEEDINGLY CALM ABOUT THE WHOLE THING...?
THERE MUST BE MORE GOING ON...
WHAT AREN'T THEY TELLING ME...?!!

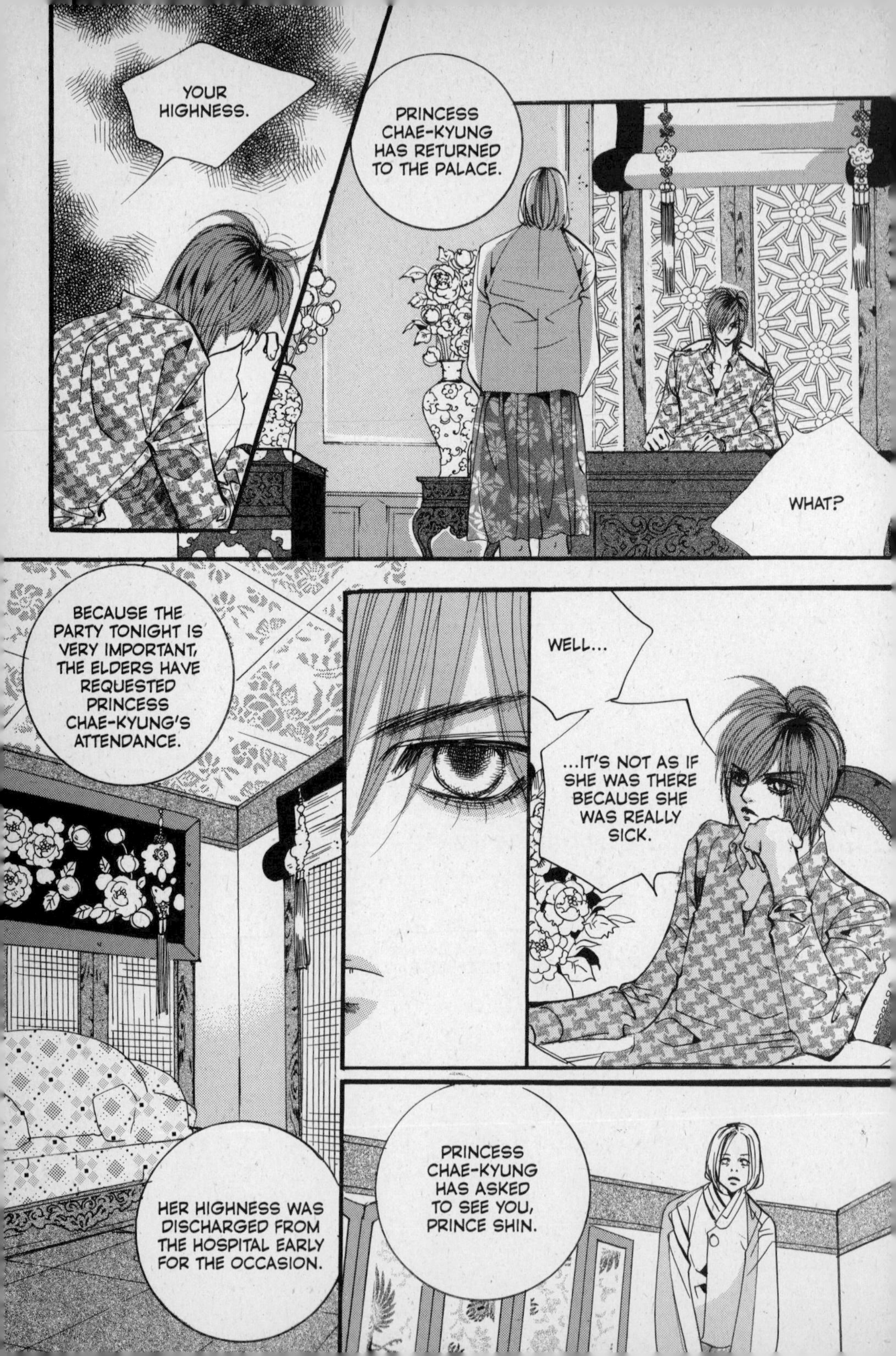
YOUR HIGHNESS.
PRINCESS CHAE-KYUNG HAS RETURNED TO THE PALACE.
WHAT?
BECAUSE THE PARTY TONIGHT IS VERY IMPORTANT, THE ELDERS HAVE REQUESTED PRINCESS CHAE-KYUNG'S ATTENDANCE.
WELL...
...IT'S NOT AS IF SHE WAS THERE BECAUSE SHE WAS REALLY SICK.
HER HIGHNESS WAS DISCHARGED FROM THE HOSPITAL EARLY FOR THE OCCASION.
PRINCESS CHAE-KYUNG HAS ASKED TO SEE YOU, PRINCE SHIN.

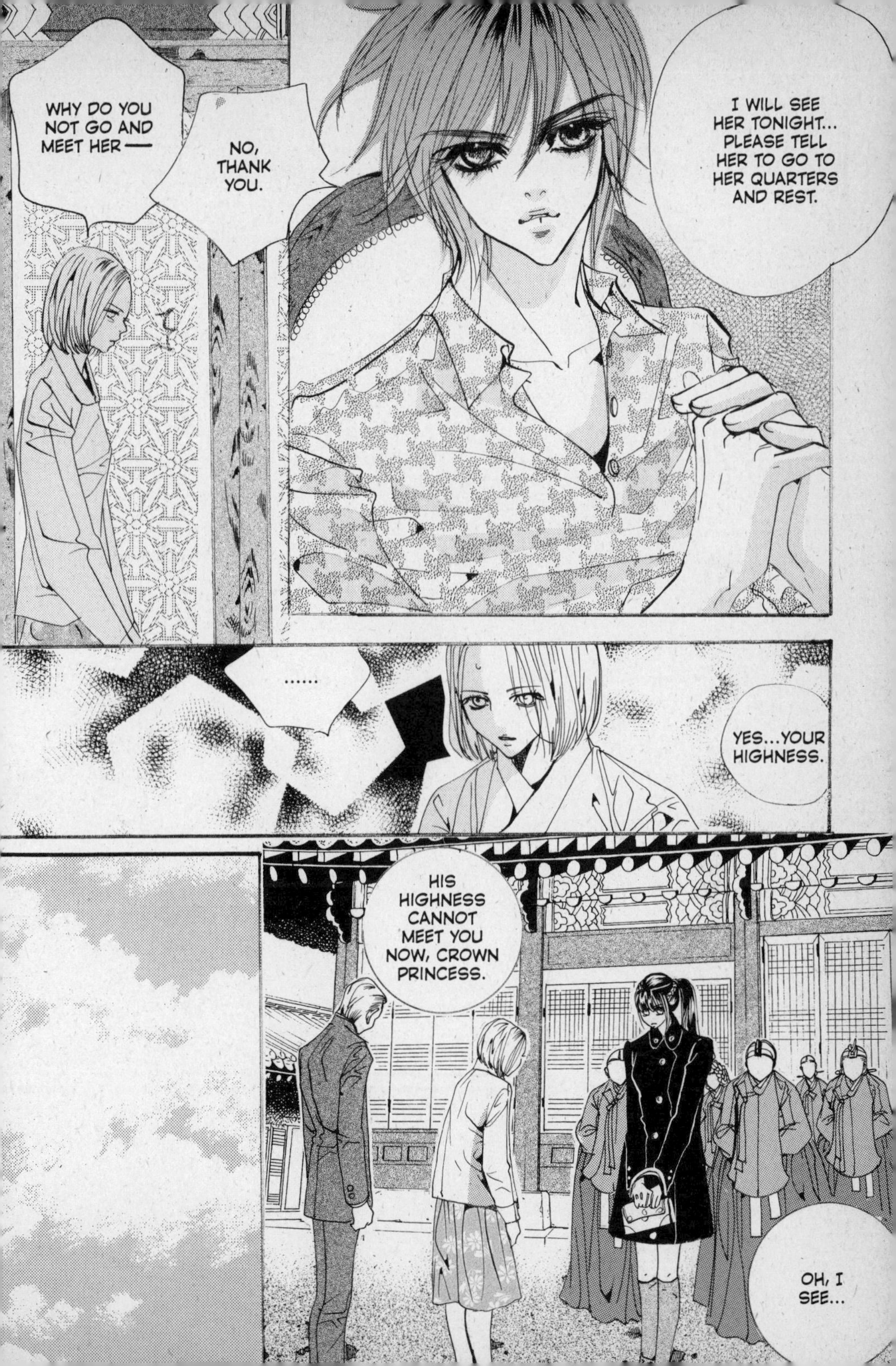
I WILL SEE HER TONIGHT... PLEASE TELL HER TO GO TO HER QUARTERS AND REST.
NO, THANK YOU.
WHY DO YOU NOT GO AND MEET HER—
YES...YOUR HIGHNESS.
......
HIS HIGHNESS CANNOT MEET YOU NOW, CROWN PRINCESS.
OH, I SEE...

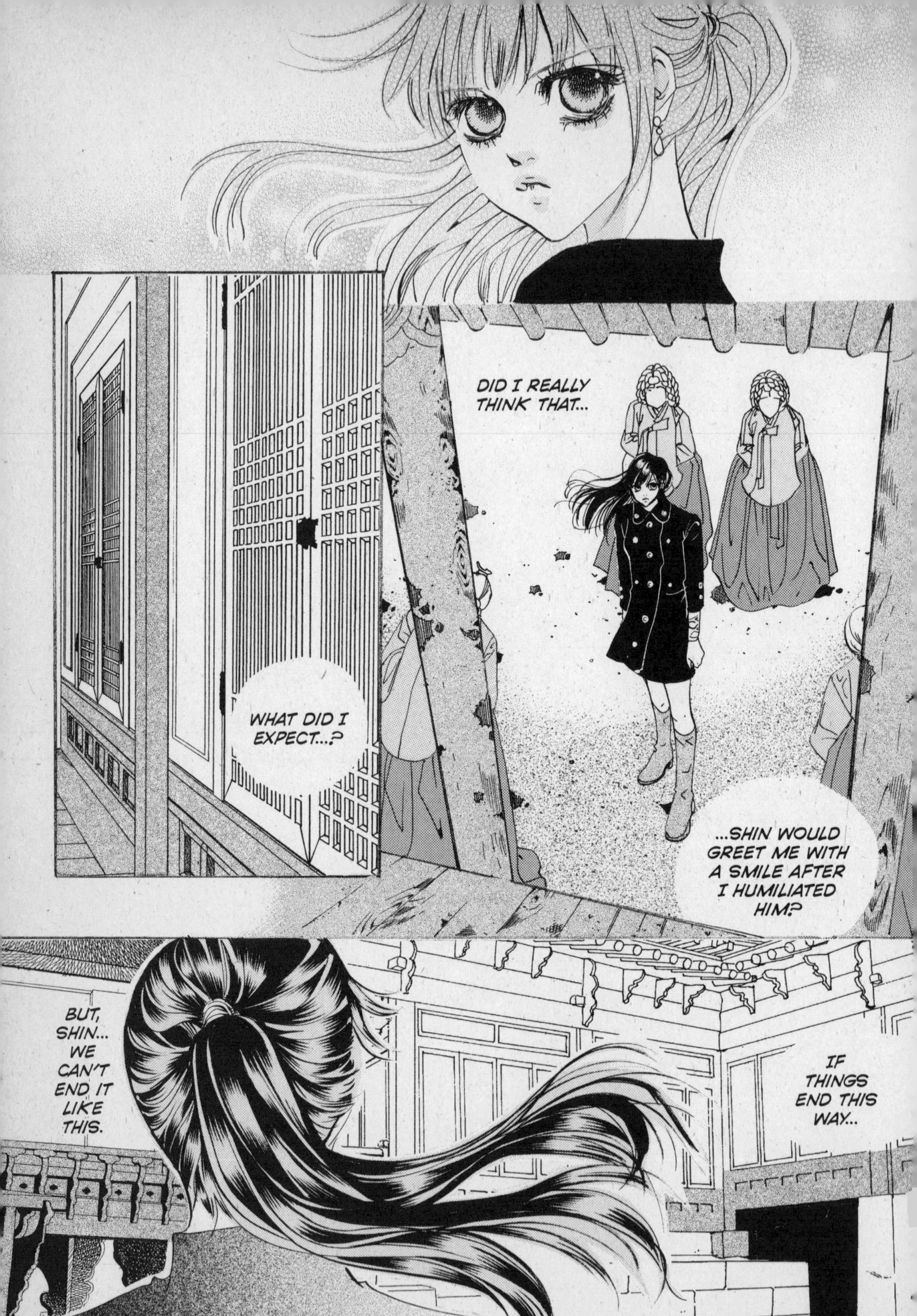
DID I REALLY THINK THAT...
WHAT DID I EXPECT...?
...SHIN WOULD GREET ME WITH A SMILE AFTER I HUMILIATED HIM?
BUT, SHIN... WE CAN'T END IT LIKE THIS.
IF THINGS END THIS WAY...

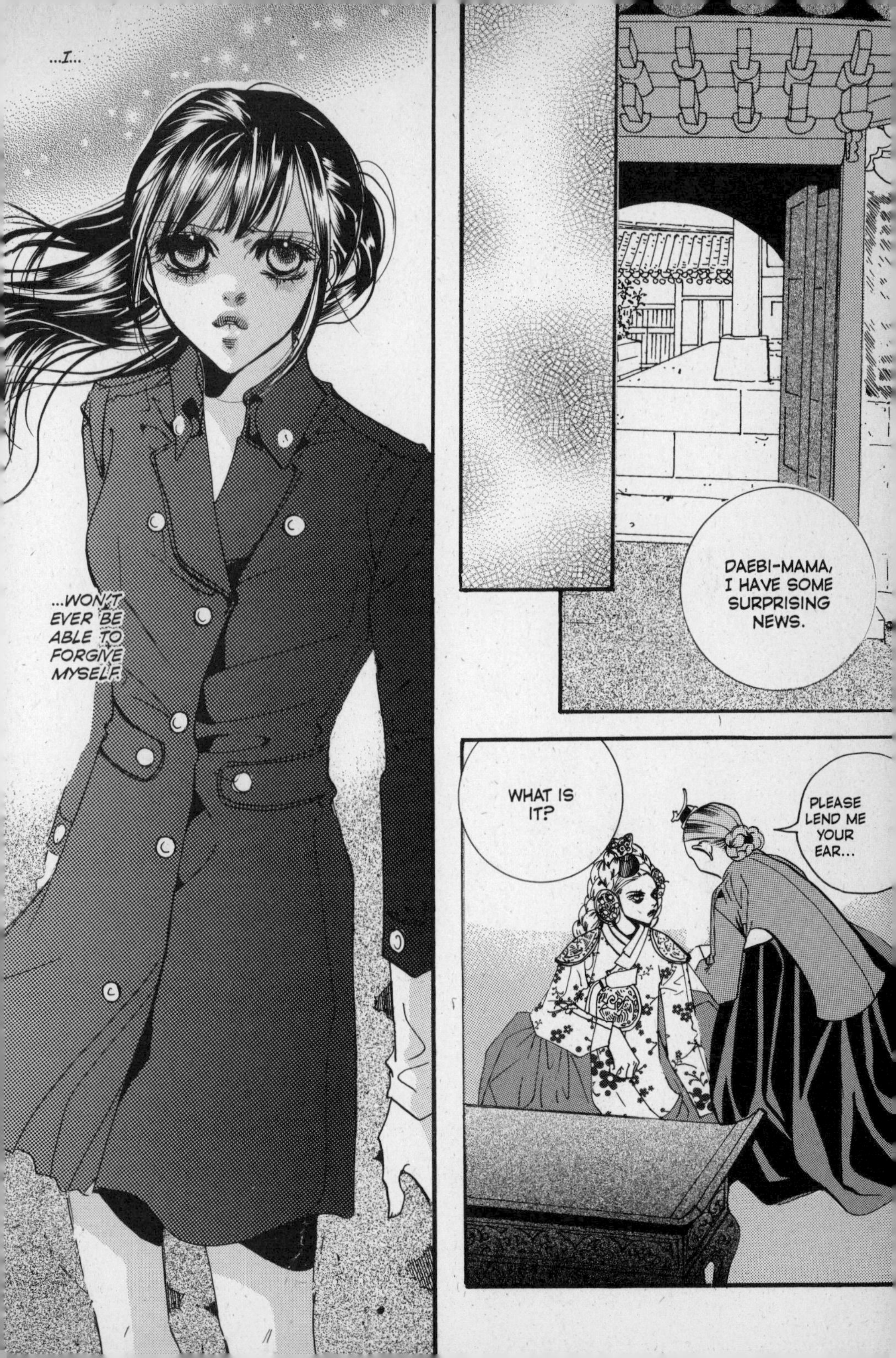
...I...
...WON'T EVER BE ABLE TO FORGIVE MYSELF.
DAEBI-MAMA, I HAVE SOME SURPRISING NEWS.
PLEASE LEND ME YOUR EAR...
WHAT IS IT?

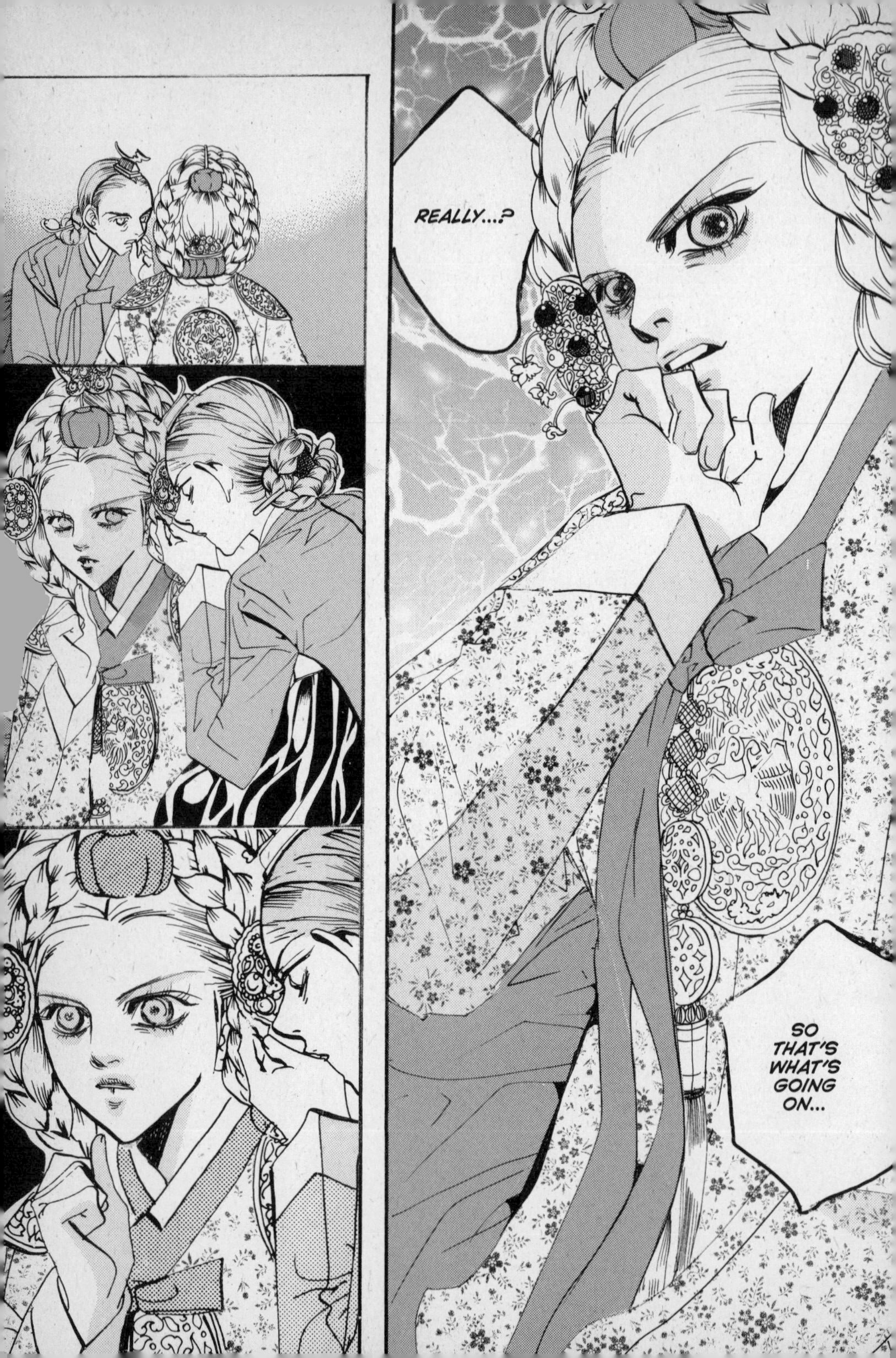
REALLY...?
SO THAT'S WHAT'S GOING ON...

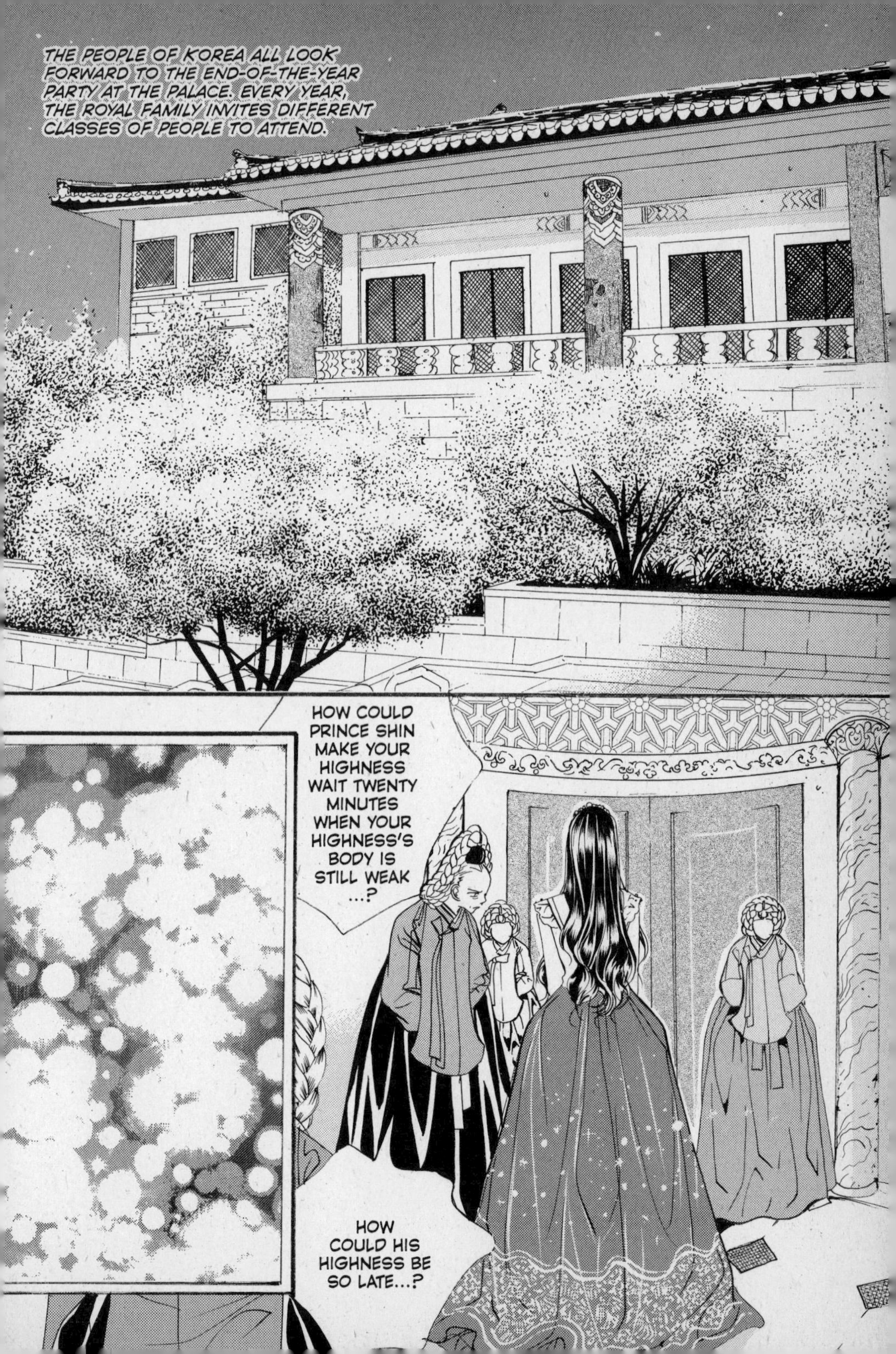
THE PEOPLE OF KOREA ALL LOOK FORWARD TO THE END-OF-THE-YEAR PARTY AT THE PALACE. EVERY YEAR, THE ROYAL FAMILY INVITES DIFFERENT CLASSES OF PEOPLE TO ATTEND.
HOW COULD PRINCE SHIN MAKE YOUR HIGHNESS WAIT TWENTY MINUTES WHEN YOUR HIGHNESS'S BODY IS STILL WEAK ...?
HOW COULD HIS HIGHNESS BE SO LATE...?

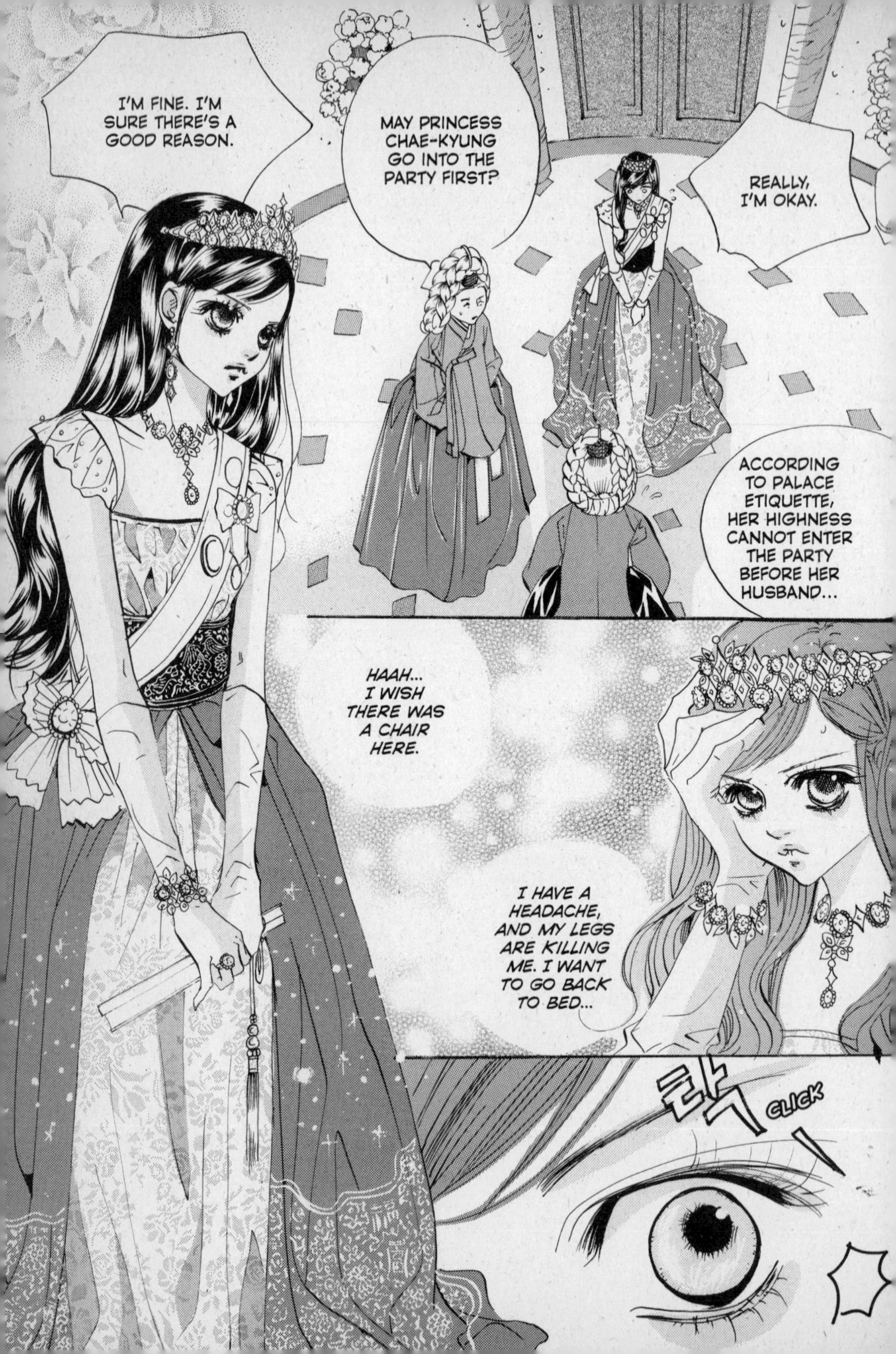
I'M FINE. I'M SURE THERE'S A GOOD REASON.
MAY PRINCESS CHAE-KYUNG GO INTO THE PARTY FIRST?
REALLY, I'M OKAY.
ACCORDING TO PALACE ETIQUETTE, HER HIGHNESS CANNOT ENTER THE PARTY BEFORE HER HUSBAND...
HAAH... I WISH THERE WAS A CHAIR HERE.
I HAVE A HEADACHE, AND MY LEGS ARE KILLING ME. I WANT TO GO BACK TO BED...
CLICK

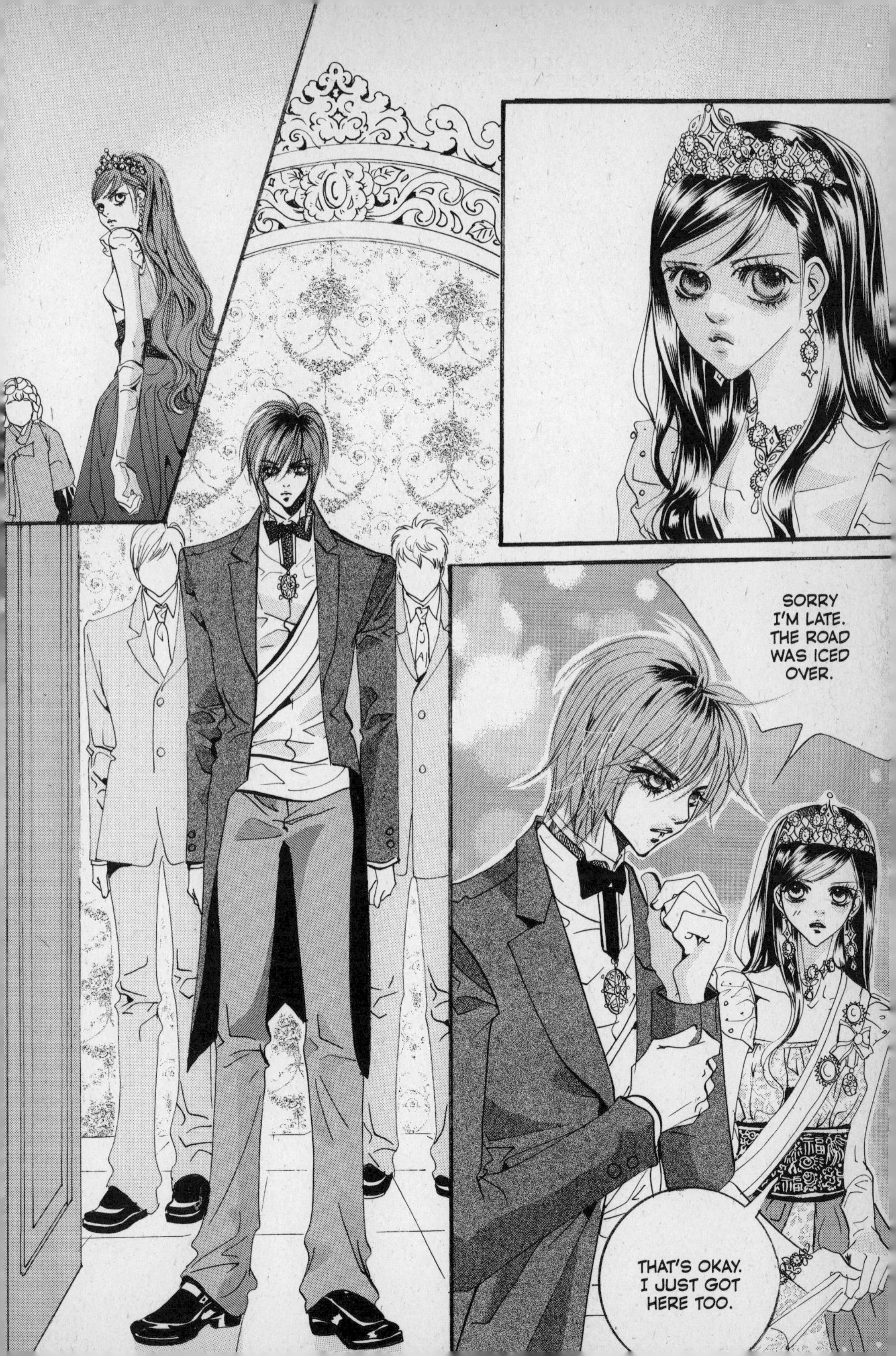
SORRY I'M LATE. THE ROAD WAS ICED OVER.
THAT'S OKAY. I JUST GOT HERE TOO.

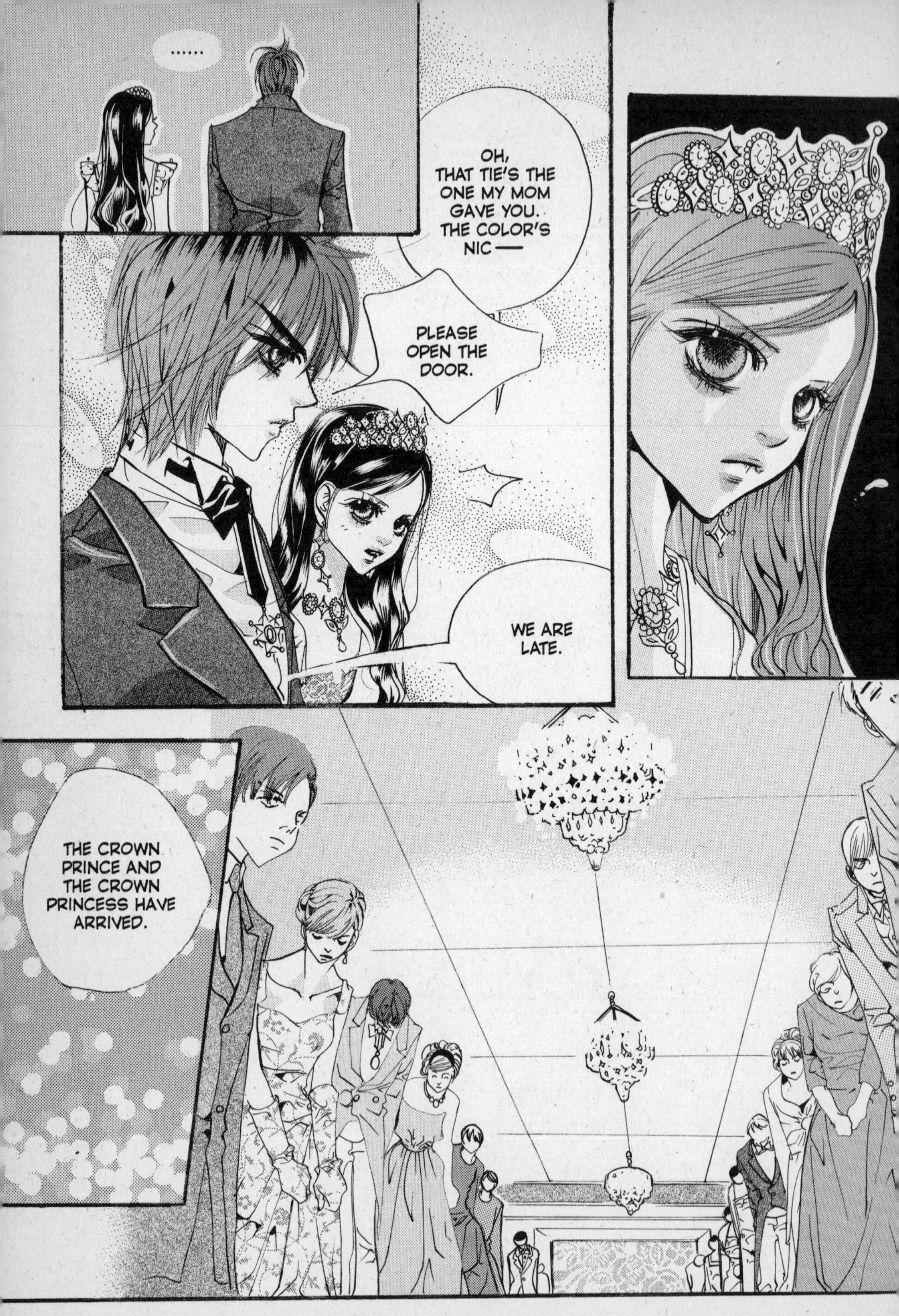
......
OH, THAT TIE'S THE ONE MY MOM GAVE YOU. THE COLOR'S NIC—
PLEASE OPEN THE DOOR.
WE ARE LATE.
THE CROWN PRINCE AND THE CROWN PRINCESS HAVE ARRIVED.

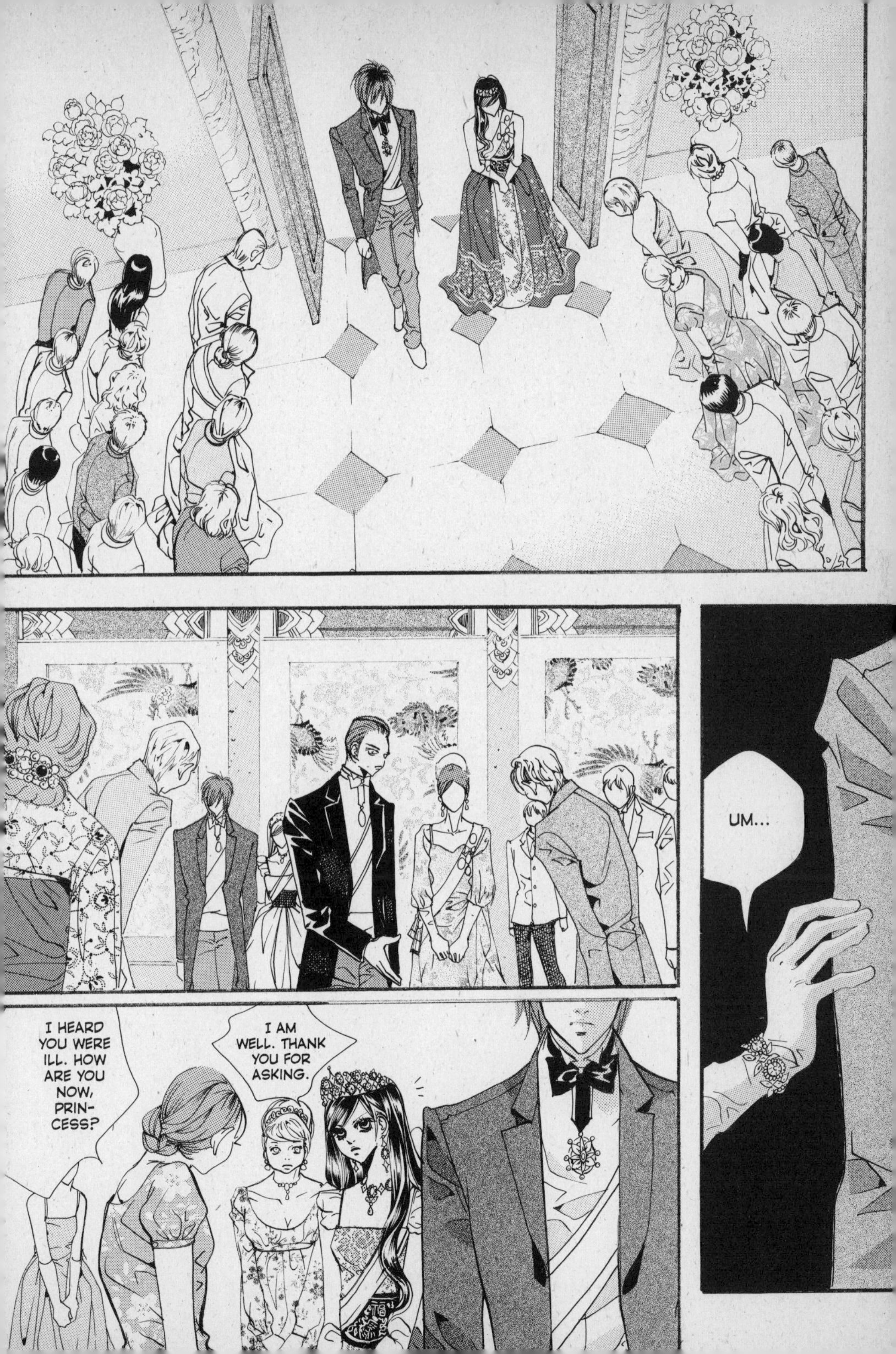
UM...
I AM WELL. THANK YOU FOR ASKING.
I HEARD YOU WERE ILL. HOW ARE YOU NOW, PRIN-CESS?

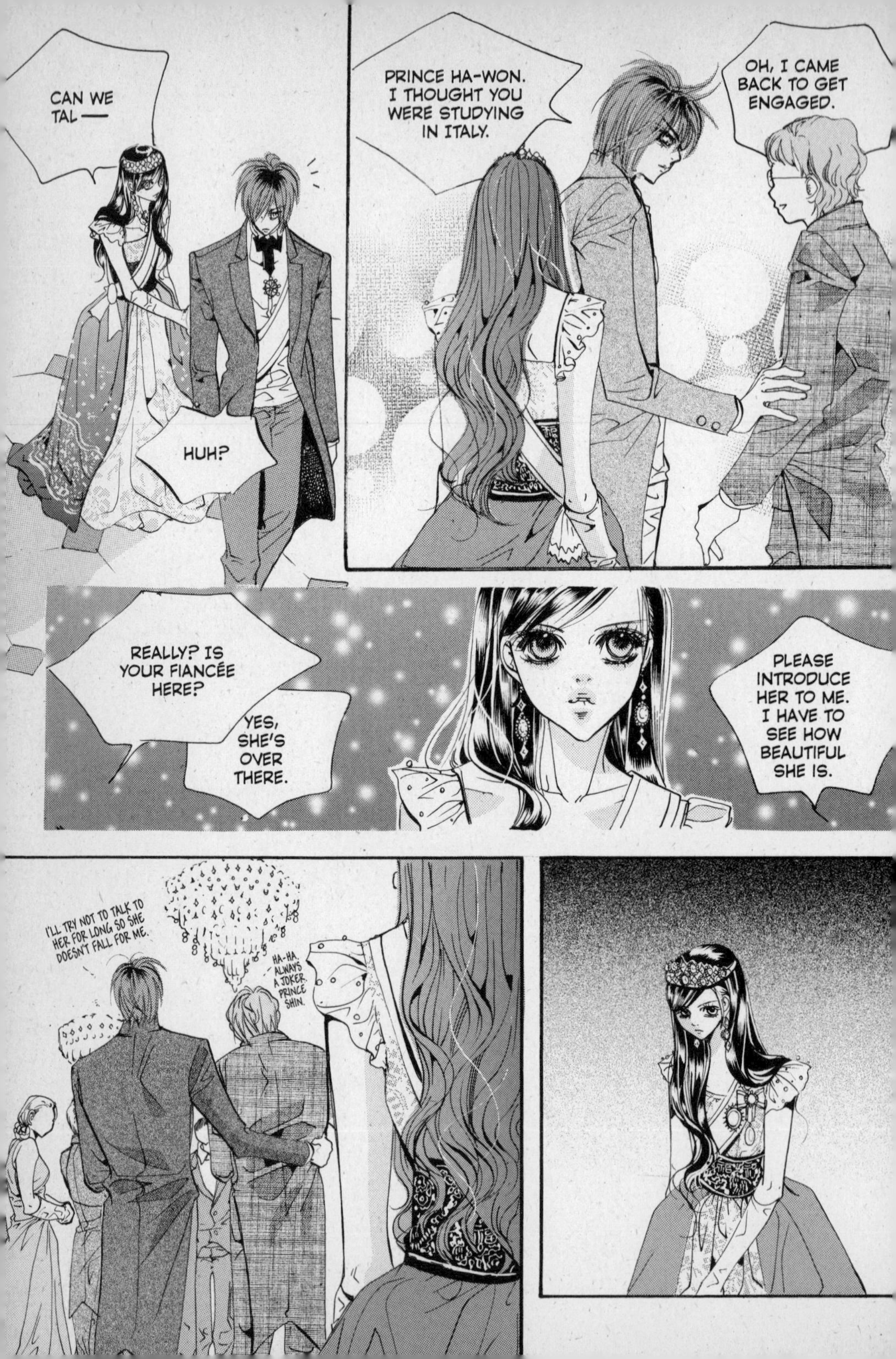
CAN WE TAL—
HUH?
PRINCE HA-WON. I THOUGHT YOU WERE STUDYING IN ITALY.
OH, I CAME BACK TO GET ENGAGED.
REALLY? IS YOUR FIANCÉE HERE?
YES, SHE'S OVER THERE.
PLEASE INTRODUCE HER TO ME. I HAVE TO SEE HOW BEAUTIFUL SHE IS.
I'LL TRY NOT TO TALK TO HER FOR LONG SO SHE DOESN'T FALL FOR ME.
HA-HA. ALWAYS A JOKER, PRINCE SHIN.

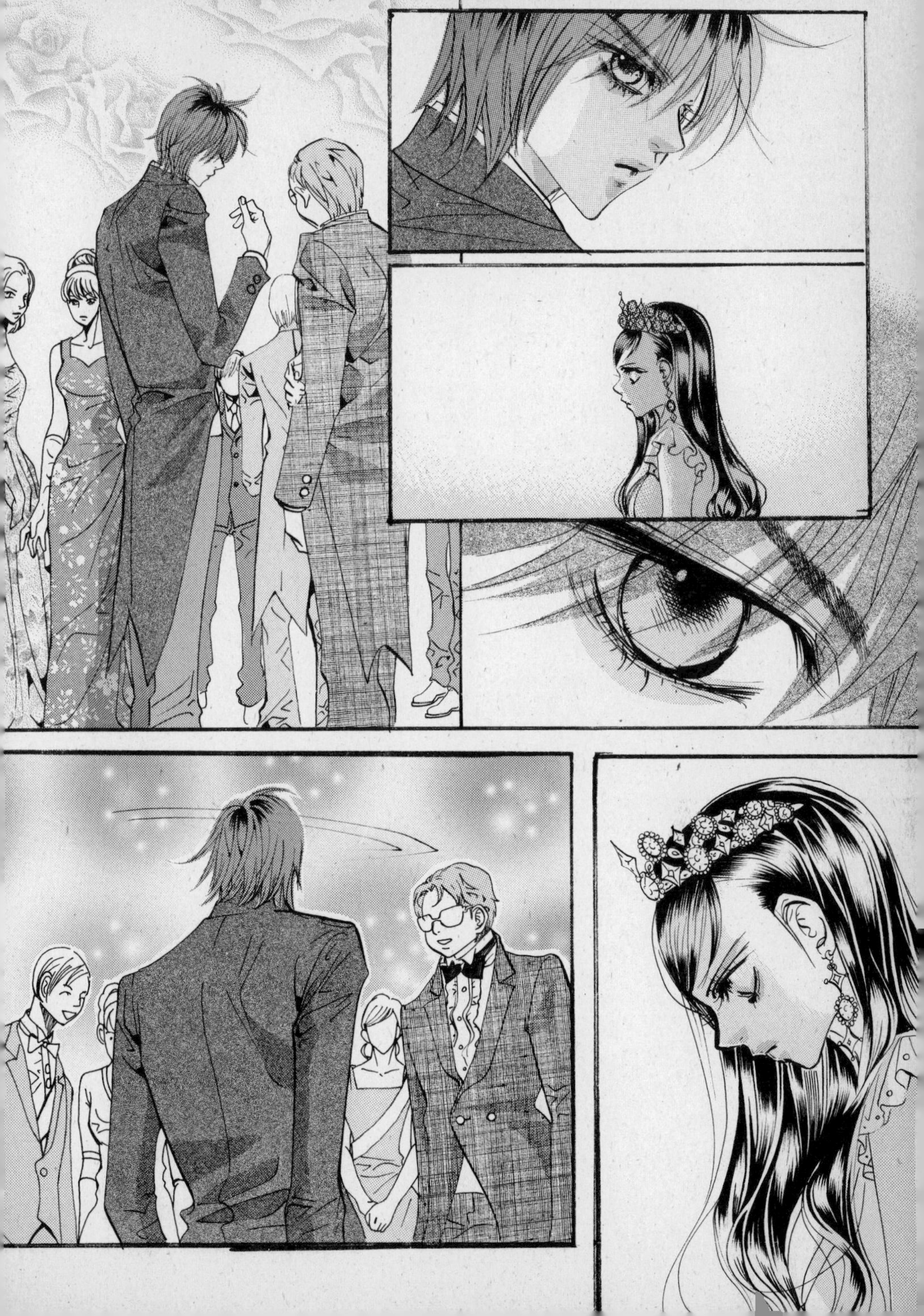

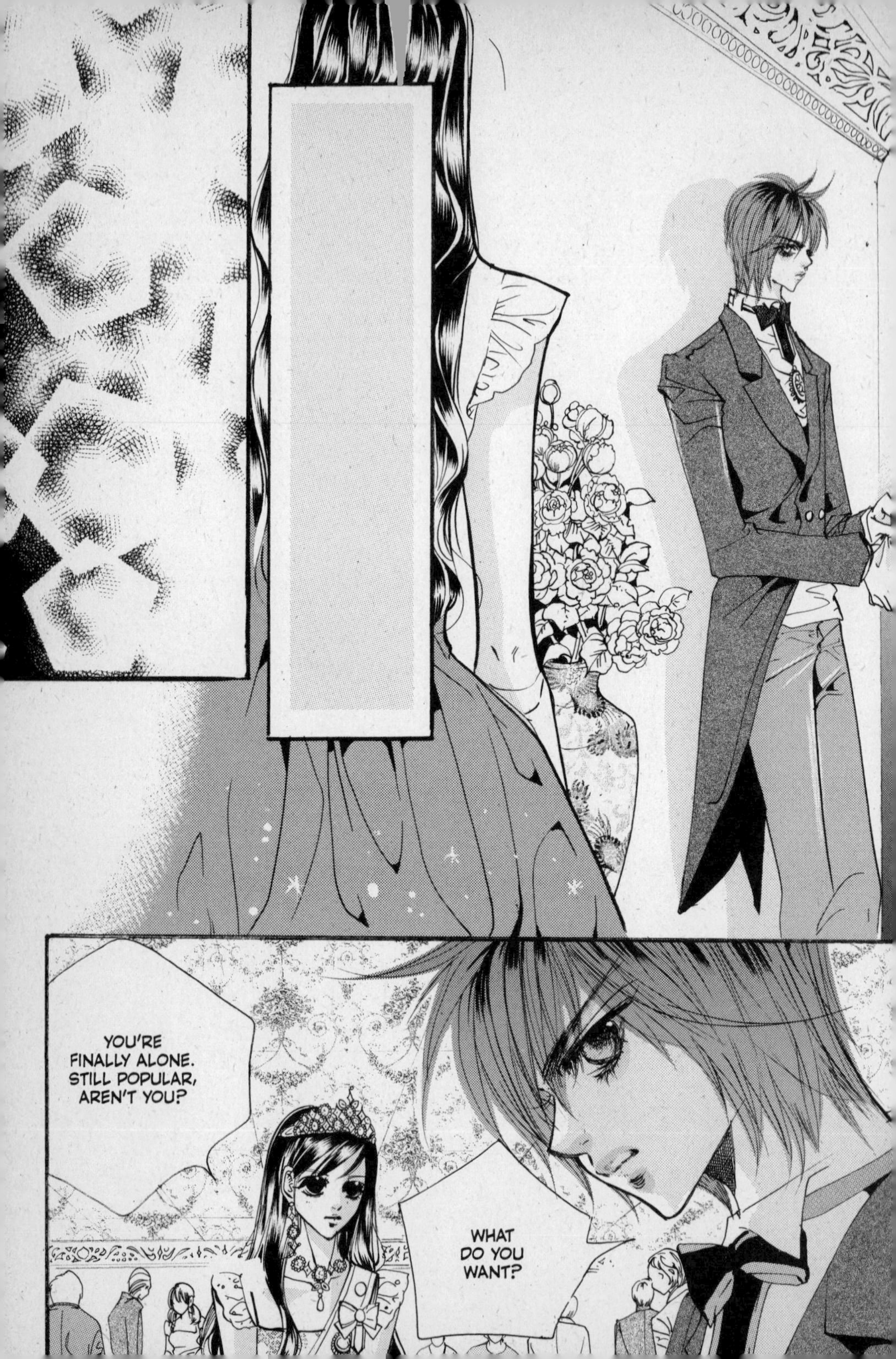
YOU'RE FINALLY ALONE. STILL POPULAR, AREN'T YOU?
WHAT DO YOU WANT?

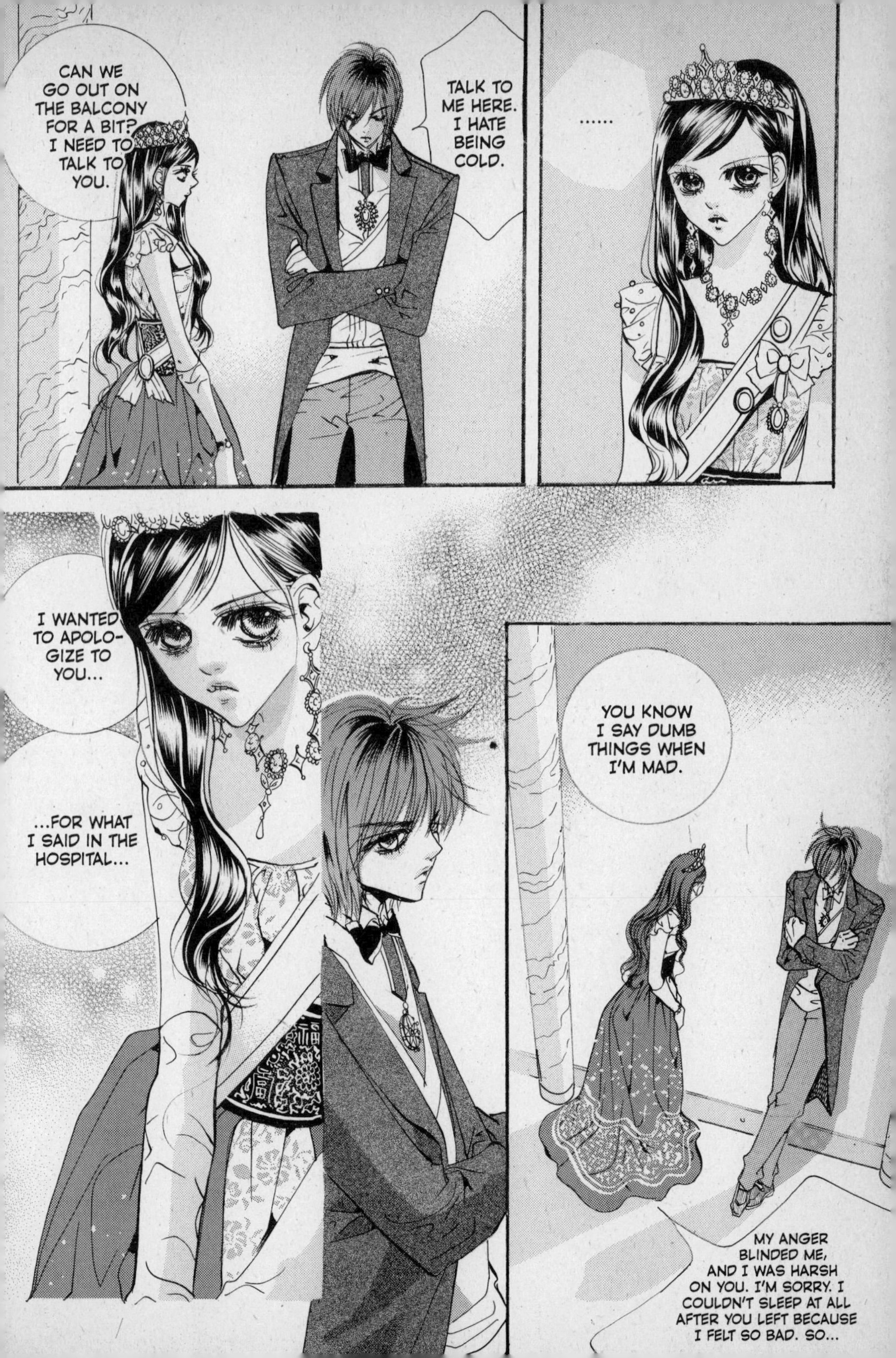
CAN WE GO OUT ON THE BALCONY FOR A BIT? I NEED TO TALK TO YOU.
TALK TO ME HERE. I HATE BEING COLD.
......
I WANTED TO APOLO-GIZE TO YOU...
...FOR WHAT I SAID IN THE HOSPITAL...
YOU KNOW I SAY DUMB THINGS WHEN I'M MAD.
MY ANGER BLINDED ME, AND I WAS HARSH ON YOU. I'M SORRY. I COULDN'T SLEEP AT ALL AFTER YOU LEFT BECAUSE I FELT SO BAD. SO...

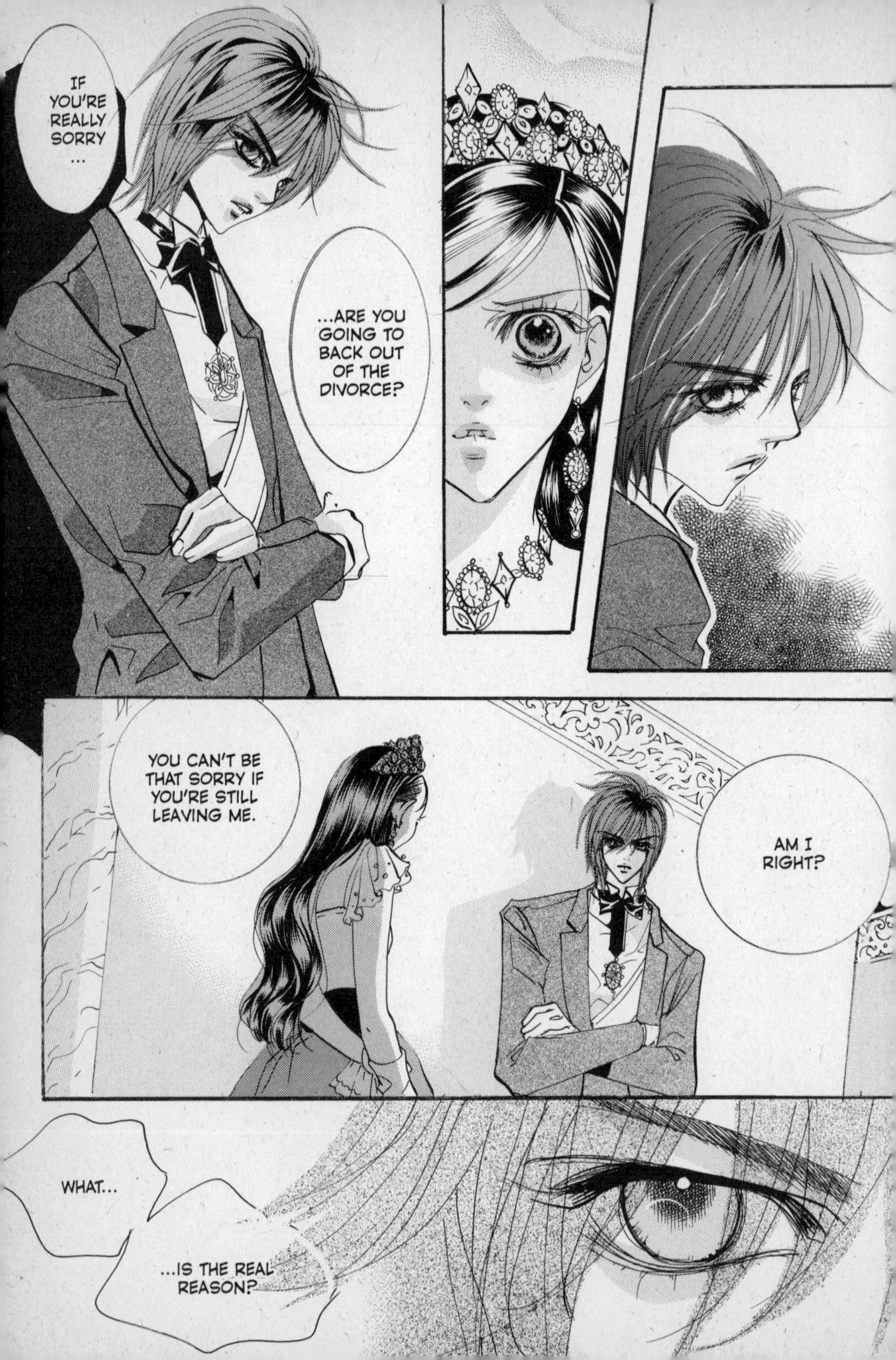

IF YOU'RE REALLY SORRY ...
...ARE YOU GOING TO BACK OUT OF THE DIVORCE?
YOU CAN'T BE THAT SORRY IF YOU'RE STILL LEAVING ME.
AM I RIGHT?
WHAT...
...IS THE REAL REASON?

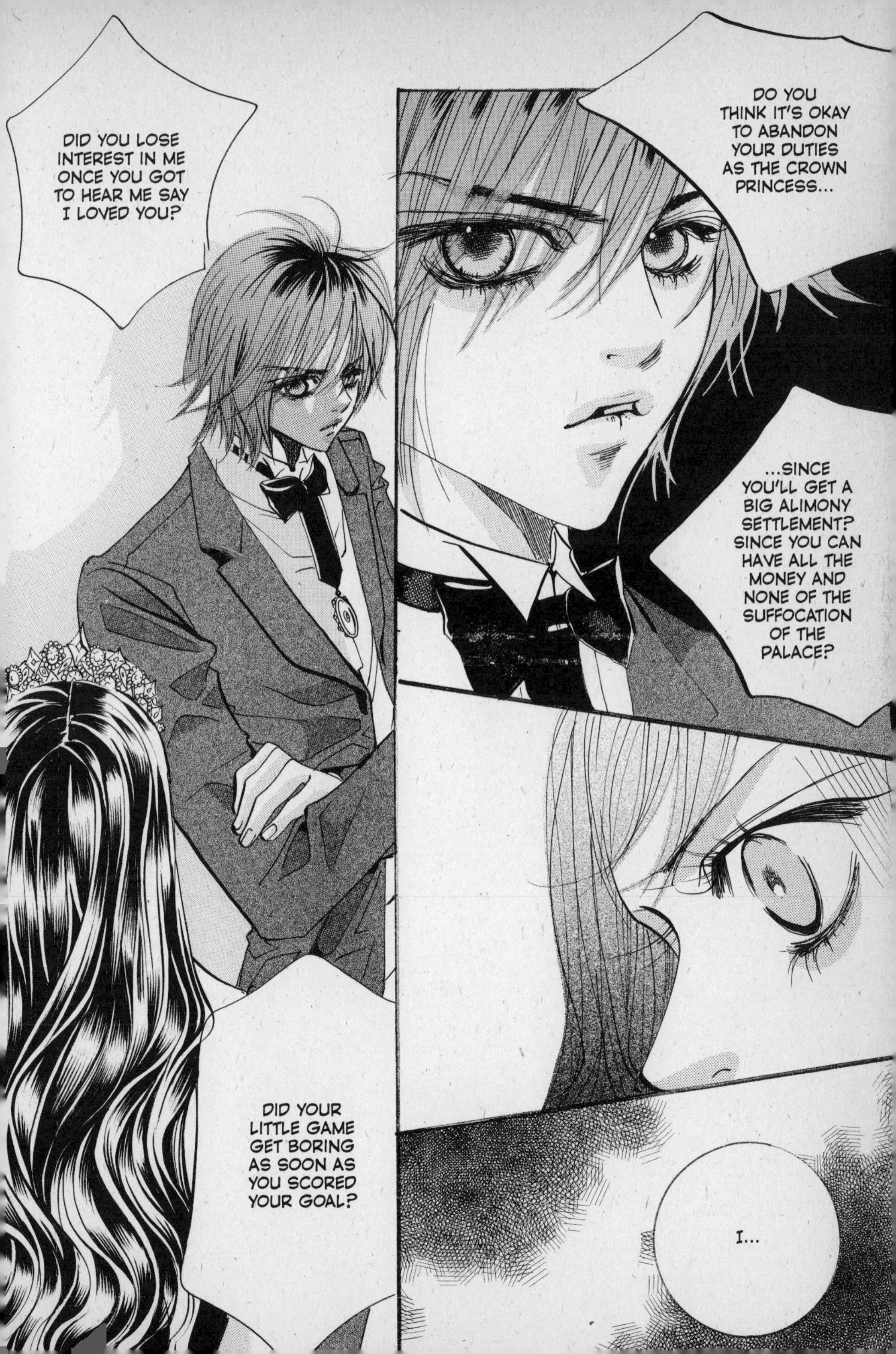
DO YOU THINK IT'S OKAY TO ABANDON YOUR DUTIES AS THE CROWN PRINCESS...
...SINCE YOU'LL GET A BIG ALIMONY SETTLEMENT? SINCE YOU CAN HAVE ALL THE MONEY AND NONE OF THE SUFFOCATION OF THE PALACE?
DID YOU LOSE INTEREST IN ME ONCE YOU GOT TO HEAR ME SAY I LOVED YOU?
DID YOUR LITTLE GAME GET BORING AS SOON AS YOU SCORED YOUR GOAL?
I...

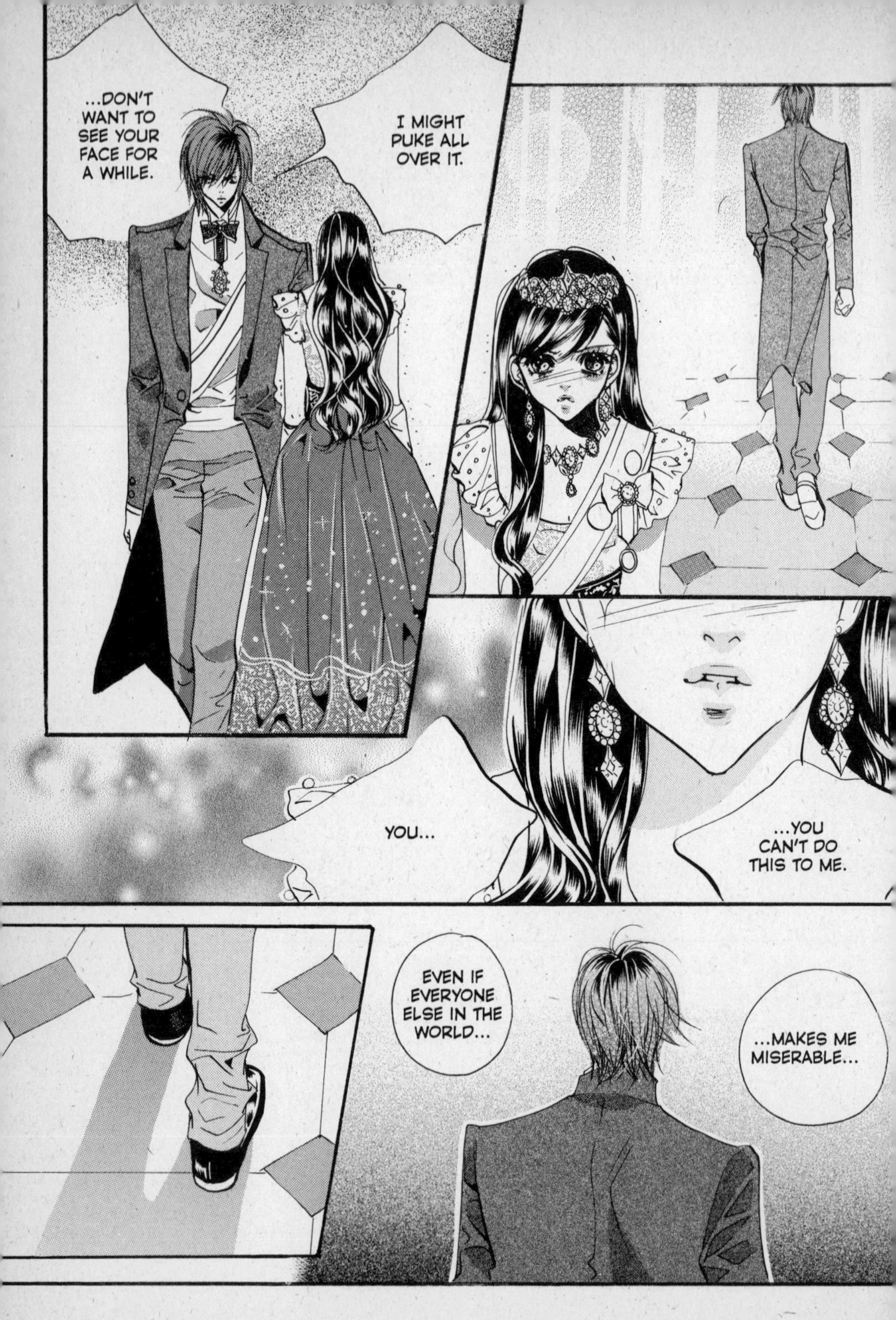
...DON'T WANT TO SEE YOUR FACE FOR A WHILE.
I MIGHT PUKE ALL OVER IT.
YOU...
...YOU CAN'T DO THIS TO ME.
EVEN IF EVERYONE ELSE IN THE WORLD...
...MAKES ME MISERABLE...

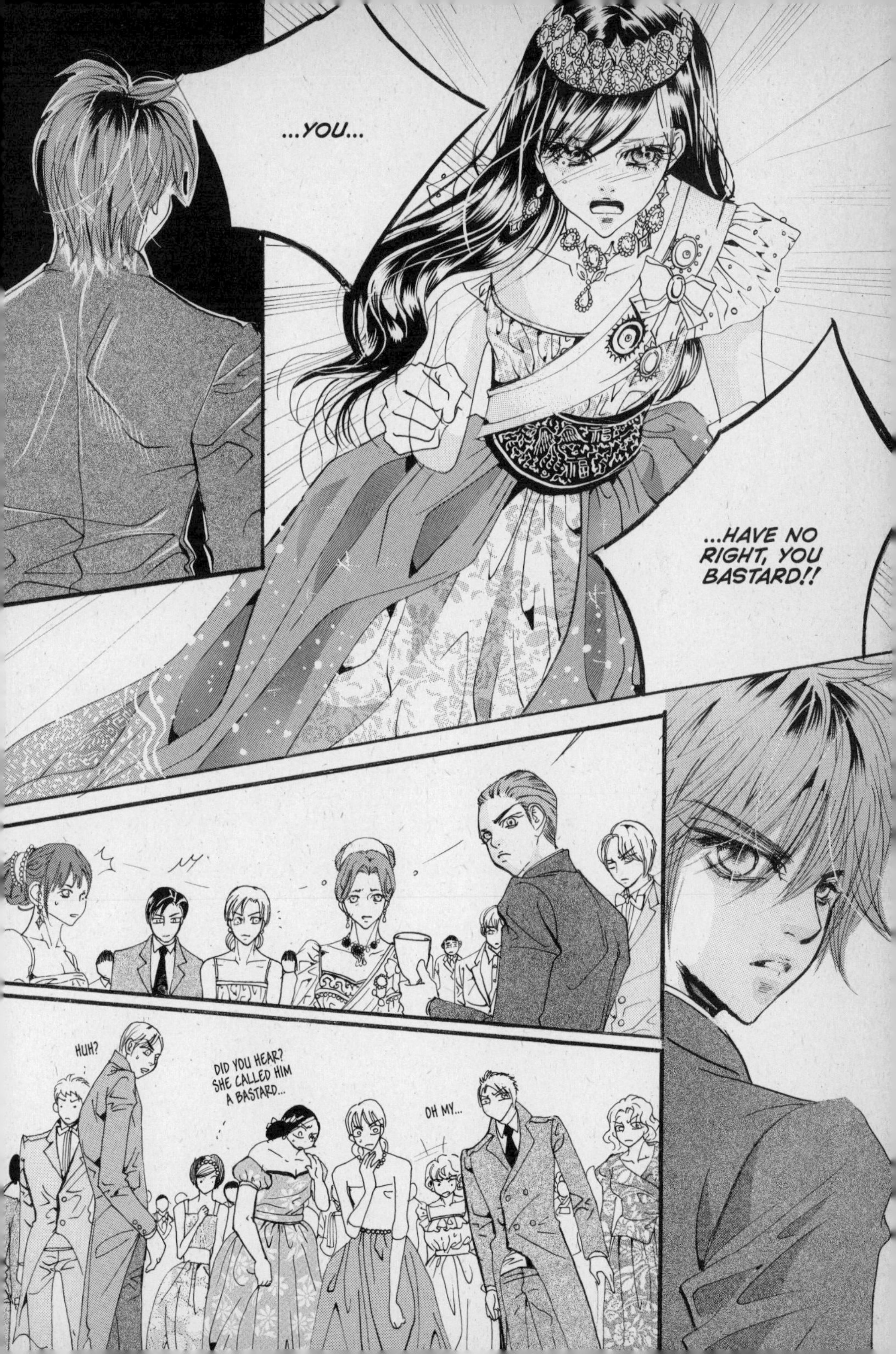
...YOU...
...HAVE NO RIGHT, YOU BASTARD!!
HUH?
DID YOU HEAR? SHE CALLED HIM A BASTARD...
OH MY...

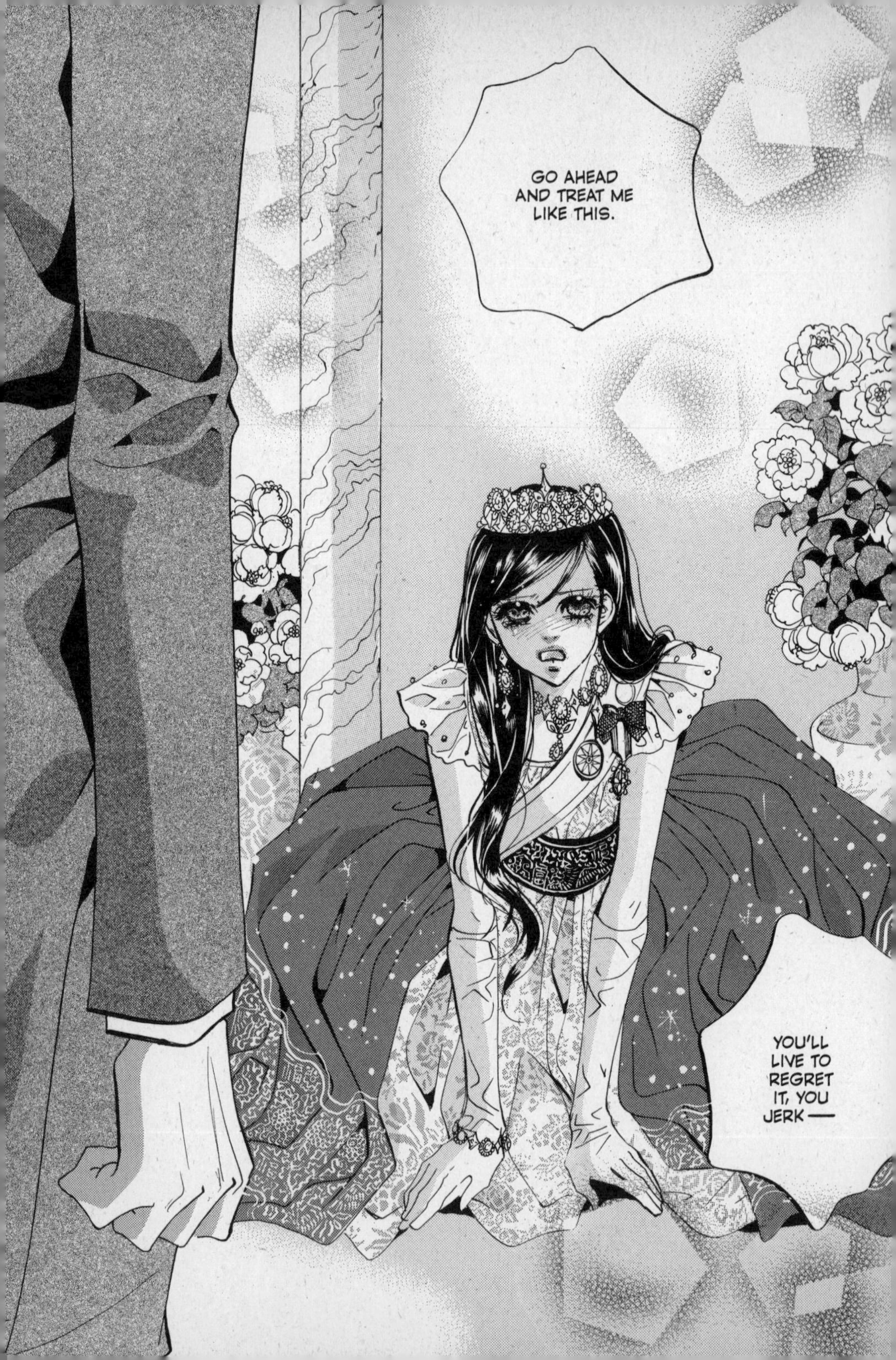
GO AHEAD AND TREAT ME LIKE THIS.
YOU'LL LIVE TO REGRET IT, YOU JERK—

THE ROYAL PALACE

Goong

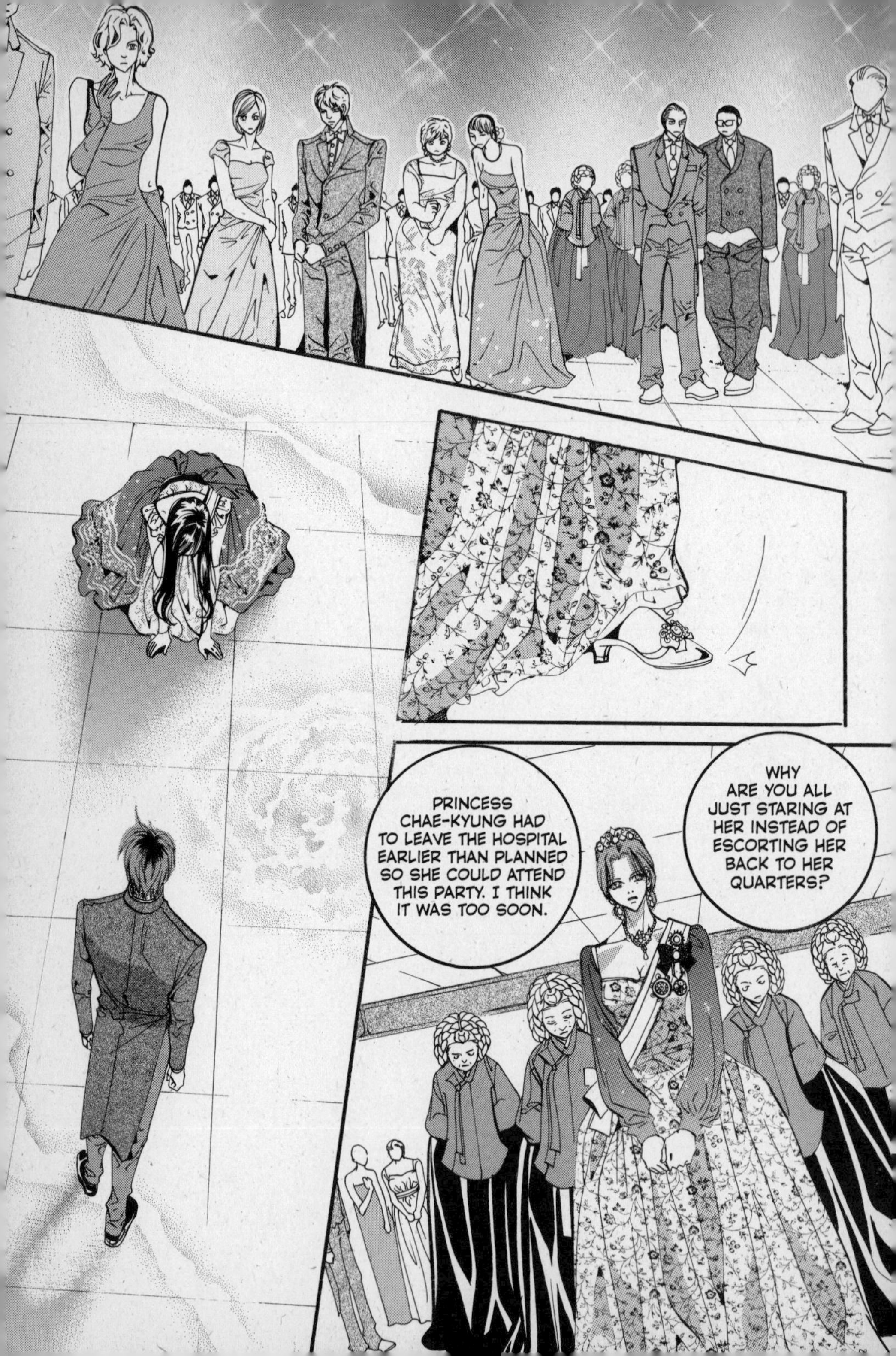
WHY ARE YOU ALL JUST STARING AT HER INSTEAD OF ESCORTING HER BACK TO HER QUARTERS?
PRINCESS CHAE-KYUNG HAD TO LEAVE THE HOSPITAL EARLIER THAN PLANNED SO SHE COULD ATTEND THIS PARTY. I THINK IT WAS TOO SOON.

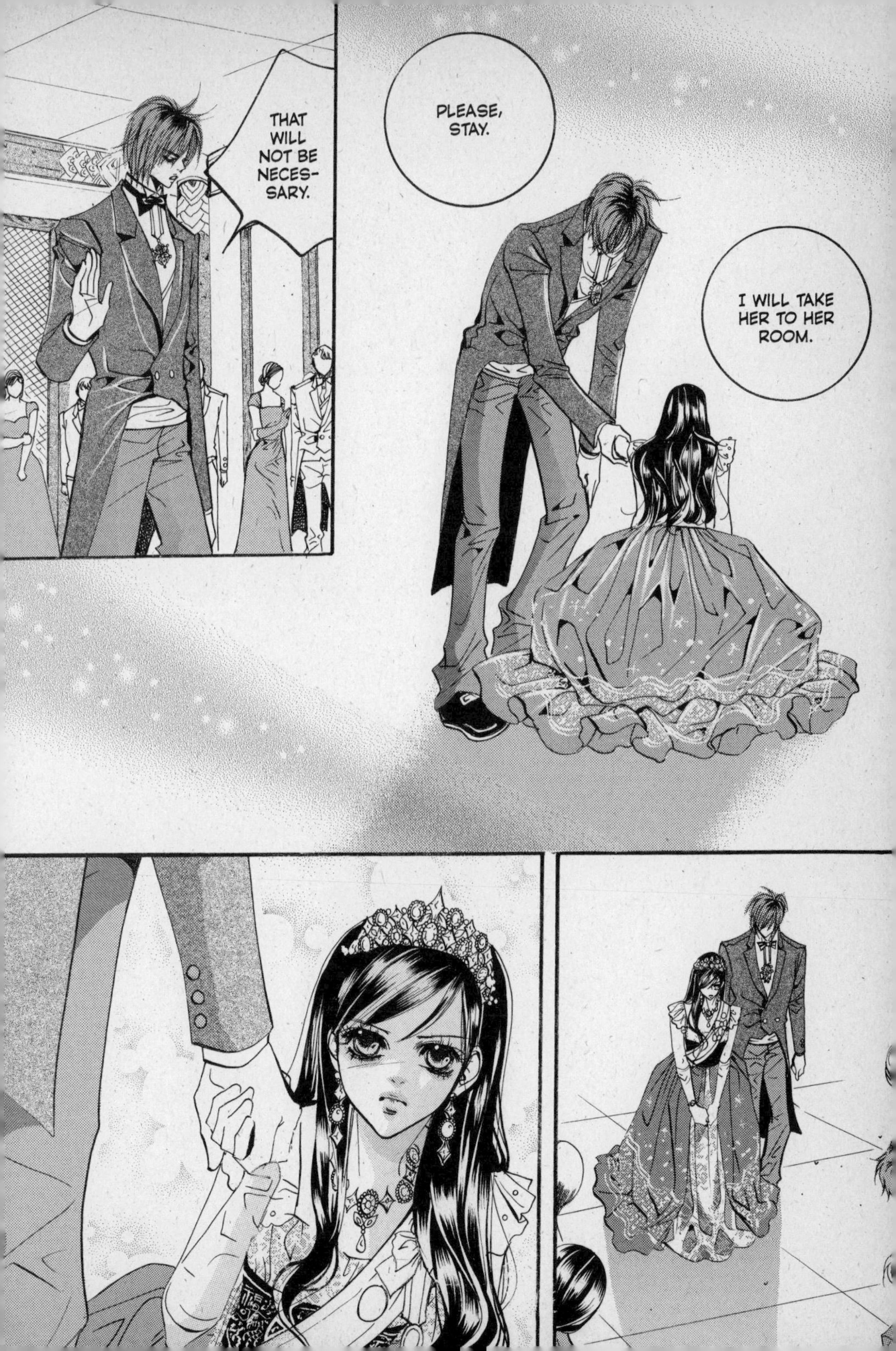
PLEASE, STAY.
I WILL TAKE HER TO HER ROOM.
THAT WILL NOT BE NECES-SARY.

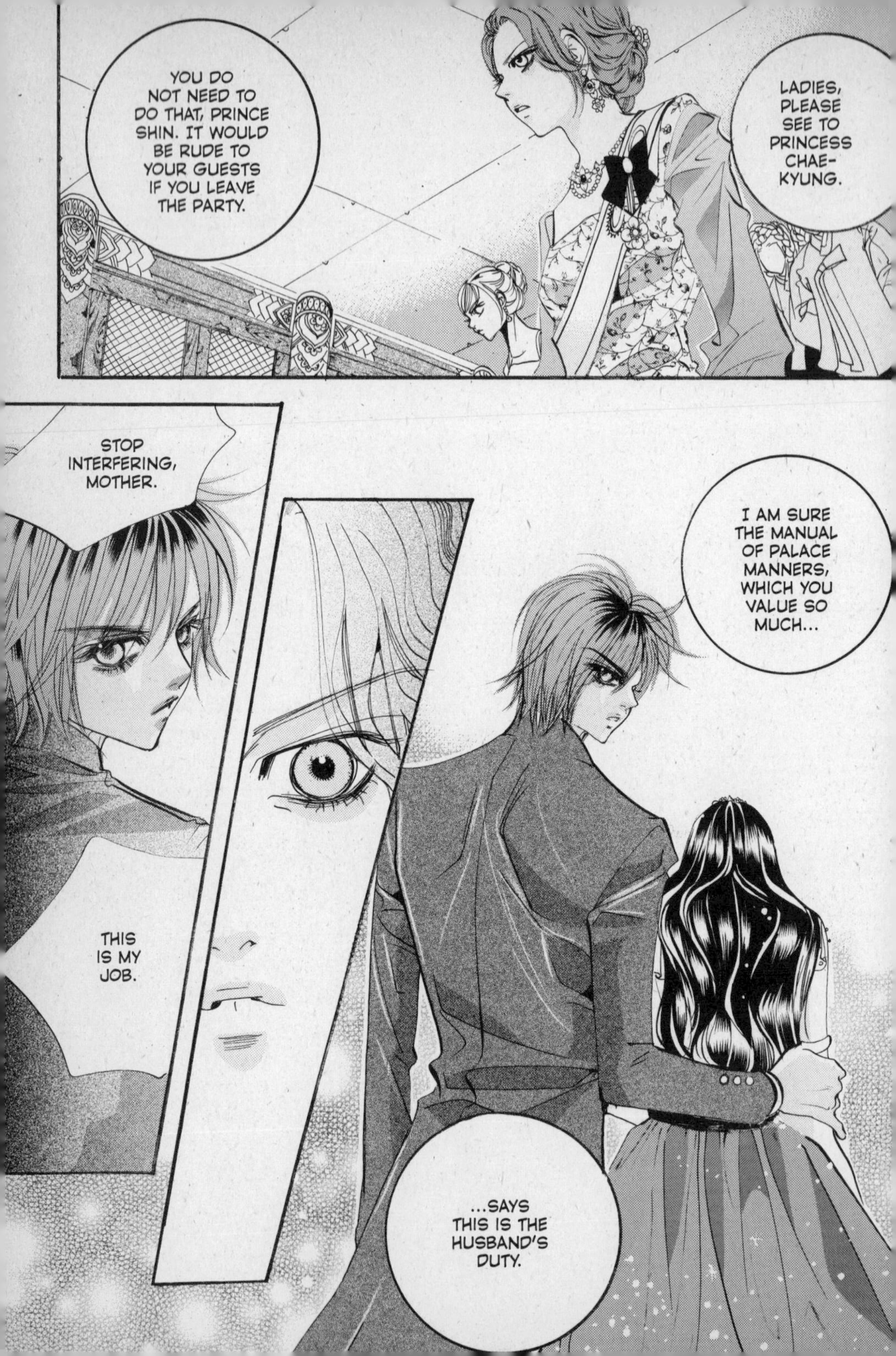
YOU DO NOT NEED TO DO THAT, PRINCE SHIN. IT WOULD BE RUDE TO YOUR GUESTS IF YOU LEAVE THE PARTY.
LADIES, PLEASE SEE TO PRINCESS CHAE-KYUNG.
STOP INTERFERING, MOTHER.
THIS IS MY JOB.
I AM SURE THE MANUAL OF PALACE MANNERS, WHICH YOU VALUE SO MUCH...
...SAYS THIS IS THE HUSBAND'S DUTY.

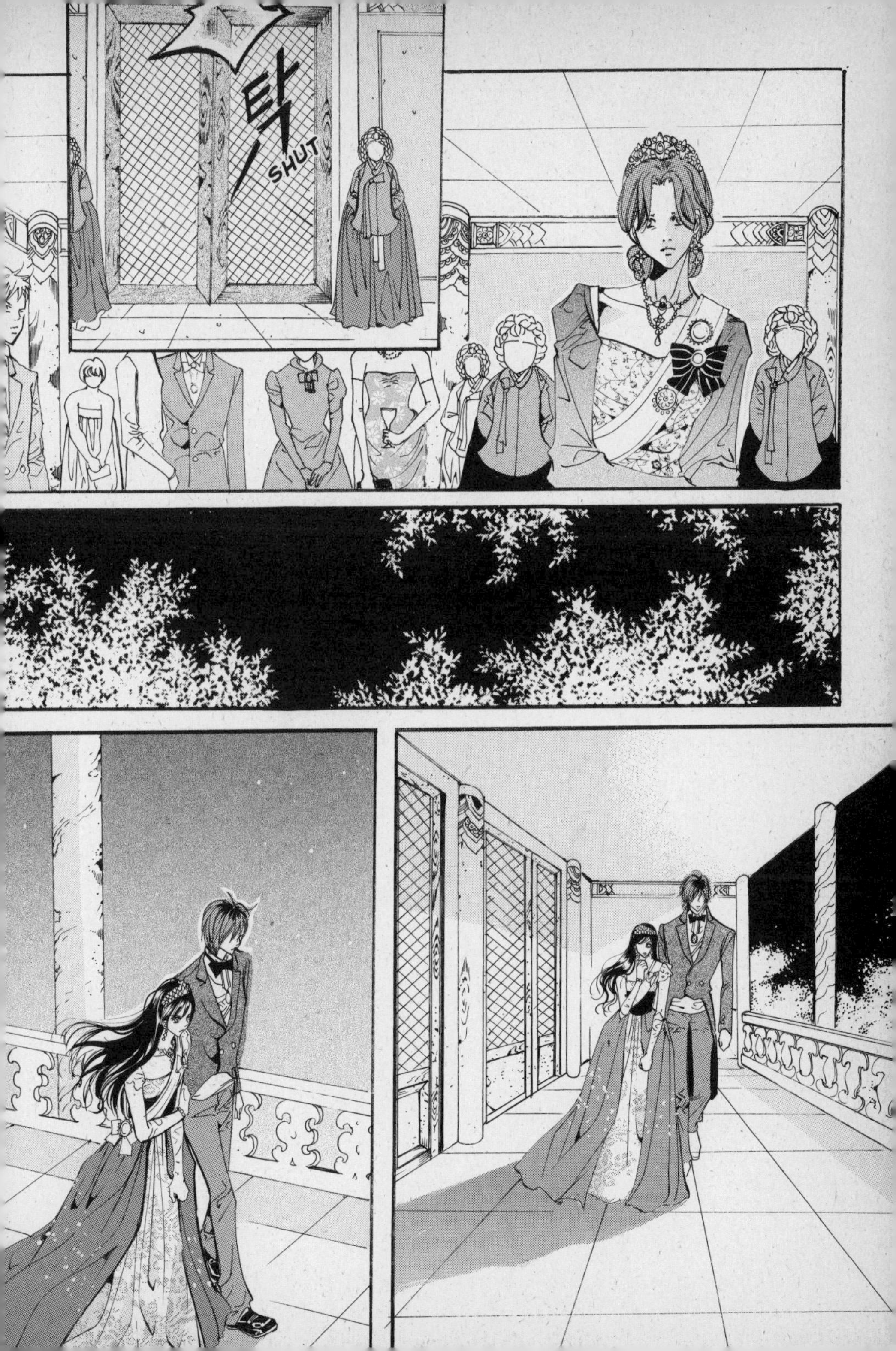
탁
SHUT

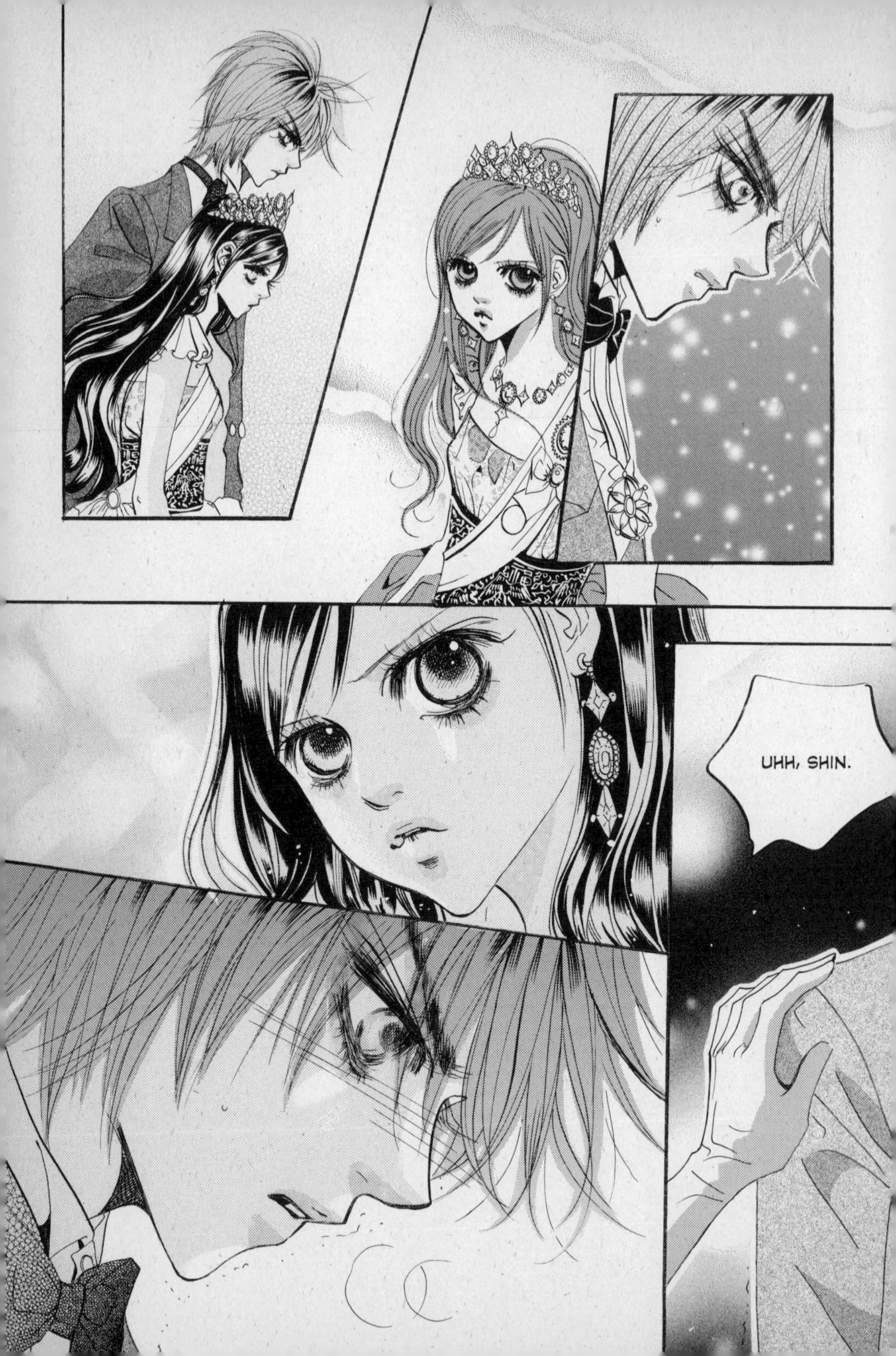
UHH, SHIN.

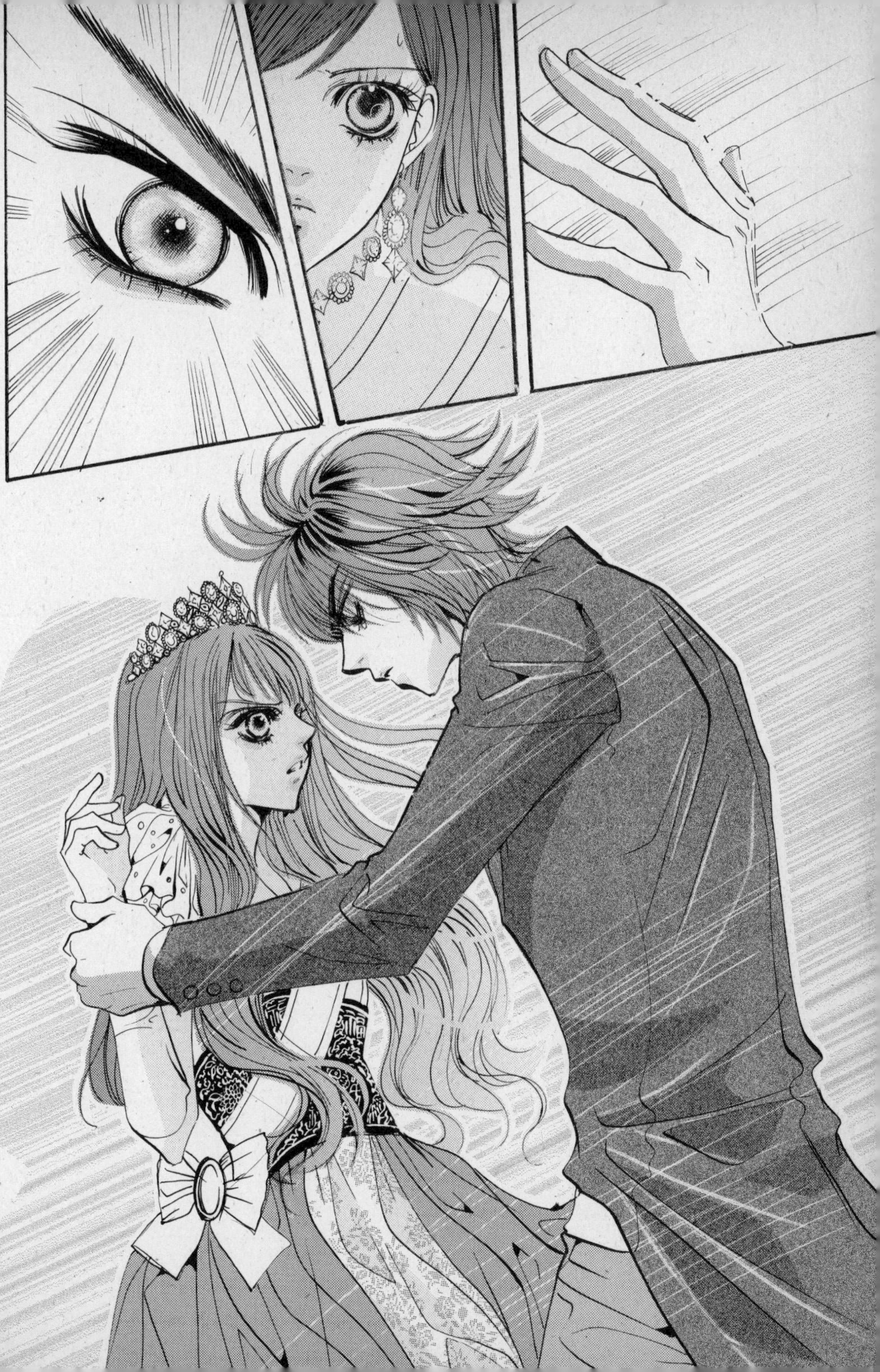

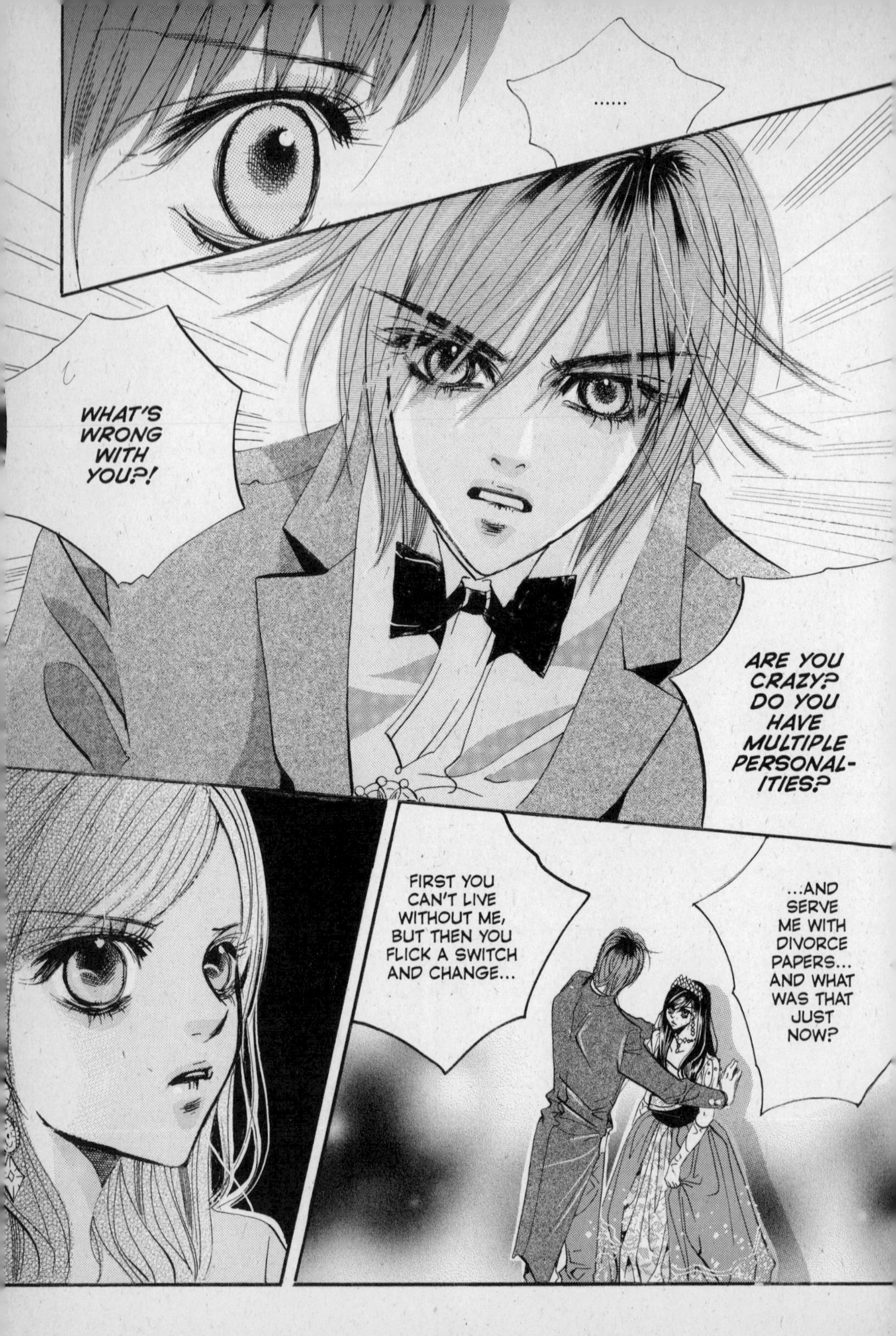
......
WHAT'S WRONG WITH YOU?!
ARE YOU CRAZY? DO YOU HAVE MULTIPLE PERSONAL-ITIES?
...AND SERVE ME WITH DIVORCE PAPERS... AND WHAT WAS THAT JUST NOW?
FIRST YOU CAN'T LIVE WITHOUT ME, BUT THEN YOU FLICK A SWITCH AND CHANGE...

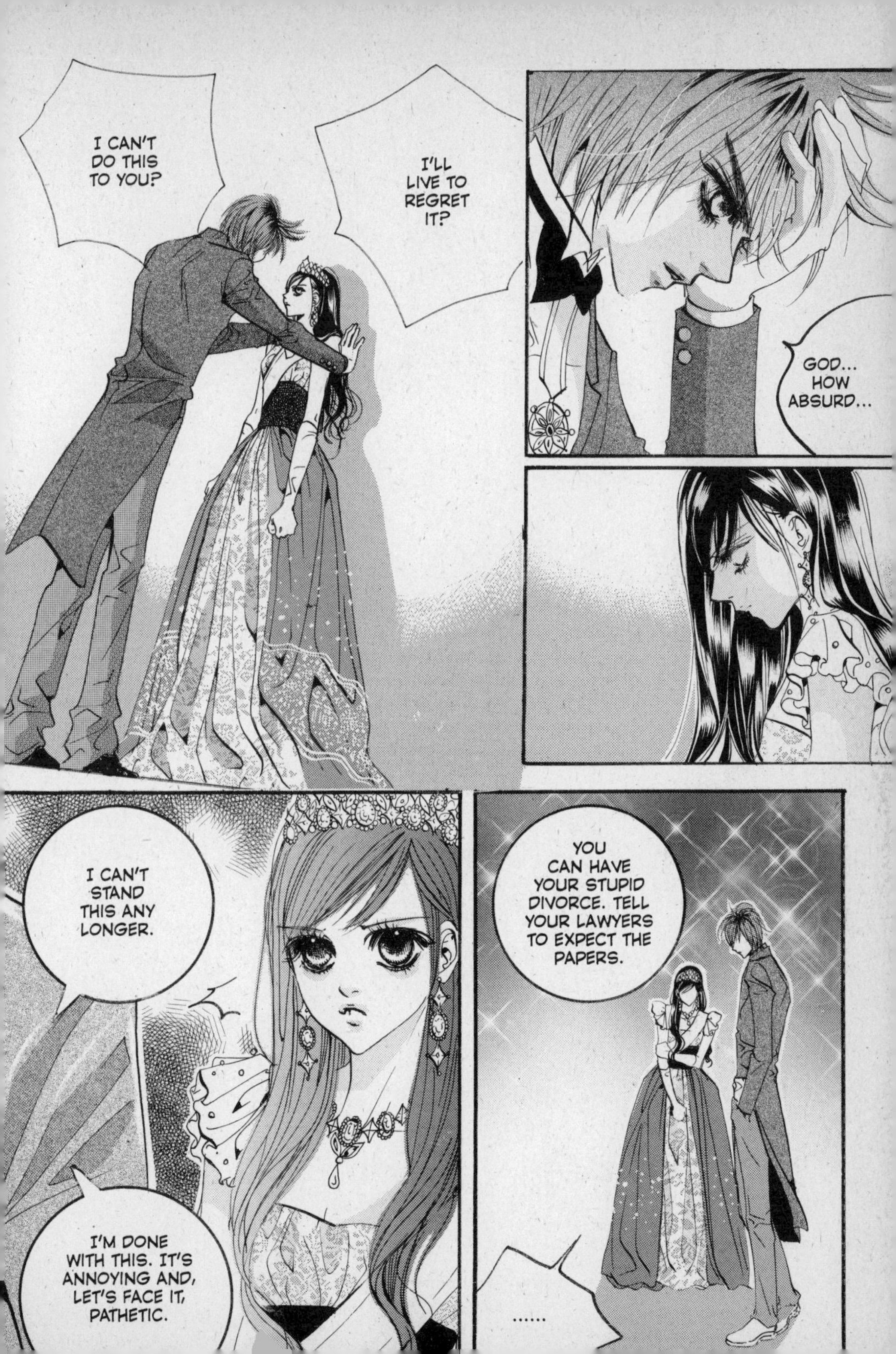
I CAN'T DO THIS TO YOU?
I'LL LIVE TO REGRET IT?
GOD... HOW ABSURD...
I CAN'T STAND THIS ANY LONGER.
I'M DONE WITH THIS. IT'S ANNOYING AND, LET'S FACE IT, PATHETIC.
YOU CAN HAVE YOUR STUPID DIVORCE. TELL YOUR LAWYERS TO EXPECT THE PAPERS.
......

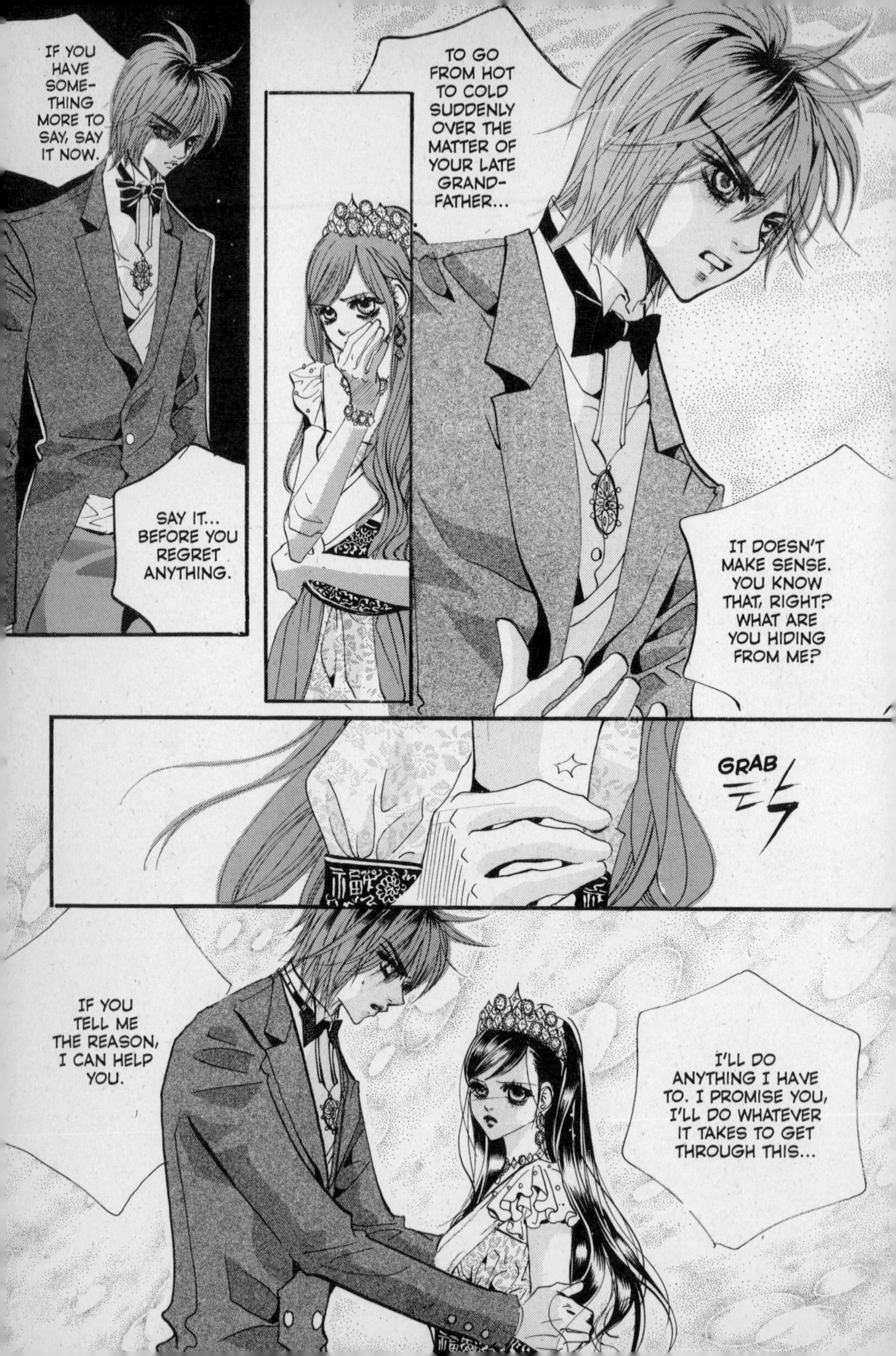
IF YOU HAVE SOME-THING MORE TO SAY, SAY IT NOW.
SAY IT... BEFORE YOU REGRET ANYTHING.
TO GO FROM HOT TO COLD SUDDENLY OVER THE MATTER OF YOUR LATE GRAND-FATHER...
IT DOESN'T MAKE SENSE. YOU KNOW THAT, RIGHT? WHAT ARE YOU HIDING FROM ME?
GRAB
IF YOU TELL ME THE REASON, I CAN HELP YOU.
I'LL DO ANYTHING I HAVE TO. I PROMISE YOU, I'LL DO WHATEVER IT TAKES TO GET THROUGH THIS...

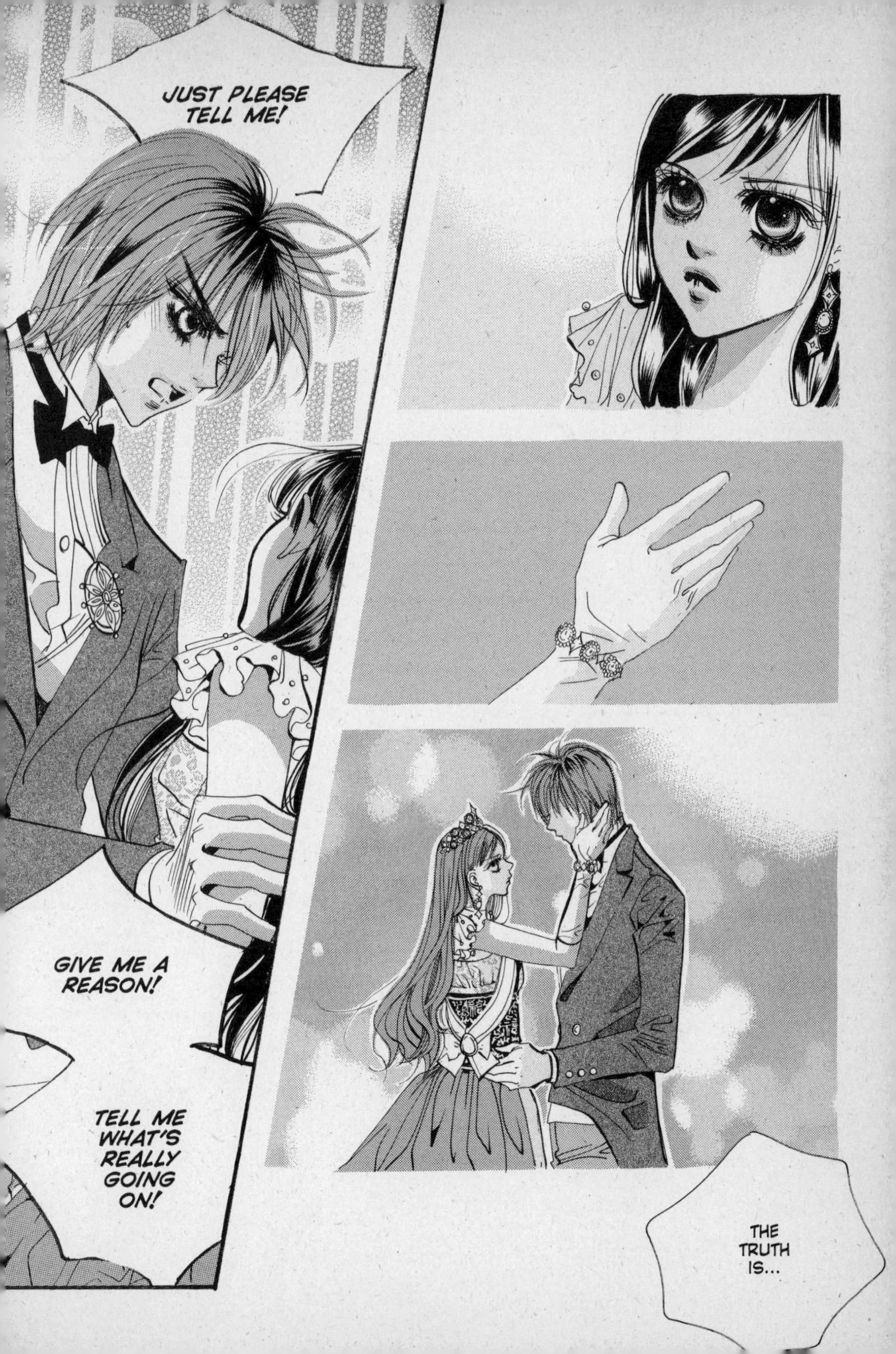
JUST PLEASE TELL ME!
GIVE ME A REASON!
TELL ME WHAT'S REALLY GOING ON!
THE TRUTH IS...

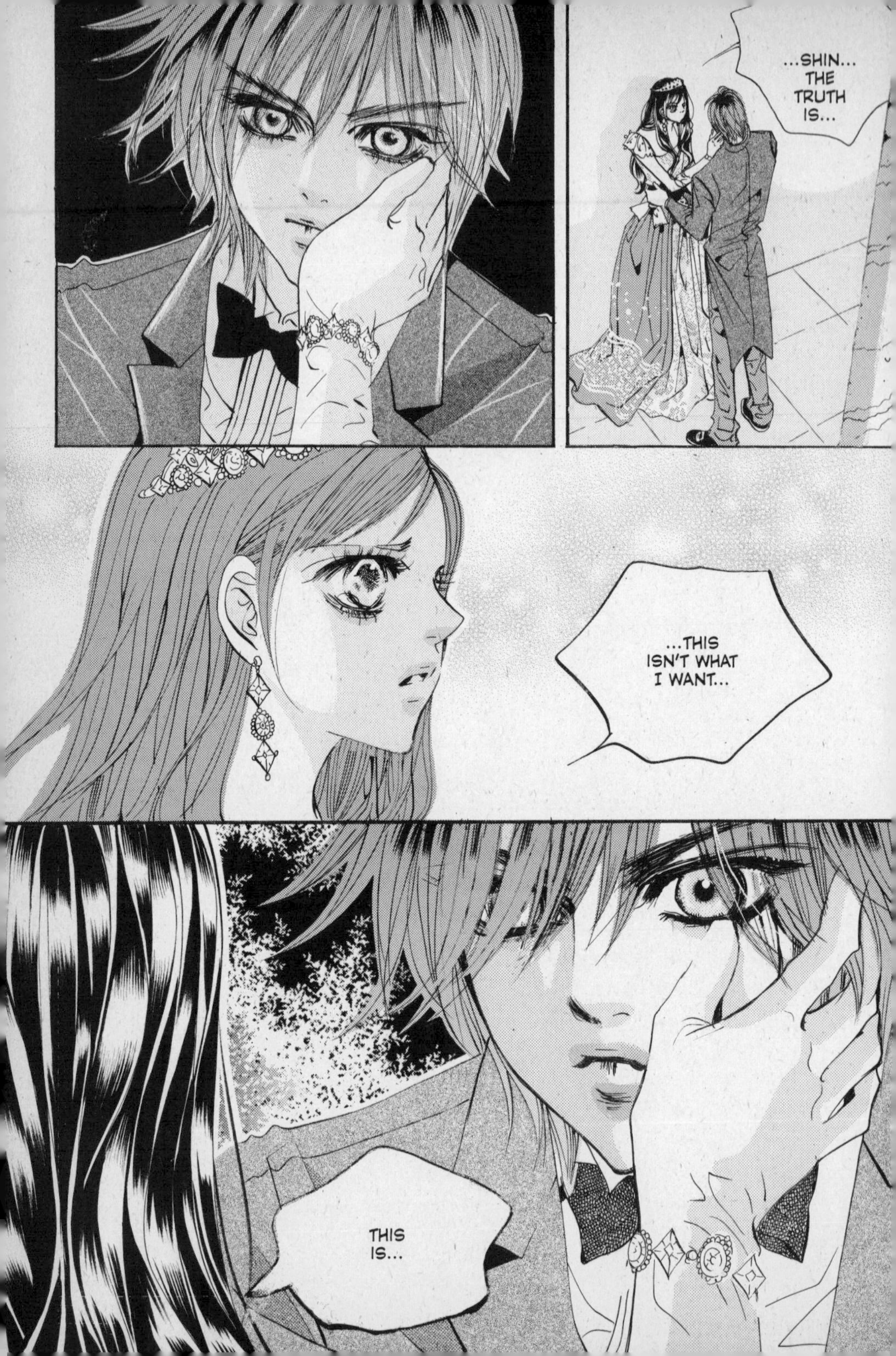
...SHIN... THE TRUTH IS...
...THIS ISN'T WHAT I WANT...
THIS IS...

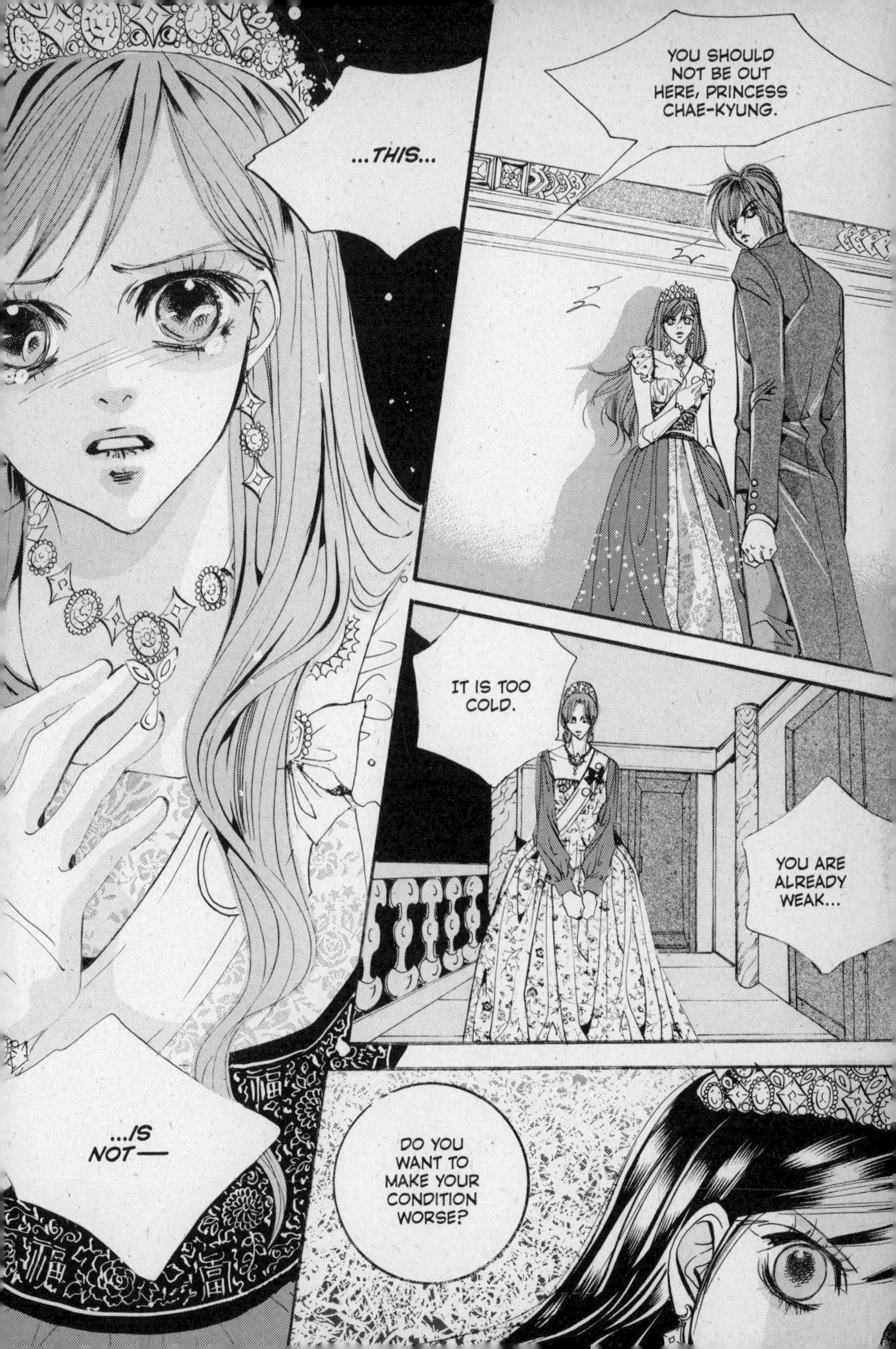
YOU SHOULD NOT BE OUT HERE, PRINCESS CHAE-KYUNG.
...THIS...
IT IS TOO COLD.
YOU ARE ALREADY WEAK...
...IS NOT—
DO YOU WANT TO MAKE YOUR CONDITION WORSE?

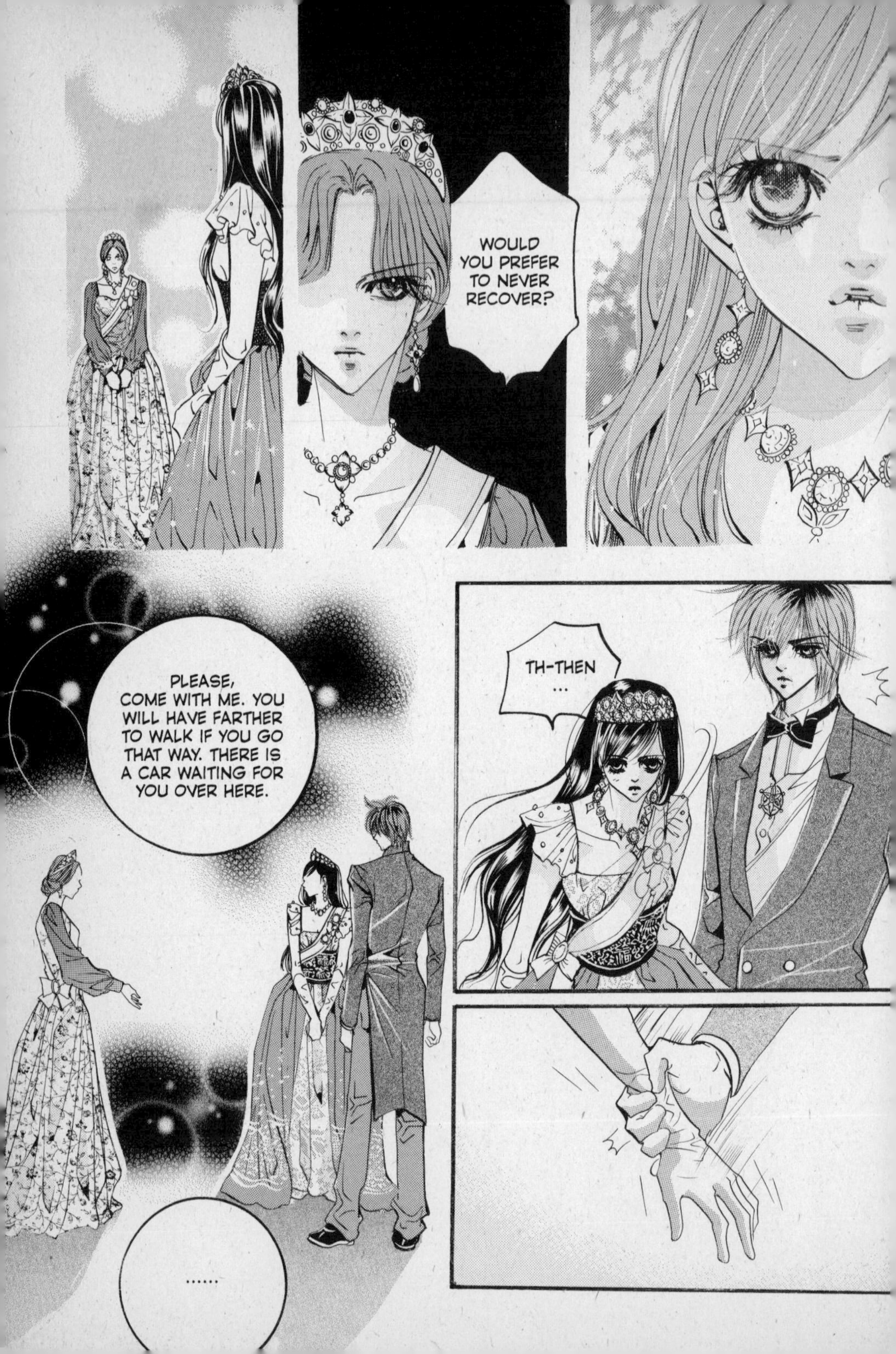
WOULD YOU PREFER TO NEVER RECOVER?
PLEASE, COME WITH ME. YOU WILL HAVE FARTHER TO WALK IF YOU GO THAT WAY. THERE IS A CAR WAITING FOR YOU OVER HERE.
TH-THEN ...
......

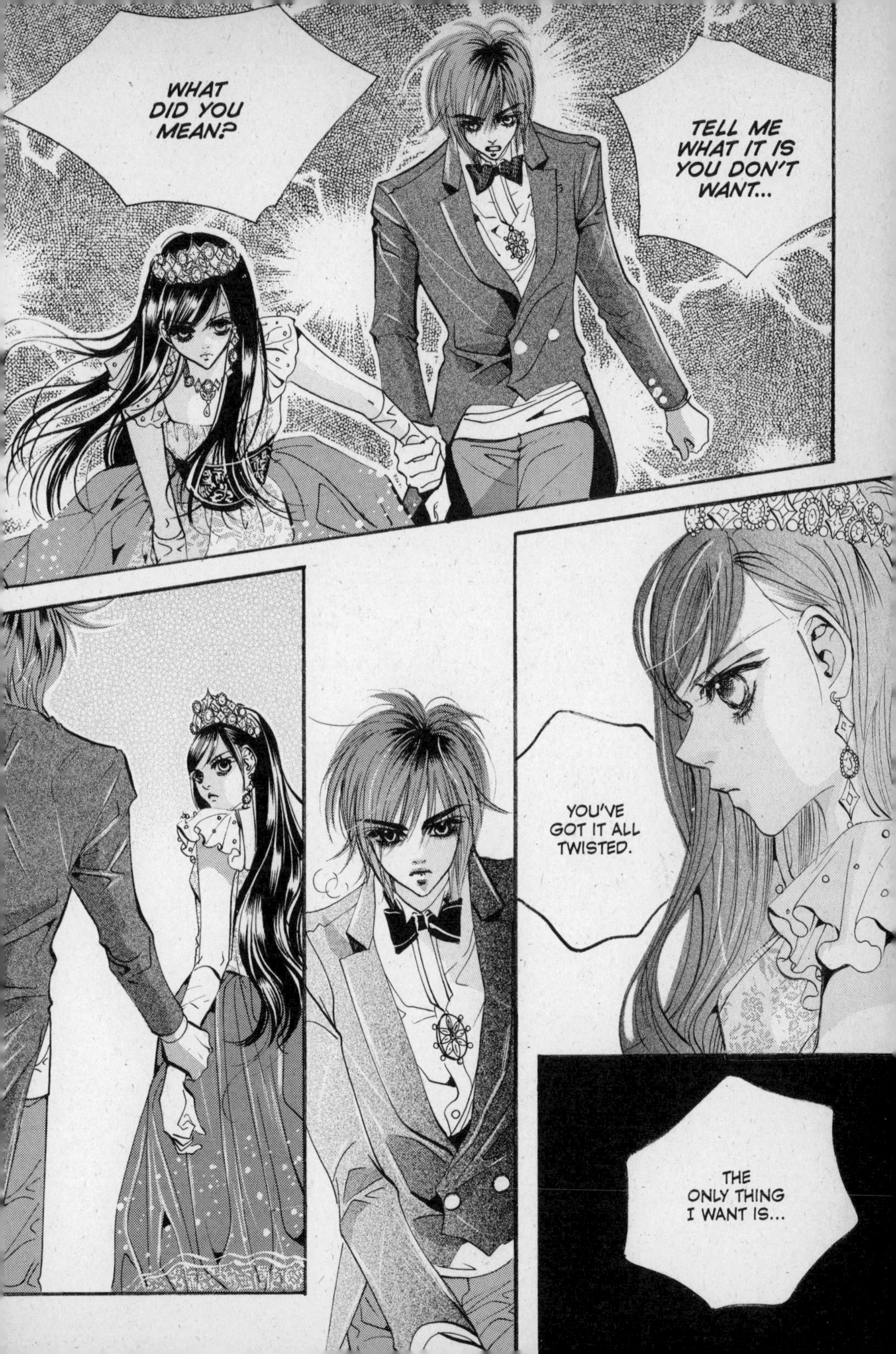
WHAT DID YOU MEAN?
TELL ME WHAT IT IS YOU DON'T WANT...
YOU'VE GOT IT ALL TWISTED.
THE ONLY THING I WANT IS...

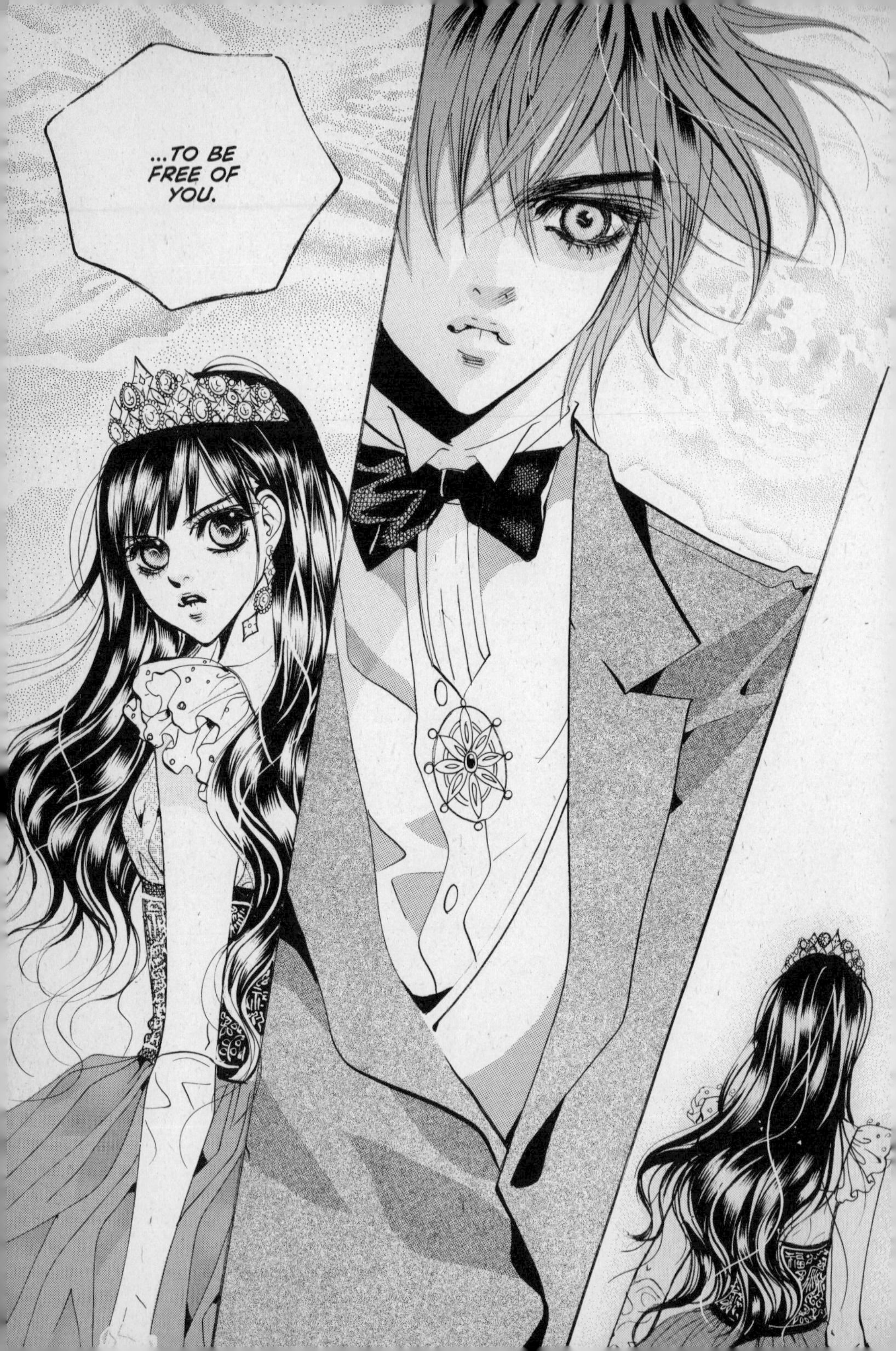
...TO BE FREE OF YOU.

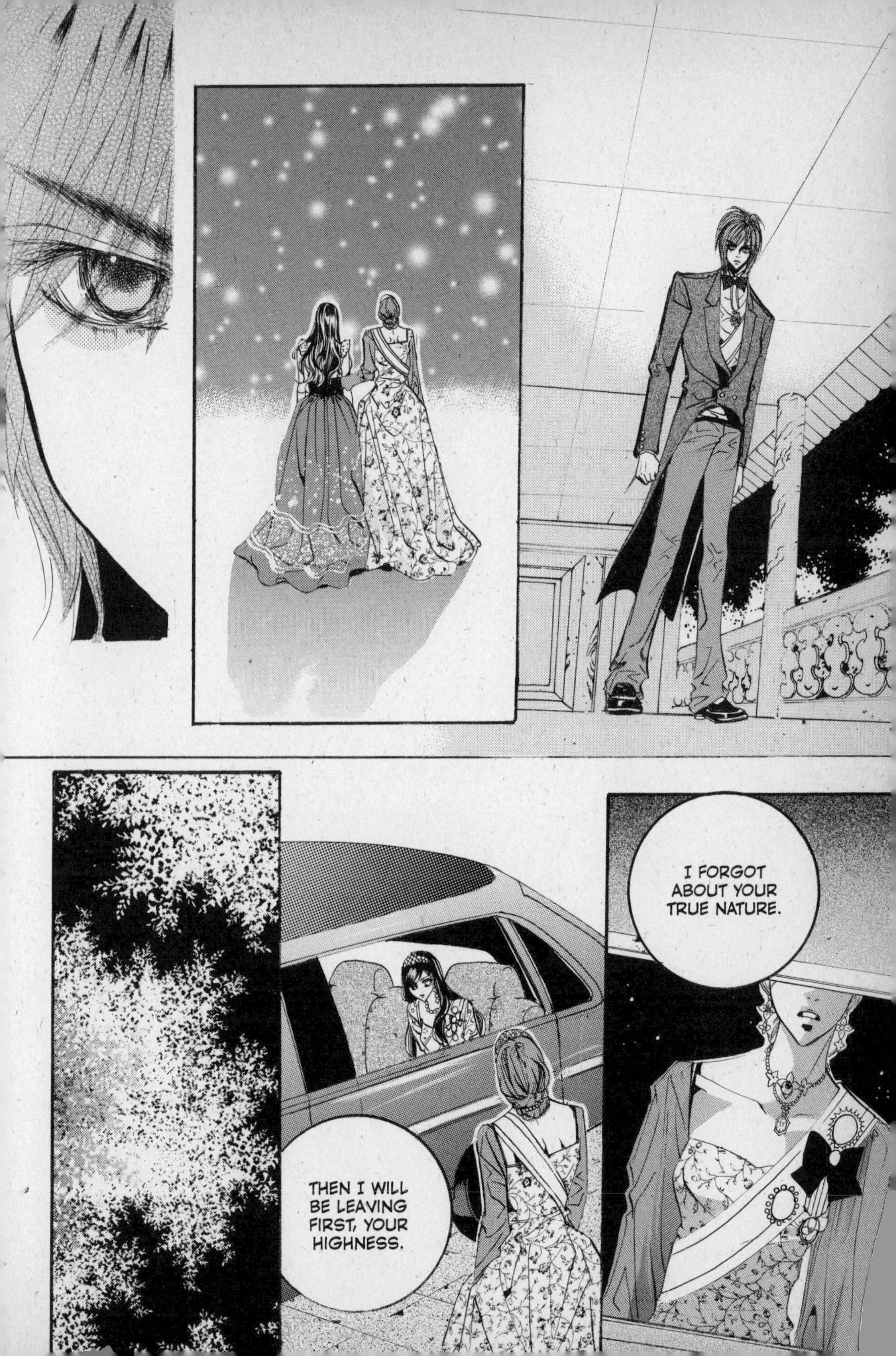
THEN I WILL BE LEAVING FIRST, YOUR HIGHNESS.
I FORGOT ABOUT YOUR TRUE NATURE.

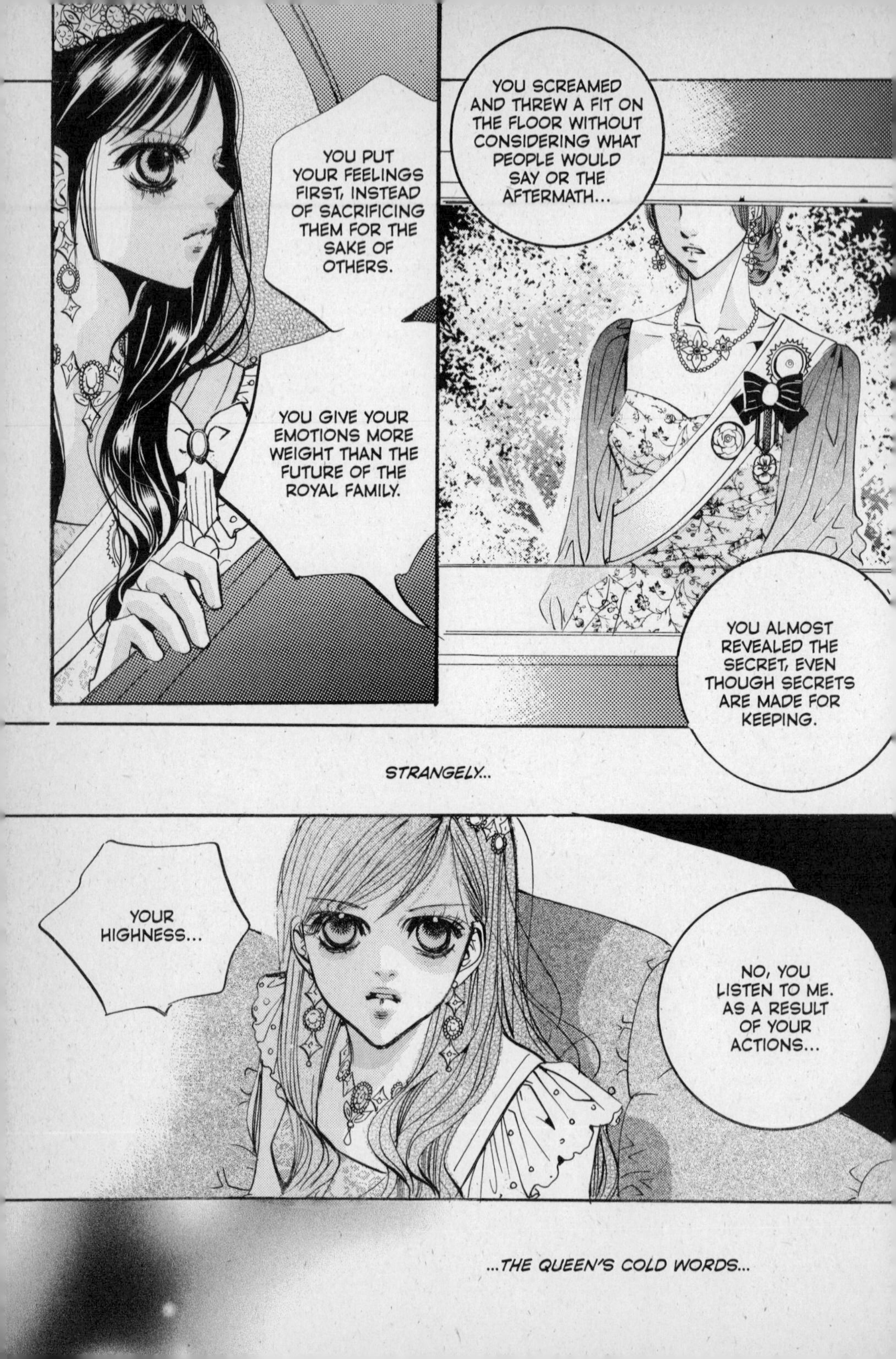
YOU PUT YOUR FEELINGS FIRST, INSTEAD OF SACRIFICING THEM FOR THE SAKE OF OTHERS.
YOU GIVE YOUR EMOTIONS MORE WEIGHT THAN THE FUTURE OF THE ROYAL FAMILY.
YOU SCREAMED AND THREW A FIT ON THE FLOOR WITHOUT CONSIDERING WHAT PEOPLE WOULD SAY OR THE AFTERMATH...
YOU ALMOST REVEALED THE SECRET, EVEN THOUGH SECRETS ARE MADE FOR KEEPING.
STRANGELY...
YOUR HIGHNESS...
NO, YOU LISTEN TO ME. AS A RESULT OF YOUR ACTIONS...
...THE QUEEN'S COLD WORDS...

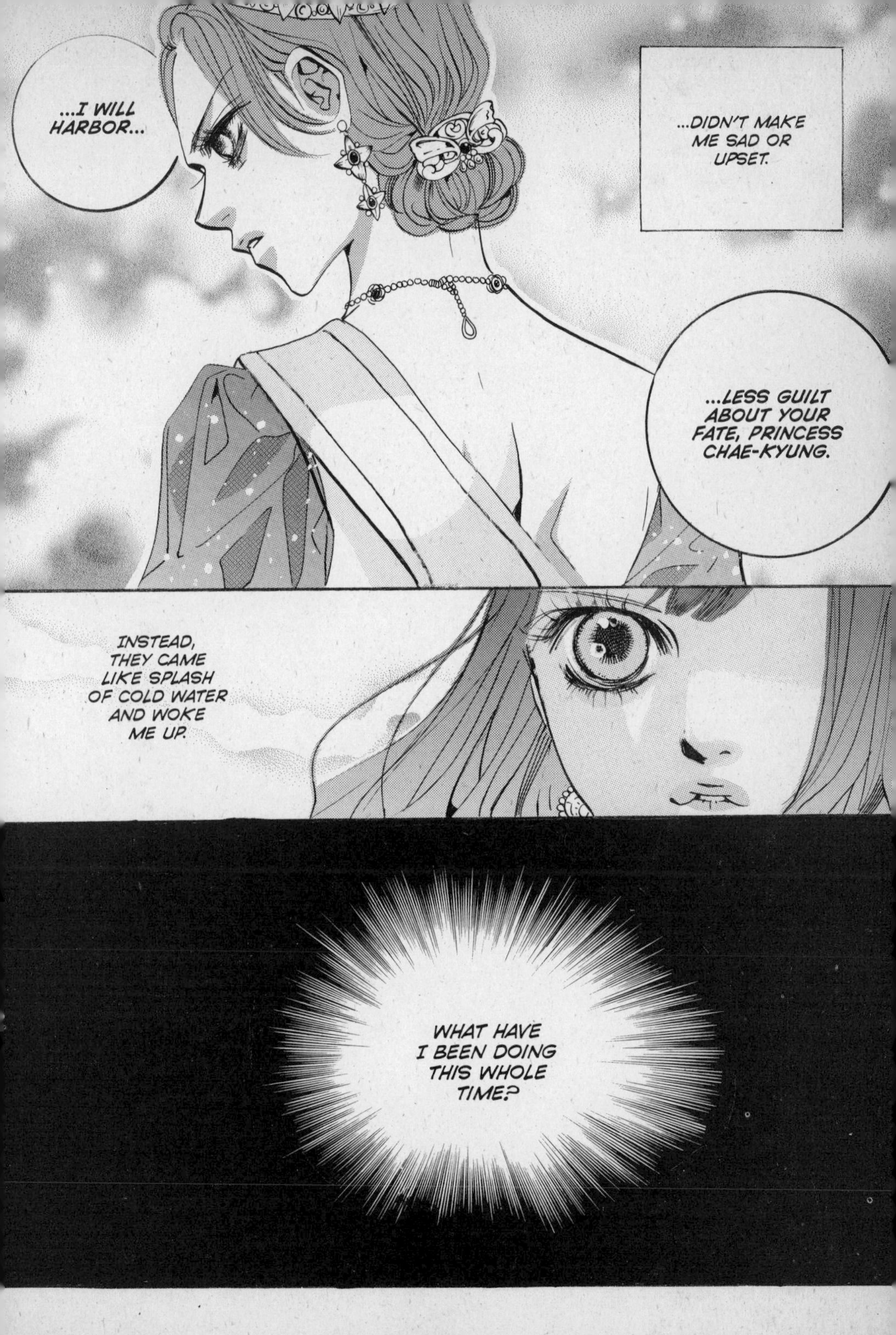
...DIDN'T MAKE ME SAD OR UPSET.
...I WILL HARBOR...
...LESS GUILT ABOUT YOUR FATE, PRINCESS CHAE-KYUNG.
INSTEAD, THEY CAME LIKE SPLASH OF COLD WATER AND WOKE ME UP.
WHAT HAVE I BEEN DOING THIS WHOLE TIME?

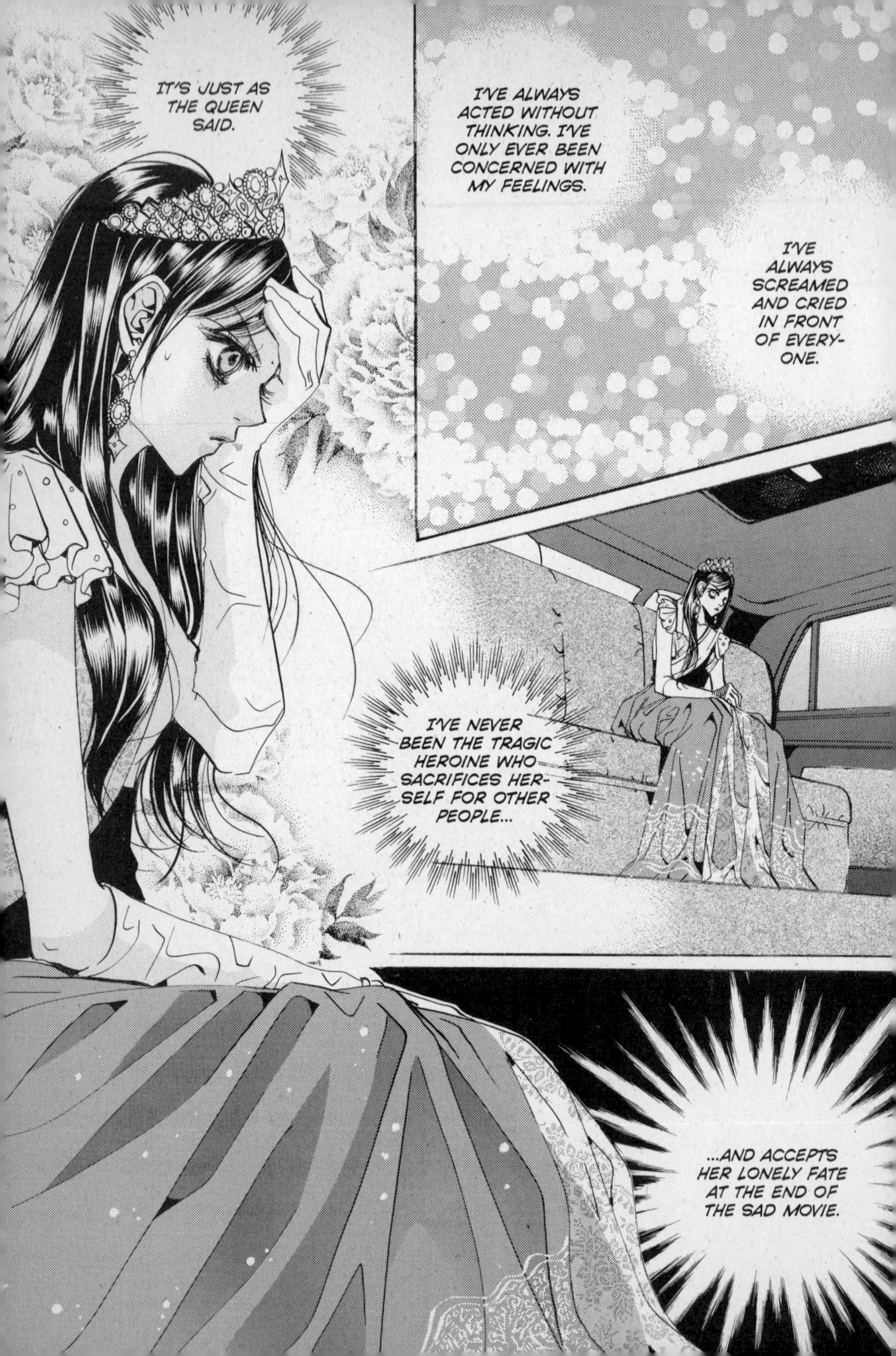
IT'S JUST AS THE QUEEN SAID.
I'VE ALWAYS ACTED WITHOUT THINKING. I'VE ONLY EVER BEEN CONCERNED WITH MY FEELINGS.
I'VE ALWAYS SCREAMED AND CRIED IN FRONT OF EVERY-ONE.
I'VE NEVER BEEN THE TRAGIC HEROINE WHO SACRIFICES HER-SELF FOR OTHER PEOPLE...
...AND ACCEPTS HER LONELY FATE AT THE END OF THE SAD MOVIE.

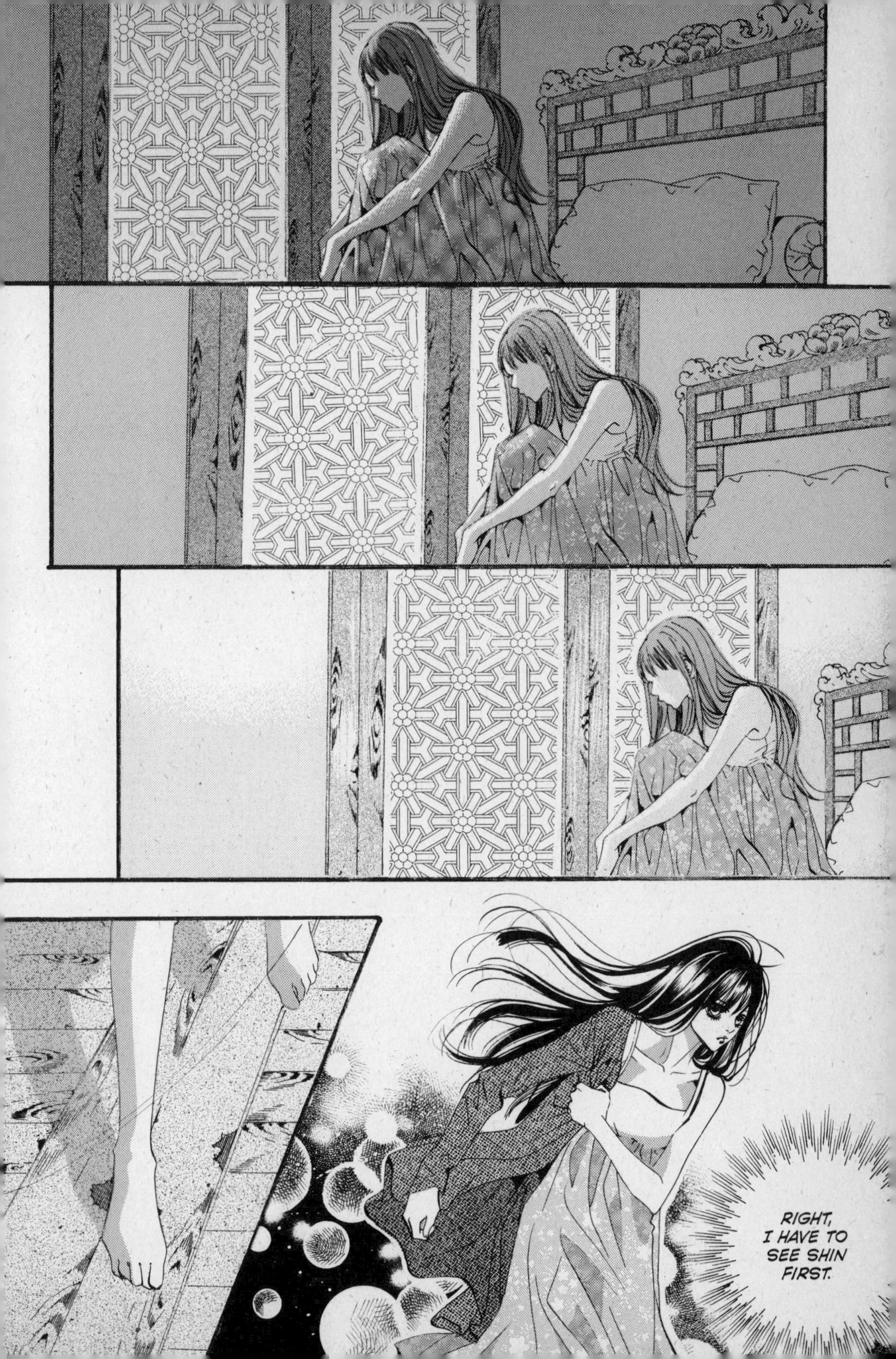
RIGHT, I HAVE TO SEE SHIN FIRST.

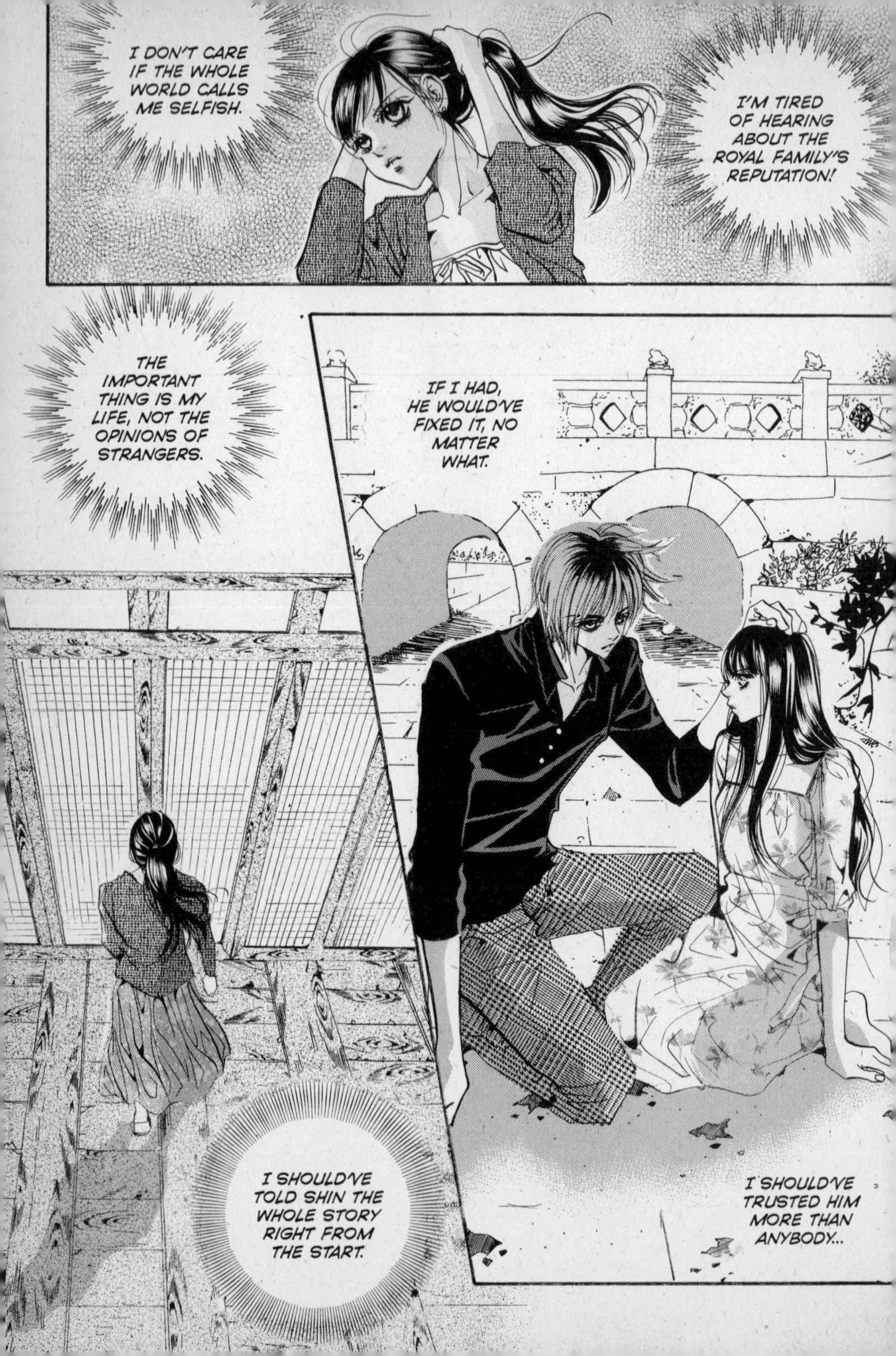
I'M TIRED OF HEARING ABOUT THE ROYAL FAMILY'S REPUTATION!
I DON'T CARE IF THE WHOLE WORLD CALLS ME SELFISH.
THE IMPORTANT THING IS MY LIFE, NOT THE OPINIONS OF STRANGERS.
IF I HAD, HE WOULD'VE FIXED IT, NO MATTER WHAT.
I SHOULD'VE TRUSTED HIM MORE THAN ANYBODY...
I SHOULD'VE TOLD SHIN THE WHOLE STORY RIGHT FROM THE START.

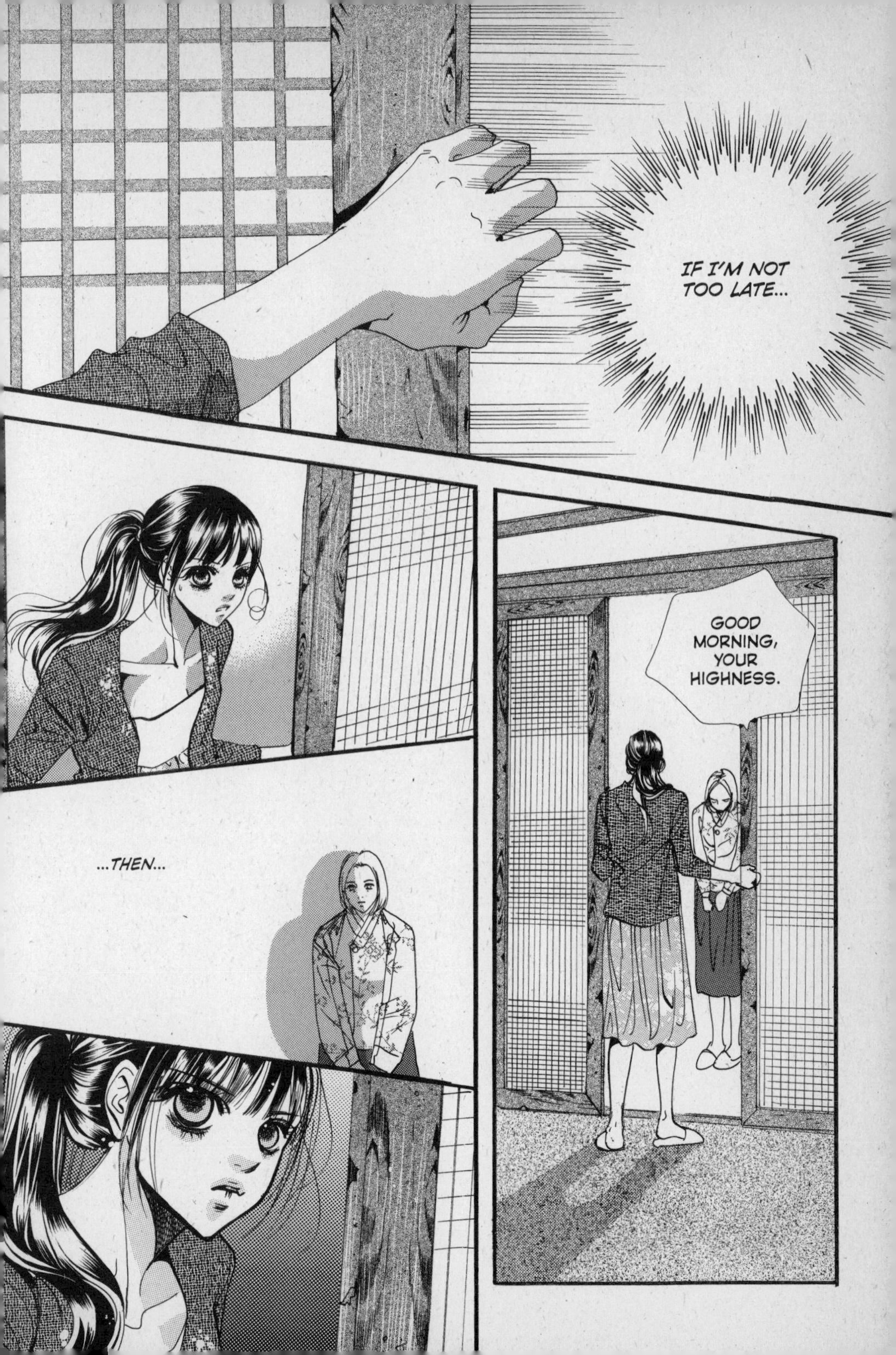
IF I'M NOT TOO LATE...
GOOD MORNING, YOUR HIGHNESS.
...THEN...

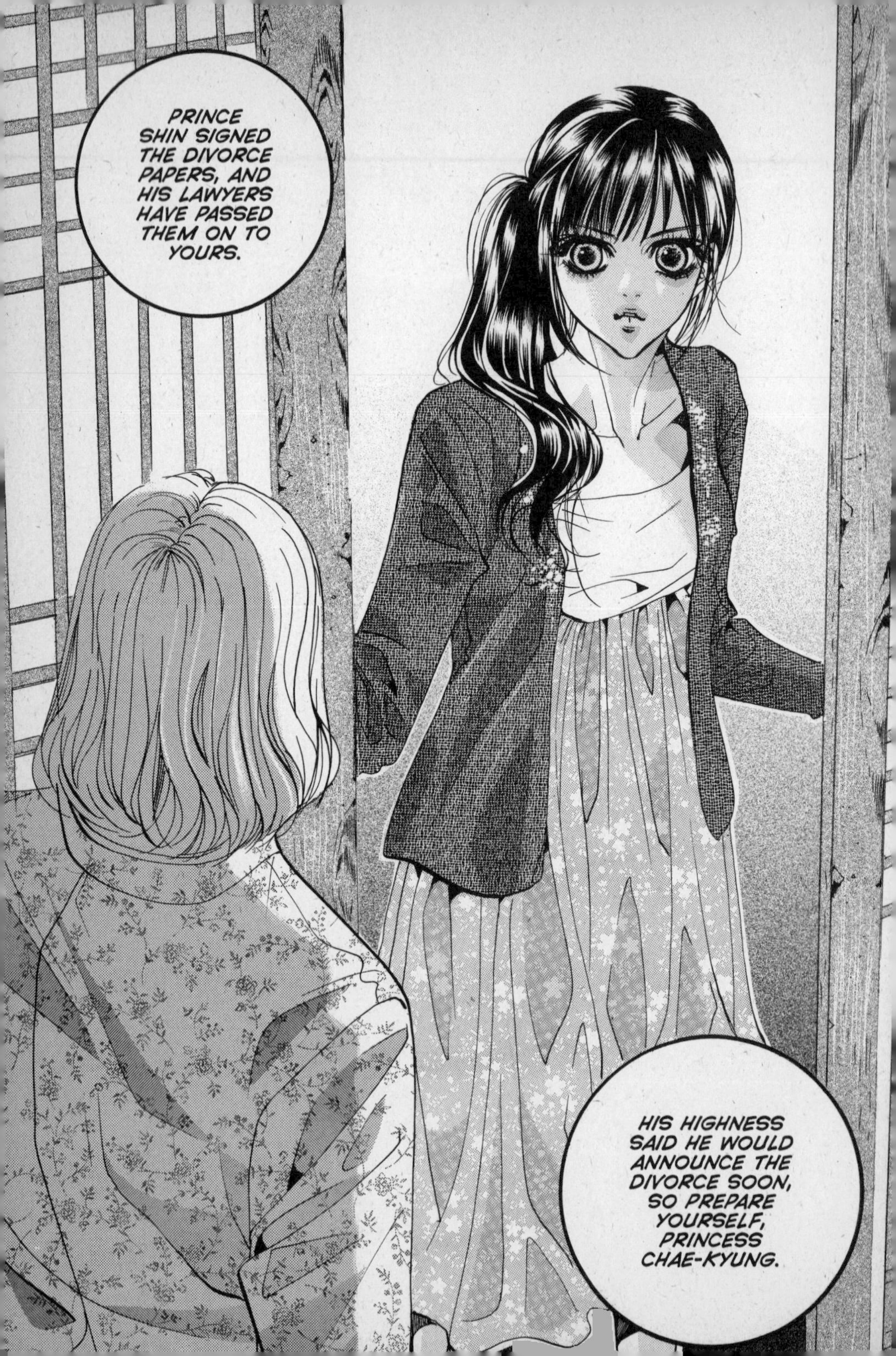
PRINCE SHIN SIGNED THE DIVORCE PAPERS, AND HIS LAWYERS HAVE PASSED THEM ON TO YOURS.
HIS HIGHNESS SAID HE WOULD ANNOUNCE THE DIVORCE SOON, SO PREPARE YOURSELF, PRINCESS CHAE-KYUNG.

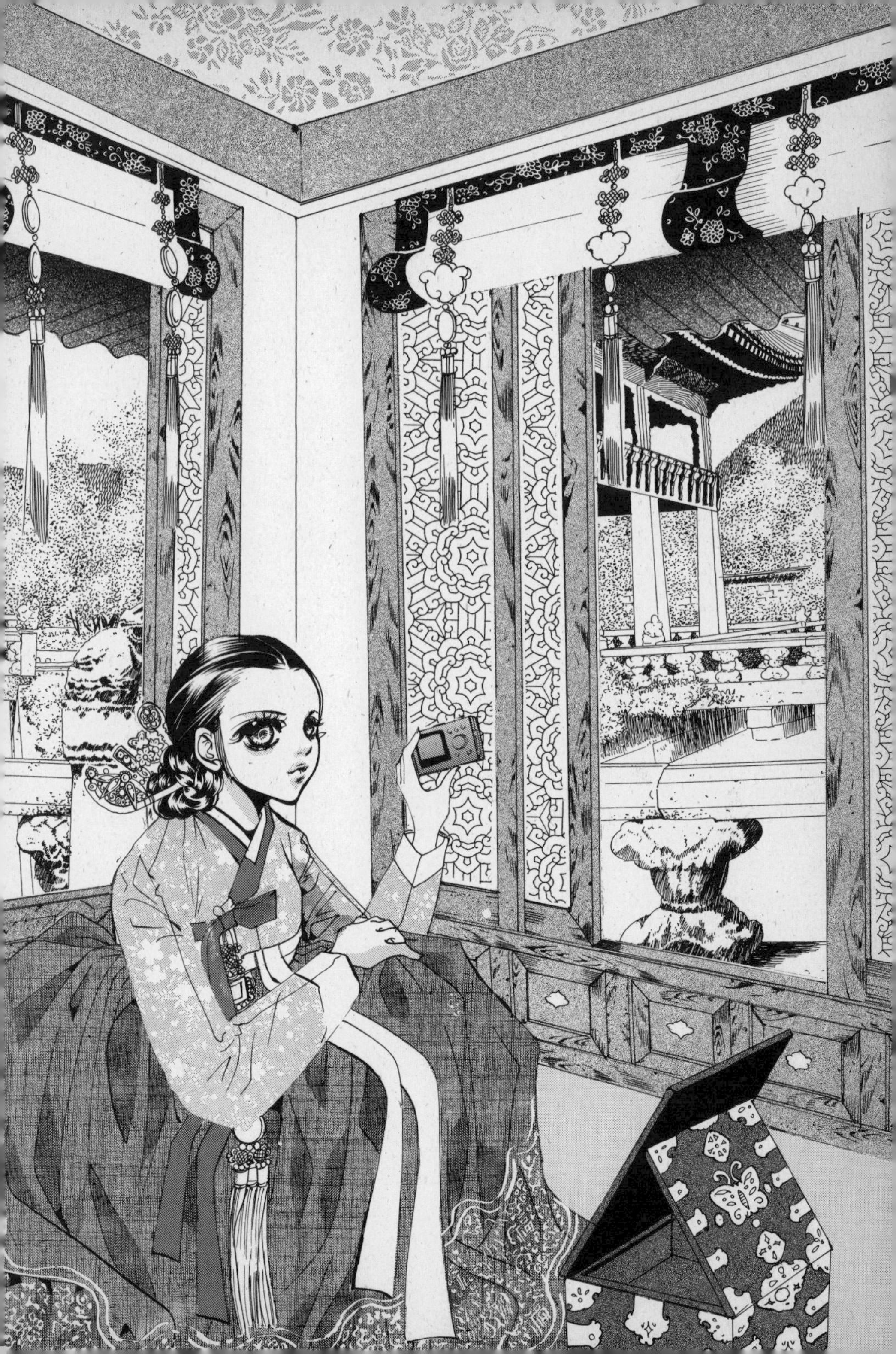

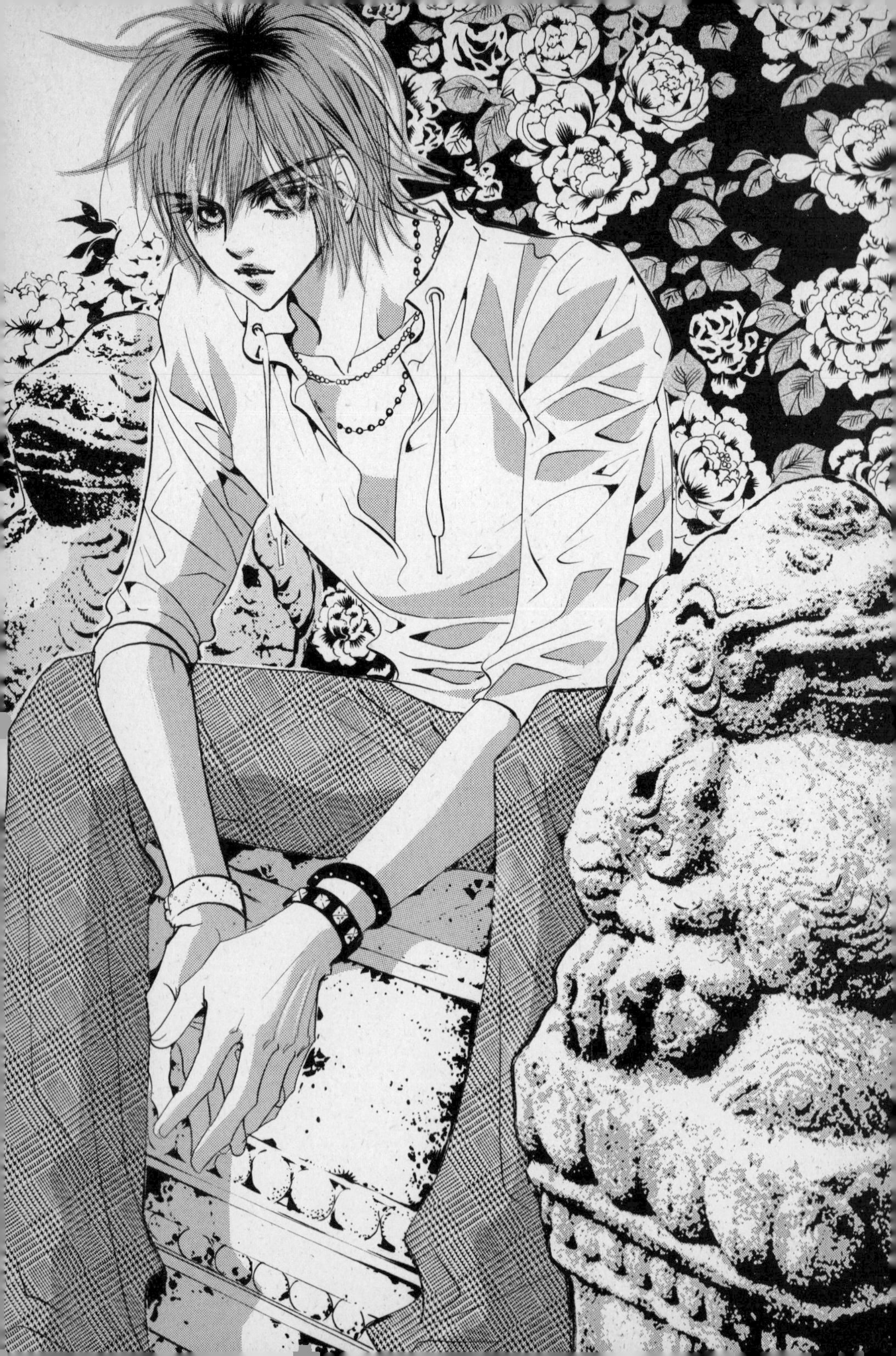

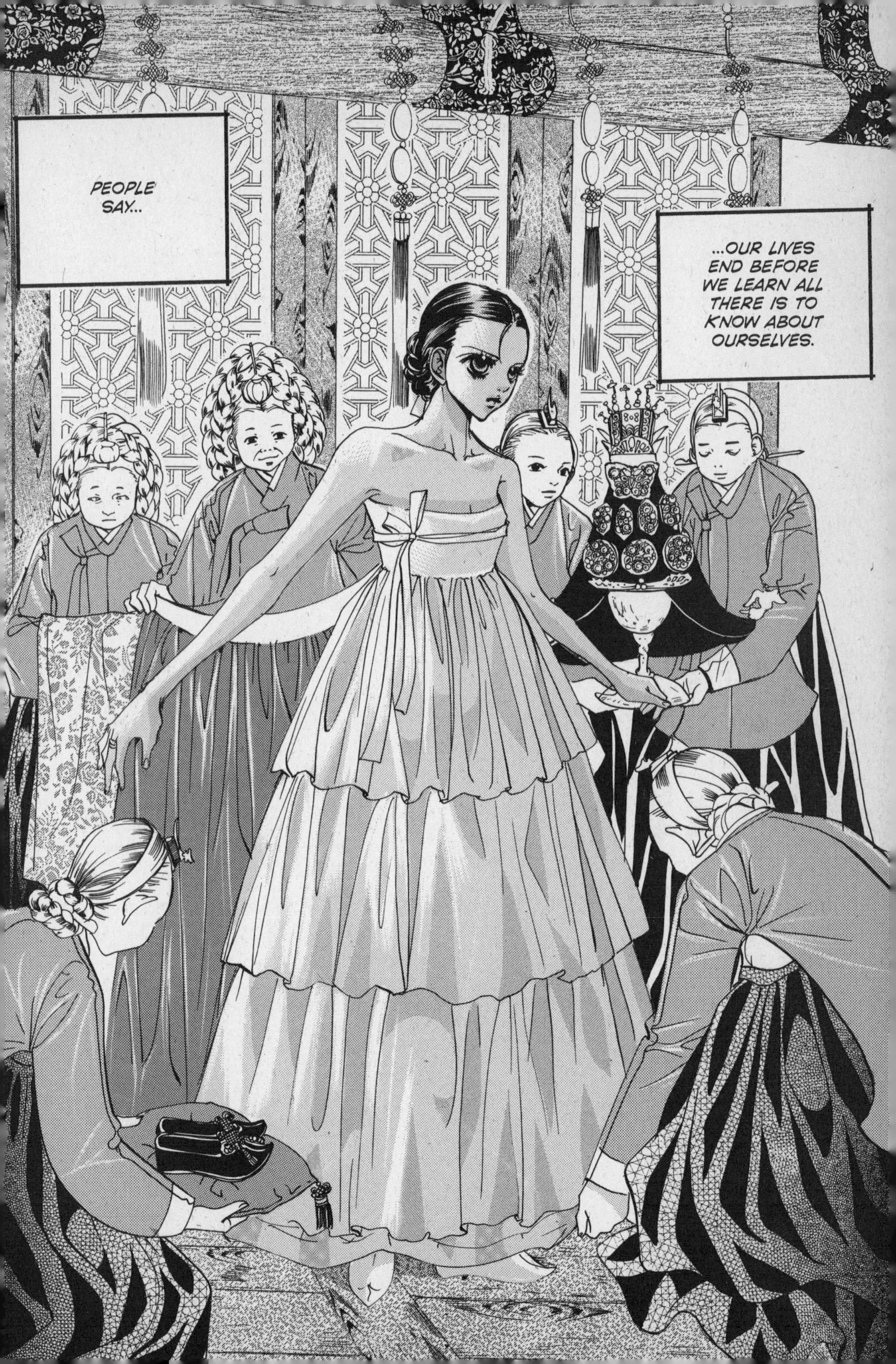
PEOPLE SAY...
...OUR LIVES END BEFORE WE LEARN ALL THERE IS TO KNOW ABOUT OURSELVES.

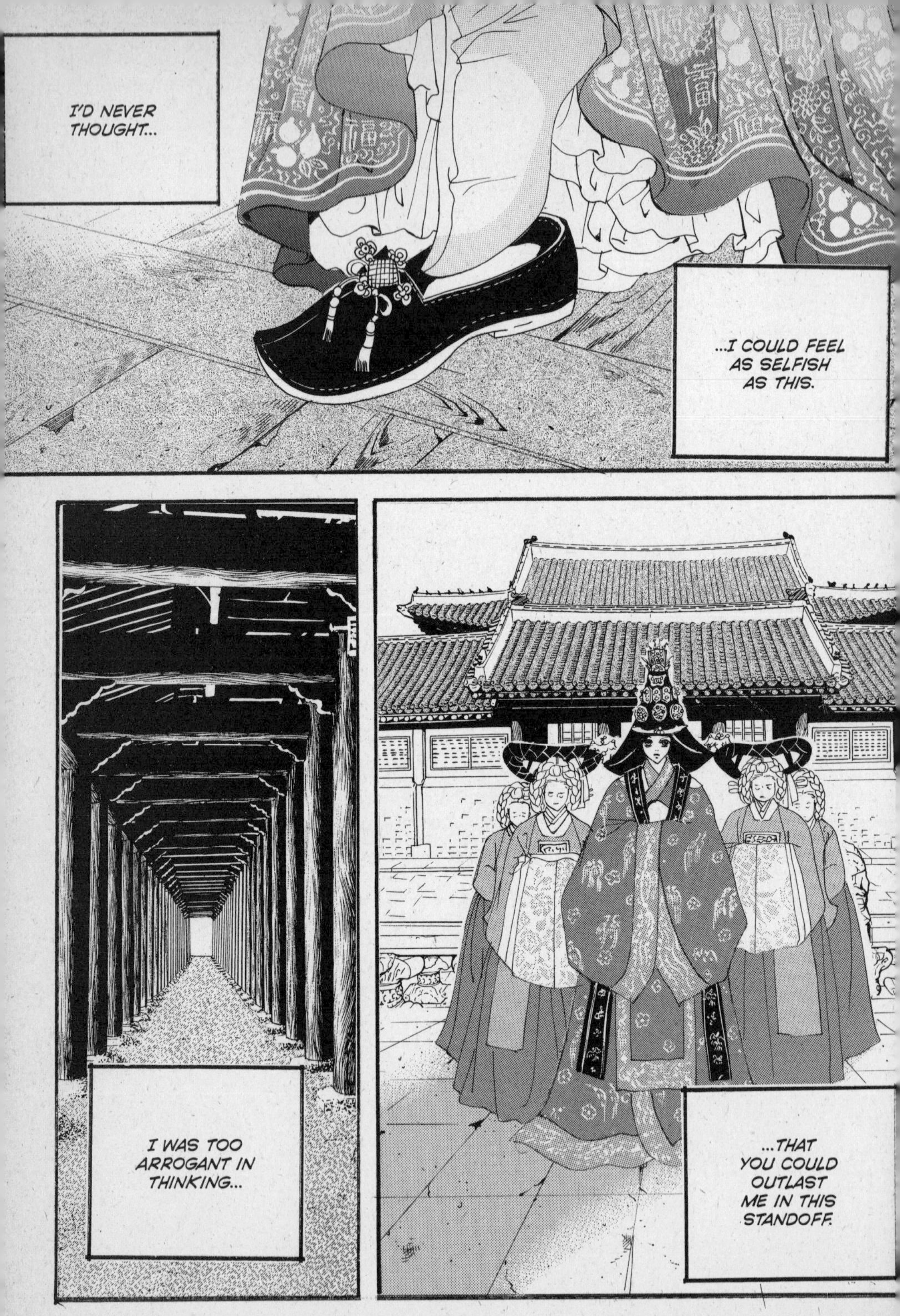
I'D NEVER THOUGHT...
...I COULD FEEL AS SELFISH AS THIS.
I WAS TOO ARROGANT IN THINKING...
...THAT YOU COULD OUTLAST ME IN THIS STANDOFF.

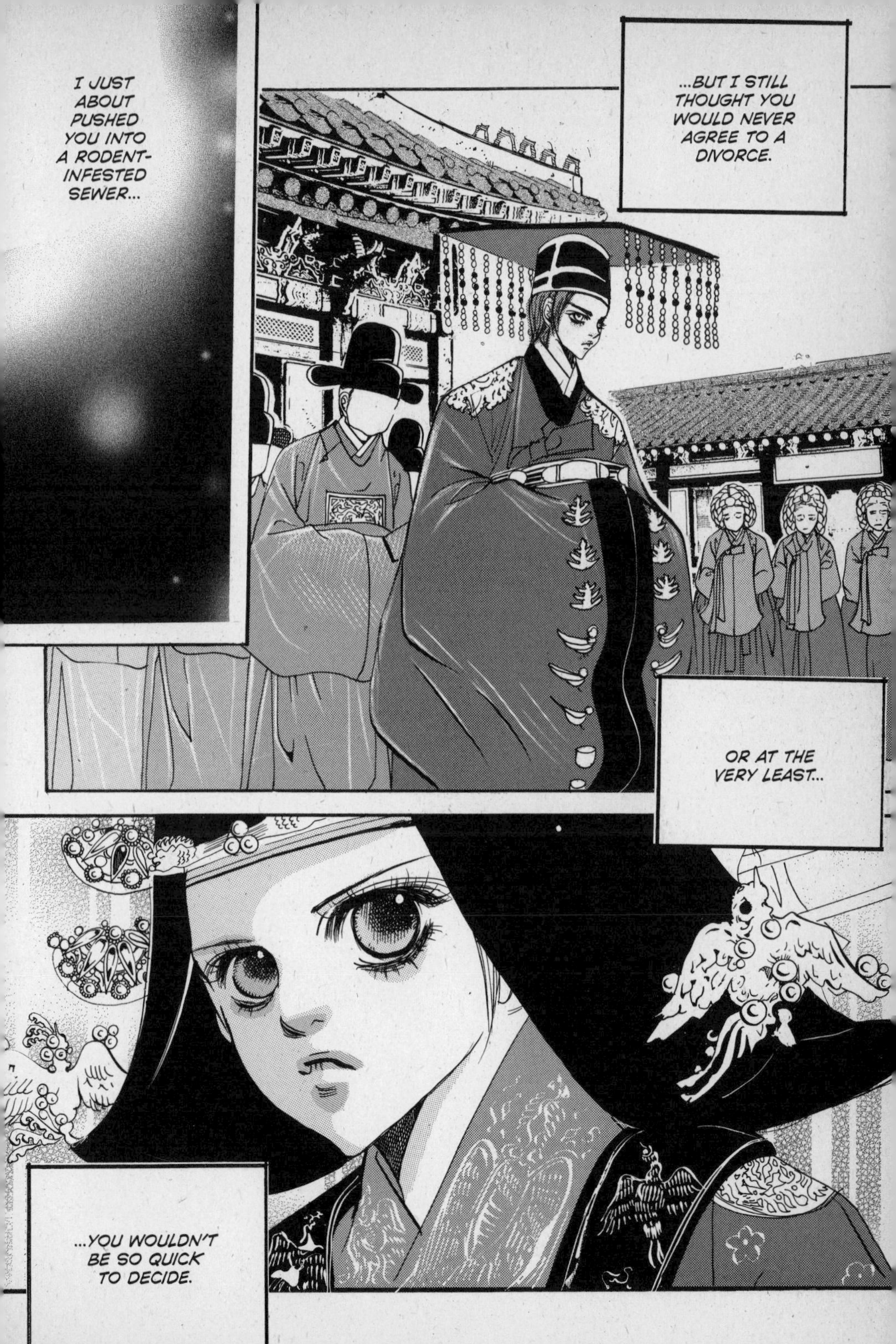

I JUST ABOUT PUSHED YOU INTO A RODENT-INFESTED SEWER...
...BUT I STILL THOUGHT YOU WOULD NEVER AGREE TO A DIVORCE.
OR AT THE VERY LEAST...
...YOU WOULDN'T BE SO QUICK TO DECIDE.

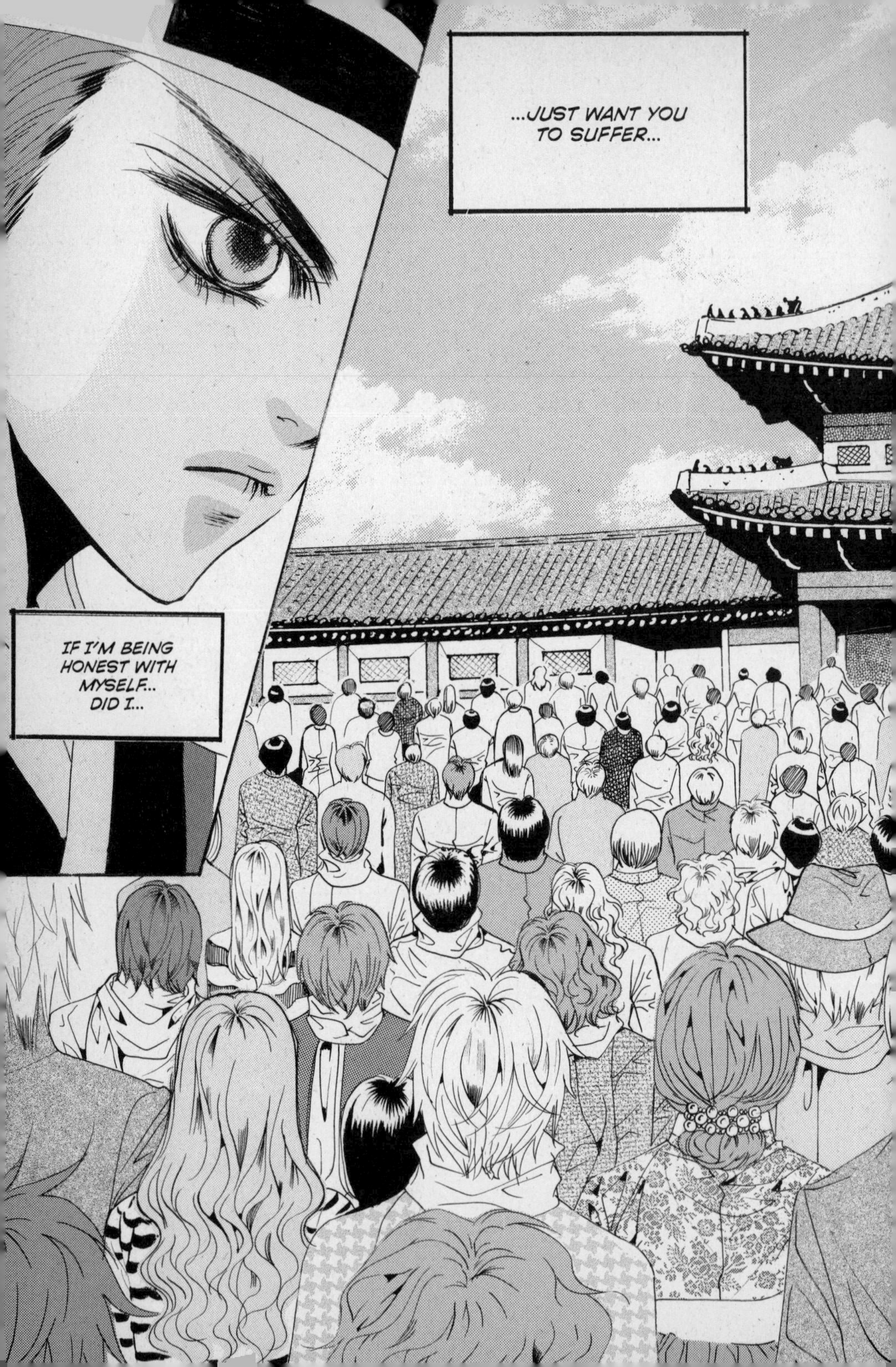
...JUST WANT YOU TO SUFFER...
IF I'M BEING HONEST WITH MYSELF... DID I...

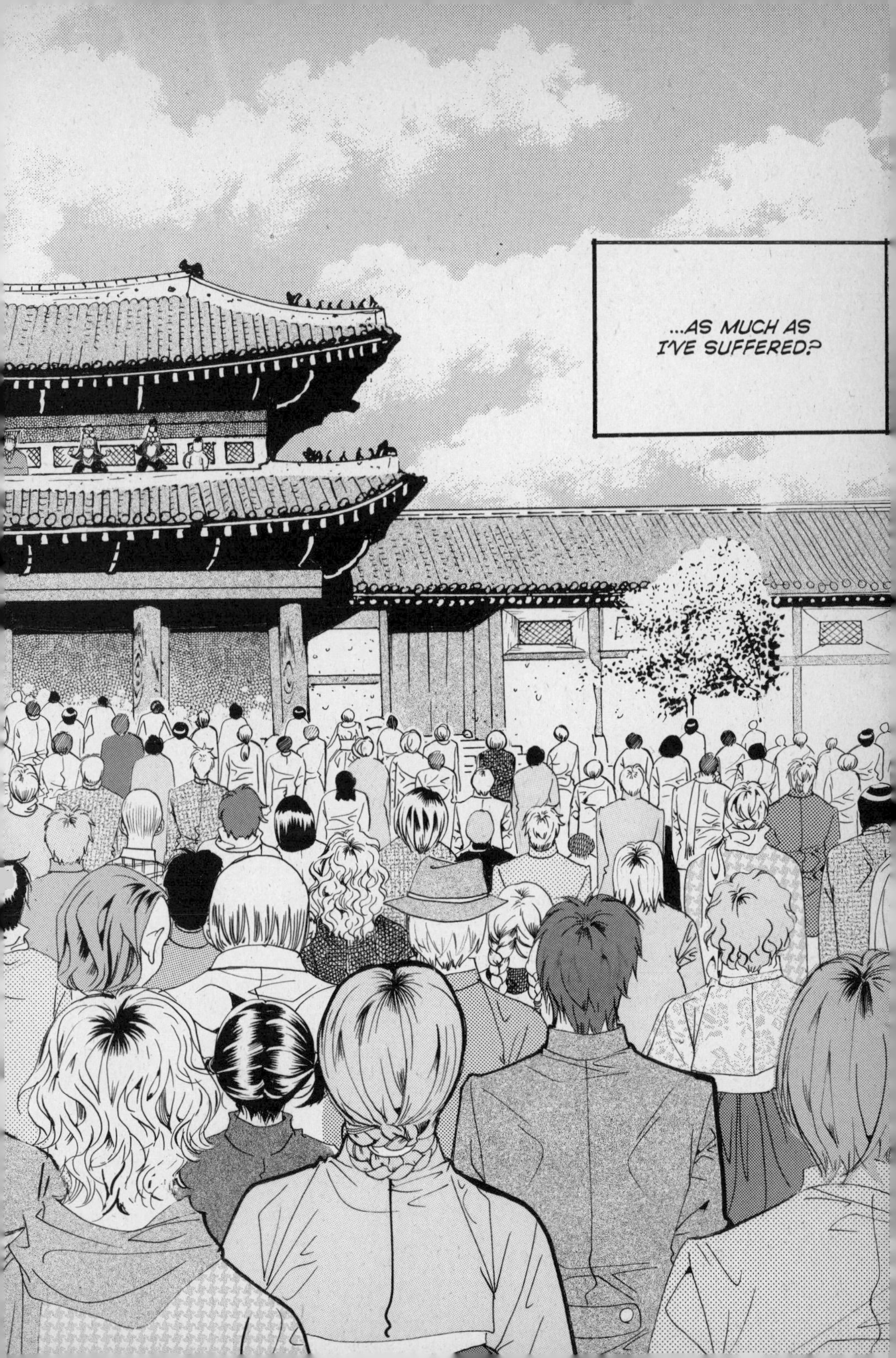
...AS MUCH AS I'VE SUFFERED?

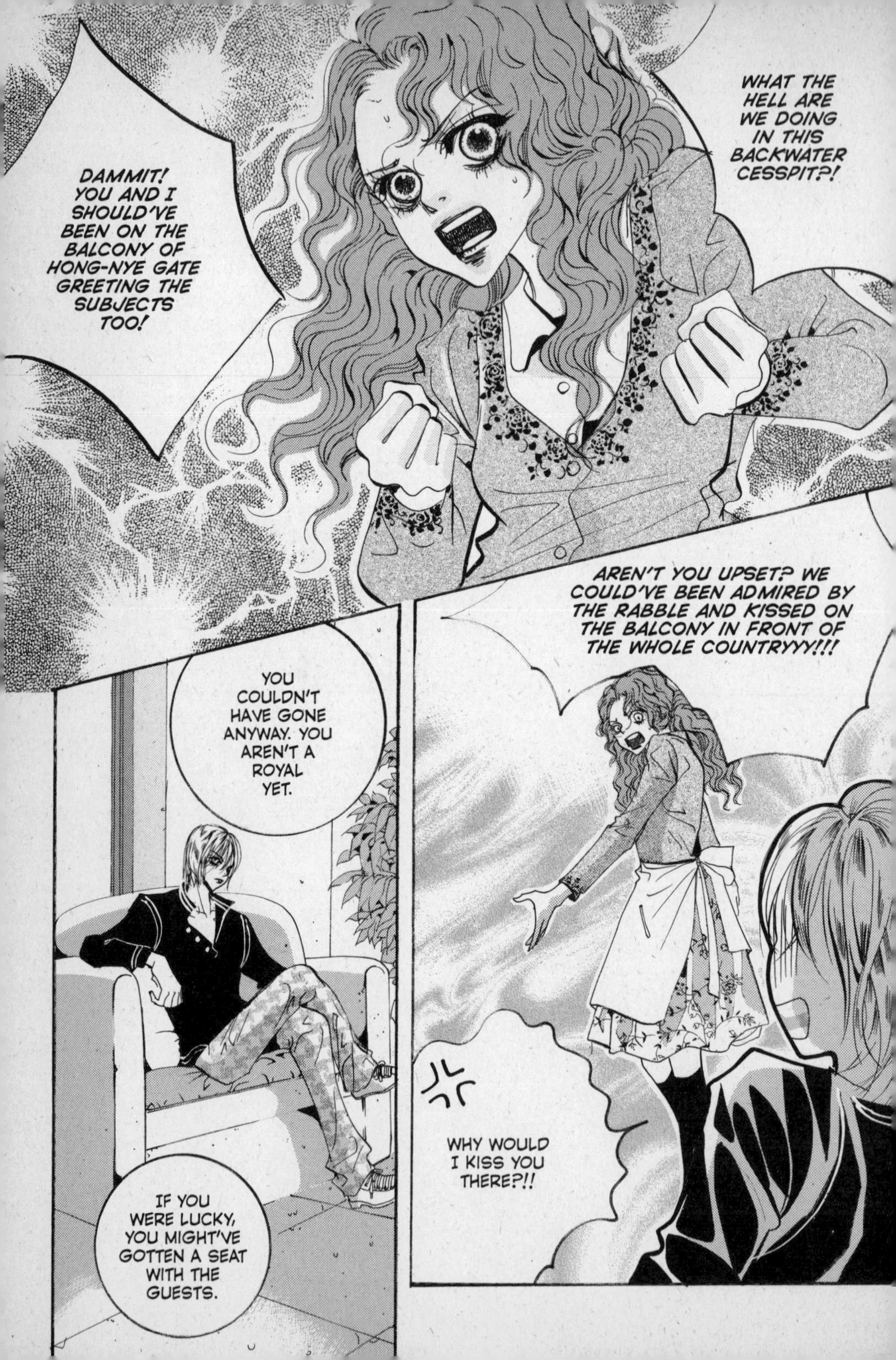
WHAT THE HELL ARE WE DOING IN THIS BACKWATER CESSPIT?!
DAMMIT! YOU AND I SHOULD'VE BEEN ON THE BALCONY OF HONG-NYE GATE GREETING THE SUBJECTS TOO!
AREN'T YOU UPSET? WE COULD'VE BEEN ADMIRED BY THE RABBLE AND KISSED ON THE BALCONY IN FRONT OF THE WHOLE COUNTRYYY!!!
YOU COULDN'T HAVE GONE ANYWAY. YOU AREN'T A ROYAL YET.
WHY WOULD I KISS YOU THERE?!!
IF YOU WERE LUCKY, YOU MIGHT'VE GOTTEN A SEAT WITH THE GUESTS.

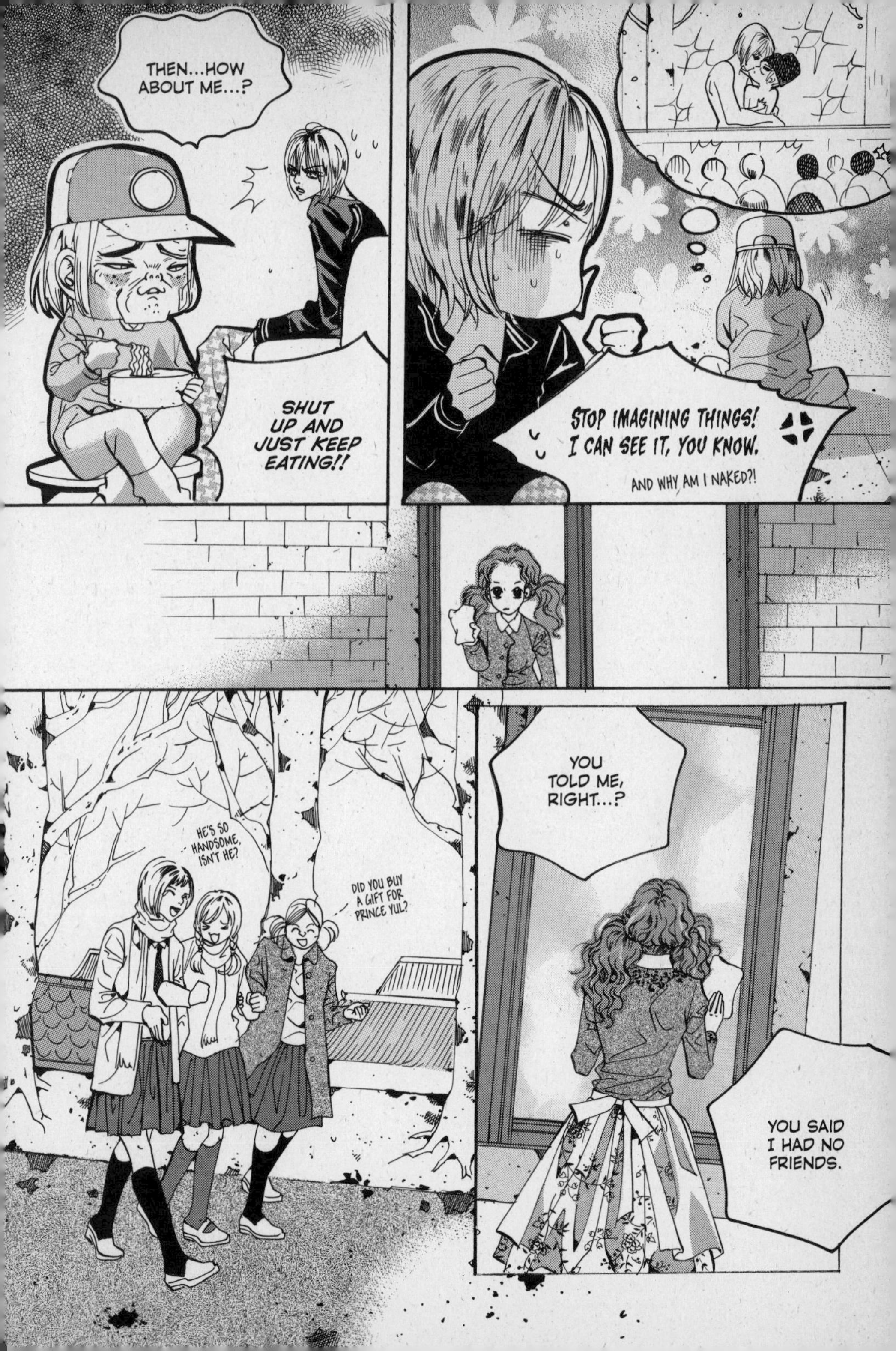
THEN...HOW ABOUT ME...?
SHUT UP AND JUST KEEP EATING!!
STOP IMAGINING THINGS! I CAN SEE IT, YOU KNOW.
AND WHY AM I NAKED?!
HE'S SO HANDSOME, ISN'T HE?
DID YOU BUY A GIFT FOR PRINCE YUL?
YOU TOLD ME, RIGHT...?
YOU SAID I HAD NO FRIENDS.

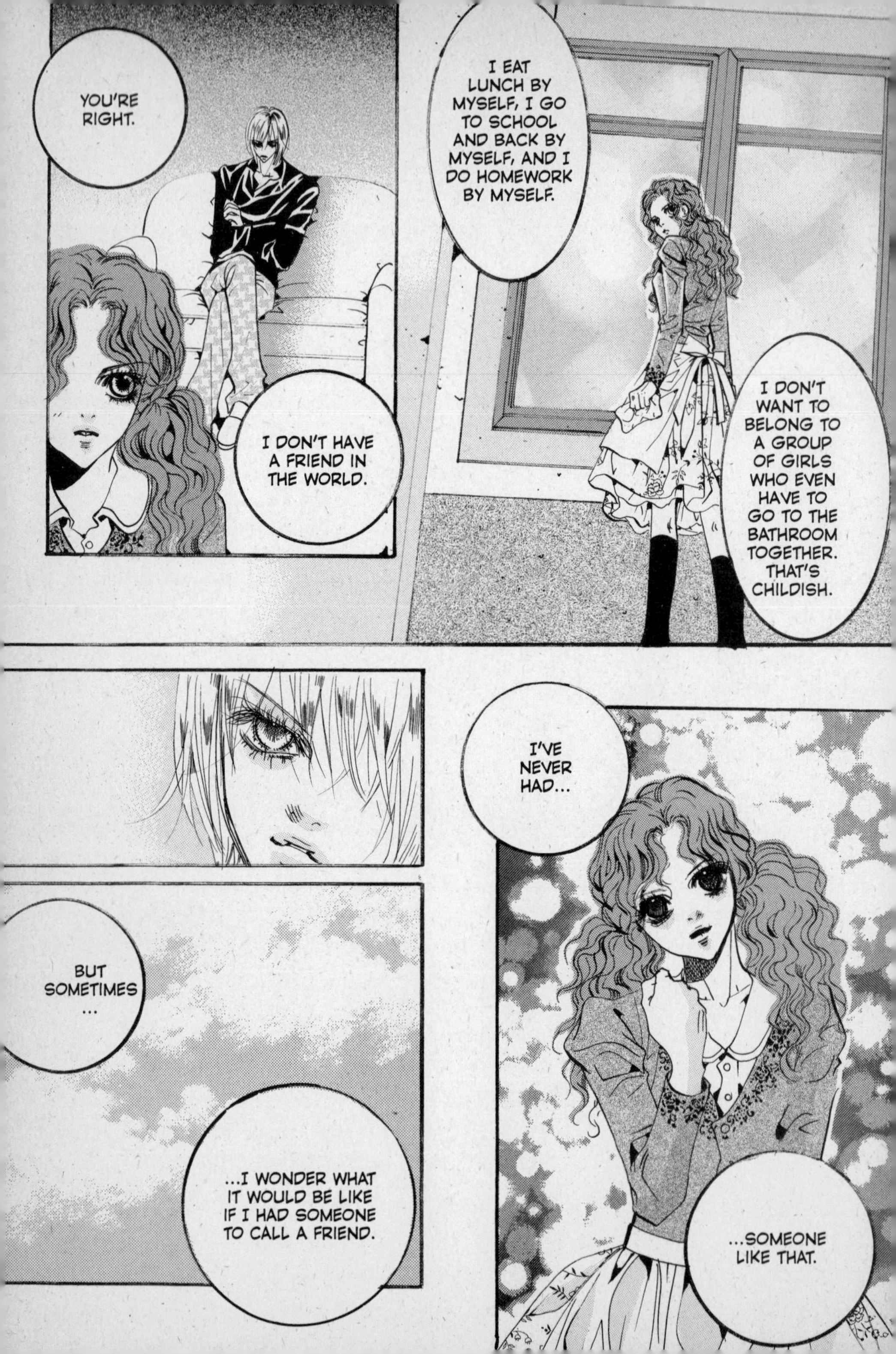
YOU'RE RIGHT.
I DON'T HAVE A FRIEND IN THE WORLD.
I EAT LUNCH BY MYSELF, I GO TO SCHOOL AND BACK BY MYSELF, AND I DO HOMEWORK BY MYSELF.
I DON'T WANT TO BELONG TO A GROUP OF GIRLS WHO EVEN HAVE TO GO TO THE BATHROOM TOGETHER. THAT'S CHILDISH.
BUT SOMETIMES ...
...I WONDER WHAT IT WOULD BE LIKE IF I HAD SOMEONE TO CALL A FRIEND.
I'VE NEVER HAD...
...SOMEONE LIKE THAT.

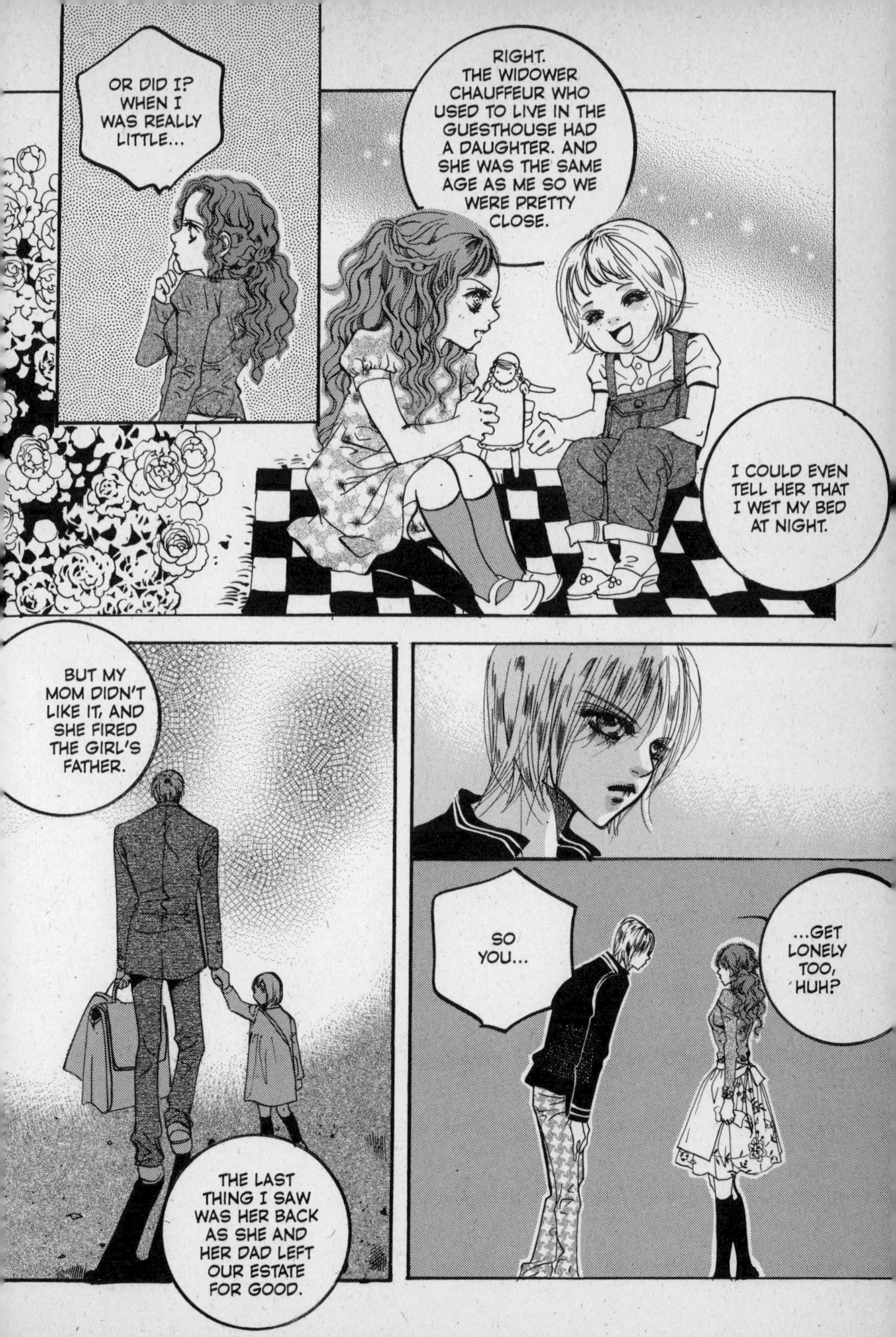

OR DID I? WHEN I WAS REALLY LITTLE...
RIGHT. THE WIDOWER CHAUFFEUR WHO USED TO LIVE IN THE GUESTHOUSE HAD A DAUGHTER. AND SHE WAS THE SAME AGE AS ME SO WE WERE PRETTY CLOSE.
I COULD EVEN TELL HER THAT I WET MY BED AT NIGHT.
BUT MY MOM DIDN'T LIKE IT, AND SHE FIRED THE GIRL'S FATHER.
THE LAST THING I SAW WAS HER BACK AS SHE AND HER DAD LEFT OUR ESTATE FOR GOOD.
SO YOU...
...GET LONELY TOO, HUH?

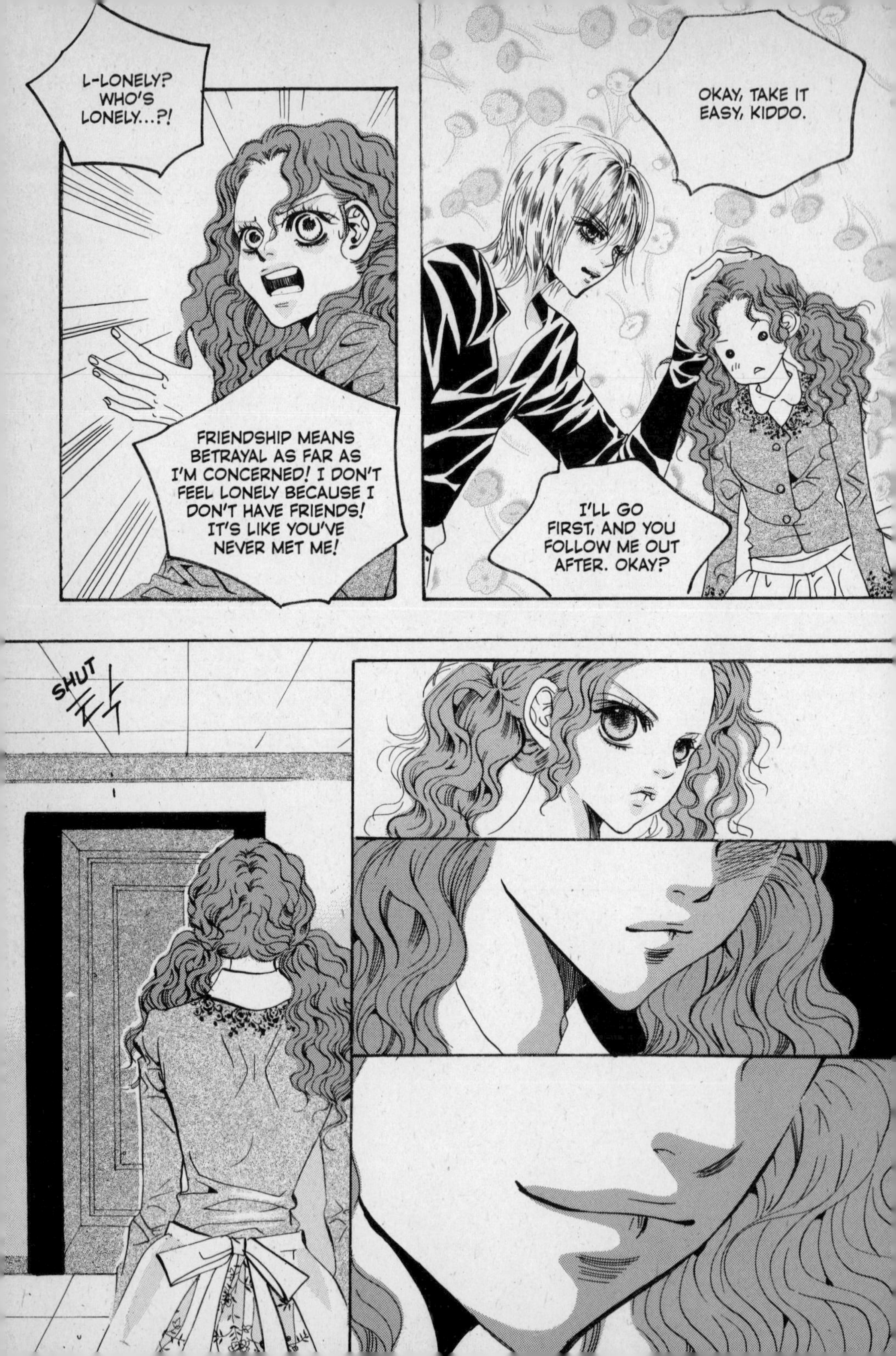
L-LONELY? WHO'S LONELY...?!
FRIENDSHIP MEANS BETRAYAL AS FAR AS I'M CONCERNED! I DON'T FEEL LONELY BECAUSE I DON'T HAVE FRIENDS! IT'S LIKE YOU'VE NEVER MET ME!
OKAY, TAKE IT EASY, KIDDO.
I'LL GO FIRST, AND YOU FOLLOW ME OUT AFTER. OKAY?
SHUT

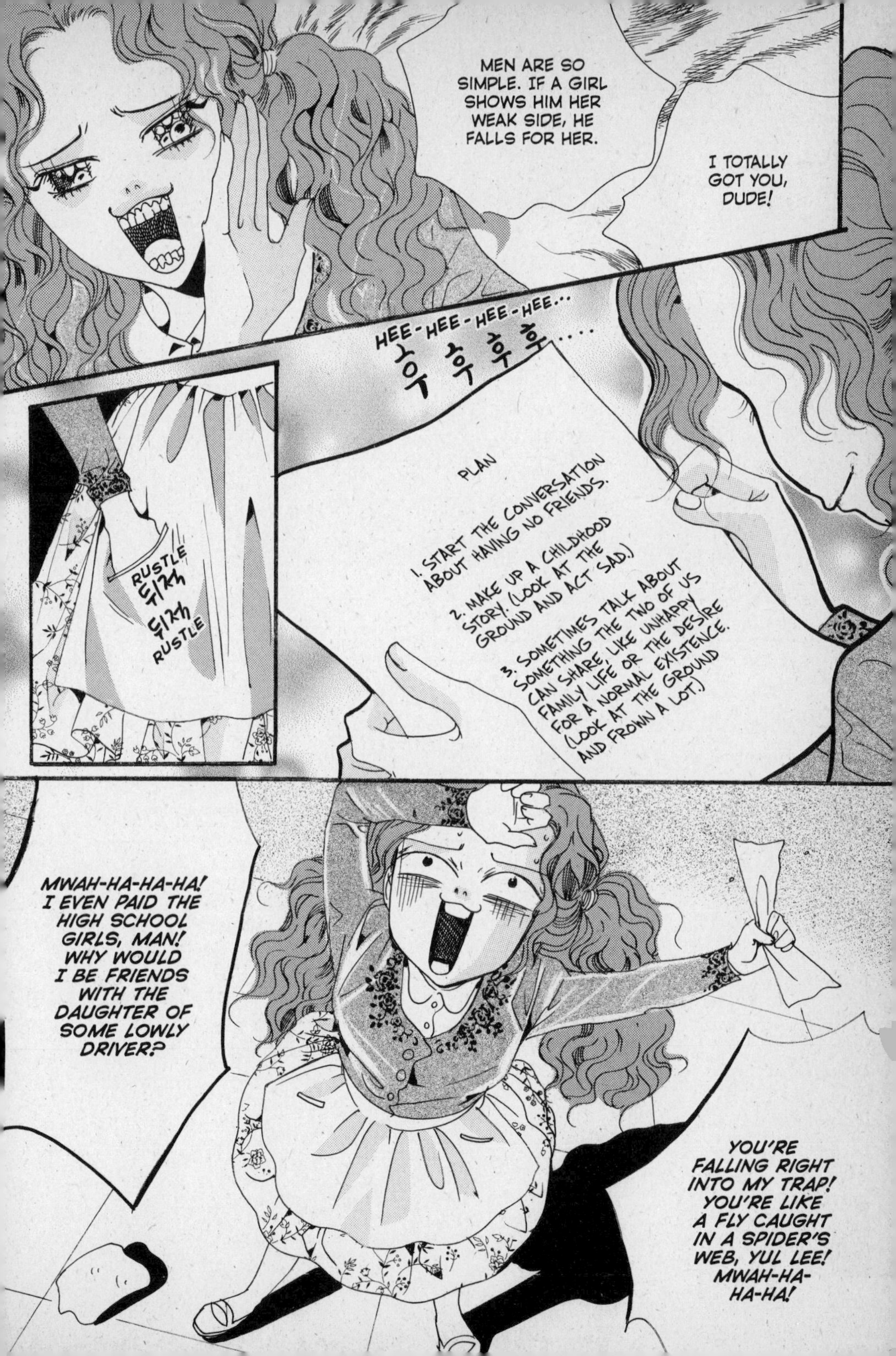
MEN ARE SO SIMPLE. IF A GIRL SHOWS HIM HER WEAK SIDE, HE FALLS FOR HER.
I TOTALLY GOT YOU, DUDE!
HEE-HEE-HEE-HEE...
후후후후....
RUSTLE 뒤적
뒤적 RUSTLE
PLAN
1. START THE CONVERSATION ABOUT HAVING NO FRIENDS.
2. MAKE UP A CHILDHOOD STORY. (LOOK AT THE GROUND AND ACT SAD.)
3. SOMETIMES TALK ABOUT SOMETHING THE TWO OF US CAN SHARE, LIKE UNHAPPY FAMILY LIFE OR THE DESIRE FOR A NORMAL EXISTENCE. (LOOK AT THE GROUND AND FROWN A LOT.)
MWAH-HA-HA-HA! I EVEN PAID THE HIGH SCHOOL GIRLS, MAN! WHY WOULD I BE FRIENDS WITH THE DAUGHTER OF SOME LOWLY DRIVER?
YOU'RE FALLING RIGHT INTO MY TRAP! YOU'RE LIKE A FLY CAUGHT IN A SPIDER'S WEB, YUL LEE! MWAH-HA-HA-HA!

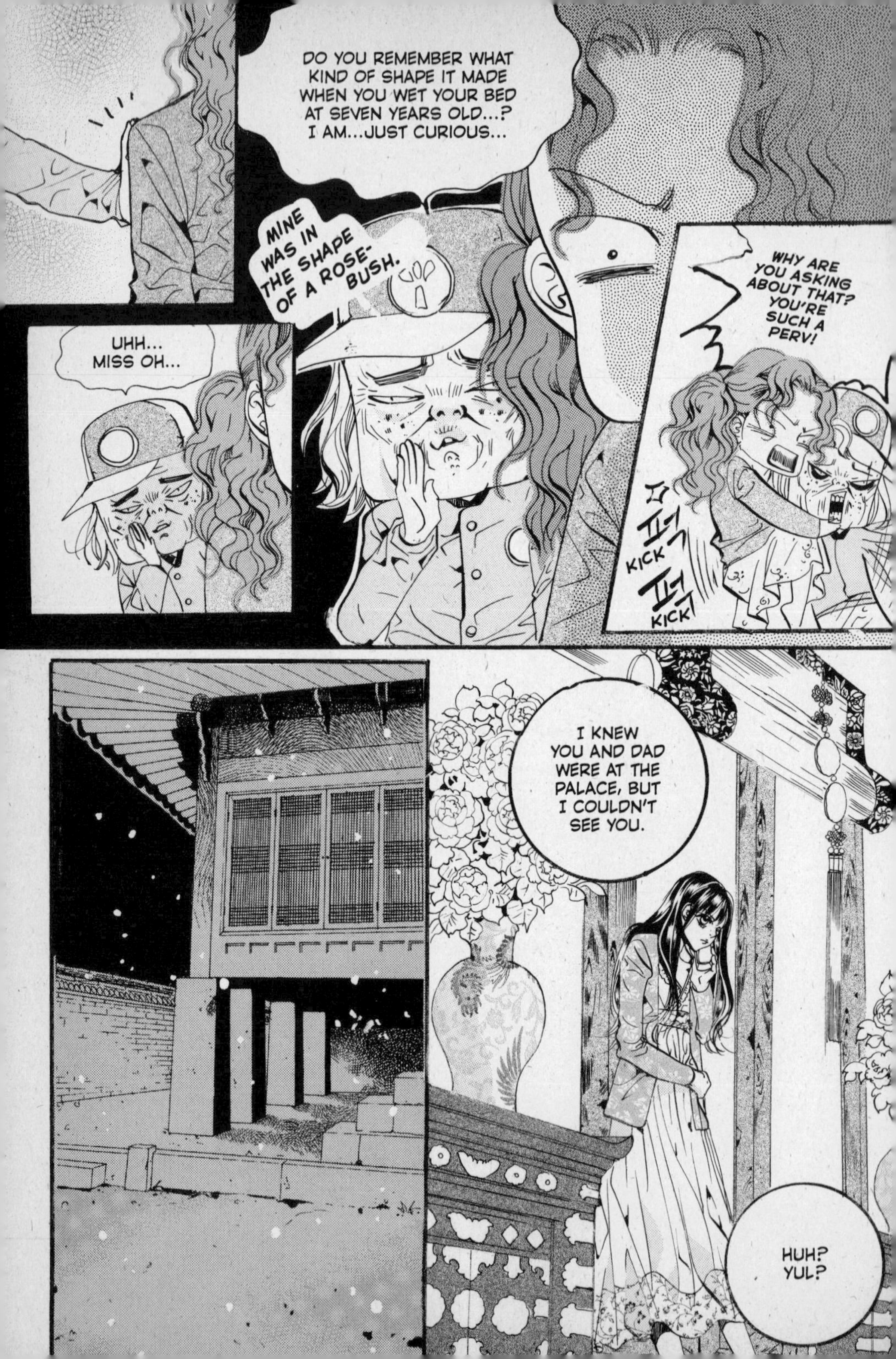
DO YOU REMEMBER WHAT KIND OF SHAPE IT MADE WHEN YOU WET YOUR BED AT SEVEN YEARS OLD...? I AM...JUST CURIOUS...
MINE WAS IN THE SHAPE OF A ROSE-BUSH.
UHH... MISS OH...
WHY ARE YOU ASKING ABOUT THAT? YOU'RE SUCH A PERV!
KICK
KICK
I KNEW YOU AND DAD WERE AT THE PALACE, BUT I COULDN'T SEE YOU.
HUH? YUL?

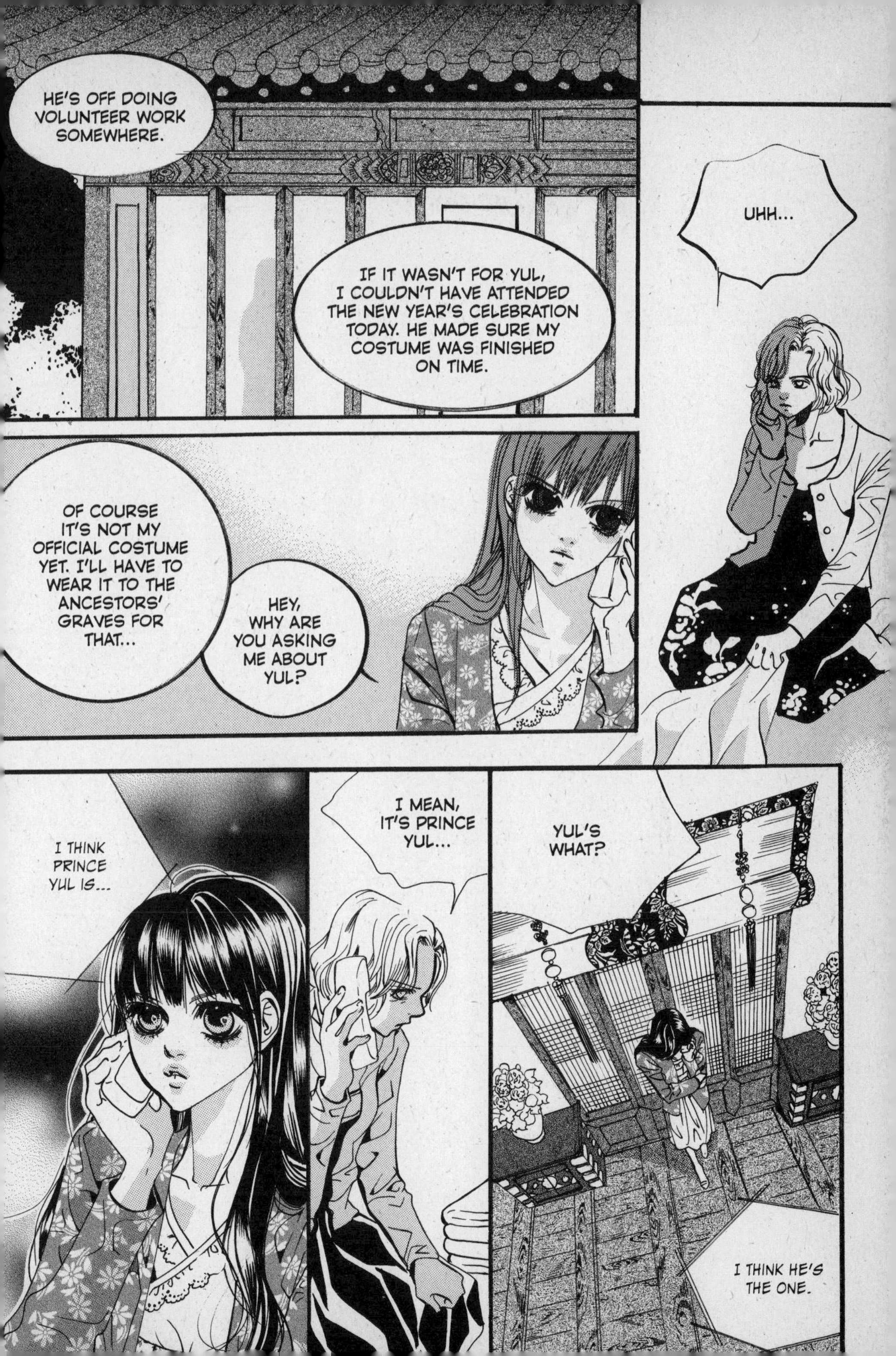
HE'S OFF DOING VOLUNTEER WORK SOMEWHERE.
UHH...
IF IT WASN'T FOR YUL, I COULDN'T HAVE ATTENDED THE NEW YEAR'S CELEBRATION TODAY. HE MADE SURE MY COSTUME WAS FINISHED ON TIME.
OF COURSE IT'S NOT MY OFFICIAL COSTUME YET. I'LL HAVE TO WEAR IT TO THE ANCESTORS' GRAVES FOR THAT...
HEY, WHY ARE YOU ASKING ME ABOUT YUL?
YUL'S WHAT?
I MEAN, IT'S PRINCE YUL...
I THINK PRINCE YUL IS...
I THINK HE'S THE ONE.

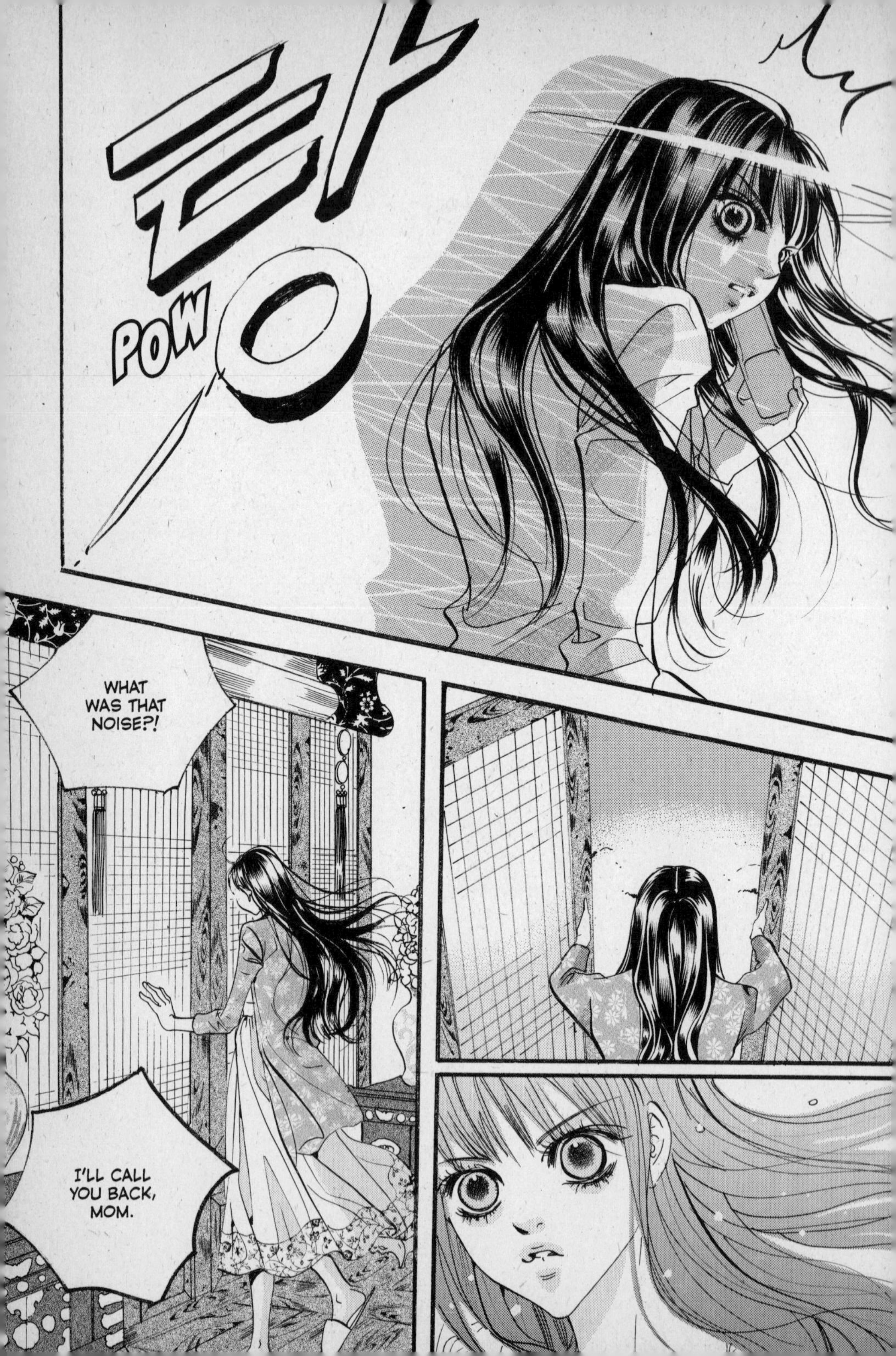
POW
WHAT WAS THAT NOISE?!
I'LL CALL YOU BACK, MOM.

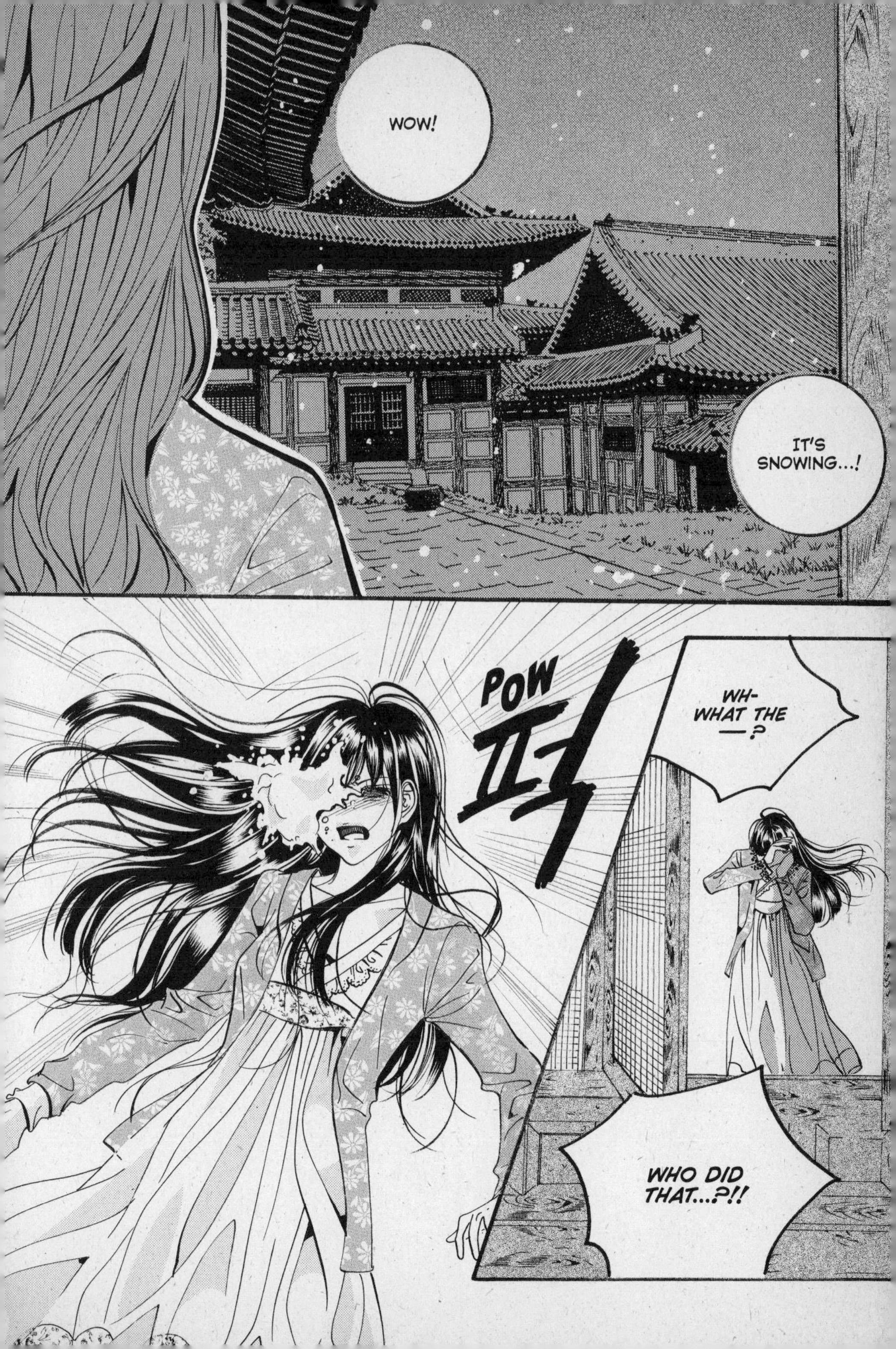

WOW!
IT'S SNOWING...!
POW
퍽
WH- WHAT THE —?
WHO DID THAT...?!!

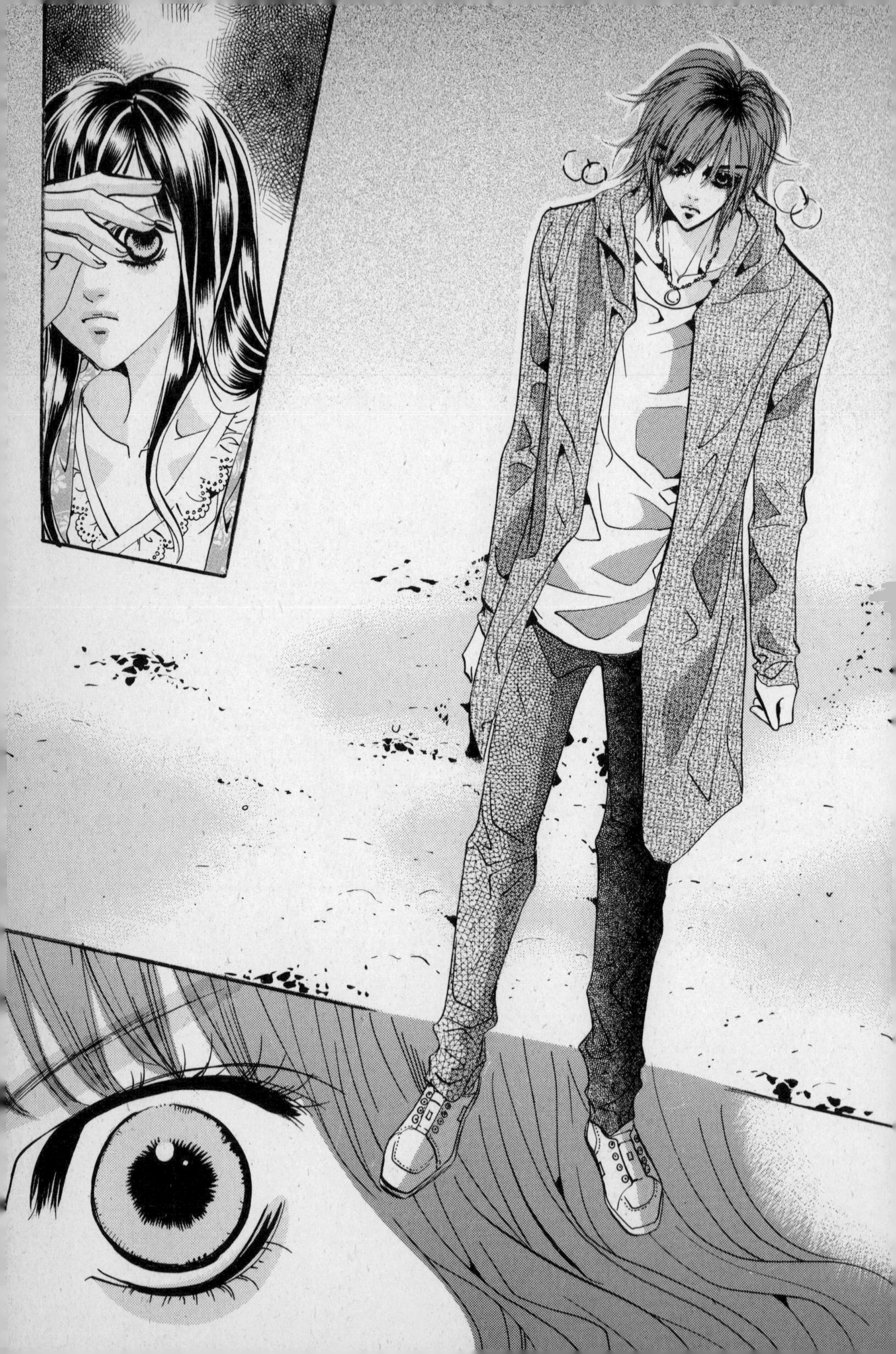

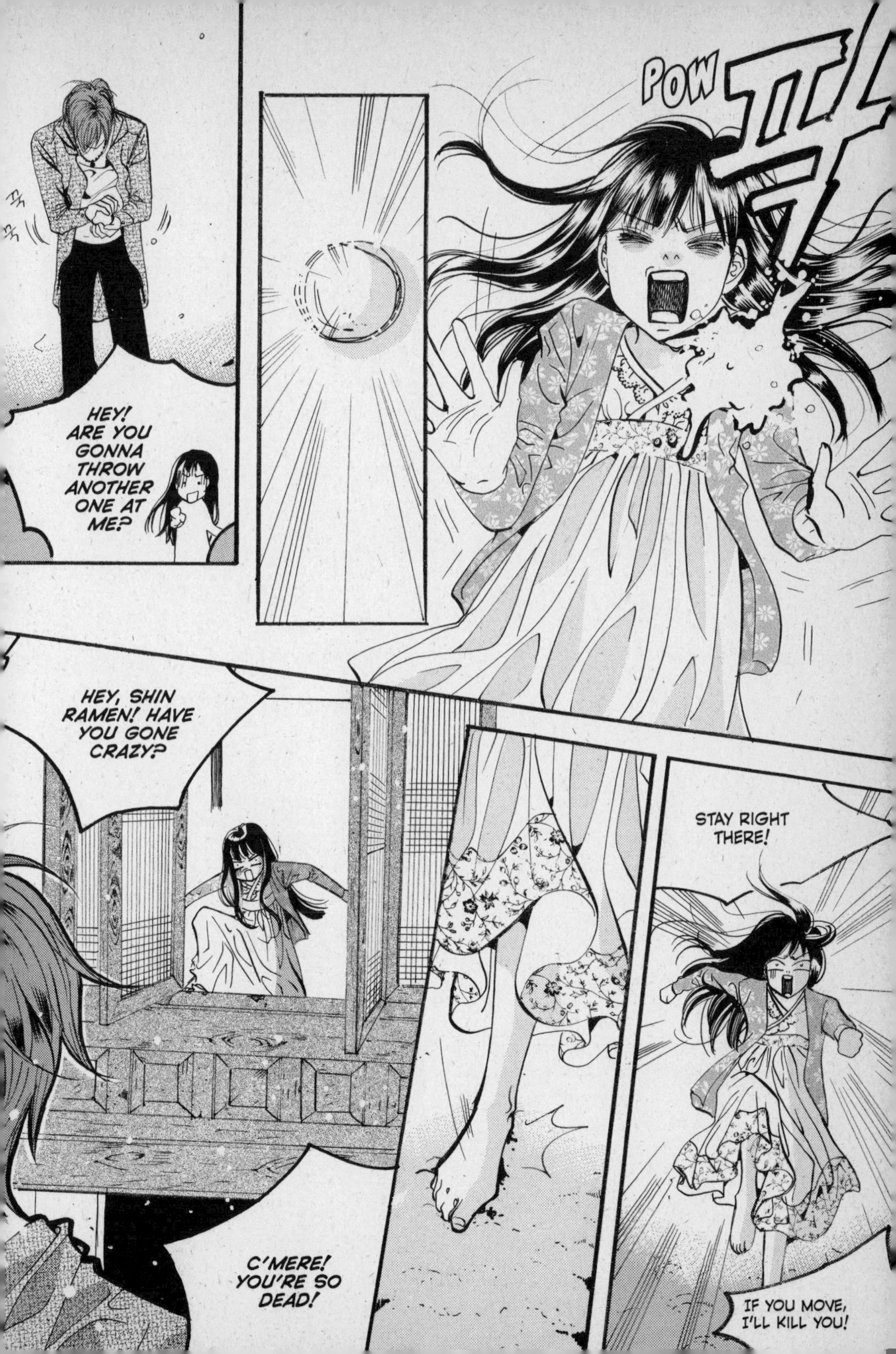
HEY! ARE YOU GONNA THROW ANOTHER ONE AT ME?
POW
HEY, SHIN RAMEN! HAVE YOU GONE CRAZY?
C'MERE! YOU'RE SO DEAD!
STAY RIGHT THERE!
IF YOU MOVE, I'LL KILL YOU!

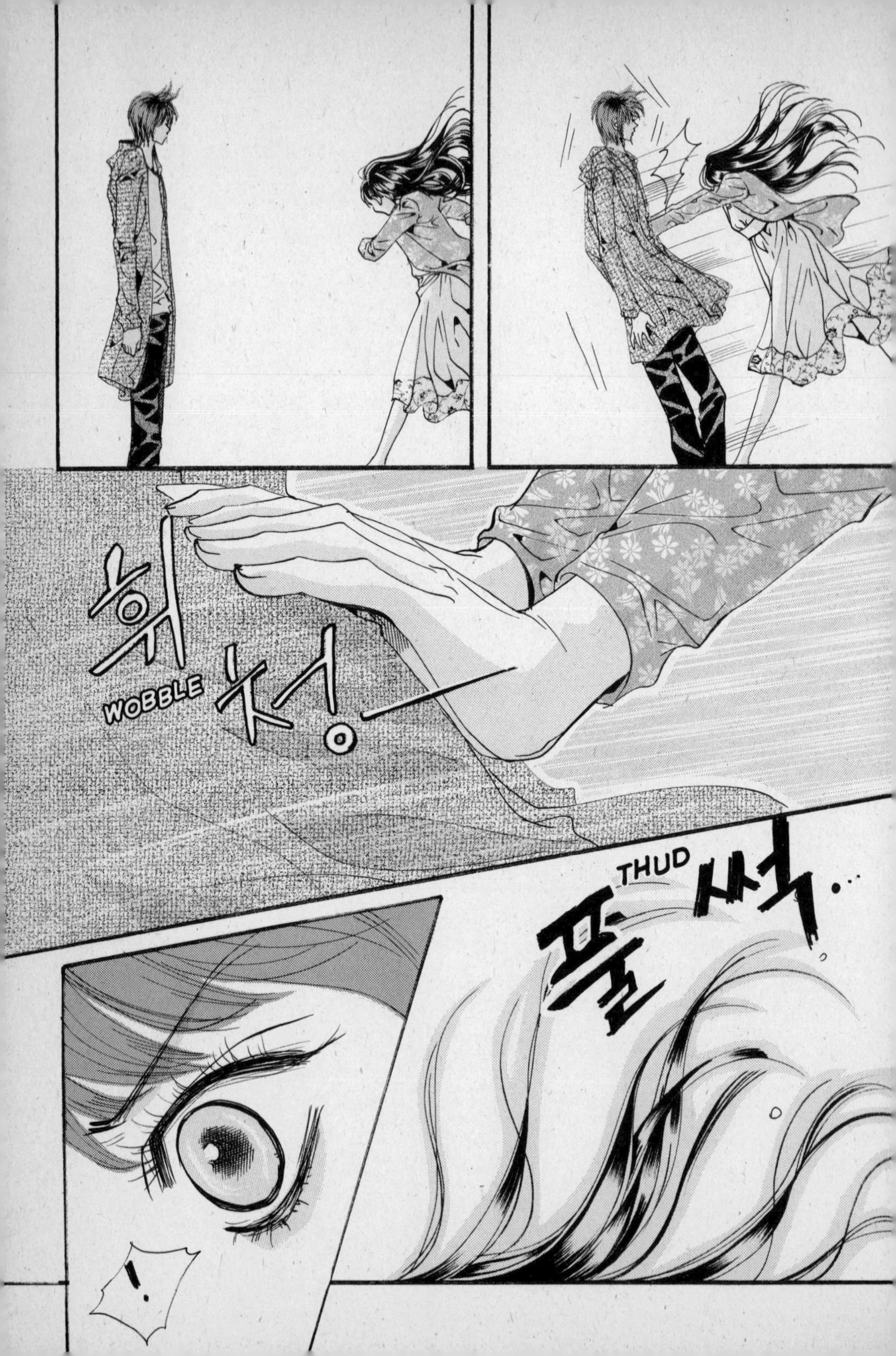

휘청
WOBBLE
풀썩...
THUD
!

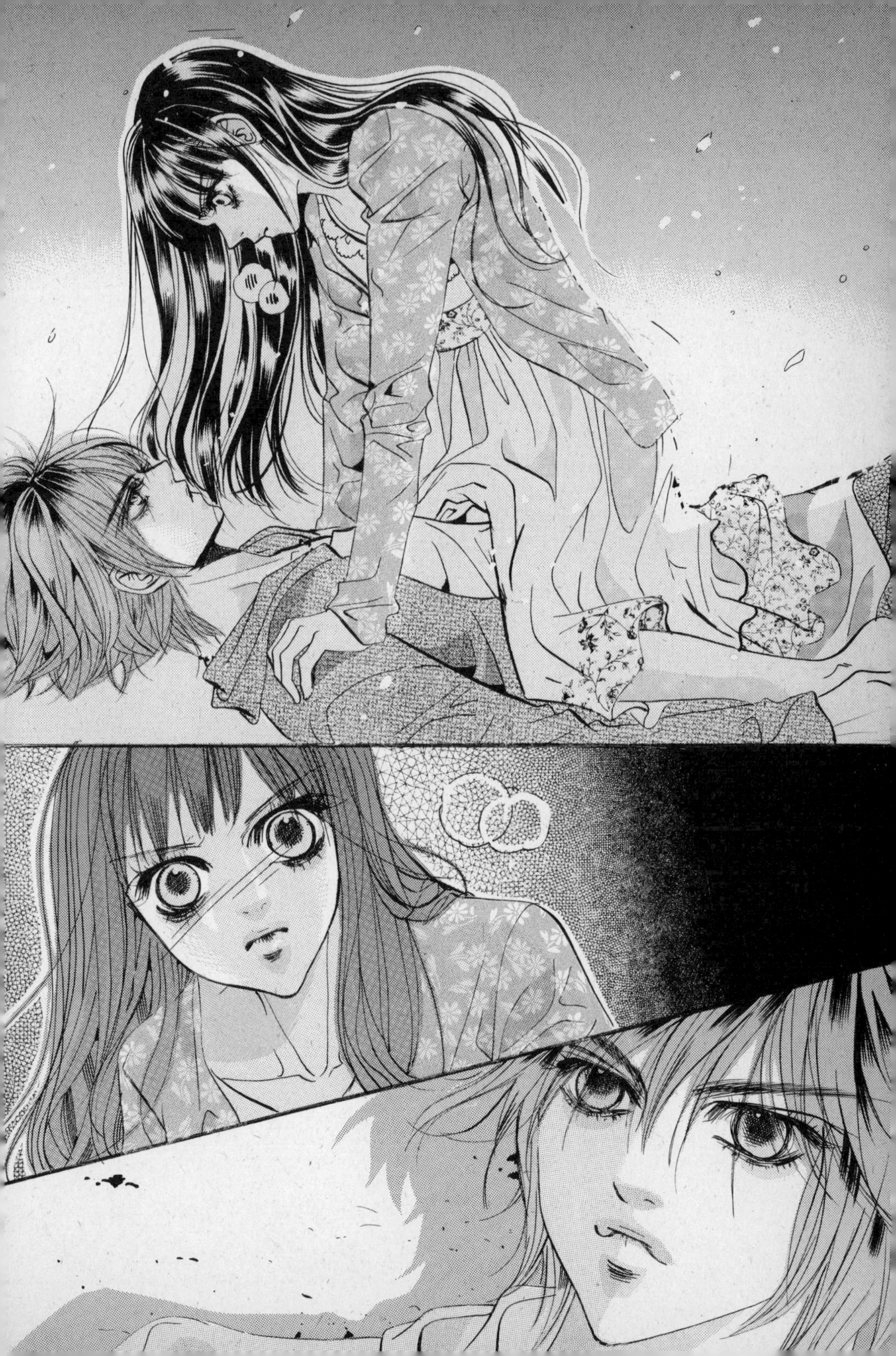

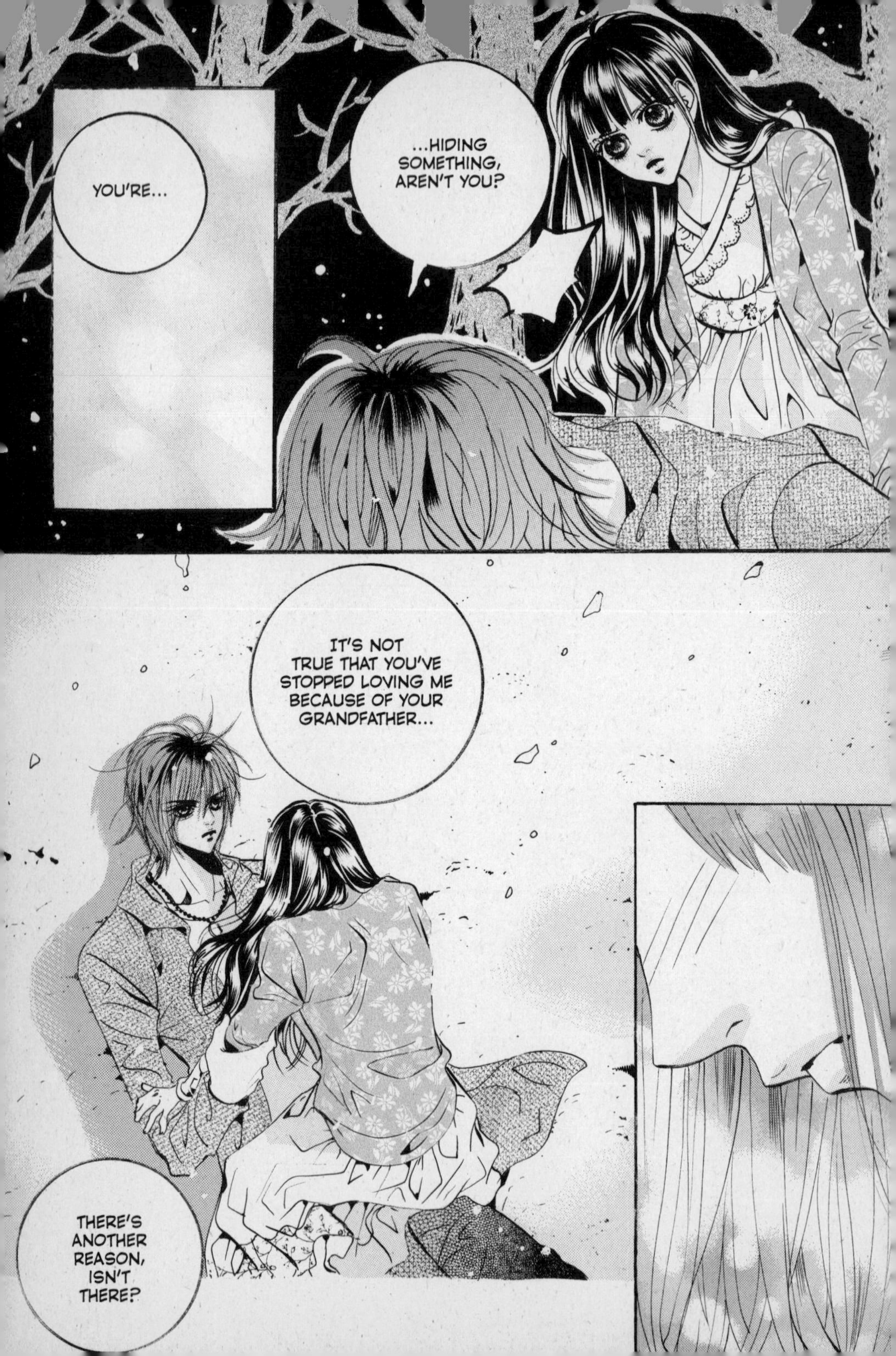
...HIDING SOMETHING, AREN'T YOU?
YOU'RE...
IT'S NOT TRUE THAT YOU'VE STOPPED LOVING ME BECAUSE OF YOUR GRANDFATHER...
THERE'S ANOTHER REASON, ISN'T THERE?

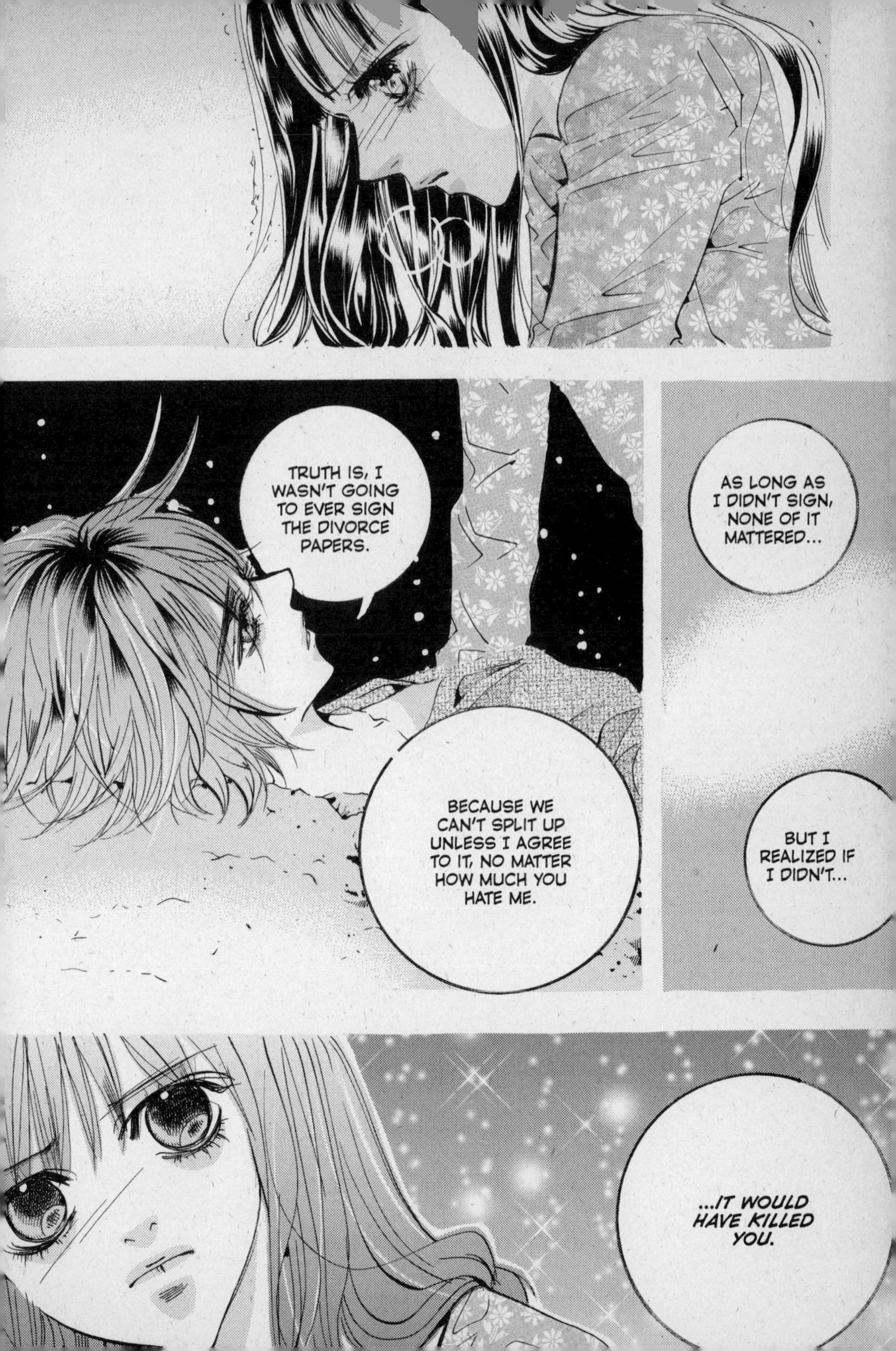
TRUTH IS, I WASN'T GOING TO EVER SIGN THE DIVORCE PAPERS.
BECAUSE WE CAN'T SPLIT UP UNLESS I AGREE TO IT, NO MATTER HOW MUCH YOU HATE ME.
AS LONG AS I DIDN'T SIGN, NONE OF IT MATTERED...
BUT I REALIZED IF I DIDN'T...
...IT WOULD HAVE KILLED YOU.

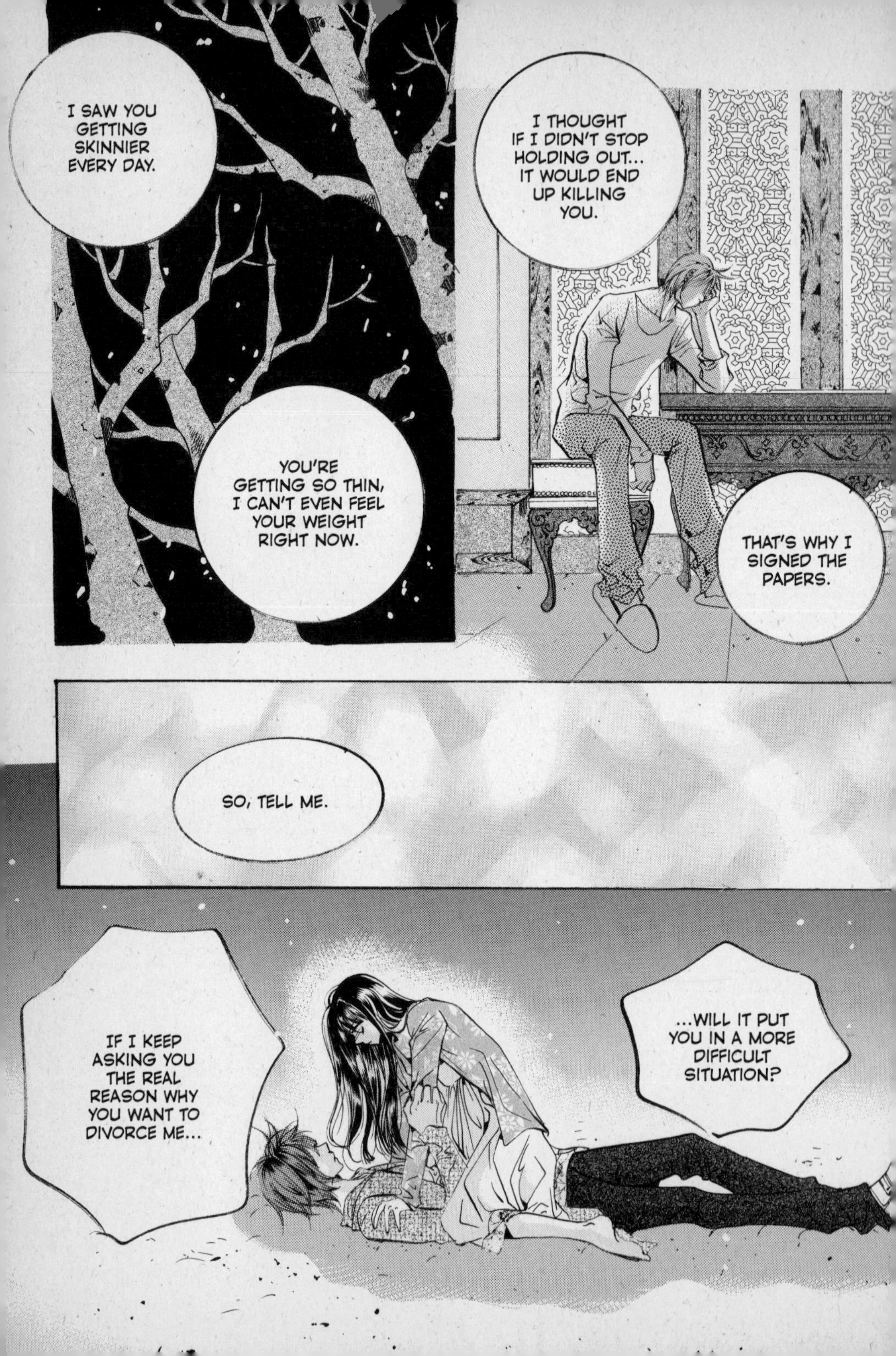
I SAW YOU GETTING SKINNIER EVERY DAY.
YOU'RE GETTING SO THIN, I CAN'T EVEN FEEL YOUR WEIGHT RIGHT NOW.
I THOUGHT IF I DIDN'T STOP HOLDING OUT... IT WOULD END UP KILLING YOU.
THAT'S WHY I SIGNED THE PAPERS.
SO, TELL ME.
IF I KEEP ASKING YOU THE REAL REASON WHY YOU WANT TO DIVORCE ME...
...WILL IT PUT YOU IN A MORE DIFFICULT SITUATION?

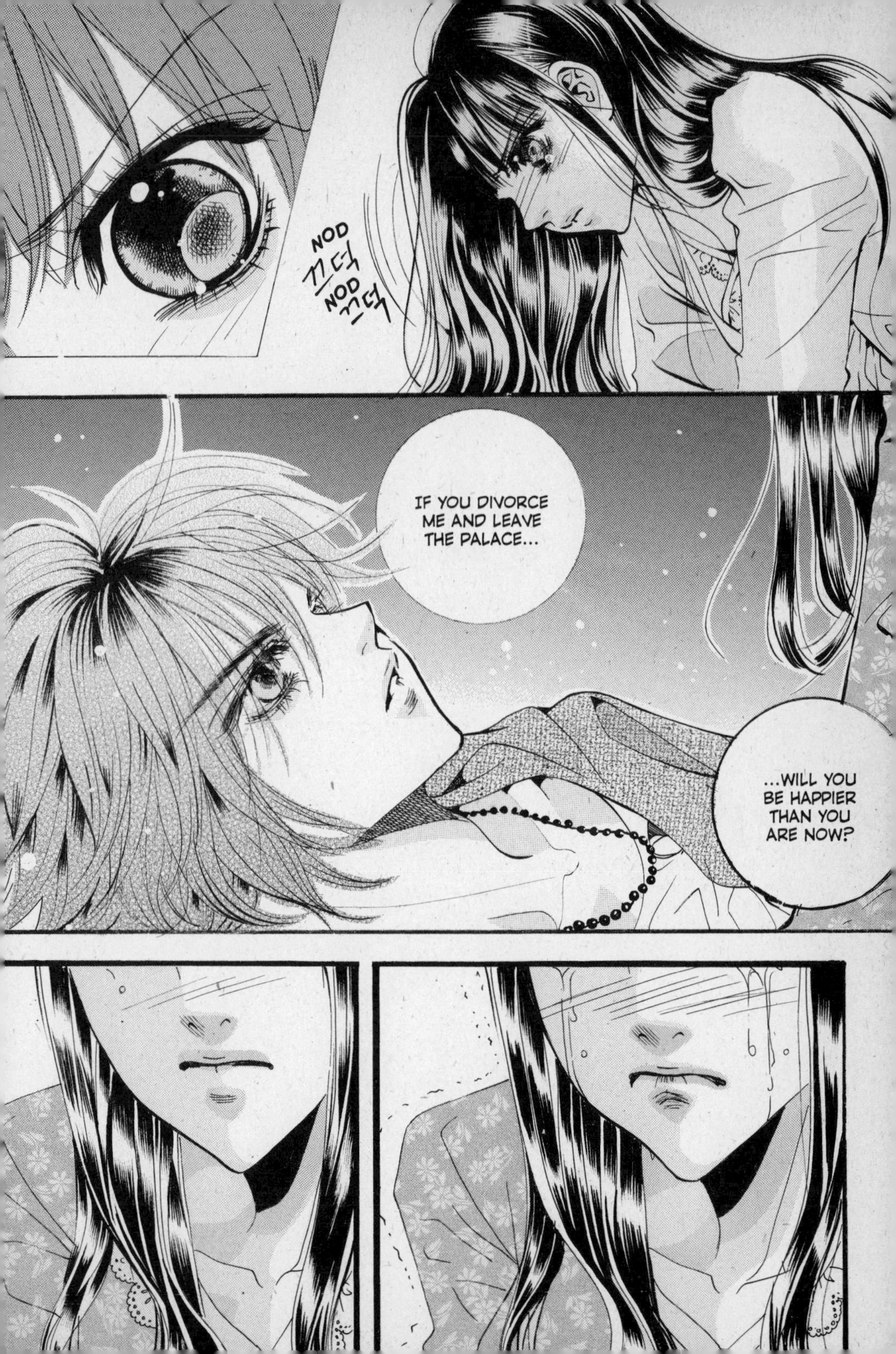
NOD
끄덕
NOD
끄덕
IF YOU DIVORCE ME AND LEAVE THE PALACE...
...WILL YOU BE HAPPIER THAN YOU ARE NOW?

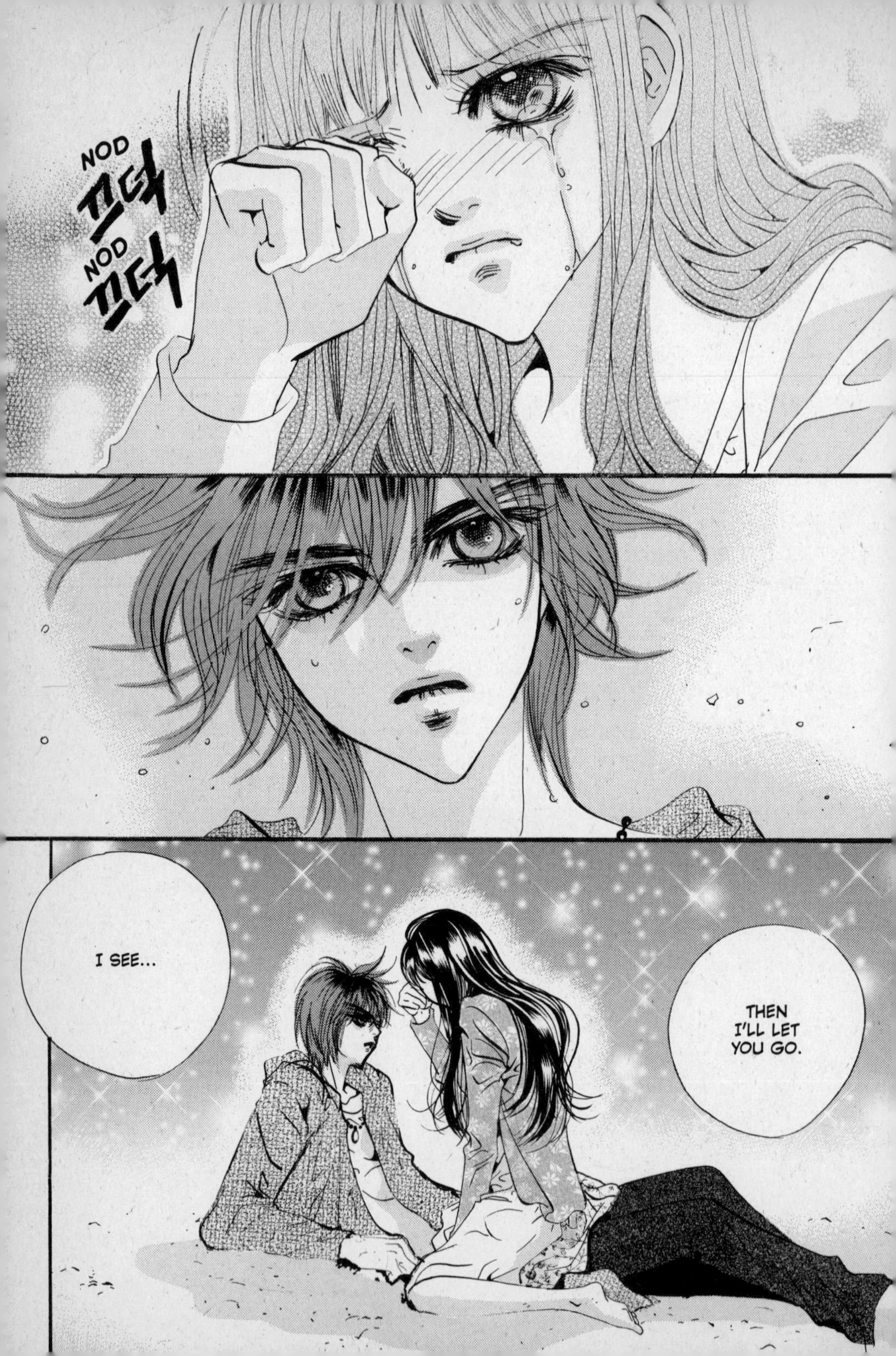

NOD
끄덕
NOD
끄덕
THEN I'LL LET YOU GO.
I SEE...

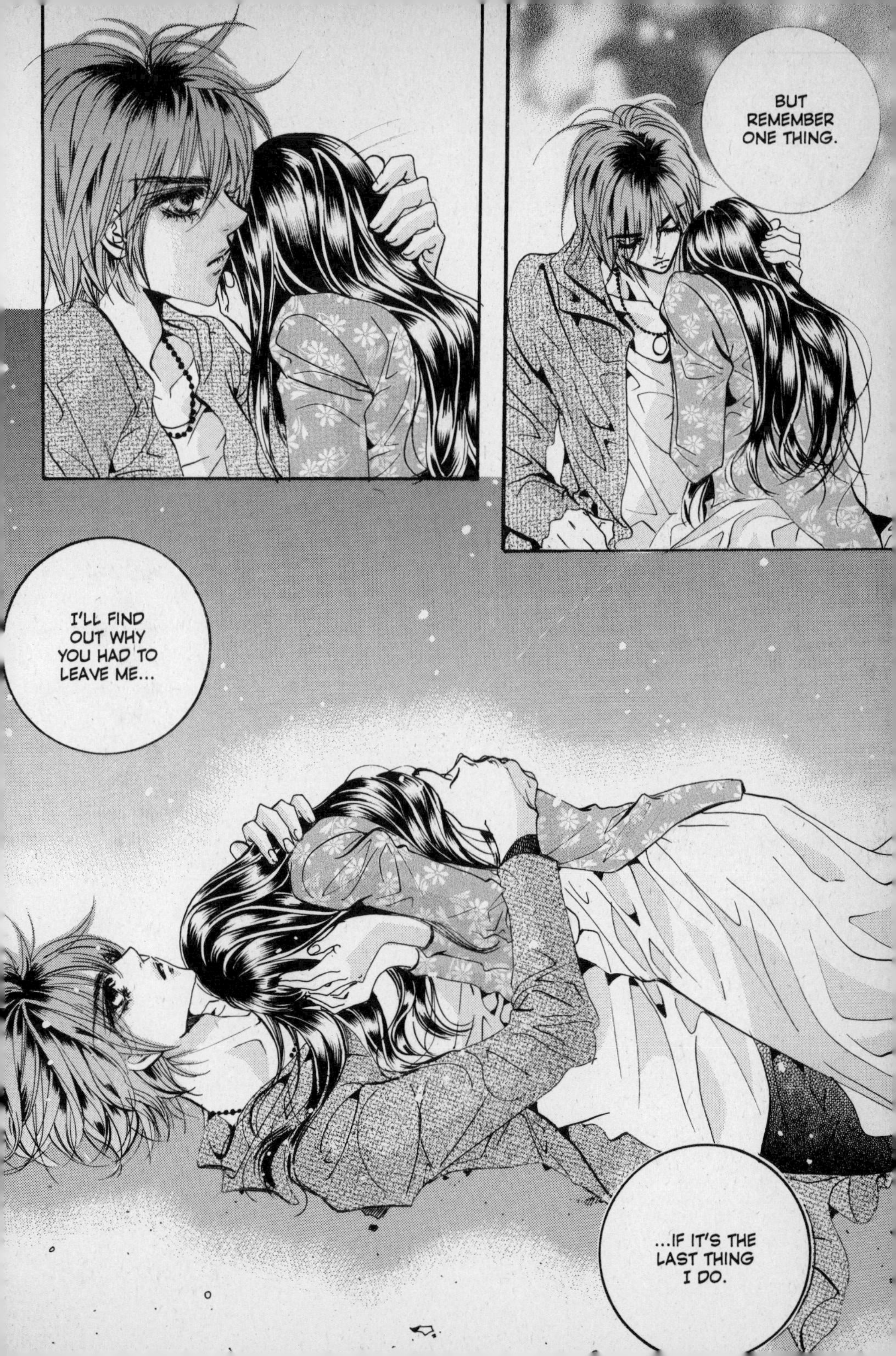
BUT REMEMBER ONE THING.
I'LL FIND OUT WHY YOU HAD TO LEAVE ME...
...IF IT'S THE LAST THING I DO.

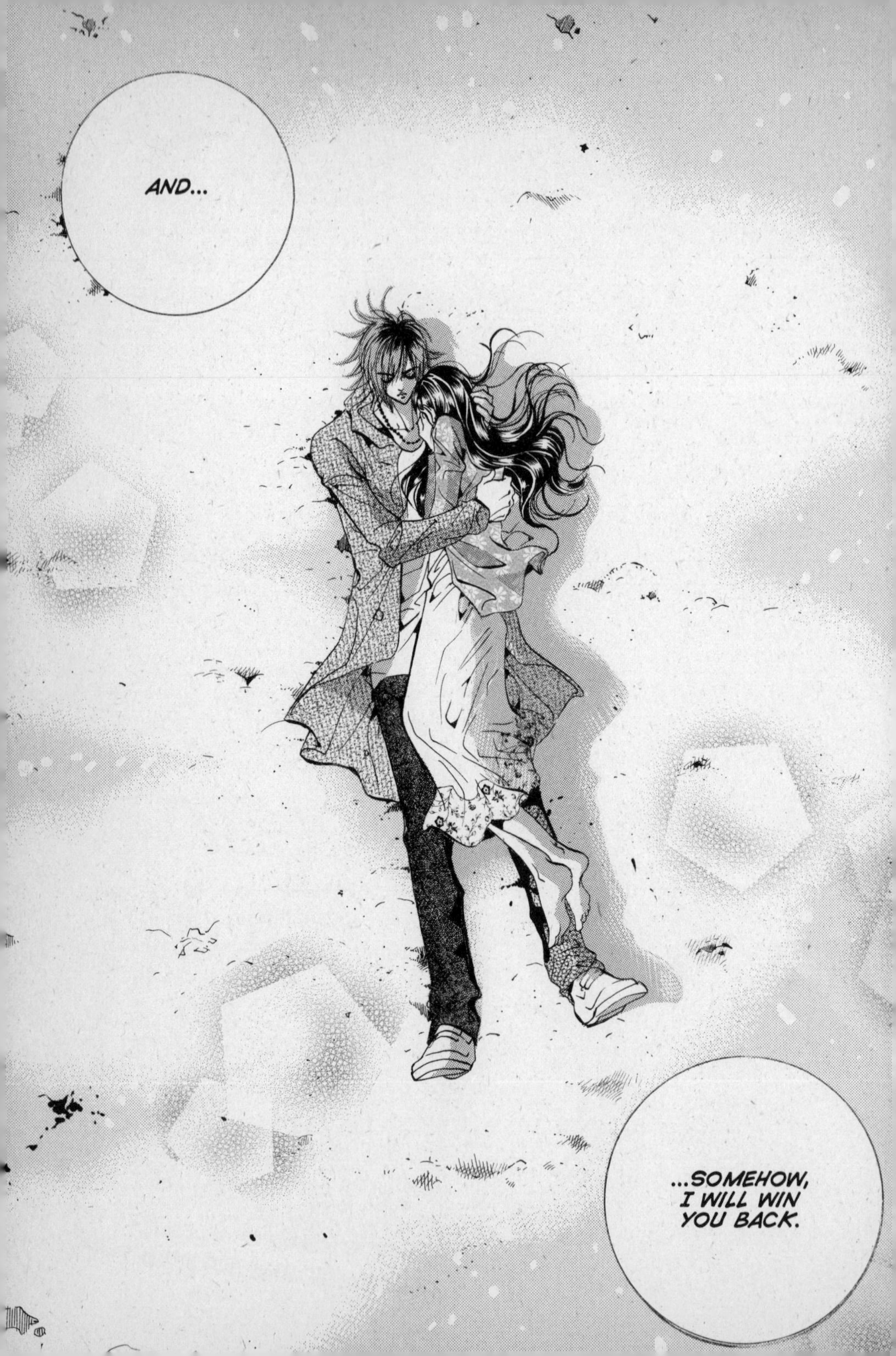
AND...
...SOMEHOW, I WILL WIN YOU BACK.

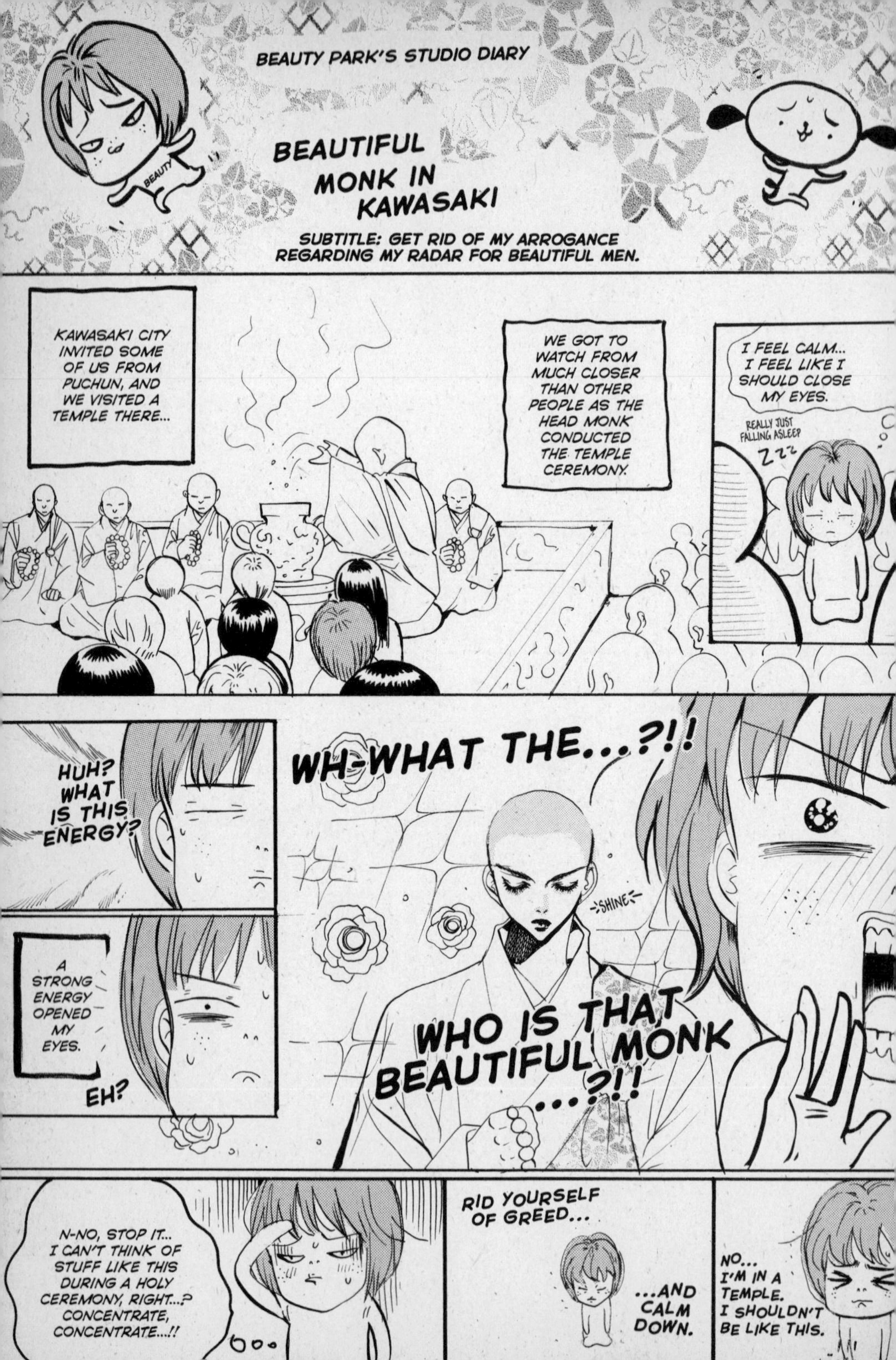

BEAUTY PARK'S STUDIO DIARY
BEAUTY
BEAUTIFUL MONK IN KAWASAKI
SUBTITLE: GET RID OF MY ARROGANCE REGARDING MY RADAR FOR BEAUTIFUL MEN.
KAWASAKI CITY INVITED SOME OF US FROM PUCHUN, AND WE VISITED A TEMPLE THERE...
WE GOT TO WATCH FROM MUCH CLOSER THAN OTHER PEOPLE AS THE HEAD MONK CONDUCTED THE TEMPLE CEREMONY.
I FEEL CALM... I FEEL LIKE I SHOULD CLOSE MY EYES.
REALLY JUST FALLING ASLEEP
ZZZ
HUH? WHAT IS THIS ENERGY?
A STRONG ENERGY OPENED MY EYES.
EH?
WH-WHAT THE...?!!
SHINE
WHO IS THAT BEAUTIFUL MONK ...?!!
N-NO, STOP IT... I CAN'T THINK OF STUFF LIKE THIS DURING A HOLY CEREMONY, RIGHT...? CONCENTRATE, CONCENTRATE...!!
RID YOURSELF OF GREED...
...AND CALM DOWN.
NO... I'M IN A TEMPLE. I SHOULDN'T BE LIKE THIS.

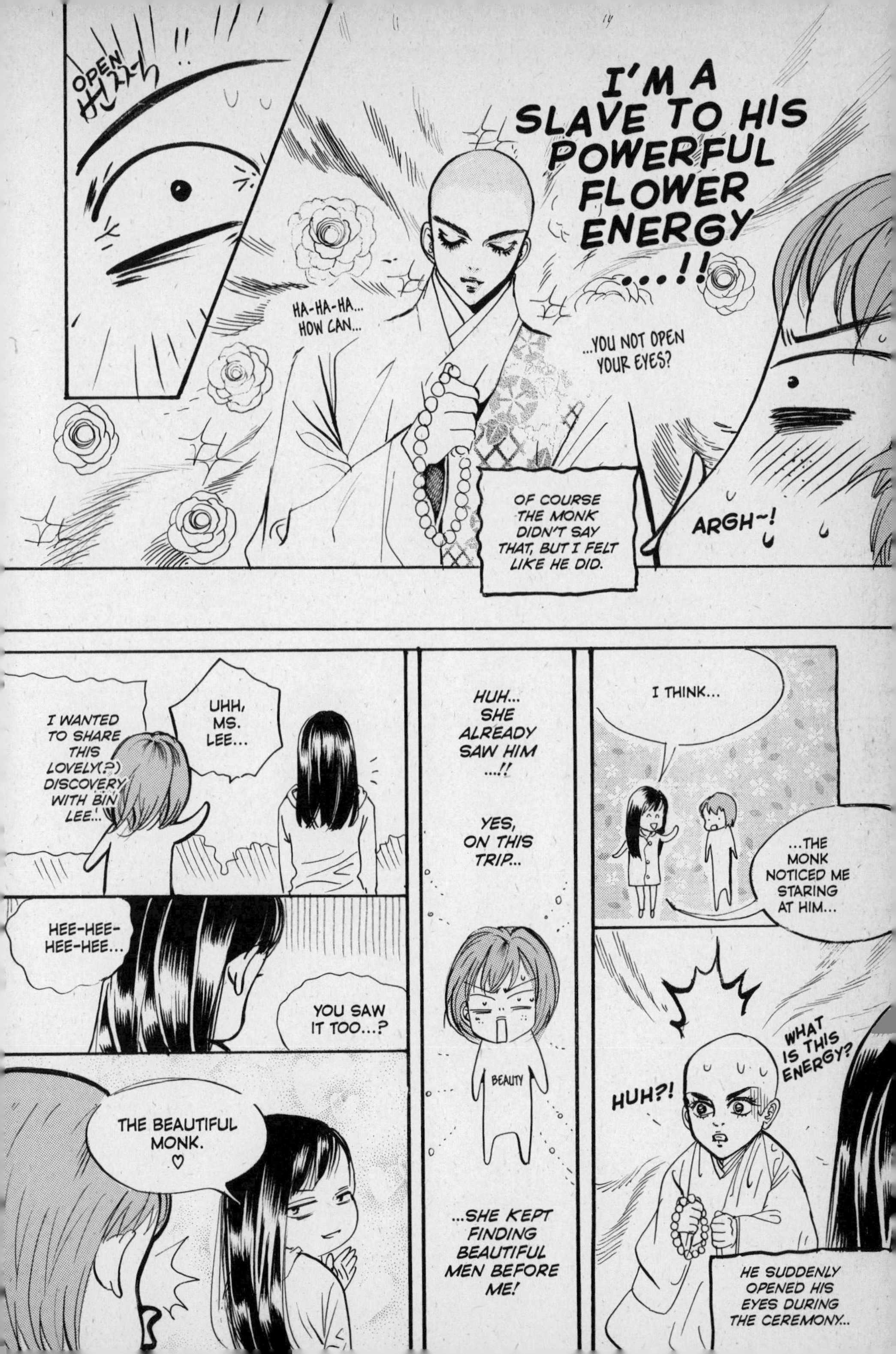
OPEN
I'M A SLAVE TO HIS POWERFUL FLOWER ENERGY ...!!
HA-HA-HA... HOW CAN...
...YOU NOT OPEN YOUR EYES?
OF COURSE THE MONK DIDN'T SAY THAT, BUT I FELT LIKE HE DID.
ARGH~!
I WANTED TO SHARE THIS LOVELY(?) DISCOVERY WITH BIN LEE...
UHH, MS. LEE...
HEE-HEE-HEE-HEE...
YOU SAW IT TOO...?
THE BEAUTIFUL MONK. ♡
HUH... SHE ALREADY SAW HIM ...!!
YES, ON THIS TRIP...
BEAUTY
...SHE KEPT FINDING BEAUTIFUL MEN BEFORE ME!
I THINK...
...THE MONK NOTICED ME STARING AT HIM...
HUH?!
WHAT IS THIS ENERGY?
HE SUDDENLY OPENED HIS EYES DURING THE CEREMONY...

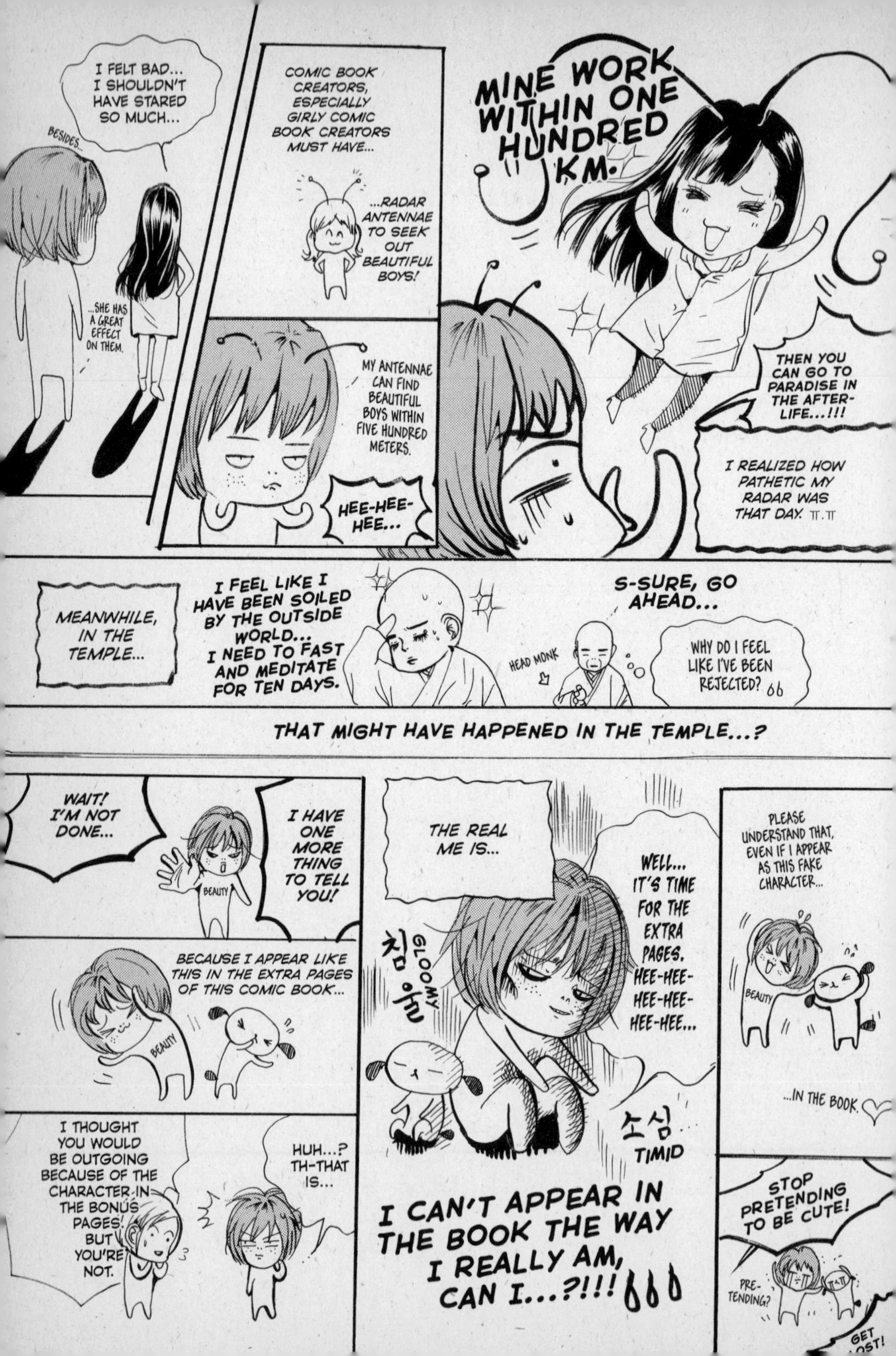
I FELT BAD... I SHOULDN'T HAVE STARED SO MUCH...
BESIDES...
...SHE HAS A GREAT EFFECT ON THEM.
COMIC BOOK CREATORS, ESPECIALLY GIRLY COMIC BOOK CREATORS MUST HAVE...
...RADAR ANTENNAE TO SEEK OUT BEAUTIFUL BOYS!
MY ANTENNAE CAN FIND BEAUTIFUL BOYS WITHIN FIVE HUNDRED METERS.
HEE-HEE-HEE...
MINE WORK WITHIN ONE HUNDRED KM.
THEN YOU CAN GO TO PARADISE IN THE AFTER-LIFE...!!!
I REALIZED HOW PATHETIC MY RADAR WAS THAT DAY. ㅠ.ㅠ
MEANWHILE, IN THE TEMPLE...
I FEEL LIKE I HAVE BEEN SOILED BY THE OUTSIDE WORLD... I NEED TO FAST AND MEDITATE FOR TEN DAYS.
S-SURE, GO AHEAD...
HEAD MONK
WHY DO I FEEL LIKE I'VE BEEN REJECTED?
THAT MIGHT HAVE HAPPENED IN THE TEMPLE...?
WAIT! I'M NOT DONE...
BEAUTY
I HAVE ONE MORE THING TO TELL YOU!
BECAUSE I APPEAR LIKE THIS IN THE EXTRA PAGES OF THIS COMIC BOOK...
BEAUTY
I THOUGHT YOU WOULD BE OUTGOING BECAUSE OF THE CHARACTER IN THE BONUS PAGES! BUT YOU'RE NOT.
HUH...? TH-THAT IS...
THE REAL ME IS...
WELL... IT'S TIME FOR THE EXTRA PAGES. HEE-HEE-HEE-HEE-HEE-HEE...
침울 GLOOMY
소심 TIMID
I CAN'T APPEAR IN THE BOOK THE WAY I REALLY AM, CAN I...?!!!
PLEASE UNDERSTAND THAT, EVEN IF I APPEAR AS THIS FAKE CHARACTER...
BEAUTY
...IN THE BOOK.
STOP PRETENDING TO BE CUTE!
PRE-TENDING?
GET LOST!

THE ROYAL PALACE

Goong

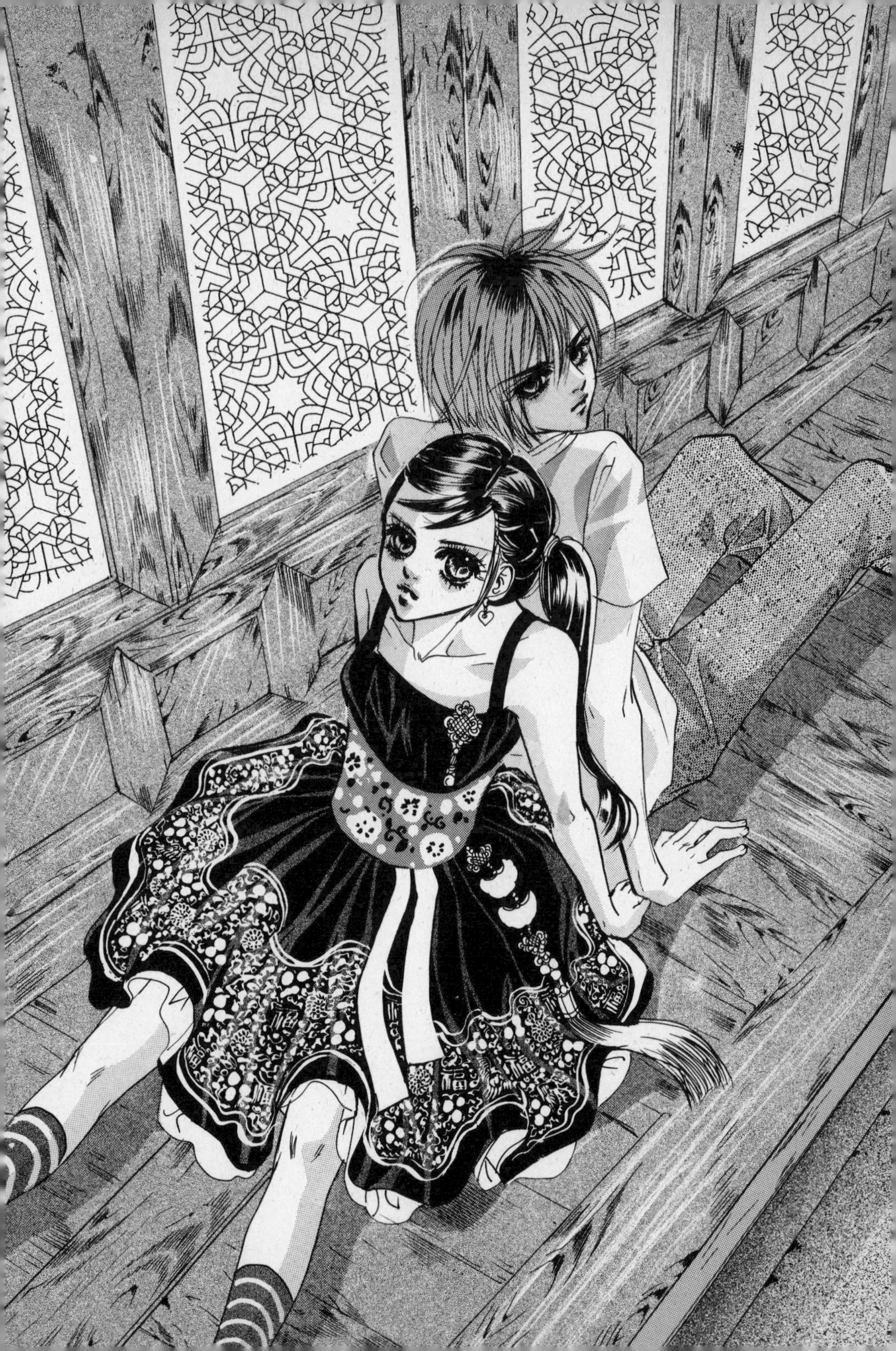

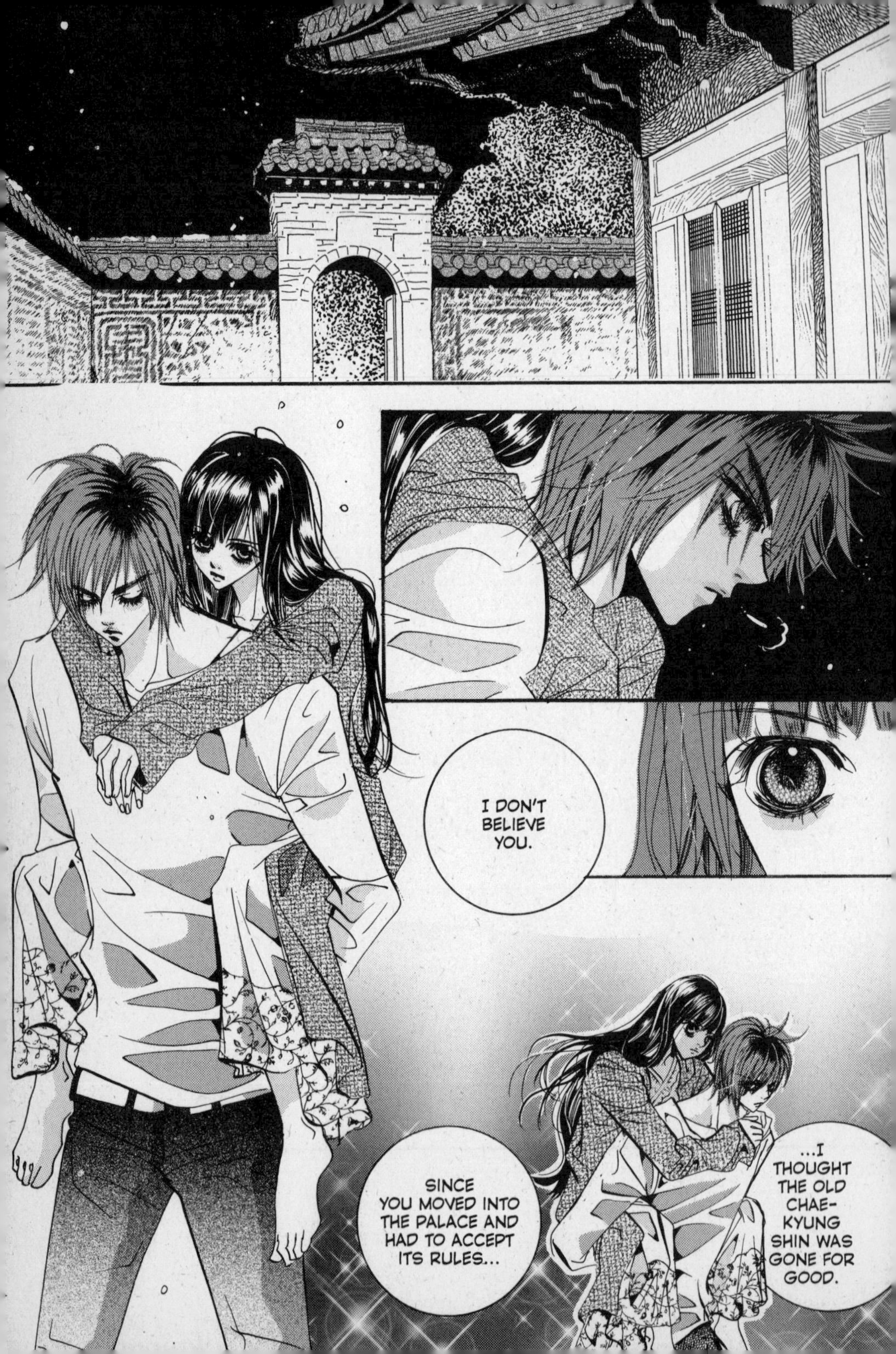
I DON'T BELIEVE YOU.
SINCE YOU MOVED INTO THE PALACE AND HAD TO ACCEPT ITS RULES...
...I THOUGHT THE OLD CHAE-KYUNG SHIN WAS GONE FOR GOOD.

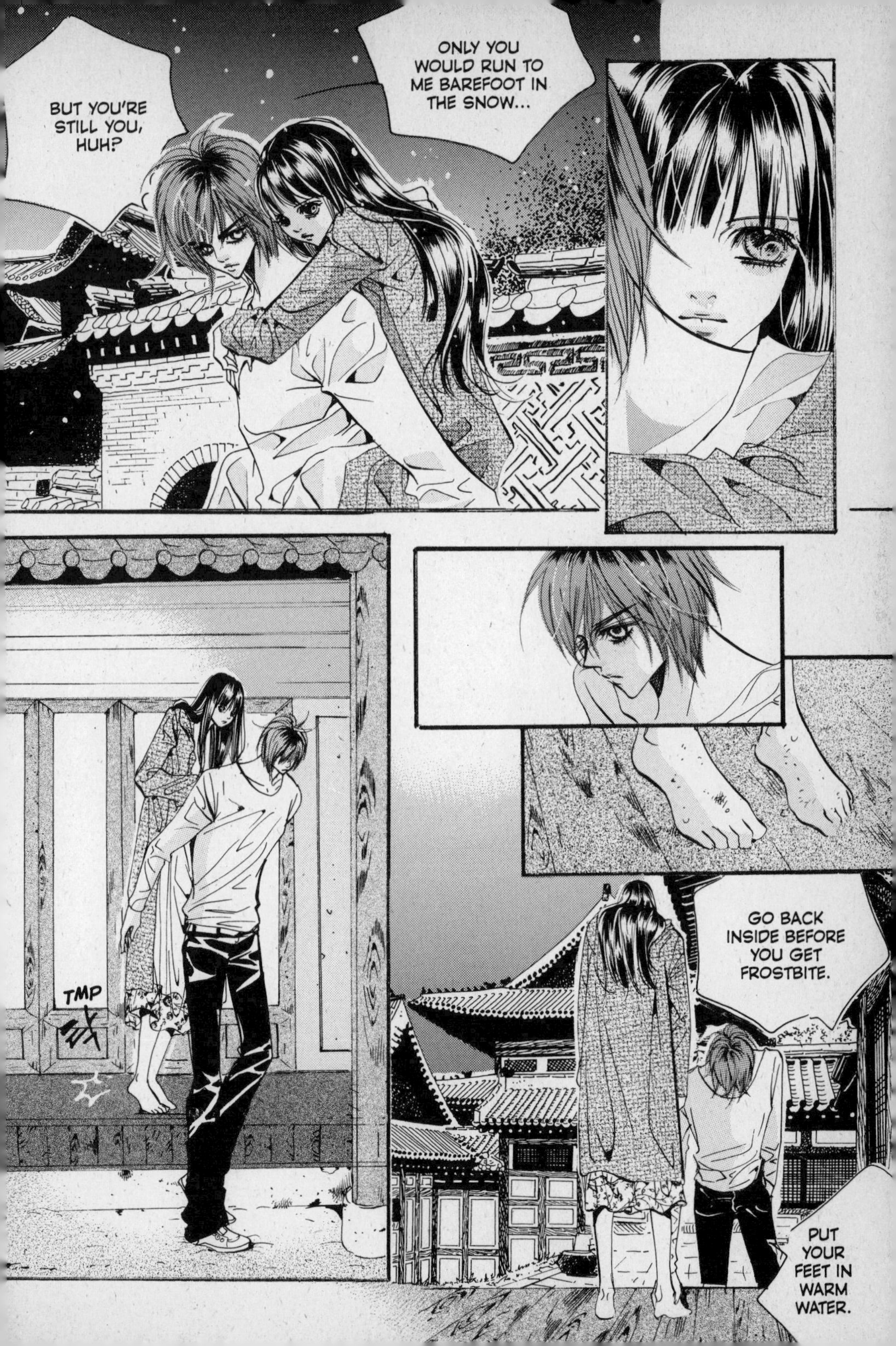
BUT YOU'RE STILL YOU, HUH?
ONLY YOU WOULD RUN TO ME BAREFOOT IN THE SNOW...
TMP
GO BACK INSIDE BEFORE YOU GET FROSTBITE.
PUT YOUR FEET IN WARM WATER.

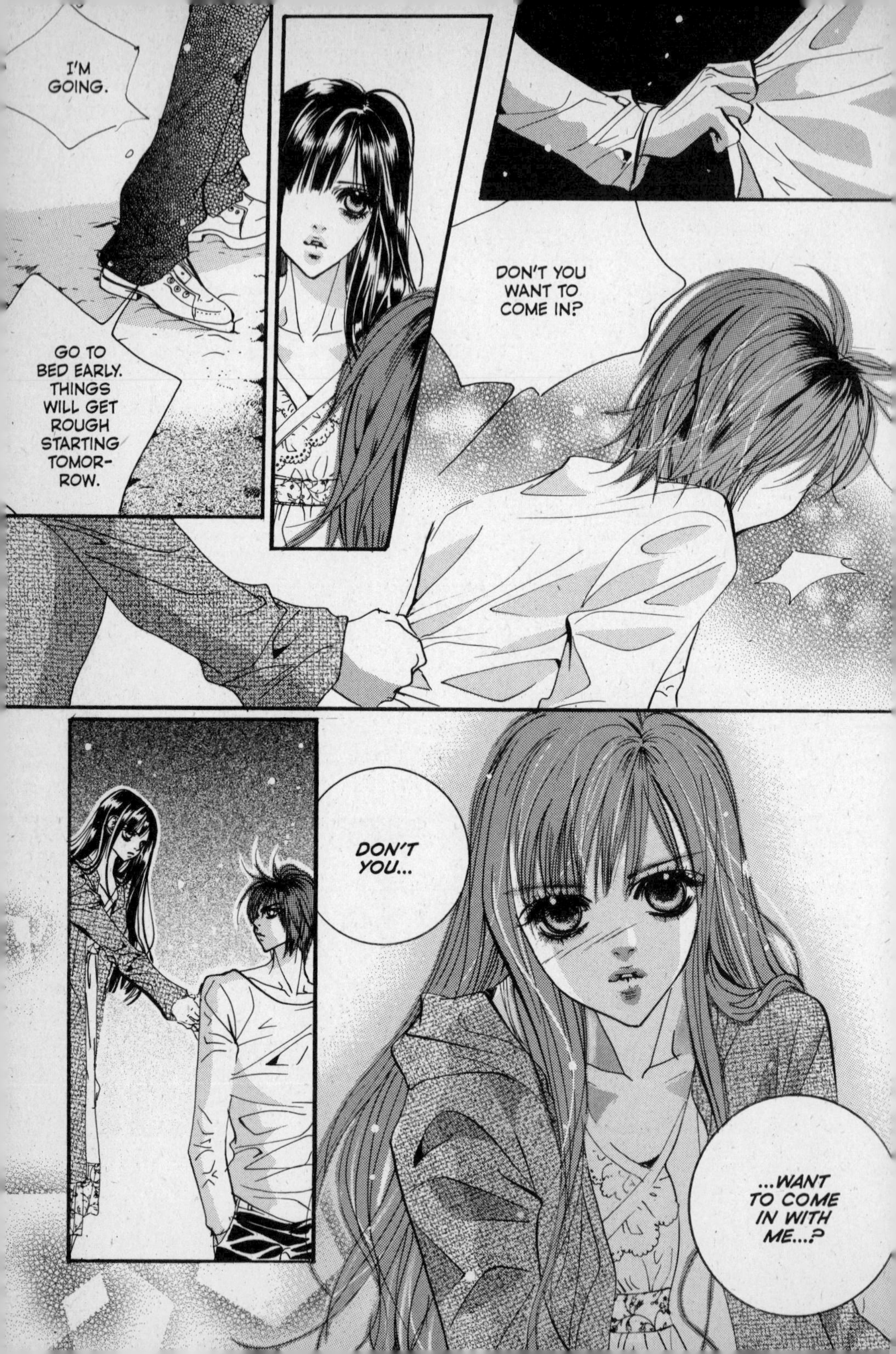
I'M GOING.
GO TO BED EARLY. THINGS WILL GET ROUGH STARTING TOMORROW.
DON'T YOU WANT TO COME IN?
DON'T YOU...
...WANT TO COME IN WITH ME...?

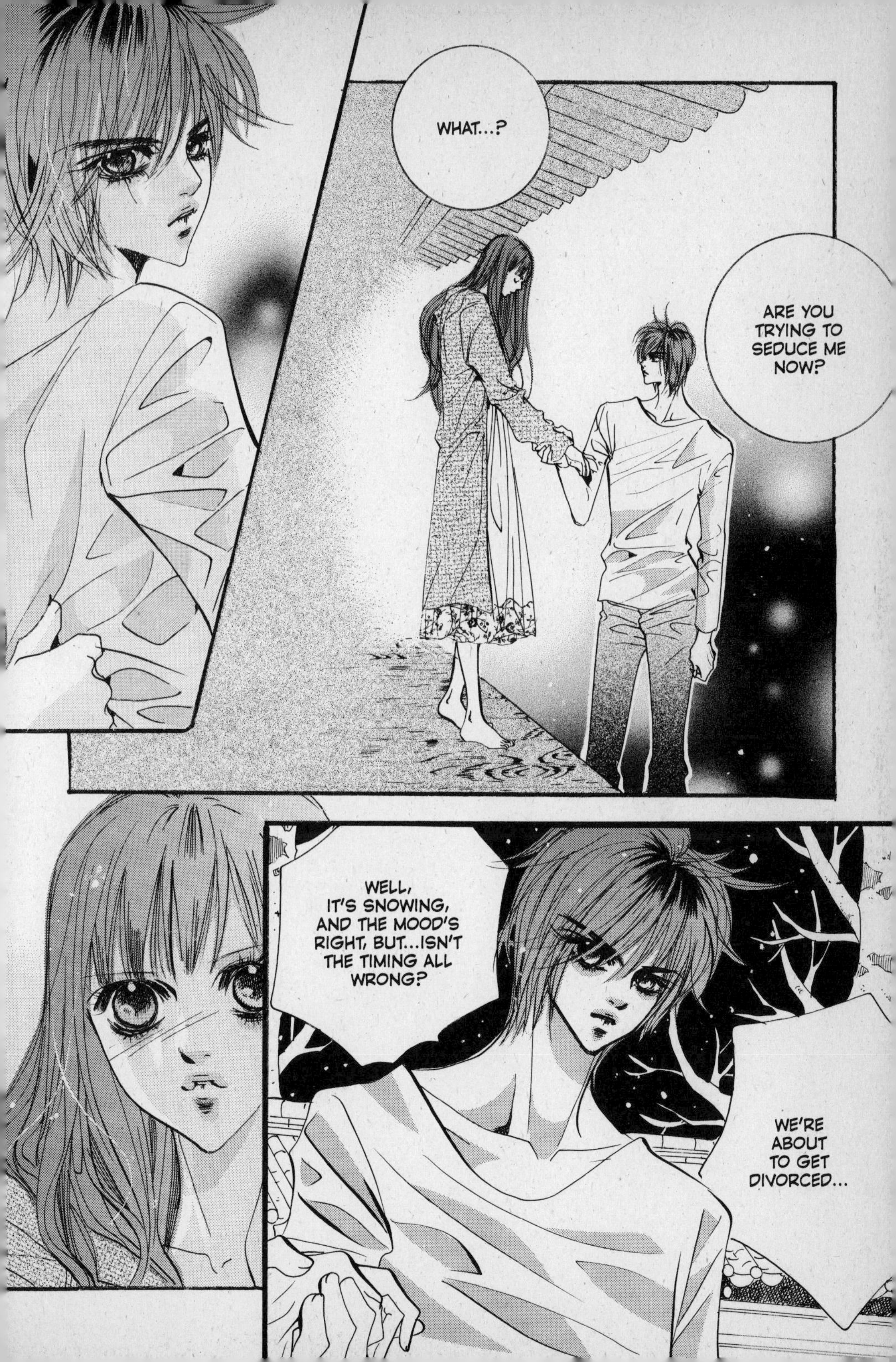
WHAT...?
ARE YOU TRYING TO SEDUCE ME NOW?
WELL, IT'S SNOWING, AND THE MOOD'S RIGHT, BUT...ISN'T THE TIMING ALL WRONG?
WE'RE ABOUT TO GET DIVORCED...

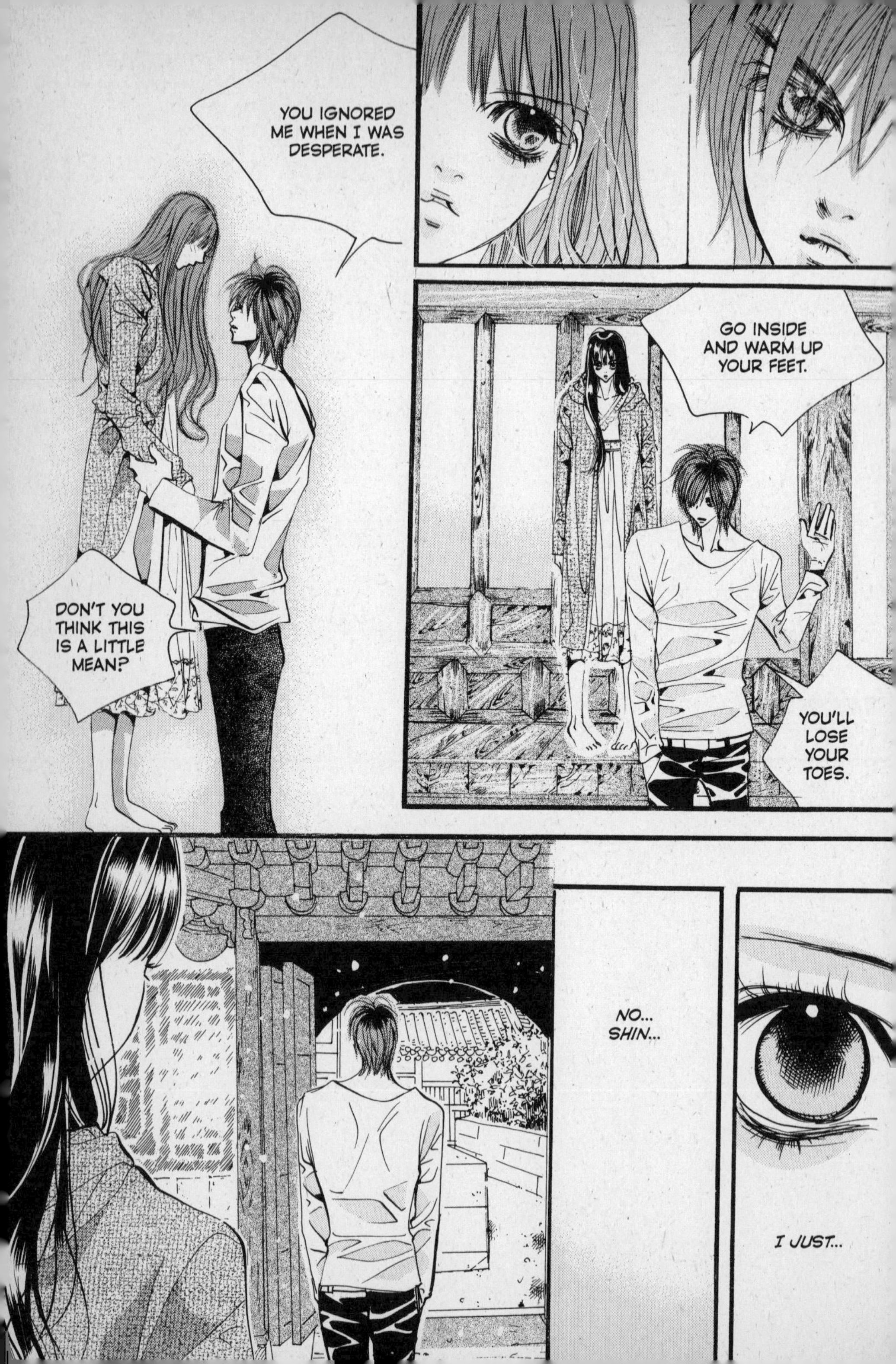
YOU IGNORED ME WHEN I WAS DESPERATE.
GO INSIDE AND WARM UP YOUR FEET.
YOU'LL LOSE YOUR TOES.
DON'T YOU THINK THIS IS A LITTLE MEAN?
I JUST...
NO... SHIN...

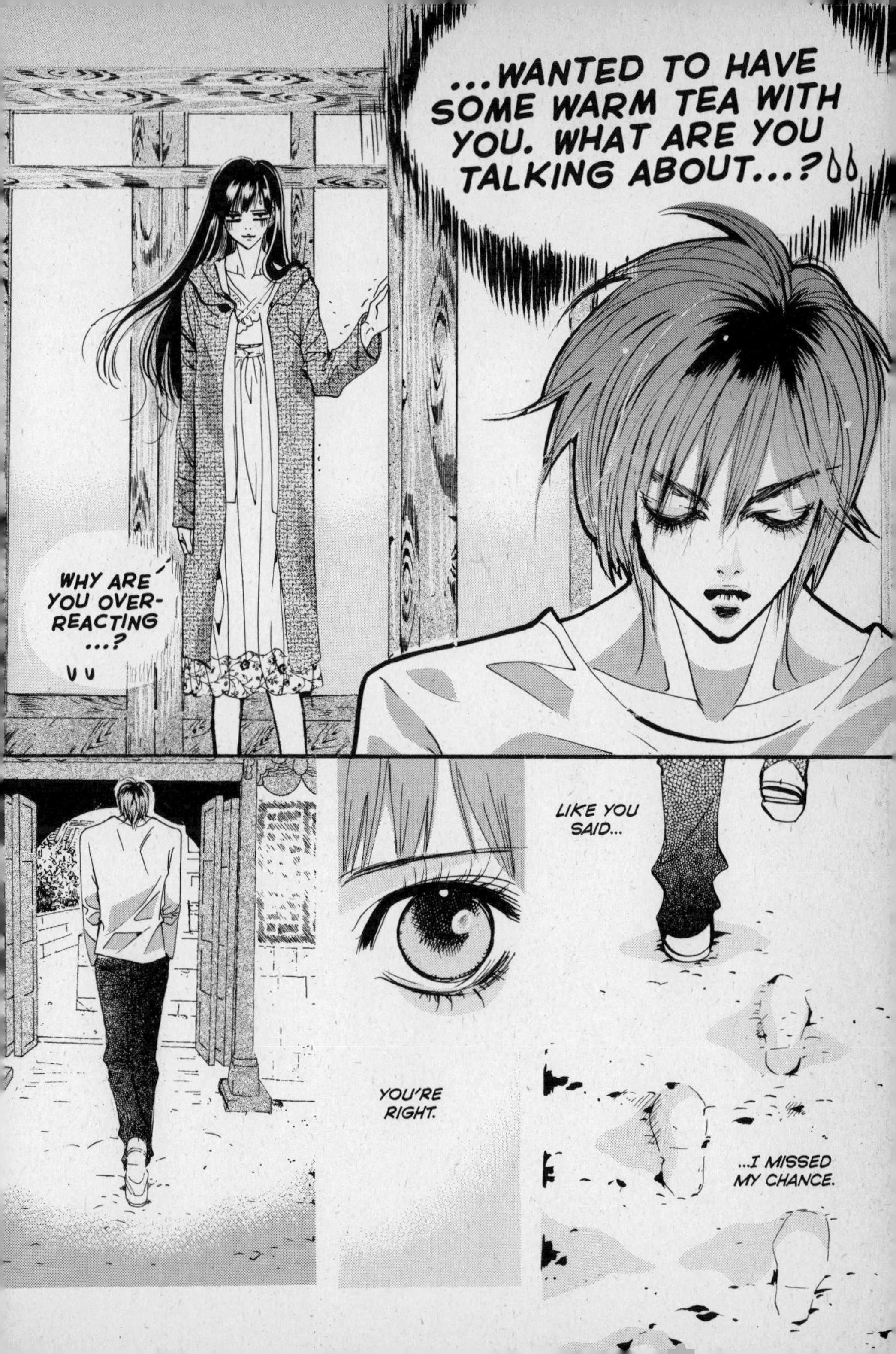
...WANTED TO HAVE SOME WARM TEA WITH YOU. WHAT ARE YOU TALKING ABOUT...?
WHY ARE YOU OVER-REACTING ...?
LIKE YOU SAID...
YOU'RE RIGHT.
...I MISSED MY CHANCE.

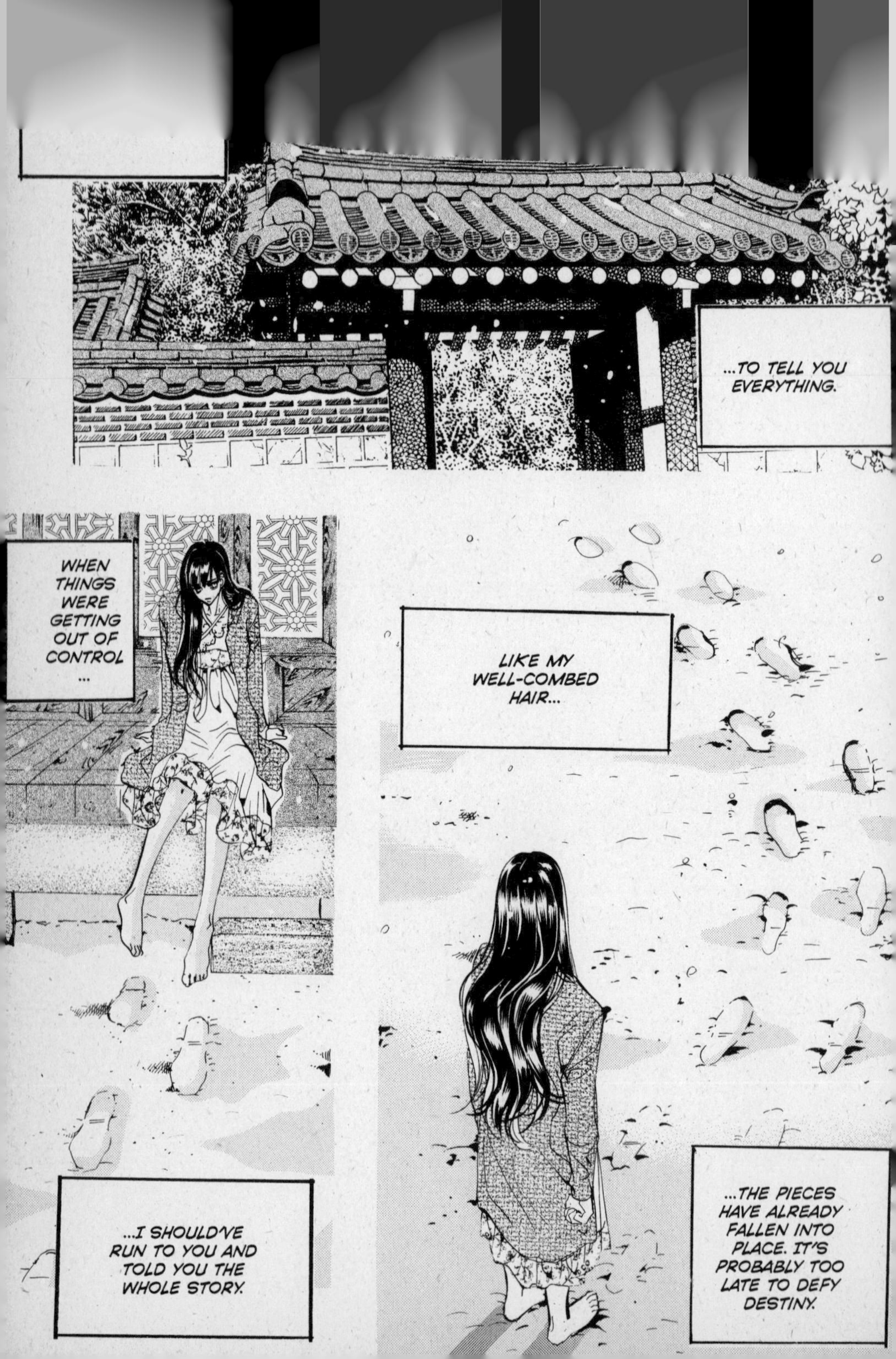
...TO TELL YOU EVERYTHING.
WHEN THINGS WERE GETTING OUT OF CONTROL ...
...I SHOULD'VE RUN TO YOU AND TOLD YOU THE WHOLE STORY.
LIKE MY WELL-COMBED HAIR...
...THE PIECES HAVE ALREADY FALLEN INTO PLACE. IT'S PROBABLY TOO LATE TO DEFY DESTINY.

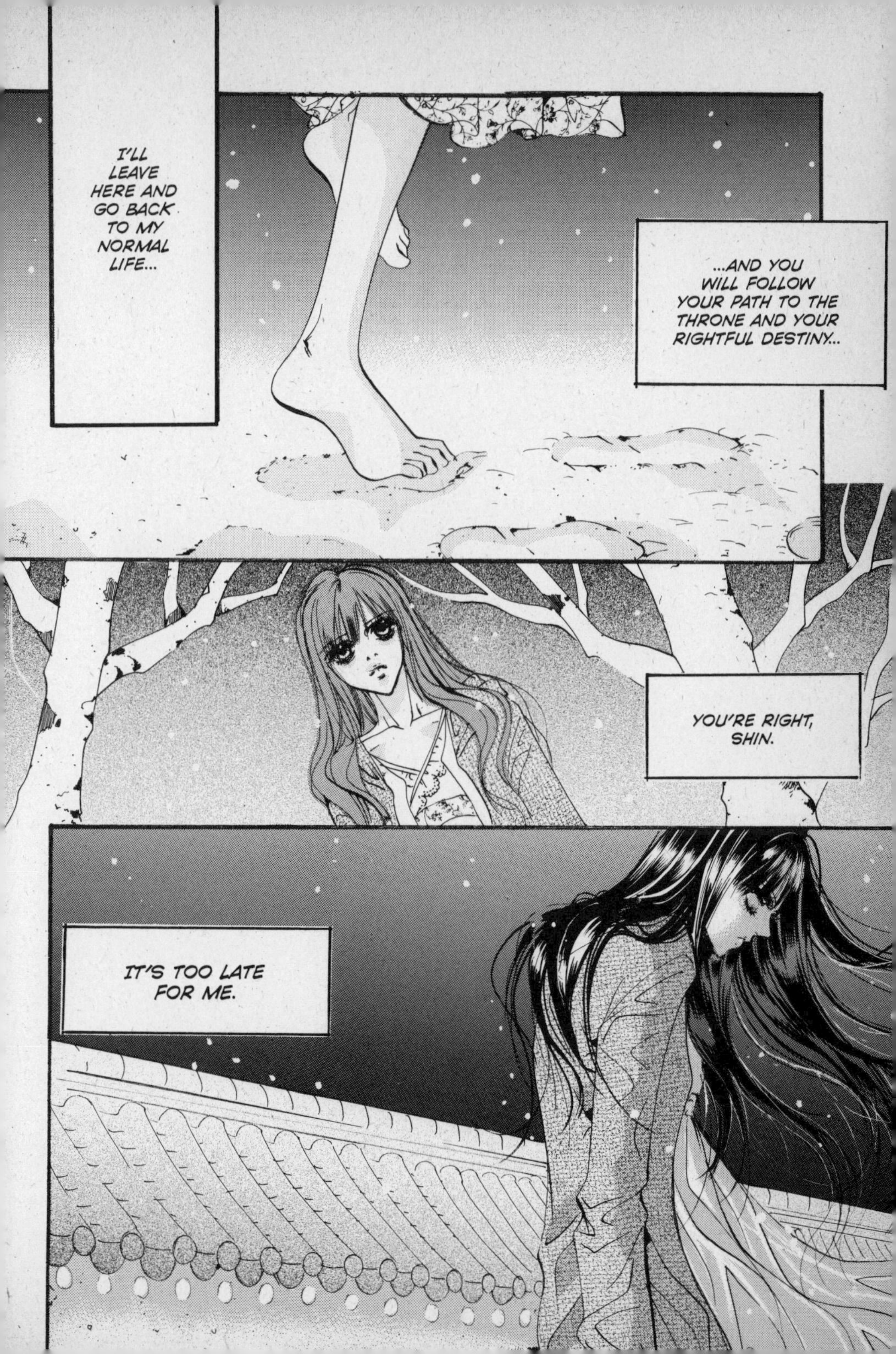
I'LL LEAVE HERE AND GO BACK TO MY NORMAL LIFE...
...AND YOU WILL FOLLOW YOUR PATH TO THE THRONE AND YOUR RIGHTFUL DESTINY...
YOU'RE RIGHT, SHIN.
IT'S TOO LATE FOR ME.

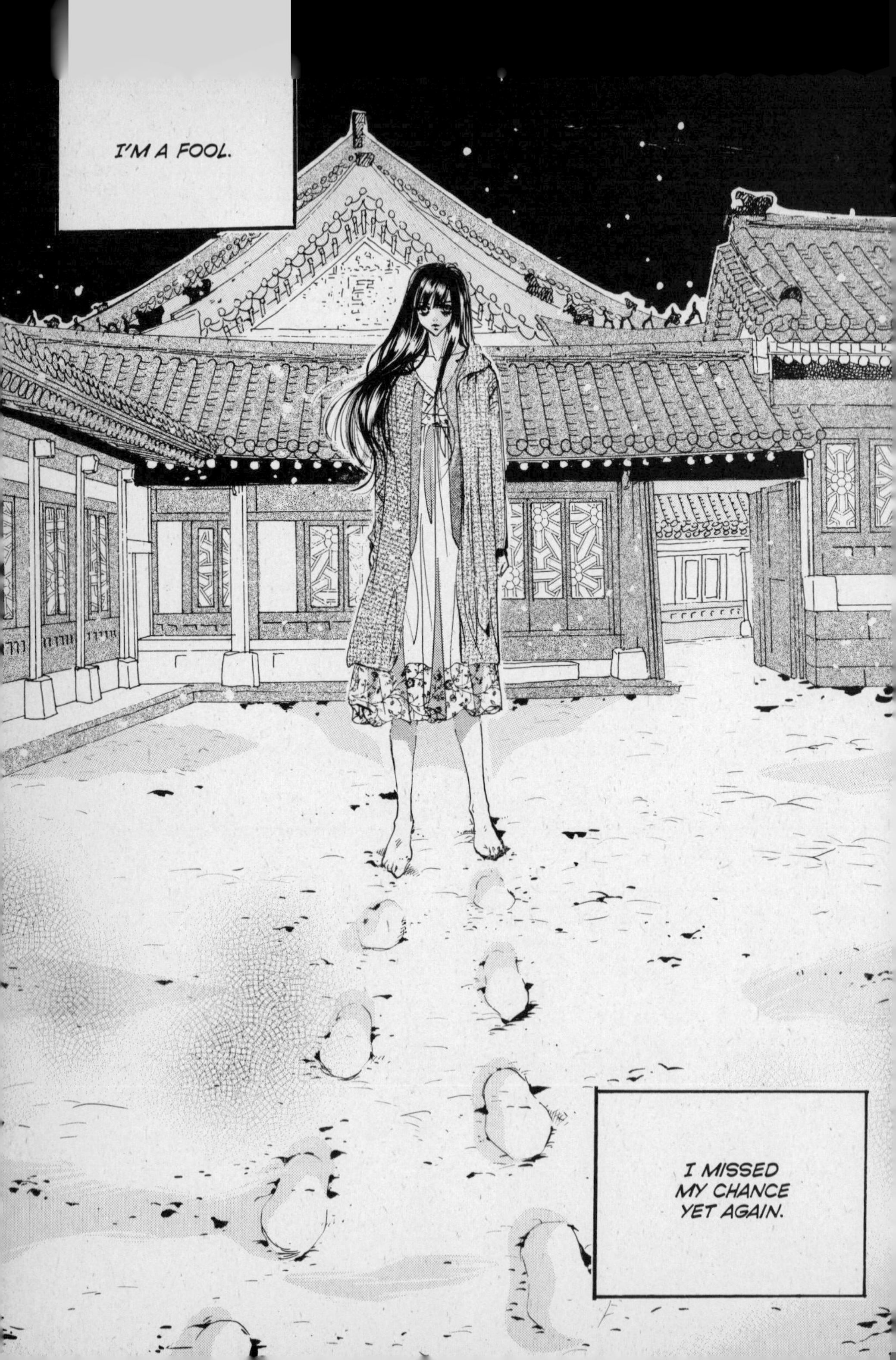
I'M A FOOL.
I MISSED MY CHANCE YET AGAIN.

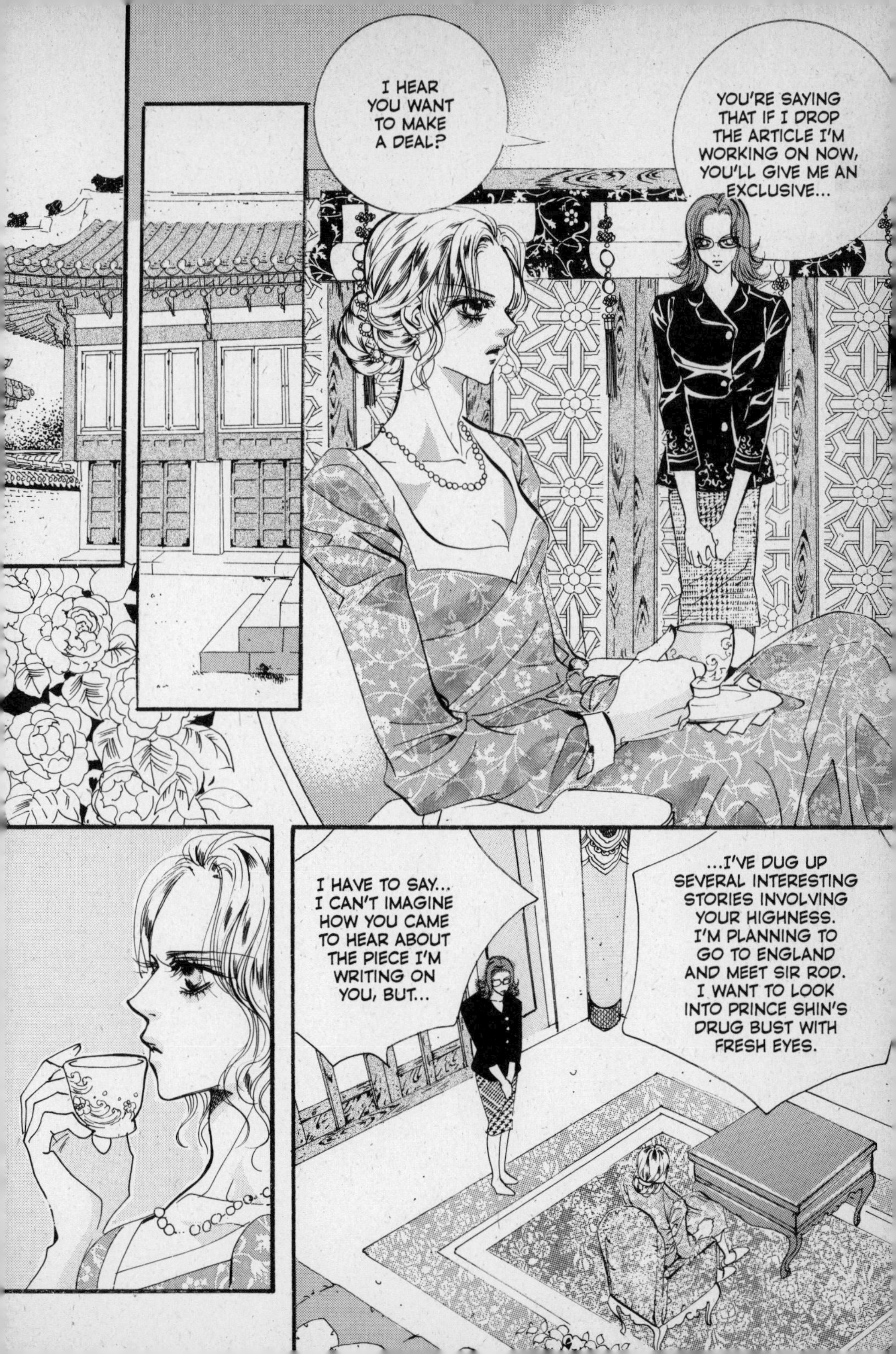
I HEAR YOU WANT TO MAKE A DEAL?
YOU'RE SAYING THAT IF I DROP THE ARTICLE I'M WORKING ON NOW, YOU'LL GIVE ME AN EXCLUSIVE...
I HAVE TO SAY... I CAN'T IMAGINE HOW YOU CAME TO HEAR ABOUT THE PIECE I'M WRITING ON YOU, BUT...
...I'VE DUG UP SEVERAL INTERESTING STORIES INVOLVING YOUR HIGHNESS. I'M PLANNING TO GO TO ENGLAND AND MEET SIR ROD. I WANT TO LOOK INTO PRINCE SHIN'S DRUG BUST WITH FRESH EYES.

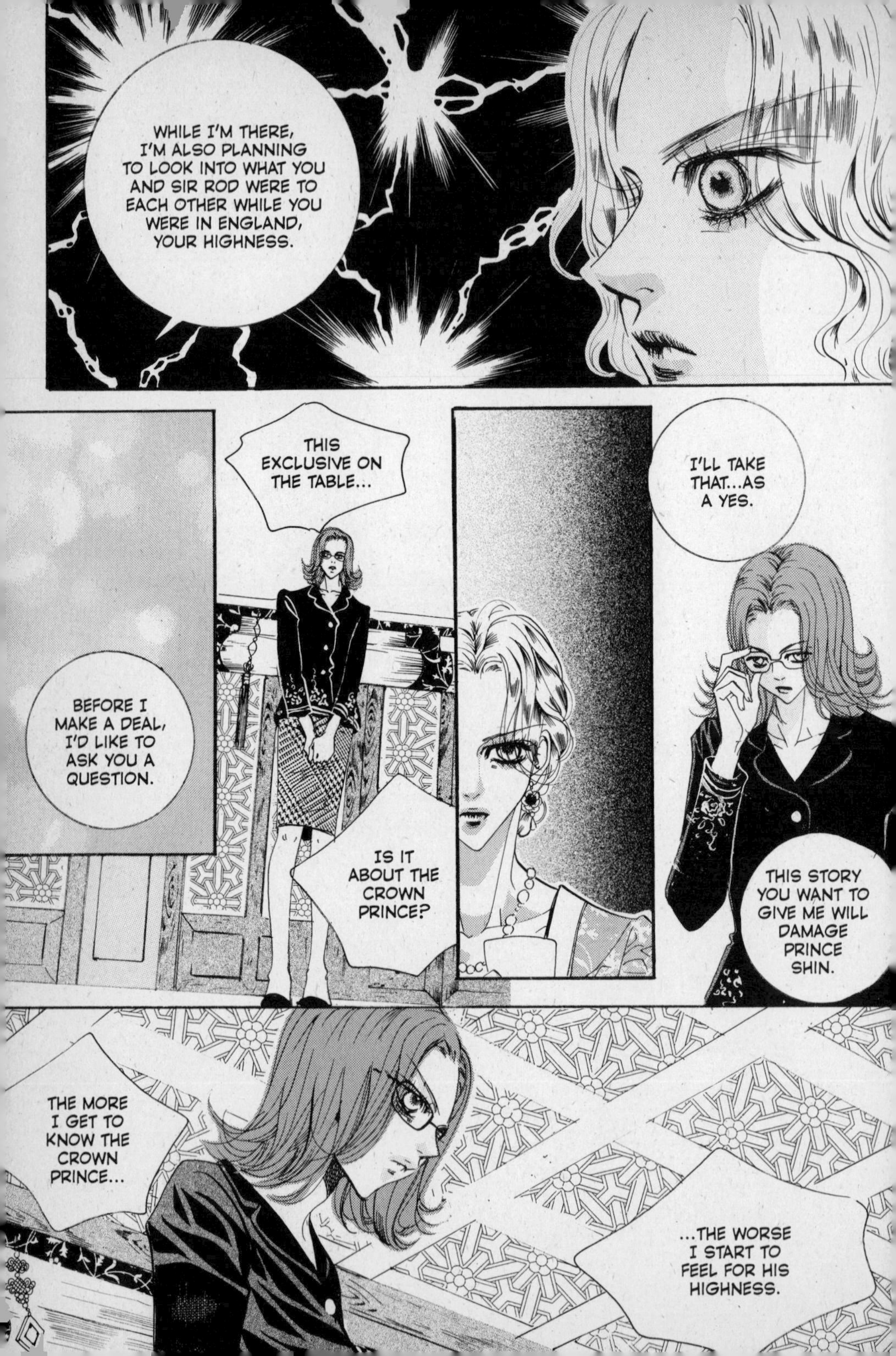
WHILE I'M THERE, I'M ALSO PLANNING TO LOOK INTO WHAT YOU AND SIR ROD WERE TO EACH OTHER WHILE YOU WERE IN ENGLAND, YOUR HIGHNESS.
THIS EXCLUSIVE ON THE TABLE...
BEFORE I MAKE A DEAL, I'D LIKE TO ASK YOU A QUESTION.
IS IT ABOUT THE CROWN PRINCE?
I'LL TAKE THAT...AS A YES.
THIS STORY YOU WANT TO GIVE ME WILL DAMAGE PRINCE SHIN.
THE MORE I GET TO KNOW THE CROWN PRINCE...
...THE WORSE I START TO FEEL FOR HIS HIGHNESS.

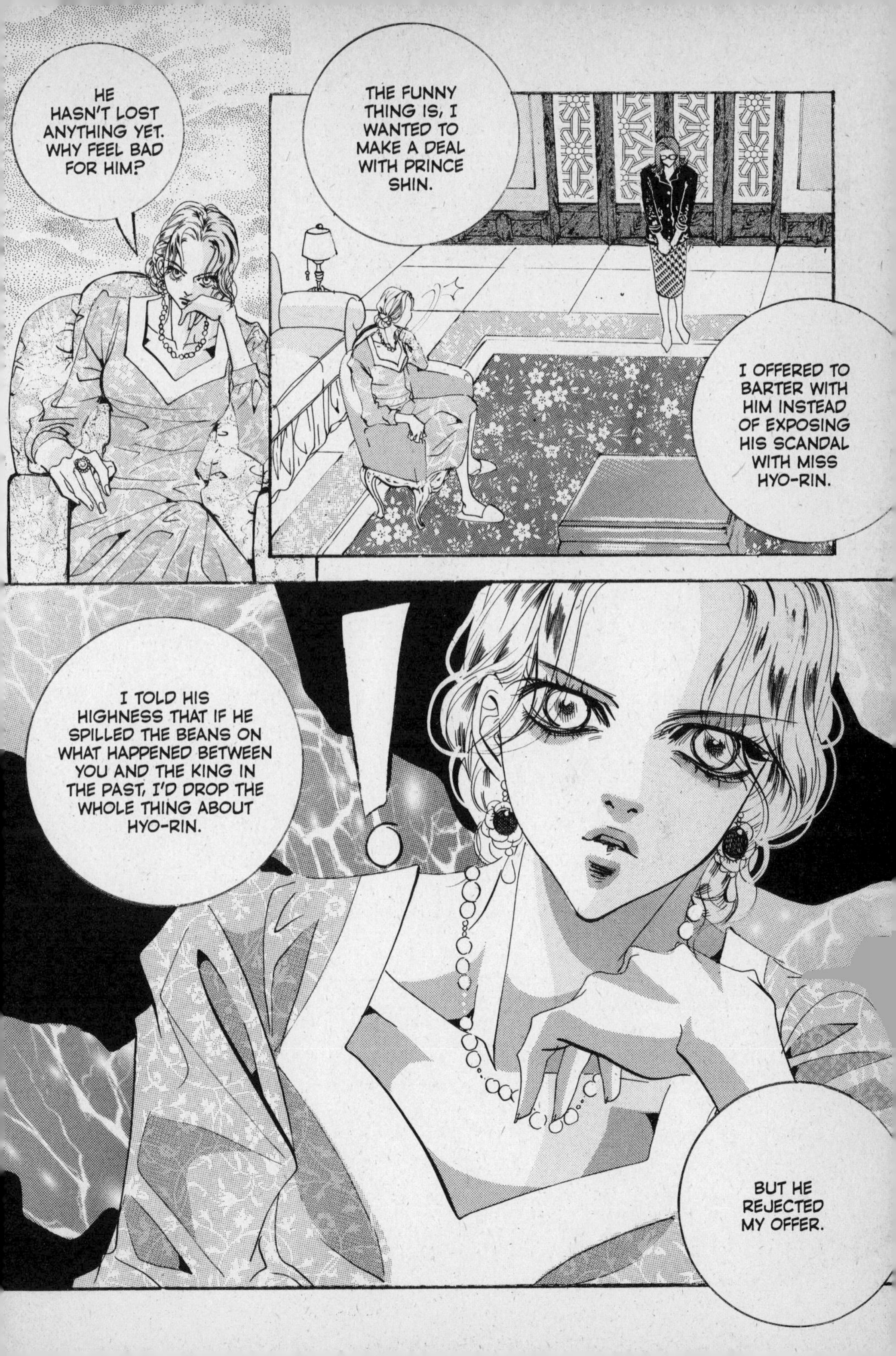

HE HASN'T LOST ANYTHING YET. WHY FEEL BAD FOR HIM?
THE FUNNY THING IS, I WANTED TO MAKE A DEAL WITH PRINCE SHIN.
I OFFERED TO BARTER WITH HIM INSTEAD OF EXPOSING HIS SCANDAL WITH MISS HYO-RIN.
I TOLD HIS HIGHNESS THAT IF HE SPILLED THE BEANS ON WHAT HAPPENED BETWEEN YOU AND THE KING IN THE PAST, I'D DROP THE WHOLE THING ABOUT HYO-RIN.
BUT HE REJECTED MY OFFER.

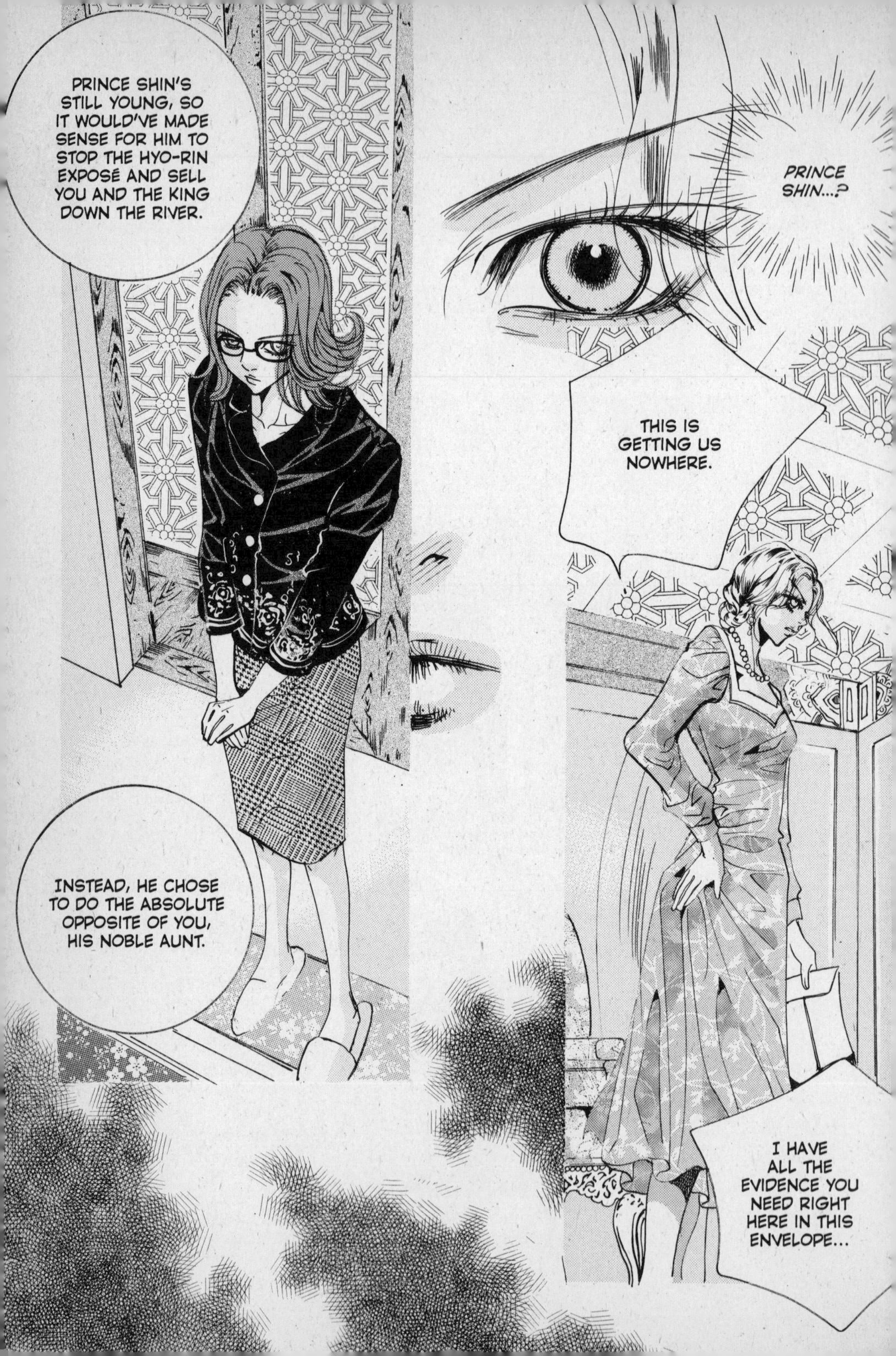
PRINCE SHIN'S STILL YOUNG, SO IT WOULD'VE MADE SENSE FOR HIM TO STOP THE HYO-RIN EXPOSÉ AND SELL YOU AND THE KING DOWN THE RIVER.
INSTEAD, HE CHOSE TO DO THE ABSOLUTE OPPOSITE OF YOU, HIS NOBLE AUNT.
PRINCE SHIN...?
THIS IS GETTING US NOWHERE.
I HAVE ALL THE EVIDENCE YOU NEED RIGHT HERE IN THIS ENVELOPE...

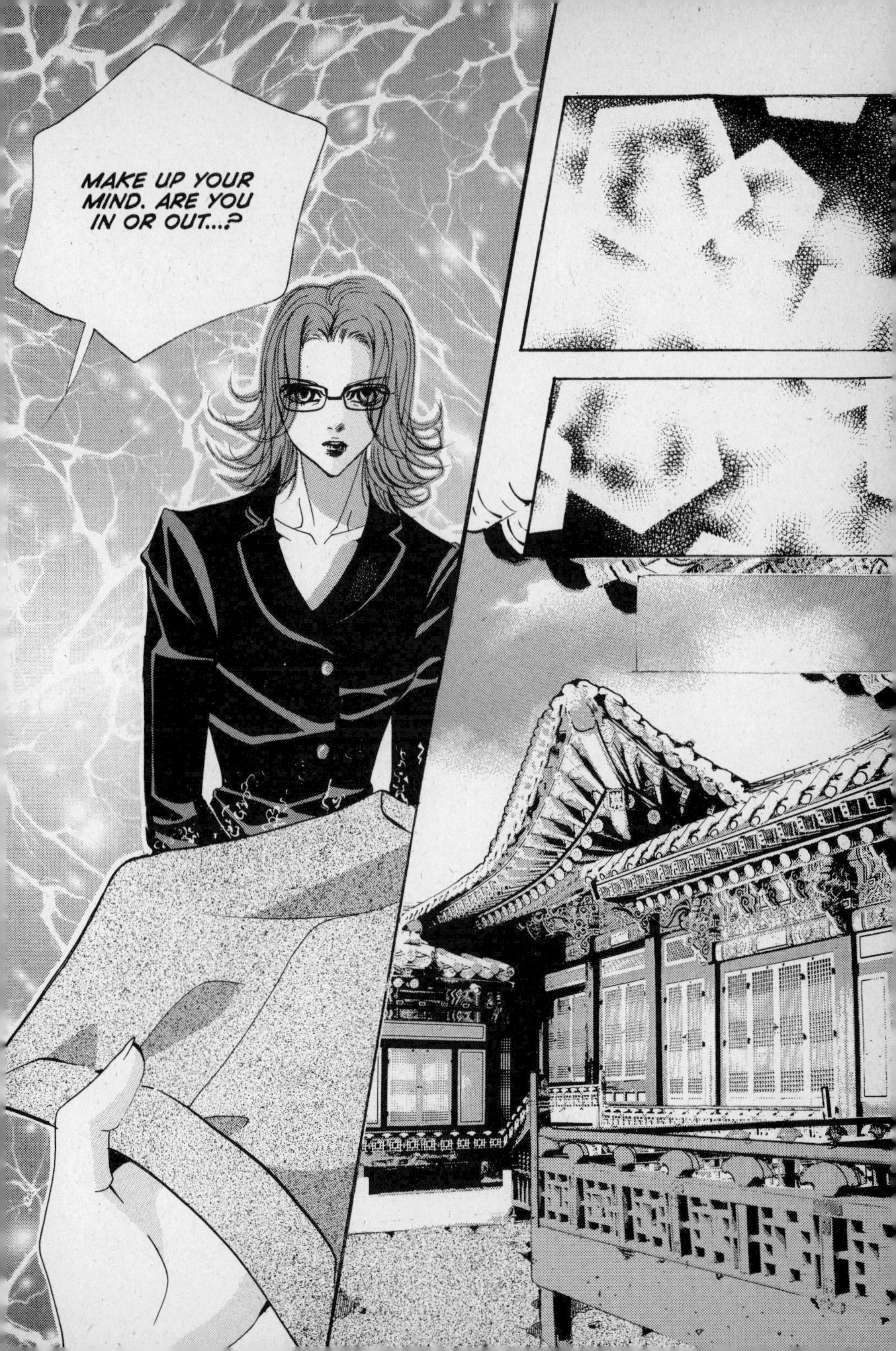
MAKE UP YOUR MIND. ARE YOU IN OR OUT...?

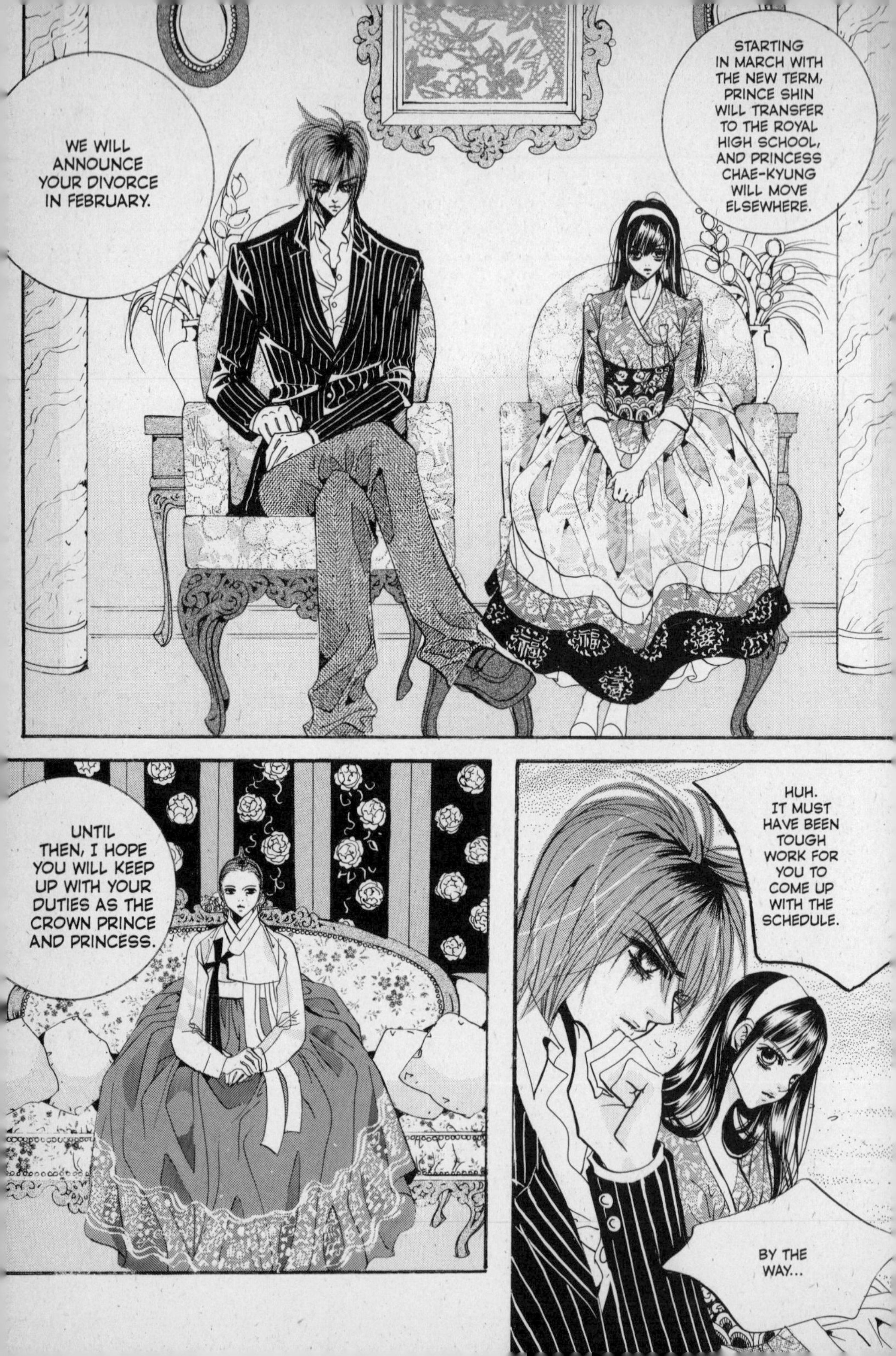
STARTING IN MARCH WITH THE NEW TERM, PRINCE SHIN WILL TRANSFER TO THE ROYAL HIGH SCHOOL, AND PRINCESS CHAE-KYUNG WILL MOVE ELSEWHERE.
WE WILL ANNOUNCE YOUR DIVORCE IN FEBRUARY.
UNTIL THEN, I HOPE YOU WILL KEEP UP WITH YOUR DUTIES AS THE CROWN PRINCE AND PRINCESS.
HUH. IT MUST HAVE BEEN TOUGH WORK FOR YOU TO COME UP WITH THE SCHEDULE.
BY THE WAY...

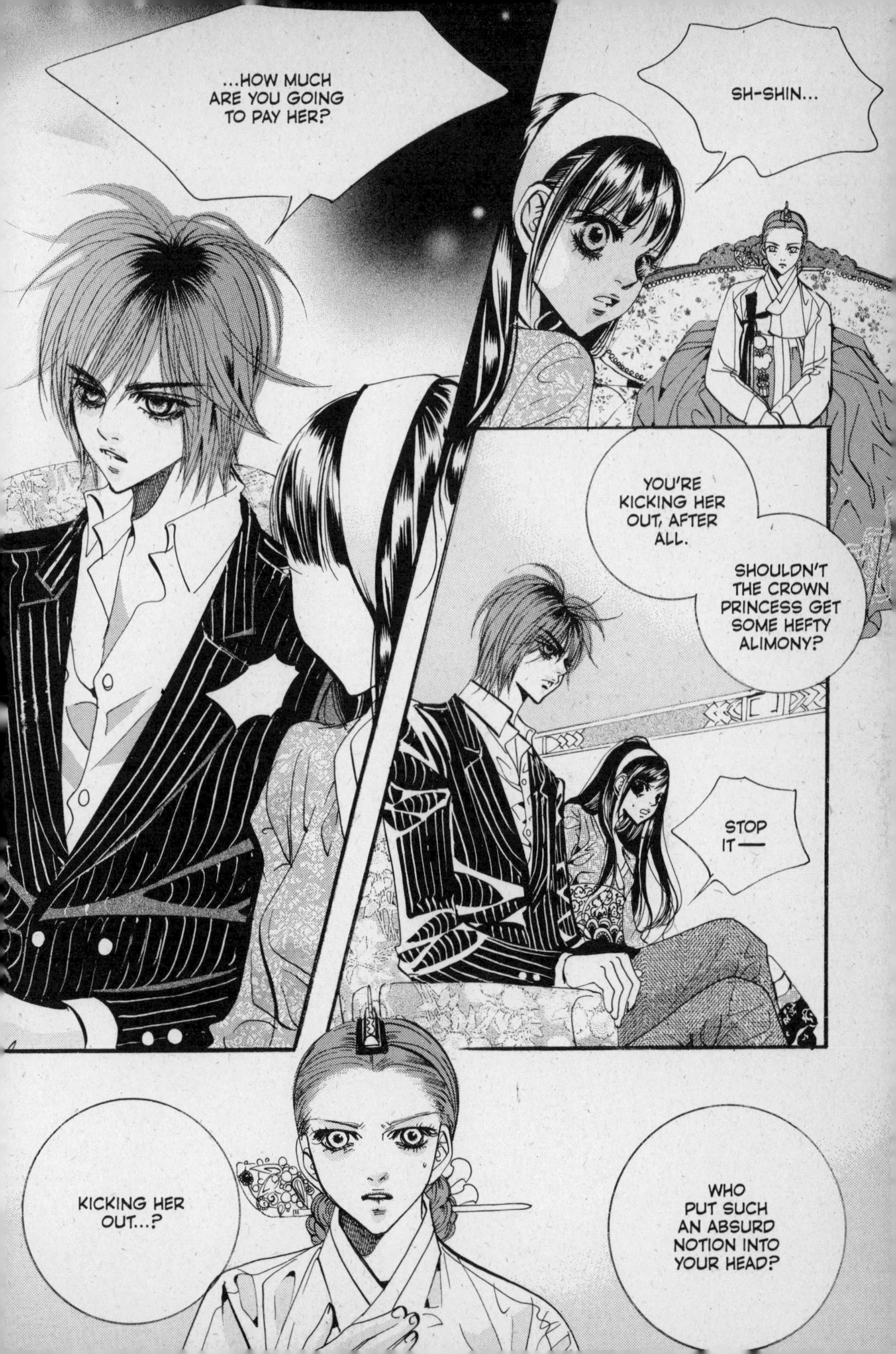
...HOW MUCH ARE YOU GOING TO PAY HER?
SH-SHIN...
YOU'RE KICKING HER OUT, AFTER ALL.
SHOULDN'T THE CROWN PRINCESS GET SOME HEFTY ALIMONY?
STOP IT—
KICKING HER OUT...?
WHO PUT SUCH AN ABSURD NOTION INTO YOUR HEAD?

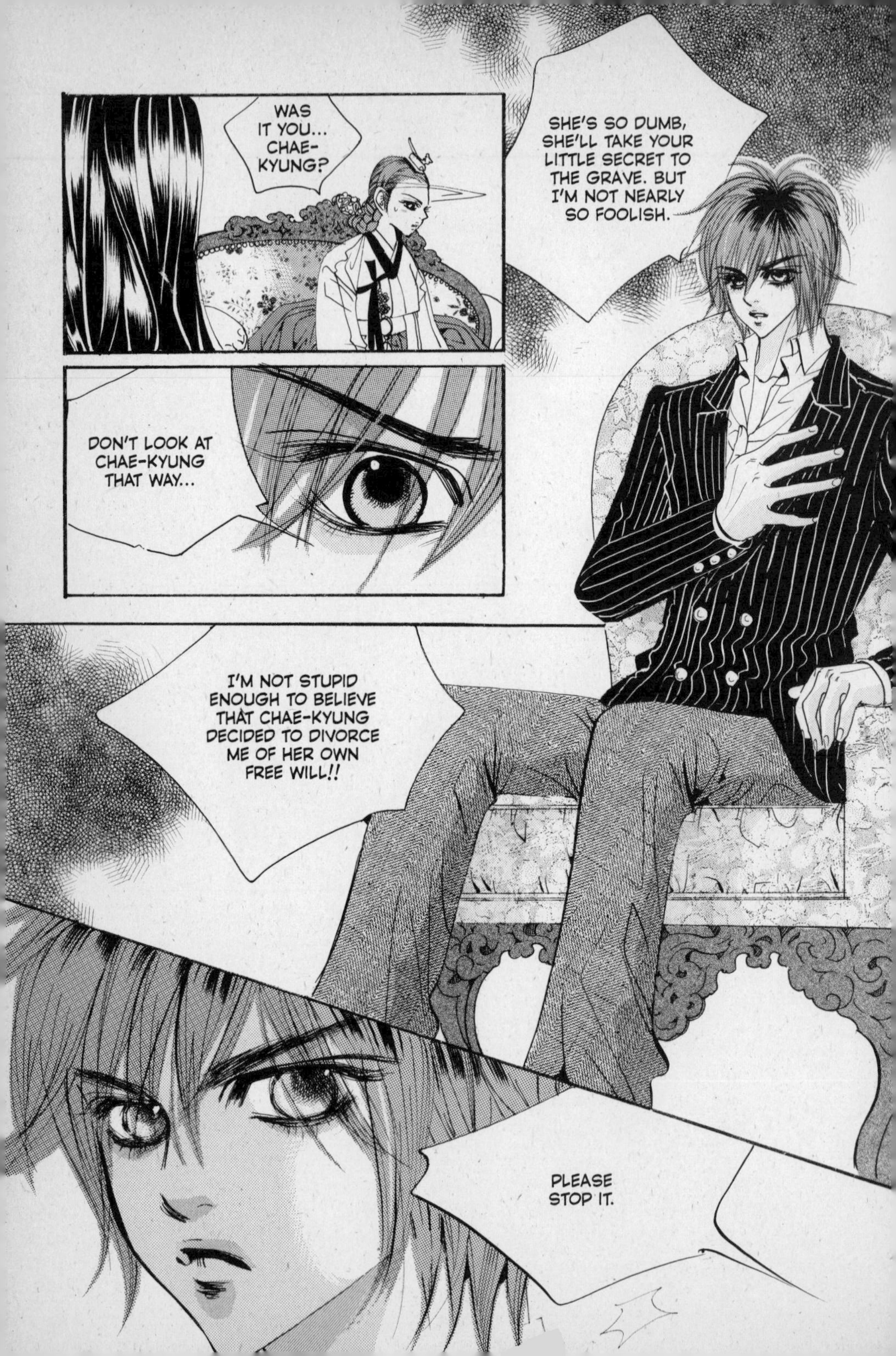
SHE'S SO DUMB, SHE'LL TAKE YOUR LITTLE SECRET TO THE GRAVE. BUT I'M NOT NEARLY SO FOOLISH.
WAS IT YOU... CHAE-KYUNG?
DON'T LOOK AT CHAE-KYUNG THAT WAY...
I'M NOT STUPID ENOUGH TO BELIEVE THAT CHAE-KYUNG DECIDED TO DIVORCE ME OF HER OWN FREE WILL!!
PLEASE STOP IT.

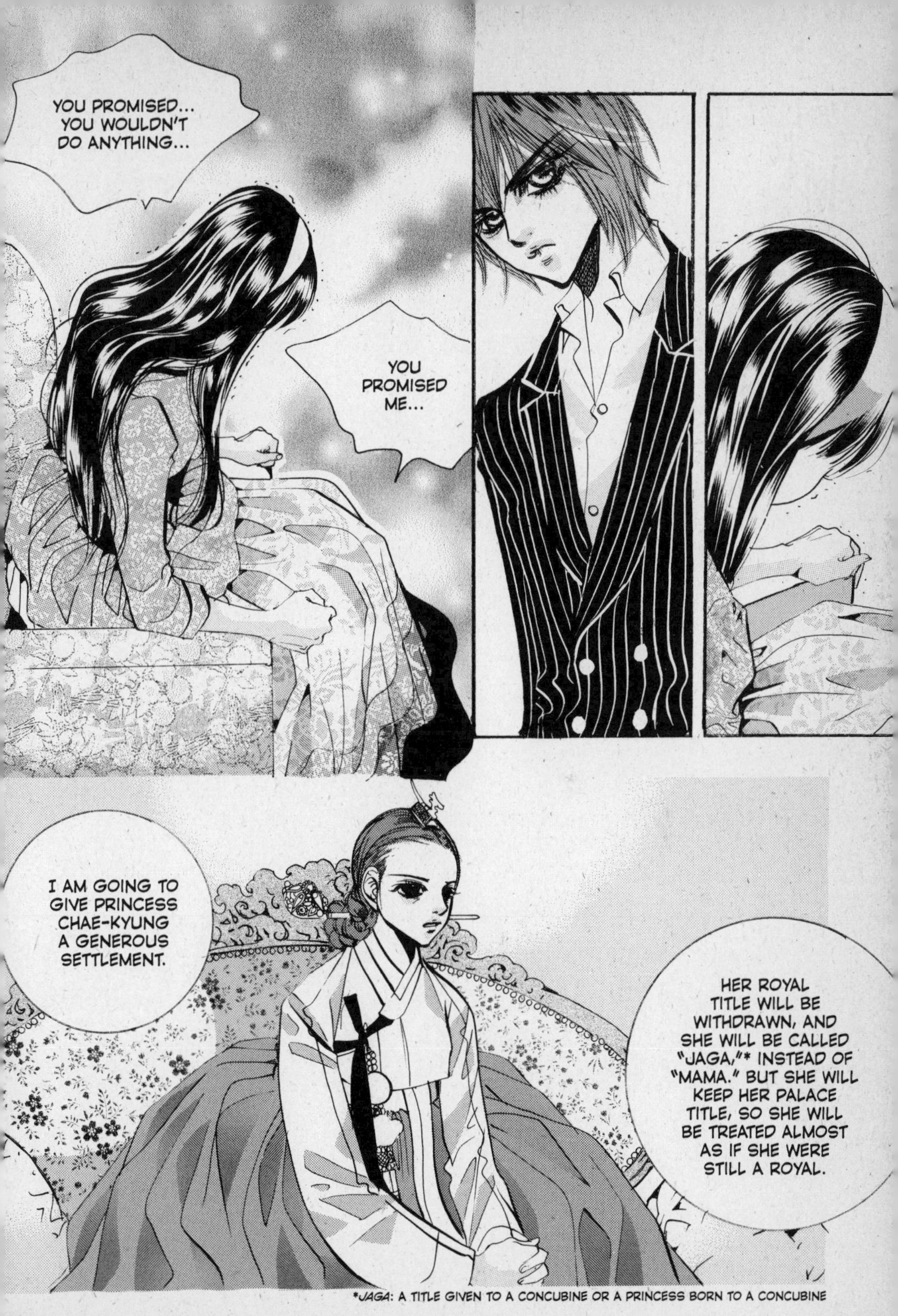
YOU PROMISED... YOU WOULDN'T DO ANYTHING...
YOU PROMISED ME...
I AM GOING TO GIVE PRINCESS CHAE-KYUNG A GENEROUS SETTLEMENT.
HER ROYAL TITLE WILL BE WITHDRAWN, AND SHE WILL BE CALLED "JAGA,"* INSTEAD OF "MAMA." BUT SHE WILL KEEP HER PALACE TITLE, SO SHE WILL BE TREATED ALMOST AS IF SHE WERE STILL A ROYAL.

**JAGA*: A TITLE GIVEN TO A CONCUBINE OR A PRINCESS BORN TO A CONCUBINE

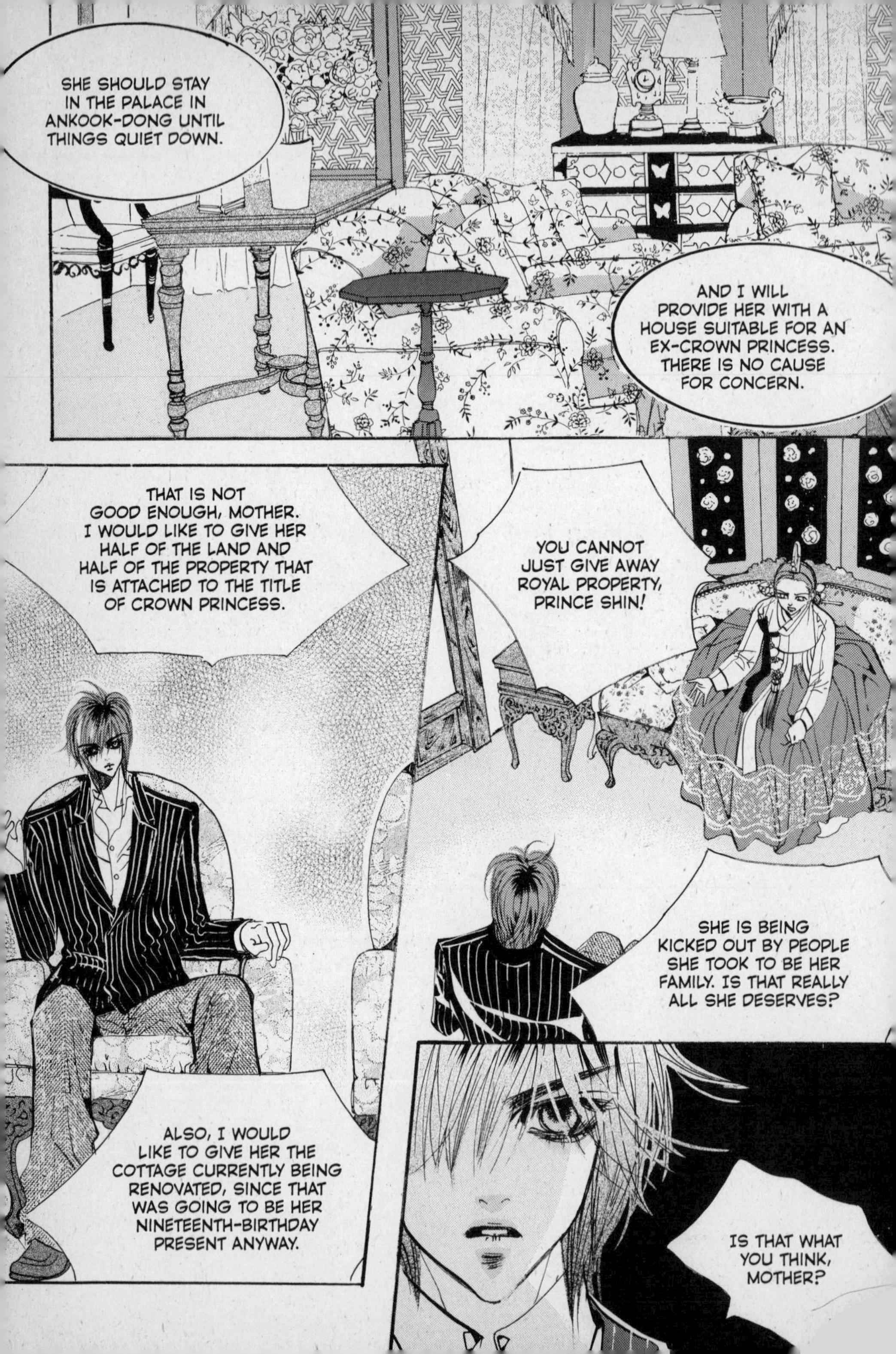
SHE SHOULD STAY IN THE PALACE IN ANKOOK-DONG UNTIL THINGS QUIET DOWN.
AND I WILL PROVIDE HER WITH A HOUSE SUITABLE FOR AN EX-CROWN PRINCESS. THERE IS NO CAUSE FOR CONCERN.
THAT IS NOT GOOD ENOUGH, MOTHER. I WOULD LIKE TO GIVE HER HALF OF THE LAND AND HALF OF THE PROPERTY THAT IS ATTACHED TO THE TITLE OF CROWN PRINCESS.
YOU CANNOT JUST GIVE AWAY ROYAL PROPERTY, PRINCE SHIN!
ALSO, I WOULD LIKE TO GIVE HER THE COTTAGE CURRENTLY BEING RENOVATED, SINCE THAT WAS GOING TO BE HER NINETEENTH-BIRTHDAY PRESENT ANYWAY.
SHE IS BEING KICKED OUT BY PEOPLE SHE TOOK TO BE HER FAMILY. IS THAT REALLY ALL SHE DESERVES?
IS THAT WHAT YOU THINK, MOTHER?

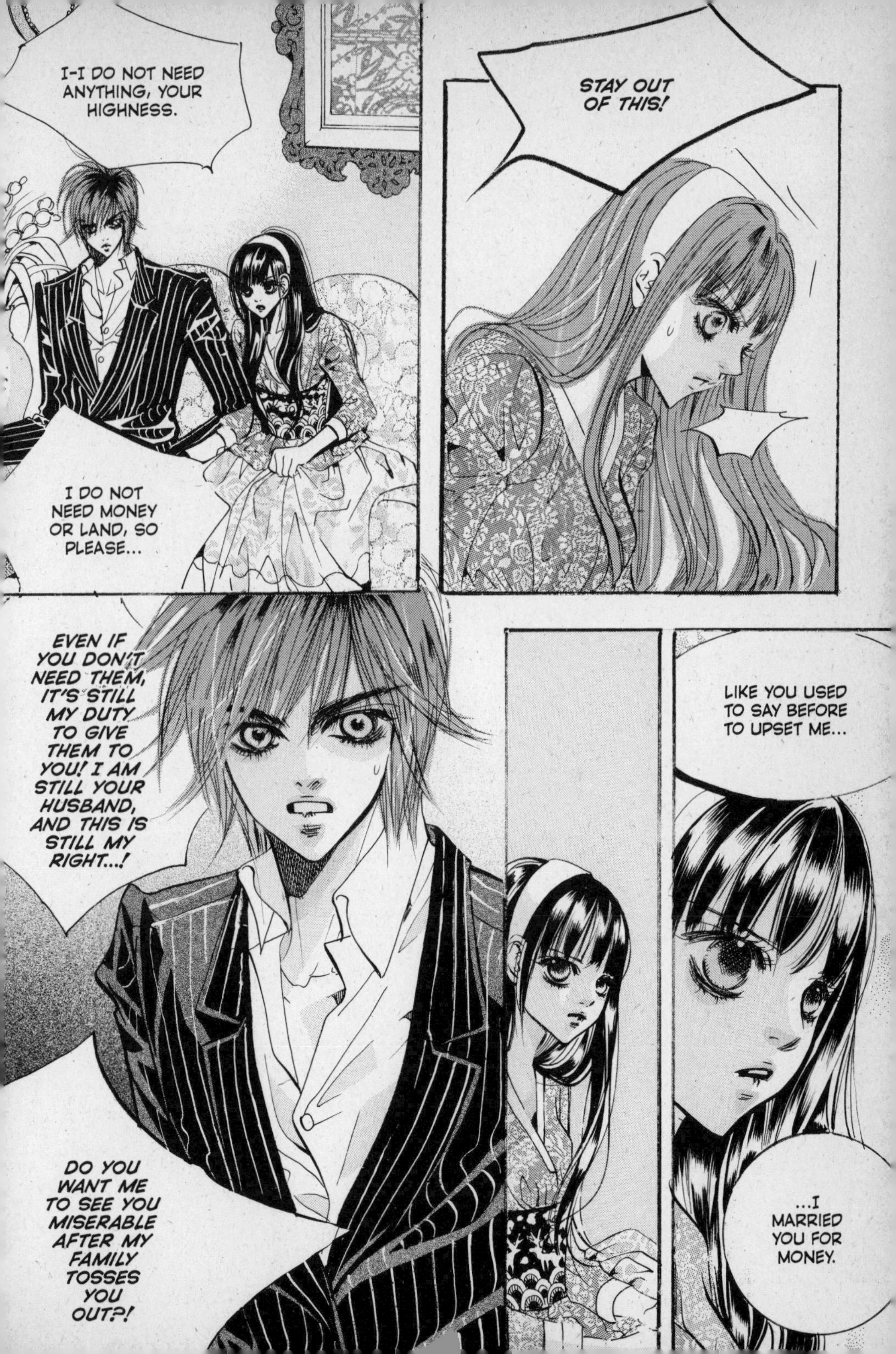
STAY OUT OF THIS!
I-I DO NOT NEED ANYTHING, YOUR HIGHNESS.
I DO NOT NEED MONEY OR LAND, SO PLEASE...
LIKE YOU USED TO SAY BEFORE TO UPSET ME...
...I MARRIED YOU FOR MONEY.
EVEN IF YOU DON'T NEED THEM, IT'S STILL MY DUTY TO GIVE THEM TO YOU! I AM STILL YOUR HUSBAND, AND THIS IS STILL MY RIGHT...!
DO YOU WANT ME TO SEE YOU MISERABLE AFTER MY FAMILY TOSSES YOU OUT?!

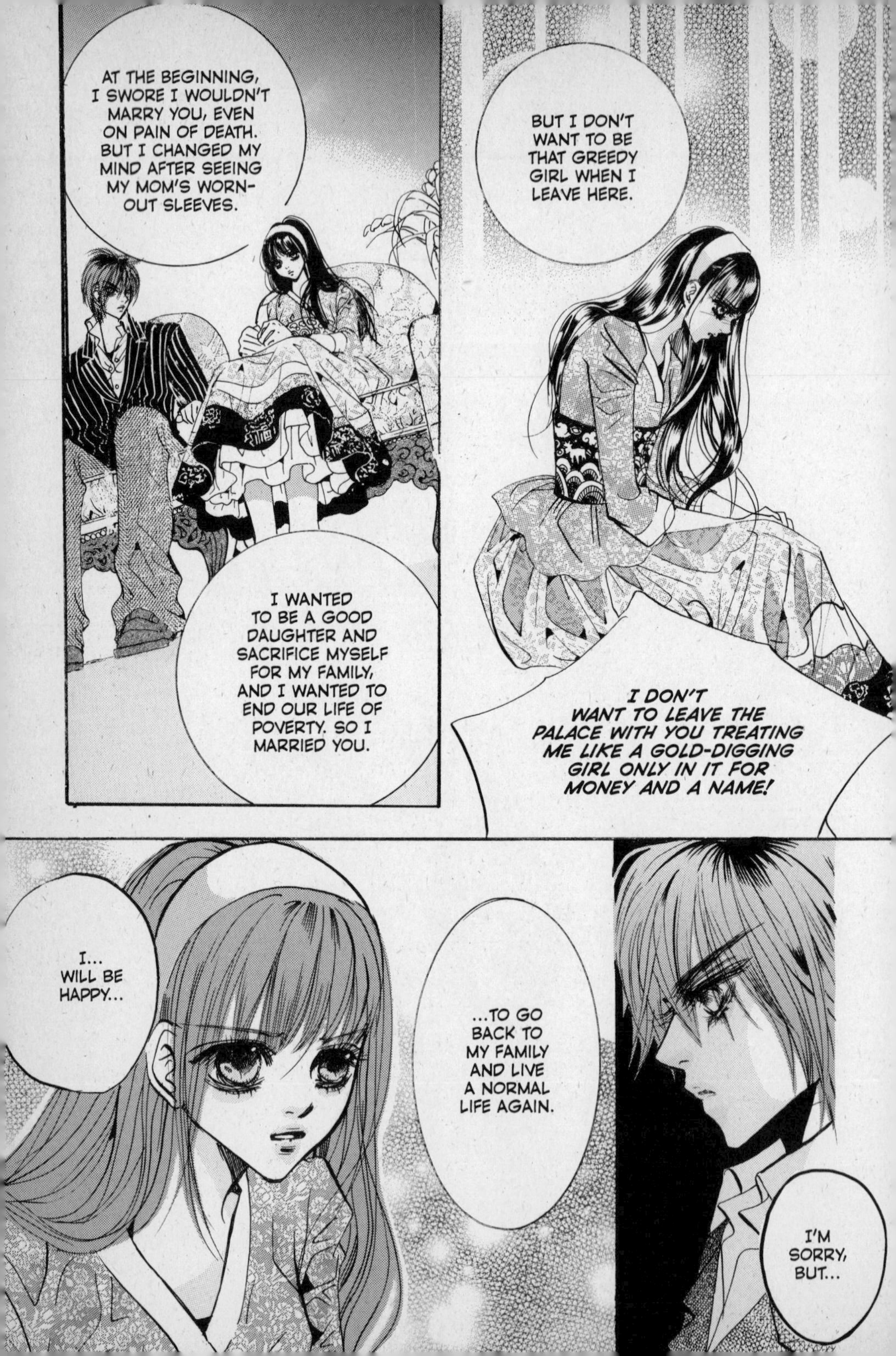
AT THE BEGINNING, I SWORE I WOULDN'T MARRY YOU, EVEN ON PAIN OF DEATH. BUT I CHANGED MY MIND AFTER SEEING MY MOM'S WORN-OUT SLEEVES.
I WANTED TO BE A GOOD DAUGHTER AND SACRIFICE MYSELF FOR MY FAMILY, AND I WANTED TO END OUR LIFE OF POVERTY. SO I MARRIED YOU.
BUT I DON'T WANT TO BE THAT GREEDY GIRL WHEN I LEAVE HERE.
I DON'T WANT TO LEAVE THE PALACE WITH YOU TREATING ME LIKE A GOLD-DIGGING GIRL ONLY IN IT FOR MONEY AND A NAME!
I... WILL BE HAPPY...
...TO GO BACK TO MY FAMILY AND LIVE A NORMAL LIFE AGAIN.
I'M SORRY, BUT...

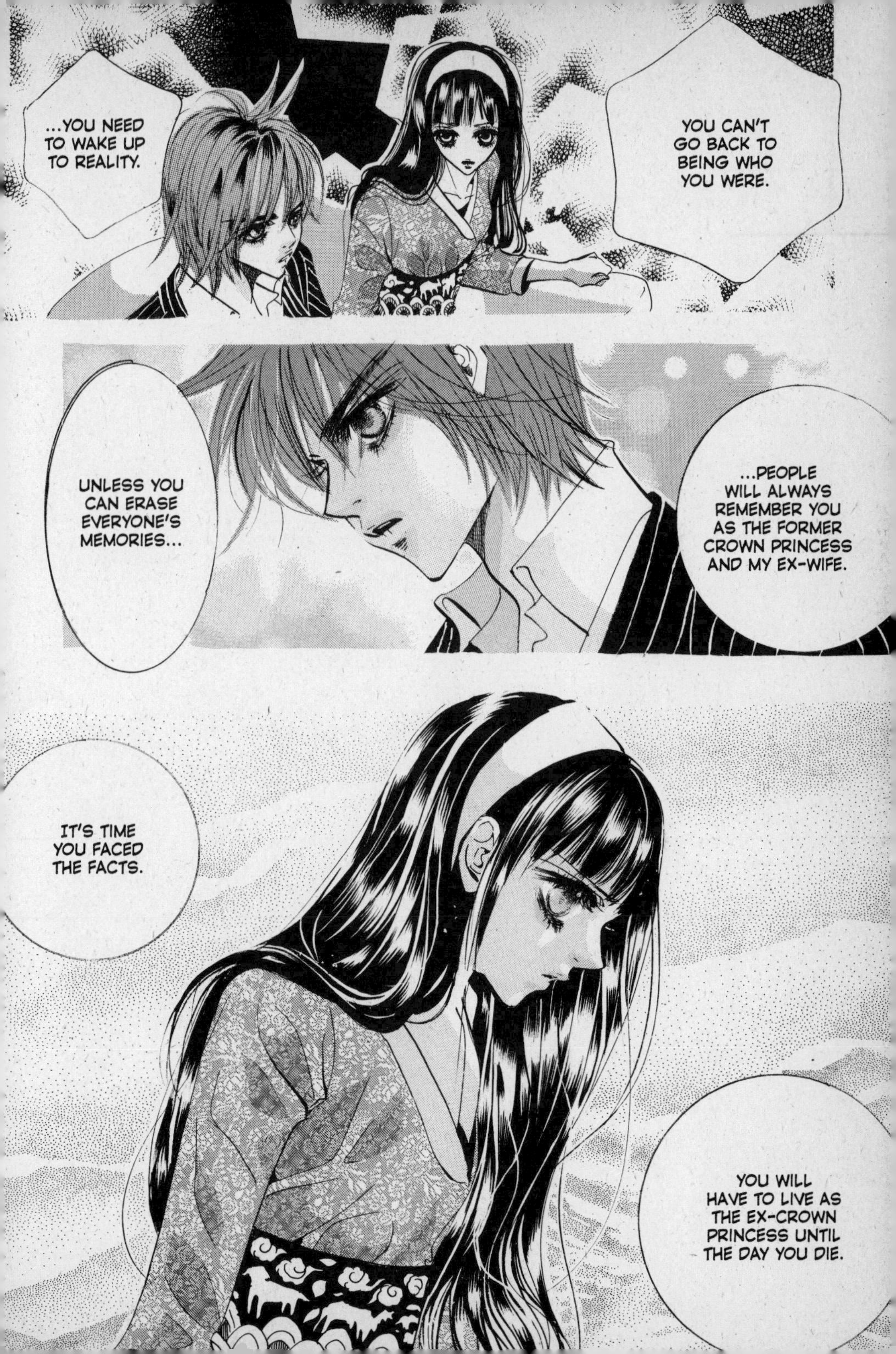
YOU CAN'T GO BACK TO BEING WHO YOU WERE.
...YOU NEED TO WAKE UP TO REALITY.
...PEOPLE WILL ALWAYS REMEMBER YOU AS THE FORMER CROWN PRINCESS AND MY EX-WIFE.
UNLESS YOU CAN ERASE EVERYONE'S MEMORIES...
YOU WILL HAVE TO LIVE AS THE EX-CROWN PRINCESS UNTIL THE DAY YOU DIE.
IT'S TIME YOU FACED THE FACTS.

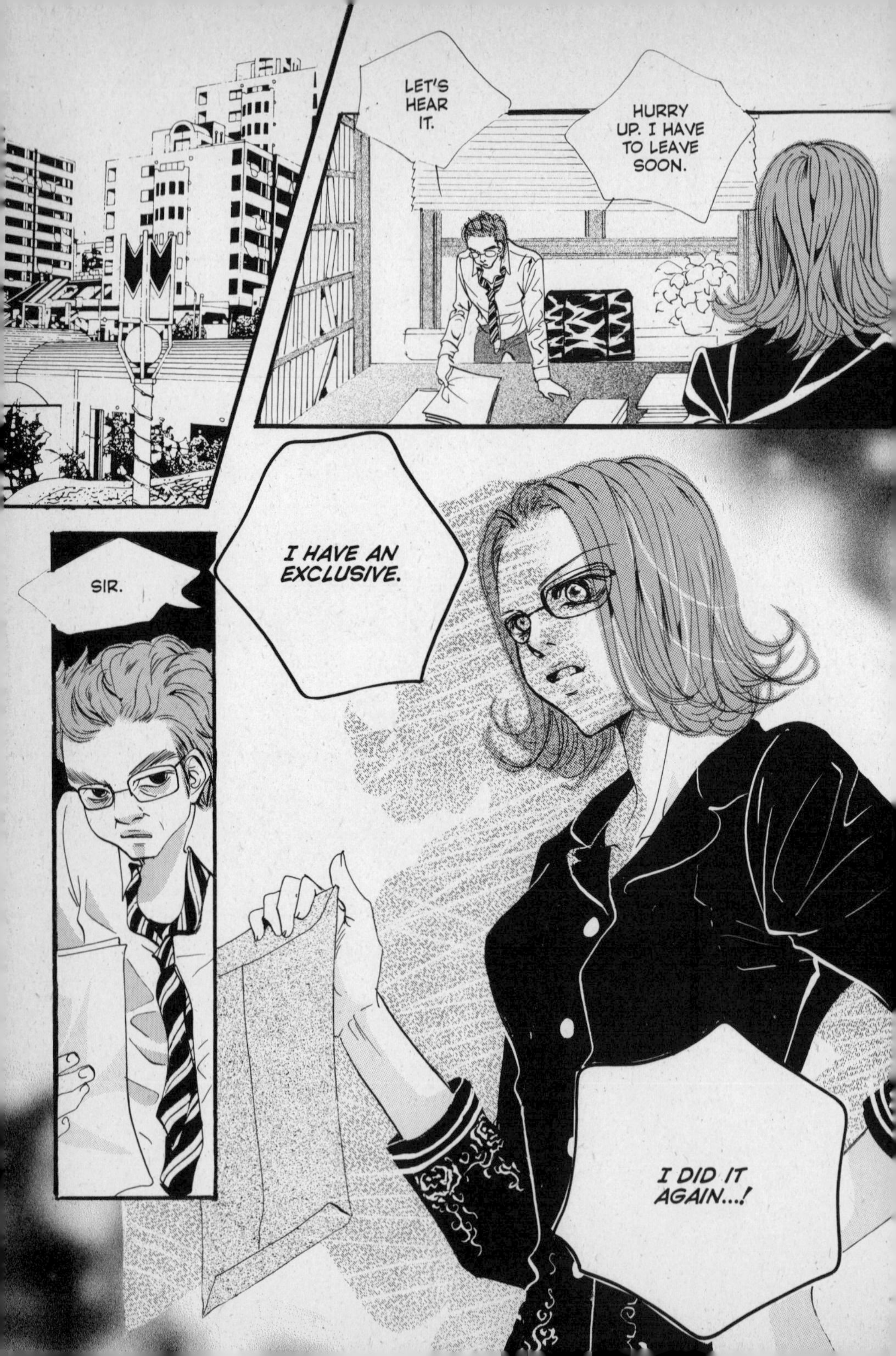
LET'S HEAR IT.
HURRY UP. I HAVE TO LEAVE SOON.
SIR.
I HAVE AN EXCLUSIVE.
I DID IT AGAIN...!

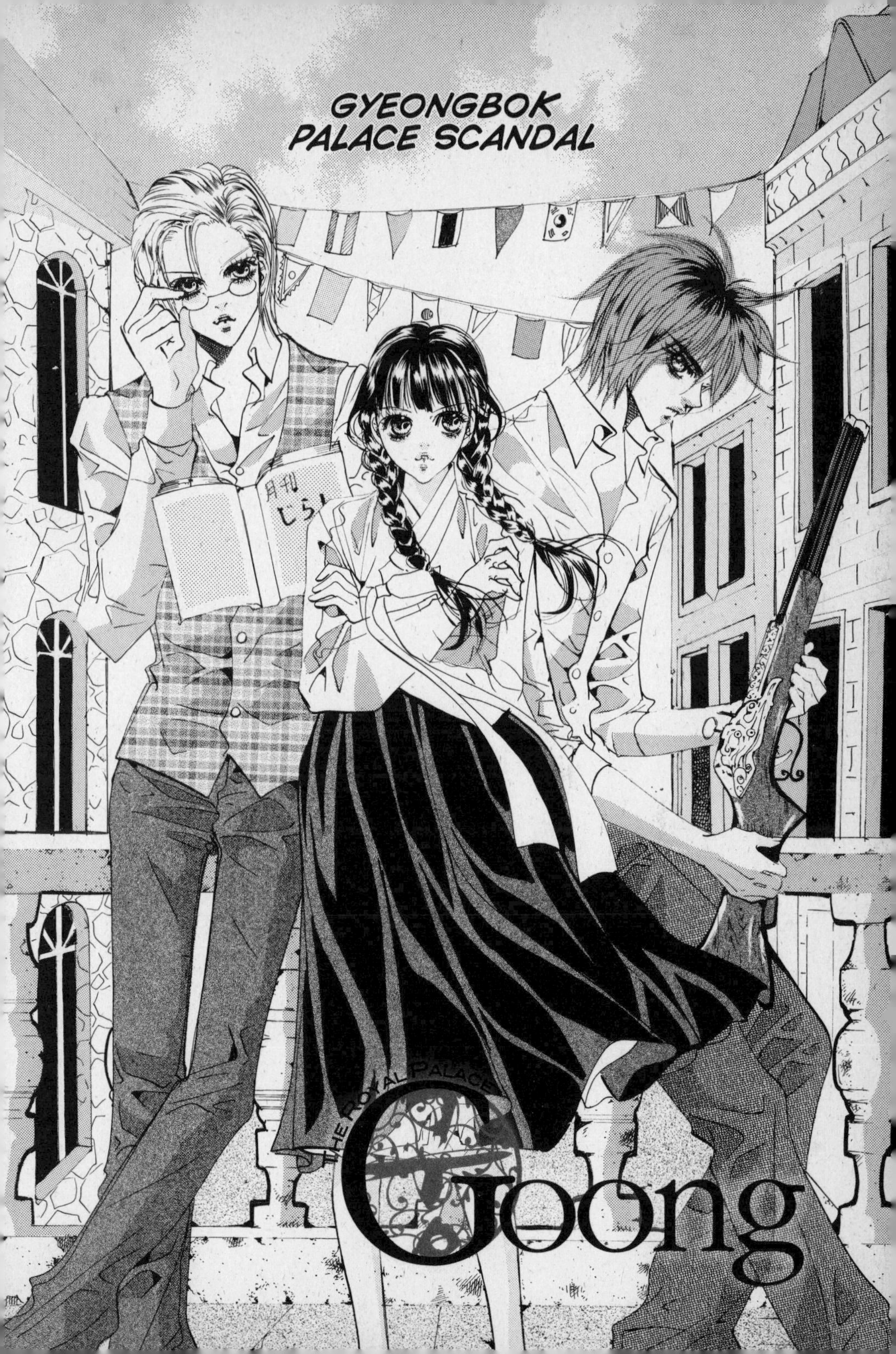
GYEONGBOK
PALACE SCANDAL
月刊
THE ROYAL PALACE
Goong

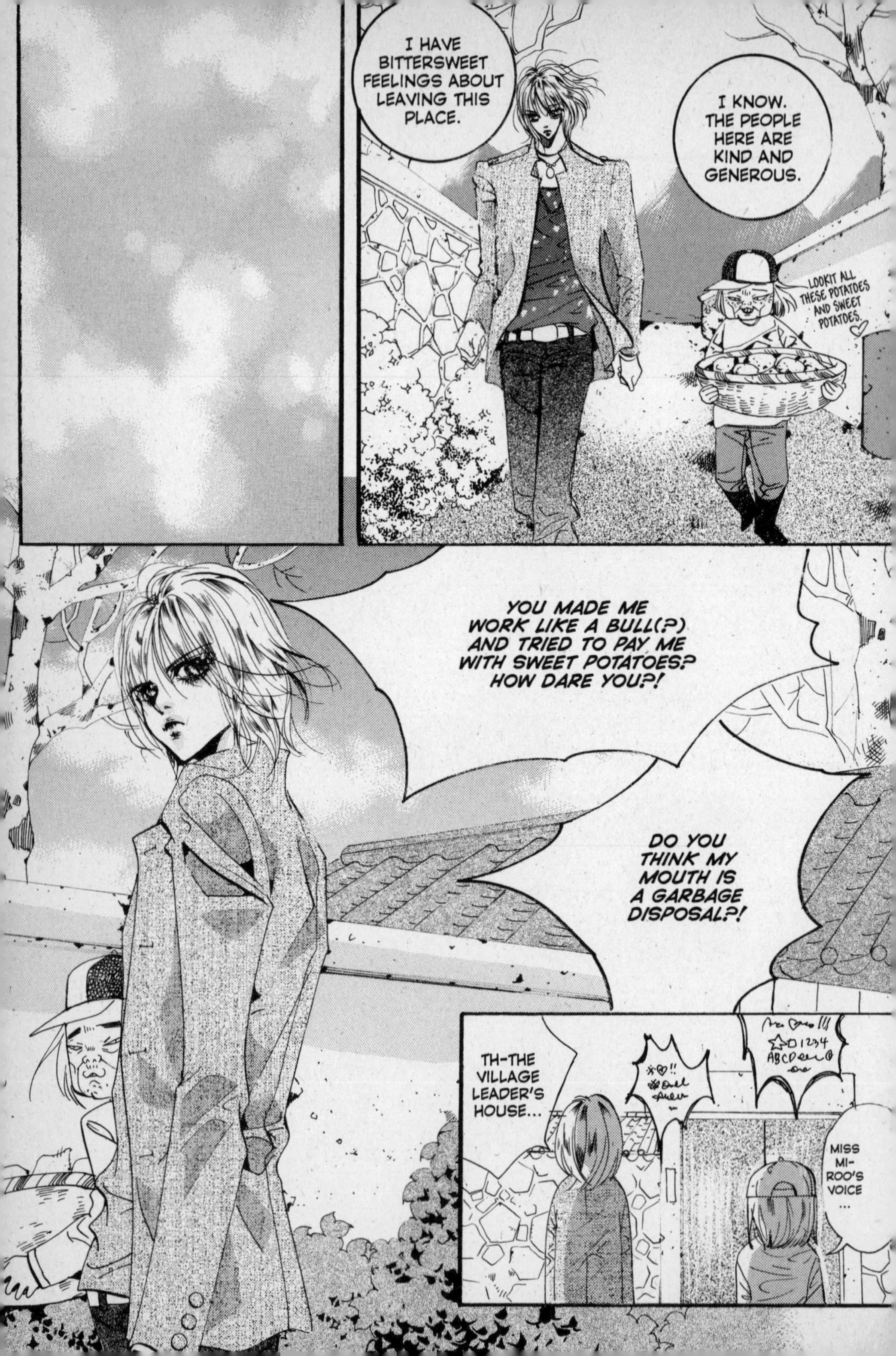
I HAVE BITTERSWEET FEELINGS ABOUT LEAVING THIS PLACE.
I KNOW. THE PEOPLE HERE ARE KIND AND GENEROUS.
LOOKIT ALL THESE POTATOES AND SWEET POTATOES.
YOU MADE ME WORK LIKE A BULL(?) AND TRIED TO PAY ME WITH SWEET POTATOES? HOW DARE YOU?!
DO YOU THINK MY MOUTH IS A GARBAGE DISPOSAL?!
TH-THE VILLAGE LEADER'S HOUSE...
MISS MI-ROO'S VOICE ...

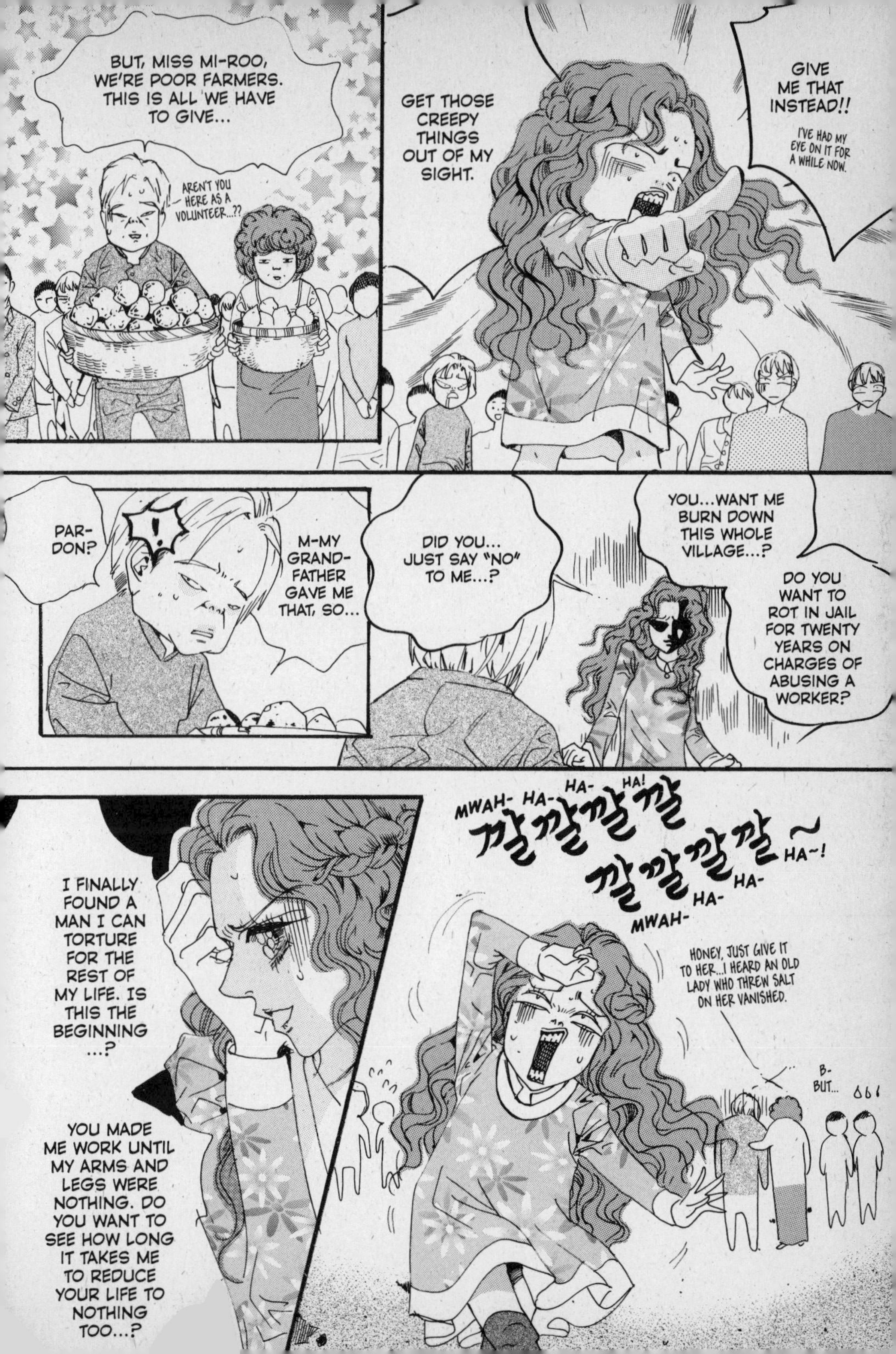
BUT, MISS MI-ROO, WE'RE POOR FARMERS. THIS IS ALL WE HAVE TO GIVE...
AREN'T YOU HERE AS A VOLUNTEER...??
GET THOSE CREEPY THINGS OUT OF MY SIGHT.
GIVE ME THAT INSTEAD!!
I'VE HAD MY EYE ON IT FOR A WHILE NOW.
PARDON?
M-MY GRANDFATHER GAVE ME THAT, SO...
DID YOU... JUST SAY "NO" TO ME...?
YOU...WANT ME BURN DOWN THIS WHOLE VILLAGE...?
DO YOU WANT TO ROT IN JAIL FOR TWENTY YEARS ON CHARGES OF ABUSING A WORKER?
I FINALLY FOUND A MAN I CAN TORTURE FOR THE REST OF MY LIFE. IS THIS THE BEGINNING ...?
YOU MADE ME WORK UNTIL MY ARMS AND LEGS WERE NOTHING. DO YOU WANT TO SEE HOW LONG IT TAKES ME TO REDUCE YOUR LIFE TO NOTHING TOO...?
MWAH- HA- HA- HA!
깔깔깔깔
깔깔깔깔~
HA-! HA- HA- MWAH-
HONEY, JUST GIVE IT TO HER...I HEARD AN OLD LADY WHO THREW SALT ON HER VANISHED.
B-BUT...

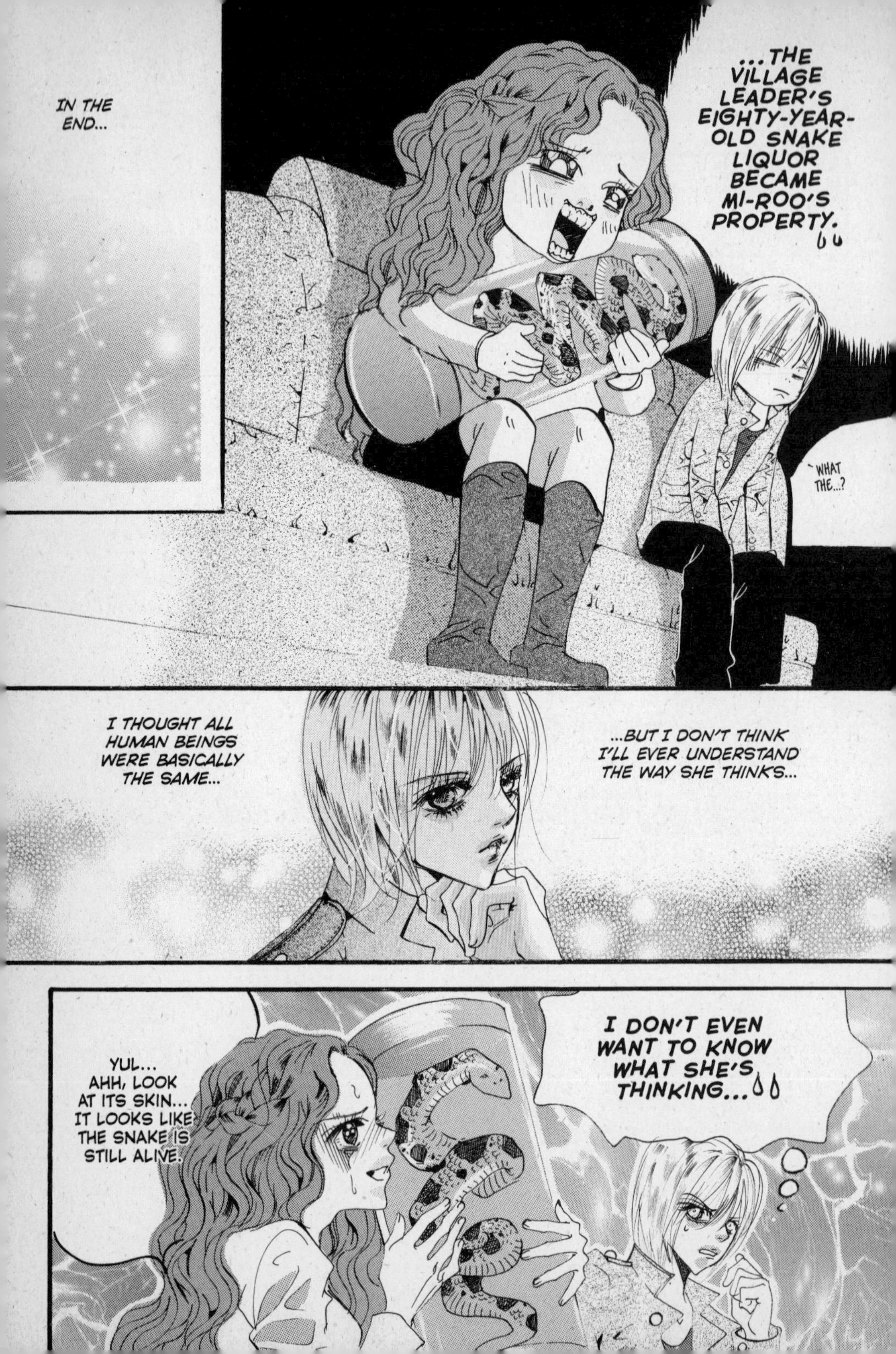
IN THE END...
...THE VILLAGE LEADER'S EIGHTY-YEAR-OLD SNAKE LIQUOR BECAME MI-ROO'S PROPERTY.
WHAT THE...?
I THOUGHT ALL HUMAN BEINGS WERE BASICALLY THE SAME...
...BUT I DON'T THINK I'LL EVER UNDERSTAND THE WAY SHE THINKS...
I DON'T EVEN WANT TO KNOW WHAT SHE'S THINKING...
YUL... AHH, LOOK AT ITS SKIN... IT LOOKS LIKE THE SNAKE IS STILL ALIVE.

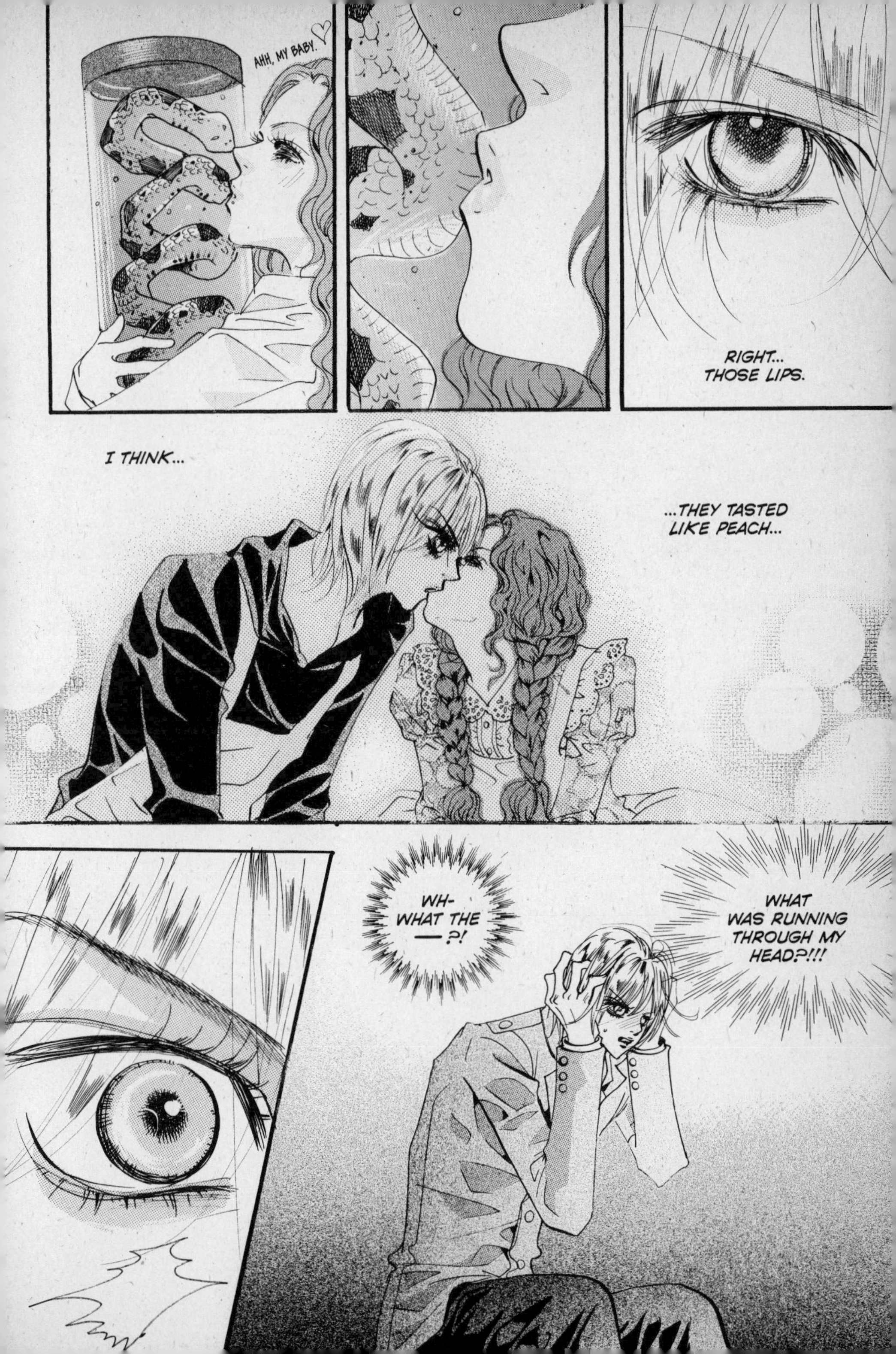
AHH, MY BABY.
RIGHT... THOSE LIPS.
I THINK...
...THEY TASTED LIKE PEACH...
WH- WHAT THE —?!
WHAT WAS RUNNING THROUGH MY HEAD?!!!

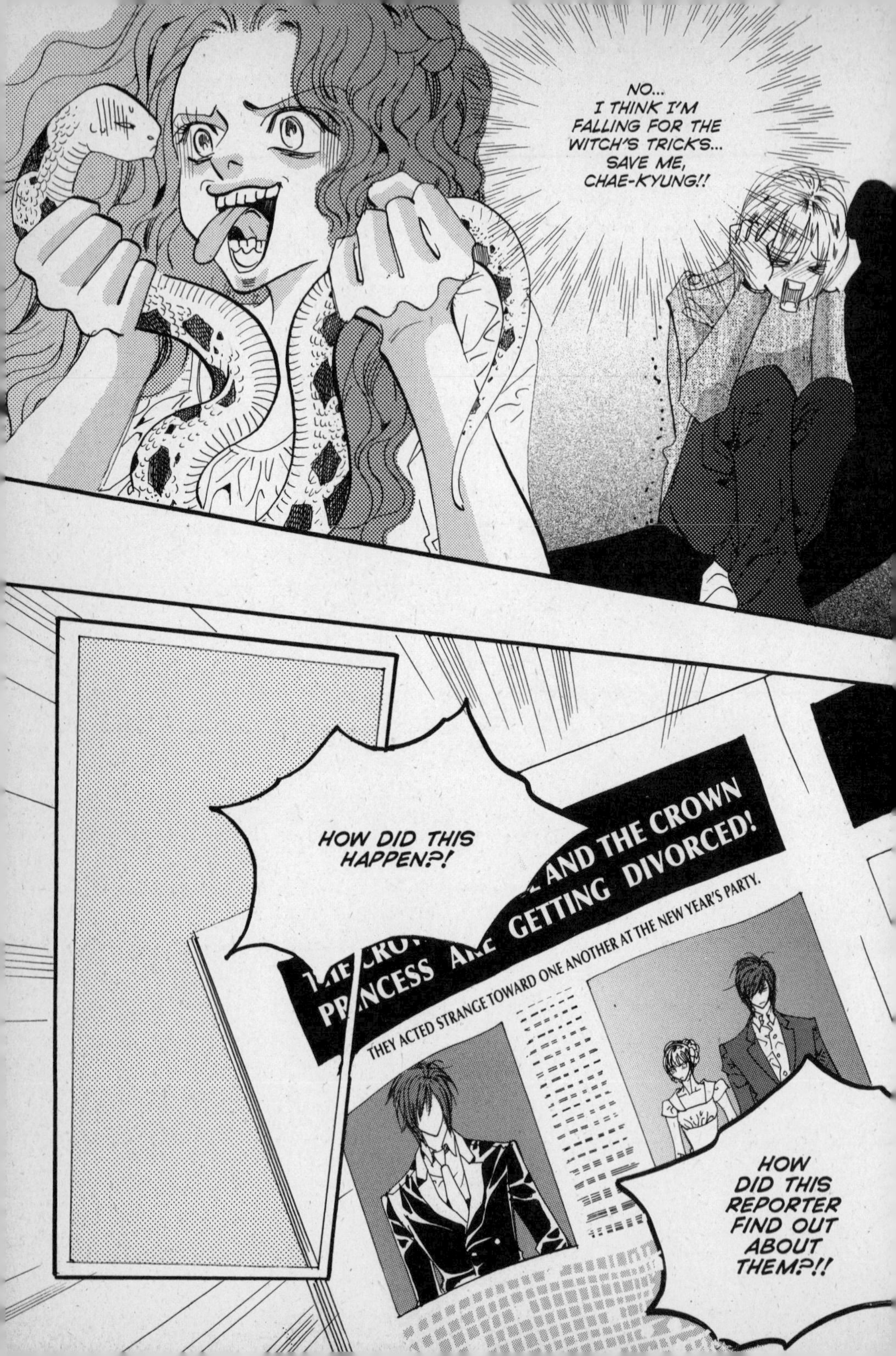
NO... I THINK I'M FALLING FOR THE WITCH'S TRICKS... SAVE ME, CHAE-KYUNG!!
HOW DID THIS HAPPEN?!
AND THE CROWN
PRINCESS
GETTING DIVORCED!
THEY ACTED STRANGE TOWARD ONE ANOTHER AT THE NEW YEAR'S PARTY.
HOW DID THIS REPORTER FIND OUT ABOUT THEM?!!

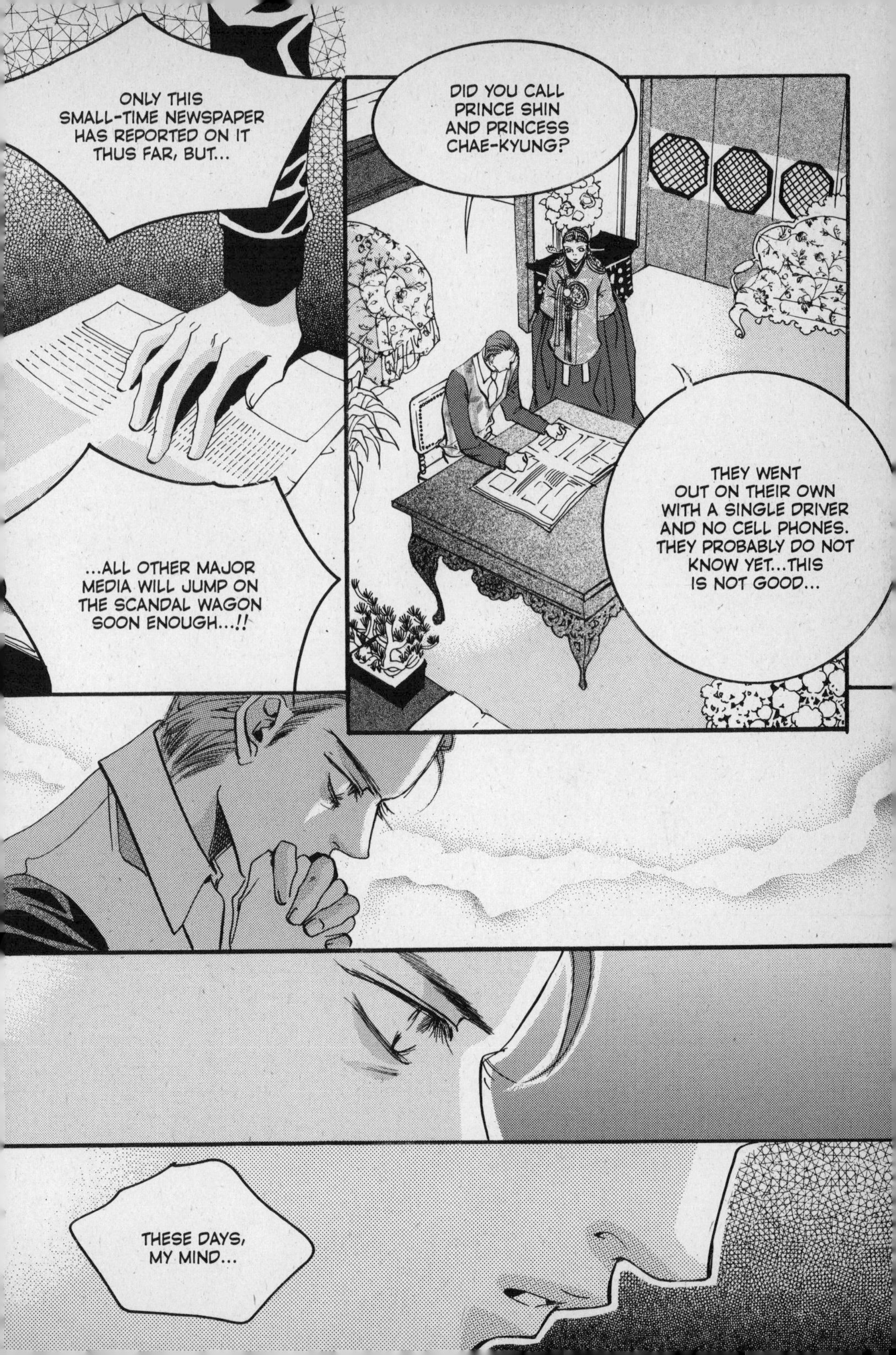
ONLY THIS SMALL-TIME NEWSPAPER HAS REPORTED ON IT THUS FAR, BUT...
...ALL OTHER MAJOR MEDIA WILL JUMP ON THE SCANDAL WAGON SOON ENOUGH...!!
DID YOU CALL PRINCE SHIN AND PRINCESS CHAE-KYUNG?
THEY WENT OUT ON THEIR OWN WITH A SINGLE DRIVER AND NO CELL PHONES. THEY PROBABLY DO NOT KNOW YET...THIS IS NOT GOOD...
THESE DAYS, MY MIND...

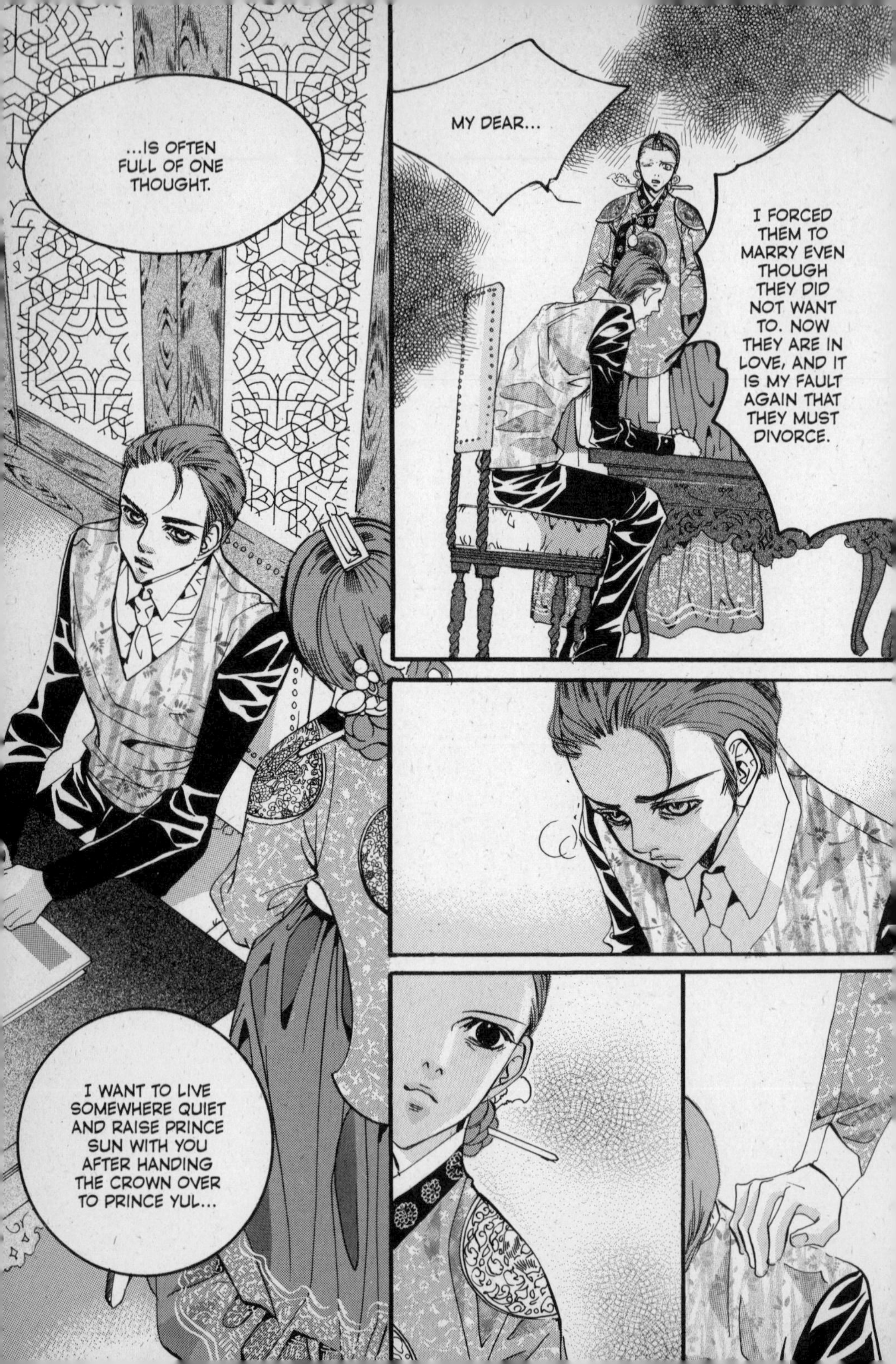
...IS OFTEN FULL OF ONE THOUGHT.
MY DEAR...
I FORCED THEM TO MARRY EVEN THOUGH THEY DID NOT WANT TO. NOW THEY ARE IN LOVE, AND IT IS MY FAULT AGAIN THAT THEY MUST DIVORCE.
I WANT TO LIVE SOMEWHERE QUIET AND RAISE PRINCE SUN WITH YOU AFTER HANDING THE CROWN OVER TO PRINCE YUL...

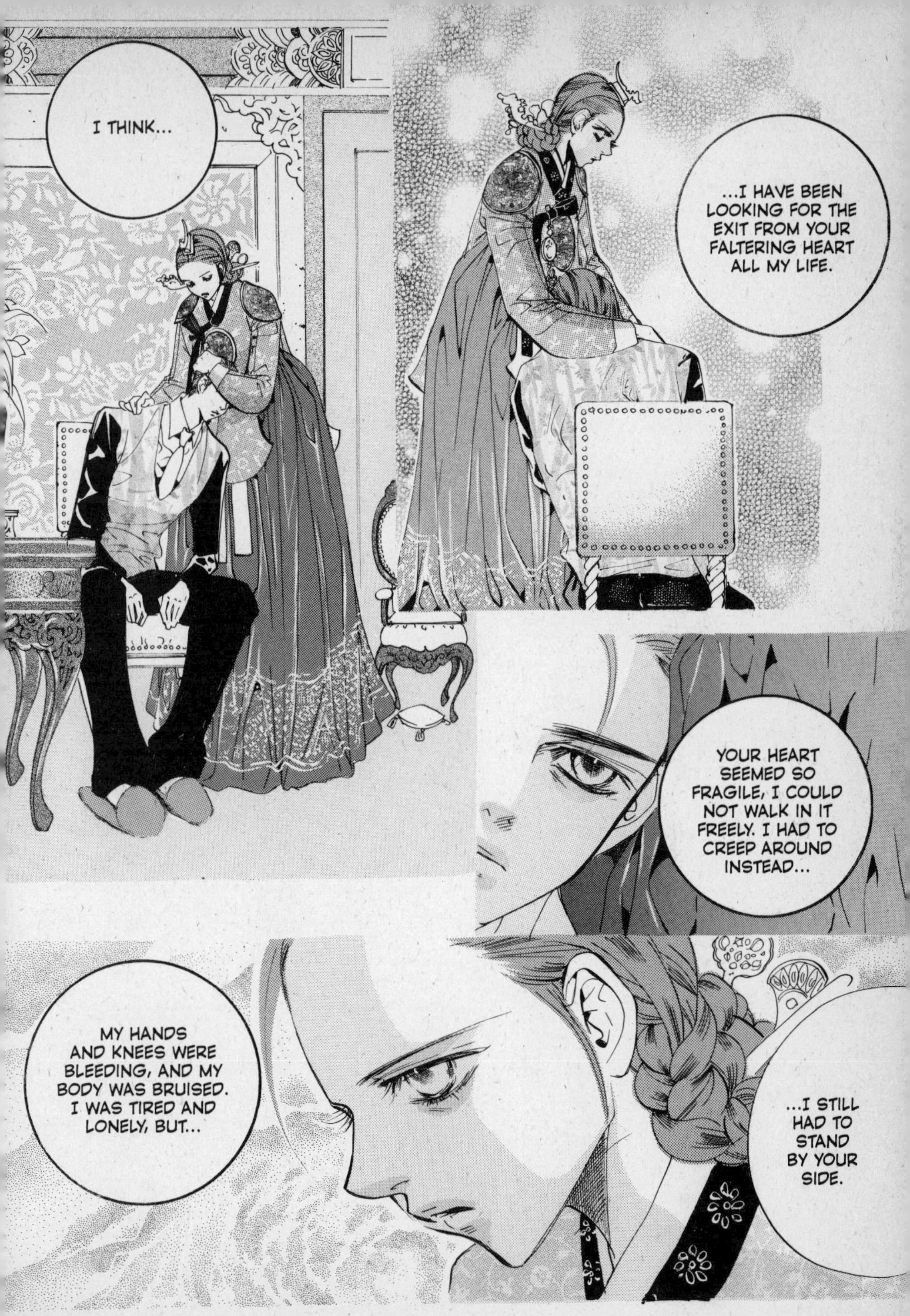
I THINK...
...I HAVE BEEN LOOKING FOR THE EXIT FROM YOUR FALTERING HEART ALL MY LIFE.
YOUR HEART SEEMED SO FRAGILE, I COULD NOT WALK IN IT FREELY. I HAD TO CREEP AROUND INSTEAD...
MY HANDS AND KNEES WERE BLEEDING, AND MY BODY WAS BRUISED. I WAS TIRED AND LONELY, BUT...
...I STILL HAD TO STAND BY YOUR SIDE.

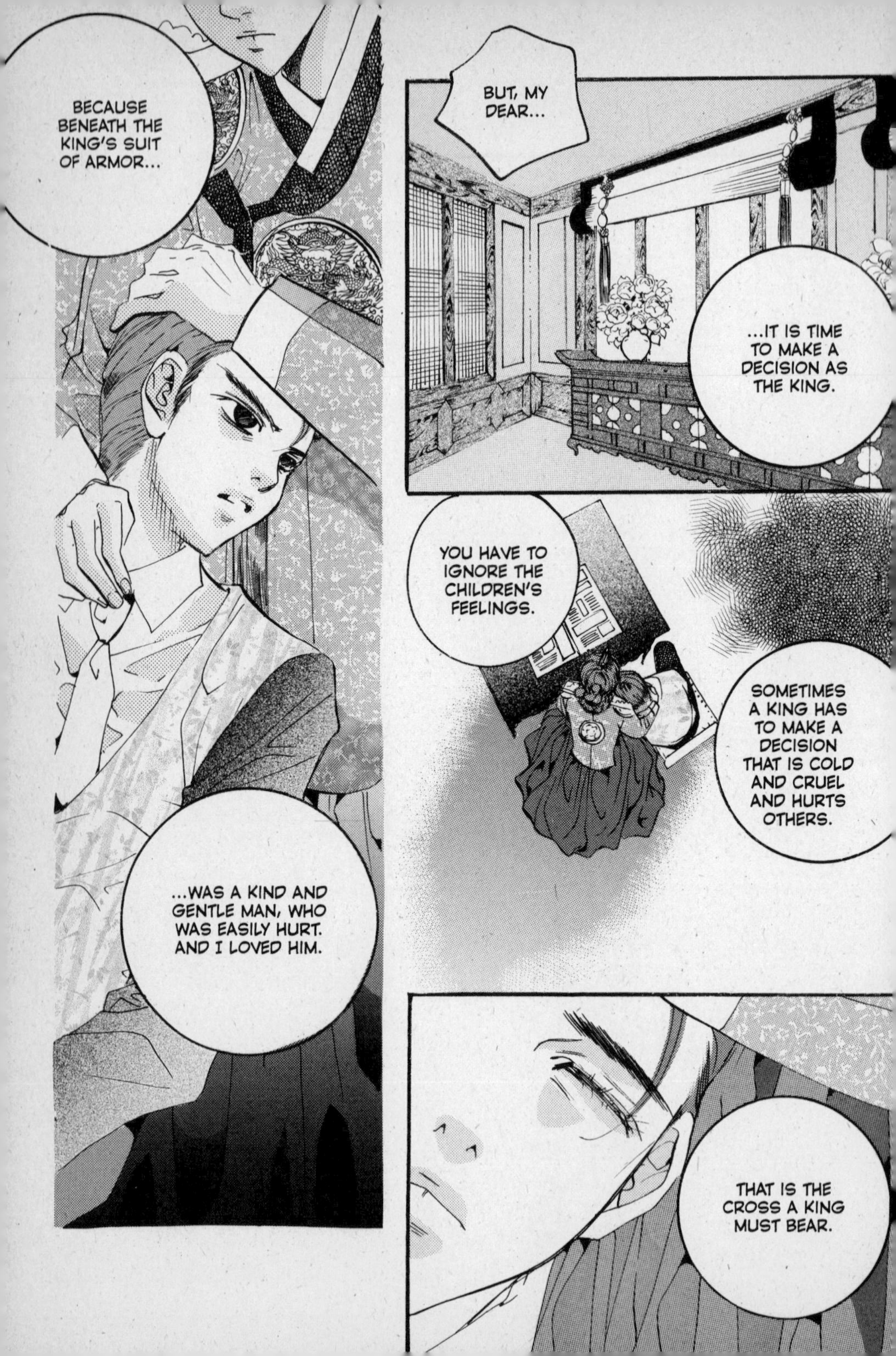
BECAUSE BENEATH THE KING'S SUIT OF ARMOR...
...WAS A KIND AND GENTLE MAN, WHO WAS EASILY HURT. AND I LOVED HIM.
BUT, MY DEAR...
...IT IS TIME TO MAKE A DECISION AS THE KING.
YOU HAVE TO IGNORE THE CHILDREN'S FEELINGS.
SOMETIMES A KING HAS TO MAKE A DECISION THAT IS COLD AND CRUEL AND HURTS OTHERS.
THAT IS THE CROSS A KING MUST BEAR.

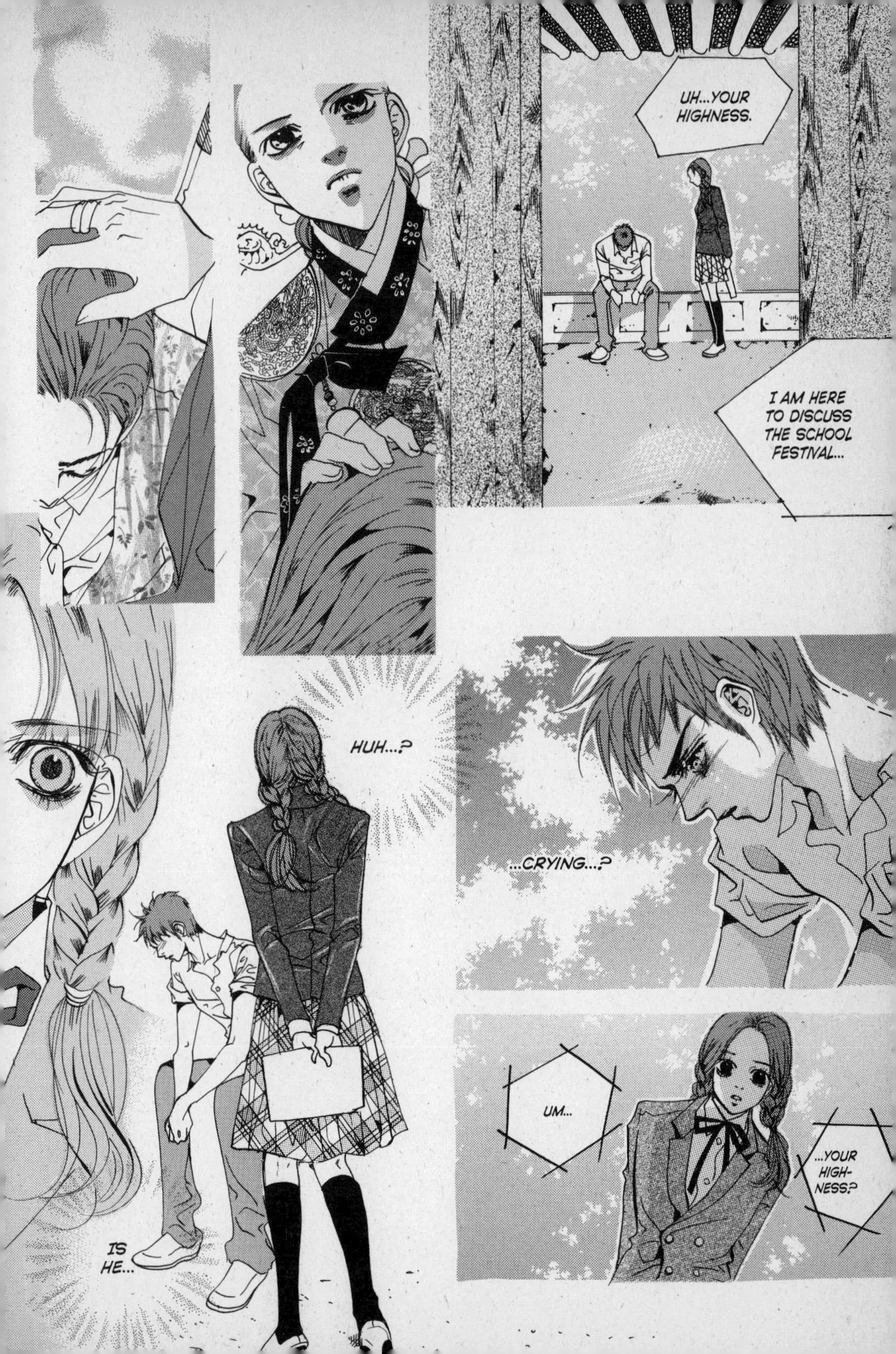
UH...YOUR HIGHNESS.
I AM HERE TO DISCUSS THE SCHOOL FESTIVAL...
HUH...?
IS HE...
...CRYING...?
UM...
...YOUR HIGH-NESS?

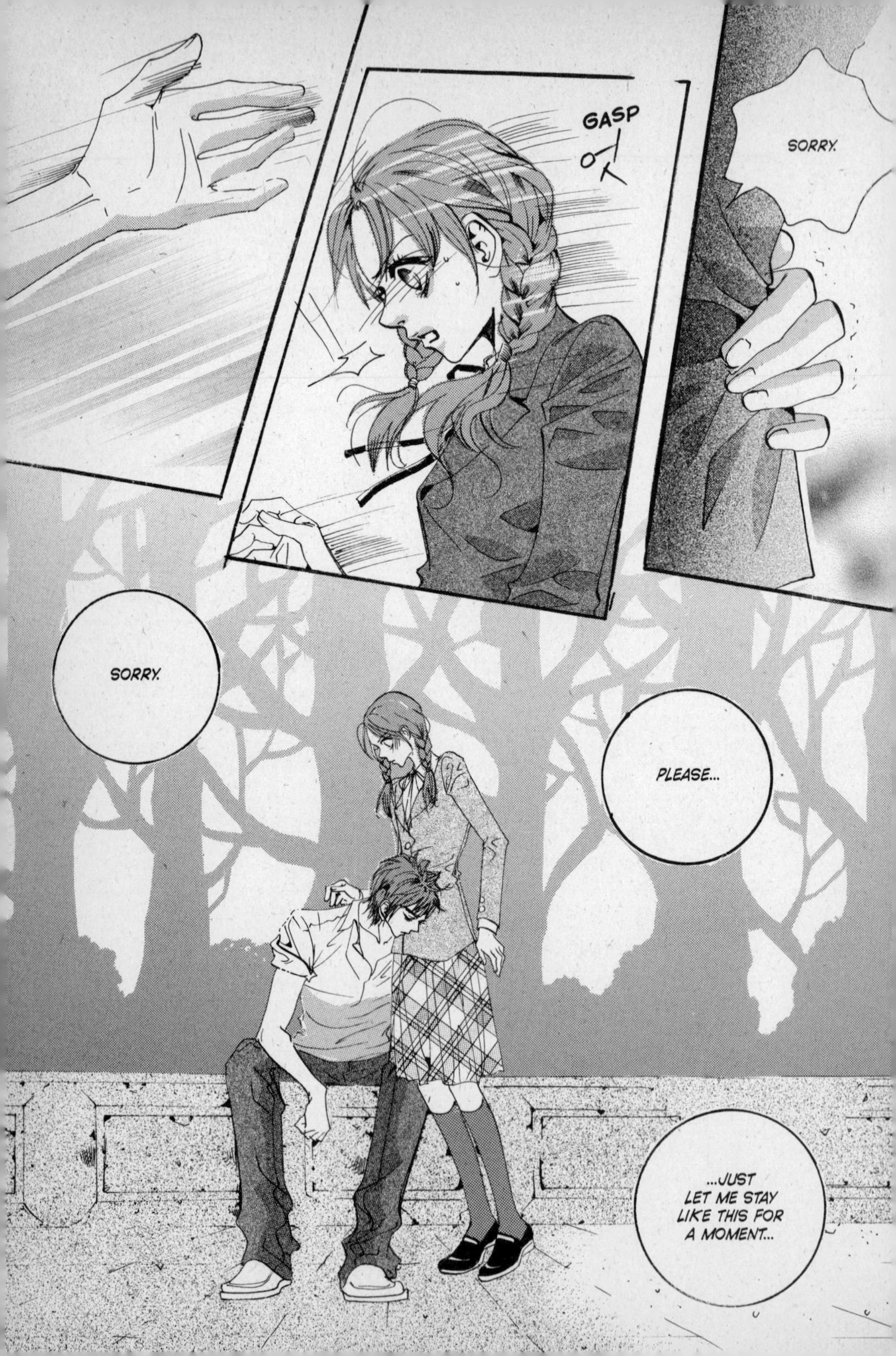
GASP
SORRY.
SORRY.
PLEASE...
...JUST LET ME STAY LIKE THIS FOR A MOMENT...

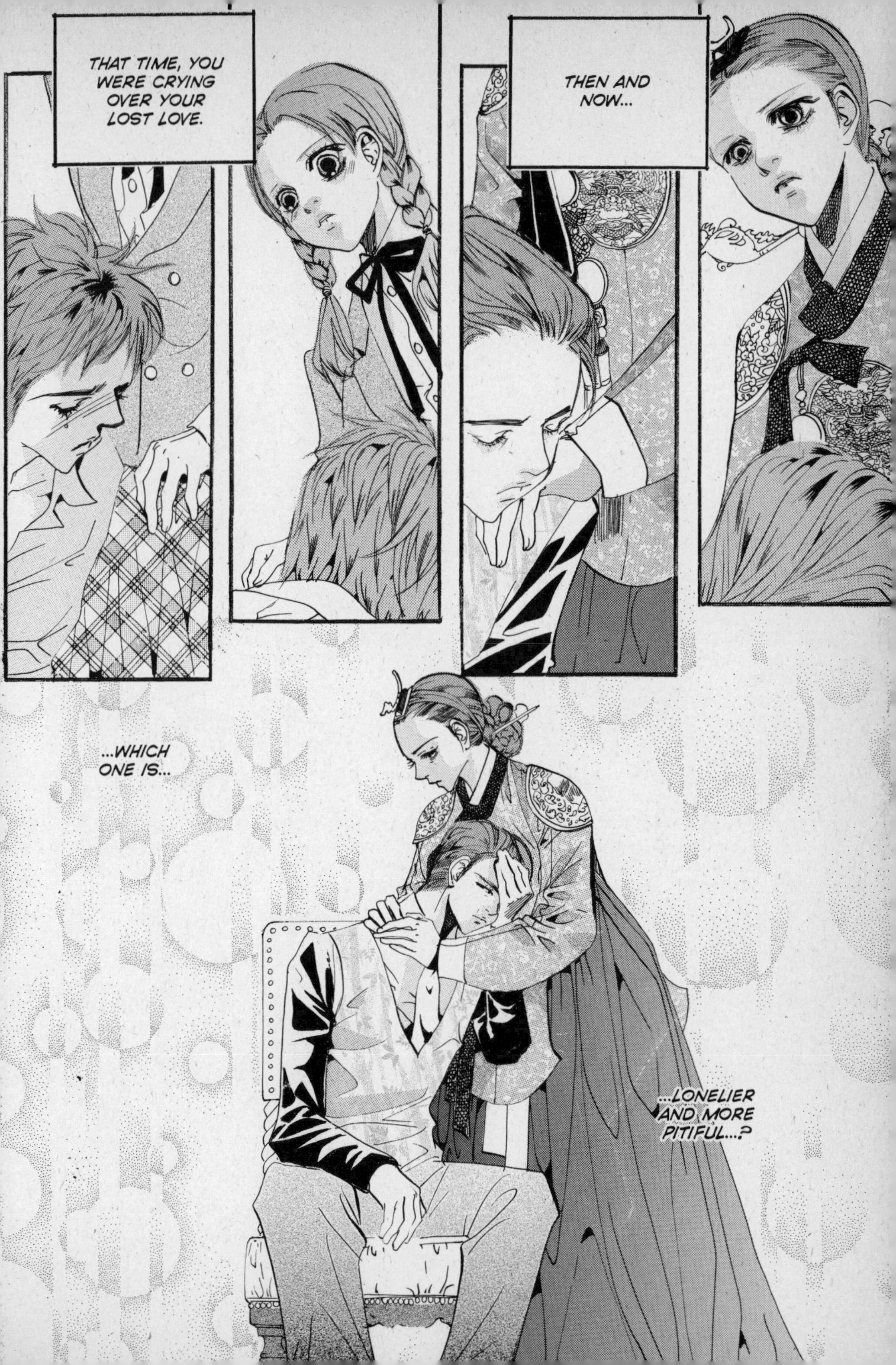
THAT TIME, YOU WERE CRYING OVER YOUR LOST LOVE.
THEN AND NOW...
...WHICH ONE IS...
...LONELIER AND MORE PITIFUL...?

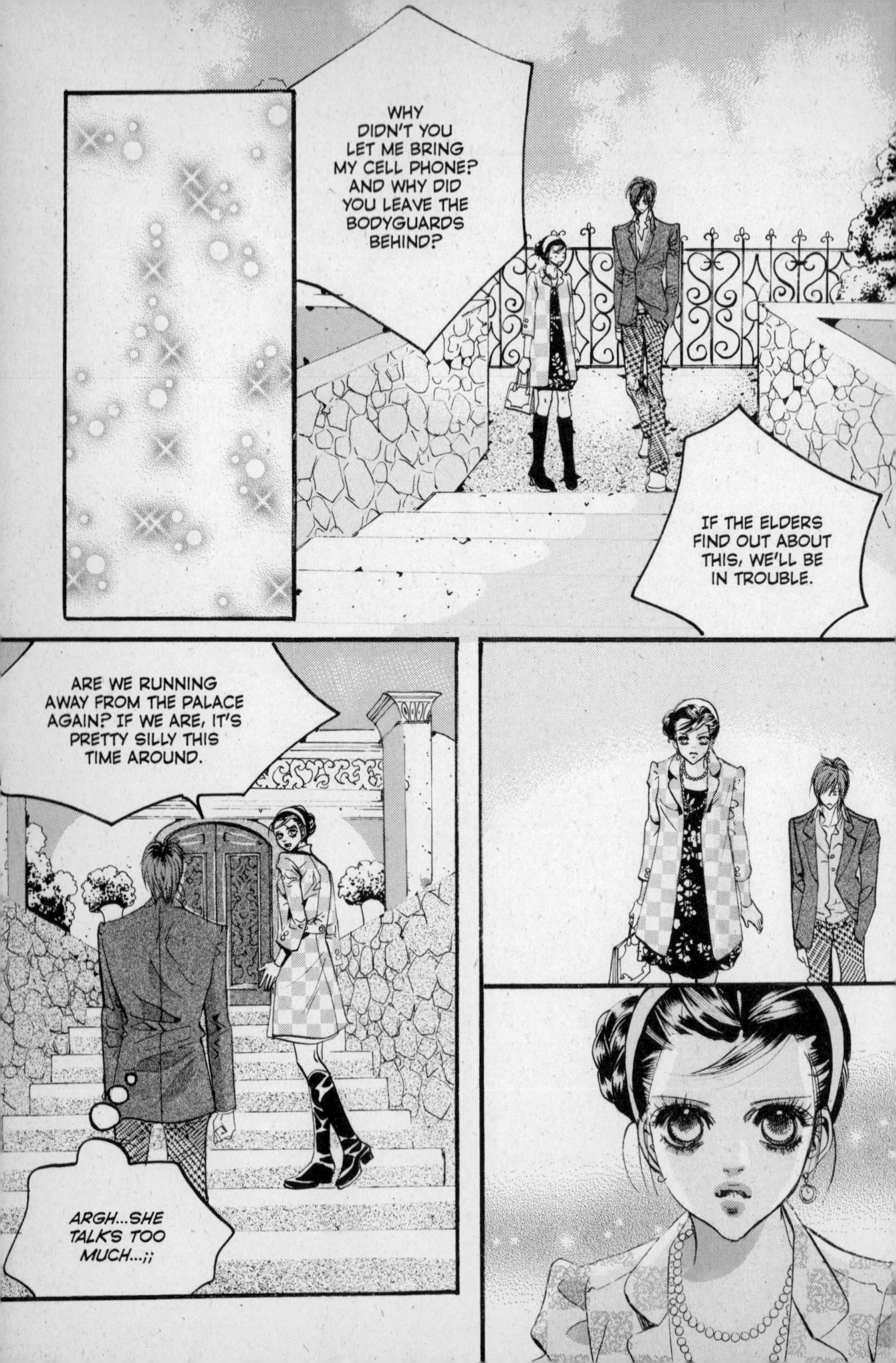
WHY DIDN'T YOU LET ME BRING MY CELL PHONE? AND WHY DID YOU LEAVE THE BODYGUARDS BEHIND?
IF THE ELDERS FIND OUT ABOUT THIS, WE'LL BE IN TROUBLE.
ARE WE RUNNING AWAY FROM THE PALACE AGAIN? IF WE ARE, IT'S PRETTY SILLY THIS TIME AROUND.
ARGH...SHE TALKS TOO MUCH...;;

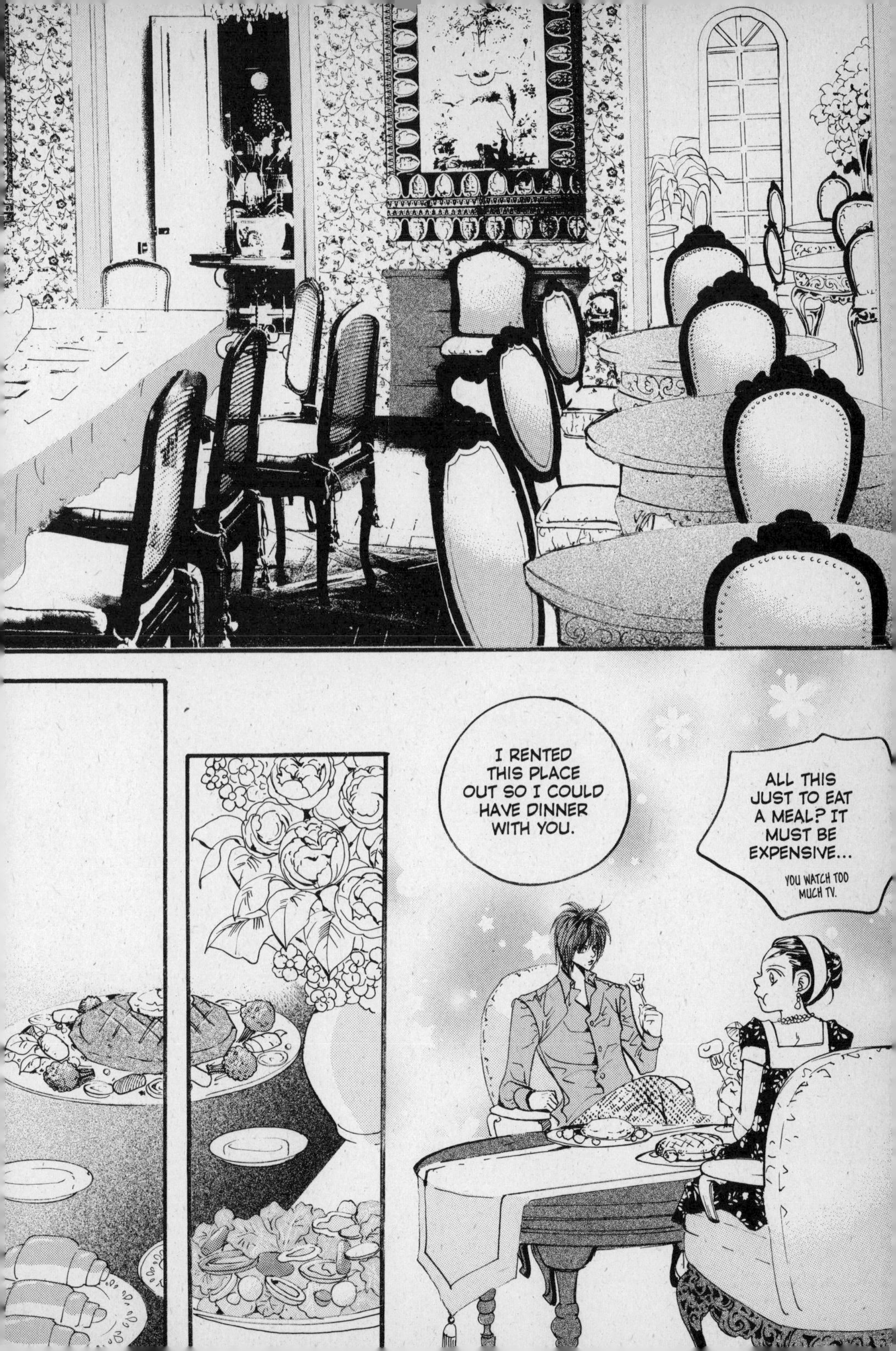
I RENTED THIS PLACE OUT SO I COULD HAVE DINNER WITH YOU.
ALL THIS JUST TO EAT A MEAL? IT MUST BE EXPENSIVE...
YOU WATCH TOO MUCH TV.

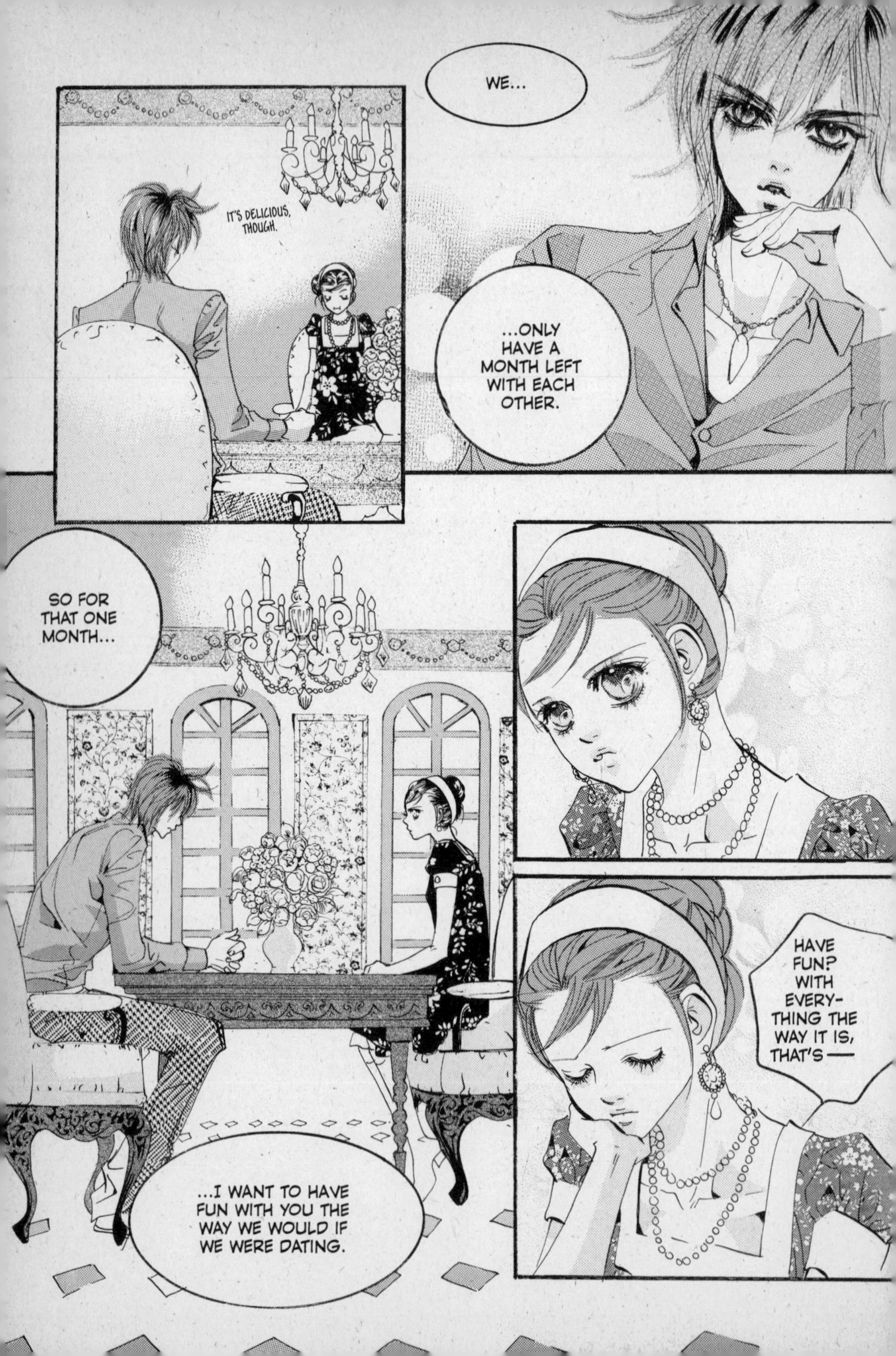
WE...
...ONLY HAVE A MONTH LEFT WITH EACH OTHER.
IT'S DELICIOUS, THOUGH.
SO FOR THAT ONE MONTH...
...I WANT TO HAVE FUN WITH YOU THE WAY WE WOULD IF WE WERE DATING.
HAVE FUN? WITH EVERY-THING THE WAY IT IS, THAT'S—

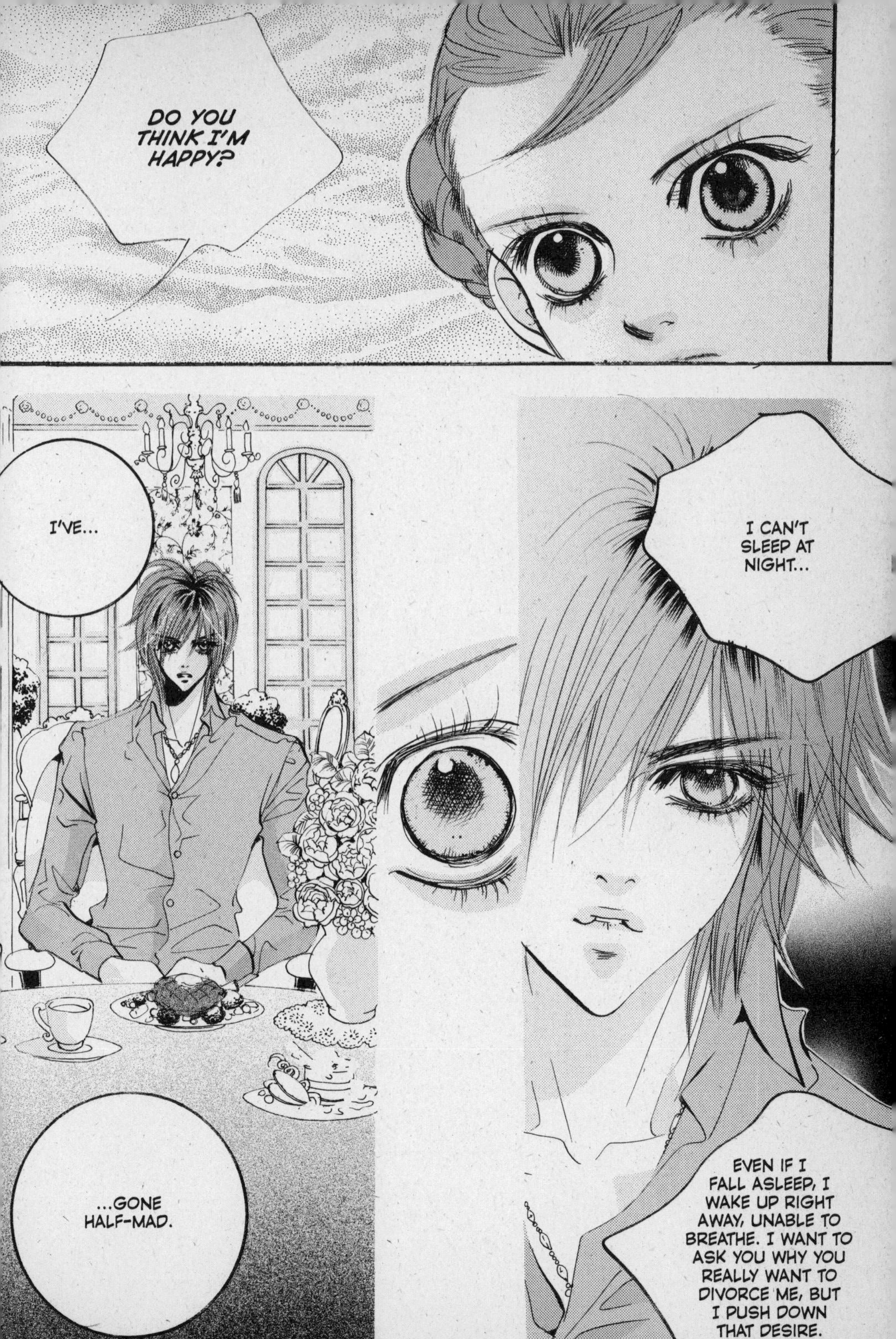
DO YOU THINK I'M HAPPY?
I CAN'T SLEEP AT NIGHT...
EVEN IF I FALL ASLEEP, I WAKE UP RIGHT AWAY, UNABLE TO BREATHE. I WANT TO ASK YOU WHY YOU REALLY WANT TO DIVORCE ME, BUT I PUSH DOWN THAT DESIRE.
I'VE...
...GONE HALF-MAD.

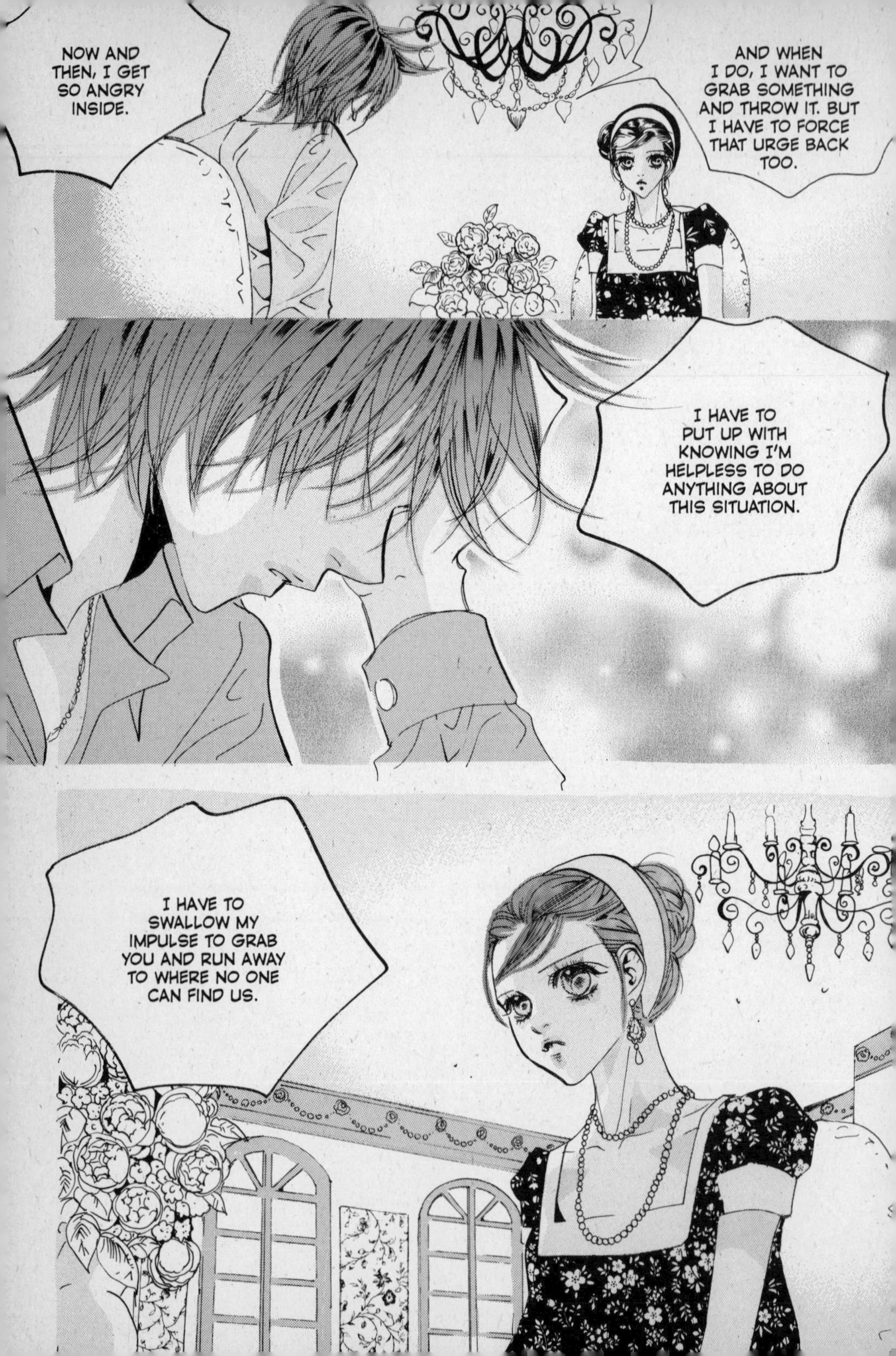
NOW AND THEN, I GET SO ANGRY INSIDE.
AND WHEN I DO, I WANT TO GRAB SOMETHING AND THROW IT. BUT I HAVE TO FORCE THAT URGE BACK TOO.
I HAVE TO PUT UP WITH KNOWING I'M HELPLESS TO DO ANYTHING ABOUT THIS SITUATION.
I HAVE TO SWALLOW MY IMPULSE TO GRAB YOU AND RUN AWAY TO WHERE NO ONE CAN FIND US.

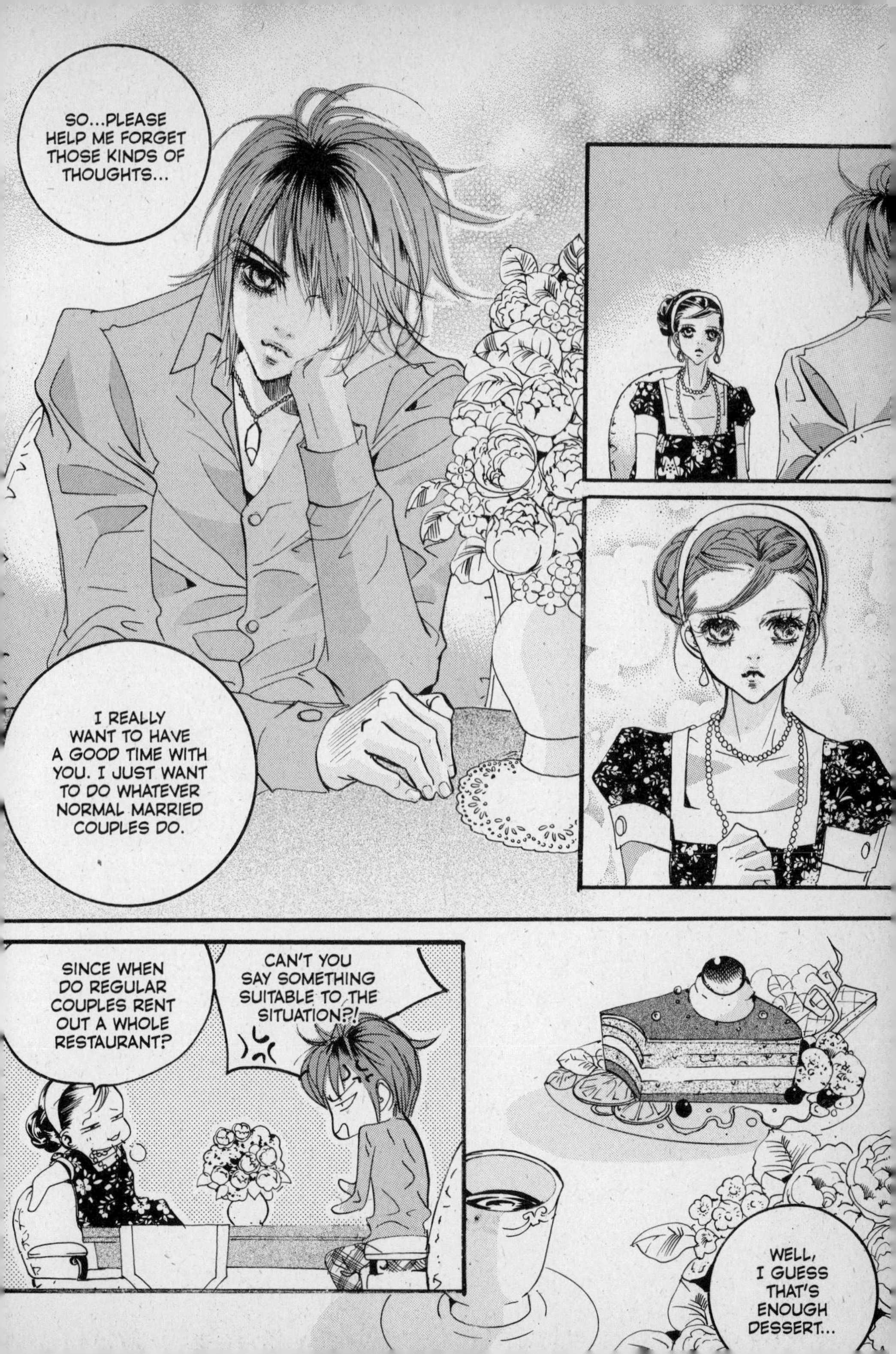
SO...PLEASE HELP ME FORGET THOSE KINDS OF THOUGHTS...
I REALLY WANT TO HAVE A GOOD TIME WITH YOU. I JUST WANT TO DO WHATEVER NORMAL MARRIED COUPLES DO.
CAN'T YOU SAY SOMETHING SUITABLE TO THE SITUATION?!
SINCE WHEN DO REGULAR COUPLES RENT OUT A WHOLE RESTAURANT?
WELL, I GUESS THAT'S ENOUGH DESSERT...

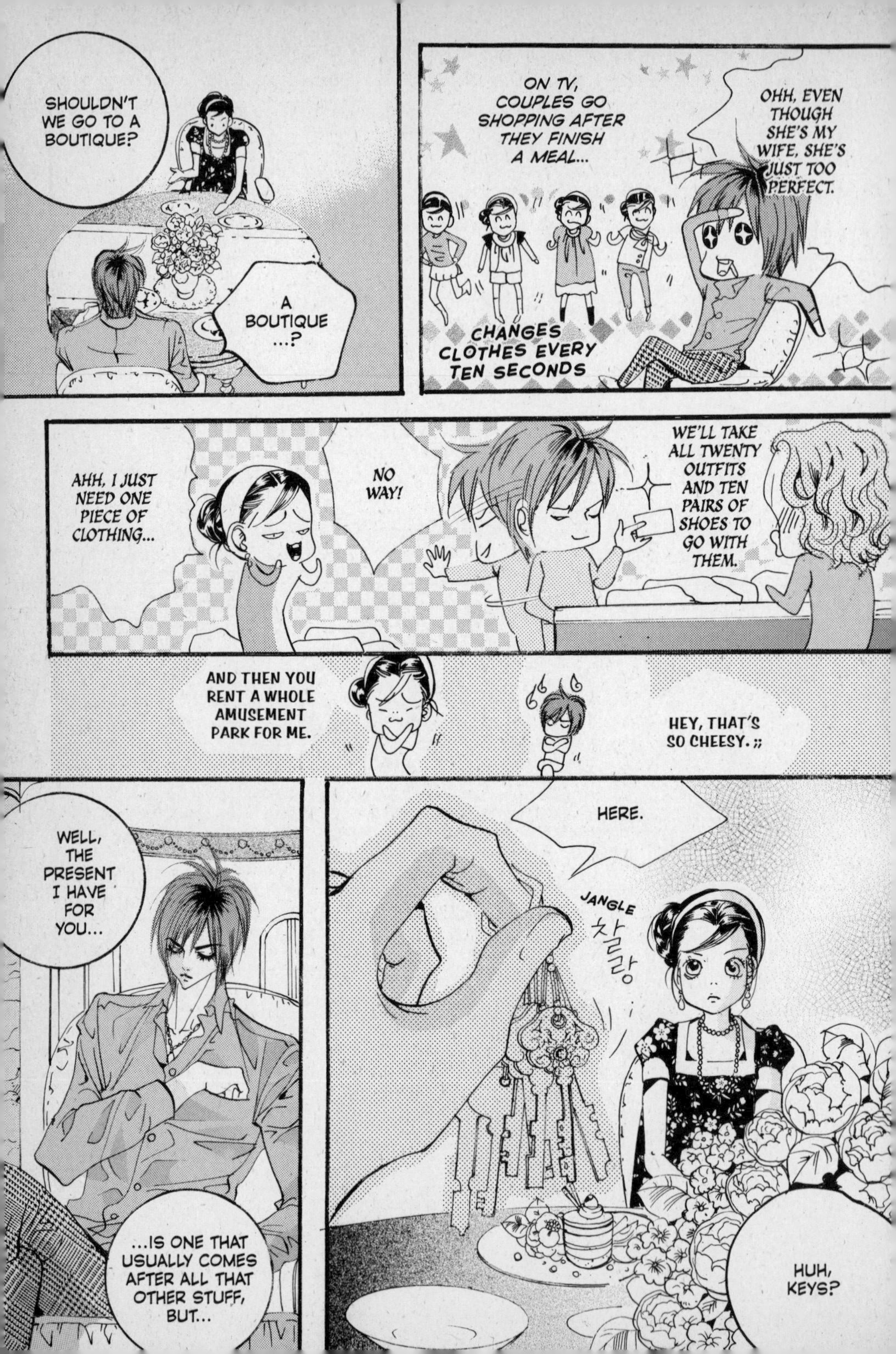
SHOULDN'T WE GO TO A BOUTIQUE?
A BOUTIQUE ...?
ON TV, COUPLES GO SHOPPING AFTER THEY FINISH A MEAL...
OHH, EVEN THOUGH SHE'S MY WIFE, SHE'S JUST TOO PERFECT.
CHANGES CLOTHES EVERY TEN SECONDS
AHH, I JUST NEED ONE PIECE OF CLOTHING...
NO WAY!
WE'LL TAKE ALL TWENTY OUTFITS AND TEN PAIRS OF SHOES TO GO WITH THEM.
AND THEN YOU RENT A WHOLE AMUSEMENT PARK FOR ME.
HEY, THAT'S SO CHEESY. ;;
WELL, THE PRESENT I HAVE FOR YOU...
...IS ONE THAT USUALLY COMES AFTER ALL THAT OTHER STUFF, BUT...
HERE.
JANGLE
찰랑
HUH, KEYS?

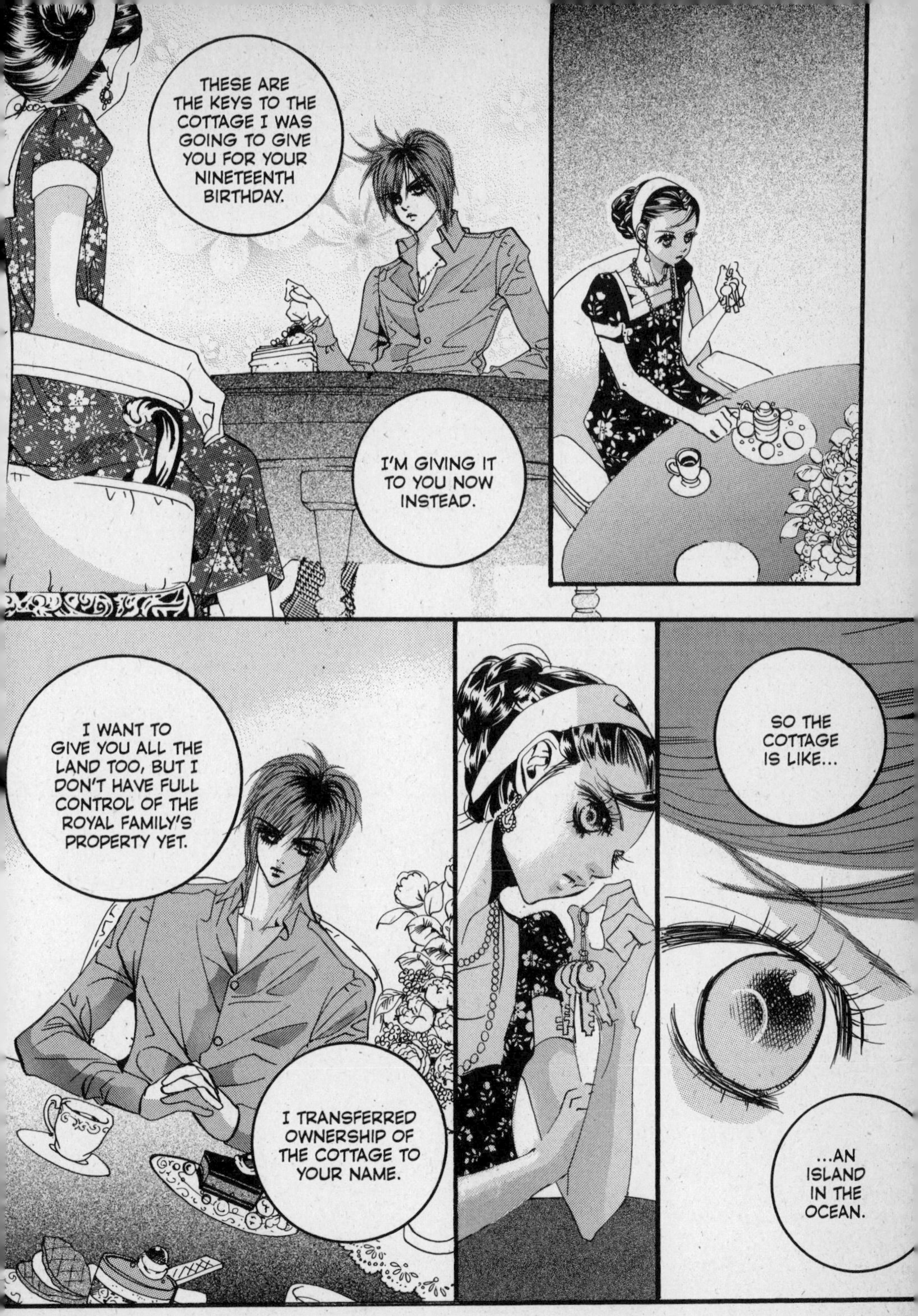
THESE ARE THE KEYS TO THE COTTAGE I WAS GOING TO GIVE YOU FOR YOUR NINETEENTH BIRTHDAY.
I'M GIVING IT TO YOU NOW INSTEAD.
I WANT TO GIVE YOU ALL THE LAND TOO, BUT I DON'T HAVE FULL CONTROL OF THE ROYAL FAMILY'S PROPERTY YET.
I TRANSFERRED OWNERSHIP OF THE COTTAGE TO YOUR NAME.
SO THE COTTAGE IS LIKE...
...AN ISLAND IN THE OCEAN.

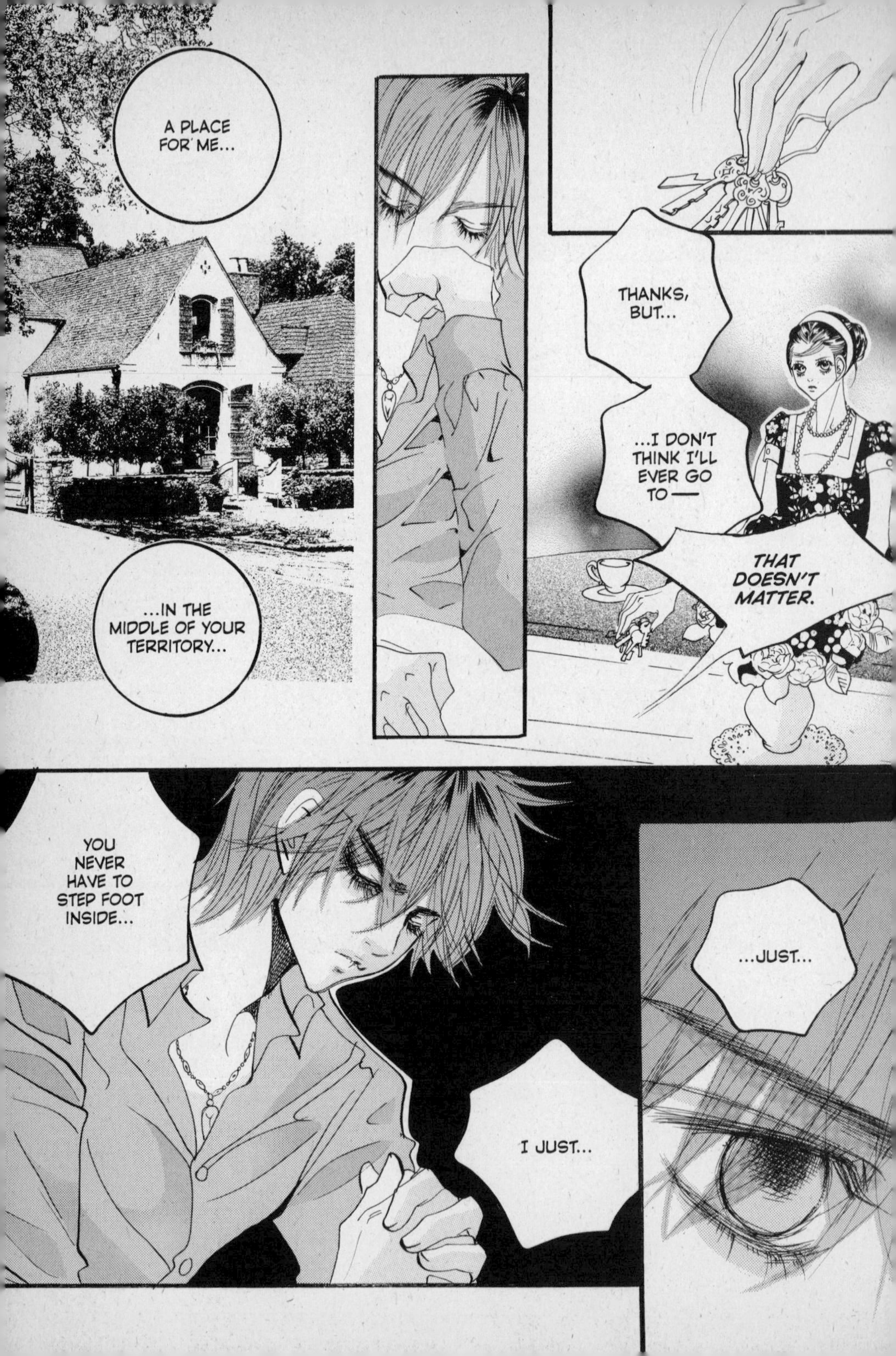
A PLACE FOR ME...
...IN THE MIDDLE OF YOUR TERRITORY...
THANKS, BUT...
...I DON'T THINK I'LL EVER GO TO—
THAT DOESN'T MATTER.
YOU NEVER HAVE TO STEP FOOT INSIDE...
I JUST...
...JUST...

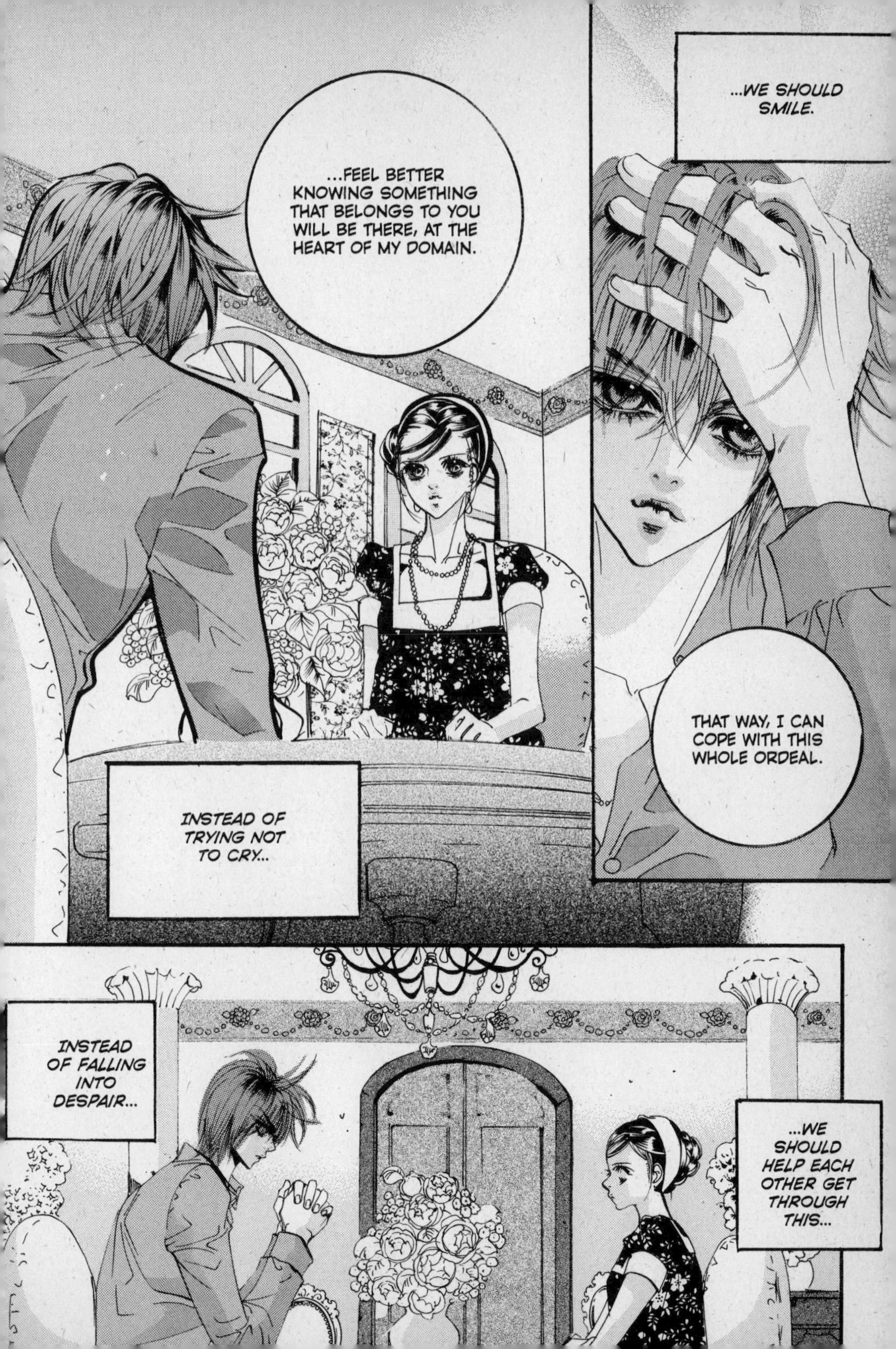
...FEEL BETTER KNOWING SOMETHING THAT BELONGS TO YOU WILL BE THERE, AT THE HEART OF MY DOMAIN.
...WE SHOULD SMILE.
INSTEAD OF TRYING NOT TO CRY...
THAT WAY, I CAN COPE WITH THIS WHOLE ORDEAL.
INSTEAD OF FALLING INTO DESPAIR...
...WE SHOULD HELP EACH OTHER GET THROUGH THIS...

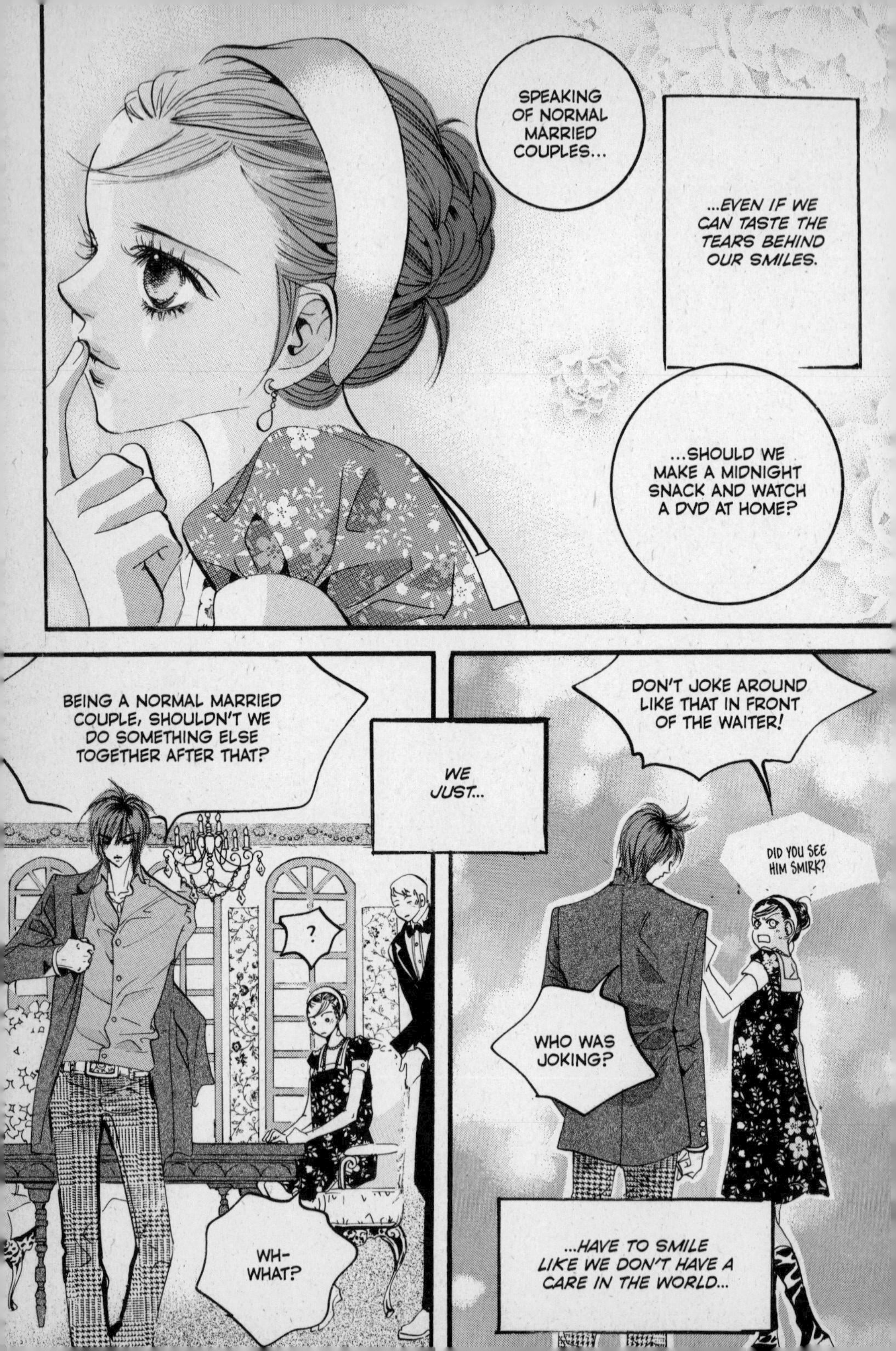
SPEAKING OF NORMAL MARRIED COUPLES...
...EVEN IF WE CAN TASTE THE TEARS BEHIND OUR SMILES.
...SHOULD WE MAKE A MIDNIGHT SNACK AND WATCH A DVD AT HOME?
BEING A NORMAL MARRIED COUPLE, SHOULDN'T WE DO SOMETHING ELSE TOGETHER AFTER THAT?
?
WH- WHAT?
WE JUST...
DON'T JOKE AROUND LIKE THAT IN FRONT OF THE WAITER!
DID YOU SEE HIM SMIRK?
WHO WAS JOKING?
...HAVE TO SMILE LIKE WE DON'T HAVE A CARE IN THE WORLD...

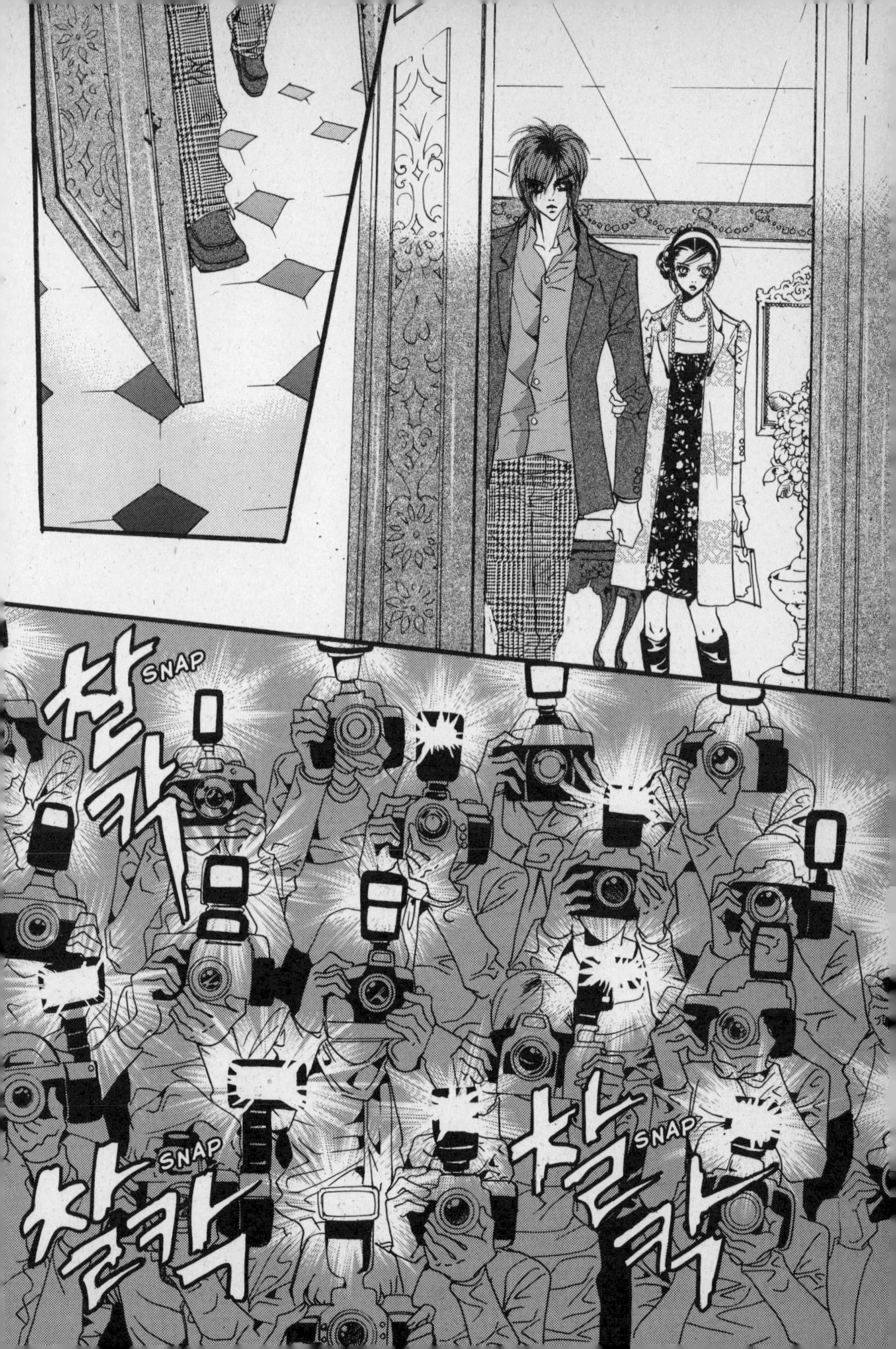

찰칵
SNAP
찰칵
SNAP
찰칵
SNAP

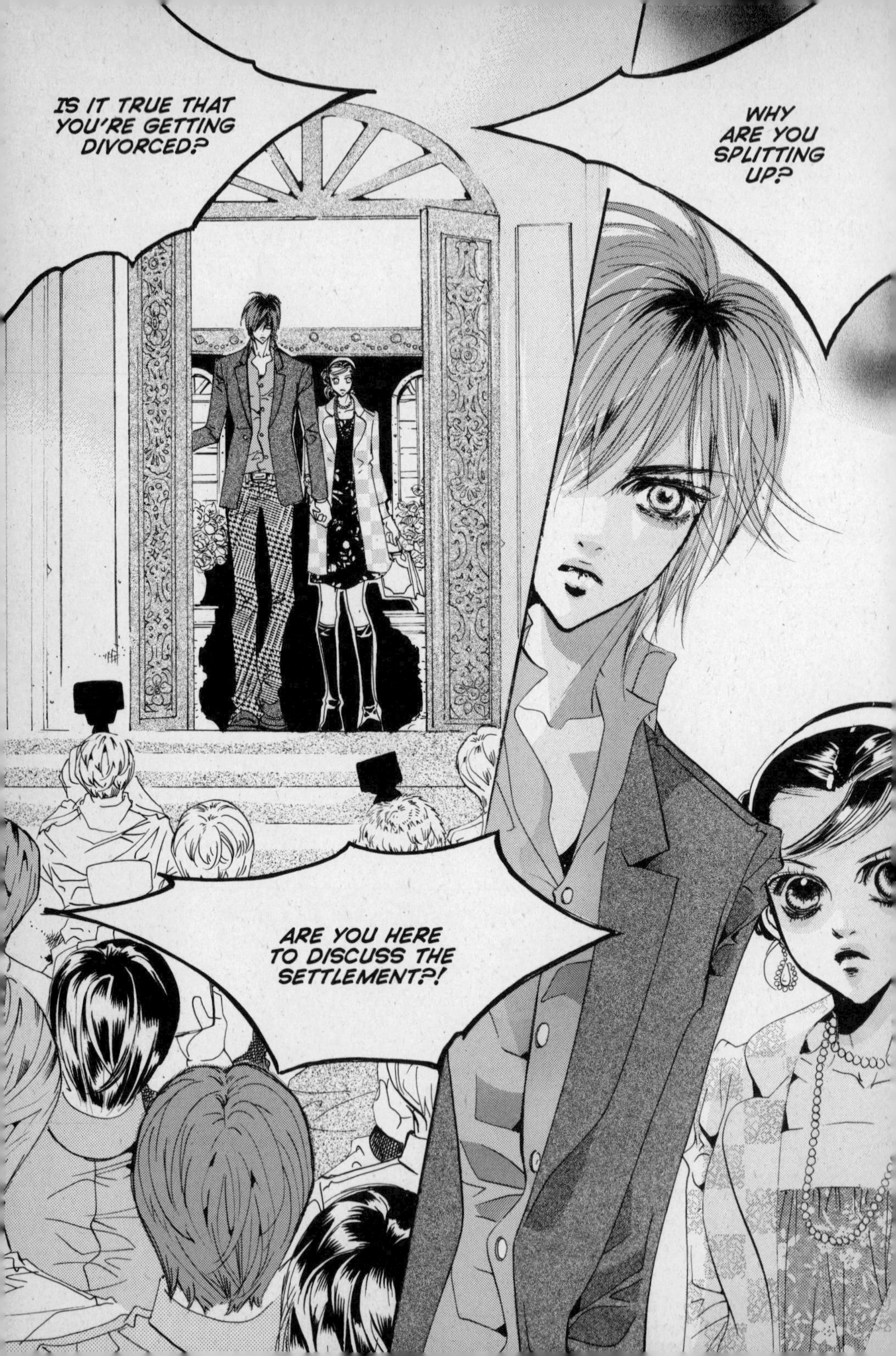
WHY ARE YOU SPLITTING UP?
IS IT TRUE THAT YOU'RE GETTING DIVORCED?
ARE YOU HERE TO DISCUSS THE SETTLEMENT?!

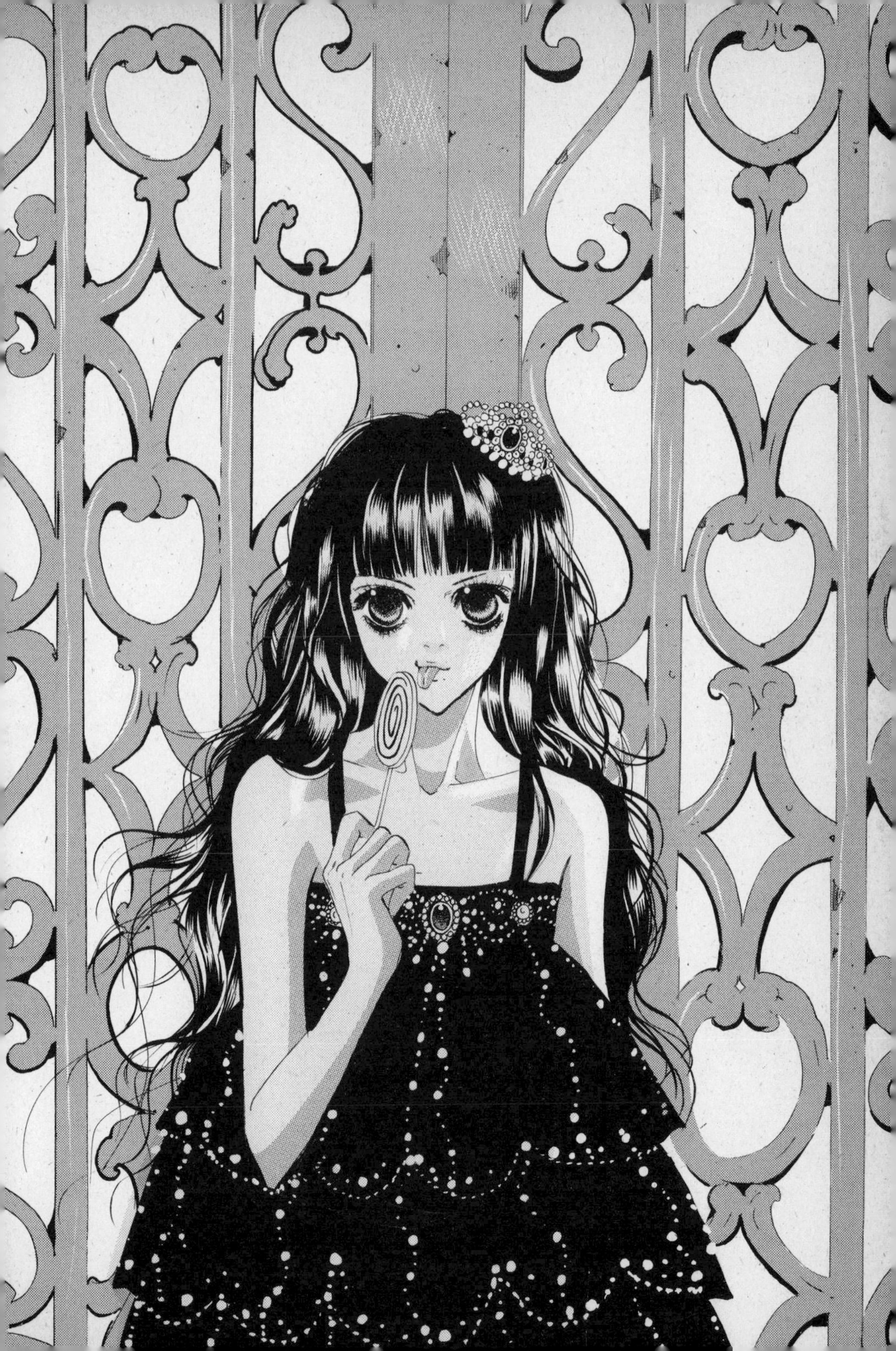

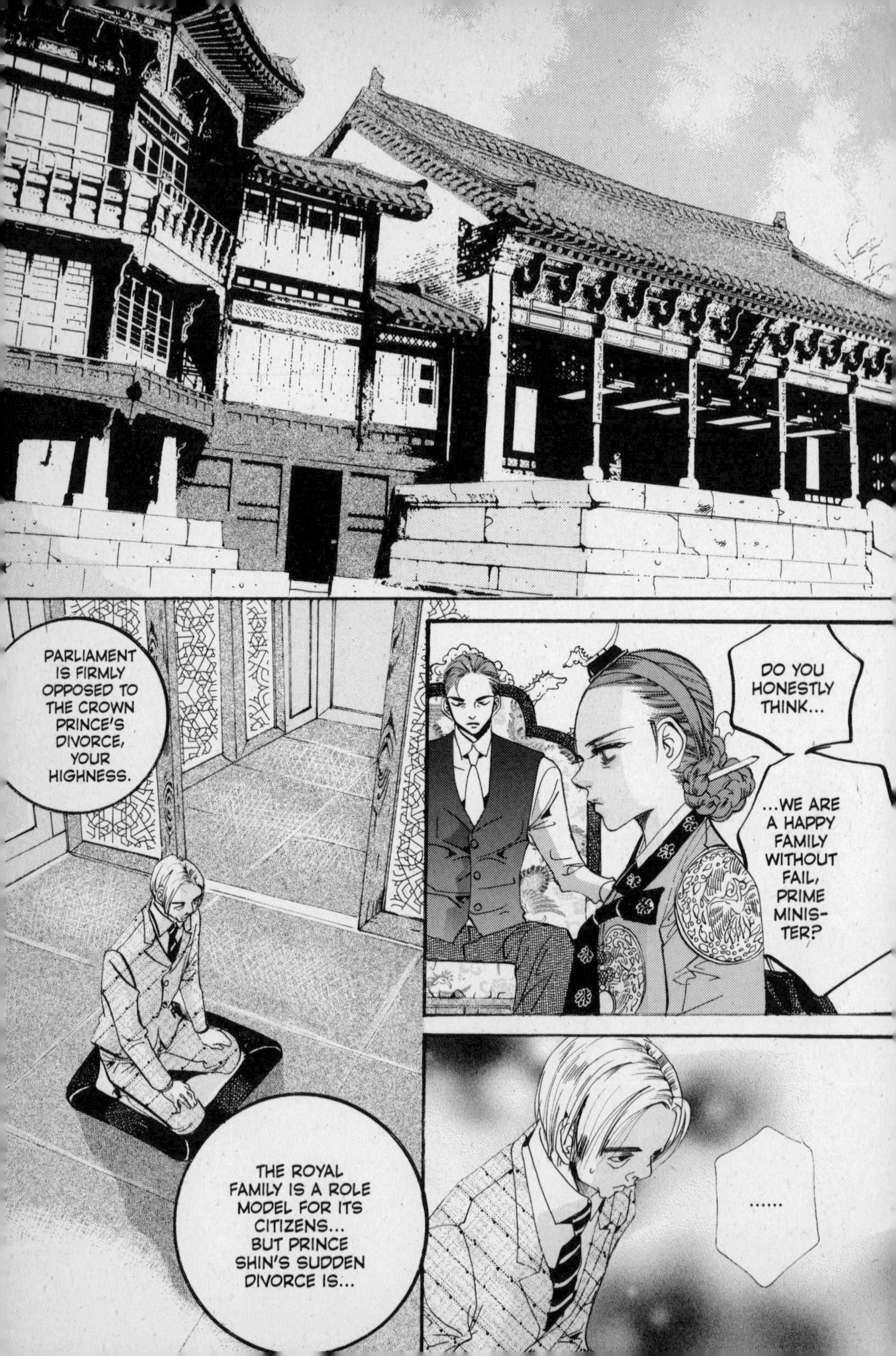
PARLIAMENT IS FIRMLY OPPOSED TO THE CROWN PRINCE'S DIVORCE, YOUR HIGHNESS.
THE ROYAL FAMILY IS A ROLE MODEL FOR ITS CITIZENS... BUT PRINCE SHIN'S SUDDEN DIVORCE IS...
DO YOU HONESTLY THINK...
...WE ARE A HAPPY FAMILY WITHOUT FAIL, PRIME MINIS-TER?
......

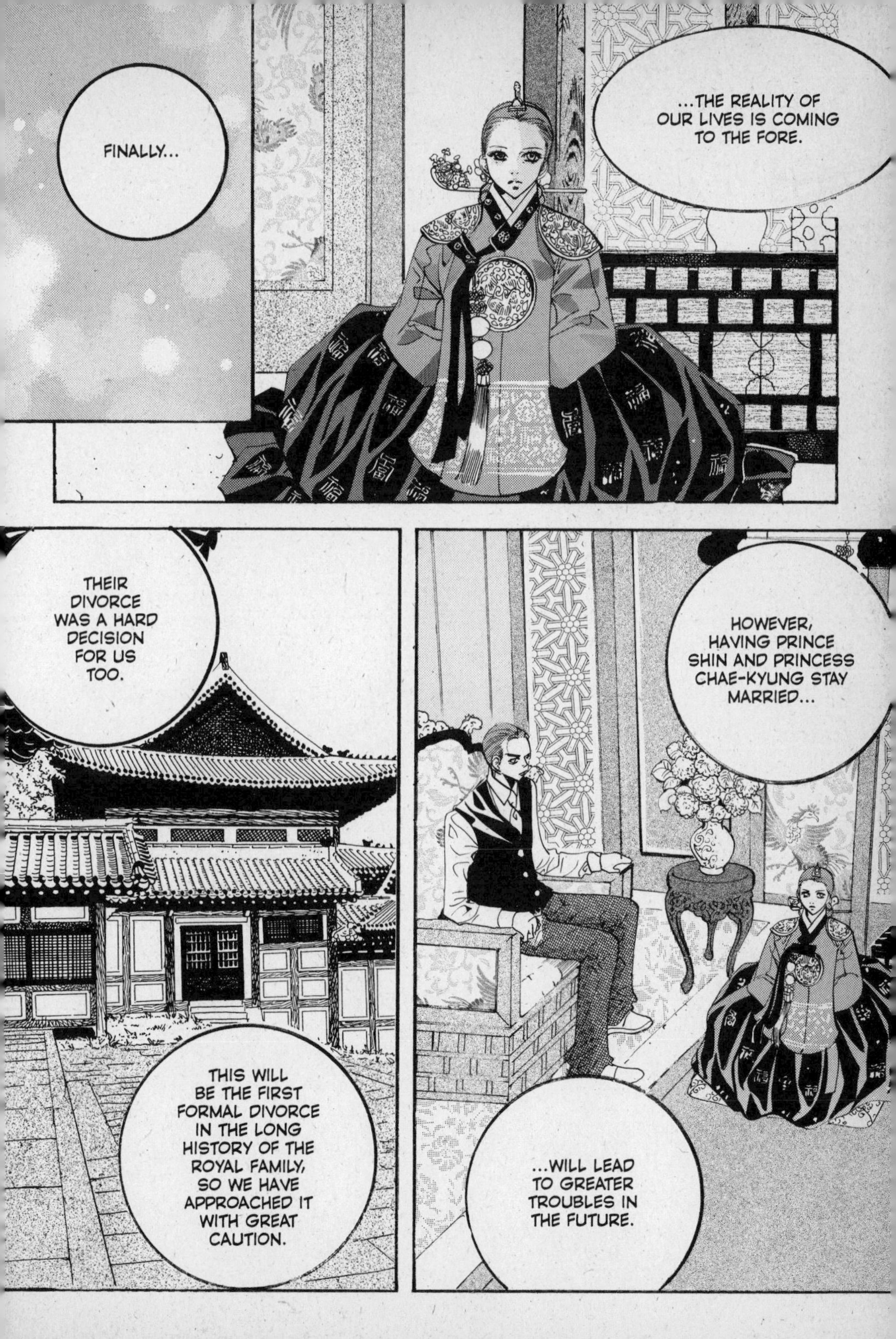
FINALLY...
...THE REALITY OF OUR LIVES IS COMING TO THE FORE.
THEIR DIVORCE WAS A HARD DECISION FOR US TOO.
THIS WILL BE THE FIRST FORMAL DIVORCE IN THE LONG HISTORY OF THE ROYAL FAMILY, SO WE HAVE APPROACHED IT WITH GREAT CAUTION.
HOWEVER, HAVING PRINCE SHIN AND PRINCESS CHAE-KYUNG STAY MARRIED...
...WILL LEAD TO GREATER TROUBLES IN THE FUTURE.

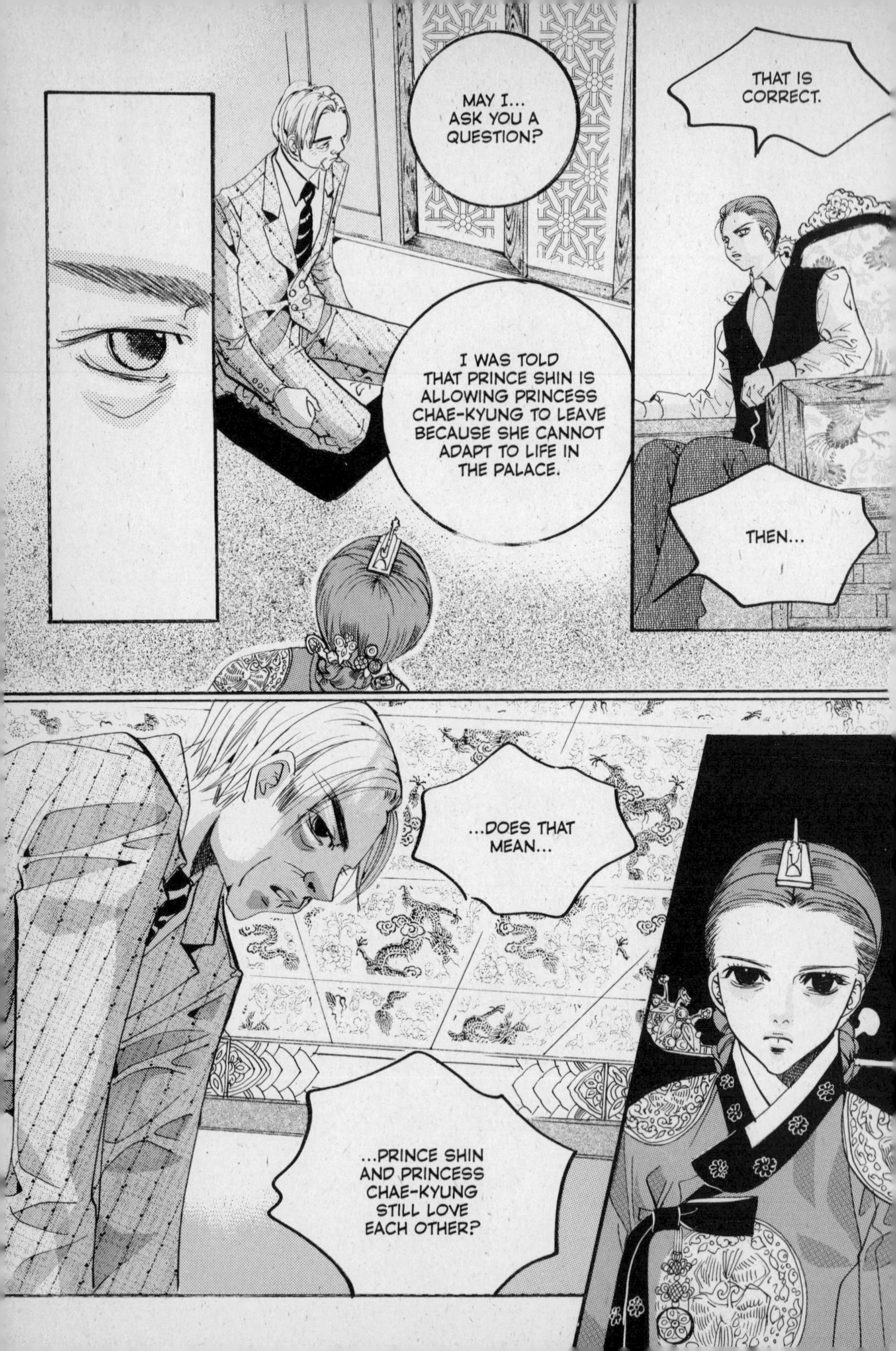
MAY I... ASK YOU A QUESTION?
THAT IS CORRECT.
I WAS TOLD THAT PRINCE SHIN IS ALLOWING PRINCESS CHAE-KYUNG TO LEAVE BECAUSE SHE CANNOT ADAPT TO LIFE IN THE PALACE.
THEN...
...DOES THAT MEAN...
...PRINCE SHIN AND PRINCESS CHAE-KYUNG STILL LOVE EACH OTHER?

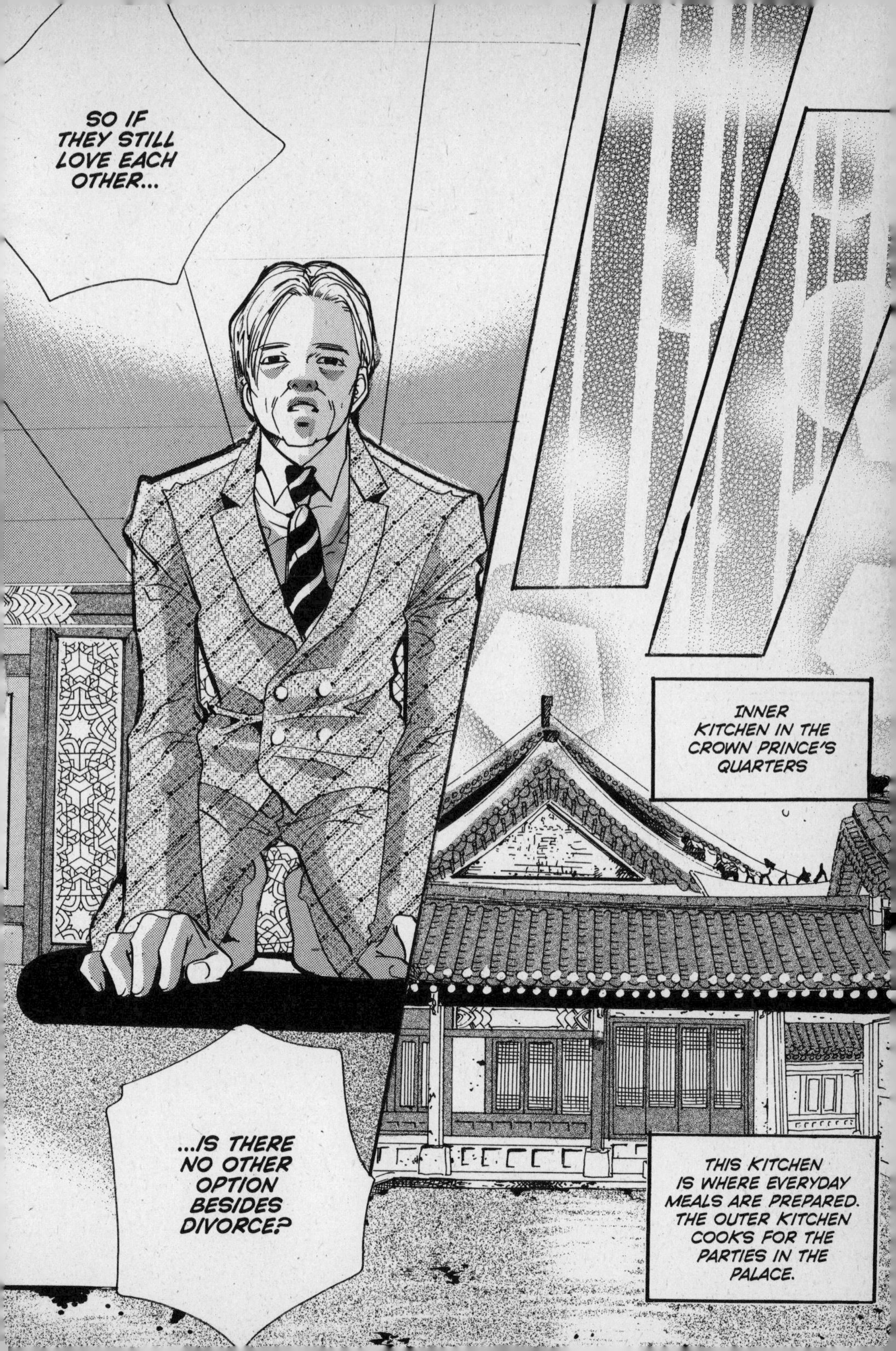
SO IF THEY STILL LOVE EACH OTHER...
INNER KITCHEN IN THE CROWN PRINCE'S QUARTERS
...IS THERE NO OTHER OPTION BESIDES DIVORCE?
THIS KITCHEN IS WHERE EVERYDAY MEALS ARE PREPARED. THE OUTER KITCHEN COOKS FOR THE PARTIES IN THE PALACE.

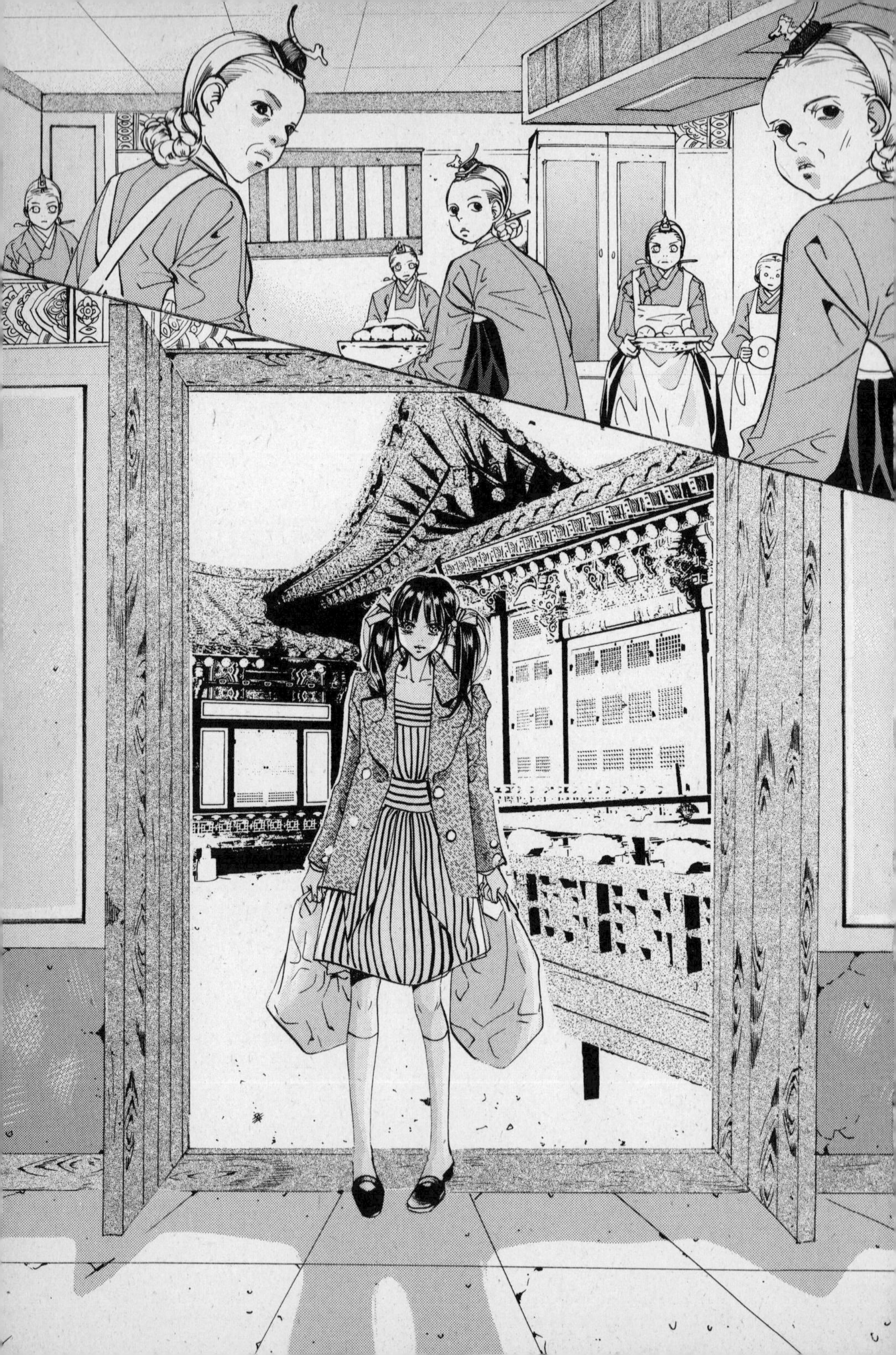

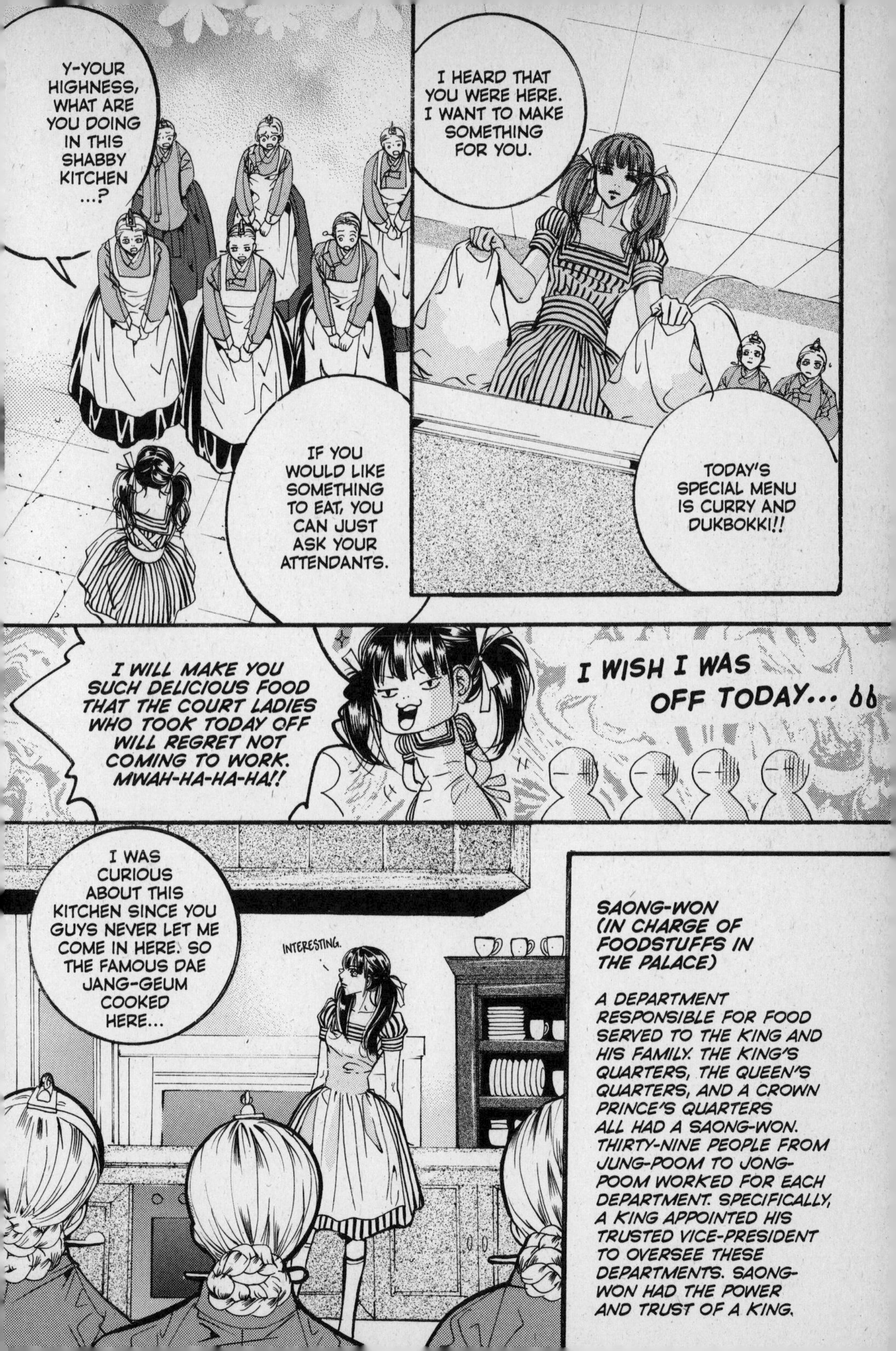
Y-YOUR HIGHNESS, WHAT ARE YOU DOING IN THIS SHABBY KITCHEN ...?
I HEARD THAT YOU WERE HERE. I WANT TO MAKE SOMETHING FOR YOU.
IF YOU WOULD LIKE SOMETHING TO EAT, YOU CAN JUST ASK YOUR ATTENDANTS.
TODAY'S SPECIAL MENU IS CURRY AND DUKBOKKI!!
I WILL MAKE YOU SUCH DELICIOUS FOOD THAT THE COURT LADIES WHO TOOK TODAY OFF WILL REGRET NOT COMING TO WORK. MWAH-HA-HA-HA!!
I WISH I WAS OFF TODAY...
I WAS CURIOUS ABOUT THIS KITCHEN SINCE YOU GUYS NEVER LET ME COME IN HERE. SO THE FAMOUS DAE JANG-GEUM COOKED HERE...
INTERESTING.
SAONG-WON (IN CHARGE OF FOODSTUFFS IN THE PALACE)
A DEPARTMENT RESPONSIBLE FOR FOOD SERVED TO THE KING AND HIS FAMILY. THE KING'S QUARTERS, THE QUEEN'S QUARTERS, AND A CROWN PRINCE'S QUARTERS ALL HAD A SAONG-WON. THIRTY-NINE PEOPLE FROM JUNG-POOM TO JONG-POOM WORKED FOR EACH DEPARTMENT. SPECIFICALLY, A KING APPOINTED HIS TRUSTED VICE-PRESIDENT TO OVERSEE THESE DEPARTMENTS. SAONG-WON HAD THE POWER AND TRUST OF A KING.

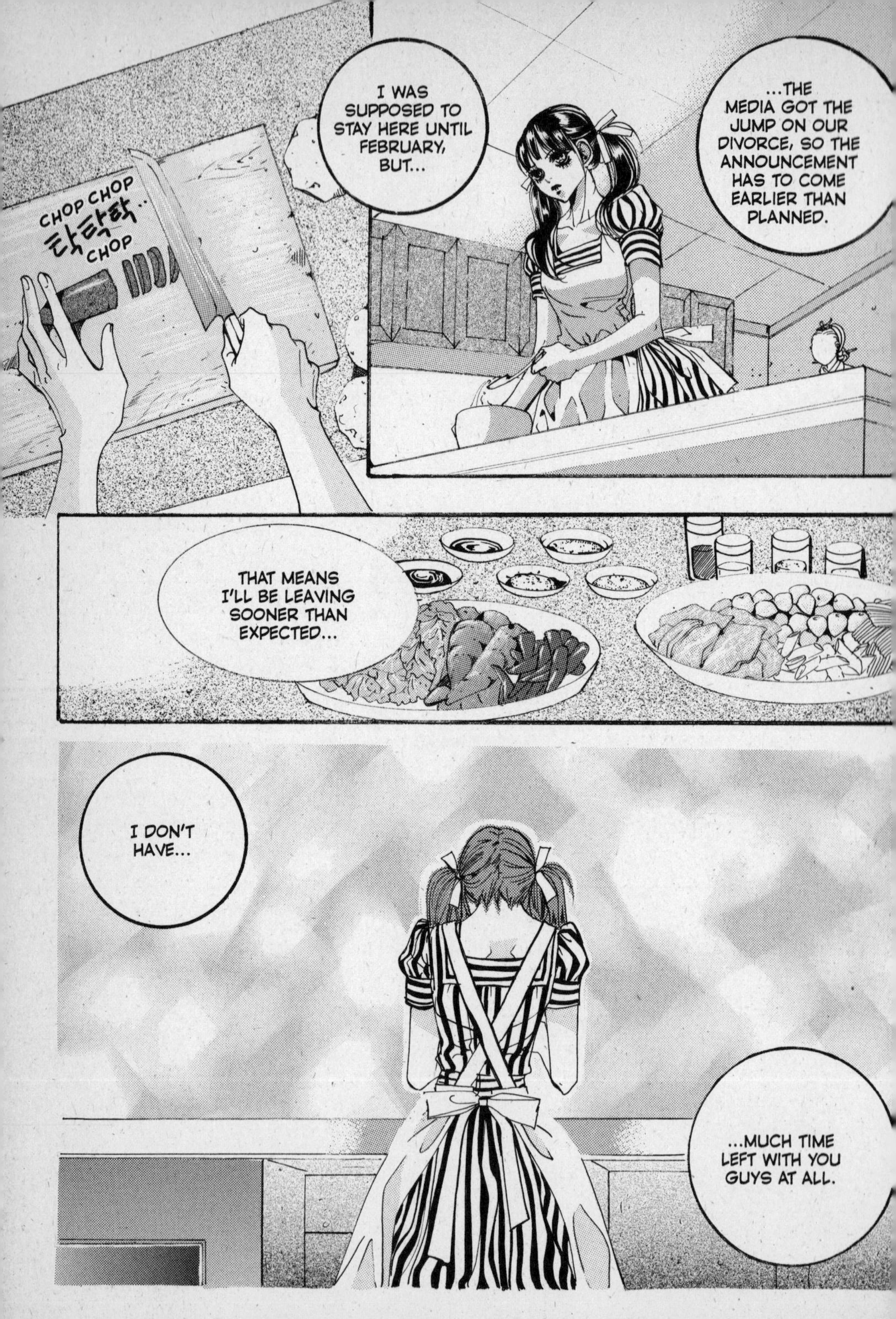
CHOP CHOP
탁탁탁..
CHOP
I WAS SUPPOSED TO STAY HERE UNTIL FEBRUARY, BUT...
...THE MEDIA GOT THE JUMP ON OUR DIVORCE, SO THE ANNOUNCEMENT HAS TO COME EARLIER THAN PLANNED.
THAT MEANS I'LL BE LEAVING SOONER THAN EXPECTED...
I DON'T HAVE...
...MUCH TIME LEFT WITH YOU GUYS AT ALL.

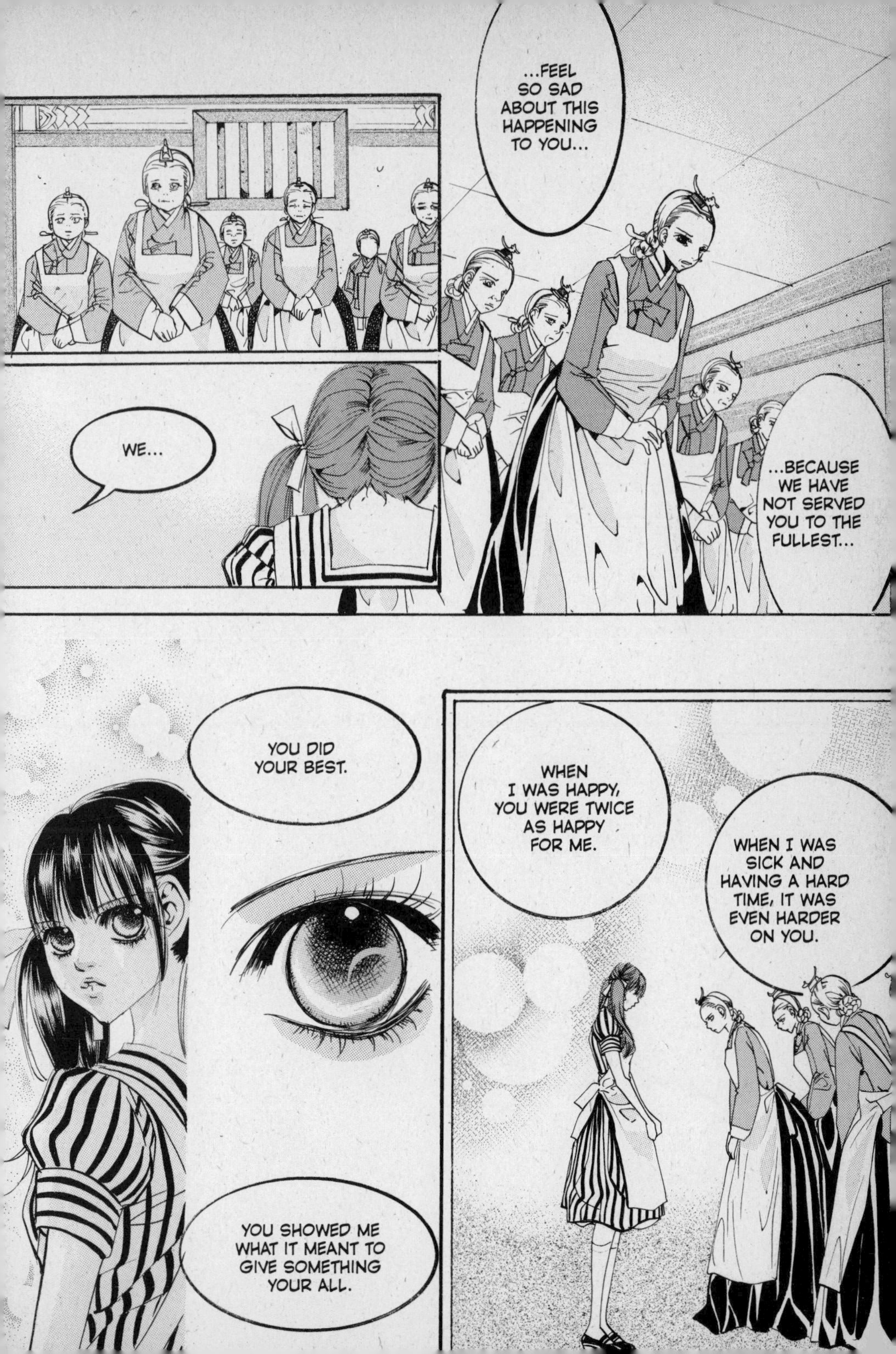
WE...
...FEEL SO SAD ABOUT THIS HAPPENING TO YOU...
...BECAUSE WE HAVE NOT SERVED YOU TO THE FULLEST...
YOU DID YOUR BEST.
YOU SHOWED ME WHAT IT MEANT TO GIVE SOMETHING YOUR ALL.
WHEN I WAS HAPPY, YOU WERE TWICE AS HAPPY FOR ME.
WHEN I WAS SICK AND HAVING A HARD TIME, IT WAS EVEN HARDER ON YOU.

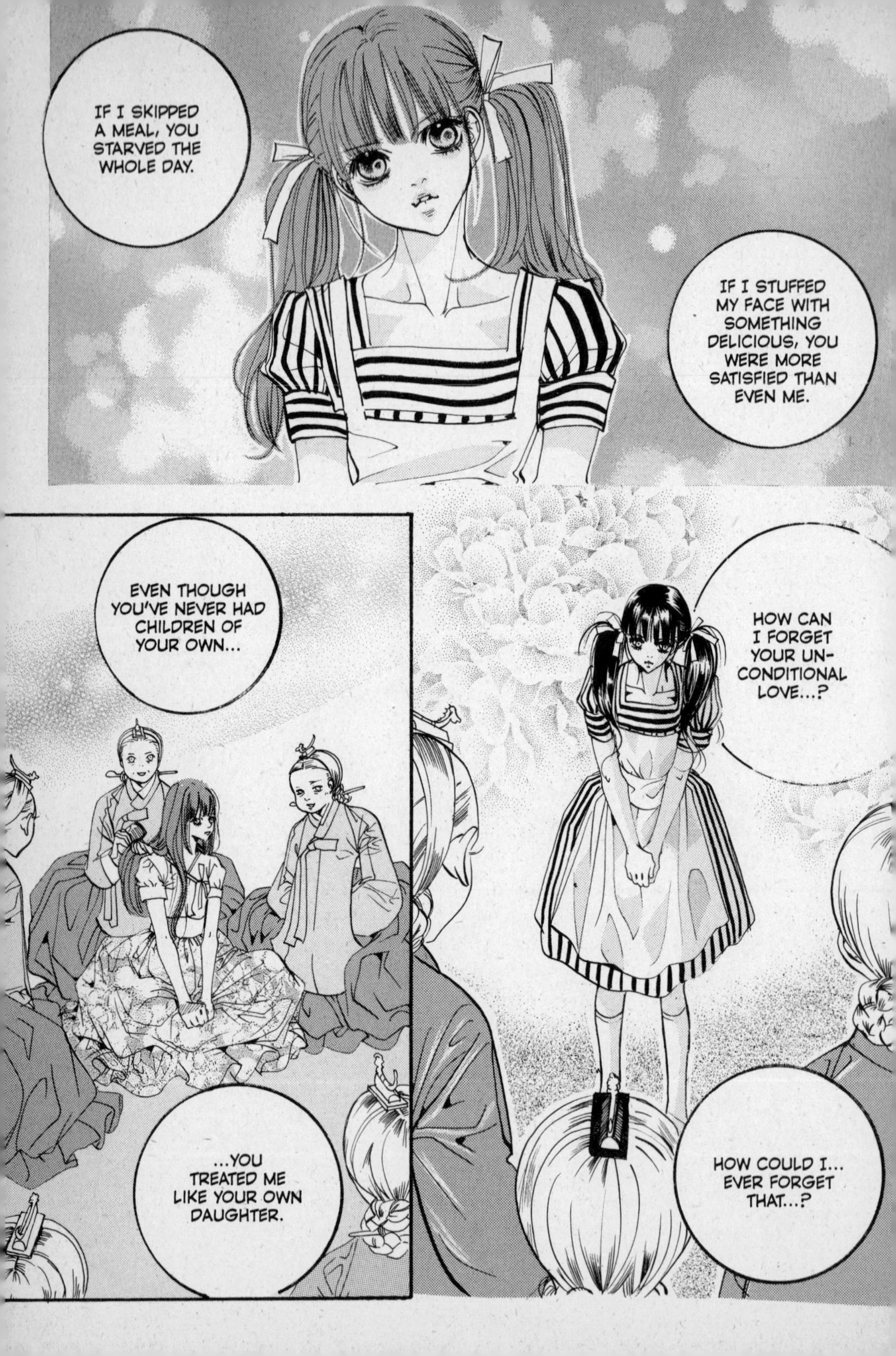
IF I SKIPPED A MEAL, YOU STARVED THE WHOLE DAY.
IF I STUFFED MY FACE WITH SOMETHING DELICIOUS, YOU WERE MORE SATISFIED THAN EVEN ME.
HOW CAN I FORGET YOUR UN-CONDITIONAL LOVE...?
EVEN THOUGH YOU'VE NEVER HAD CHILDREN OF YOUR OWN...
...YOU TREATED ME LIKE YOUR OWN DAUGHTER.
HOW COULD I... EVER FORGET THAT...?

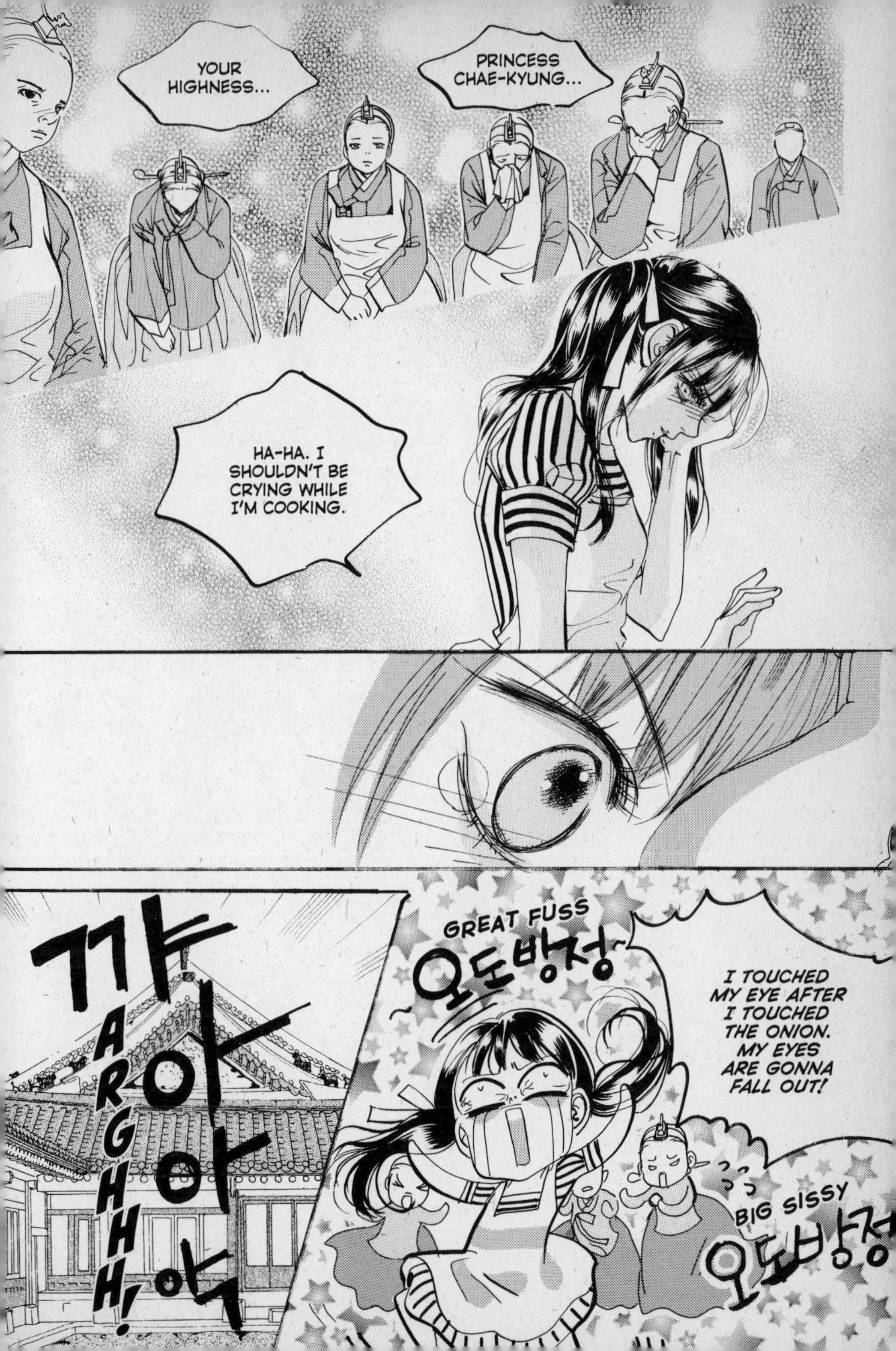
PRINCESS CHAE-KYUNG...
YOUR HIGHNESS...
HA-HA. I SHOULDN'T BE CRYING WHILE I'M COOKING.
꺄아악
ARGHHH!
GREAT FUSS
오도방정
I TOUCHED MY EYE AFTER I TOUCHED THE ONION. MY EYES ARE GONNA FALL OUT!
BIG SISSY
오도방정

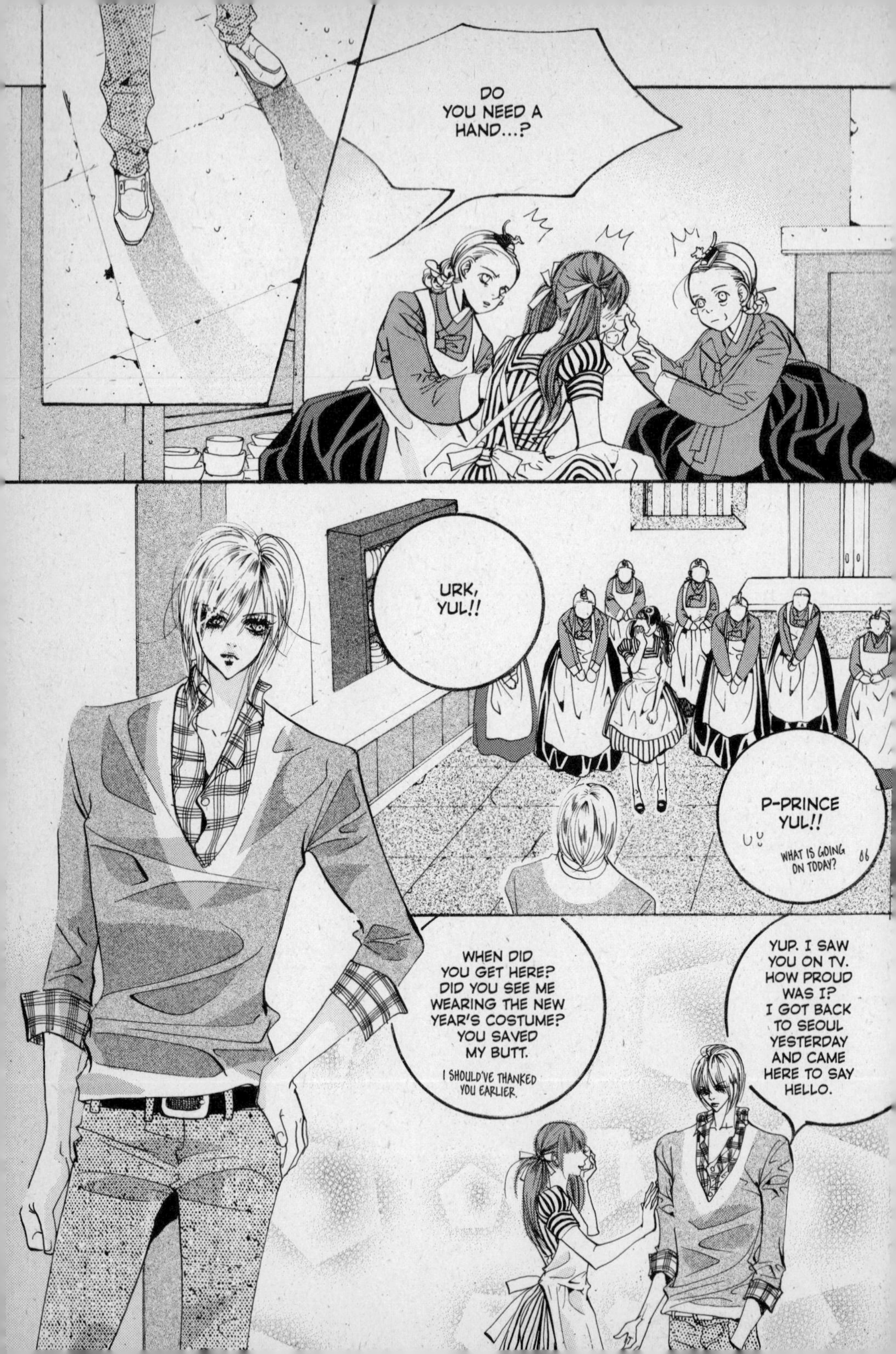
DO YOU NEED A HAND...?
URK, YUL!!
P-PRINCE YUL!!
WHAT IS GOING ON TODAY?
WHEN DID YOU GET HERE? DID YOU SEE ME WEARING THE NEW YEAR'S COSTUME? YOU SAVED MY BUTT.
I SHOULD'VE THANKED YOU EARLIER.
YUP. I SAW YOU ON TV. HOW PROUD WAS I? I GOT BACK TO SEOUL YESTERDAY AND CAME HERE TO SAY HELLO.

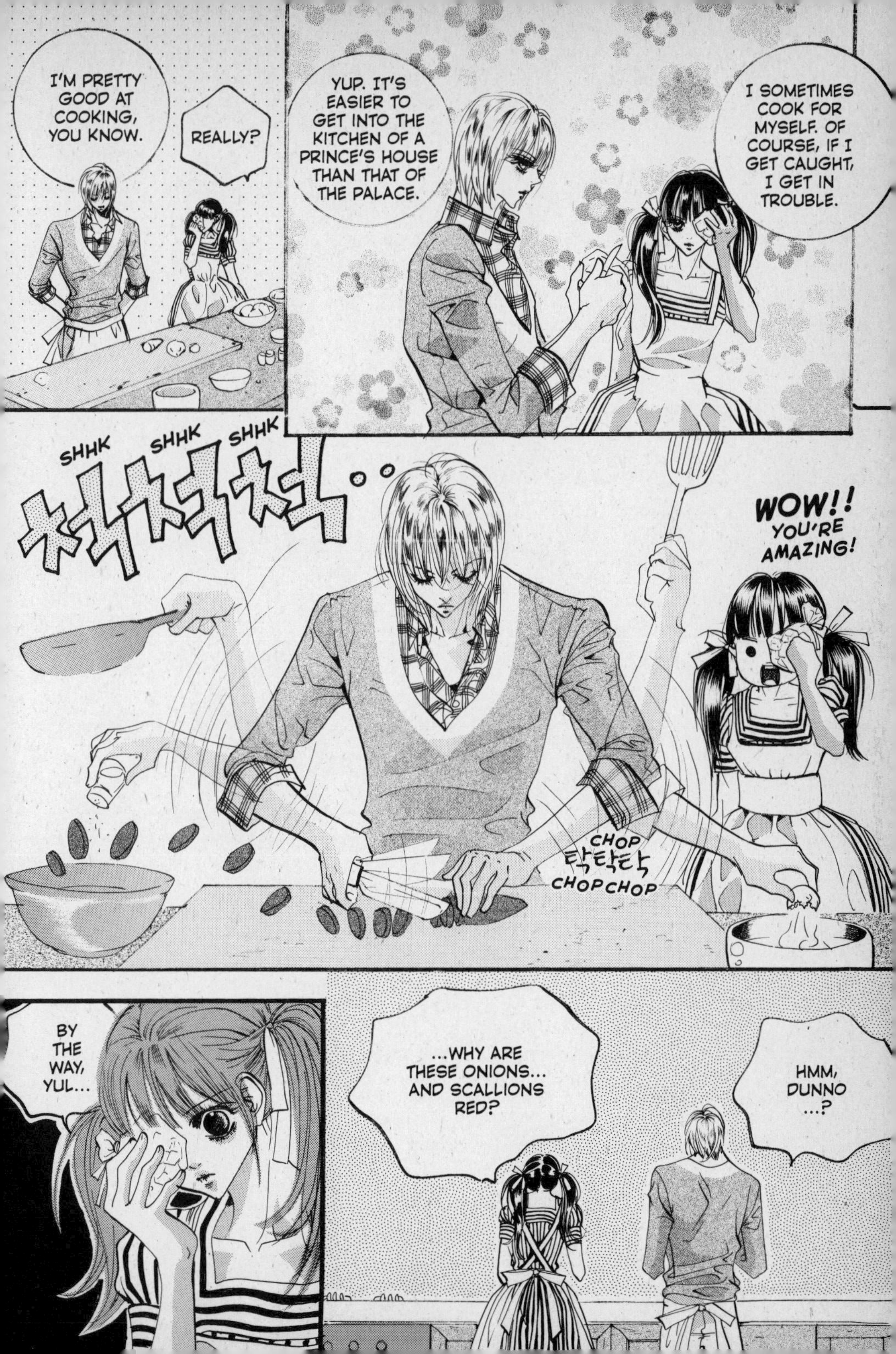
I'M PRETTY GOOD AT COOKING, YOU KNOW.
REALLY?
YUP. IT'S EASIER TO GET INTO THE KITCHEN OF A PRINCE'S HOUSE THAN THAT OF THE PALACE.
I SOMETIMES COOK FOR MYSELF. OF COURSE, IF I GET CAUGHT, I GET IN TROUBLE.
SHHK SHHK SHHK
척척척척...
WOW!! YOU'RE AMAZING!
CHOP 탁탁탁 CHOPCHOP
BY THE WAY, YUL...
...WHY ARE THESE ONIONS... AND SCALLIONS RED?
HMM, DUNNO ...?

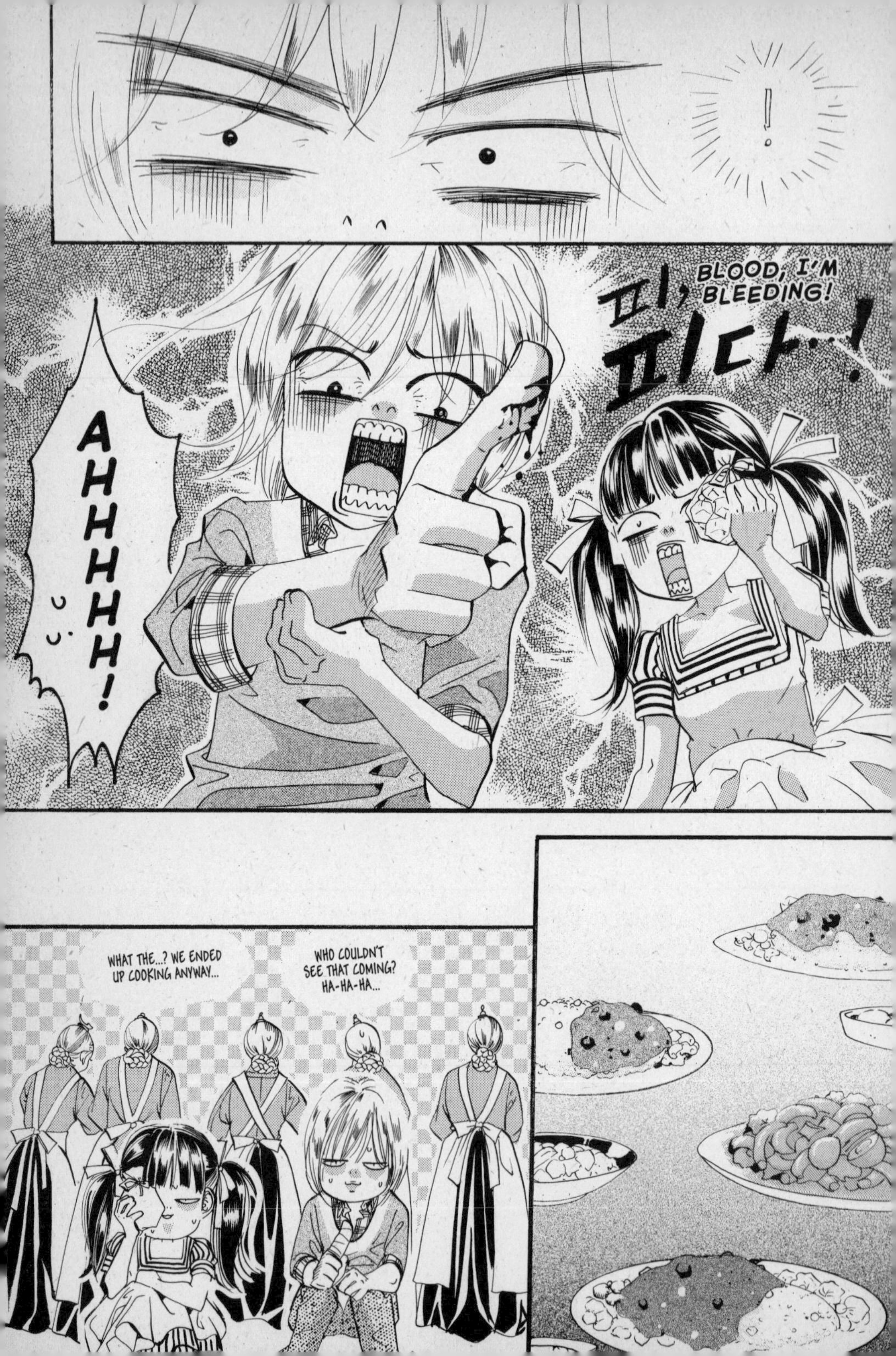
!
BLOOD, I'M BLEEDING!
피, 피다…!
AHHHHH!
WHAT THE...? WE ENDED UP COOKING ANYWAY...
WHO COULDN'T SEE THAT COMING? HA-HA-HA...

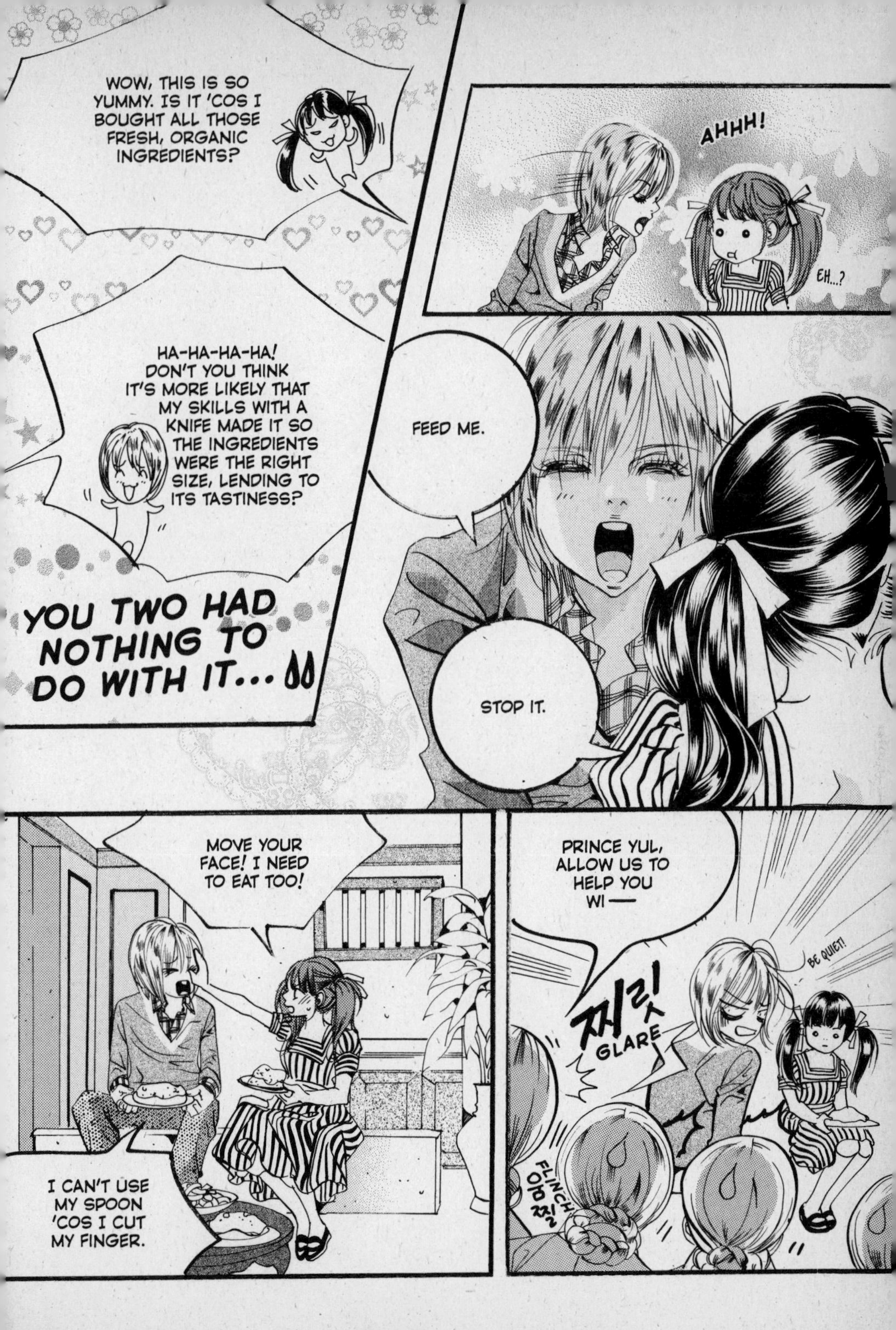
WOW, THIS IS SO YUMMY. IS IT 'COS I BOUGHT ALL THOSE FRESH, ORGANIC INGREDIENTS?
HA-HA-HA-HA! DON'T YOU THINK IT'S MORE LIKELY THAT MY SKILLS WITH A KNIFE MADE IT SO THE INGREDIENTS WERE THE RIGHT SIZE, LENDING TO ITS TASTINESS?
YOU TWO HAD NOTHING TO DO WITH IT...
AHHH!
EH...?
FEED ME.
STOP IT.
MOVE YOUR FACE! I NEED TO EAT TOO!
I CAN'T USE MY SPOON 'COS I CUT MY FINGER.
PRINCE YUL, ALLOW US TO HELP YOU WI—
째릿
GLARE
BE QUIET!
움찔
FLINCH

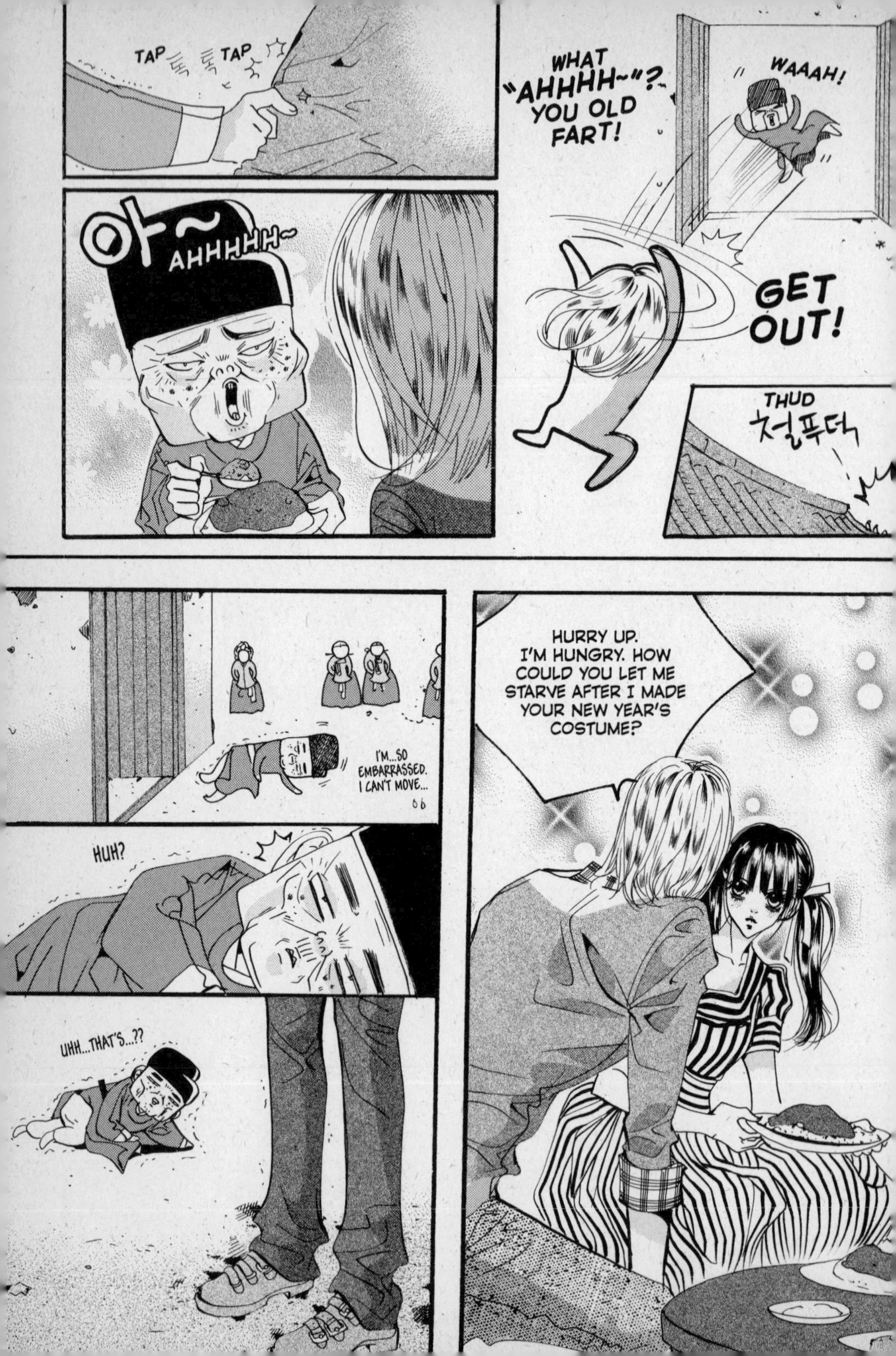
WHAT "AHHHH~"? YOU OLD FART!
WAAAH!
GET OUT!
TAP 톡 톡 TAP
아~ AHHHHH~
THUD 철푸덕
HURRY UP. I'M HUNGRY. HOW COULD YOU LET ME STARVE AFTER I MADE YOUR NEW YEAR'S COSTUME?
I'M...SO EMBARRASSED. I CAN'T MOVE...
HUH?
UHH...THAT'S...??

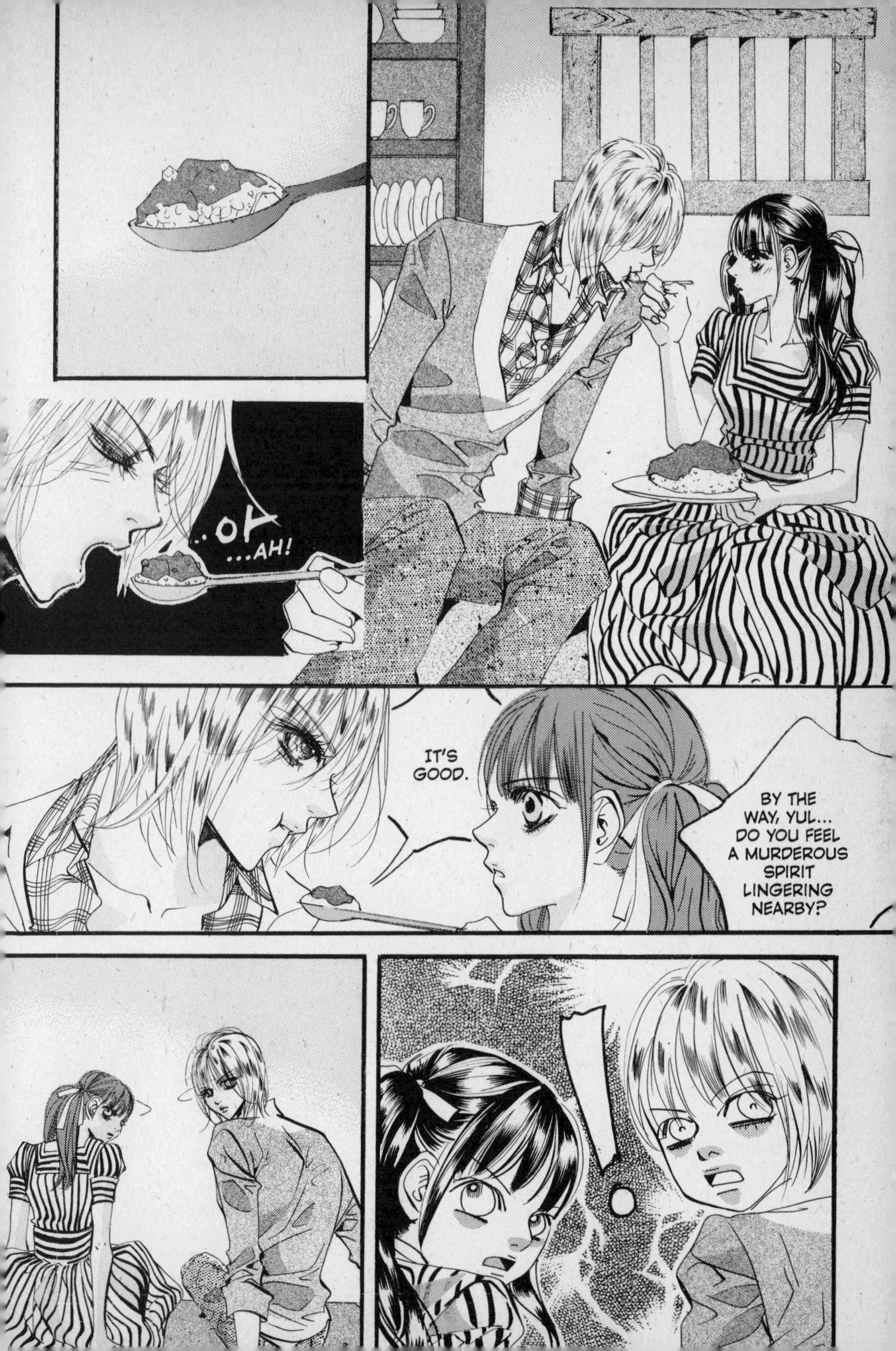
...AH!
IT'S GOOD.
BY THE WAY, YUL... DO YOU FEEL A MURDEROUS SPIRIT LINGERING NEARBY?

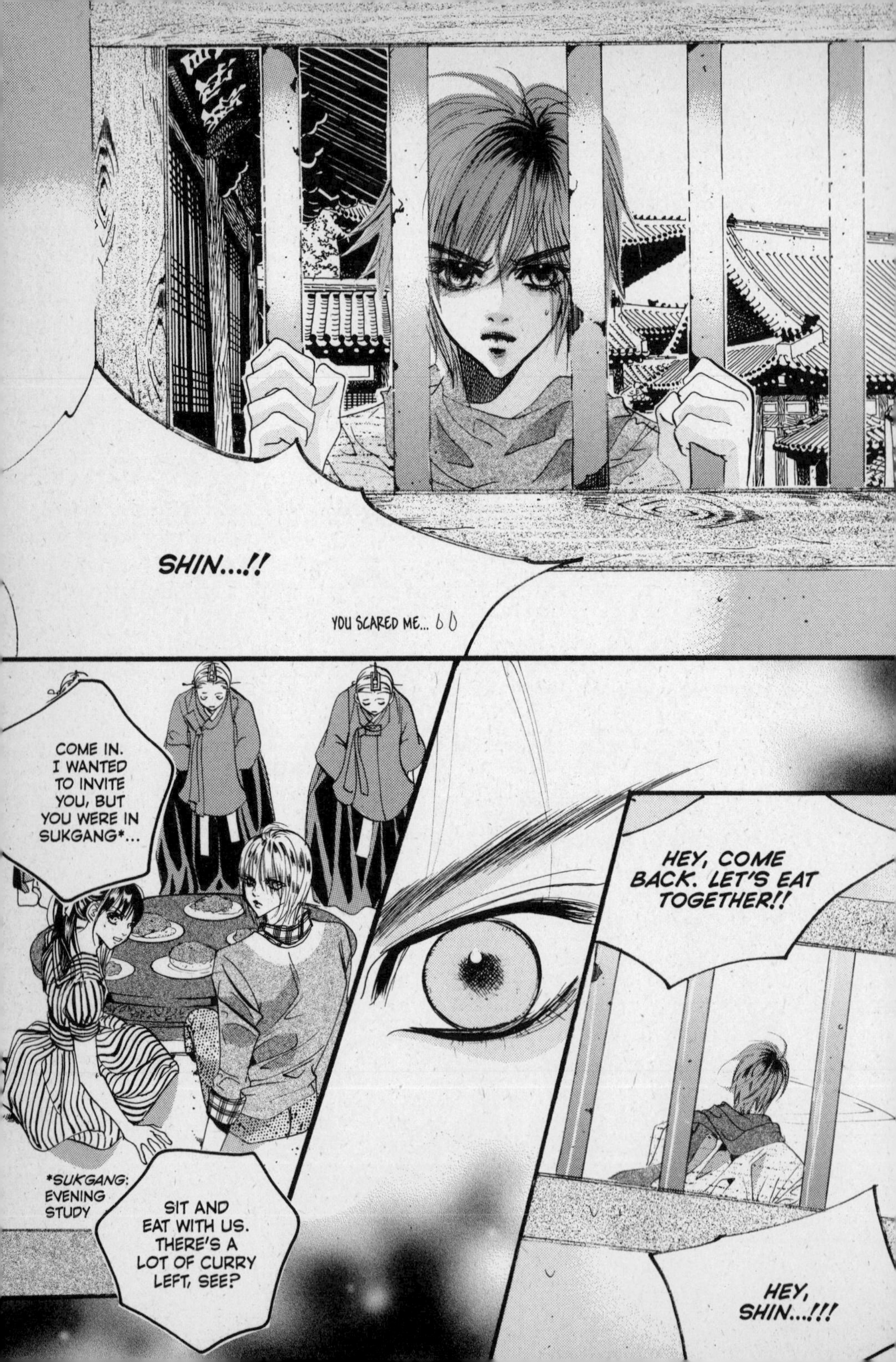
SHIN...!!
YOU SCARED ME...
COME IN. I WANTED TO INVITE YOU, BUT YOU WERE IN SUKGANG*...
SIT AND EAT WITH US. THERE'S A LOT OF CURRY LEFT, SEE?
*SUKGANG: EVENING STUDY
HEY, COME BACK. LET'S EAT TOGETHER!!
HEY, SHIN...!!!

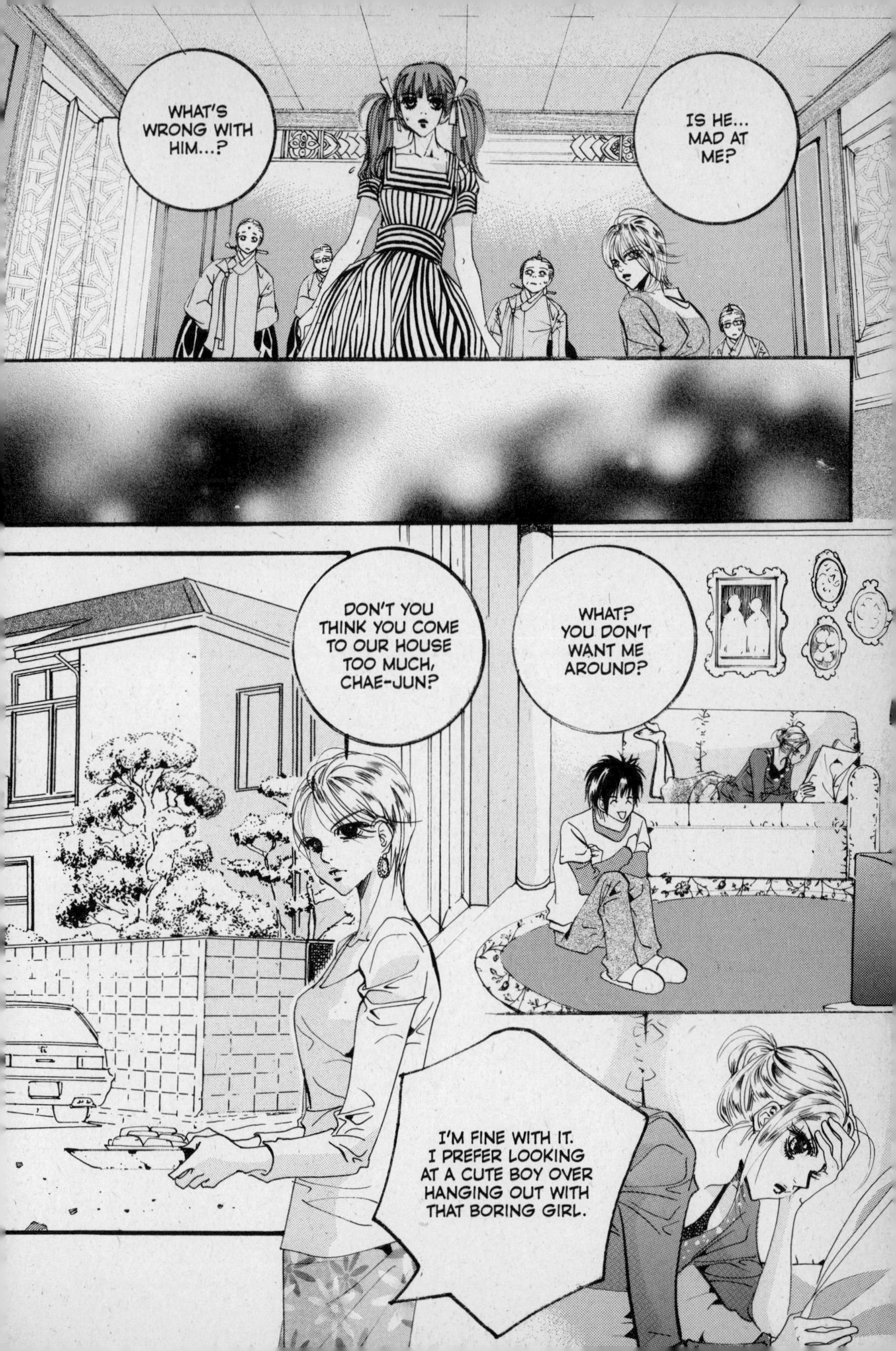
WHAT'S WRONG WITH HIM...?
IS HE... MAD AT ME?
DON'T YOU THINK YOU COME TO OUR HOUSE TOO MUCH, CHAE-JUN?
WHAT? YOU DON'T WANT ME AROUND?
I'M FINE WITH IT. I PREFER LOOKING AT A CUTE BOY OVER HANGING OUT WITH THAT BORING GIRL.

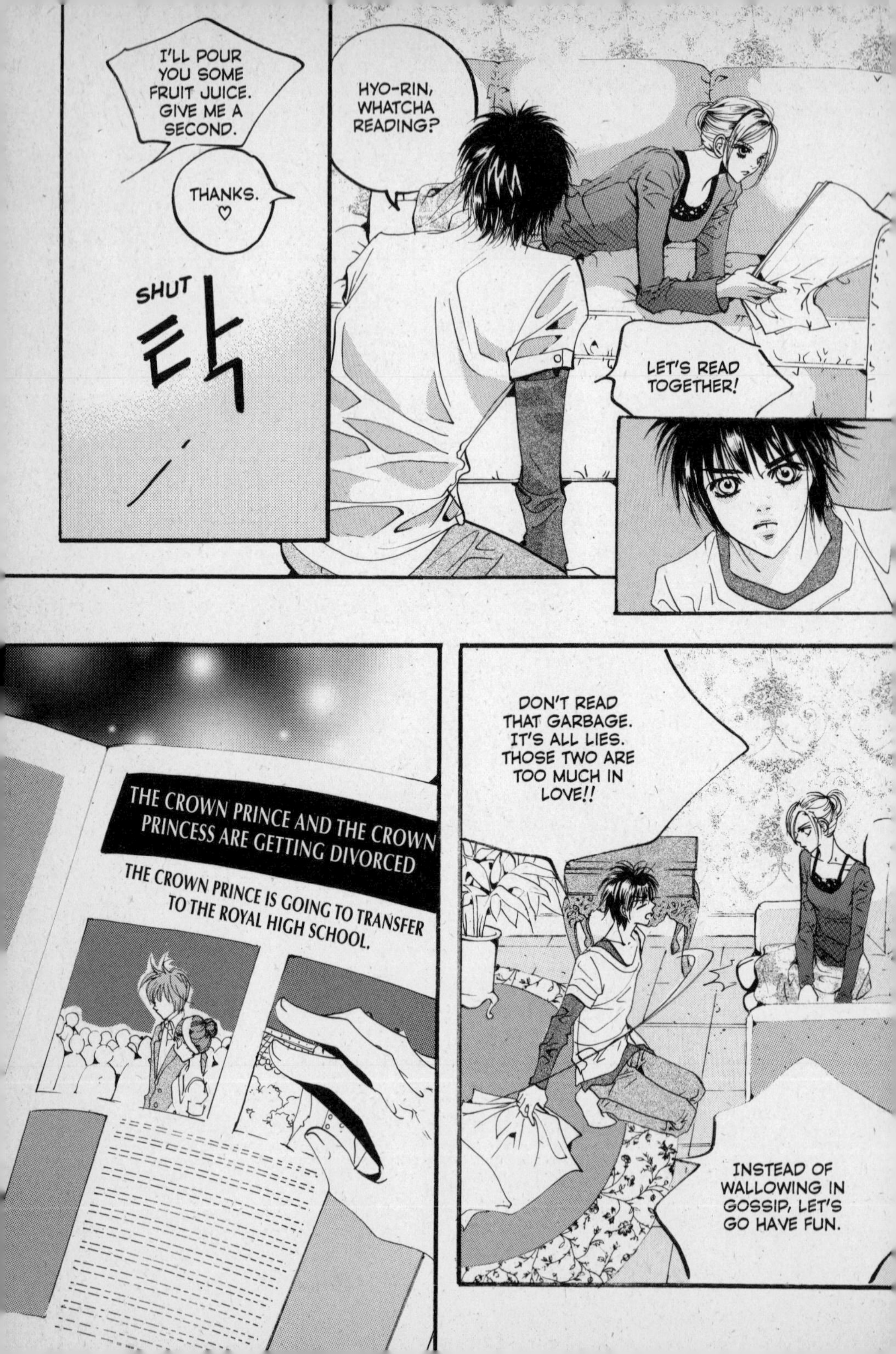
I'LL POUR YOU SOME FRUIT JUICE. GIVE ME A SECOND.
THANKS. ♡
SHUT
탁
HYO-RIN, WHATCHA READING?
LET'S READ TOGETHER!
THE CROWN PRINCE AND THE CROWN PRINCESS ARE GETTING DIVORCED
THE CROWN PRINCE IS GOING TO TRANSFER TO THE ROYAL HIGH SCHOOL.
DON'T READ THAT GARBAGE. IT'S ALL LIES. THOSE TWO ARE TOO MUCH IN LOVE!!
INSTEAD OF WALLOWING IN GOSSIP, LET'S GO HAVE FUN.

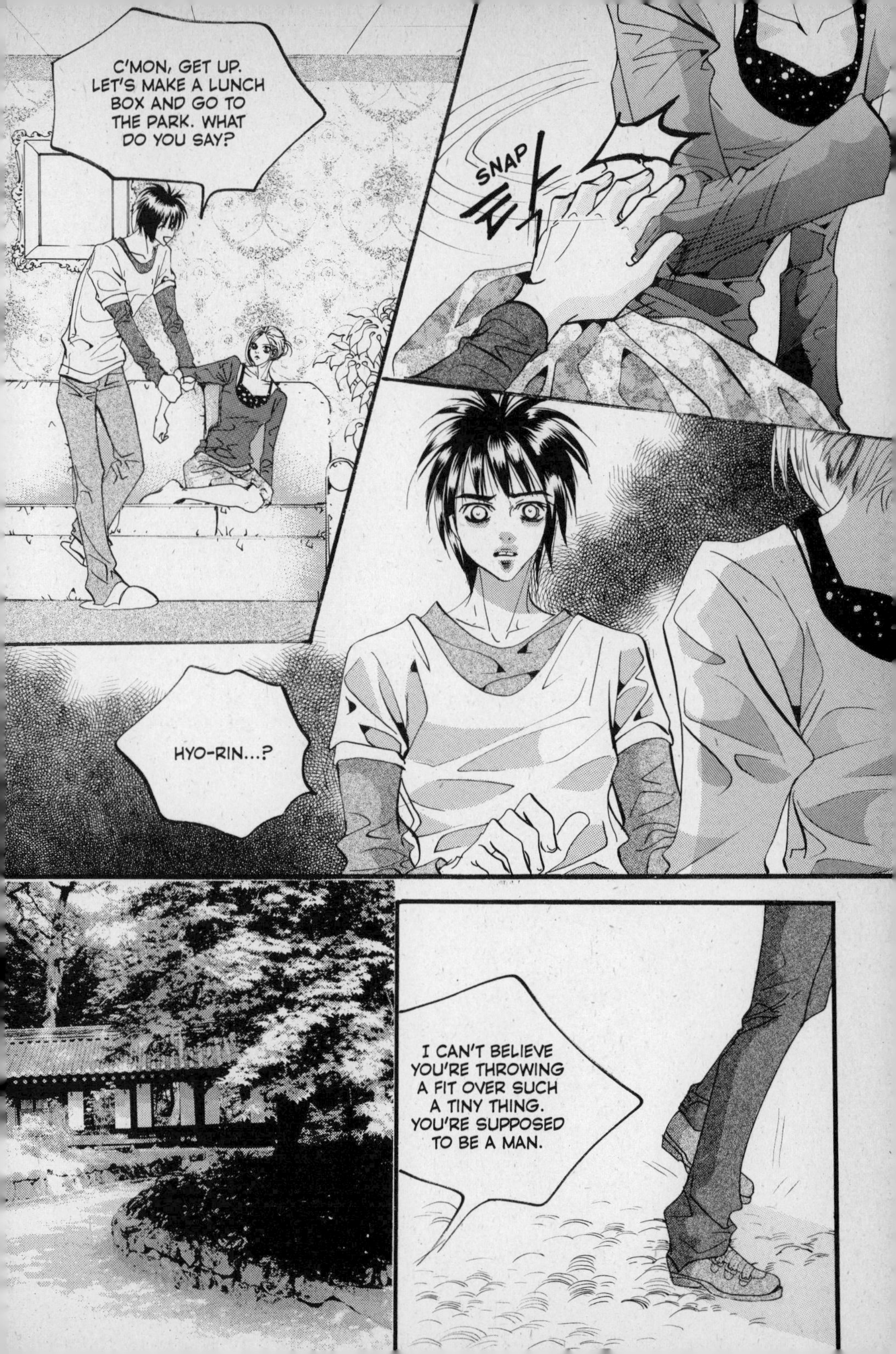

C'MON, GET UP. LET'S MAKE A LUNCH BOX AND GO TO THE PARK. WHAT DO YOU SAY?
SNAP
HYO-RIN...?
I CAN'T BELIEVE YOU'RE THROWING A FIT OVER SUCH A TINY THING. YOU'RE SUPPOSED TO BE A MAN.

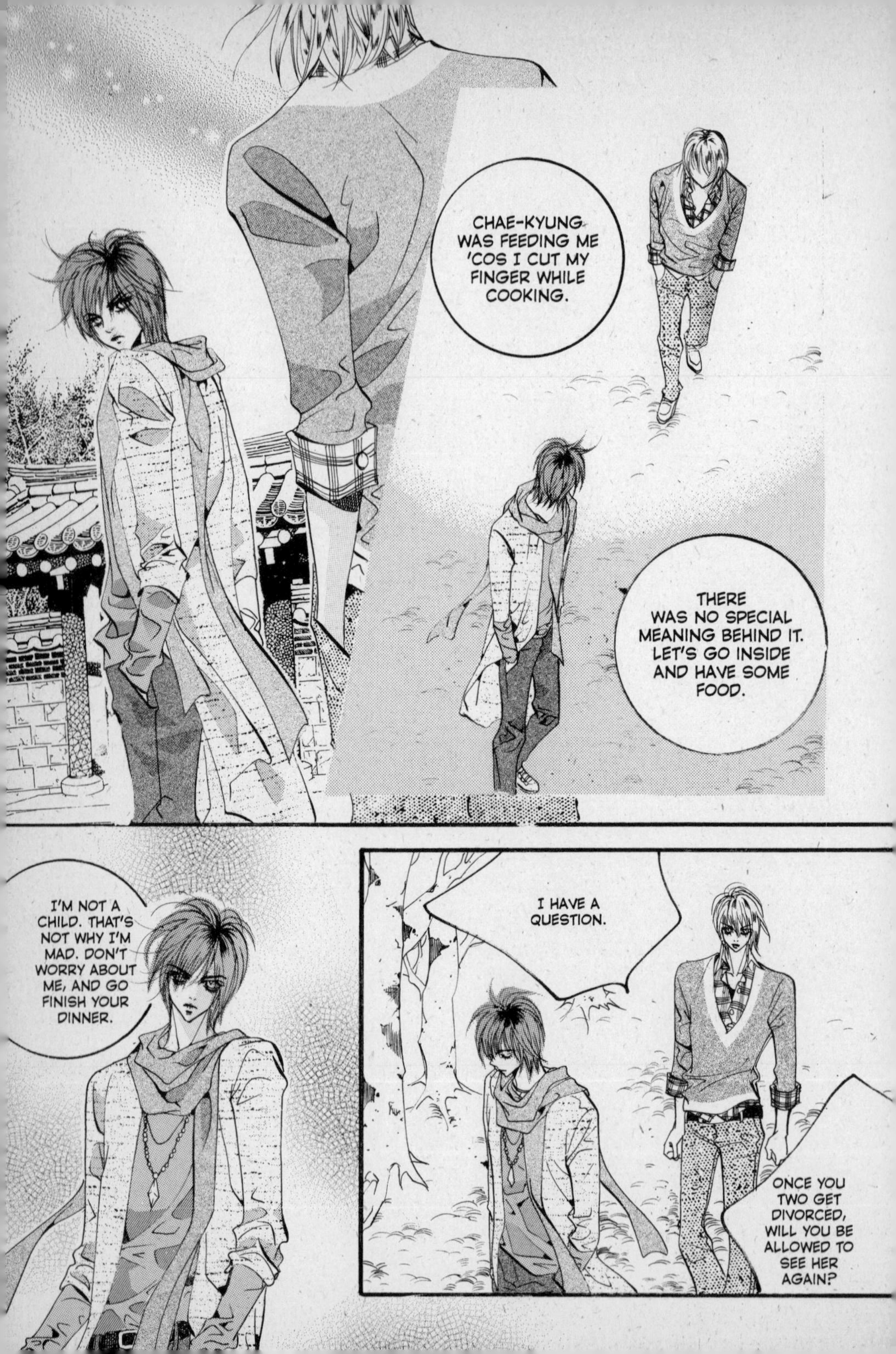
CHAE-KYUNG WAS FEEDING ME 'COS I CUT MY FINGER WHILE COOKING.
THERE WAS NO SPECIAL MEANING BEHIND IT. LET'S GO INSIDE AND HAVE SOME FOOD.
I'M NOT A CHILD. THAT'S NOT WHY I'M MAD. DON'T WORRY ABOUT ME, AND GO FINISH YOUR DINNER.
I HAVE A QUESTION.
ONCE YOU TWO GET DIVORCED, WILL YOU BE ALLOWED TO SEE HER AGAIN?

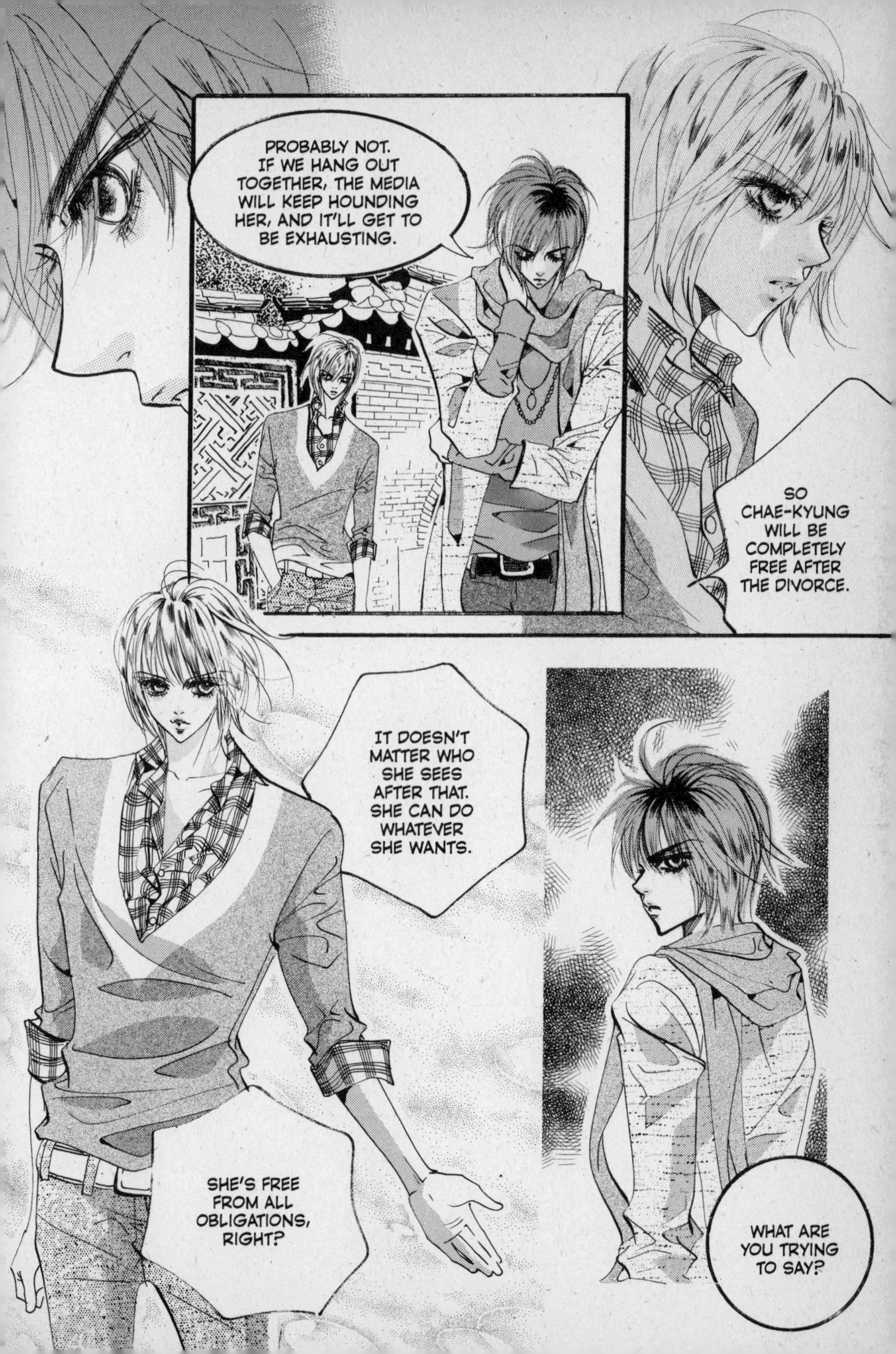
PROBABLY NOT. IF WE HANG OUT TOGETHER, THE MEDIA WILL KEEP HOUNDING HER, AND IT'LL GET TO BE EXHAUSTING.
SO CHAE-KYUNG WILL BE COMPLETELY FREE AFTER THE DIVORCE.
IT DOESN'T MATTER WHO SHE SEES AFTER THAT. SHE CAN DO WHATEVER SHE WANTS.
SHE'S FREE FROM ALL OBLIGATIONS, RIGHT?
WHAT ARE YOU TRYING TO SAY?

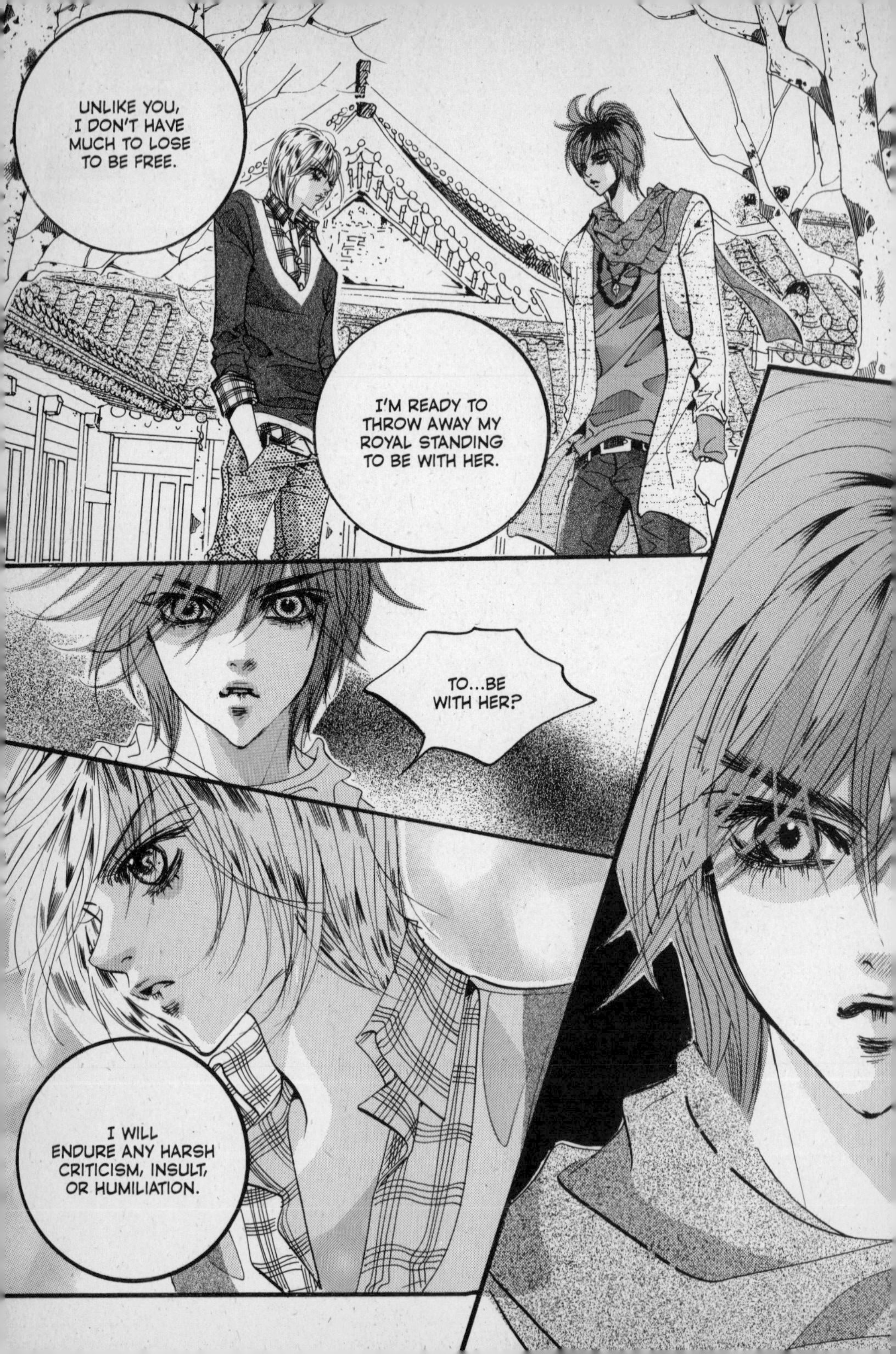
UNLIKE YOU, I DON'T HAVE MUCH TO LOSE TO BE FREE.
I'M READY TO THROW AWAY MY ROYAL STANDING TO BE WITH HER.
TO...BE WITH HER?
I WILL ENDURE ANY HARSH CRITICISM, INSULT, OR HUMILIATION.

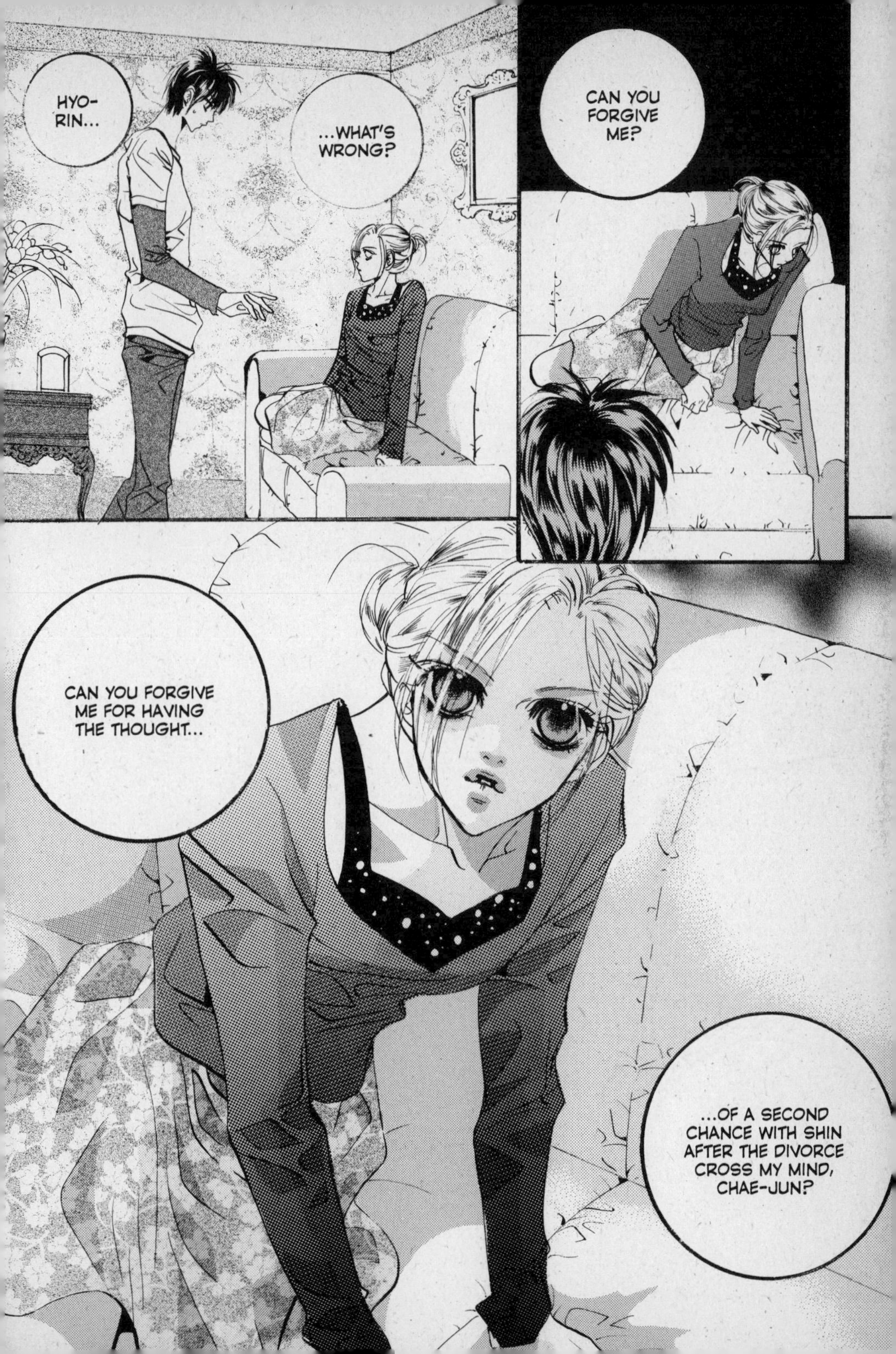
HYO-RIN...
...WHAT'S WRONG?
CAN YOU FORGIVE ME?
CAN YOU FORGIVE ME FOR HAVING THE THOUGHT...
...OF A SECOND CHANCE WITH SHIN AFTER THE DIVORCE CROSS MY MIND, CHAE-JUN?

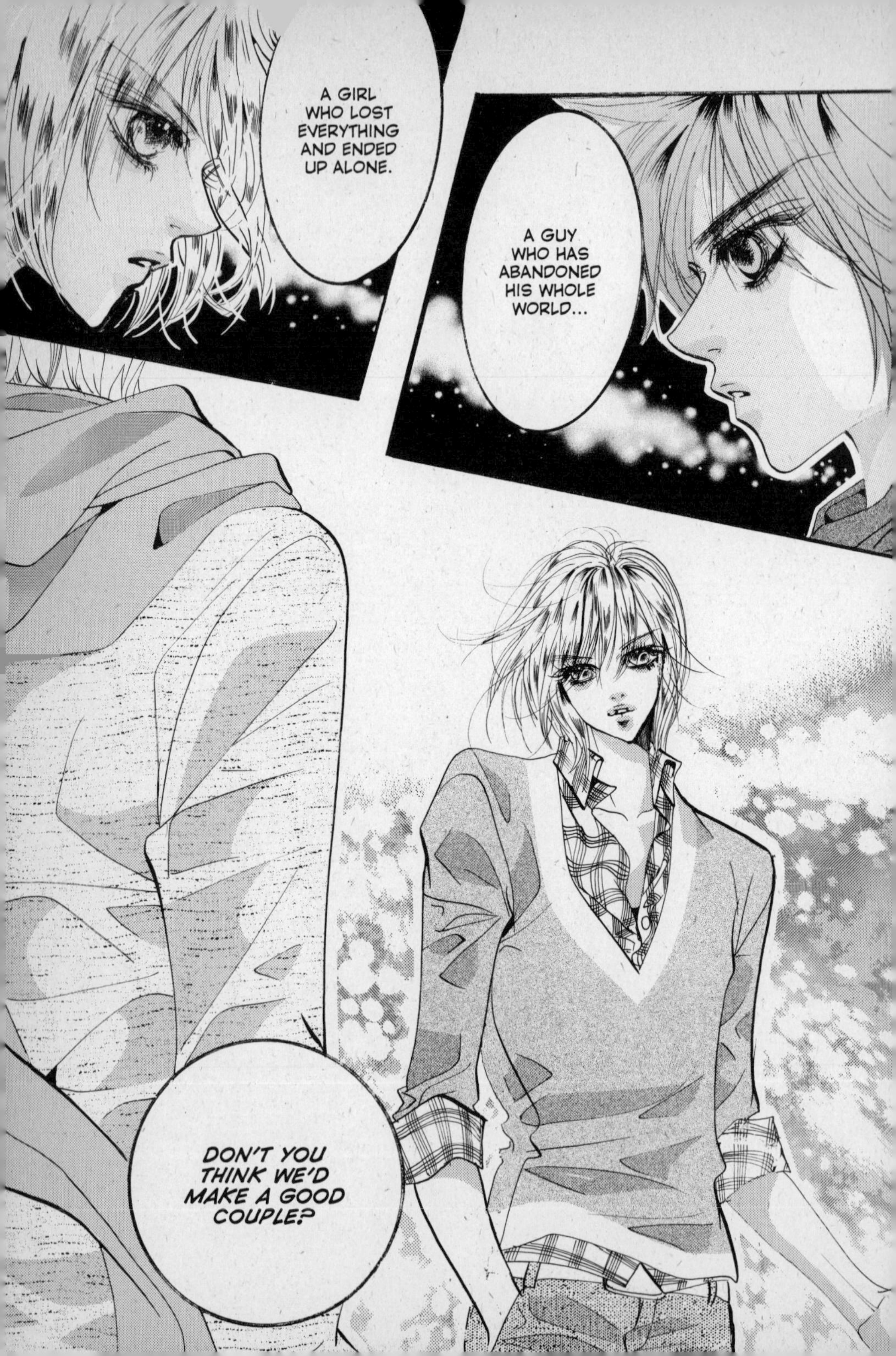
A GIRL WHO LOST EVERYTHING AND ENDED UP ALONE.
A GUY WHO HAS ABANDONED HIS WHOLE WORLD...
DON'T YOU THINK WE'D MAKE A GOOD COUPLE?

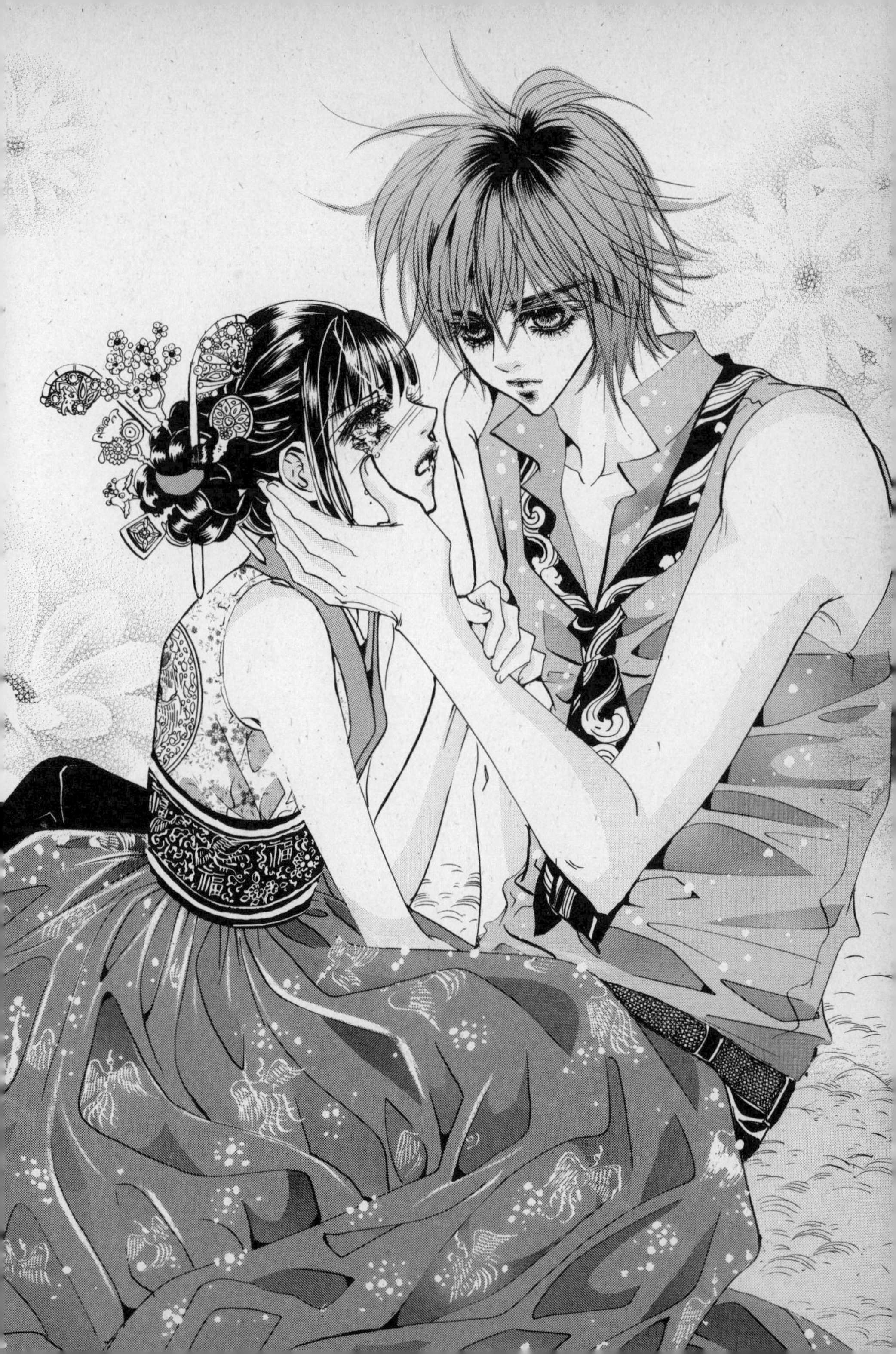

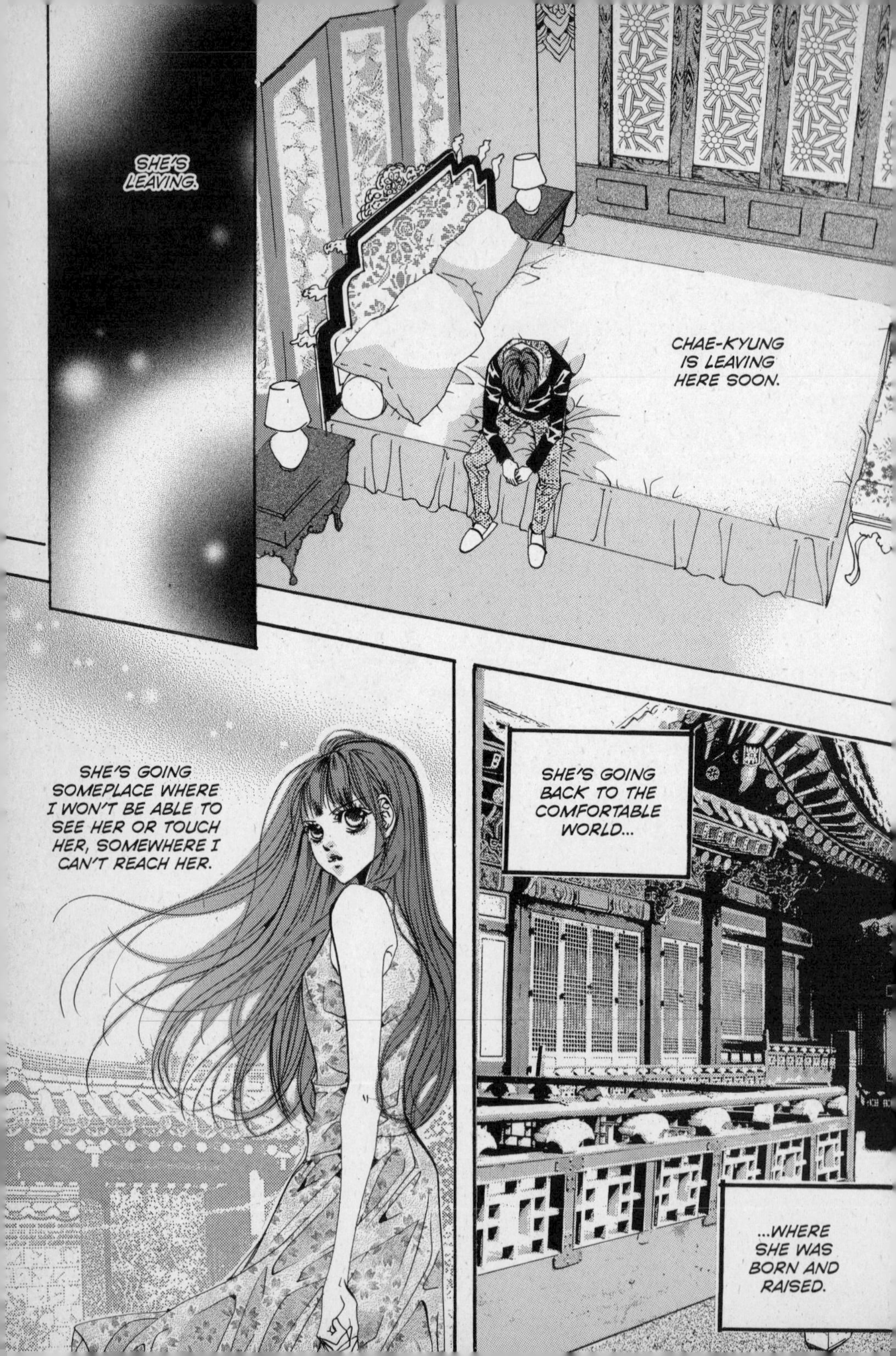
SHE'S LEAVING.
CHAE-KYUNG IS LEAVING HERE SOON.
SHE'S GOING SOMEPLACE WHERE I WON'T BE ABLE TO SEE HER OR TOUCH HER, SOMEWHERE I CAN'T REACH HER.
SHE'S GOING BACK TO THE COMFORTABLE WORLD...
...WHERE SHE WAS BORN AND RAISED.

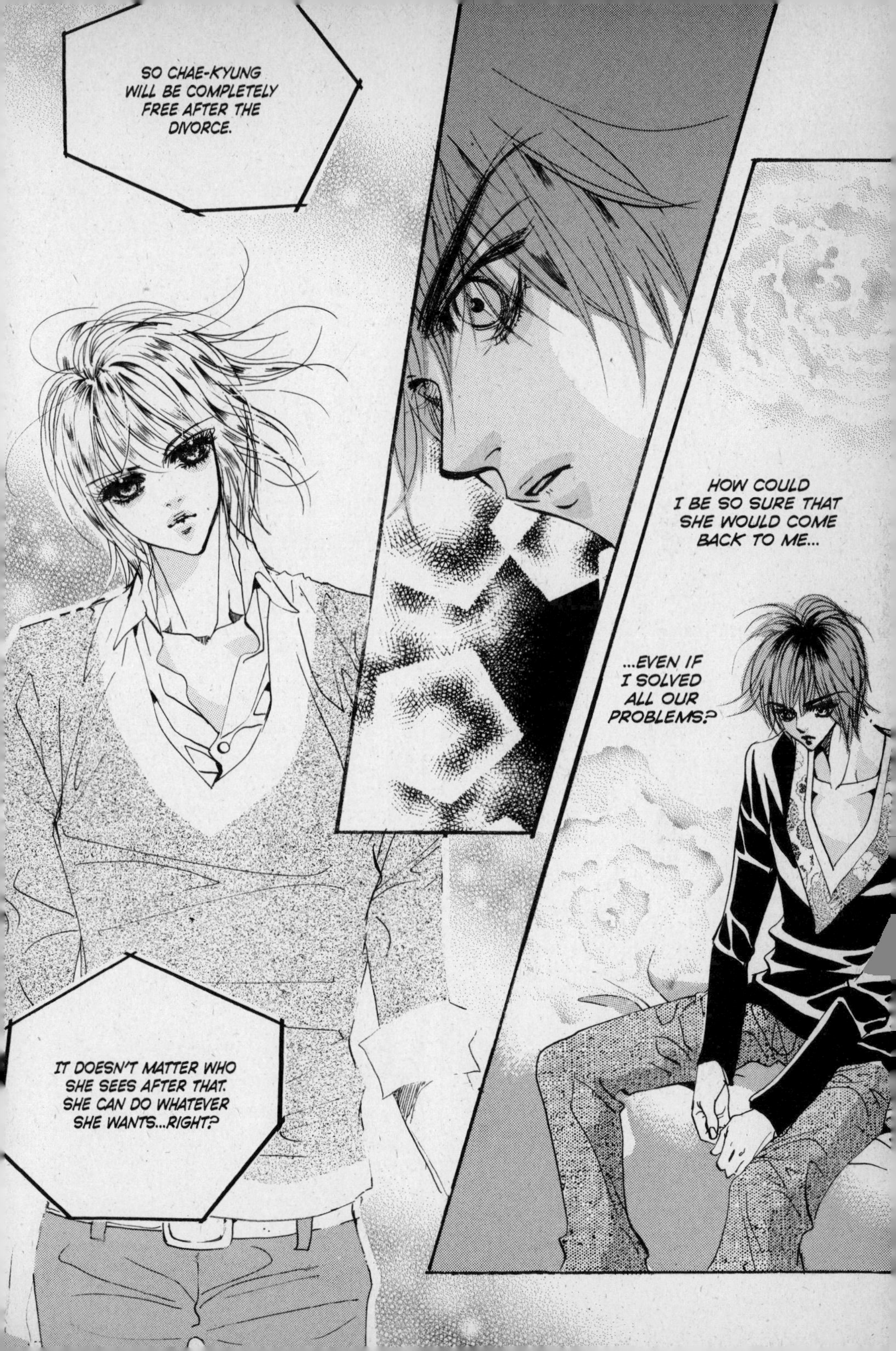
SO CHAE-KYUNG WILL BE COMPLETELY FREE AFTER THE DIVORCE.
IT DOESN'T MATTER WHO SHE SEES AFTER THAT. SHE CAN DO WHATEVER SHE WANTS...RIGHT?
HOW COULD I BE SO SURE THAT SHE WOULD COME BACK TO ME...
...EVEN IF I SOLVED ALL OUR PROBLEMS?

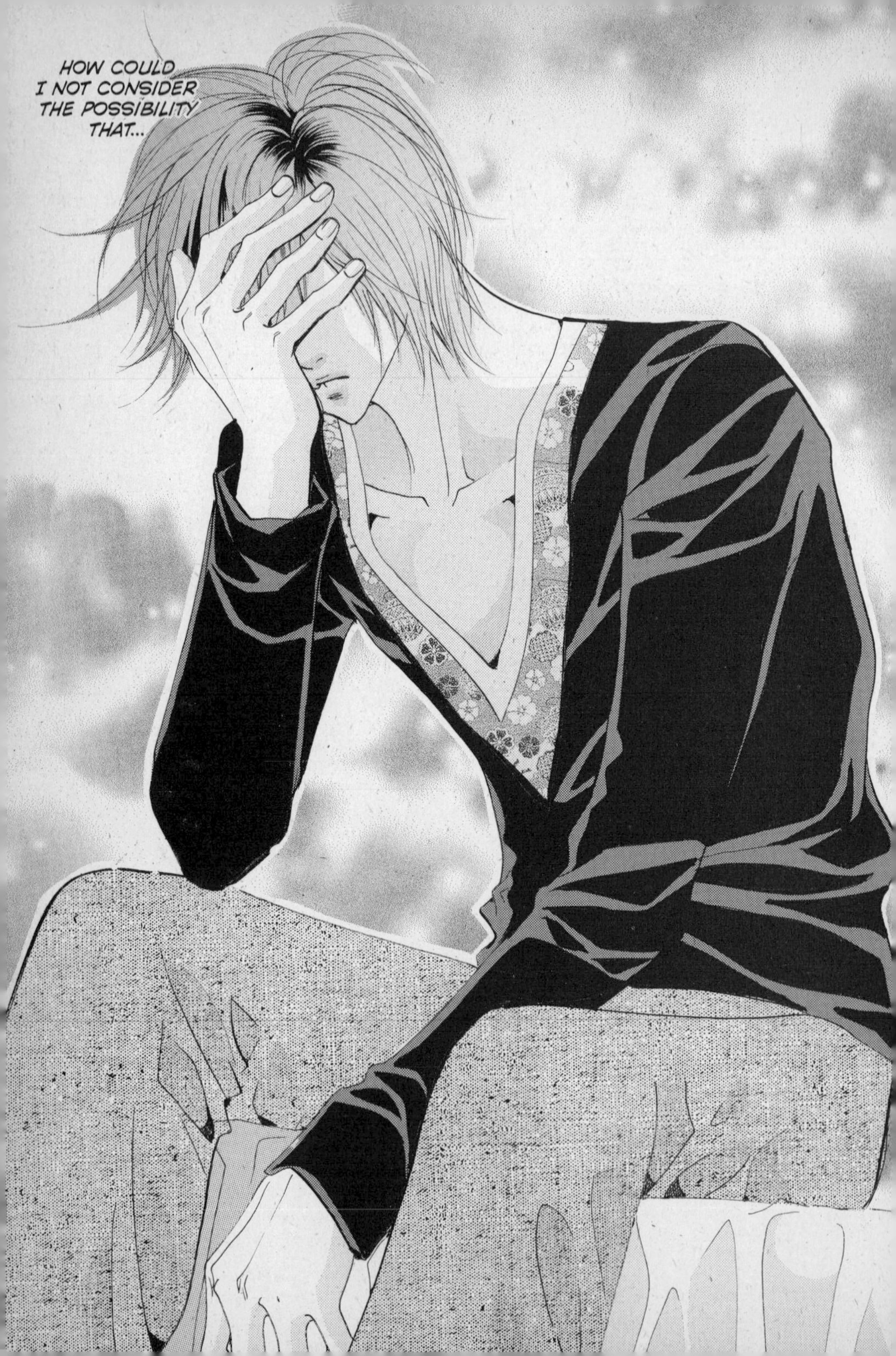
HOW COULD I NOT CONSIDER THE POSSIBILITY THAT...

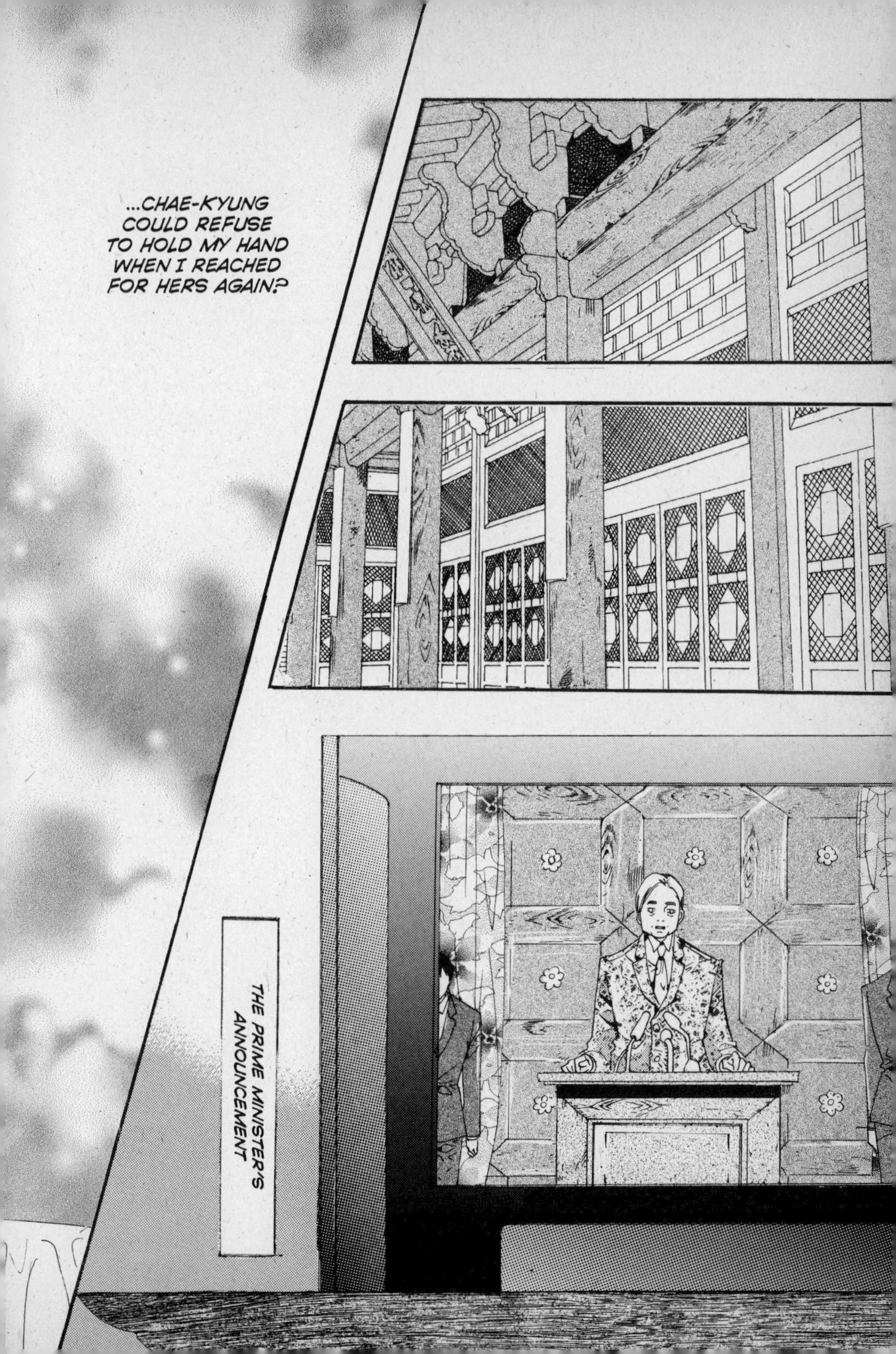
...CHAE-KYUNG COULD REFUSE TO HOLD MY HAND WHEN I REACHED FOR HERS AGAIN?
THE PRIME MINISTER'S ANNOUNCEMENT

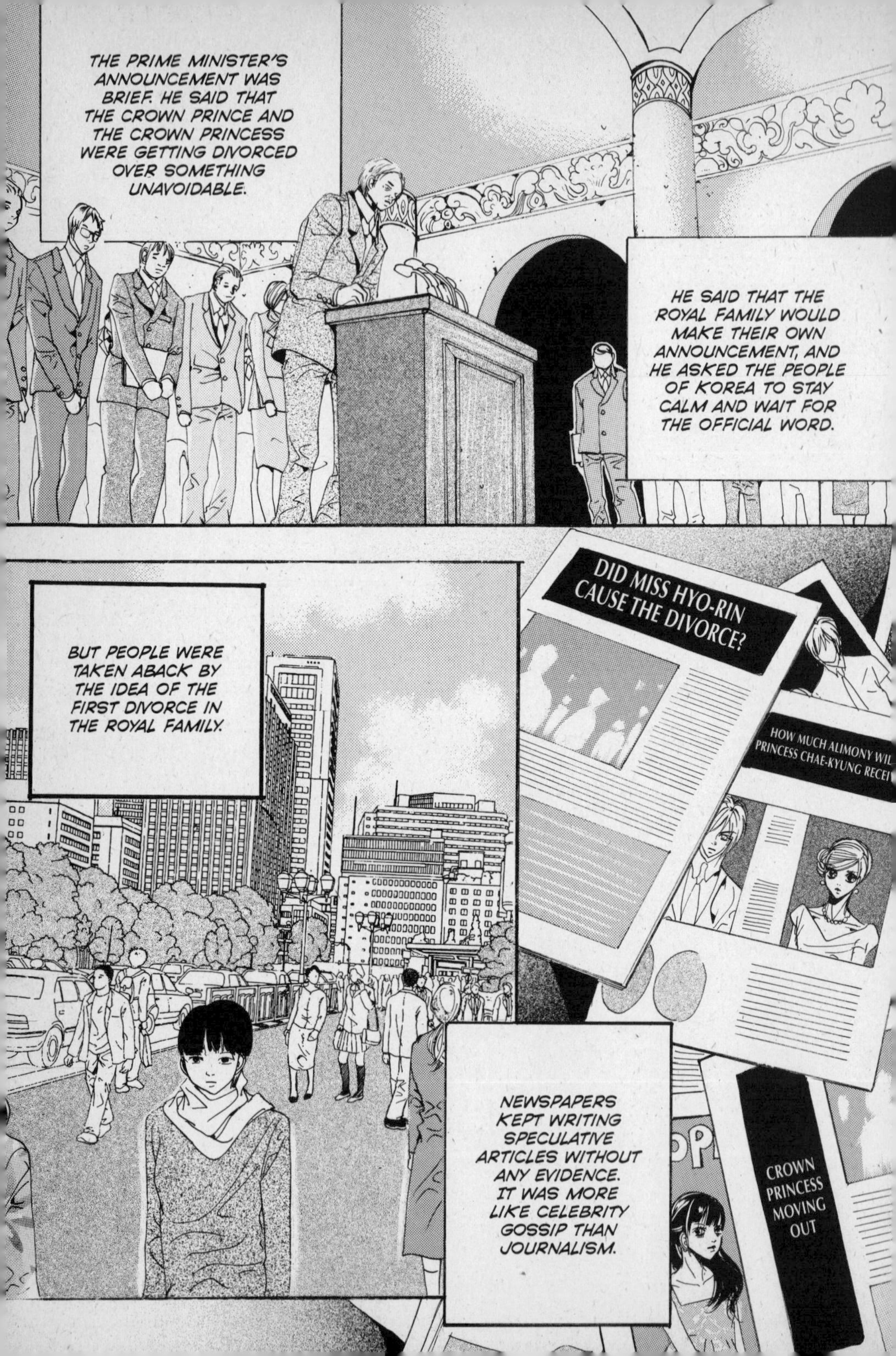
THE PRIME MINISTER'S ANNOUNCEMENT WAS BRIEF. HE SAID THAT THE CROWN PRINCE AND THE CROWN PRINCESS WERE GETTING DIVORCED OVER SOMETHING UNAVOIDABLE.
HE SAID THAT THE ROYAL FAMILY WOULD MAKE THEIR OWN ANNOUNCEMENT, AND HE ASKED THE PEOPLE OF KOREA TO STAY CALM AND WAIT FOR THE OFFICIAL WORD.
BUT PEOPLE WERE TAKEN ABACK BY THE IDEA OF THE FIRST DIVORCE IN THE ROYAL FAMILY.
DID MISS HYO-RIN CAUSE THE DIVORCE?
HOW MUCH ALIMONY WIL
PRINCESS CHAE-KYUNG RECEI
NEWSPAPERS KEPT WRITING SPECULATIVE ARTICLES WITHOUT ANY EVIDENCE. IT WAS MORE LIKE CELEBRITY GOSSIP THAN JOURNALISM.
CROWN PRINCESS MOVING OUT

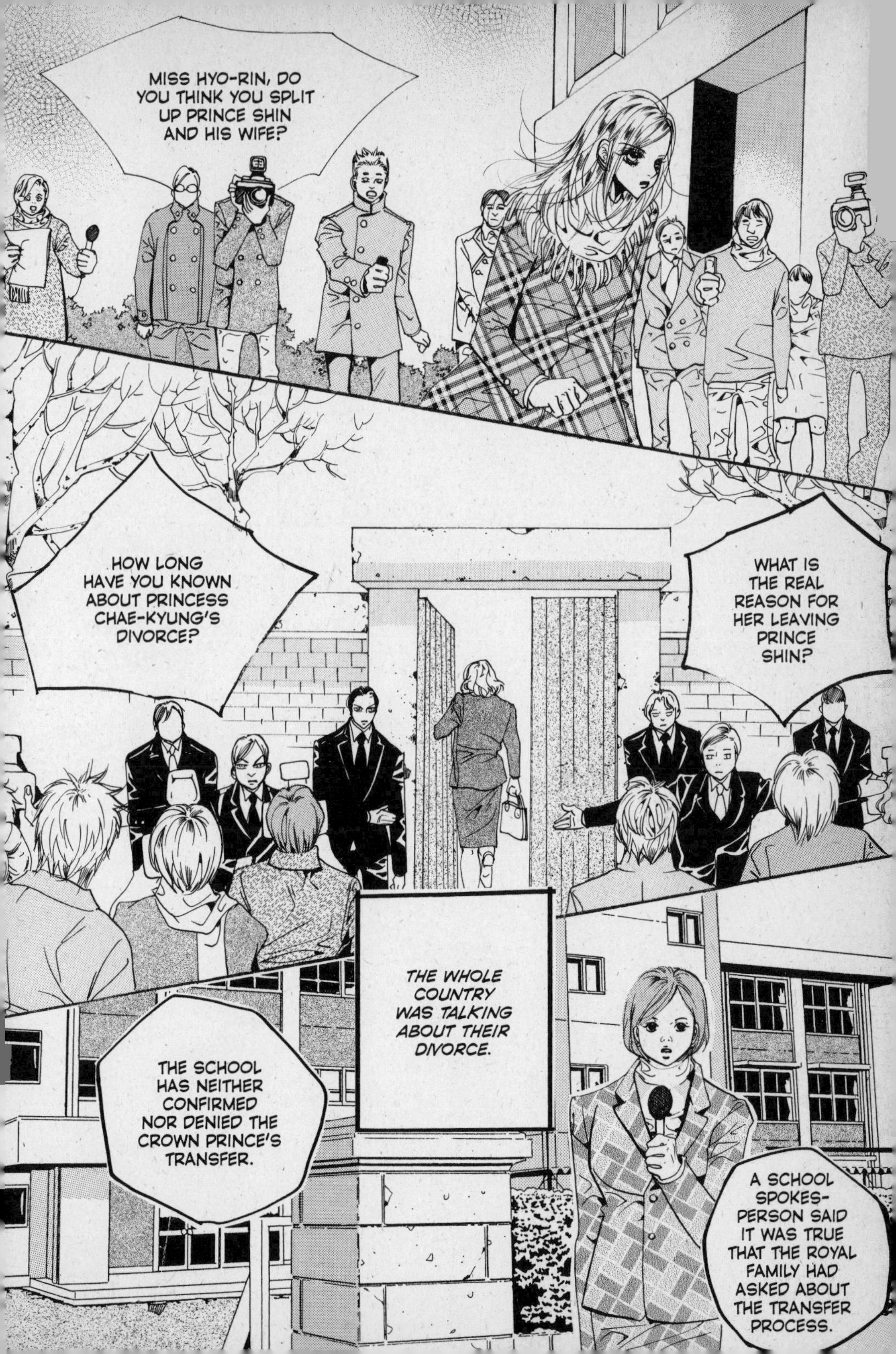
MISS HYO-RIN, DO YOU THINK YOU SPLIT UP PRINCE SHIN AND HIS WIFE?
HOW LONG HAVE YOU KNOWN ABOUT PRINCESS CHAE-KYUNG'S DIVORCE?
WHAT IS THE REAL REASON FOR HER LEAVING PRINCE SHIN?
THE WHOLE COUNTRY WAS TALKING ABOUT THEIR DIVORCE.
THE SCHOOL HAS NEITHER CONFIRMED NOR DENIED THE CROWN PRINCE'S TRANSFER.
A SCHOOL SPOKES-PERSON SAID IT WAS TRUE THAT THE ROYAL FAMILY HAD ASKED ABOUT THE TRANSFER PROCESS.

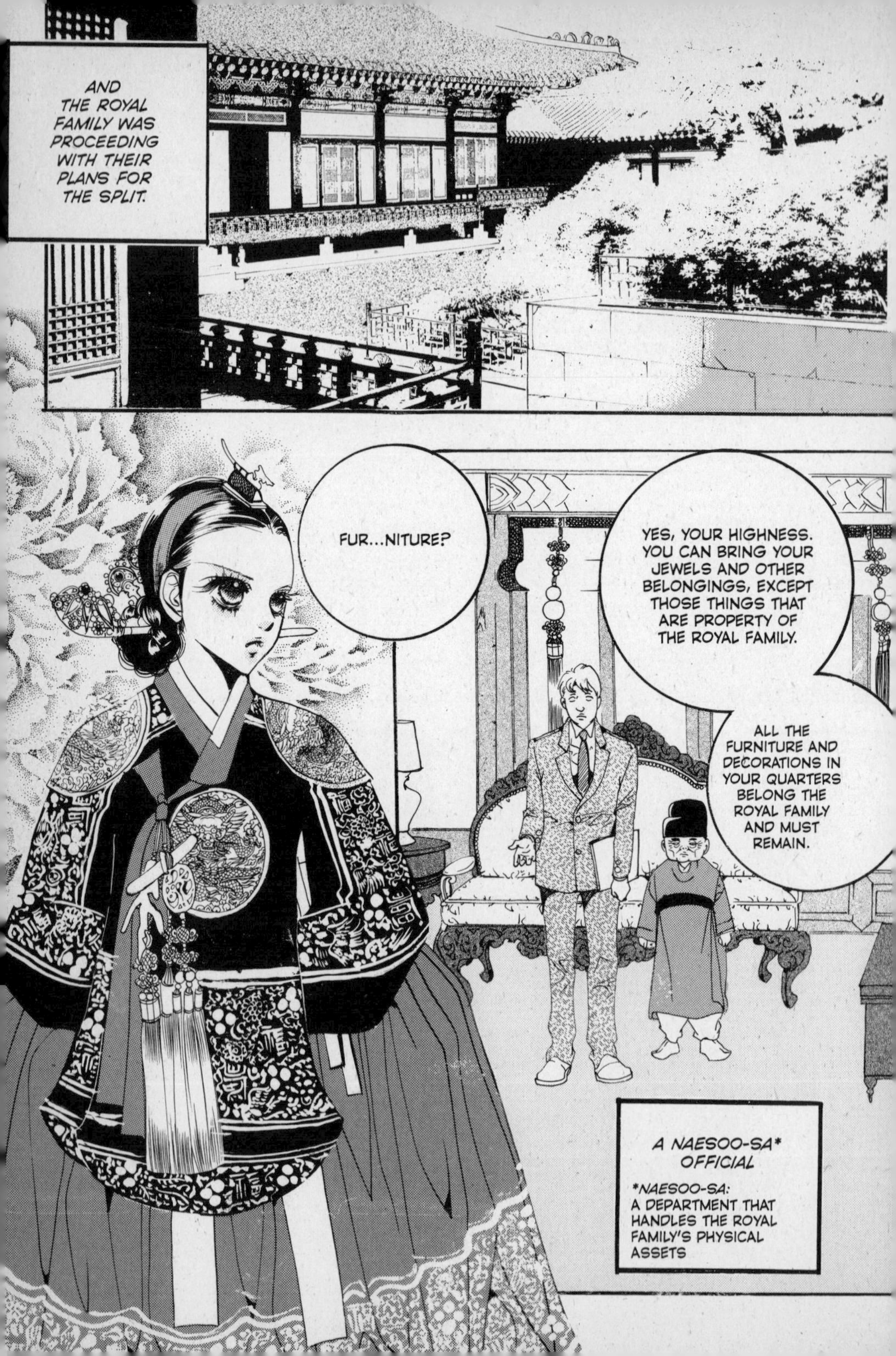
AND THE ROYAL FAMILY WAS PROCEEDING WITH THEIR PLANS FOR THE SPLIT.
FUR...NITURE?
YES, YOUR HIGHNESS. YOU CAN BRING YOUR JEWELS AND OTHER BELONGINGS, EXCEPT THOSE THINGS THAT ARE PROPERTY OF THE ROYAL FAMILY.
ALL THE FURNITURE AND DECORATIONS IN YOUR QUARTERS BELONG THE ROYAL FAMILY AND MUST REMAIN.
A NAESOO-SA* OFFICIAL
*NAESOO-SA: A DEPARTMENT THAT HANDLES THE ROYAL FAMILY'S PHYSICAL ASSETS

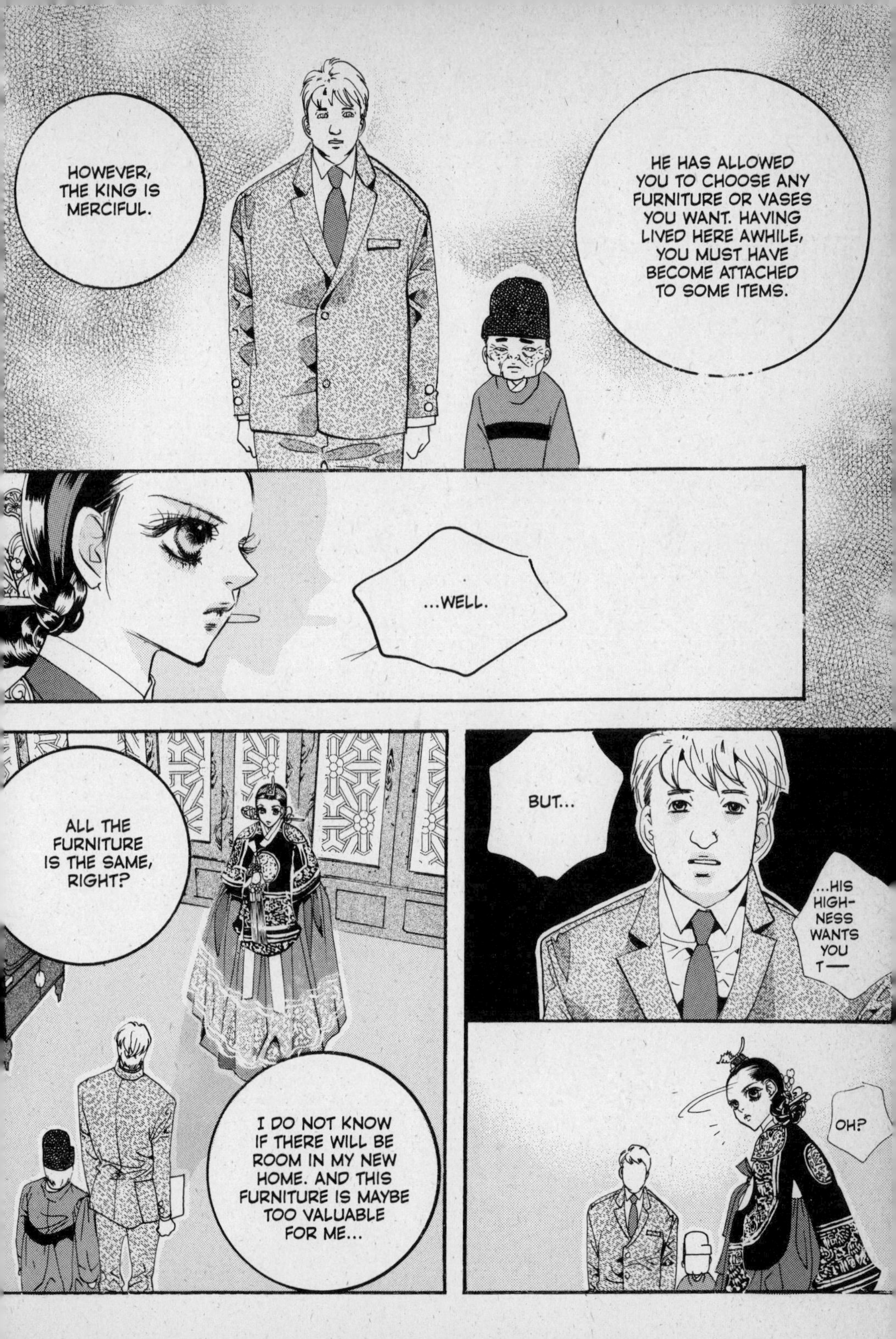
HOWEVER, THE KING IS MERCIFUL.
HE HAS ALLOWED YOU TO CHOOSE ANY FURNITURE OR VASES YOU WANT. HAVING LIVED HERE AWHILE, YOU MUST HAVE BECOME ATTACHED TO SOME ITEMS.
...WELL.
ALL THE FURNITURE IS THE SAME, RIGHT?
I DO NOT KNOW IF THERE WILL BE ROOM IN MY NEW HOME. AND THIS FURNITURE IS MAYBE TOO VALUABLE FOR ME...
BUT...
...HIS HIGH-NESS WANTS YOU T—
OH?

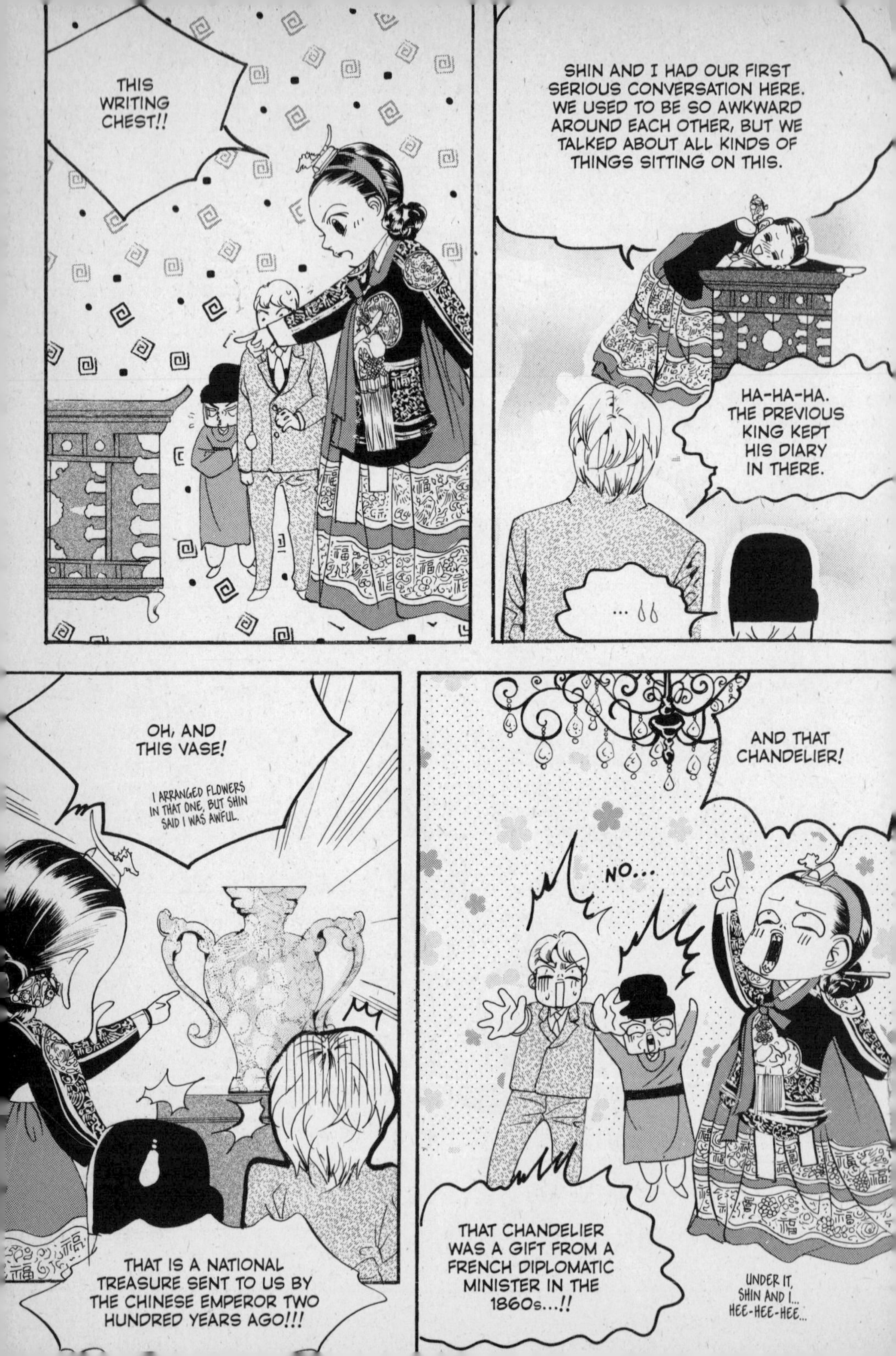
THIS WRITING CHEST!!
SHIN AND I HAD OUR FIRST SERIOUS CONVERSATION HERE. WE USED TO BE SO AWKWARD AROUND EACH OTHER, BUT WE TALKED ABOUT ALL KINDS OF THINGS SITTING ON THIS.
HA-HA-HA. THE PREVIOUS KING KEPT HIS DIARY IN THERE.
...
OH, AND THIS VASE!
I ARRANGED FLOWERS IN THAT ONE, BUT SHIN SAID I WAS AWFUL.
THAT IS A NATIONAL TREASURE SENT TO US BY THE CHINESE EMPEROR TWO HUNDRED YEARS AGO!!!
AND THAT CHANDELIER!
NO...
THAT CHANDELIER WAS A GIFT FROM A FRENCH DIPLOMATIC MINISTER IN THE 1860s...!!
UNDER IT, SHIN AND I... HEE-HEE-HEE...

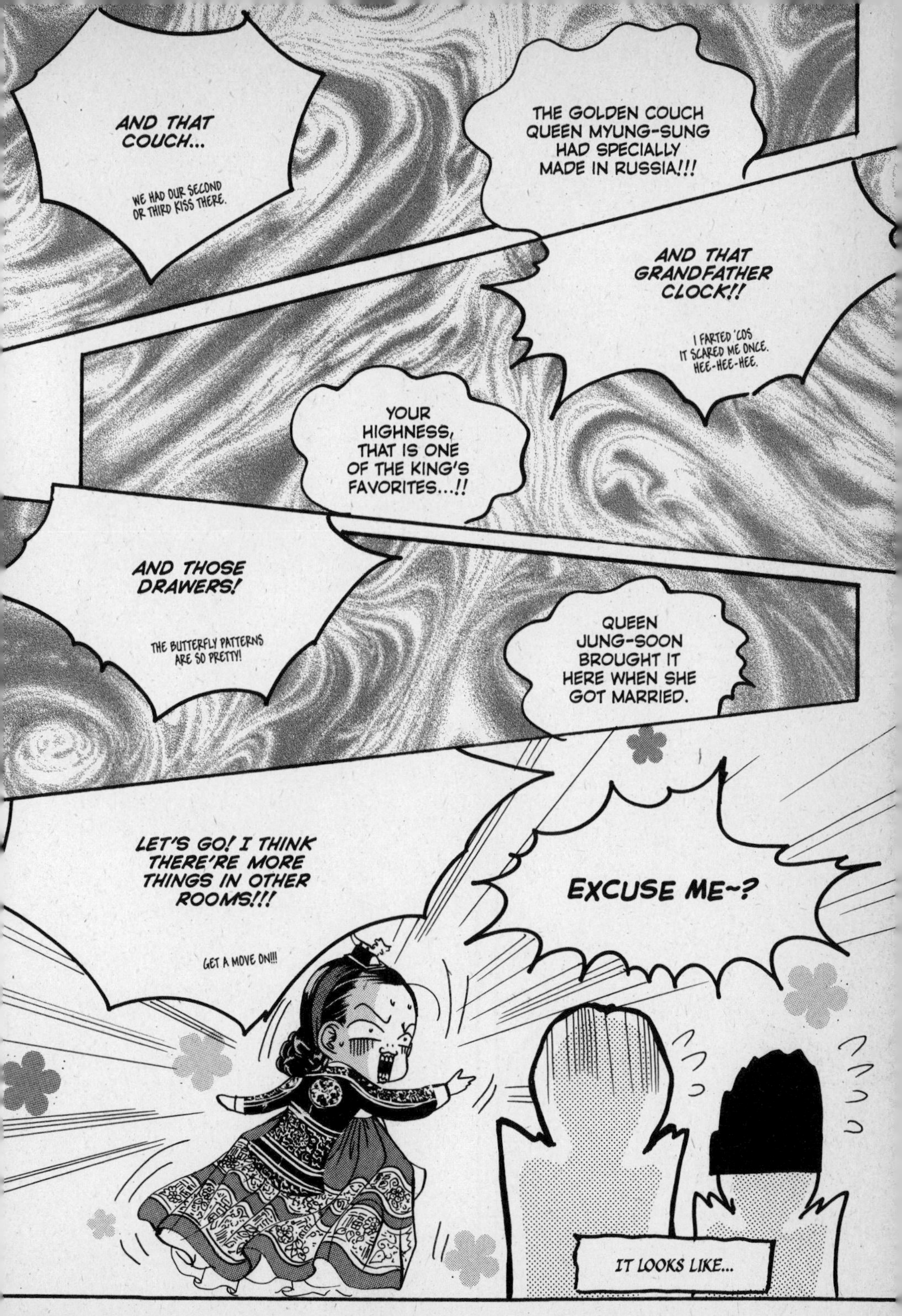
AND THAT COUCH...
WE HAD OUR SECOND OR THIRD KISS THERE.
THE GOLDEN COUCH QUEEN MYUNG-SUNG HAD SPECIALLY MADE IN RUSSIA!!!
AND THAT GRANDFATHER CLOCK!!
I FARTED 'COS IT SCARED ME ONCE. HEE-HEE-HEE.
YOUR HIGHNESS, THAT IS ONE OF THE KING'S FAVORITES...!!
AND THOSE DRAWERS!
THE BUTTERFLY PATTERNS ARE SO PRETTY!
QUEEN JUNG-SOON BROUGHT IT HERE WHEN SHE GOT MARRIED.
LET'S GO! I THINK THERE'RE MORE THINGS IN OTHER ROOMS!!!
GET A MOVE ON!!!
EXCUSE ME~?
IT LOOKS LIKE...

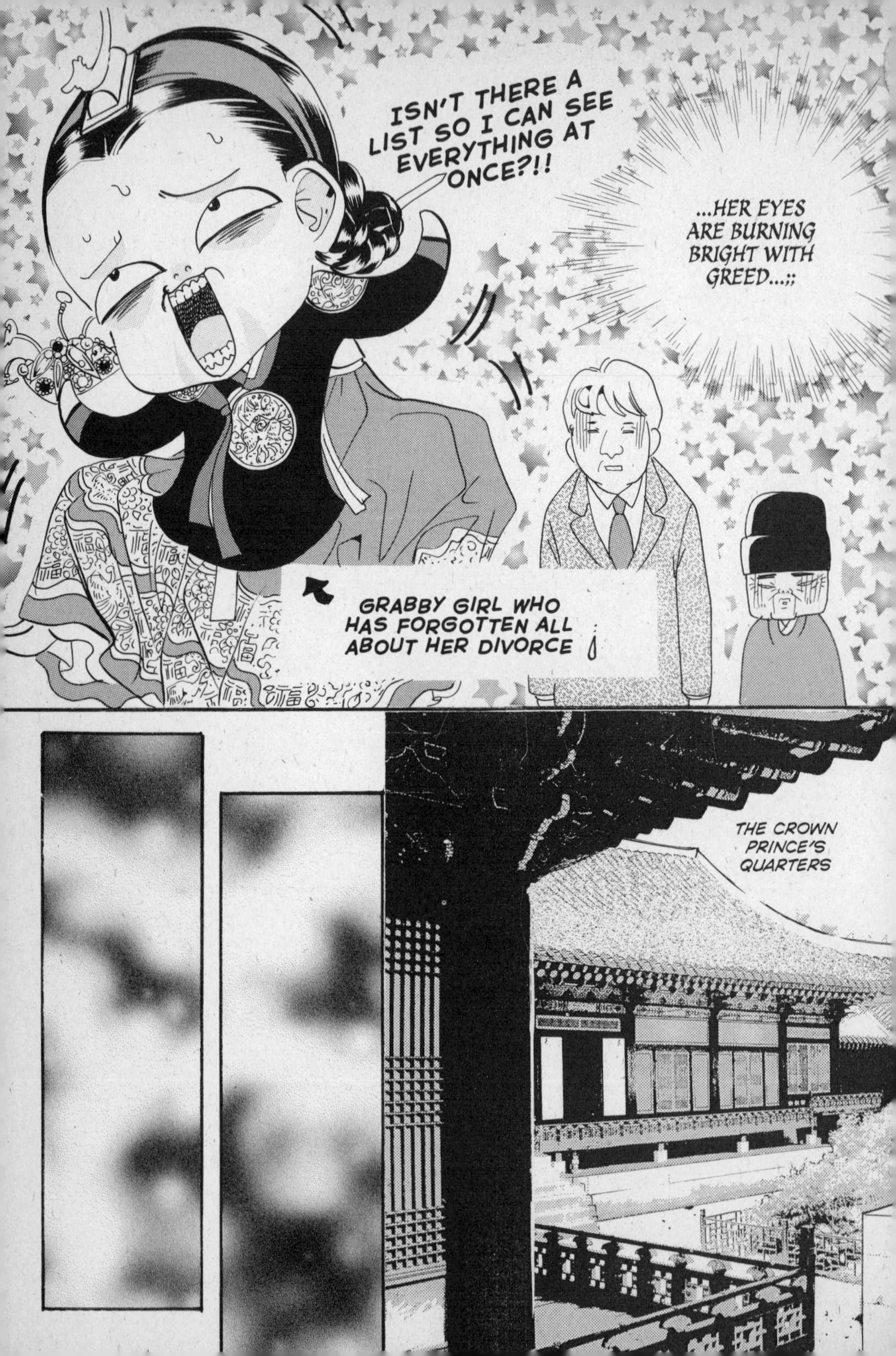
ISN'T THERE A LIST SO I CAN SEE EVERYTHING AT ONCE?!!
...HER EYES ARE BURNING BRIGHT WITH GREED...;;
GRABBY GIRL WHO HAS FORGOTTEN ALL ABOUT HER DIVORCE
THE CROWN PRINCE'S QUARTERS

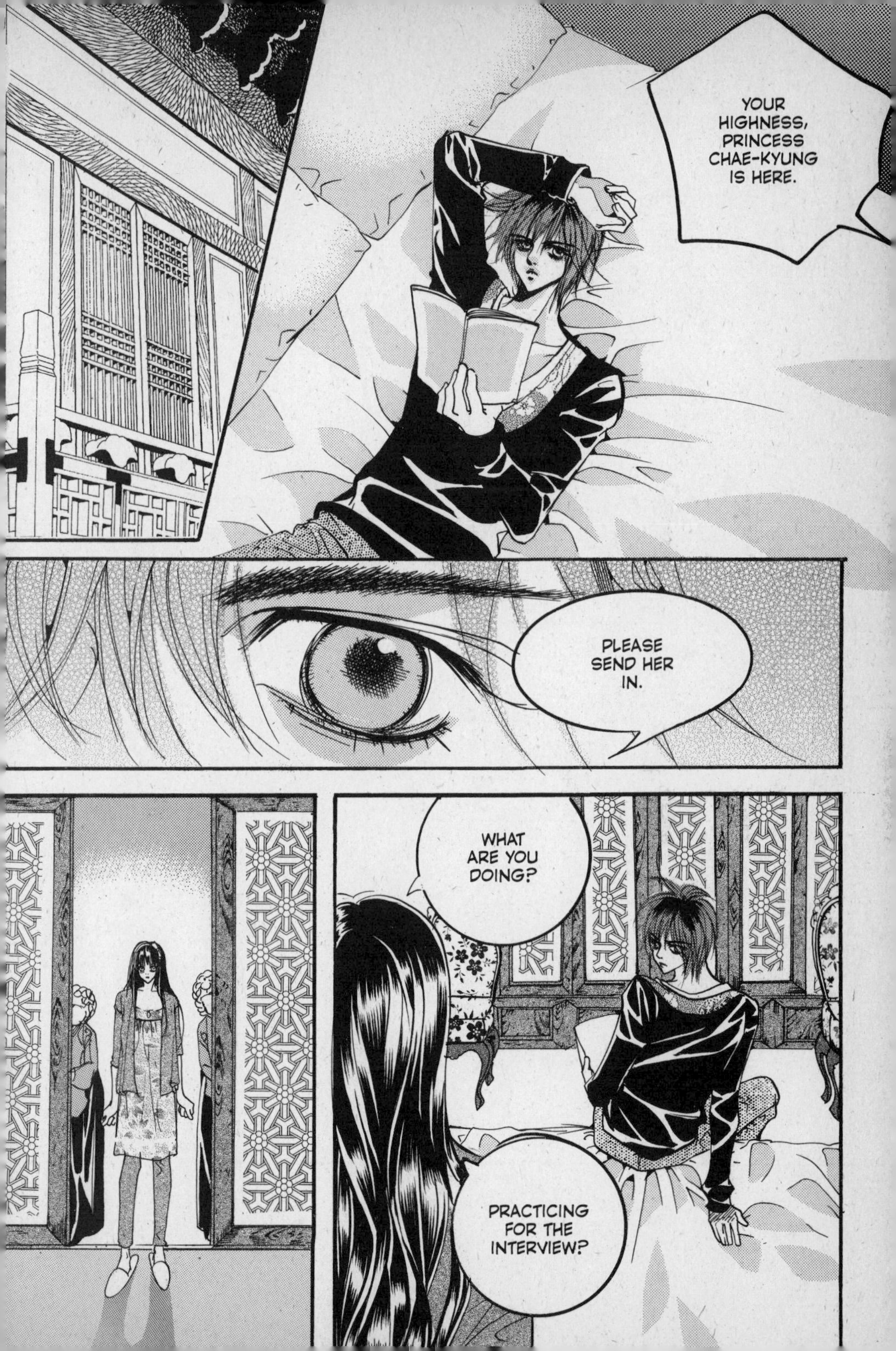
YOUR HIGHNESS, PRINCESS CHAE-KYUNG IS HERE.
PLEASE SEND HER IN.
WHAT ARE YOU DOING?
PRACTICING FOR THE INTERVIEW?

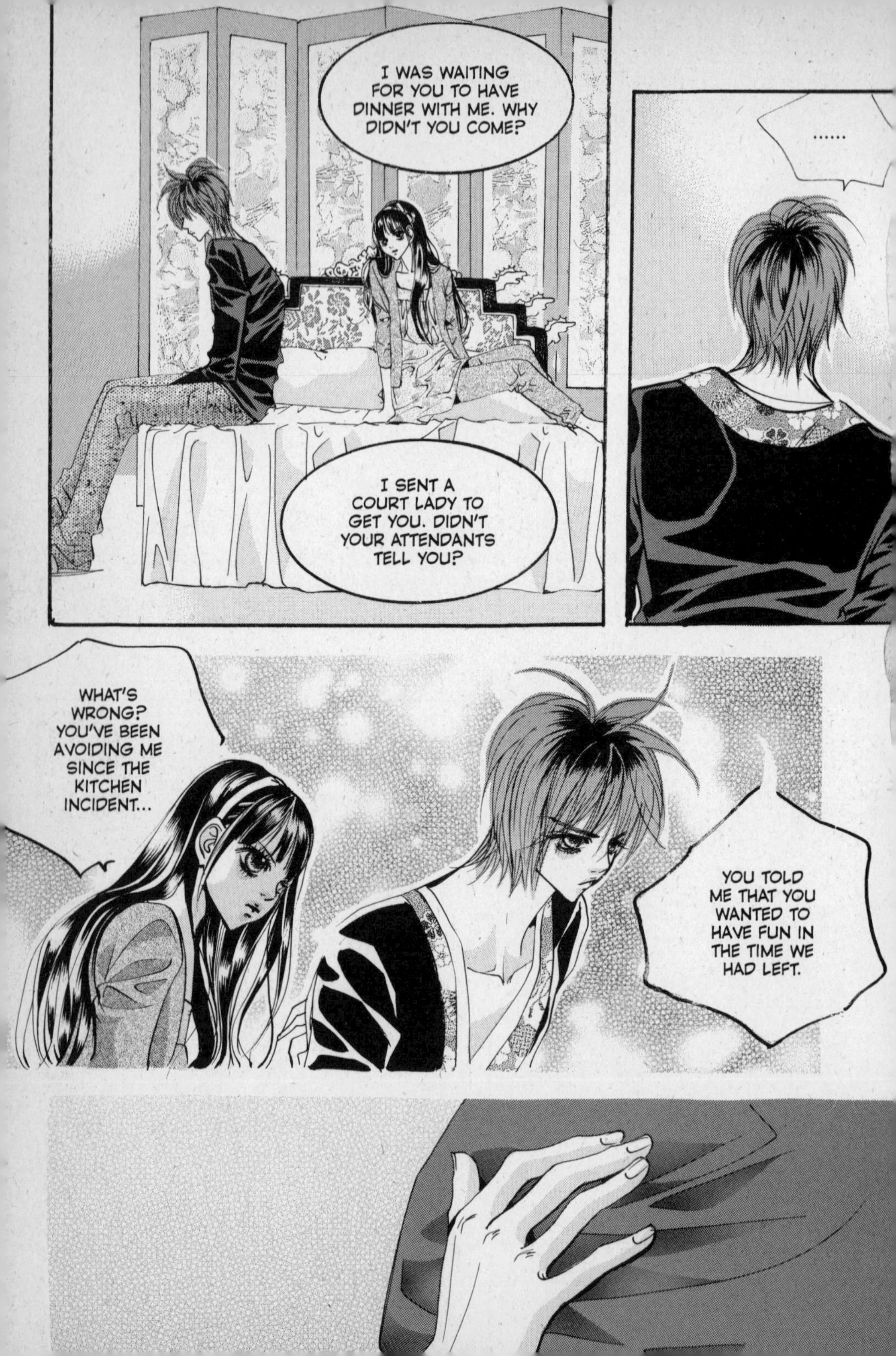
......
I WAS WAITING FOR YOU TO HAVE DINNER WITH ME. WHY DIDN'T YOU COME?
I SENT A COURT LADY TO GET YOU. DIDN'T YOUR ATTENDANTS TELL YOU?
YOU TOLD ME THAT YOU WANTED TO HAVE FUN IN THE TIME WE HAD LEFT.
WHAT'S WRONG? YOU'VE BEEN AVOIDING ME SINCE THE KITCHEN INCIDENT...

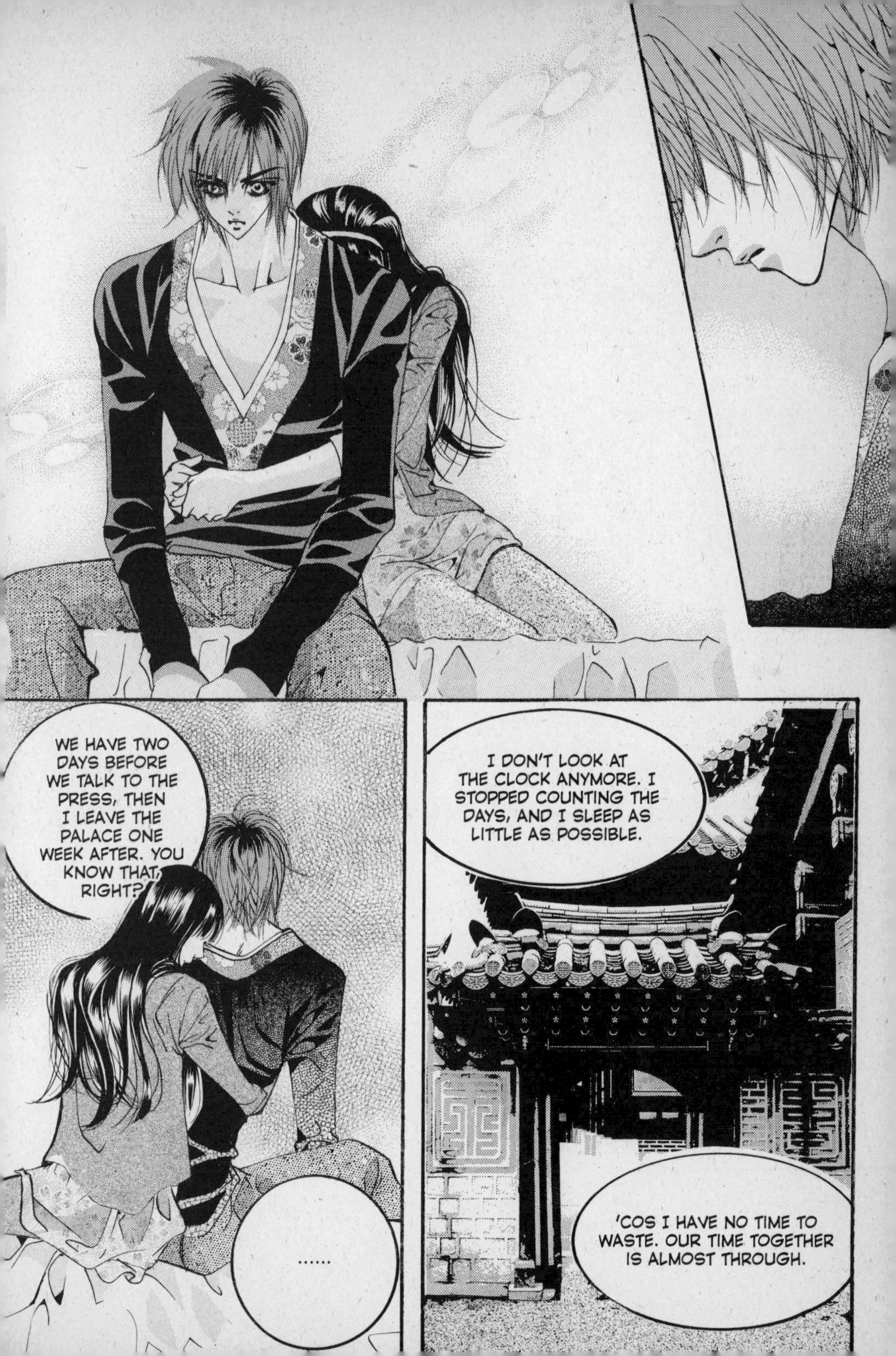
I DON'T LOOK AT THE CLOCK ANYMORE. I STOPPED COUNTING THE DAYS, AND I SLEEP AS LITTLE AS POSSIBLE.
WE HAVE TWO DAYS BEFORE WE TALK TO THE PRESS, THEN I LEAVE THE PALACE ONE WEEK AFTER. YOU KNOW THAT, RIGHT?
'COS I HAVE NO TIME TO WASTE. OUR TIME TOGETHER IS ALMOST THROUGH.
......

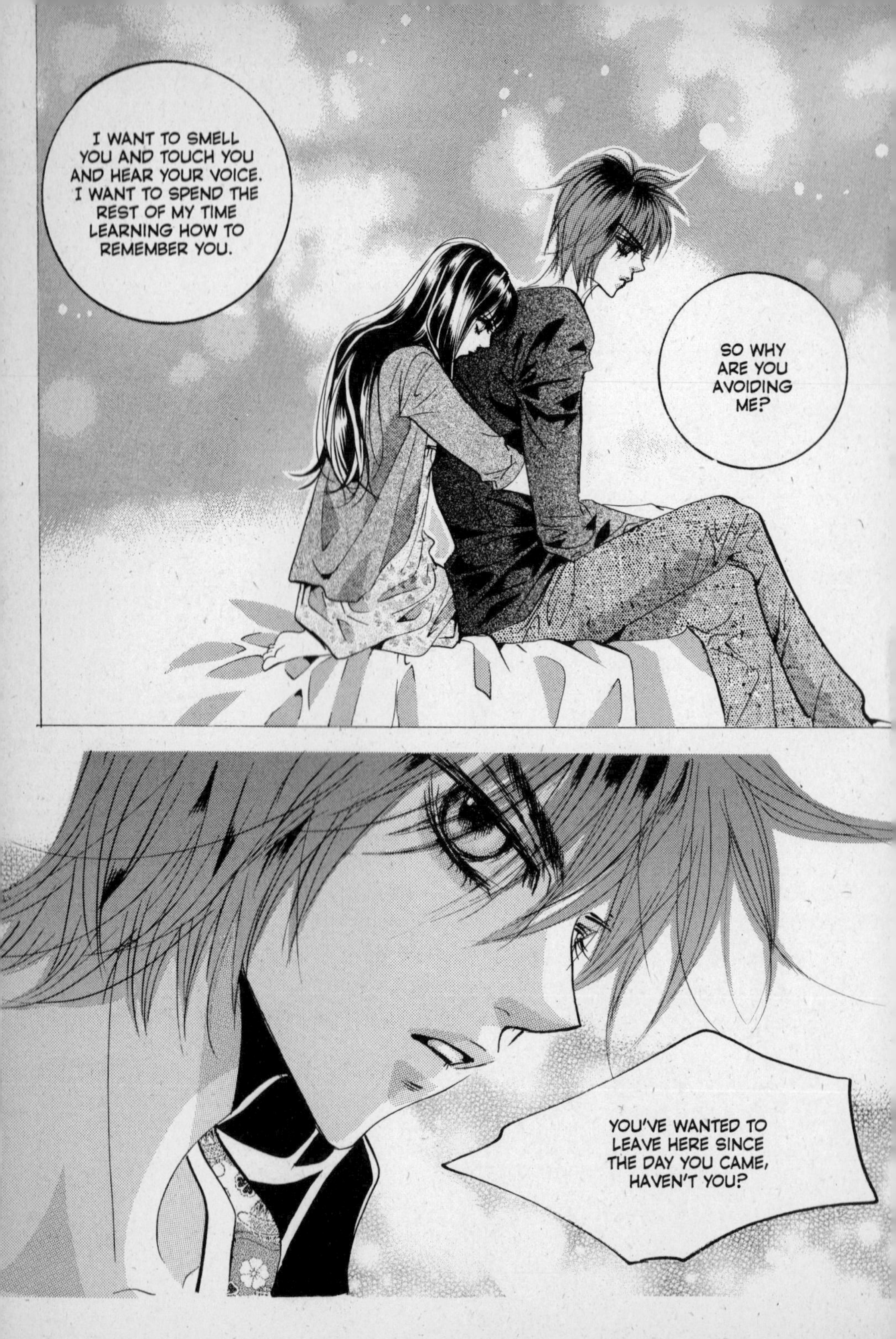
I WANT TO SMELL YOU AND TOUCH YOU AND HEAR YOUR VOICE. I WANT TO SPEND THE REST OF MY TIME LEARNING HOW TO REMEMBER YOU.
SO WHY ARE YOU AVOIDING ME?
YOU'VE WANTED TO LEAVE HERE SINCE THE DAY YOU CAME, HAVEN'T YOU?

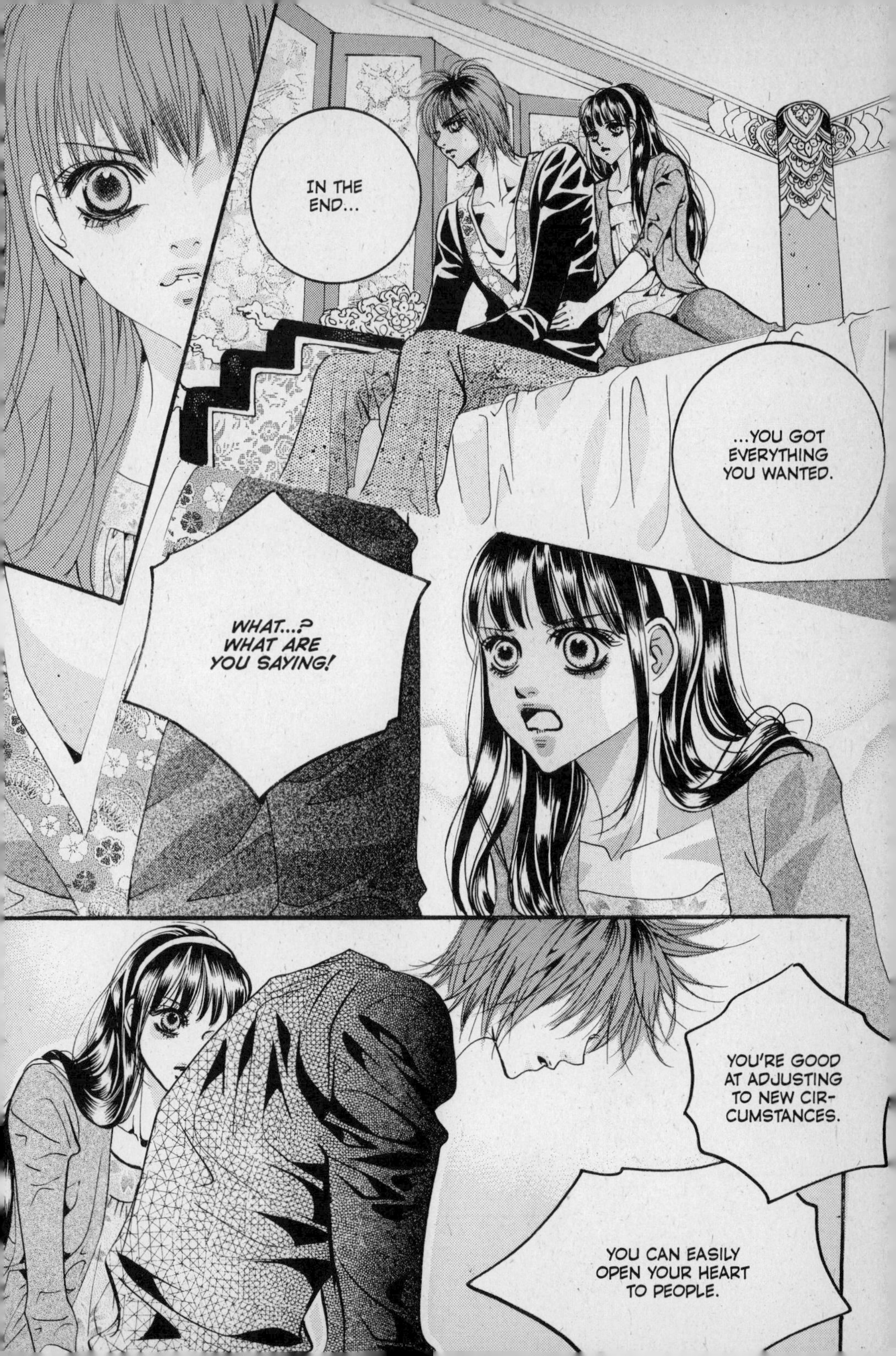

IN THE END...
...YOU GOT EVERYTHING YOU WANTED.
WHAT...? WHAT ARE YOU SAYING!
YOU'RE GOOD AT ADJUSTING TO NEW CIR-CUMSTANCES.
YOU CAN EASILY OPEN YOUR HEART TO PEOPLE.

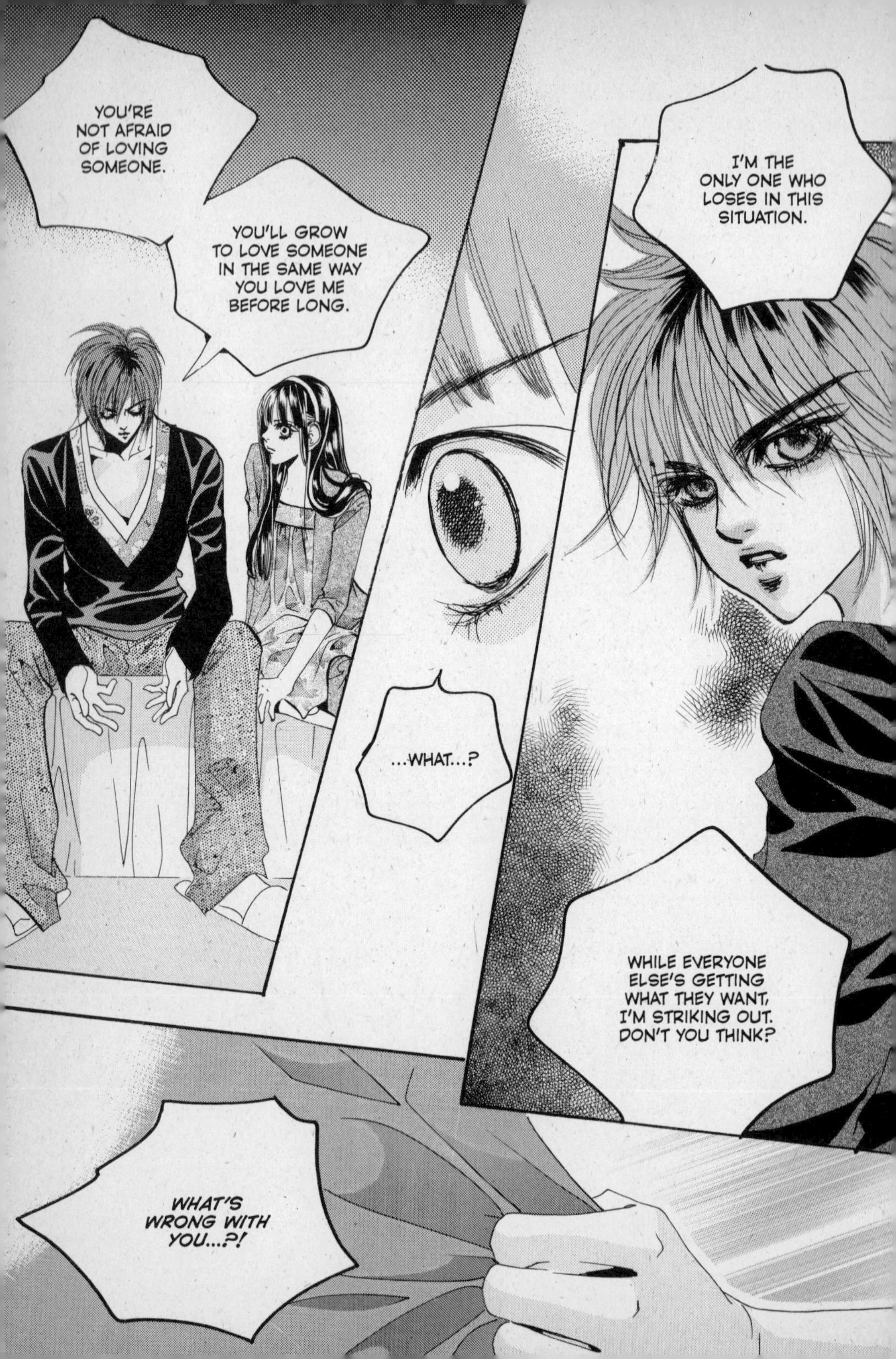
YOU'RE NOT AFRAID OF LOVING SOMEONE.
YOU'LL GROW TO LOVE SOMEONE IN THE SAME WAY YOU LOVE ME BEFORE LONG.
...WHAT...?
I'M THE ONLY ONE WHO LOSES IN THIS SITUATION.
WHILE EVERYONE ELSE'S GETTING WHAT THEY WANT, I'M STRIKING OUT. DON'T YOU THINK?
WHAT'S WRONG WITH YOU...?!

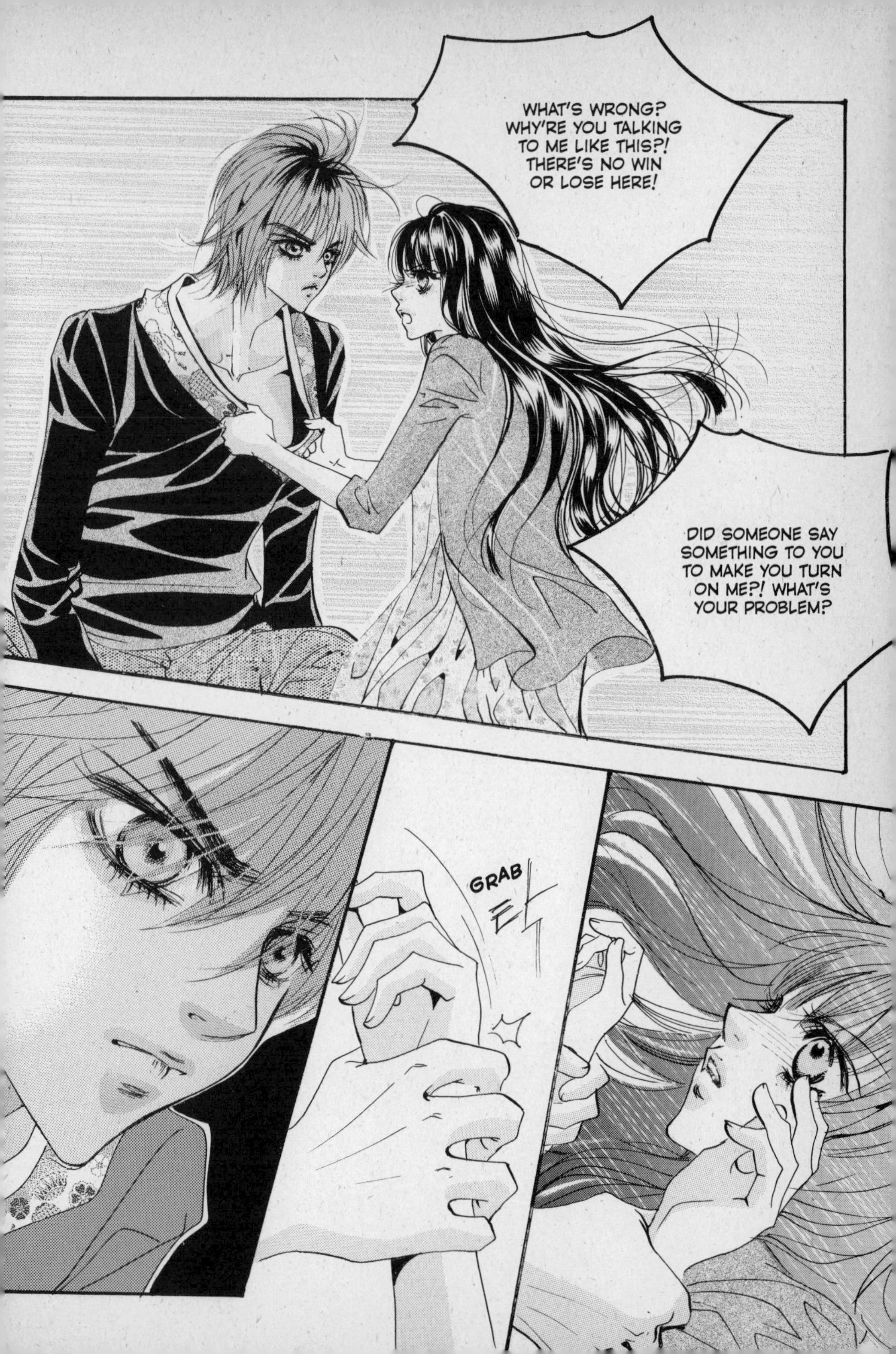
WHAT'S WRONG? WHY'RE YOU TALKING TO ME LIKE THIS?! THERE'S NO WIN OR LOSE HERE!
DID SOMEONE SAY SOMETHING TO YOU TO MAKE YOU TURN ON ME?! WHAT'S YOUR PROBLEM?
GRAB

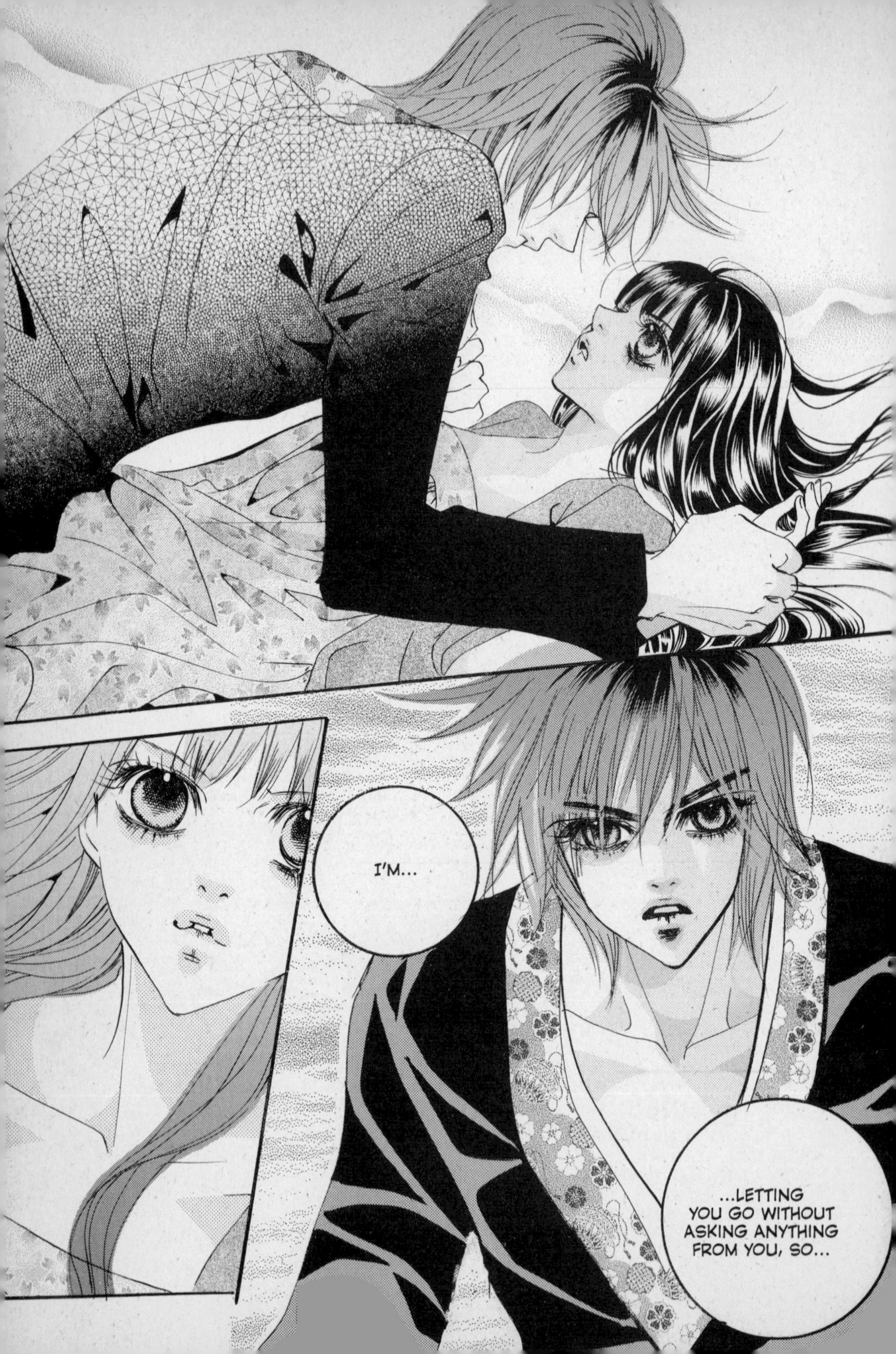
I'M...
...LETTING YOU GO WITHOUT ASKING ANYTHING FROM YOU, SO...

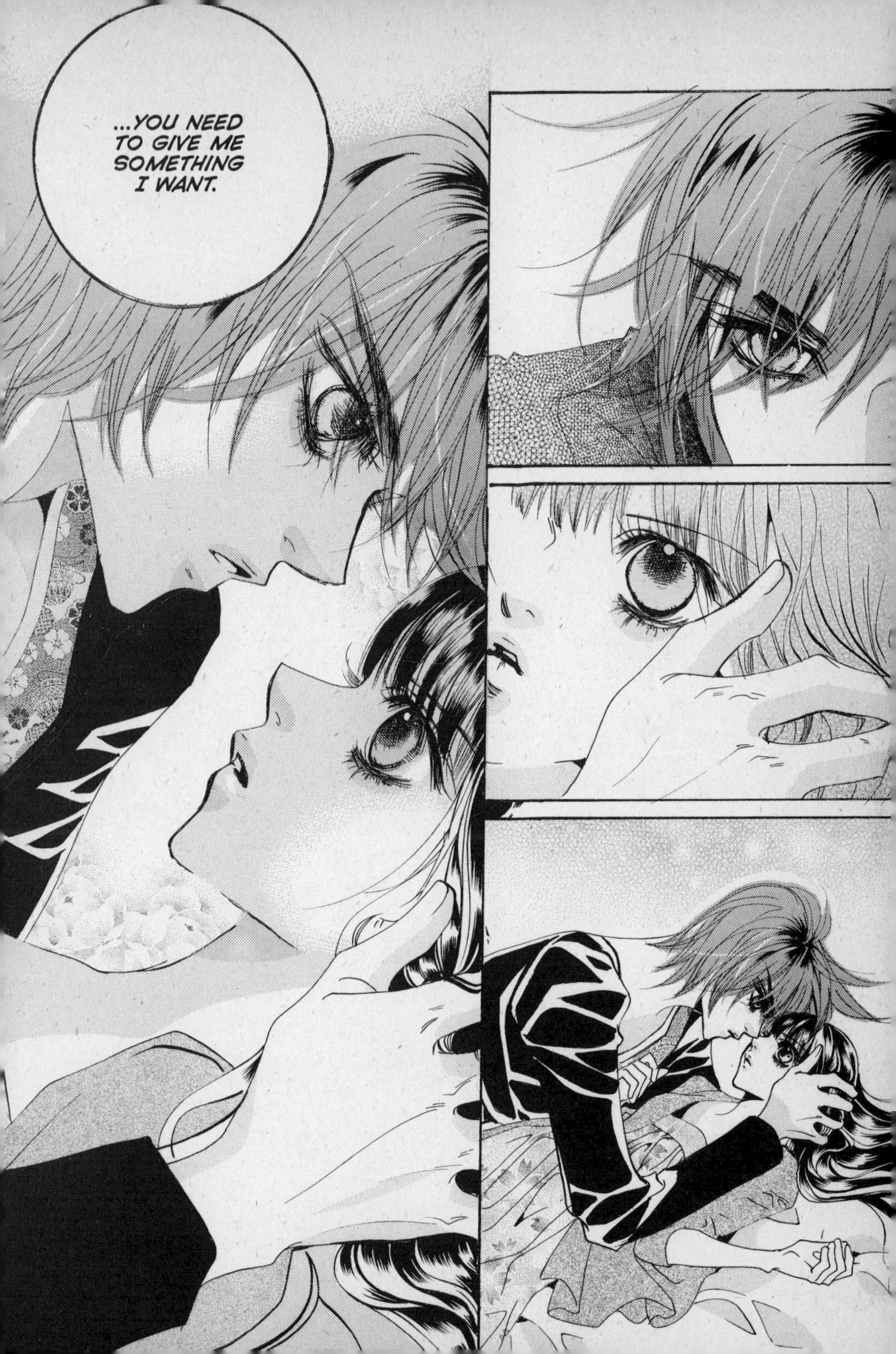
...YOU NEED TO GIVE ME SOMETHING I WANT.

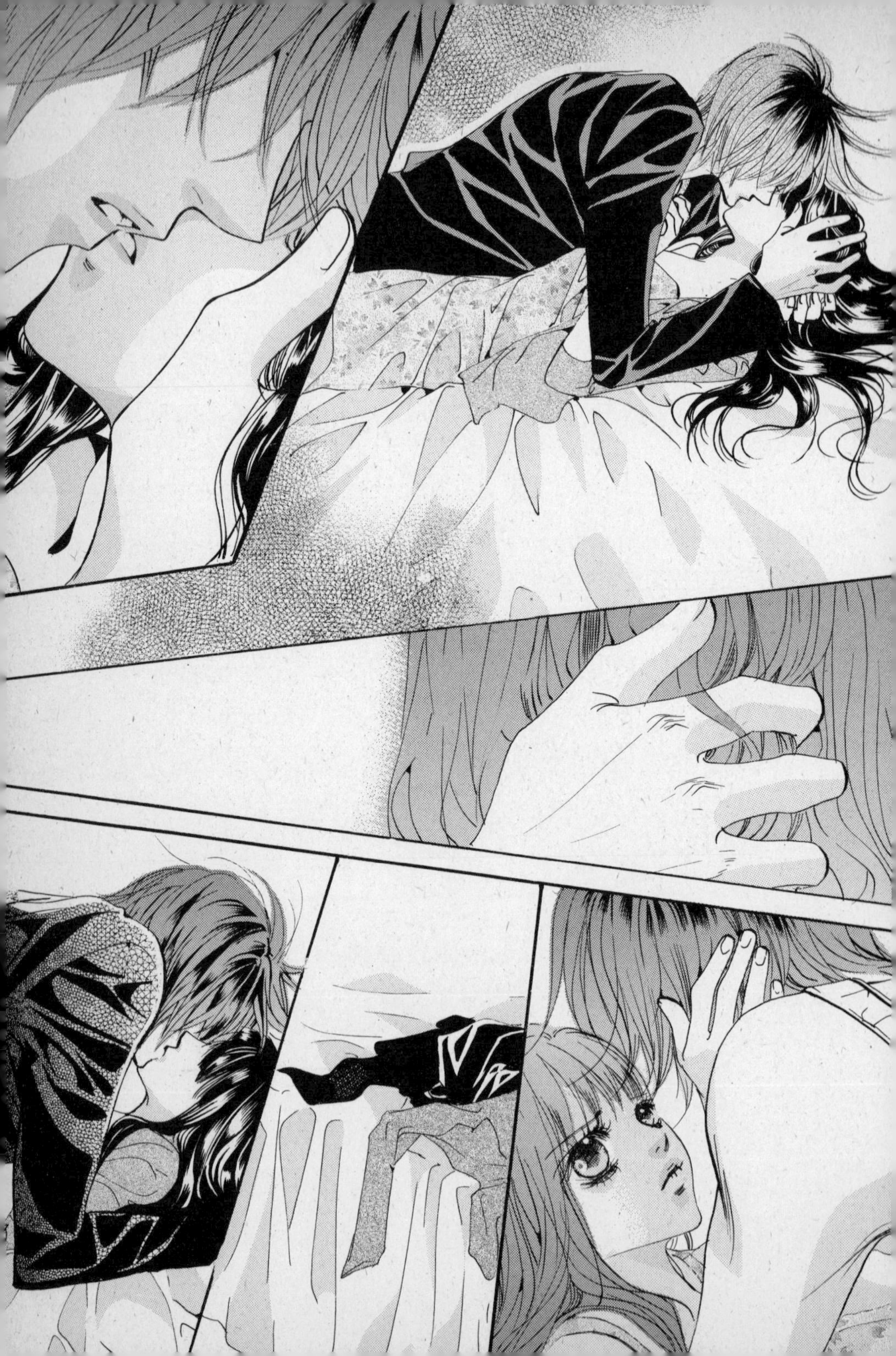

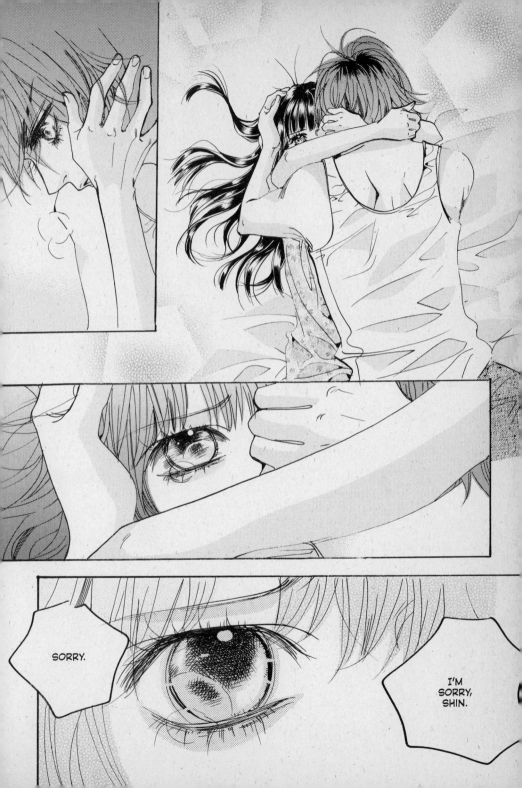

SORRY.

I'M SORRY, SHIN.

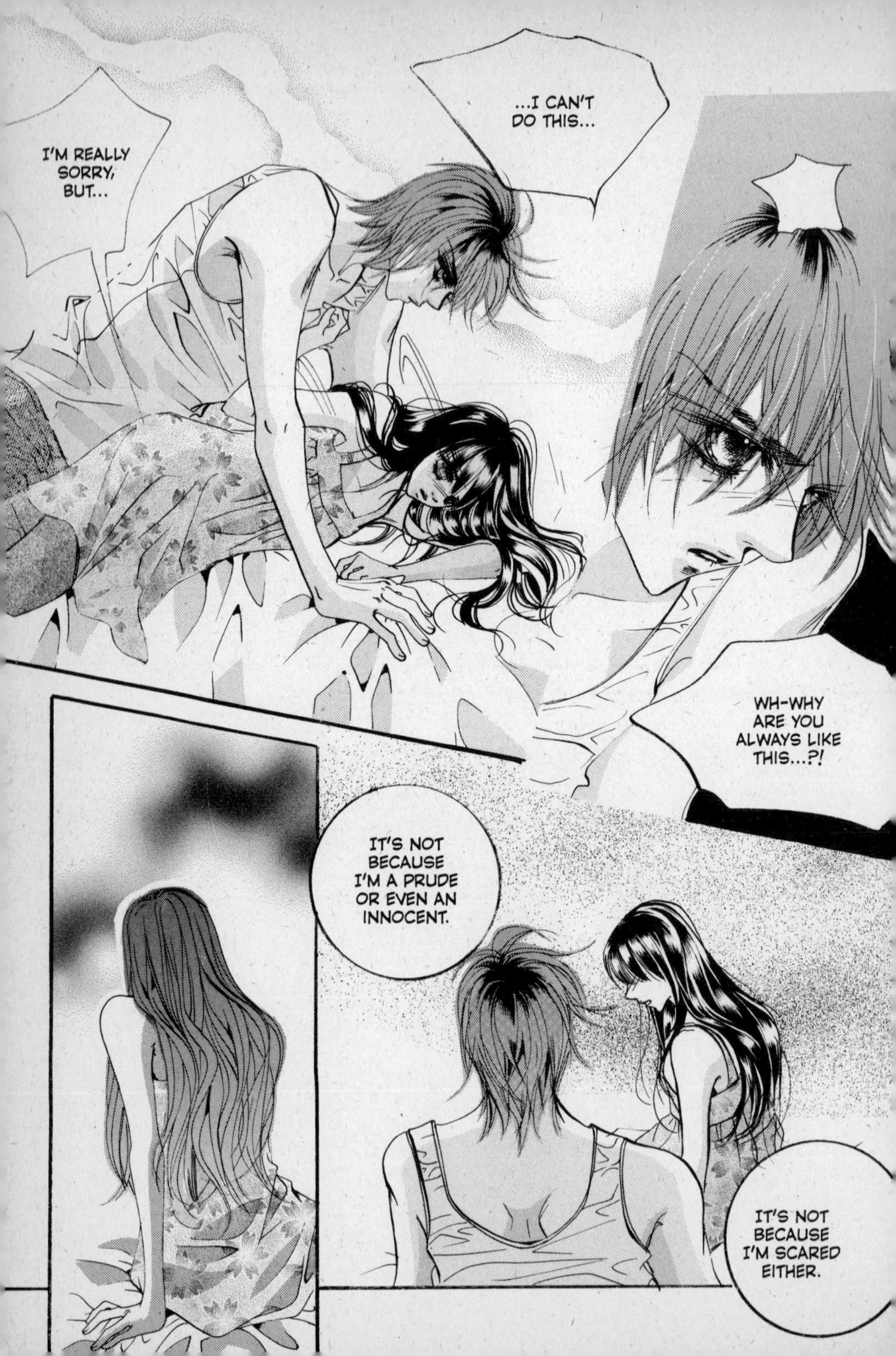
...I CAN'T DO THIS...
I'M REALLY SORRY, BUT...
WH-WHY ARE YOU ALWAYS LIKE THIS...?!
IT'S NOT BECAUSE I'M A PRUDE OR EVEN AN INNOCENT.
IT'S NOT BECAUSE I'M SCARED EITHER.

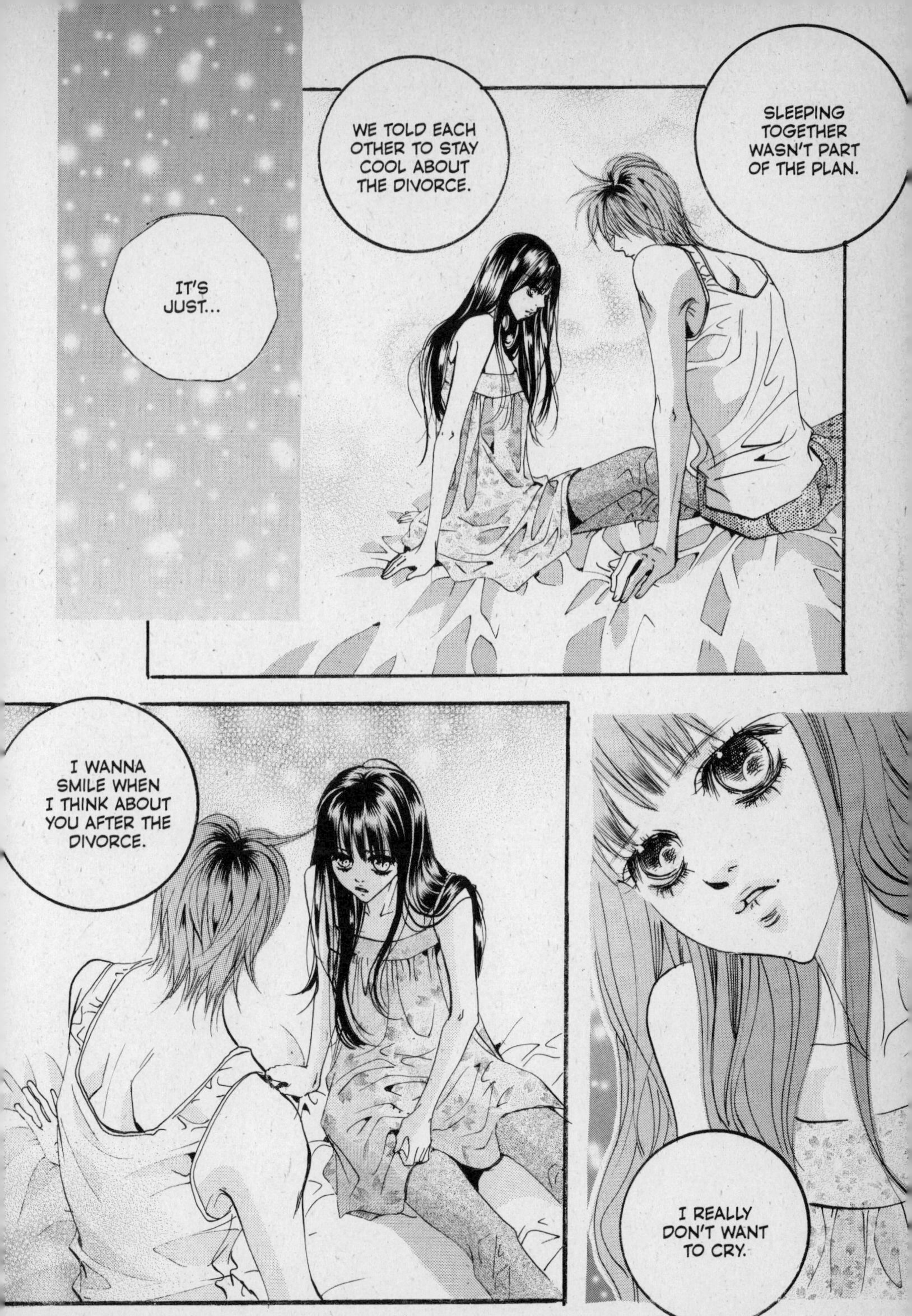
WE TOLD EACH OTHER TO STAY COOL ABOUT THE DIVORCE.
SLEEPING TOGETHER WASN'T PART OF THE PLAN.
IT'S JUST...
I WANNA SMILE WHEN I THINK ABOUT YOU AFTER THE DIVORCE.
I REALLY DON'T WANT TO CRY.

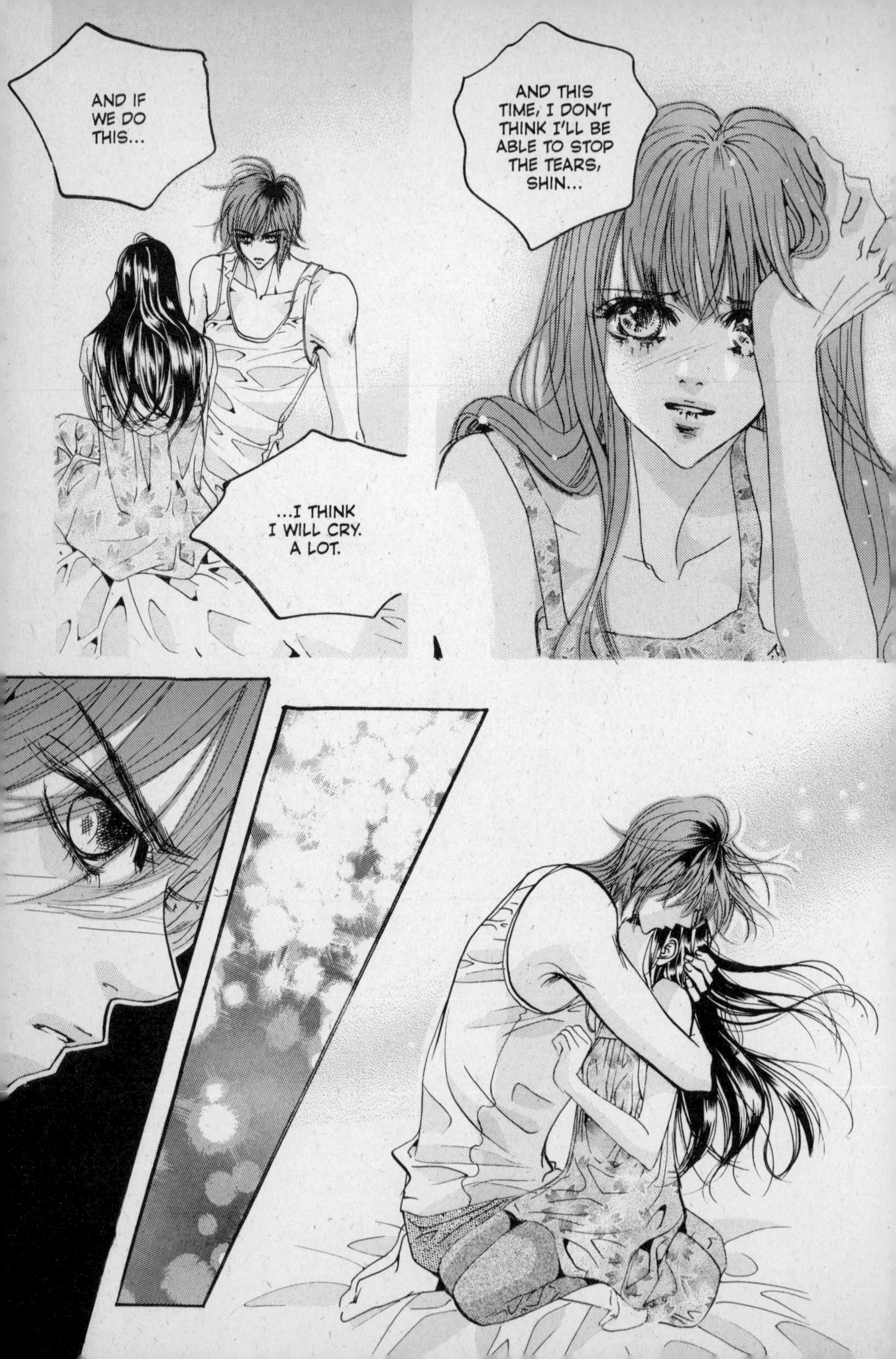
AND IF WE DO THIS...
...I THINK I WILL CRY. A LOT.
AND THIS TIME, I DON'T THINK I'LL BE ABLE TO STOP THE TEARS, SHIN...

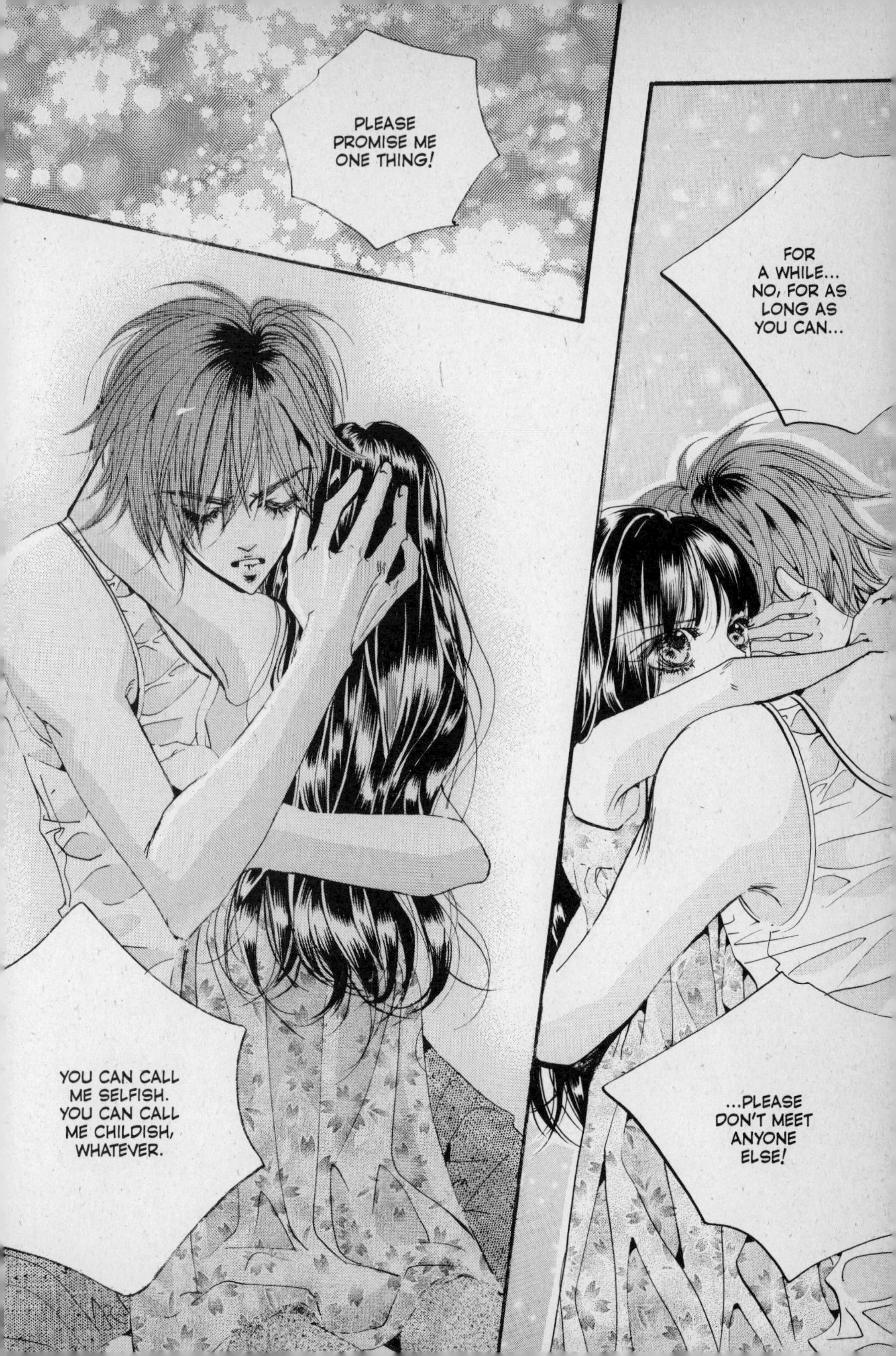
PLEASE PROMISE ME ONE THING!
FOR A WHILE... NO, FOR AS LONG AS YOU CAN...
YOU CAN CALL ME SELFISH. YOU CAN CALL ME CHILDISH, WHATEVER.
...PLEASE DON'T MEET ANYONE ELSE!

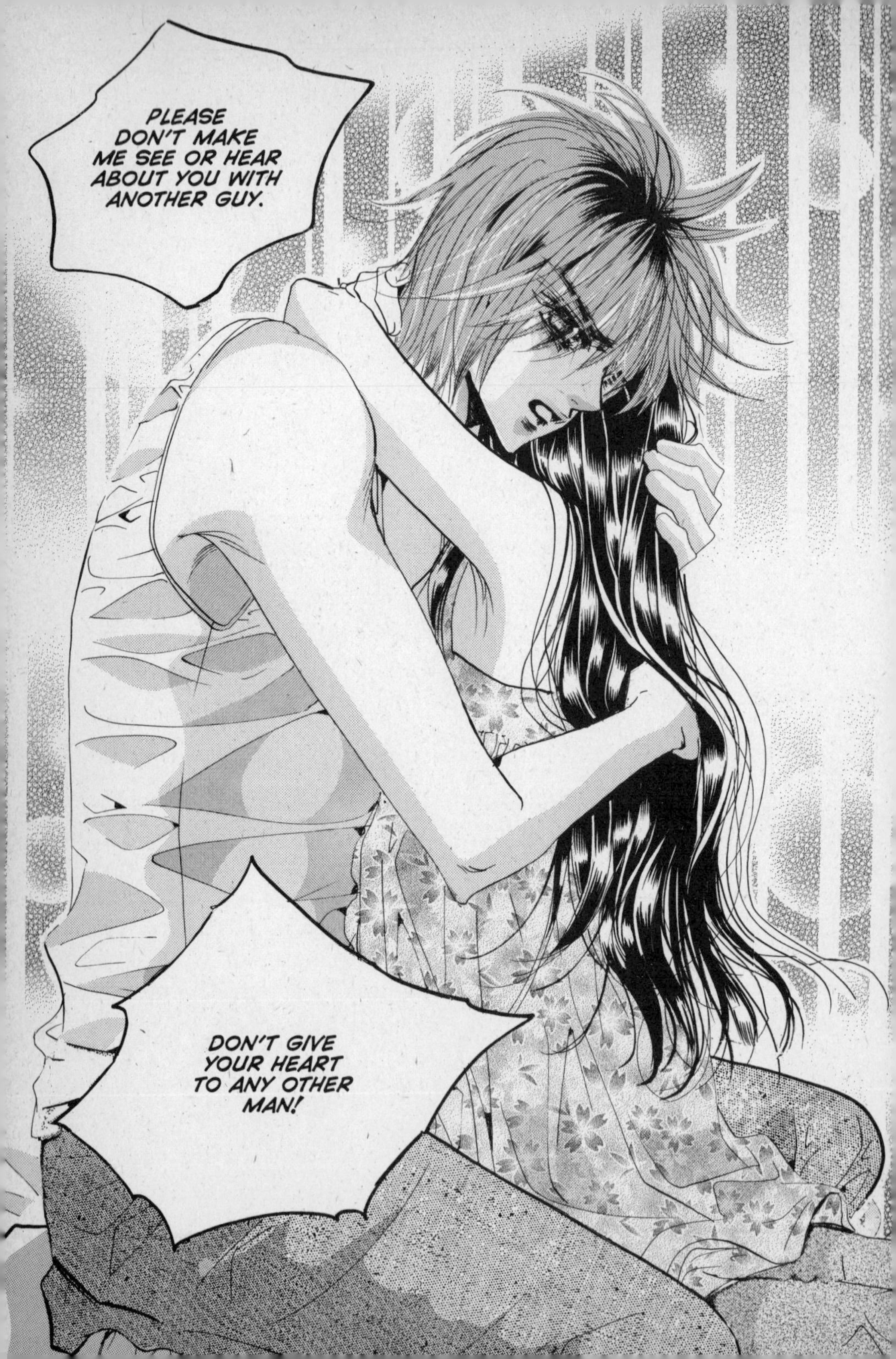
PLEASE DON'T MAKE ME SEE OR HEAR ABOUT YOU WITH ANOTHER GUY.
DON'T GIVE YOUR HEART TO ANY OTHER MAN!

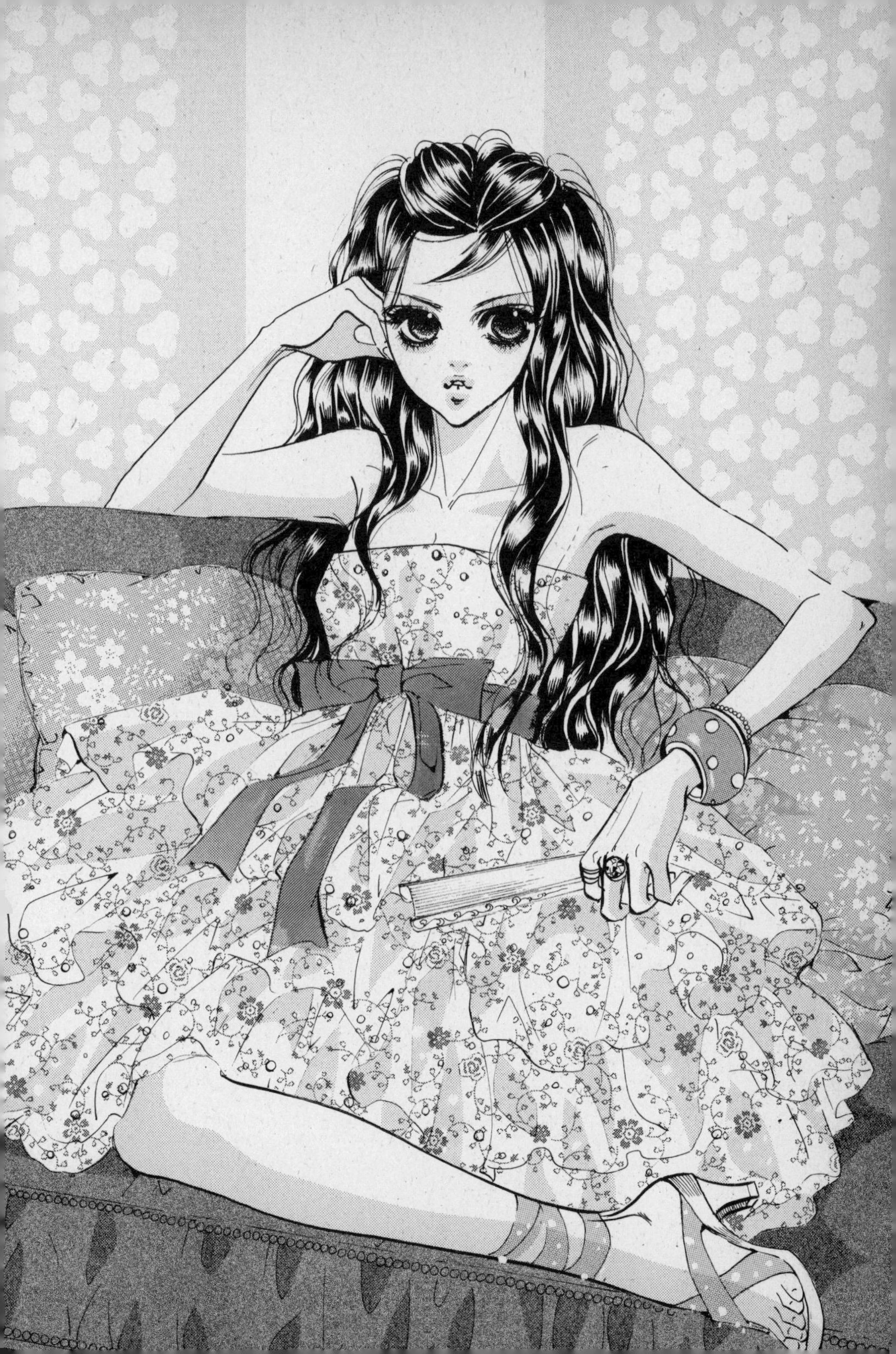

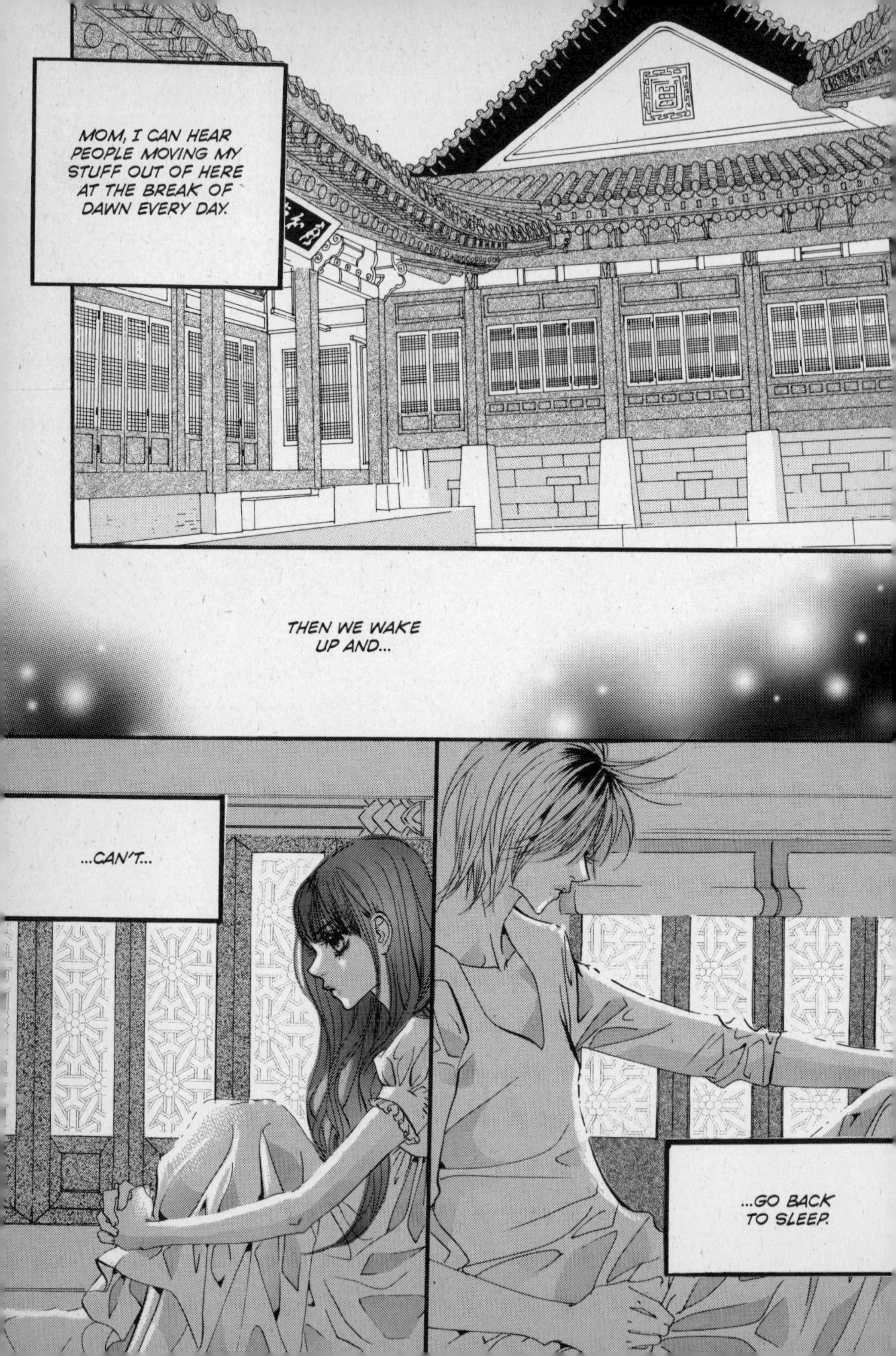
MOM, I CAN HEAR PEOPLE MOVING MY STUFF OUT OF HERE AT THE BREAK OF DAWN EVERY DAY.
THEN WE WAKE UP AND...
...CAN'T...
...GO BACK TO SLEEP.

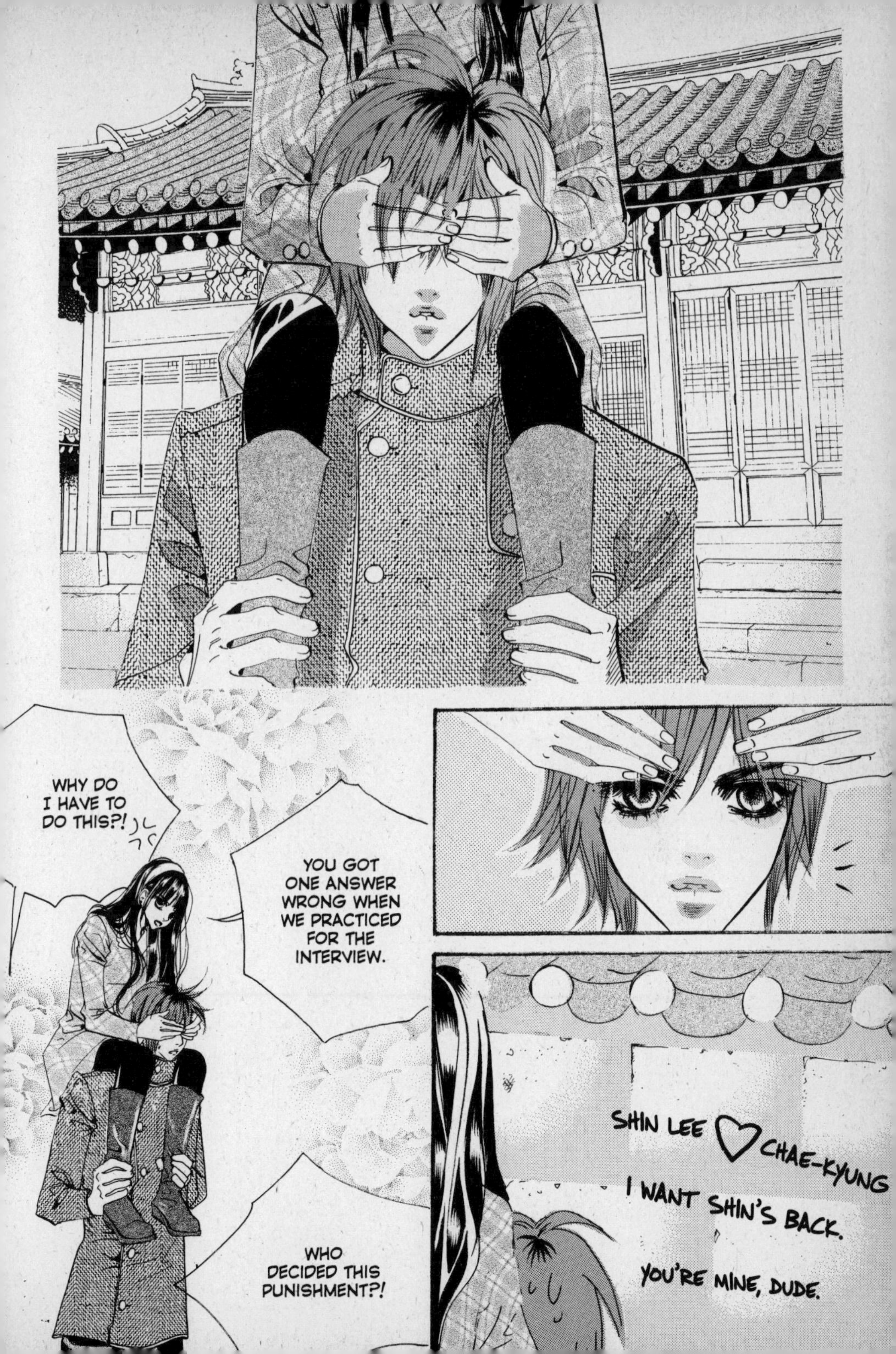
WHY DO I HAVE TO DO THIS?!
YOU GOT ONE ANSWER WRONG WHEN WE PRACTICED FOR THE INTERVIEW.
WHO DECIDED THIS PUNISHMENT?!
SHIN LEE ♡ CHAE-KYUNG
I WANT SHIN'S BACK.
YOU'RE MINE, DUDE.

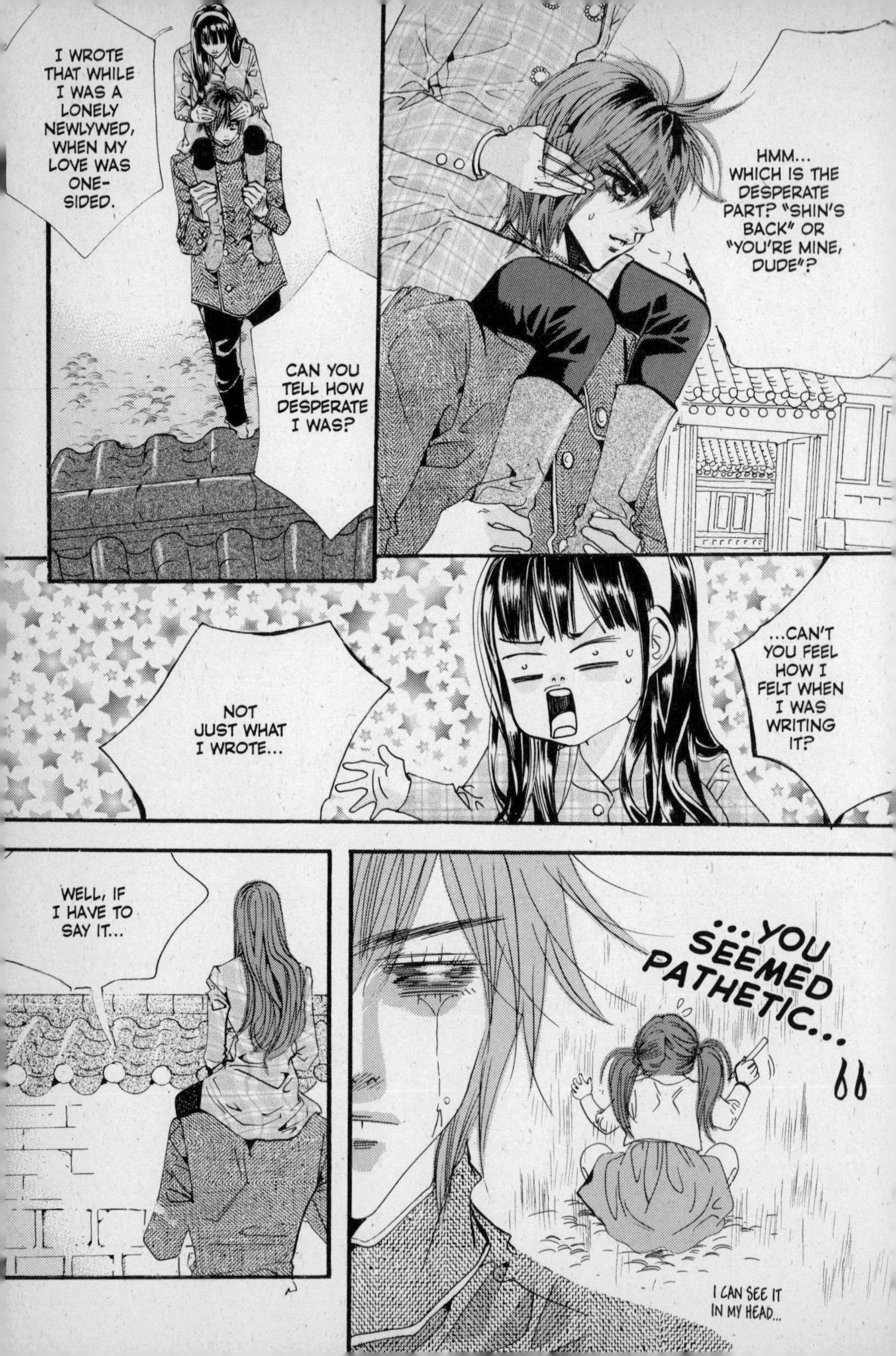
I WROTE THAT WHILE I WAS A LONELY NEWLYWED, WHEN MY LOVE WAS ONE-SIDED.
CAN YOU TELL HOW DESPERATE I WAS?
HMM... WHICH IS THE DESPERATE PART? "SHIN'S BACK" OR "YOU'RE MINE, DUDE"?
NOT JUST WHAT I WROTE...
...CAN'T YOU FEEL HOW I FELT WHEN I WAS WRITING IT?
WELL, IF I HAVE TO SAY IT...
...YOU SEEMED PATHETIC...
I CAN SEE IT IN MY HEAD...

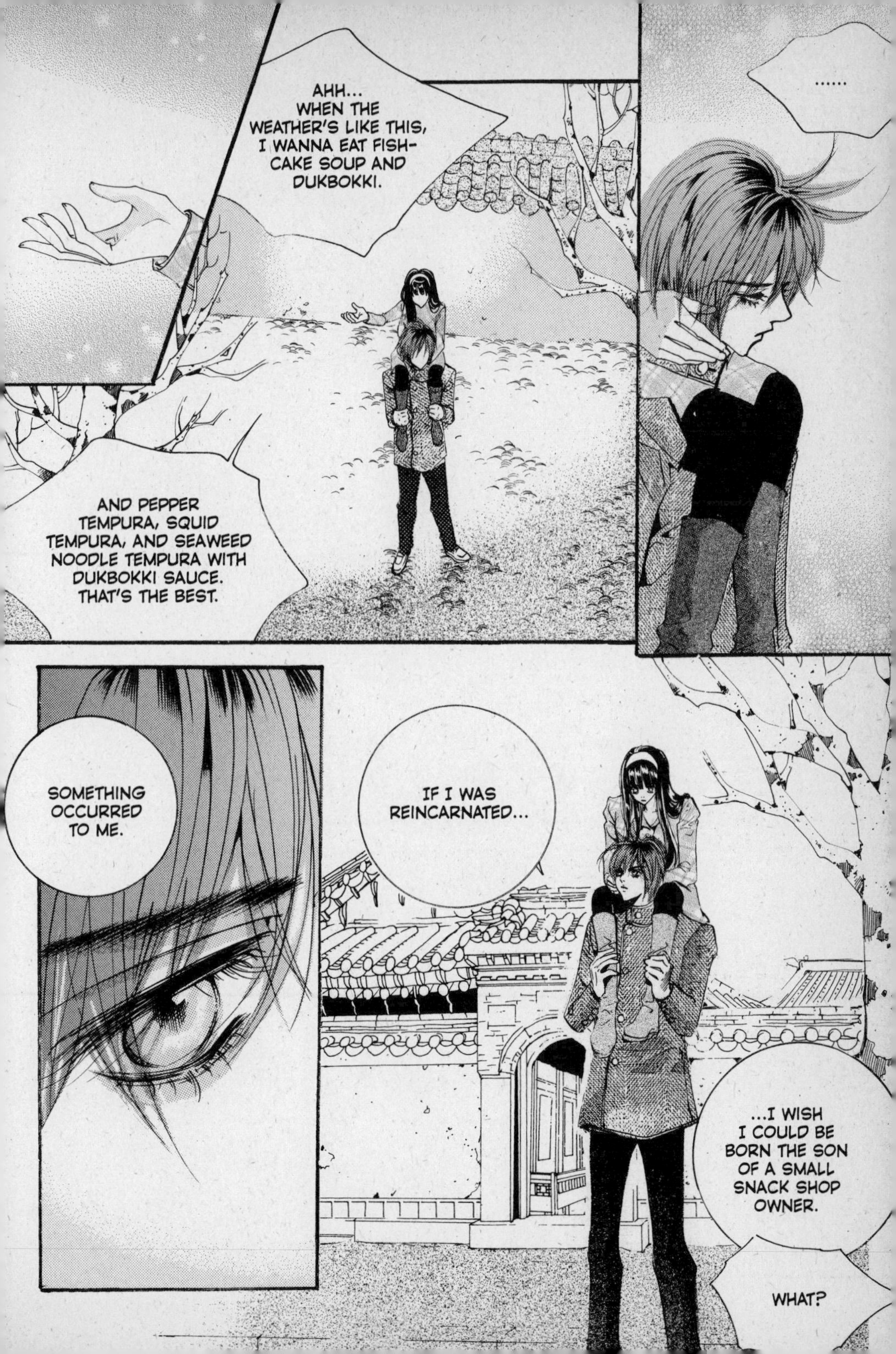
AHH... WHEN THE WEATHER'S LIKE THIS, I WANNA EAT FISH-CAKE SOUP AND DUKBOKKI.
AND PEPPER TEMPURA, SQUID TEMPURA, AND SEAWEED NOODLE TEMPURA WITH DUKBOKKI SAUCE. THAT'S THE BEST.
......
SOMETHING OCCURRED TO ME.
IF I WAS REINCARNATED...
...I WISH I COULD BE BORN THE SON OF A SMALL SNACK SHOP OWNER.
WHAT?

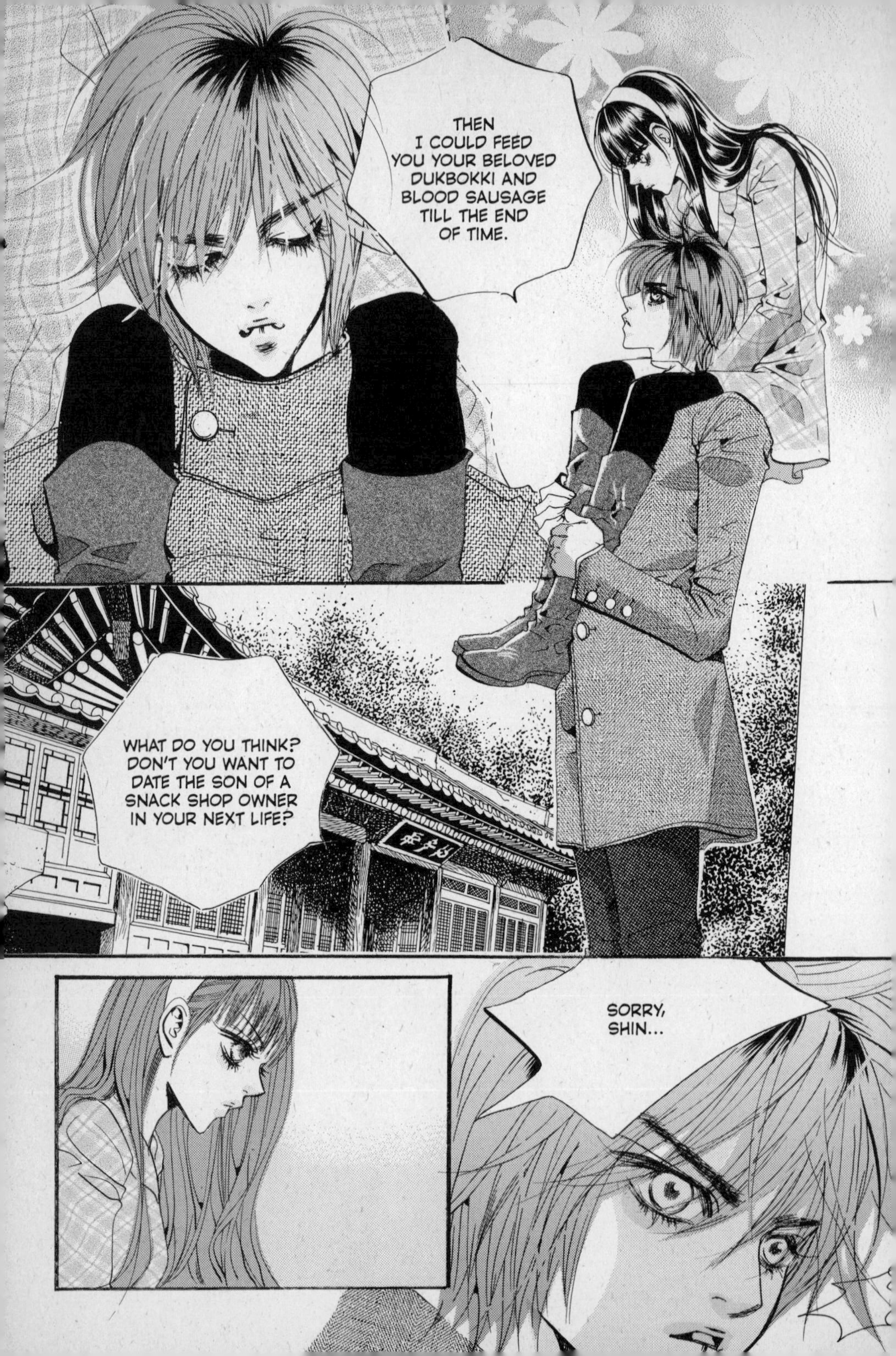
THEN I COULD FEED YOU YOUR BELOVED DUKBOKKI AND BLOOD SAUSAGE TILL THE END OF TIME.
WHAT DO YOU THINK? DON'T YOU WANT TO DATE THE SON OF A SNACK SHOP OWNER IN YOUR NEXT LIFE?
SORRY, SHIN...

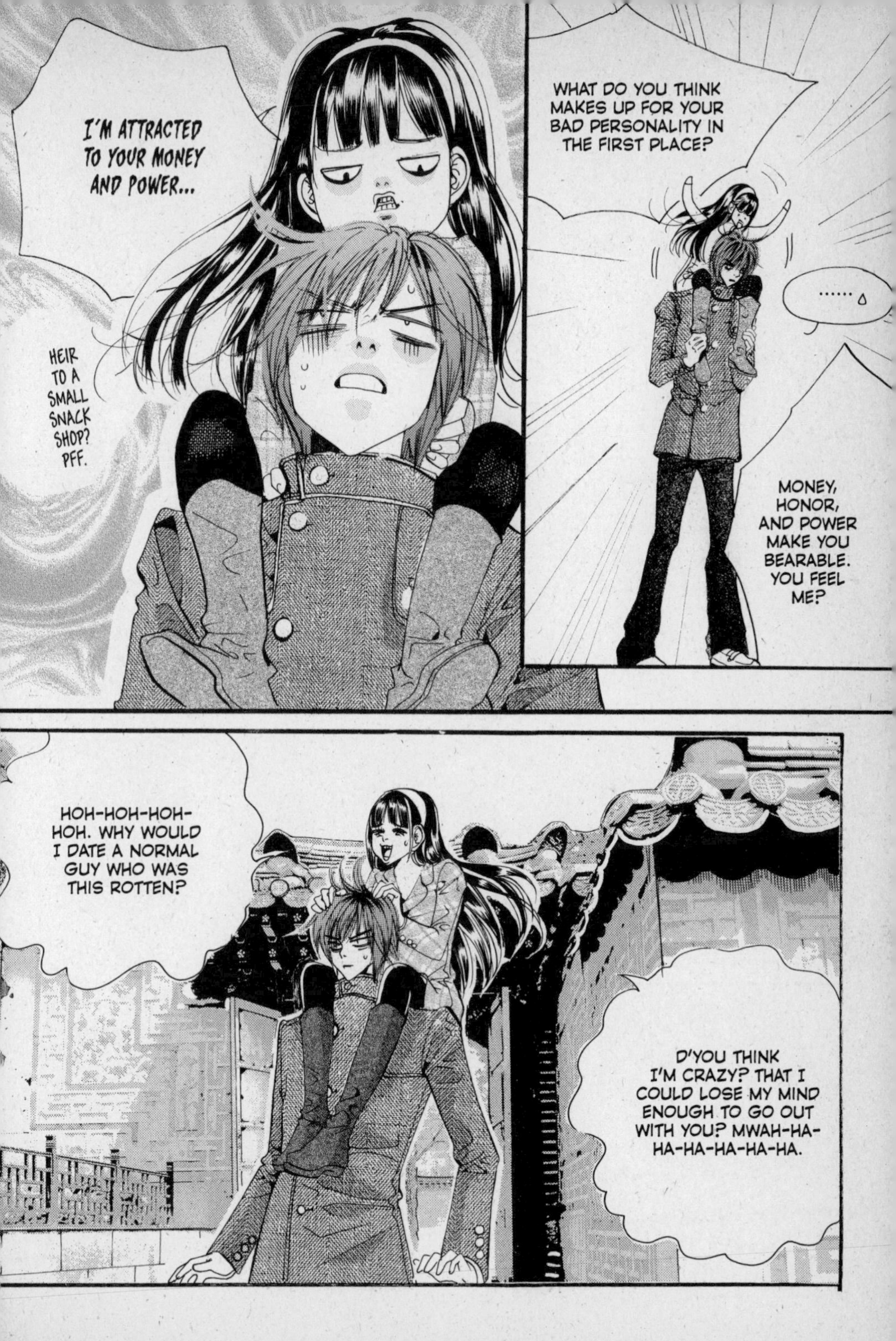
I'M ATTRACTED TO YOUR MONEY AND POWER...
HEIR TO A SMALL SNACK SHOP? PFF.
WHAT DO YOU THINK MAKES UP FOR YOUR BAD PERSONALITY IN THE FIRST PLACE?
......
MONEY, HONOR, AND POWER MAKE YOU BEARABLE. YOU FEEL ME?
HOH-HOH-HOH-HOH. WHY WOULD I DATE A NORMAL GUY WHO WAS THIS ROTTEN?
D'YOU THINK I'M CRAZY? THAT I COULD LOSE MY MIND ENOUGH TO GO OUT WITH YOU? MWAH-HA-HA-HA-HA-HA-HA.

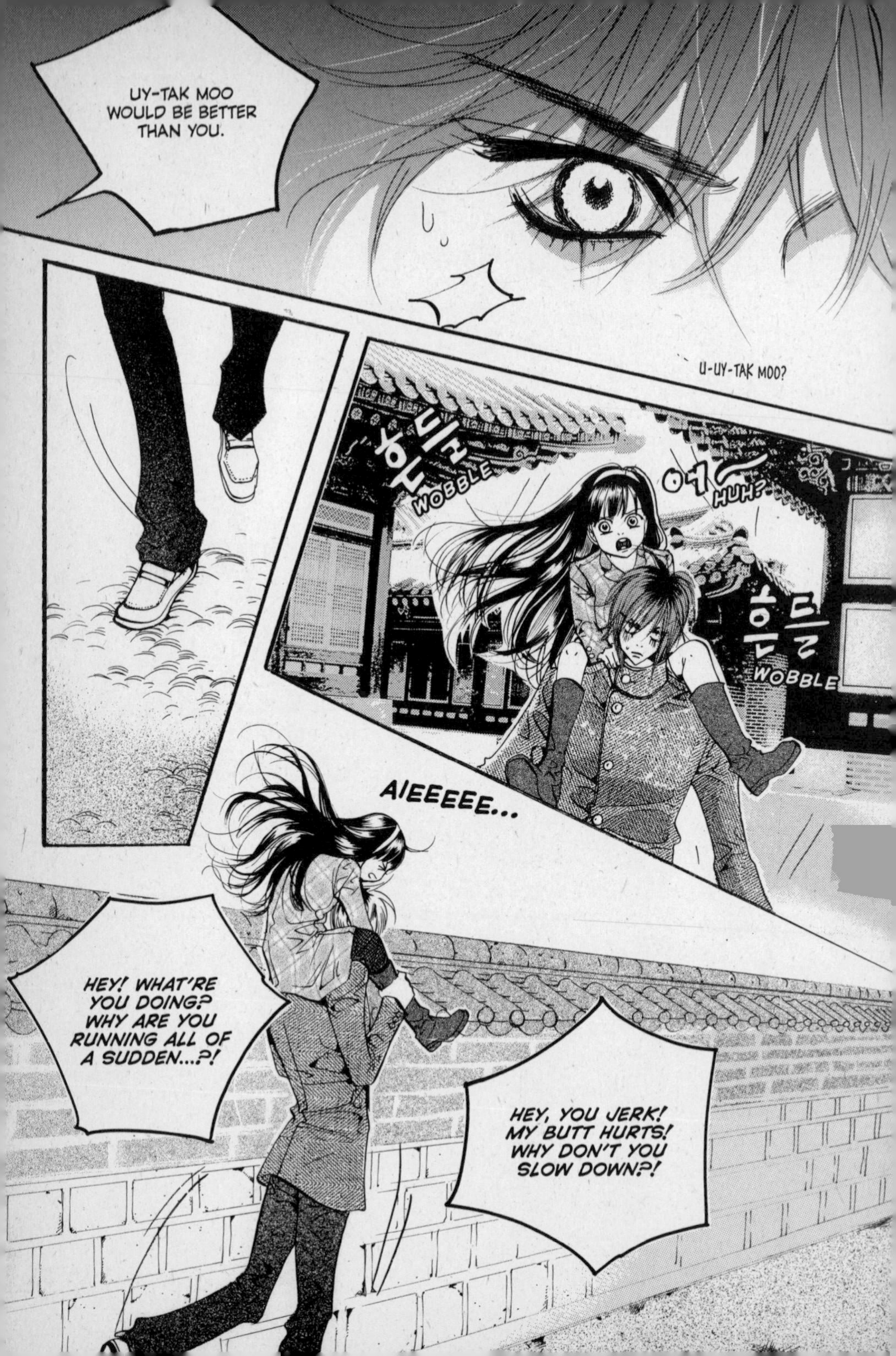
UY-TAK MOO WOULD BE BETTER THAN YOU.
U-UY-TAK MOO?
흔들
WOBBLE
어~
HUH?
흔들
WOBBLE
AIEEEEE...
HEY! WHAT'RE YOU DOING? WHY ARE YOU RUNNING ALL OF A SUDDEN...?!
HEY, YOU JERK! MY BUTT HURTS! WHY DON'T YOU SLOW DOWN?!

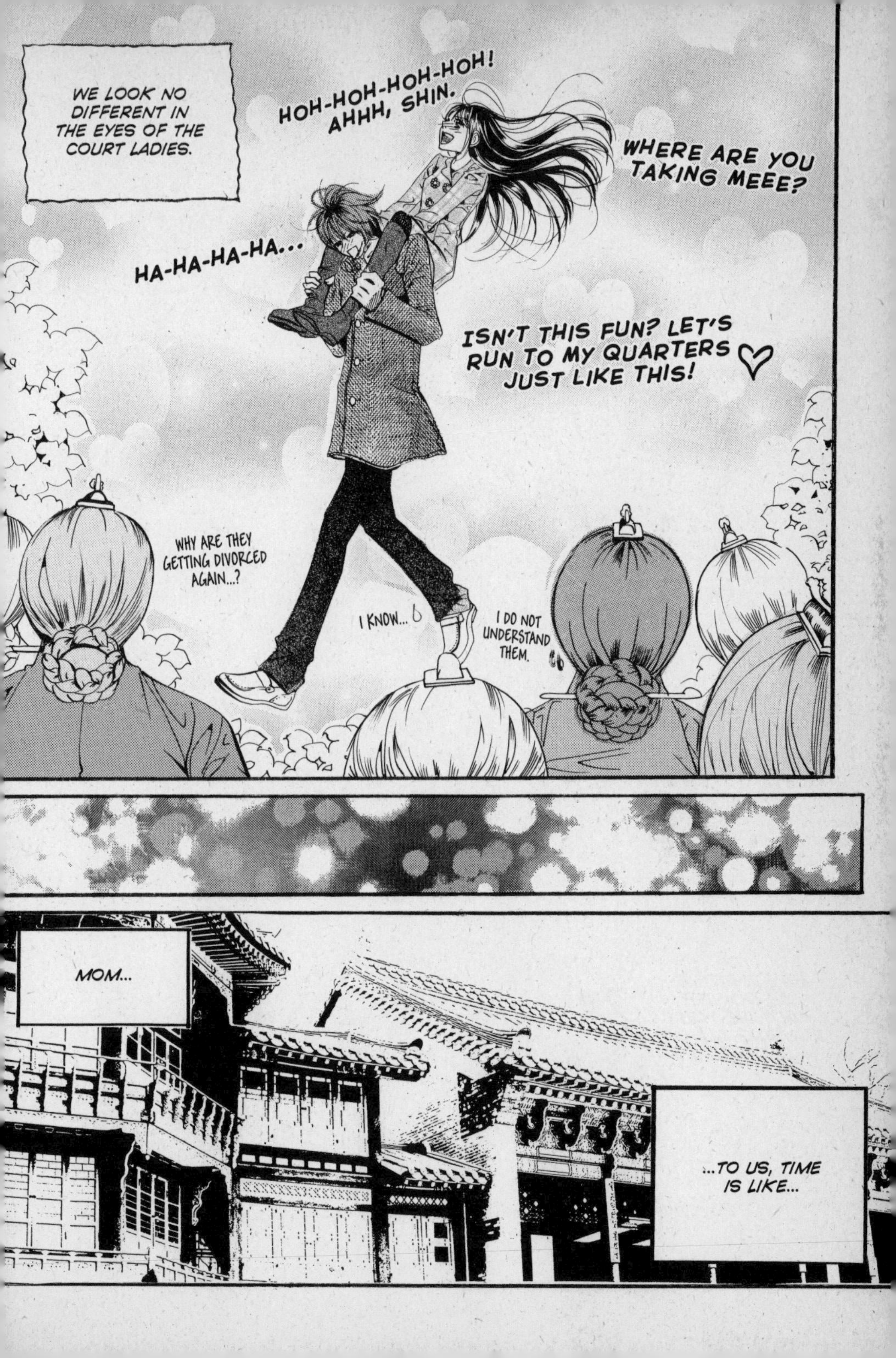
WE LOOK NO DIFFERENT IN THE EYES OF THE COURT LADIES.
HOH-HOH-HOH-HOH! AHHH, SHIN.
WHERE ARE YOU TAKING MEEE?
HA-HA-HA-HA...
ISN'T THIS FUN? LET'S RUN TO MY QUARTERS JUST LIKE THIS!
WHY ARE THEY GETTING DIVORCED AGAIN...?
I KNOW...
I DO NOT UNDERSTAND THEM.
MOM...
...TO US, TIME IS LIKE...

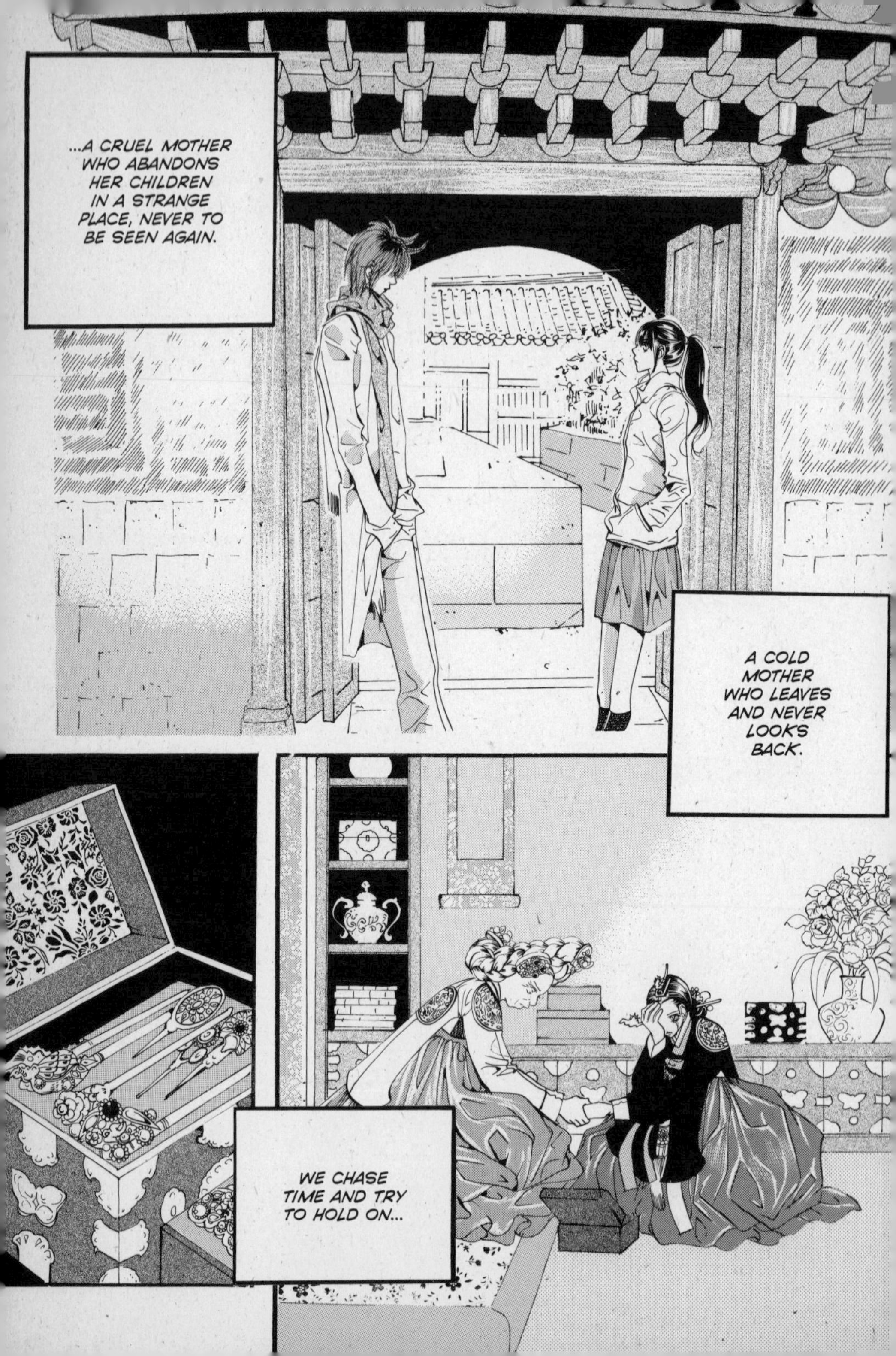
...A CRUEL MOTHER WHO ABANDONS HER CHILDREN IN A STRANGE PLACE, NEVER TO BE SEEN AGAIN.
A COLD MOTHER WHO LEAVES AND NEVER LOOKS BACK.
WE CHASE TIME AND TRY TO HOLD ON...

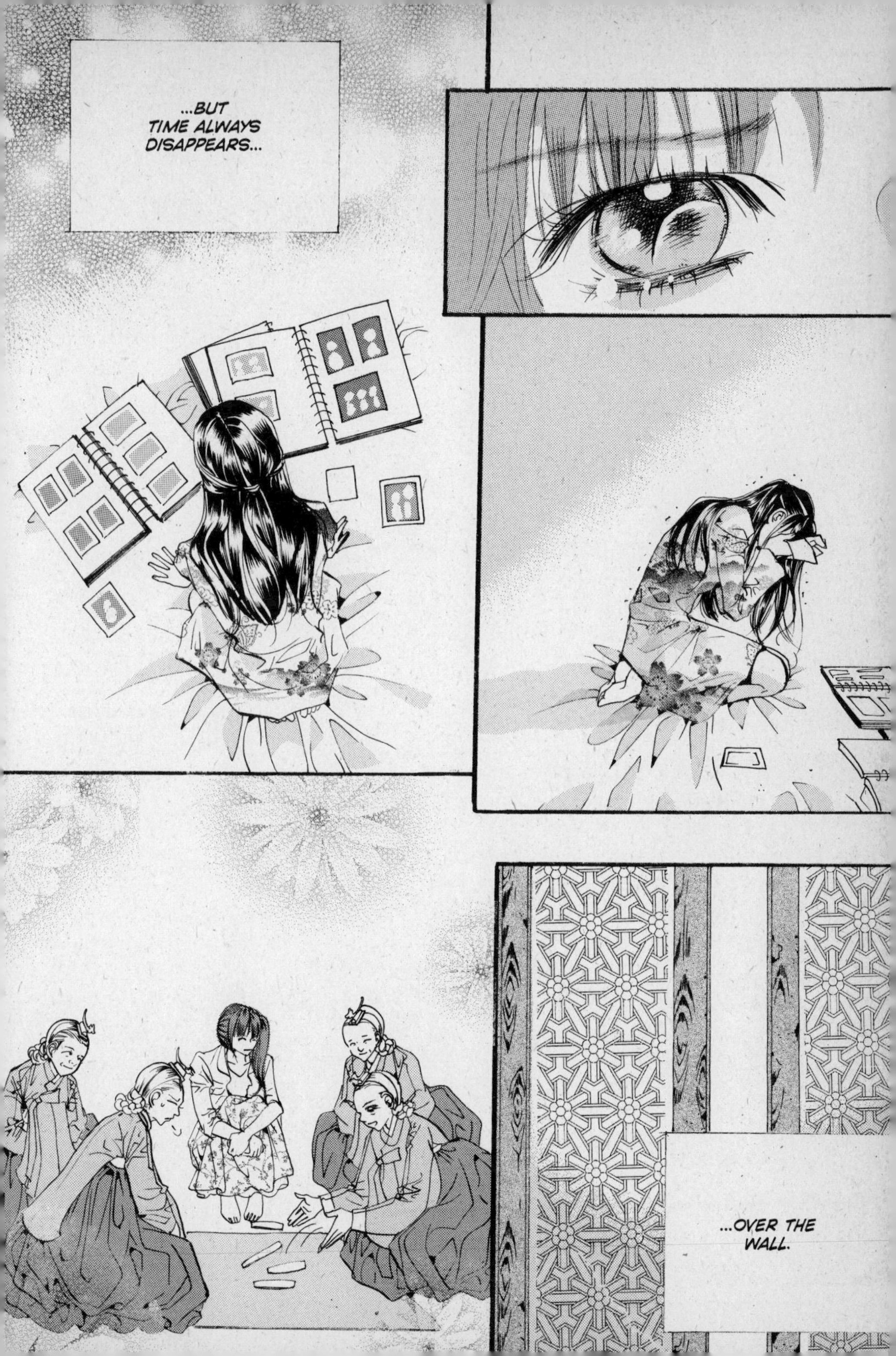
...BUT TIME ALWAYS DISAPPEARS...
...OVER THE WALL.

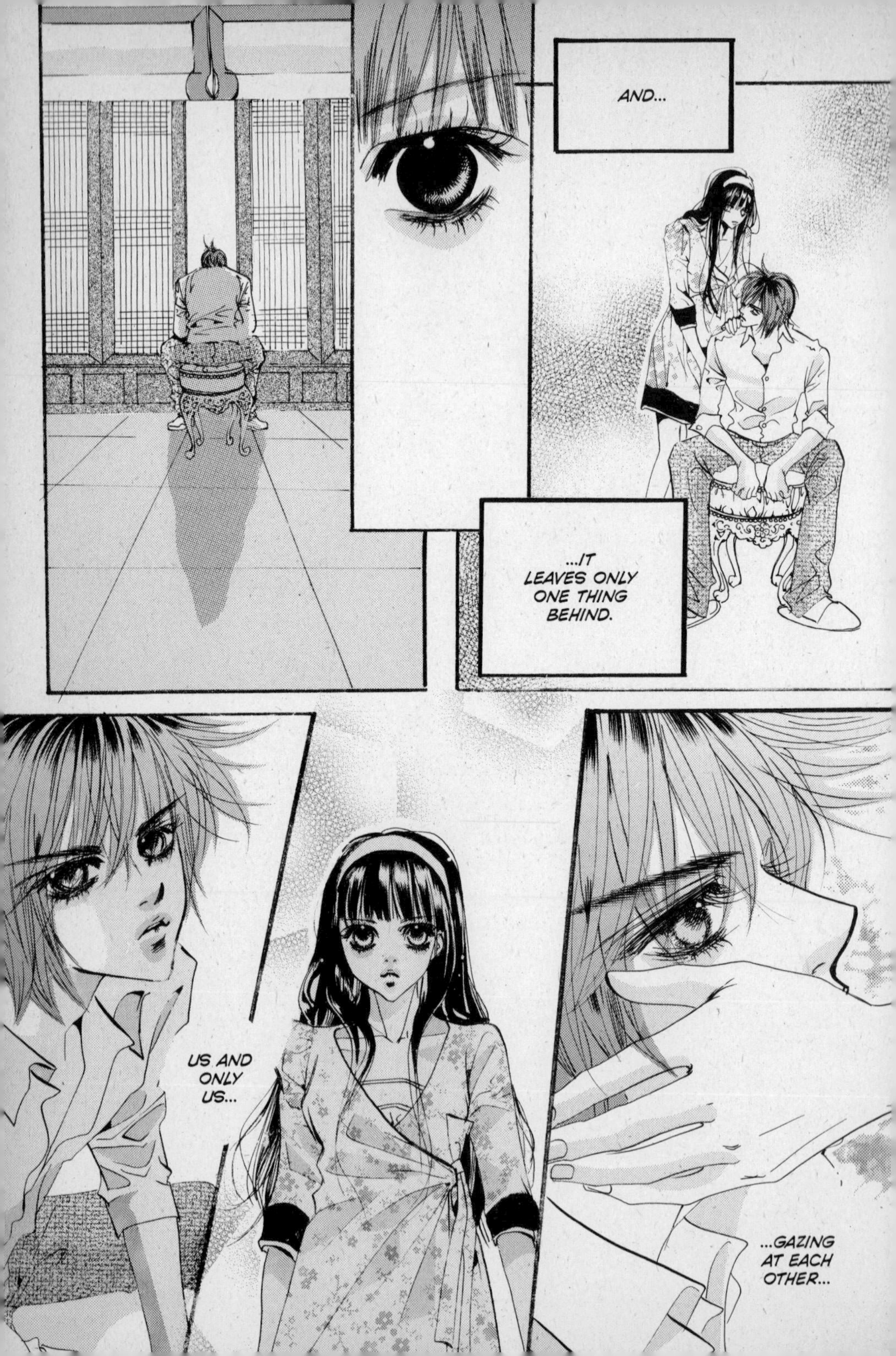
AND...
...IT LEAVES ONLY ONE THING BEHIND.
US AND ONLY US...
...GAZING AT EACH OTHER...

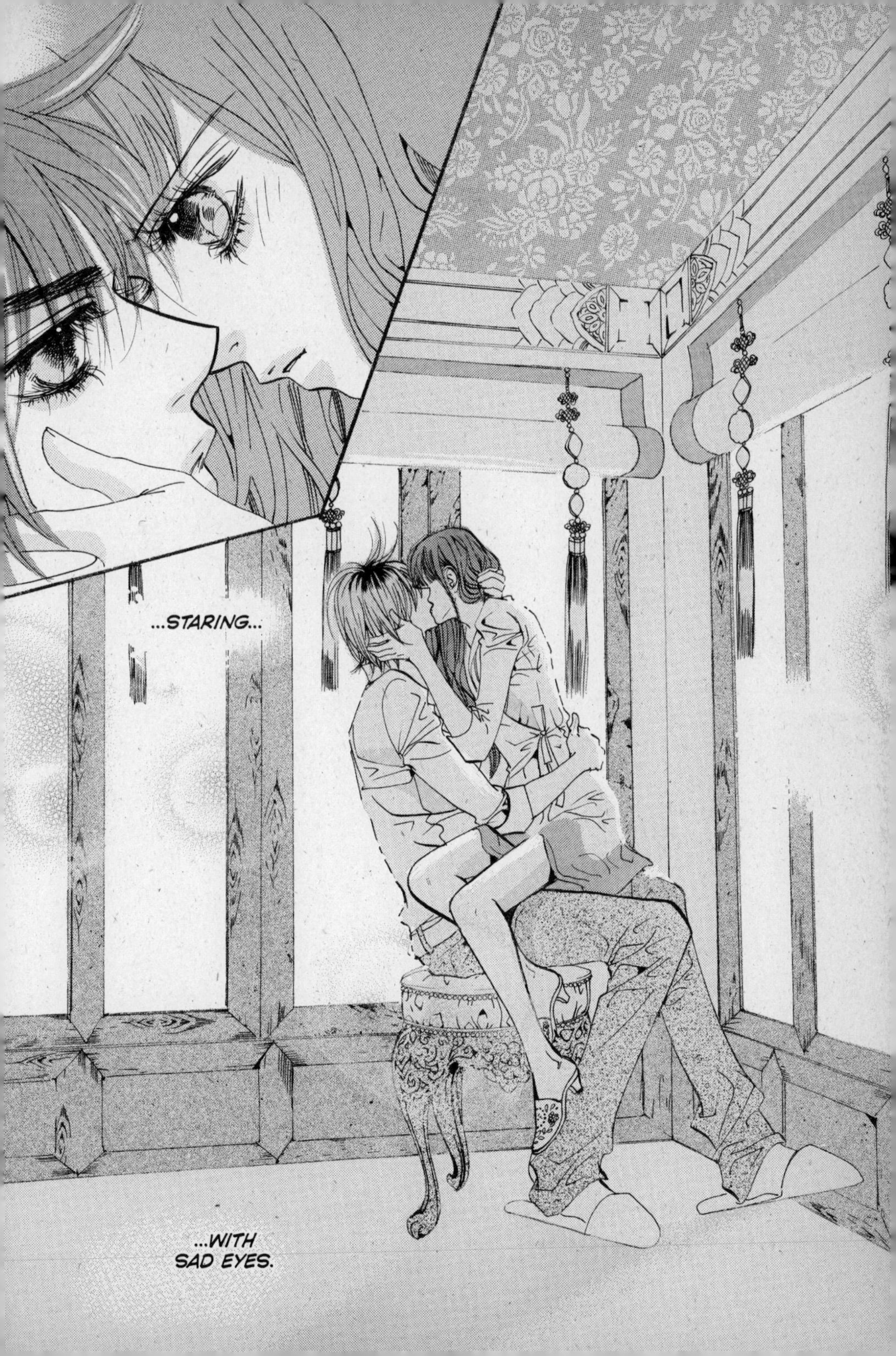
...STARING...
...WITH SAD EYES.

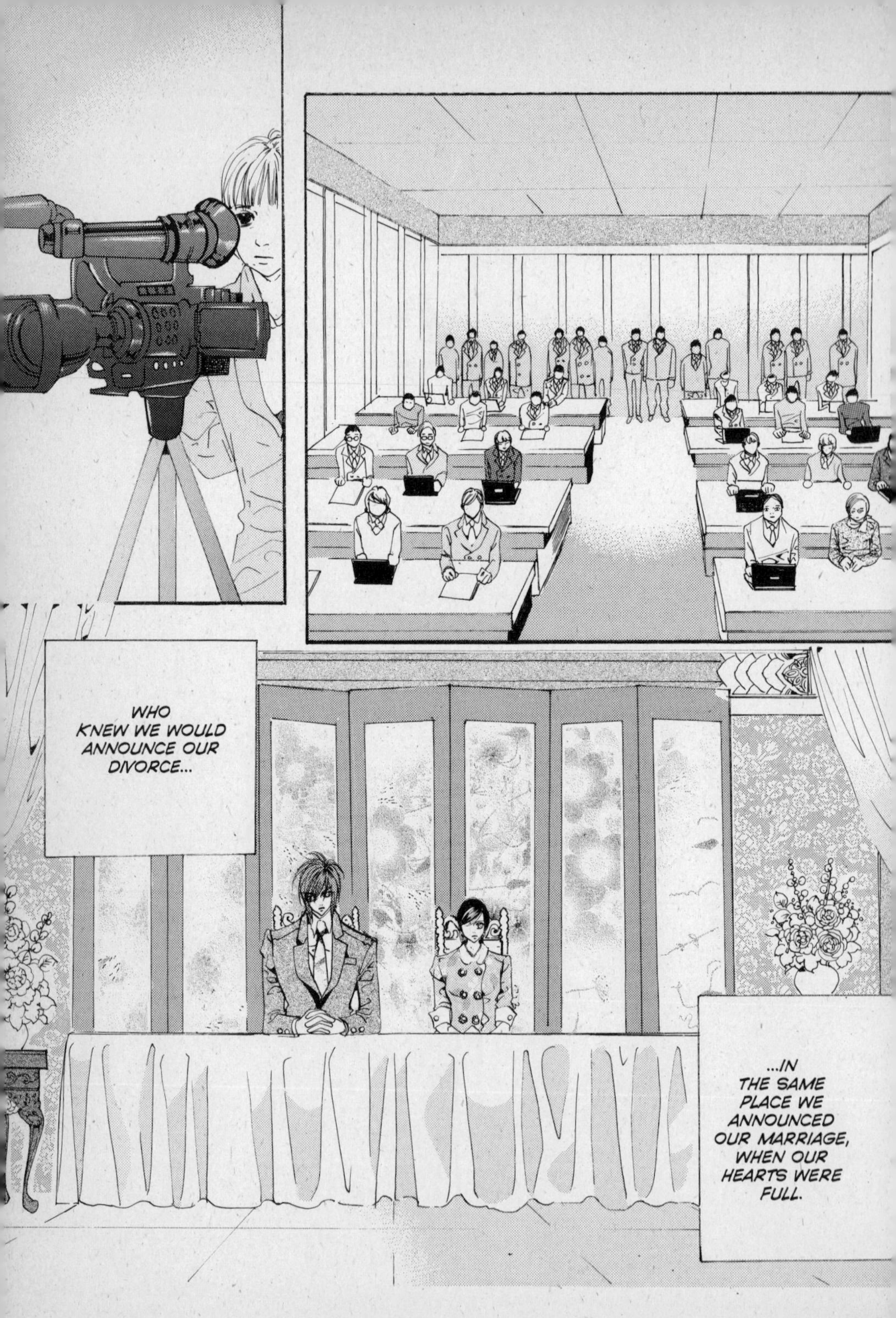

WHO KNEW WE WOULD ANNOUNCE OUR DIVORCE...
...IN THE SAME PLACE WE ANNOUNCED OUR MARRIAGE, WHEN OUR HEARTS WERE FULL.

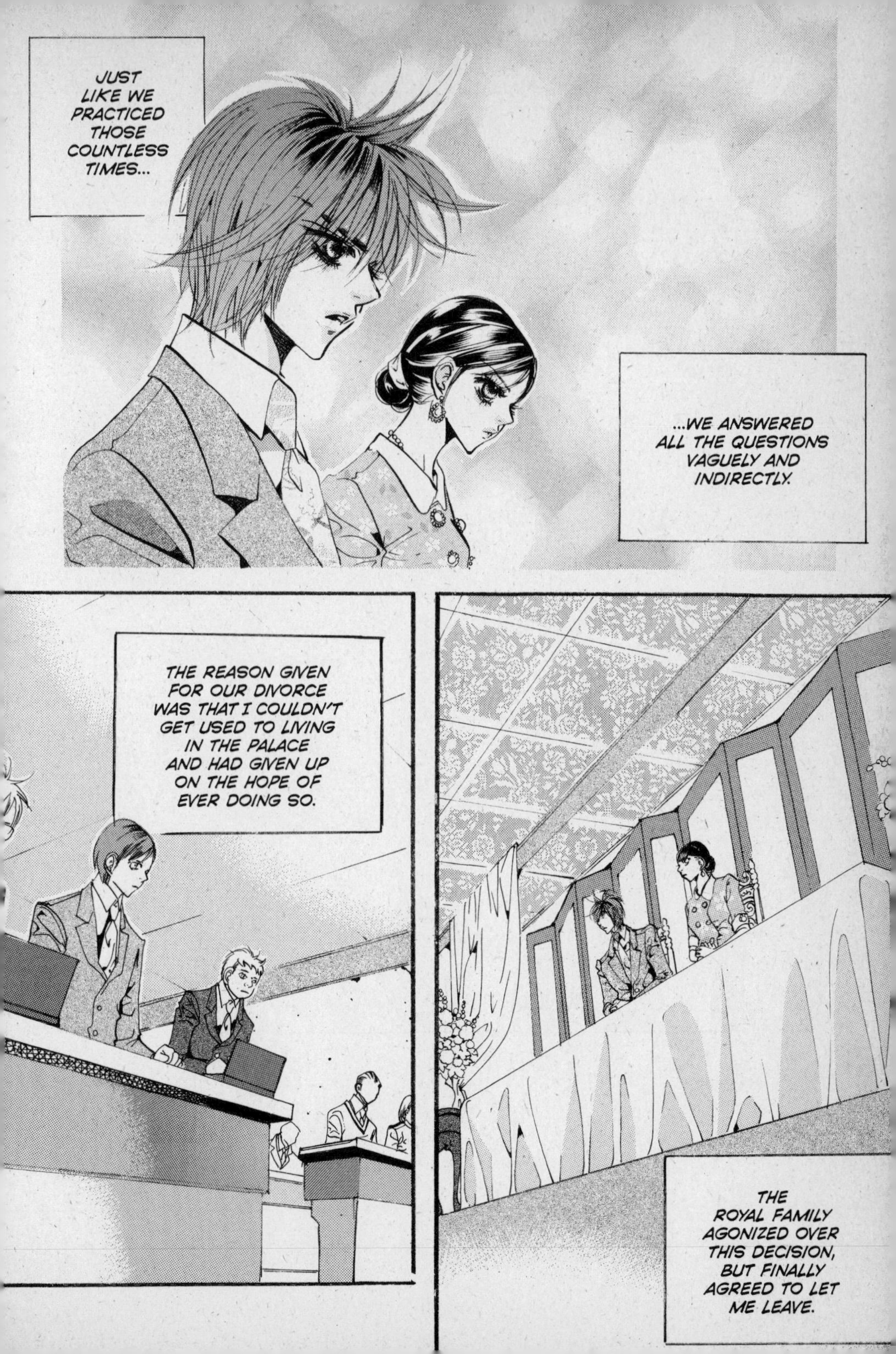
JUST LIKE WE PRACTICED THOSE COUNTLESS TIMES...
...WE ANSWERED ALL THE QUESTIONS VAGUELY AND INDIRECTLY.
THE REASON GIVEN FOR OUR DIVORCE WAS THAT I COULDN'T GET USED TO LIVING IN THE PALACE AND HAD GIVEN UP ON THE HOPE OF EVER DOING SO.
THE ROYAL FAMILY AGONIZED OVER THIS DECISION, BUT FINALLY AGREED TO LET ME LEAVE.

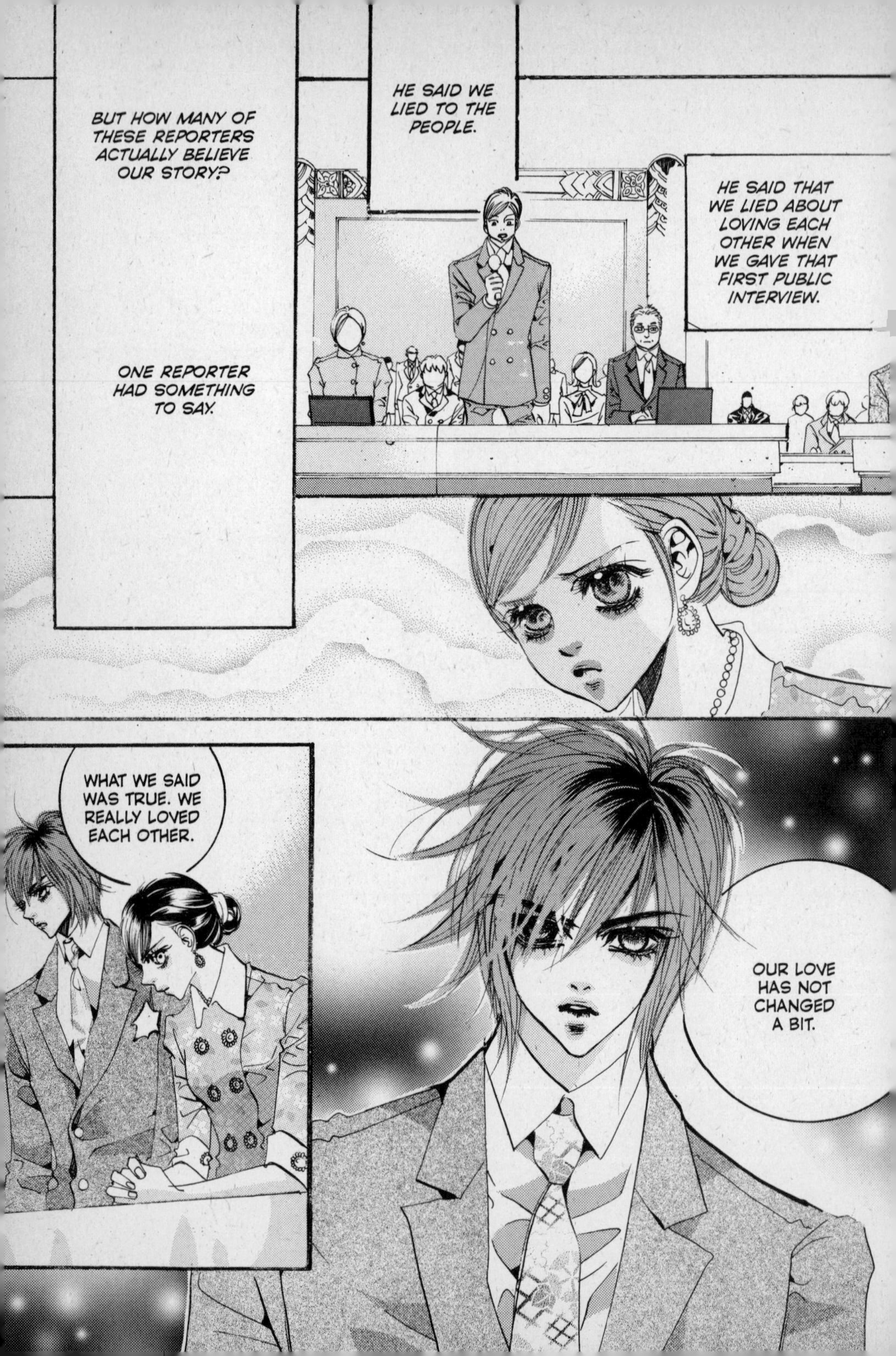
BUT HOW MANY OF THESE REPORTERS ACTUALLY BELIEVE OUR STORY?
ONE REPORTER HAD SOMETHING TO SAY.
HE SAID WE LIED TO THE PEOPLE.
HE SAID THAT WE LIED ABOUT LOVING EACH OTHER WHEN WE GAVE THAT FIRST PUBLIC INTERVIEW.
WHAT WE SAID WAS TRUE. WE REALLY LOVED EACH OTHER.
OUR LOVE HAS NOT CHANGED A BIT.

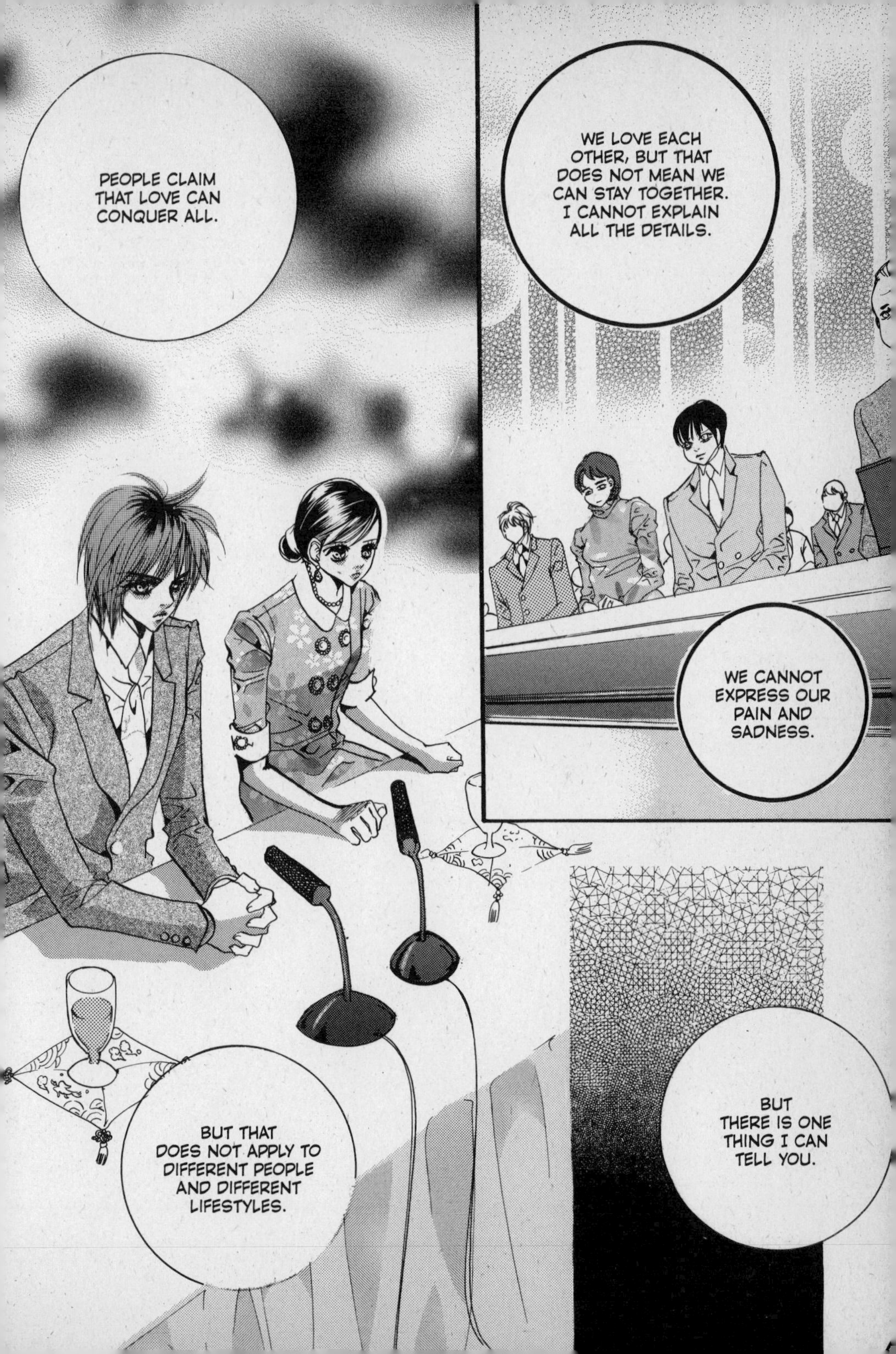
PEOPLE CLAIM THAT LOVE CAN CONQUER ALL.
BUT THAT DOES NOT APPLY TO DIFFERENT PEOPLE AND DIFFERENT LIFESTYLES.
WE LOVE EACH OTHER, BUT THAT DOES NOT MEAN WE CAN STAY TOGETHER. I CANNOT EXPLAIN ALL THE DETAILS.
WE CANNOT EXPRESS OUR PAIN AND SADNESS.
BUT THERE IS ONE THING I CAN TELL YOU.

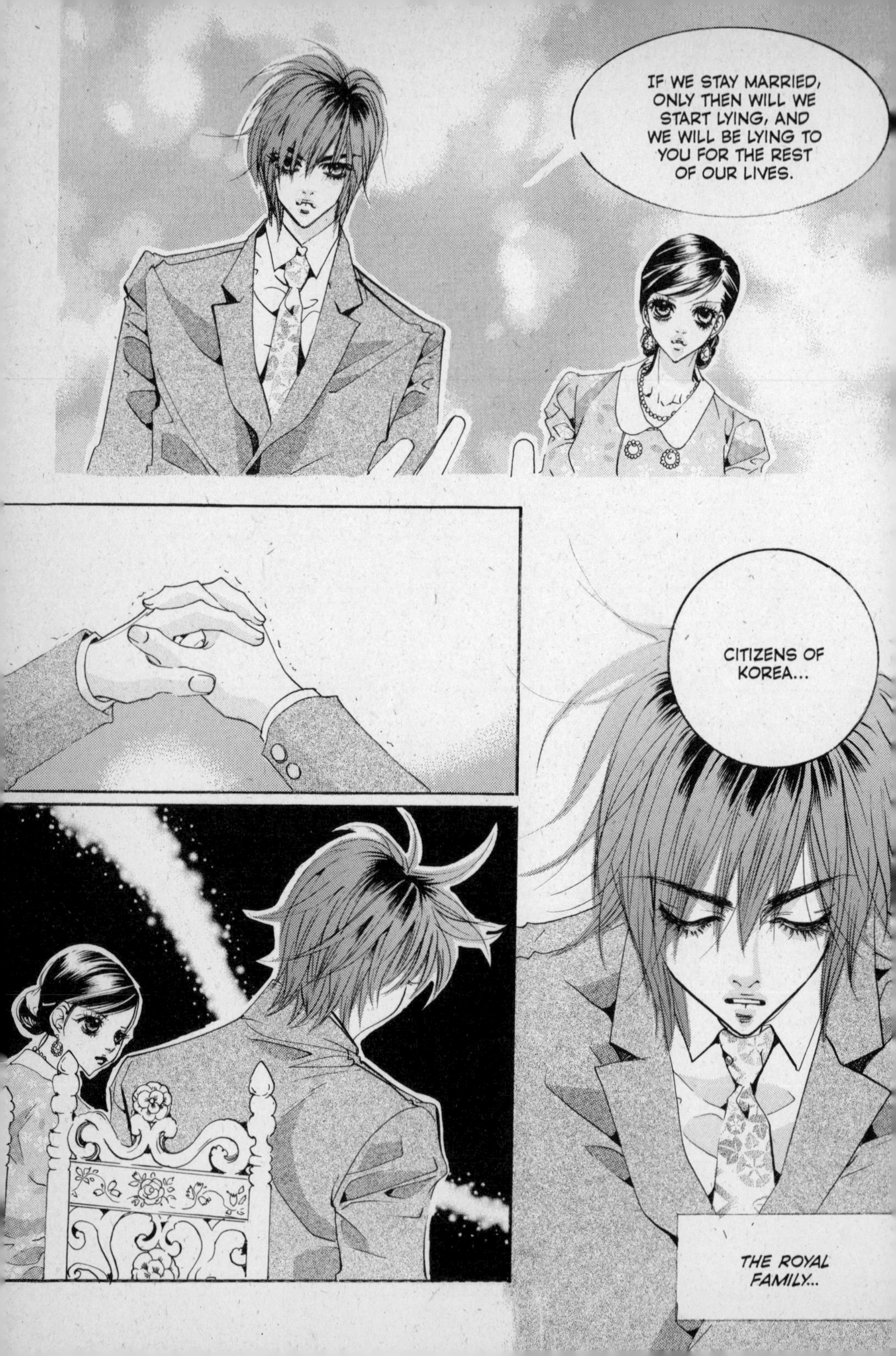
IF WE STAY MARRIED, ONLY THEN WILL WE START LYING, AND WE WILL BE LYING TO YOU FOR THE REST OF OUR LIVES.
CITIZENS OF KOREA...
THE ROYAL FAMILY...

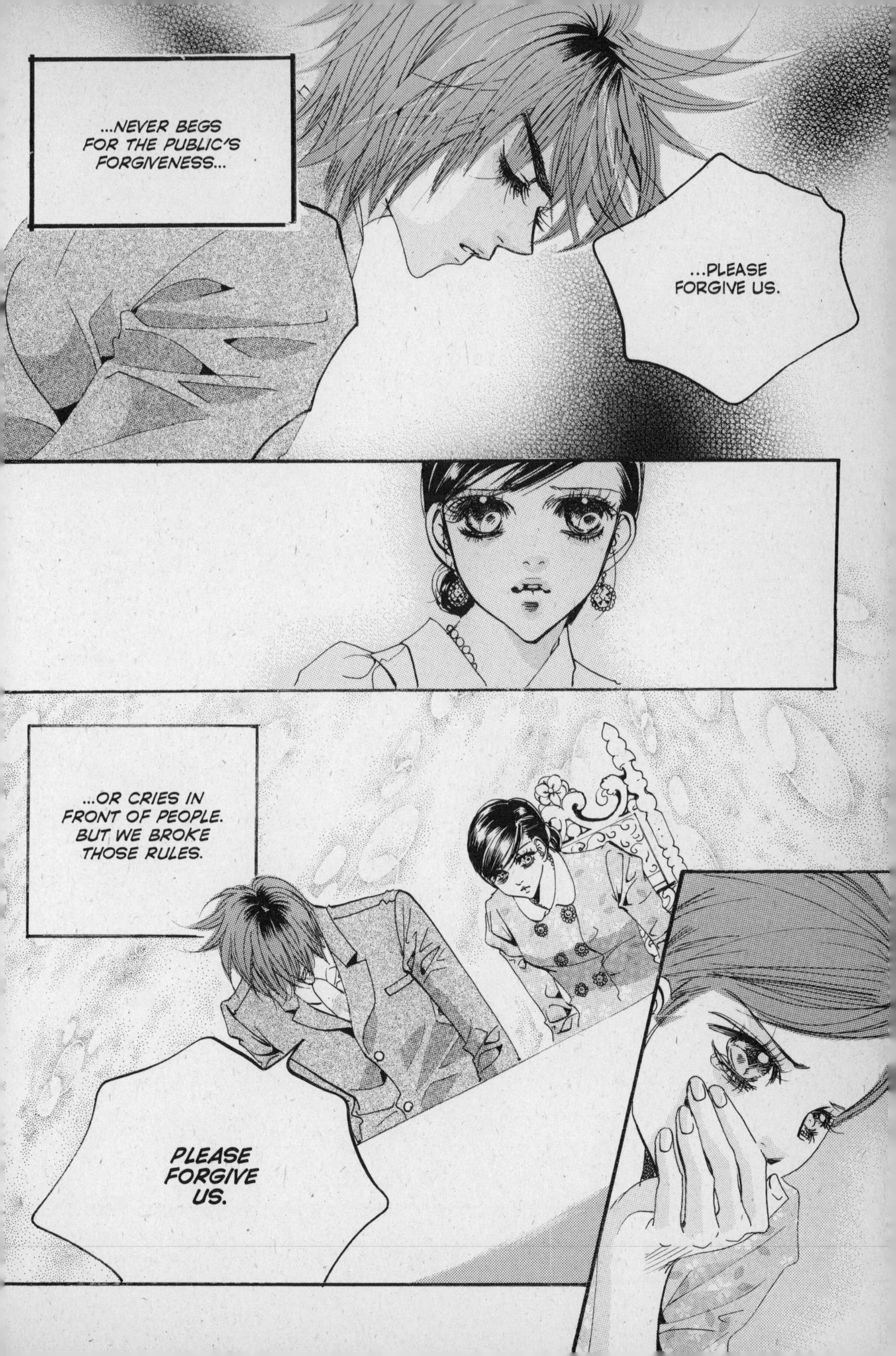
...NEVER BEGS FOR THE PUBLIC'S FORGIVENESS...
...PLEASE FORGIVE US.
...OR CRIES IN FRONT OF PEOPLE. BUT WE BROKE THOSE RULES.
PLEASE FORGIVE US.

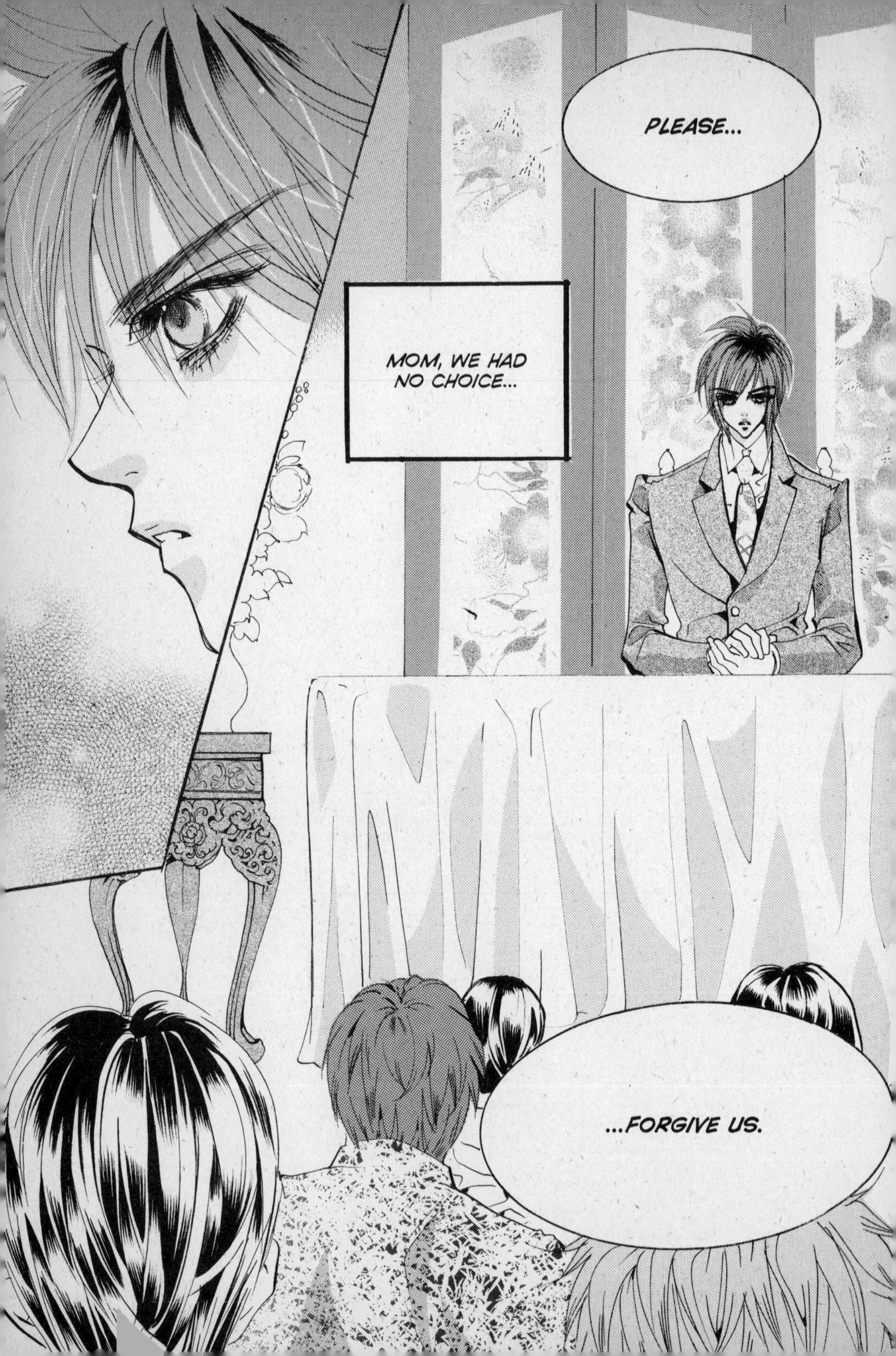
PLEASE...
MOM, WE HAD NO CHOICE...
...FORGIVE US.

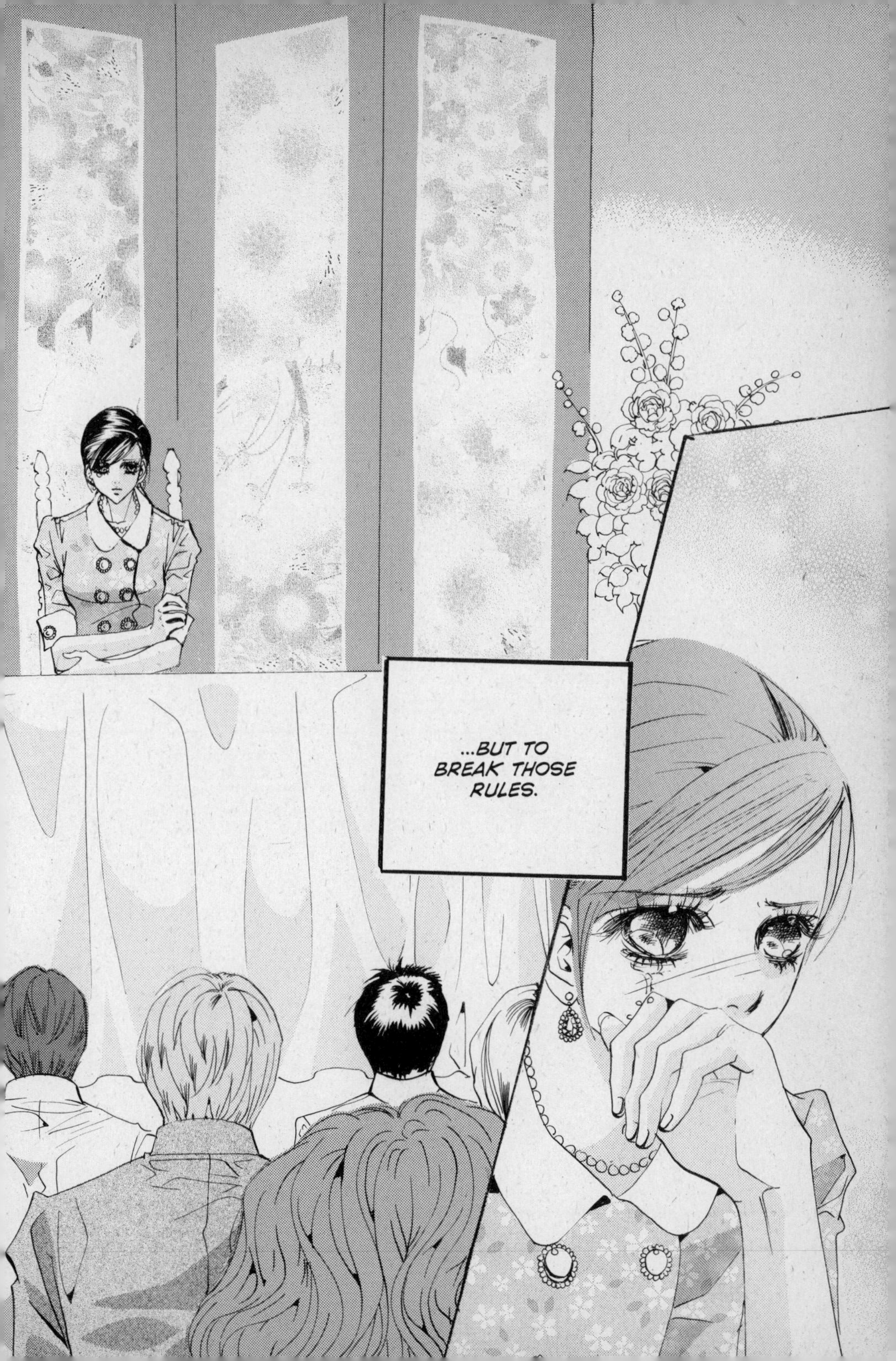
...BUT TO BREAK THOSE RULES.

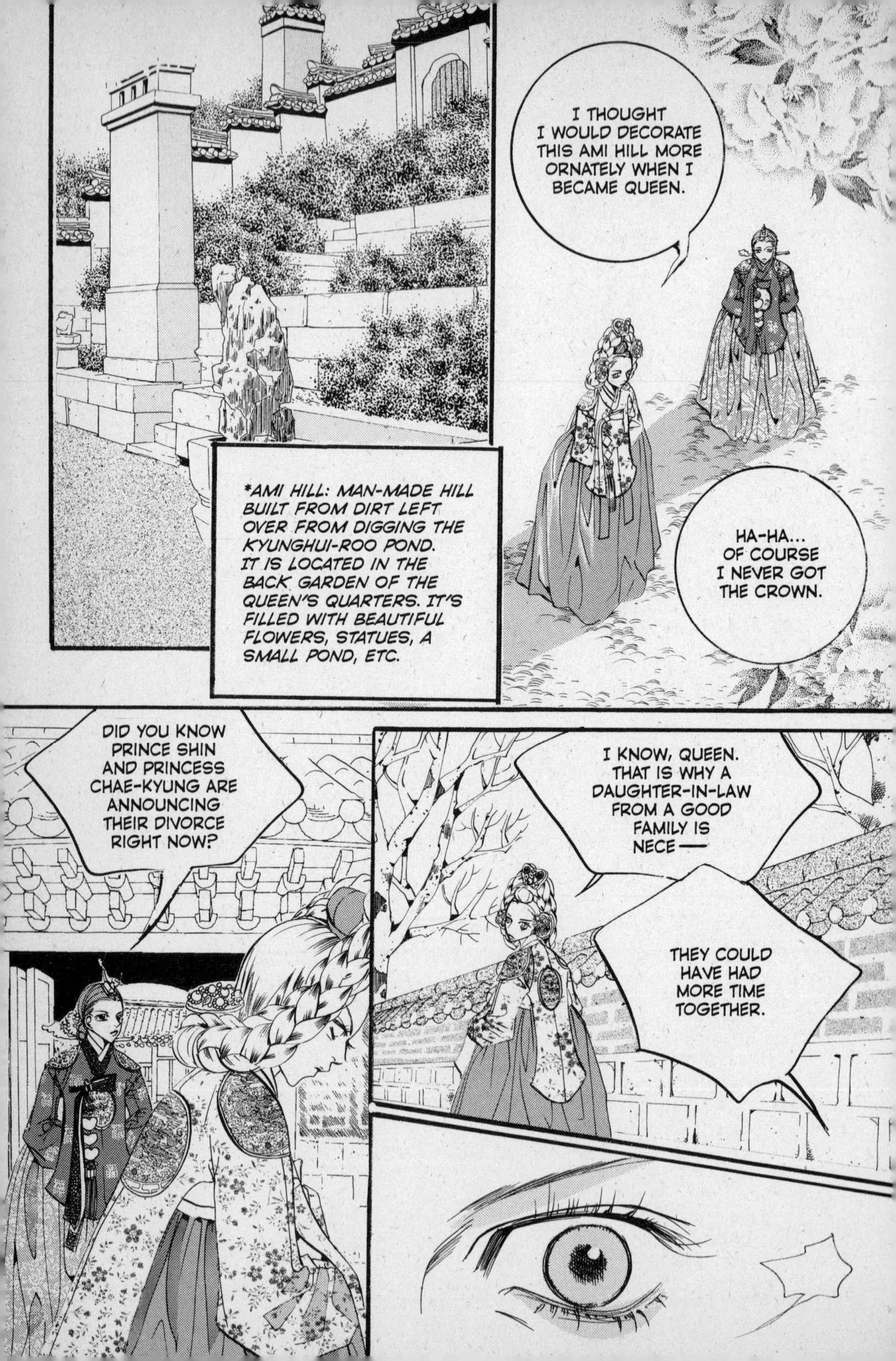
I THOUGHT I WOULD DECORATE THIS AMI HILL MORE ORNATELY WHEN I BECAME QUEEN.
*AMI HILL: MAN-MADE HILL BUILT FROM DIRT LEFT OVER FROM DIGGING THE KYUNGHUI-ROO POND. IT IS LOCATED IN THE BACK GARDEN OF THE QUEEN'S QUARTERS. IT'S FILLED WITH BEAUTIFUL FLOWERS, STATUES, A SMALL POND, ETC.
HA-HA... OF COURSE I NEVER GOT THE CROWN.
DID YOU KNOW PRINCE SHIN AND PRINCESS CHAE-KYUNG ARE ANNOUNCING THEIR DIVORCE RIGHT NOW?
I KNOW, QUEEN. THAT IS WHY A DAUGHTER-IN-LAW FROM A GOOD FAMILY IS NECE—
THEY COULD HAVE HAD MORE TIME TOGETHER.

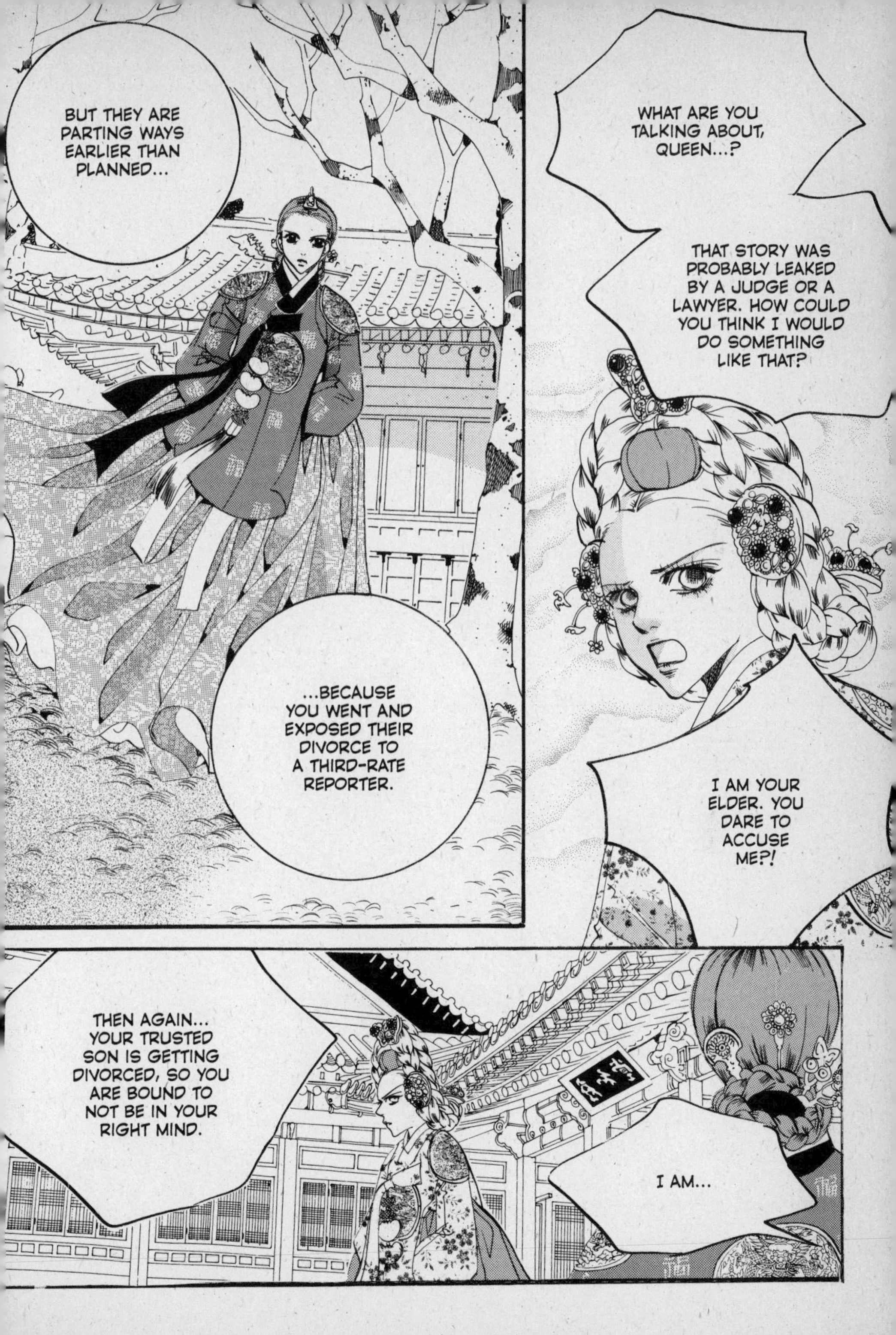
BUT THEY ARE PARTING WAYS EARLIER THAN PLANNED...
WHAT ARE YOU TALKING ABOUT, QUEEN...?
...BECAUSE YOU WENT AND EXPOSED THEIR DIVORCE TO A THIRD-RATE REPORTER.
THAT STORY WAS PROBABLY LEAKED BY A JUDGE OR A LAWYER. HOW COULD YOU THINK I WOULD DO SOMETHING LIKE THAT?
I AM YOUR ELDER. YOU DARE TO ACCUSE ME?!
THEN AGAIN... YOUR TRUSTED SON IS GETTING DIVORCED, SO YOU ARE BOUND TO NOT BE IN YOUR RIGHT MIND.
I AM...

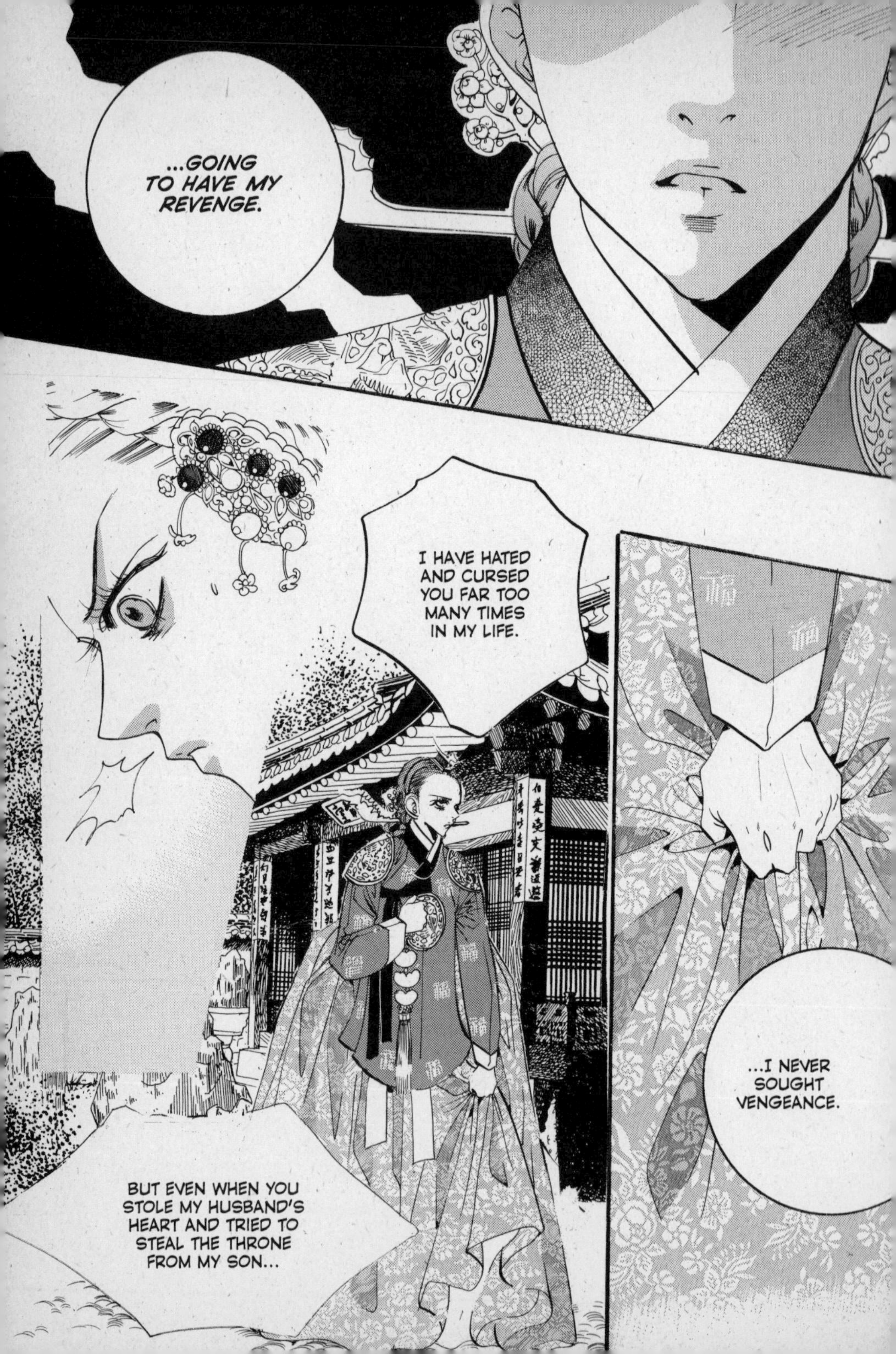
...GOING TO HAVE MY REVENGE.
I HAVE HATED AND CURSED YOU FAR TOO MANY TIMES IN MY LIFE.
BUT EVEN WHEN YOU STOLE MY HUSBAND'S HEART AND TRIED TO STEAL THE THRONE FROM MY SON...
...I NEVER SOUGHT VENGEANCE.

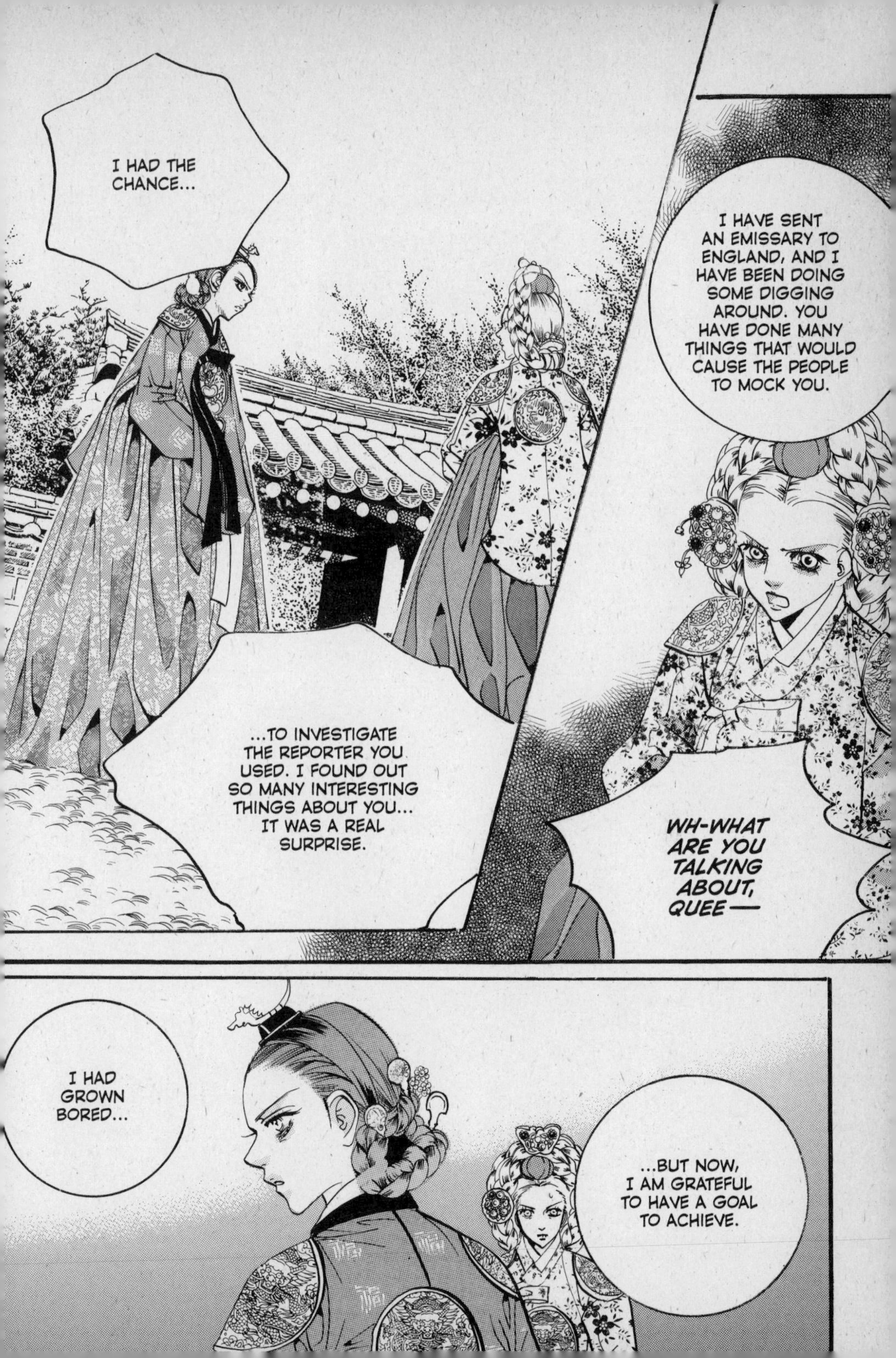
I HAD THE CHANCE...
...TO INVESTIGATE THE REPORTER YOU USED. I FOUND OUT SO MANY INTERESTING THINGS ABOUT YOU... IT WAS A REAL SURPRISE.
I HAVE SENT AN EMISSARY TO ENGLAND, AND I HAVE BEEN DOING SOME DIGGING AROUND. YOU HAVE DONE MANY THINGS THAT WOULD CAUSE THE PEOPLE TO MOCK YOU.
WH-WHAT ARE YOU TALKING ABOUT, QUEE—
I HAD GROWN BORED...
...BUT NOW, I AM GRATEFUL TO HAVE A GOAL TO ACHIEVE.

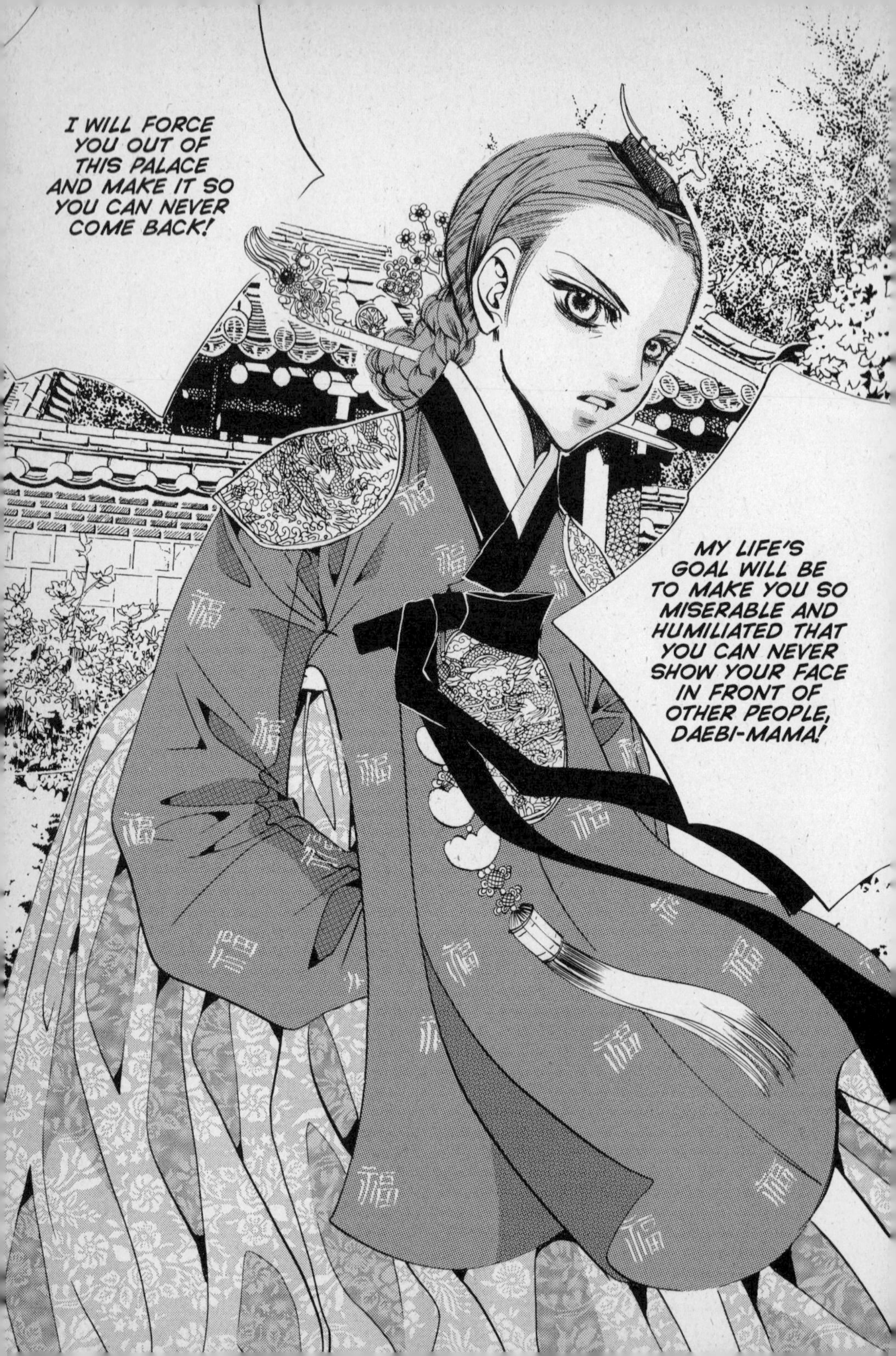
I WILL FORCE YOU OUT OF THIS PALACE AND MAKE IT SO YOU CAN NEVER COME BACK!
MY LIFE'S GOAL WILL BE TO MAKE YOU SO MISERABLE AND HUMILIATED THAT YOU CAN NEVER SHOW YOUR FACE IN FRONT OF OTHER PEOPLE, DAEBI-MAMA!

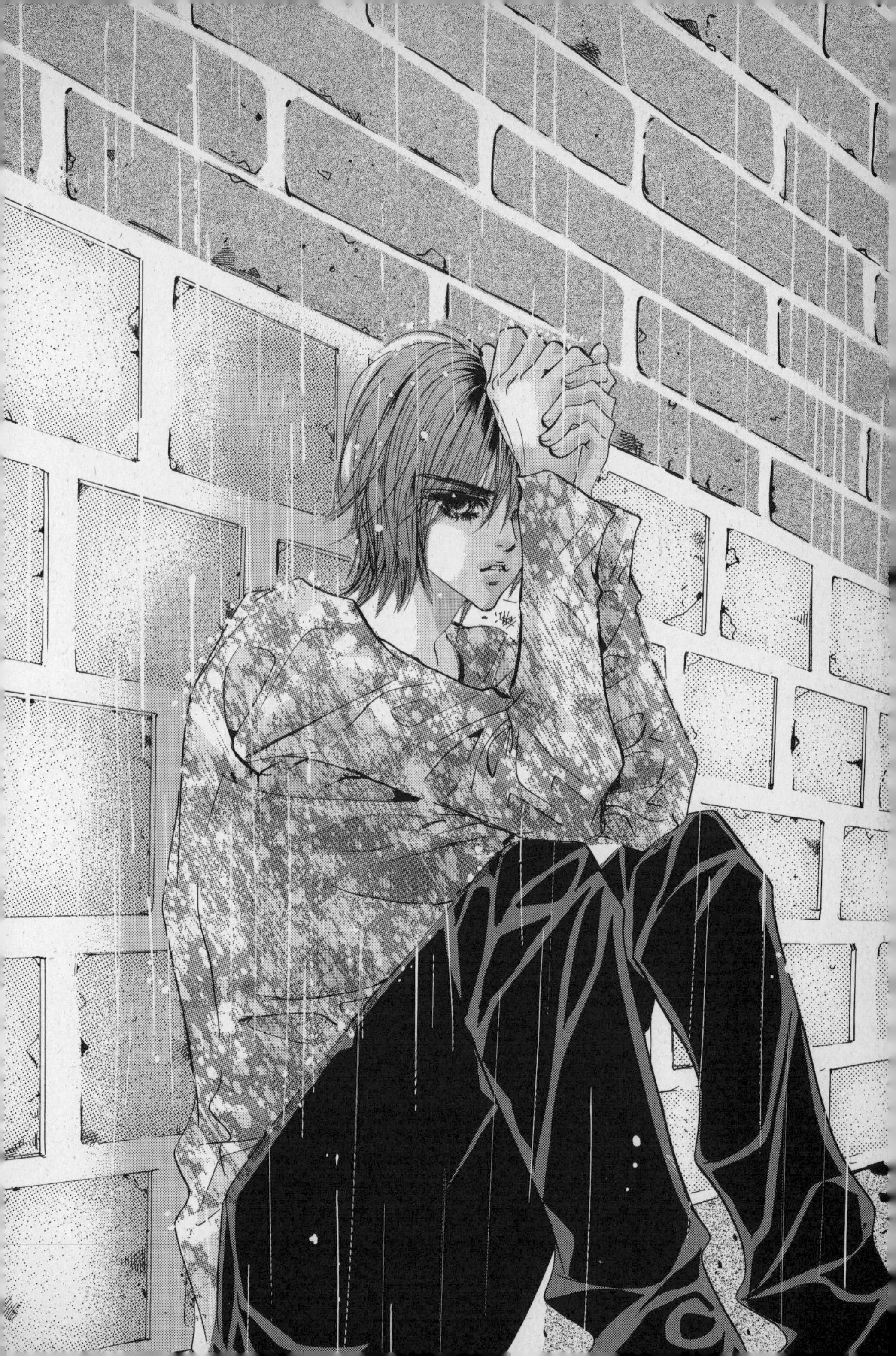

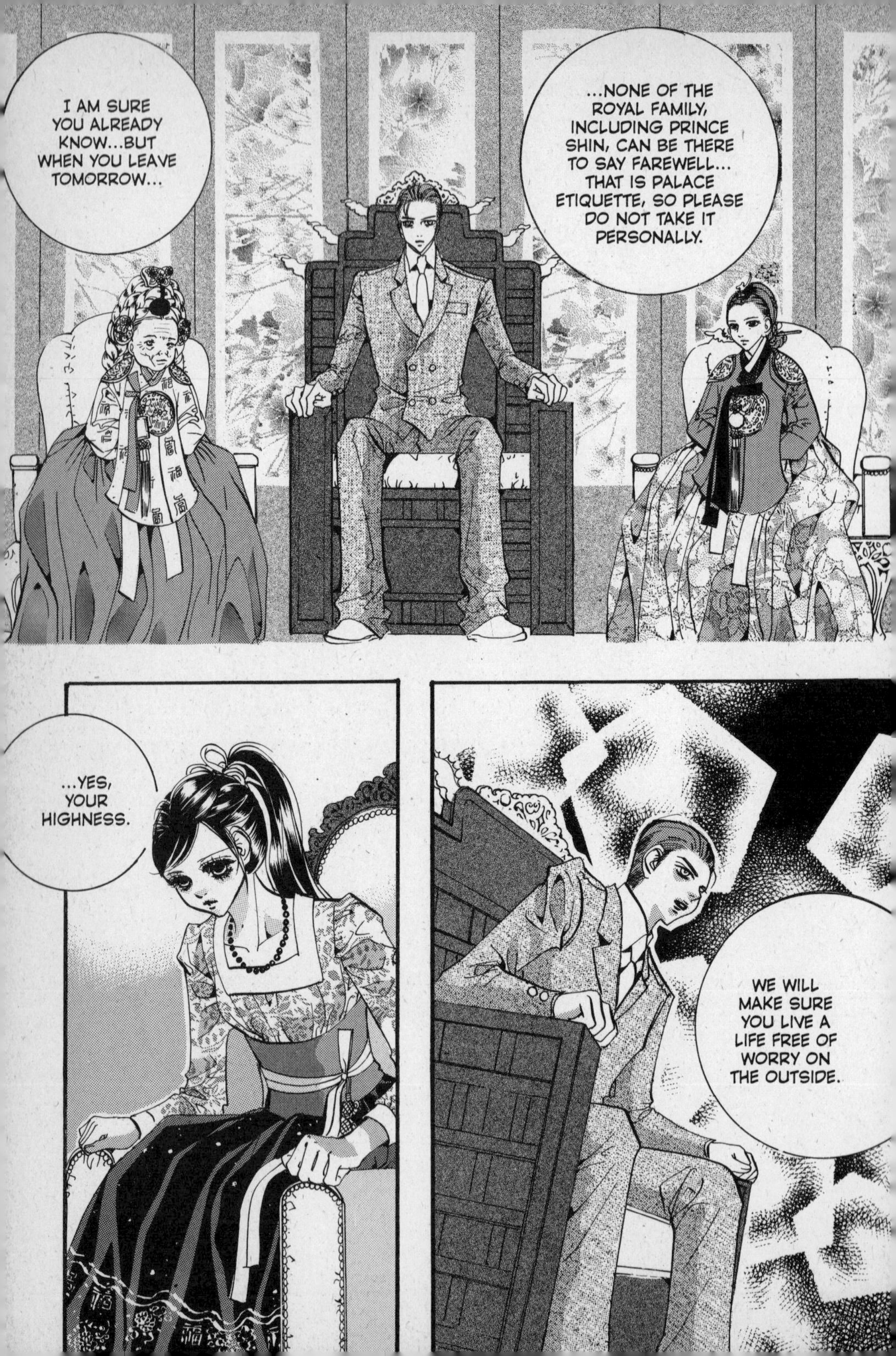
I AM SURE YOU ALREADY KNOW...BUT WHEN YOU LEAVE TOMORROW...
...NONE OF THE ROYAL FAMILY, INCLUDING PRINCE SHIN, CAN BE THERE TO SAY FAREWELL... THAT IS PALACE ETIQUETTE, SO PLEASE DO NOT TAKE IT PERSONALLY.
WE WILL MAKE SURE YOU LIVE A LIFE FREE OF WORRY ON THE OUTSIDE.
...YES, YOUR HIGHNESS.

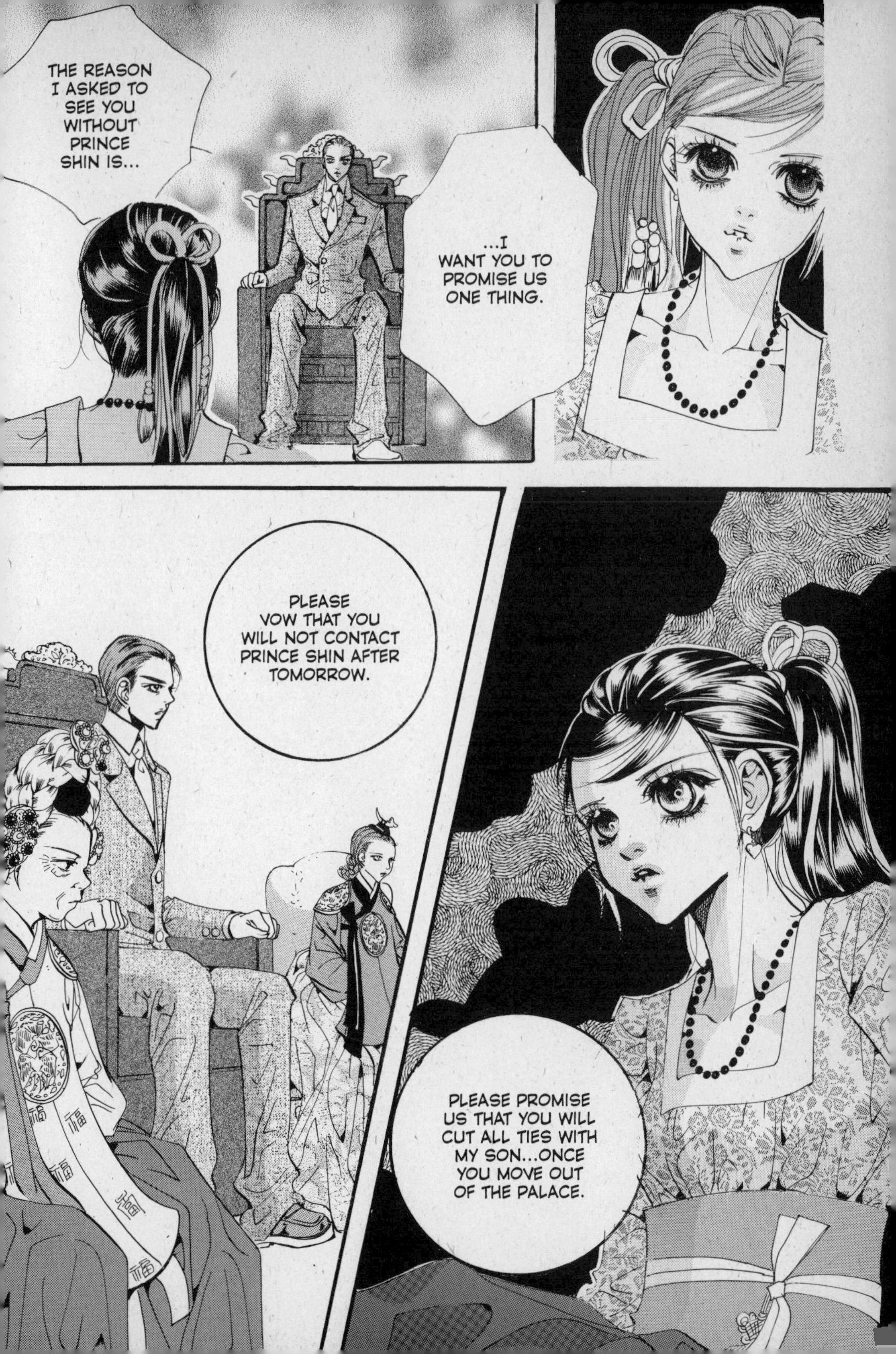
THE REASON I ASKED TO SEE YOU WITHOUT PRINCE SHIN IS...
...I WANT YOU TO PROMISE US ONE THING.
PLEASE VOW THAT YOU WILL NOT CONTACT PRINCE SHIN AFTER TOMORROW.
PLEASE PROMISE US THAT YOU WILL CUT ALL TIES WITH MY SON...ONCE YOU MOVE OUT OF THE PALACE.

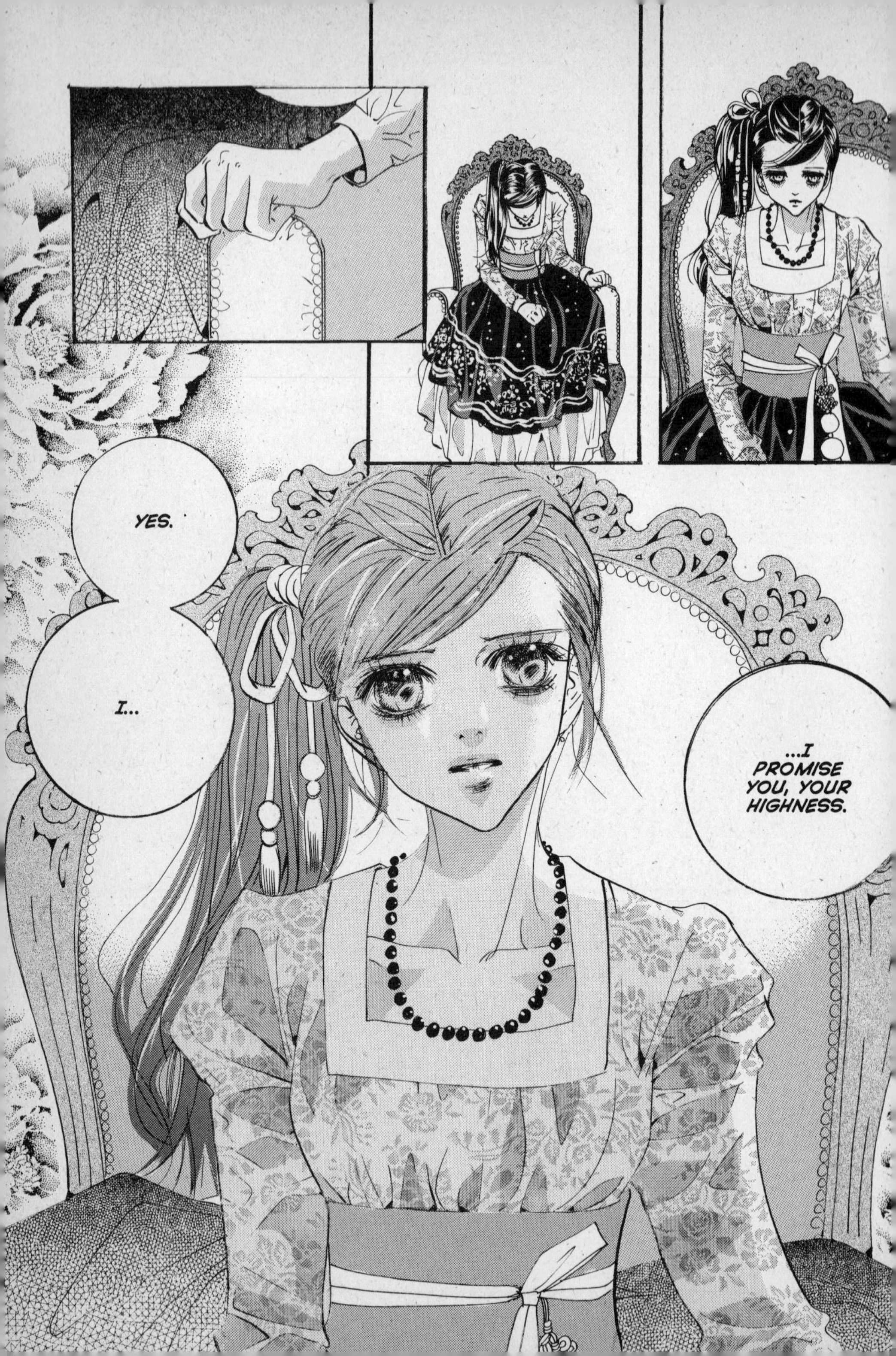
YES.
I...
...I PROMISE YOU, YOUR HIGHNESS.

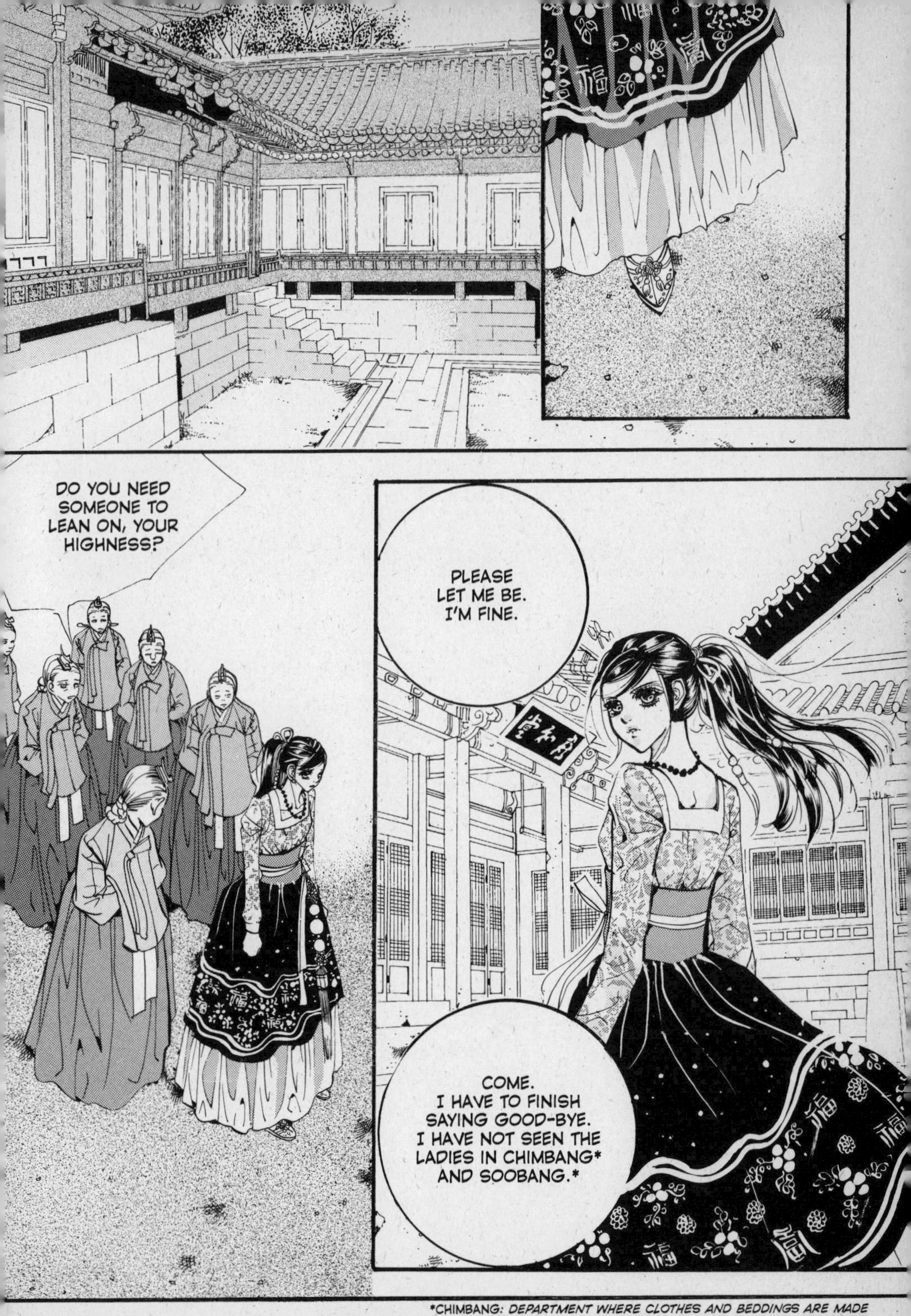
DO YOU NEED SOMEONE TO LEAN ON, YOUR HIGHNESS?
PLEASE LET ME BE. I'M FINE.
COME. I HAVE TO FINISH SAYING GOOD-BYE. I HAVE NOT SEEN THE LADIES IN CHIMBANG* AND SOOBANG.*

*CHIMBANG: *DEPARTMENT WHERE CLOTHES AND BEDDINGS ARE MADE*
*SOOBANG: *DEPARTMENT WHERE BEDDINGS, BLANKETS, AND MATS ARE EMBROIDERED*

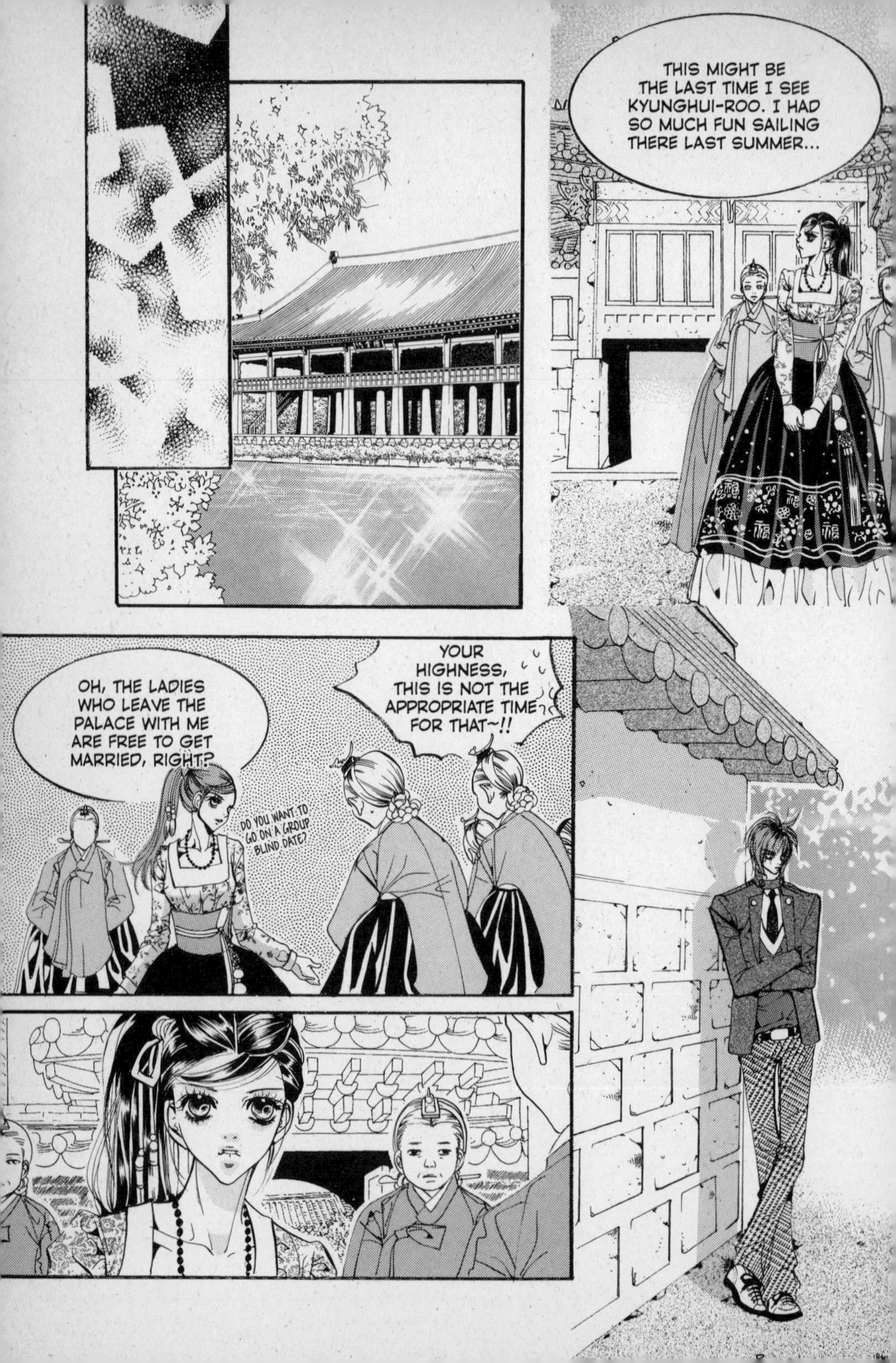
THIS MIGHT BE THE LAST TIME I SEE KYUNGHUI-ROO. I HAD SO MUCH FUN SAILING THERE LAST SUMMER...
OH, THE LADIES WHO LEAVE THE PALACE WITH ME ARE FREE TO GET MARRIED, RIGHT?
DO YOU WANT TO GO ON A GROUP BLIND DATE?
YOUR HIGHNESS, THIS IS NOT THE APPROPRIATE TIME FOR THAT~!!

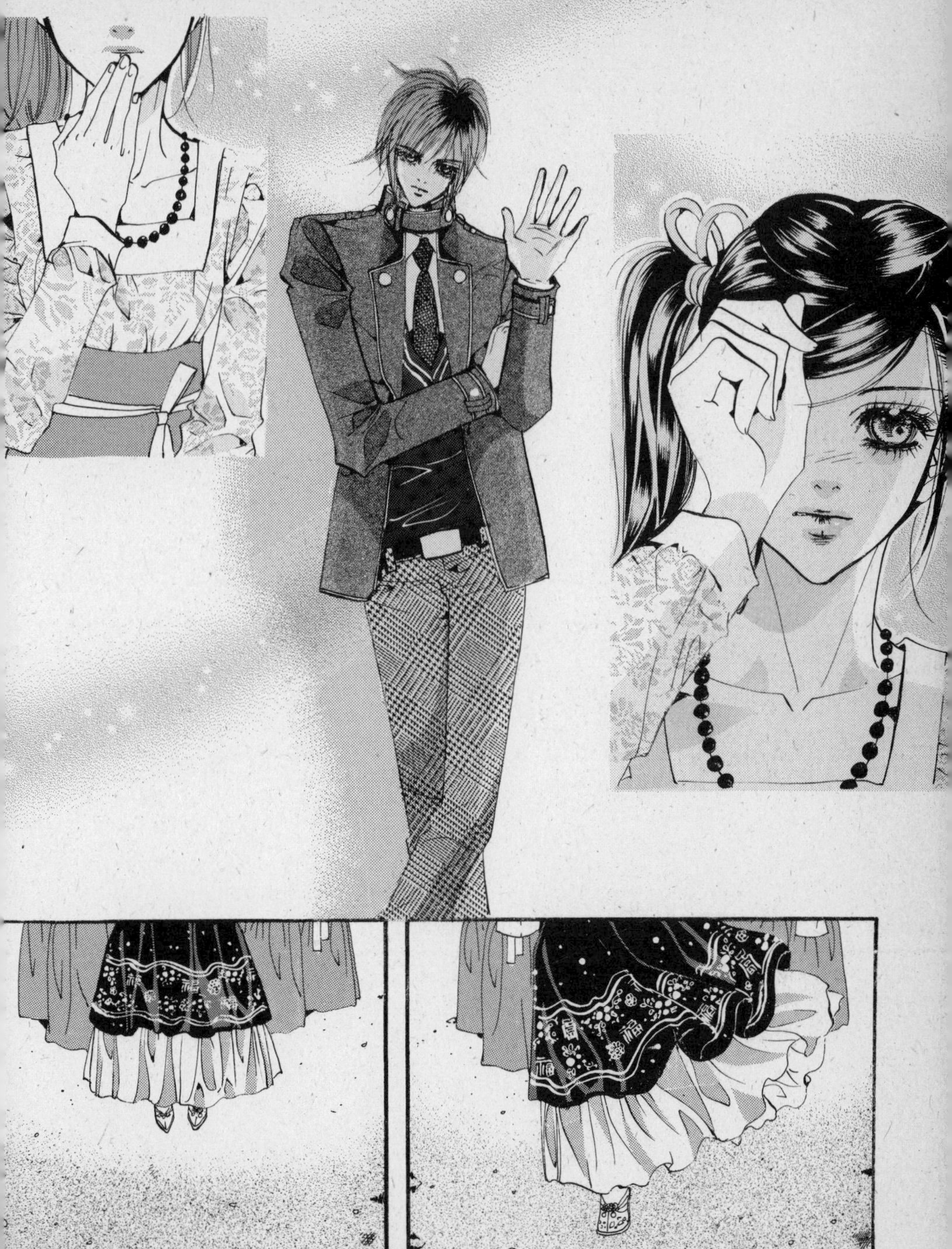

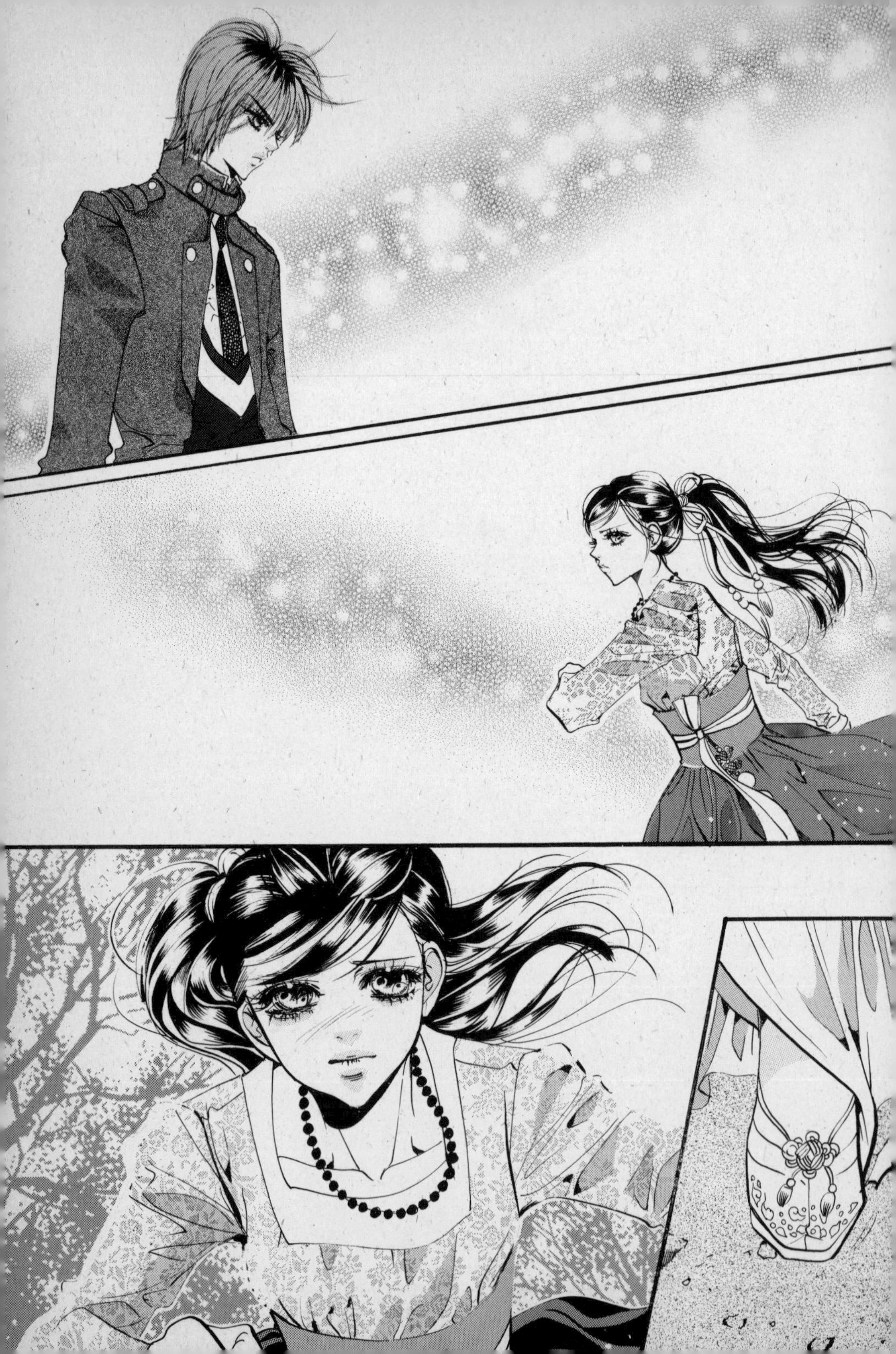

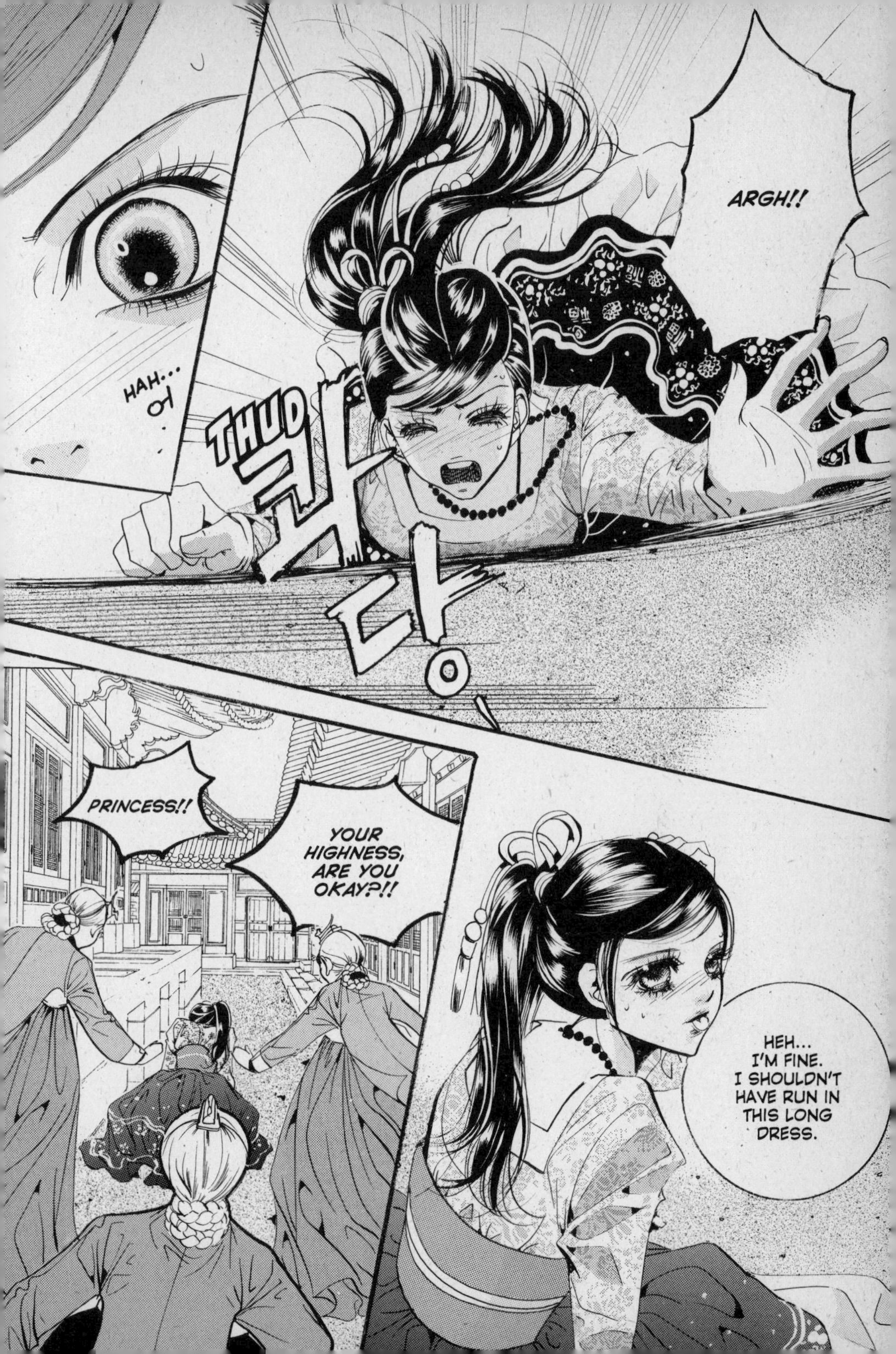

HAH... 어...
ARGH!!
THUD
콰당
PRINCESS!!
YOUR HIGHNESS, ARE YOU OKAY?!!
HEH... I'M FINE. I SHOULDN'T HAVE RUN IN THIS LONG DRESS.

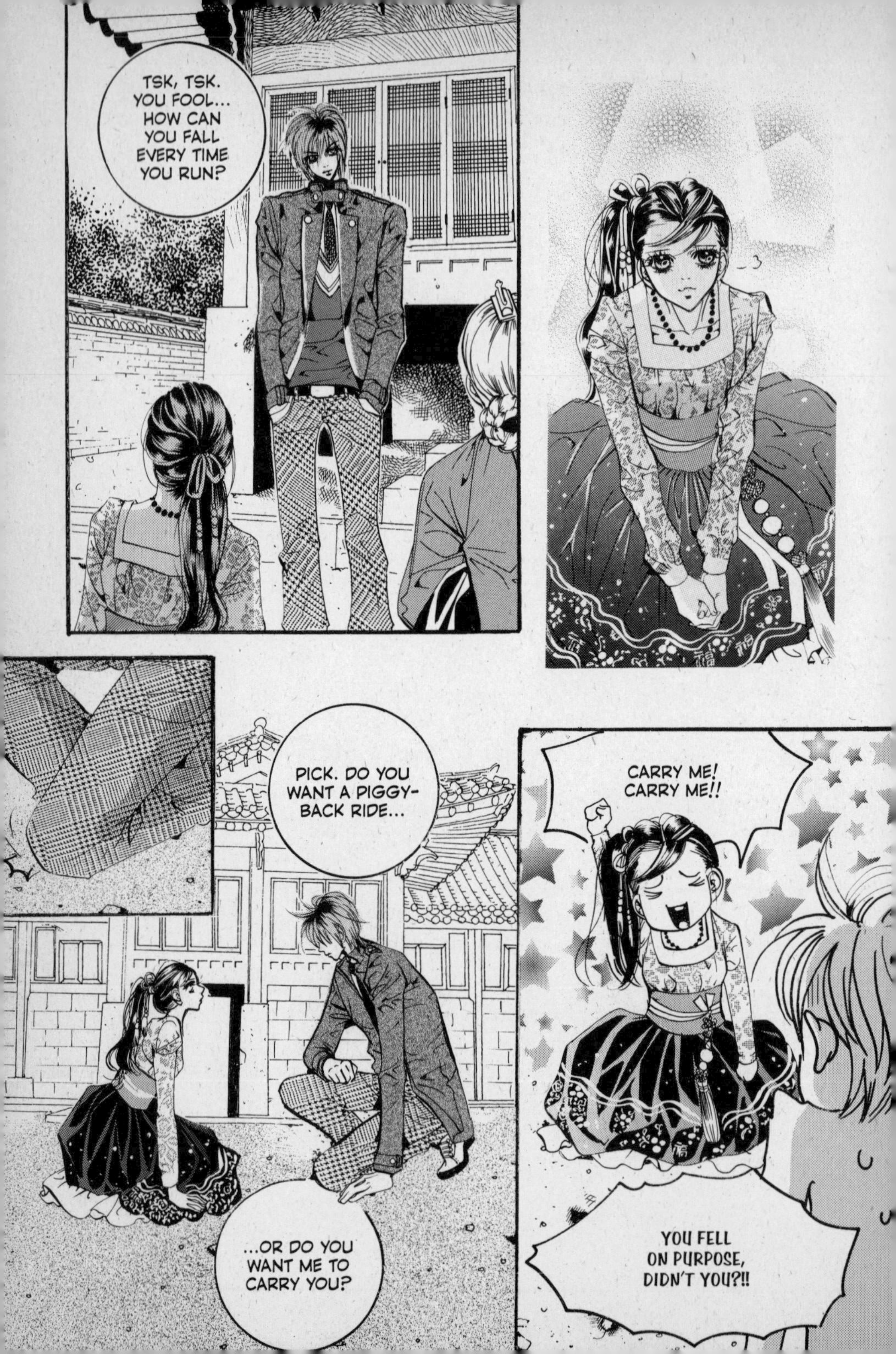
TSK, TSK. YOU FOOL... HOW CAN YOU FALL EVERY TIME YOU RUN?
PICK. DO YOU WANT A PIGGY-BACK RIDE...
...OR DO YOU WANT ME TO CARRY YOU?
CARRY ME! CARRY ME!!
YOU FELL ON PURPOSE, DIDN'T YOU?!!

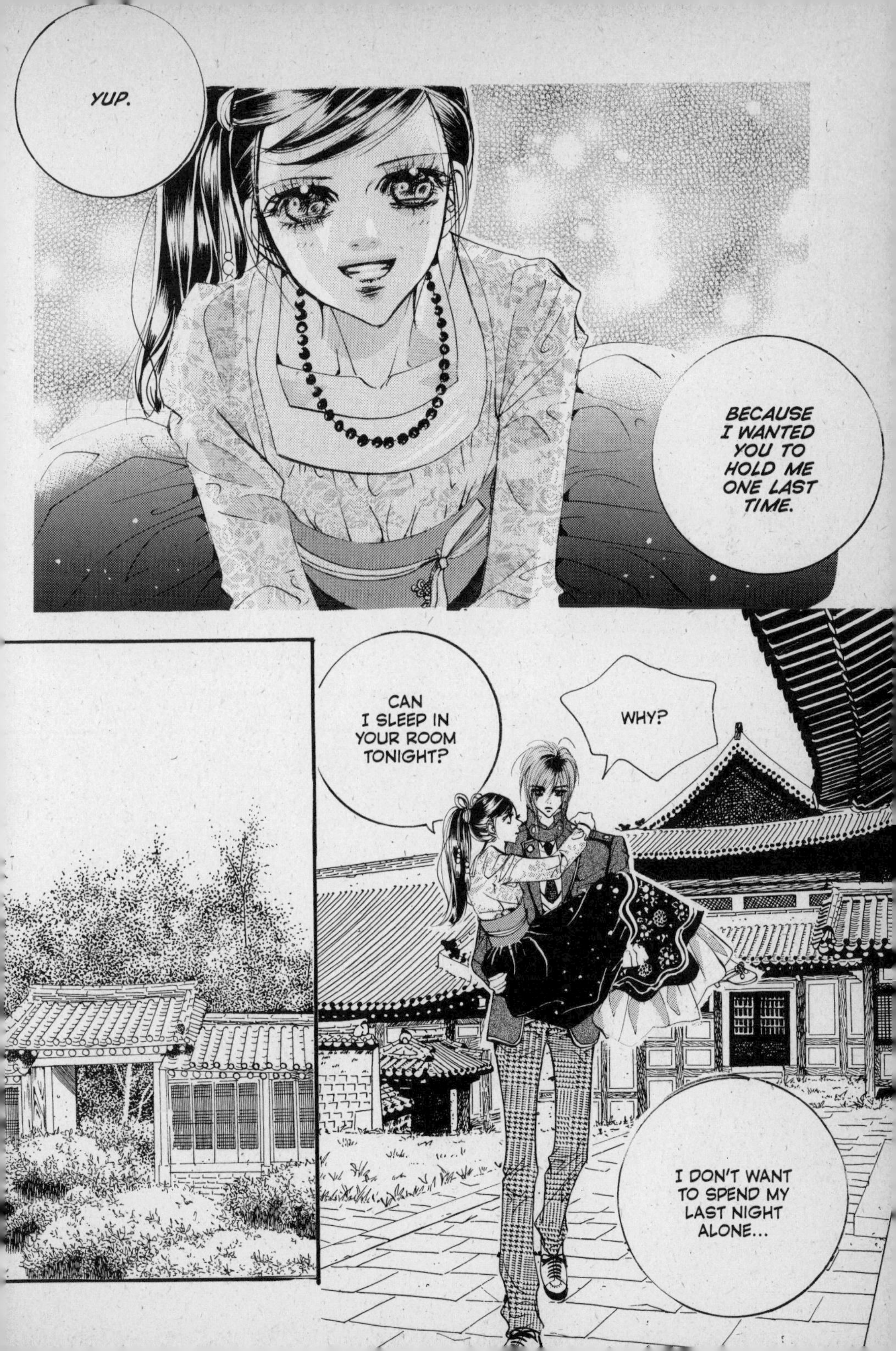
YUP.
BECAUSE I WANTED YOU TO HOLD ME ONE LAST TIME.
CAN I SLEEP IN YOUR ROOM TONIGHT?
WHY?
I DON'T WANT TO SPEND MY LAST NIGHT ALONE...

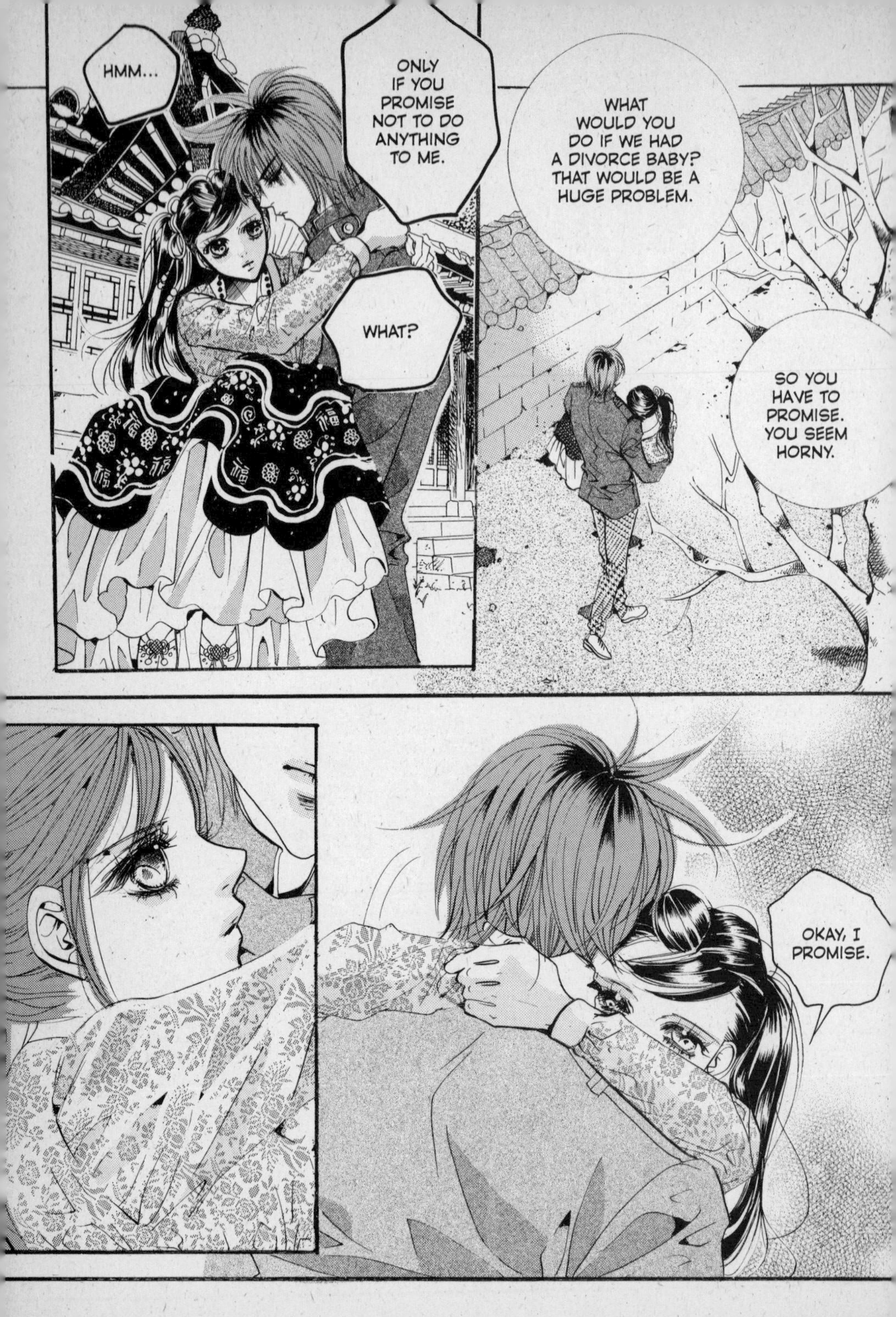
HMM...
ONLY IF YOU PROMISE NOT TO DO ANYTHING TO ME.
WHAT?
WHAT WOULD YOU DO IF WE HAD A DIVORCE BABY? THAT WOULD BE A HUGE PROBLEM.
SO YOU HAVE TO PROMISE. YOU SEEM HORNY.
OKAY, I PROMISE.

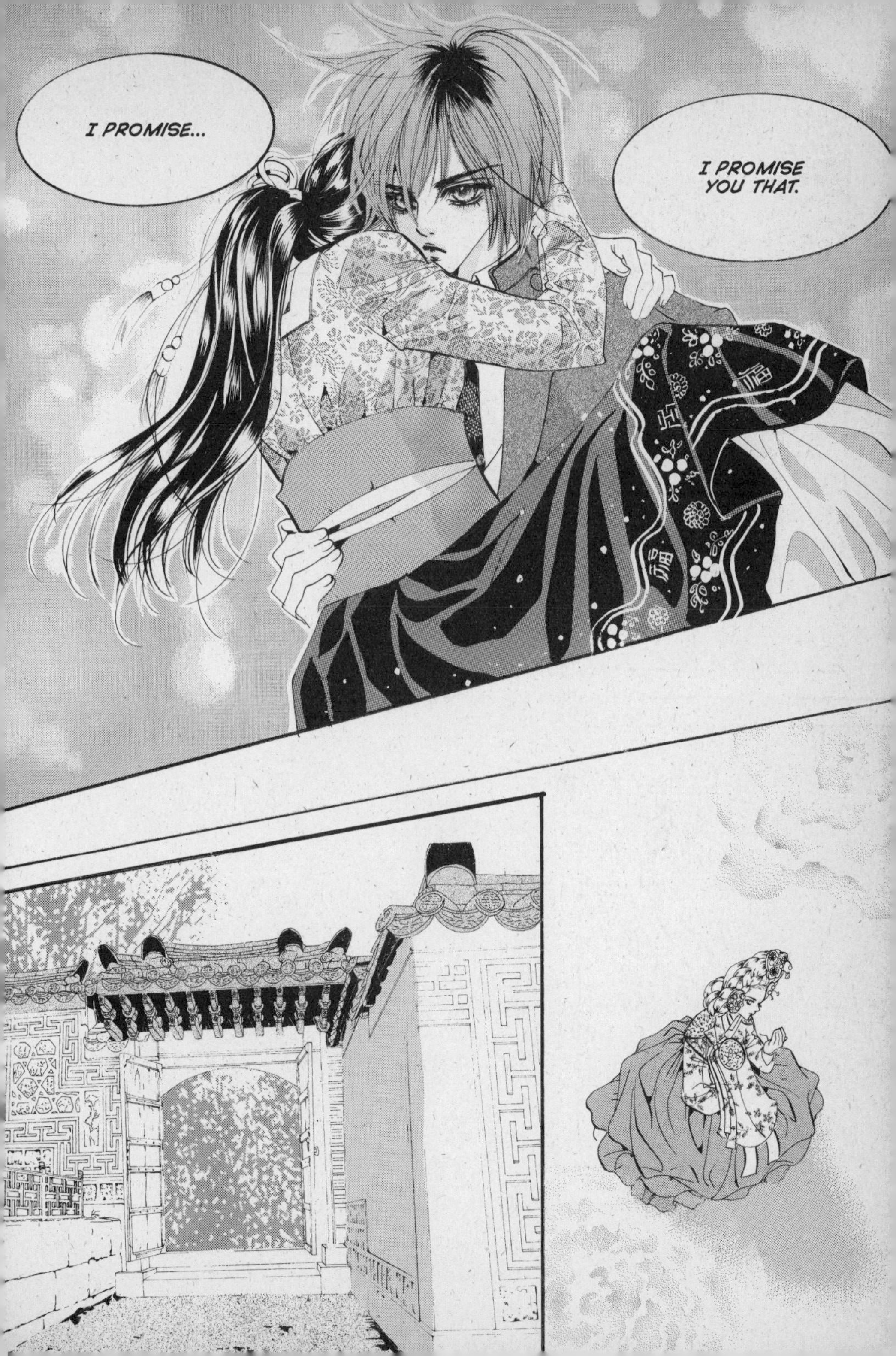
I PROMISE...
I PROMISE YOU THAT.

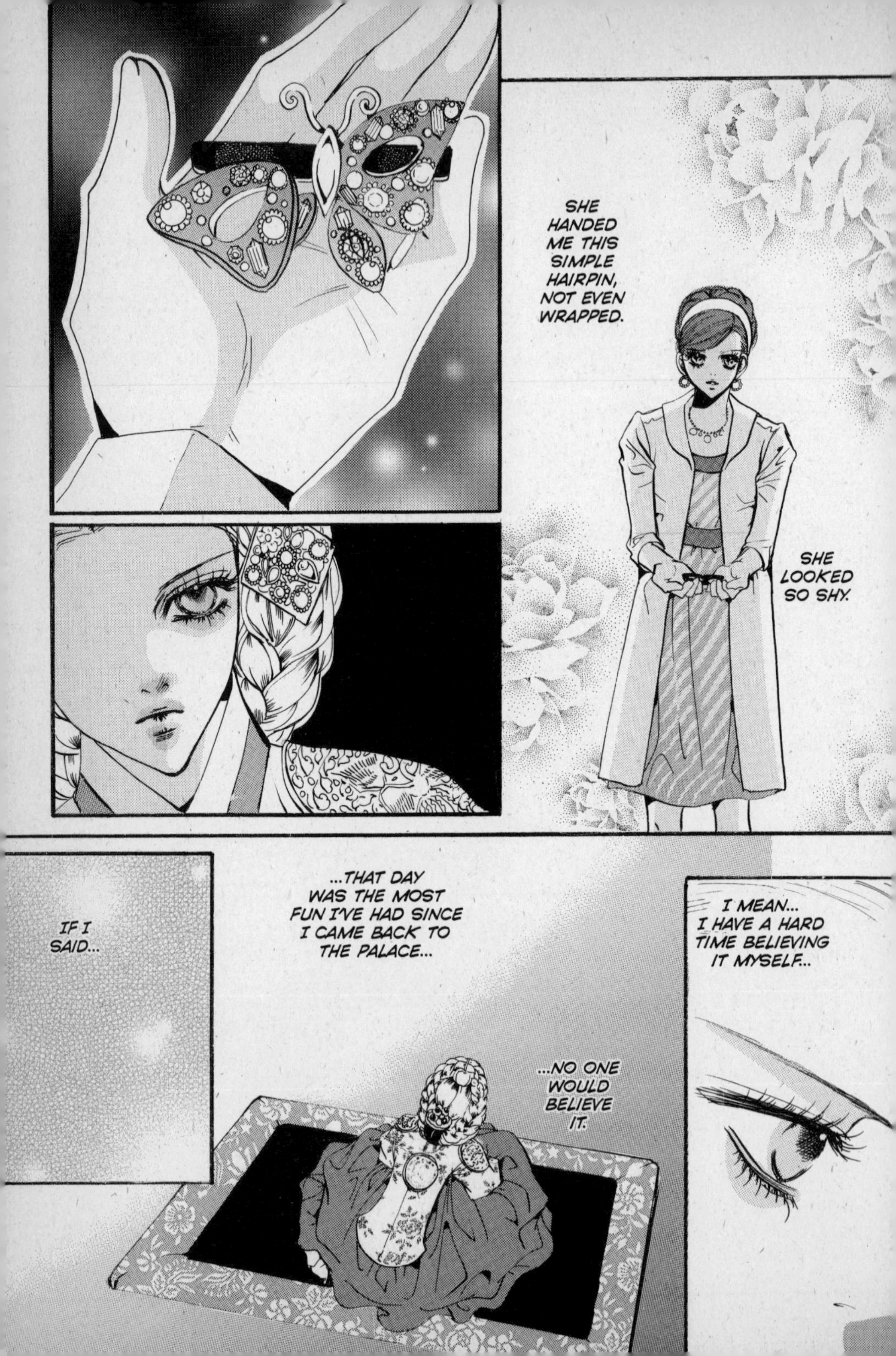
SHE HANDED ME THIS SIMPLE HAIRPIN, NOT EVEN WRAPPED.
SHE LOOKED SO SHY.
IF I SAID...
...THAT DAY WAS THE MOST FUN I'VE HAD SINCE I CAME BACK TO THE PALACE...
...NO ONE WOULD BELIEVE IT.
I MEAN... I HAVE A HARD TIME BELIEVING IT MYSELF...

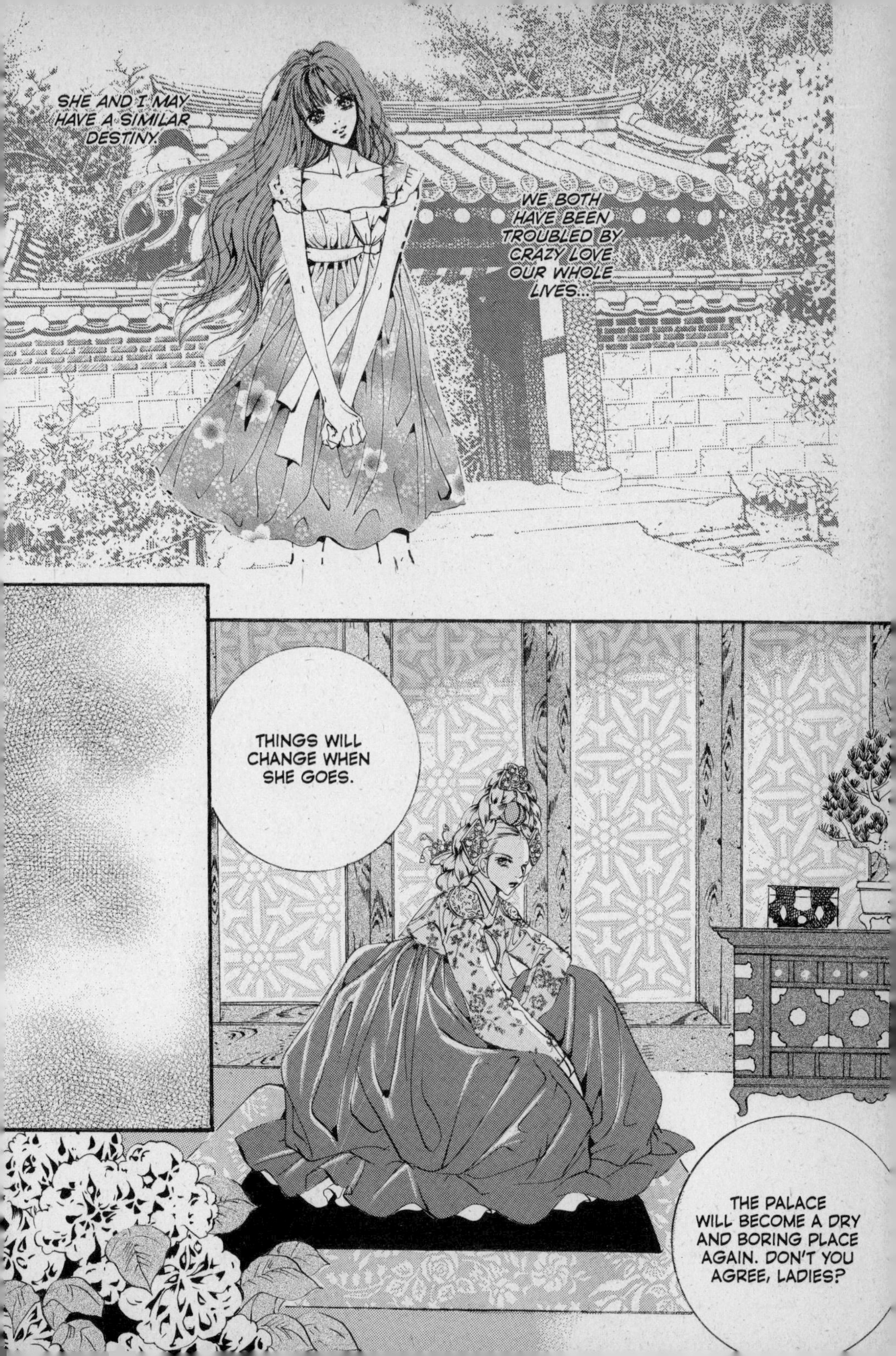
SHE AND I MAY HAVE A SIMILAR DESTINY.
WE BOTH HAVE BEEN TROUBLED BY CRAZY LOVE OUR WHOLE LIVES...
THINGS WILL CHANGE WHEN SHE GOES.
THE PALACE WILL BECOME A DRY AND BORING PLACE AGAIN. DON'T YOU AGREE, LADIES?

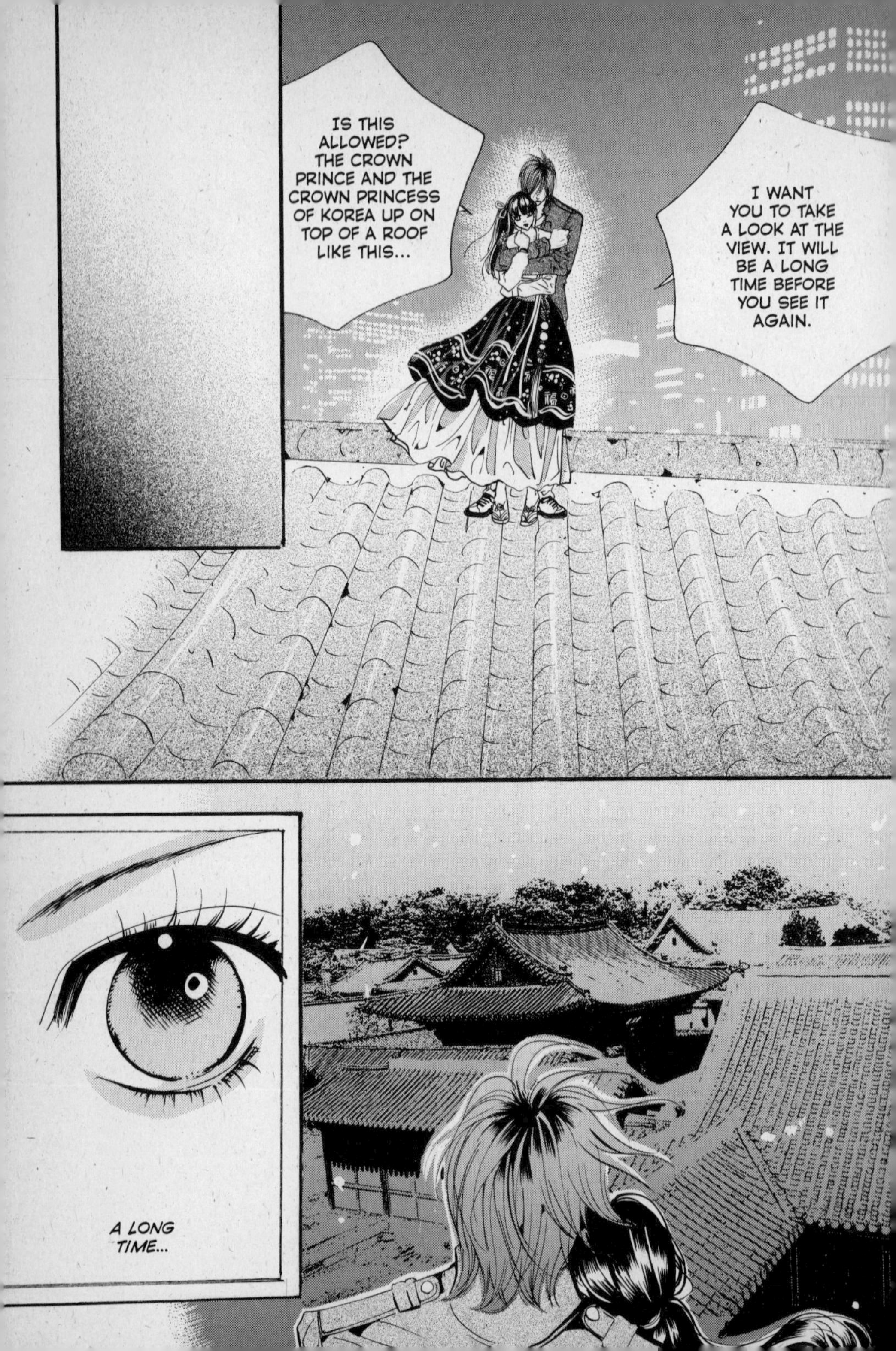
I WANT YOU TO TAKE A LOOK AT THE VIEW. IT WILL BE A LONG TIME BEFORE YOU SEE IT AGAIN.
IS THIS ALLOWED? THE CROWN PRINCE AND THE CROWN PRINCESS OF KOREA UP ON TOP OF A ROOF LIKE THIS...
A LONG TIME...

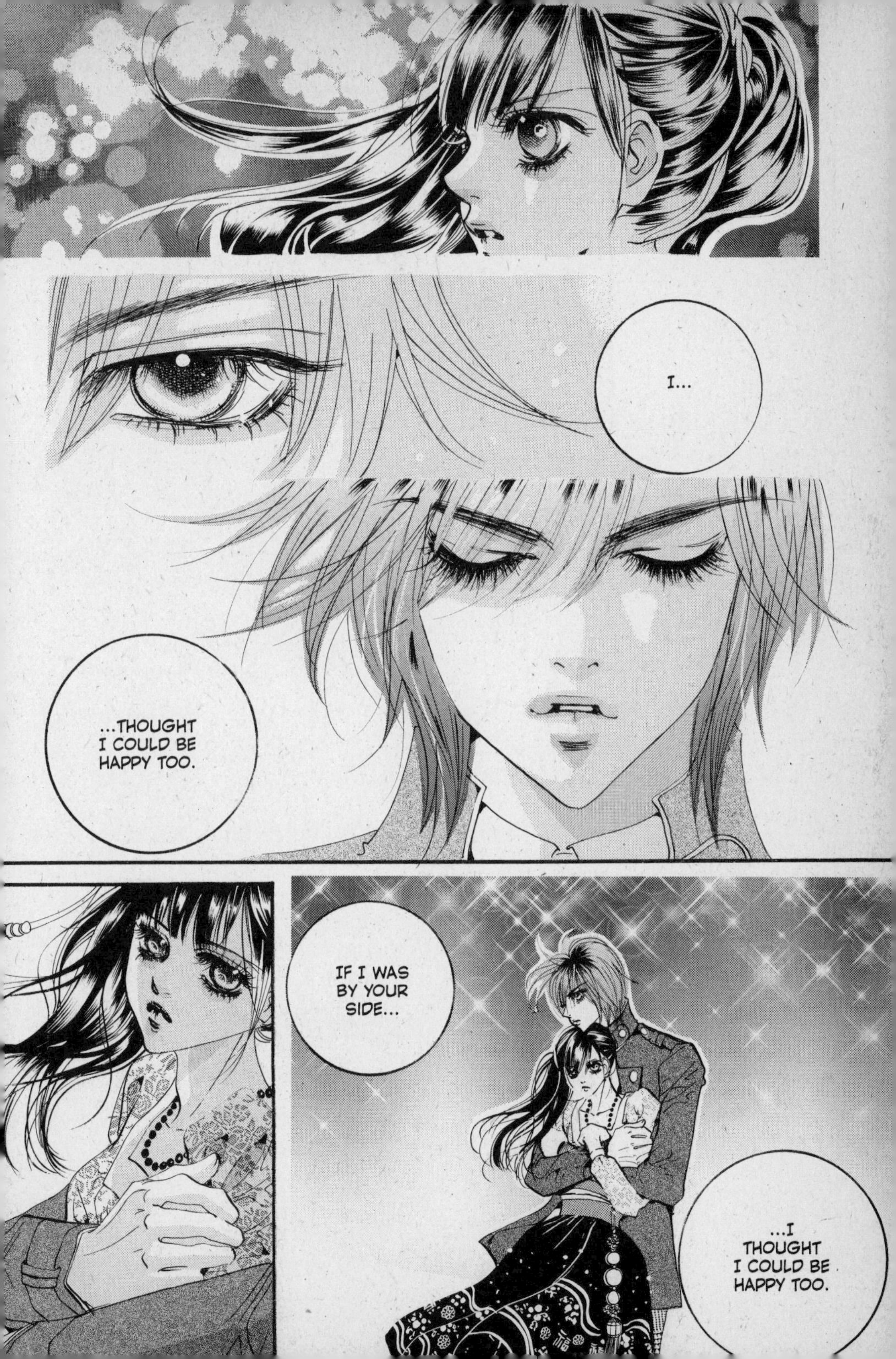
I...
...THOUGHT I COULD BE HAPPY TOO.
IF I WAS BY YOUR SIDE...
...I THOUGHT I COULD BE HAPPY TOO.

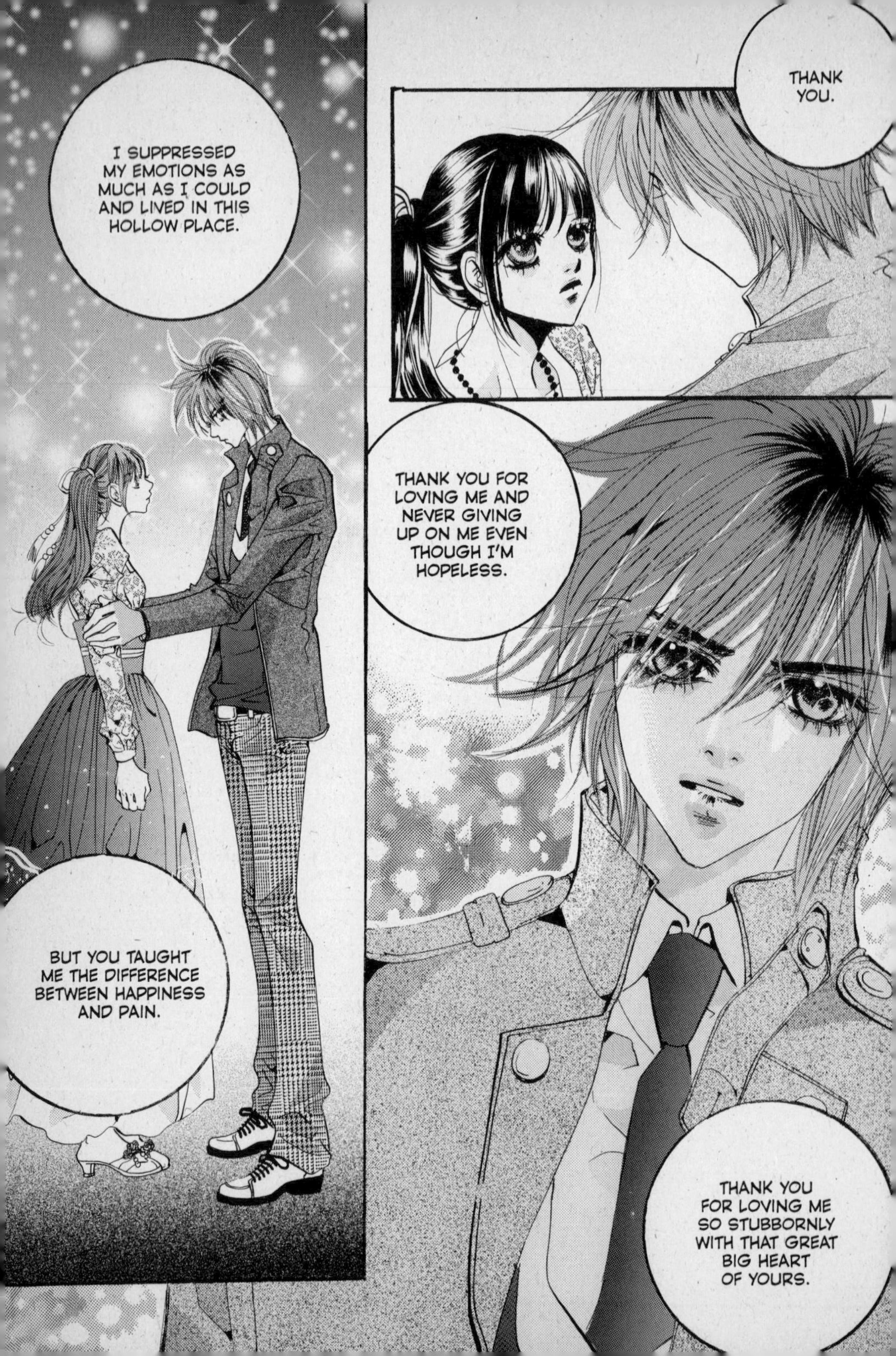
I SUPPRESSED MY EMOTIONS AS MUCH AS I COULD AND LIVED IN THIS HOLLOW PLACE.
BUT YOU TAUGHT ME THE DIFFERENCE BETWEEN HAPPINESS AND PAIN.
THANK YOU.
THANK YOU FOR LOVING ME AND NEVER GIVING UP ON ME EVEN THOUGH I'M HOPELESS.
THANK YOU FOR LOVING ME SO STUBBORNLY WITH THAT GREAT BIG HEART OF YOURS.

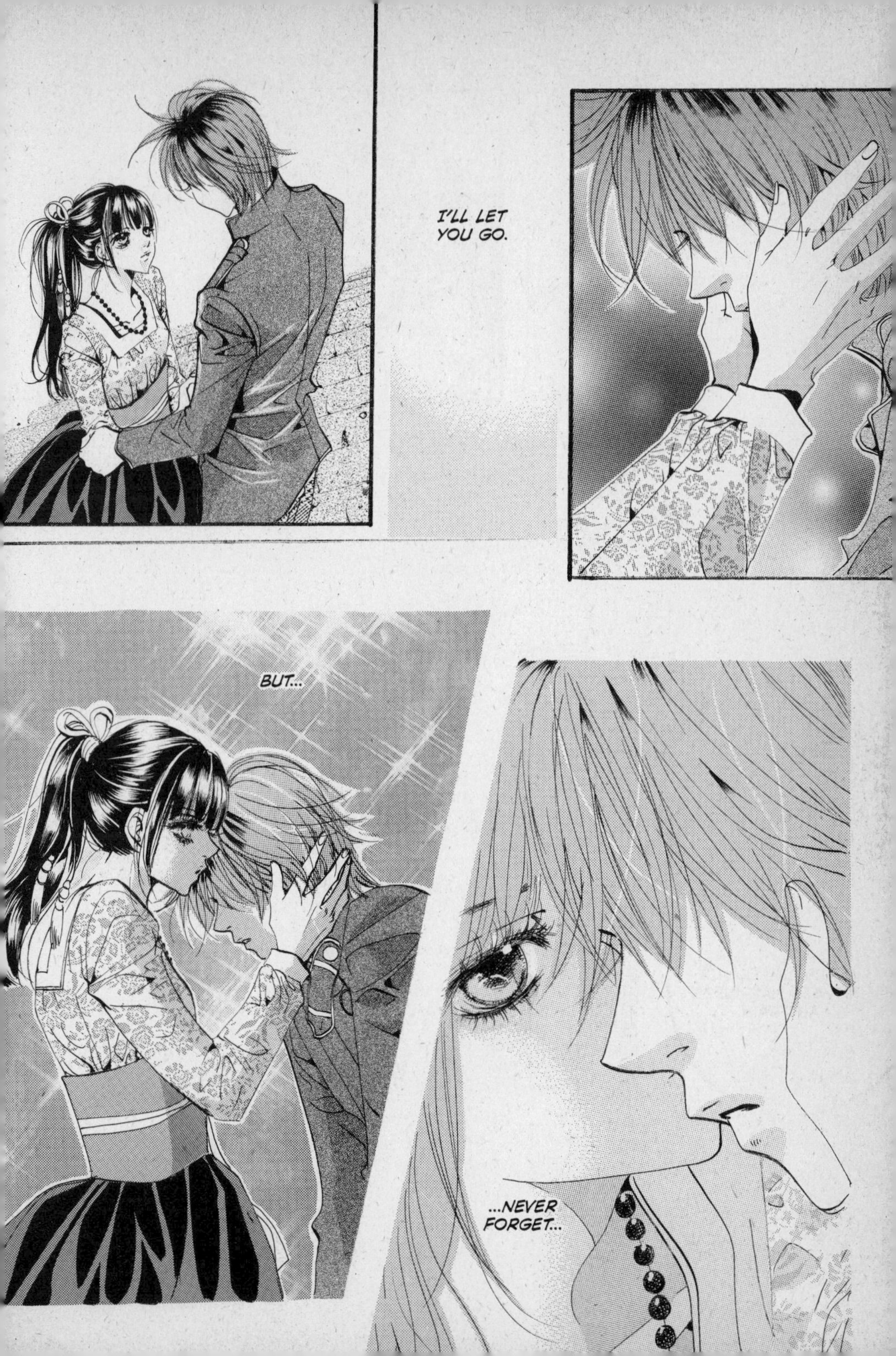
I'LL LET YOU GO.
BUT...
...NEVER FORGET...

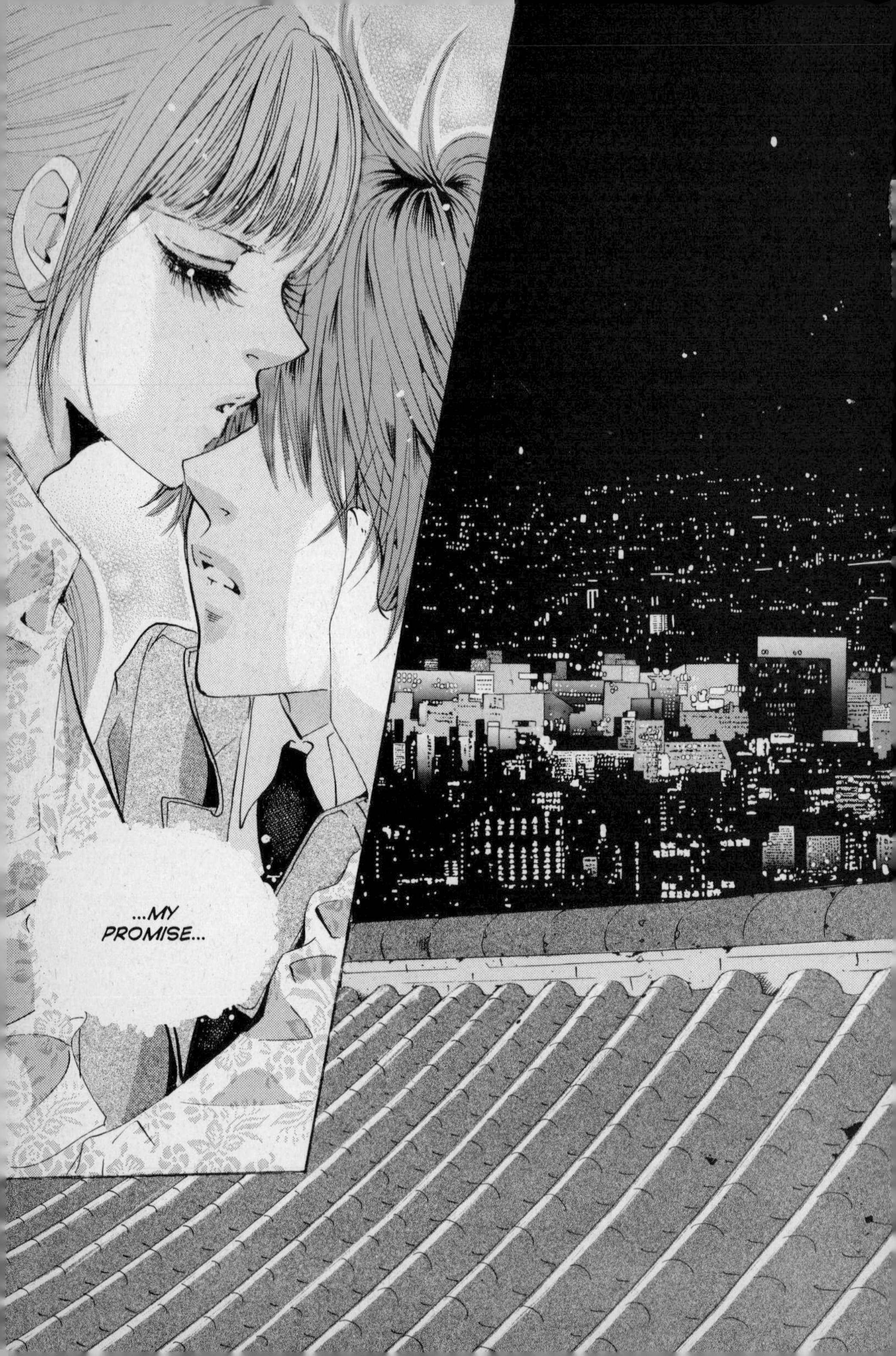
...MY PROMISE...

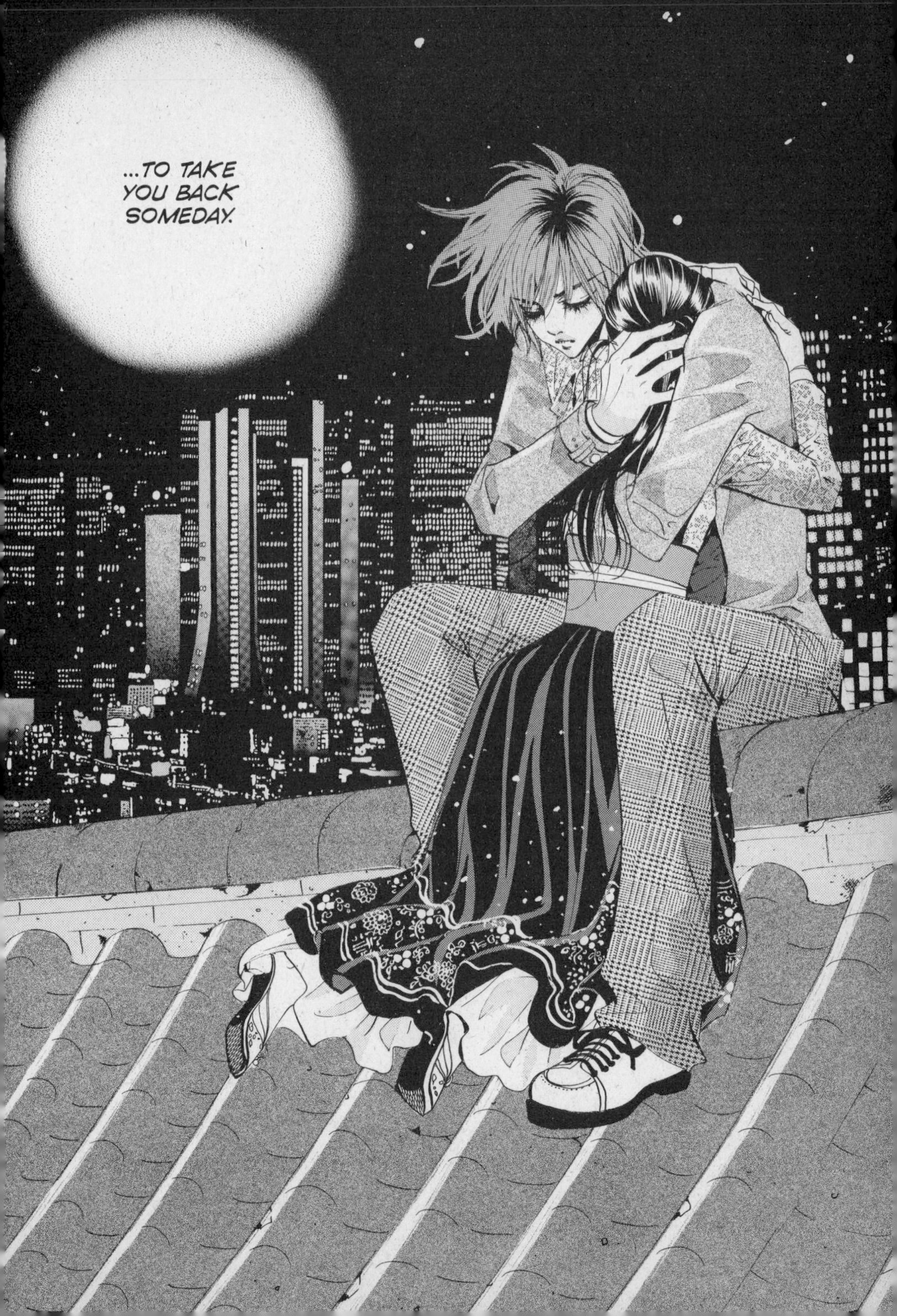
...TO TAKE YOU BACK SOMEDAY.

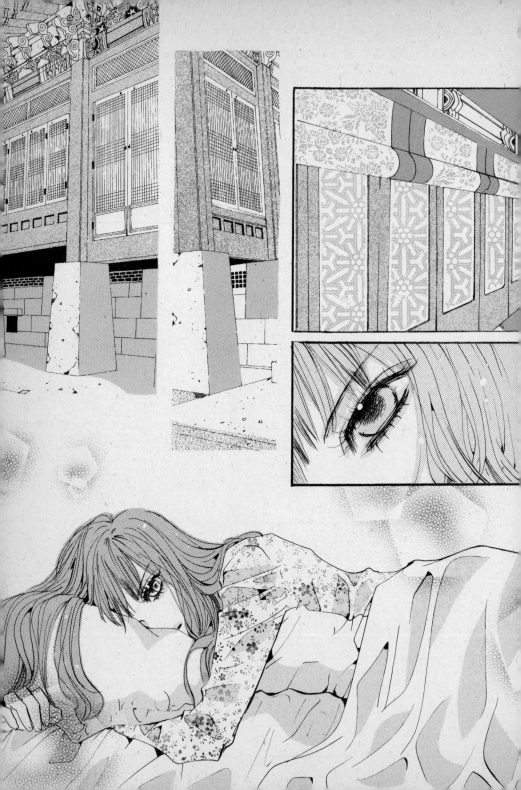

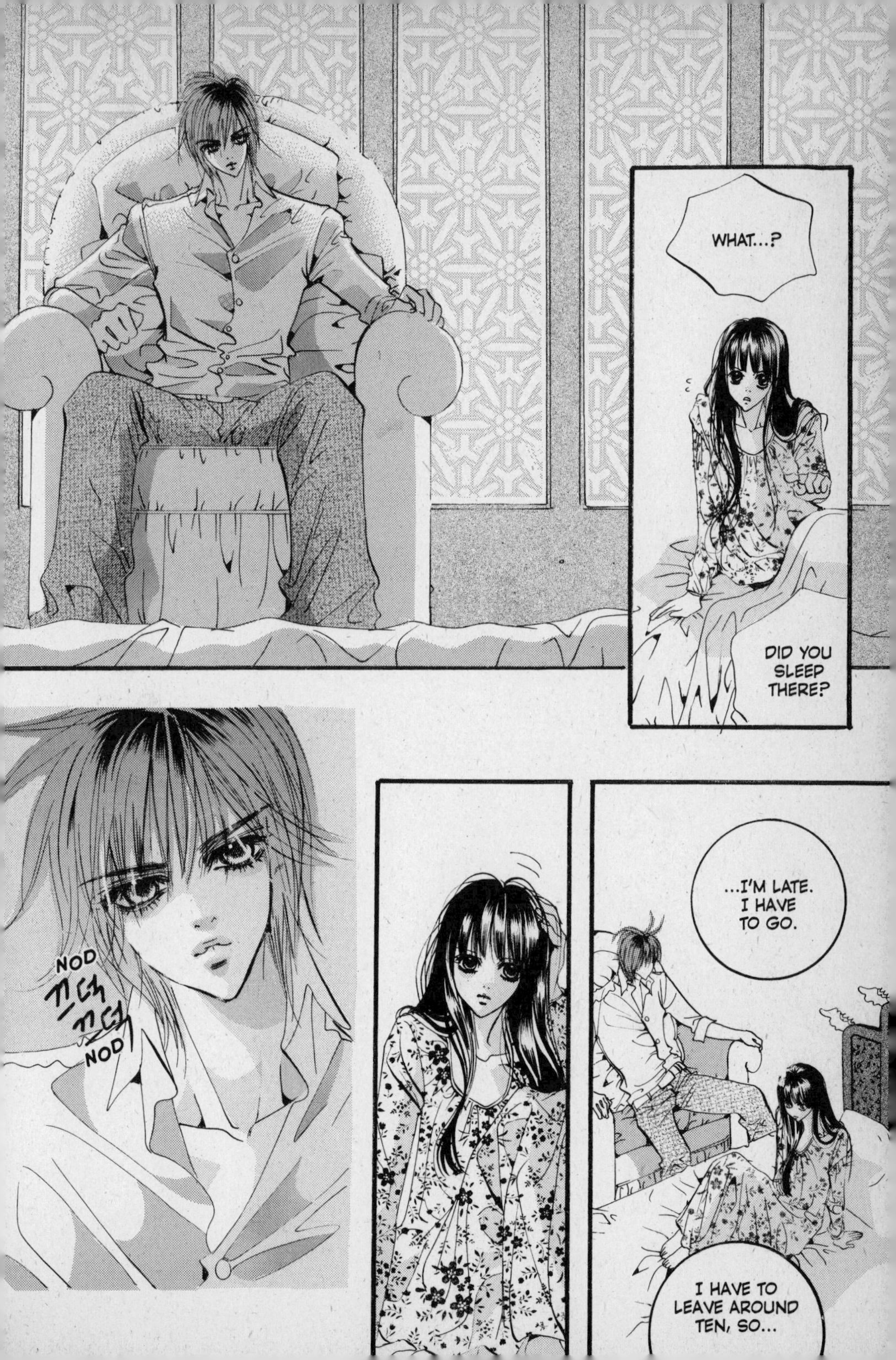

WHAT...?
DID YOU SLEEP THERE?
NOD 끄덕 끄덕 NOD
...I'M LATE. I HAVE TO GO.
I HAVE TO LEAVE AROUND TEN, SO...

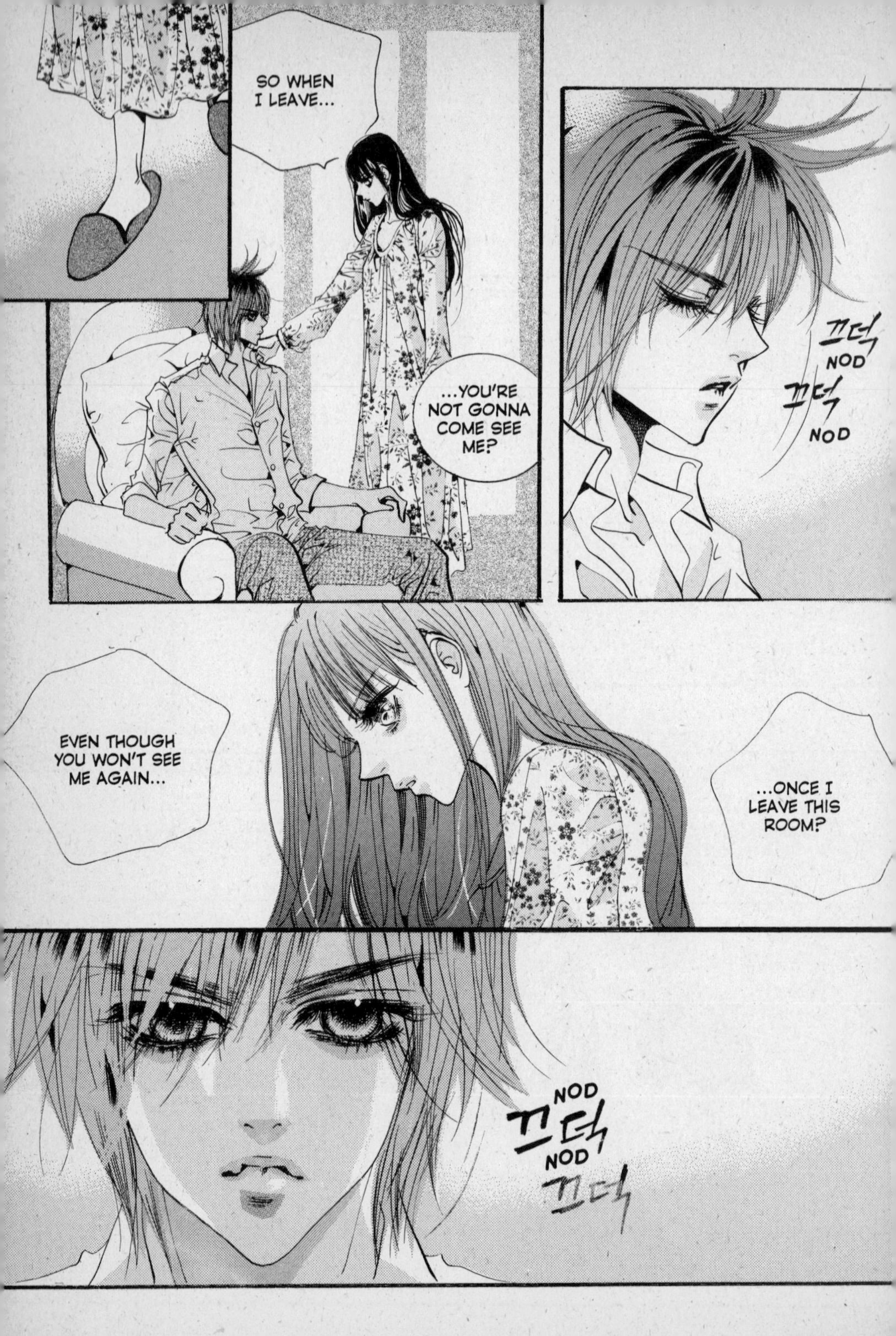
SO WHEN I LEAVE...
...YOU'RE NOT GONNA COME SEE ME?
끄덕
NOD
끄덕
NOD
EVEN THOUGH YOU WON'T SEE ME AGAIN...
...ONCE I LEAVE THIS ROOM?
NOD
끄덕
NOD
끄덕

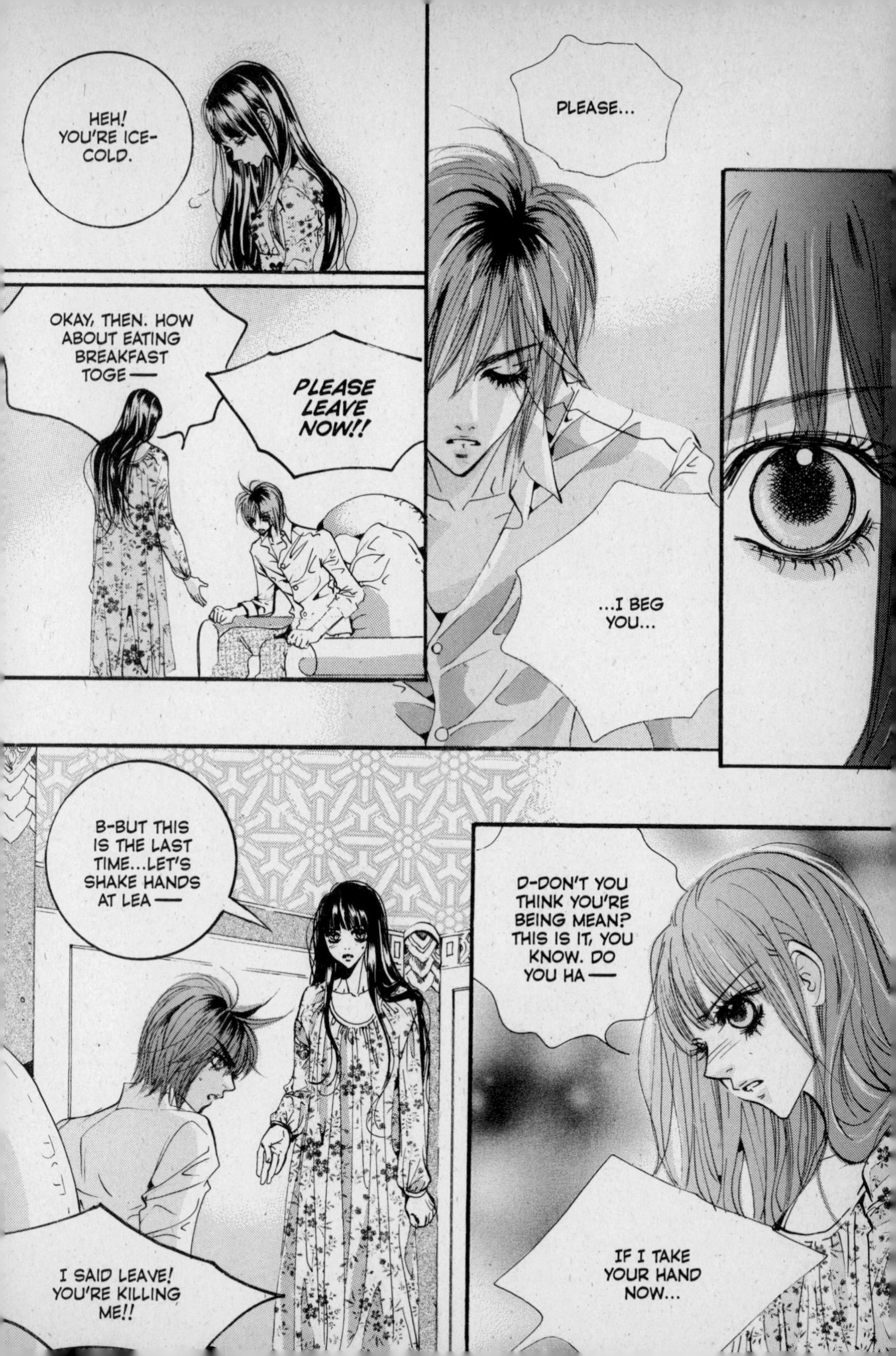
HEH! YOU'RE ICE-COLD.
OKAY, THEN. HOW ABOUT EATING BREAKFAST TOGE—
PLEASE LEAVE NOW!!
PLEASE...
...I BEG YOU...
B-BUT THIS IS THE LAST TIME...LET'S SHAKE HANDS AT LEA—
I SAID LEAVE! YOU'RE KILLING ME!!
D-DON'T YOU THINK YOU'RE BEING MEAN? THIS IS IT, YOU KNOW. DO YOU HA—
IF I TAKE YOUR HAND NOW...

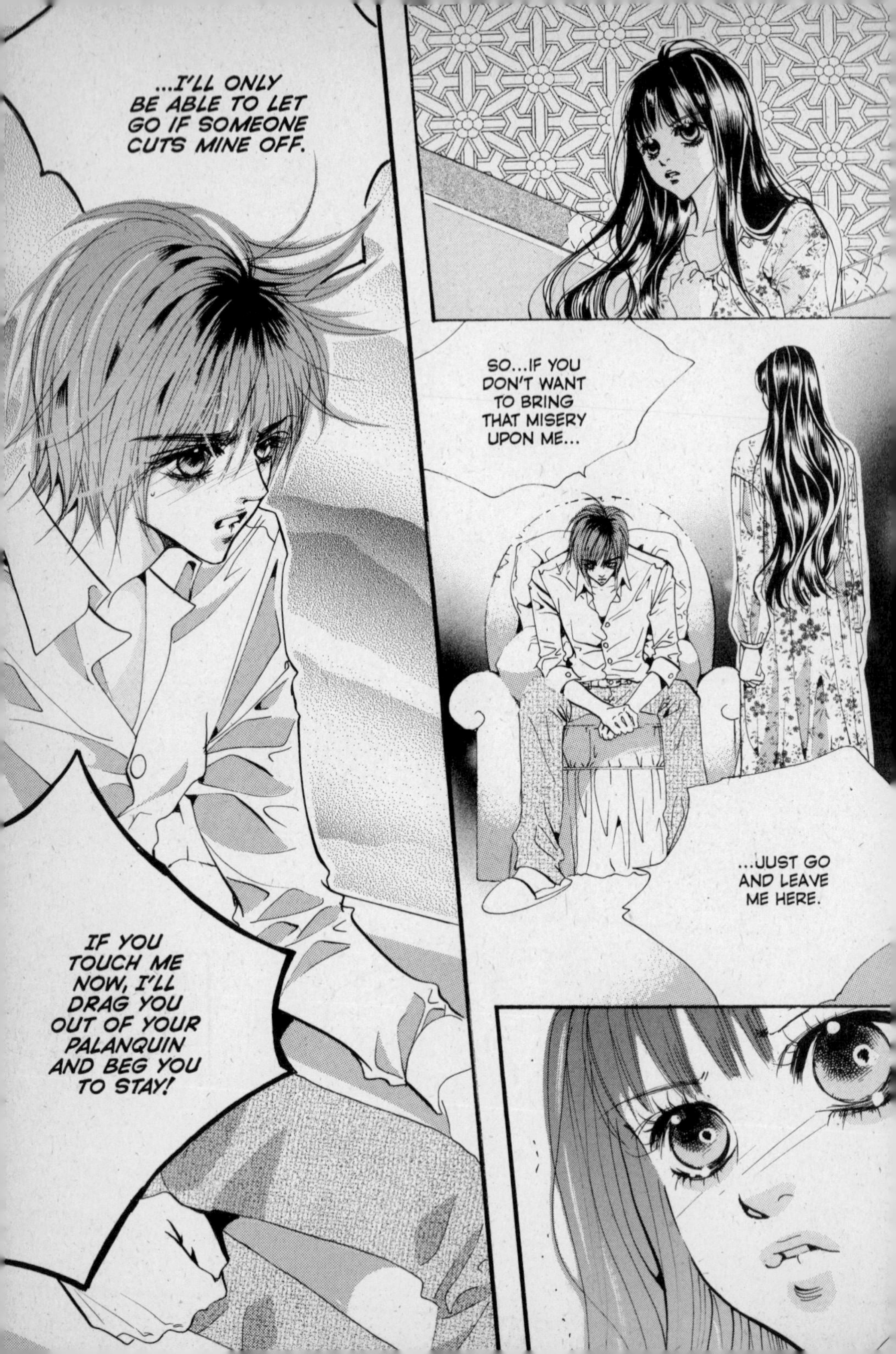

...I'LL ONLY BE ABLE TO LET GO IF SOMEONE CUTS MINE OFF.
IF YOU TOUCH ME NOW, I'LL DRAG YOU OUT OF YOUR PALANQUIN AND BEG YOU TO STAY!
SO...IF YOU DON'T WANT TO BRING THAT MISERY UPON ME...
...JUST GO AND LEAVE ME HERE.

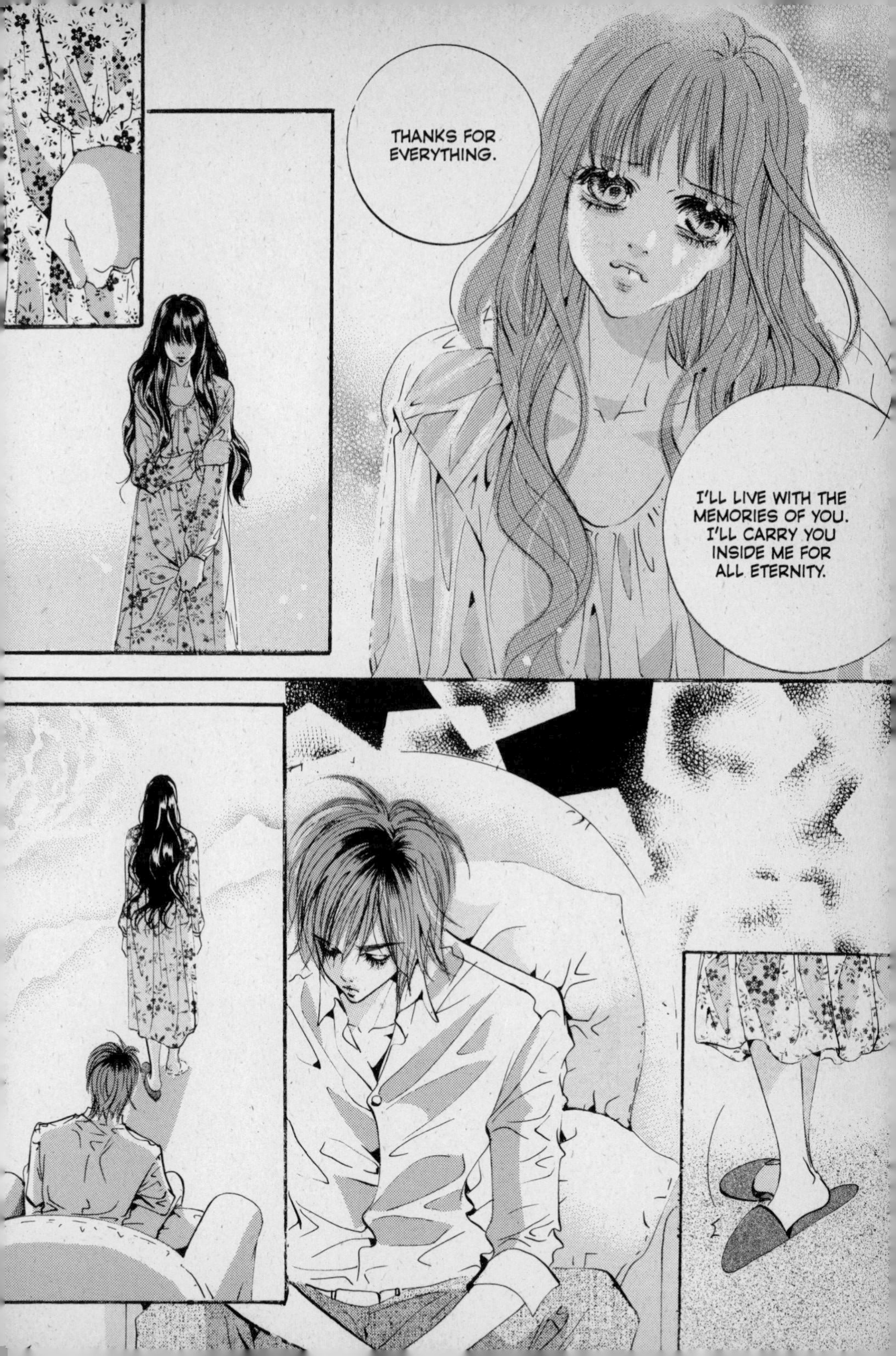
THANKS FOR EVERYTHING.
I'LL LIVE WITH THE MEMORIES OF YOU. I'LL CARRY YOU INSIDE ME FOR ALL ETERNITY.

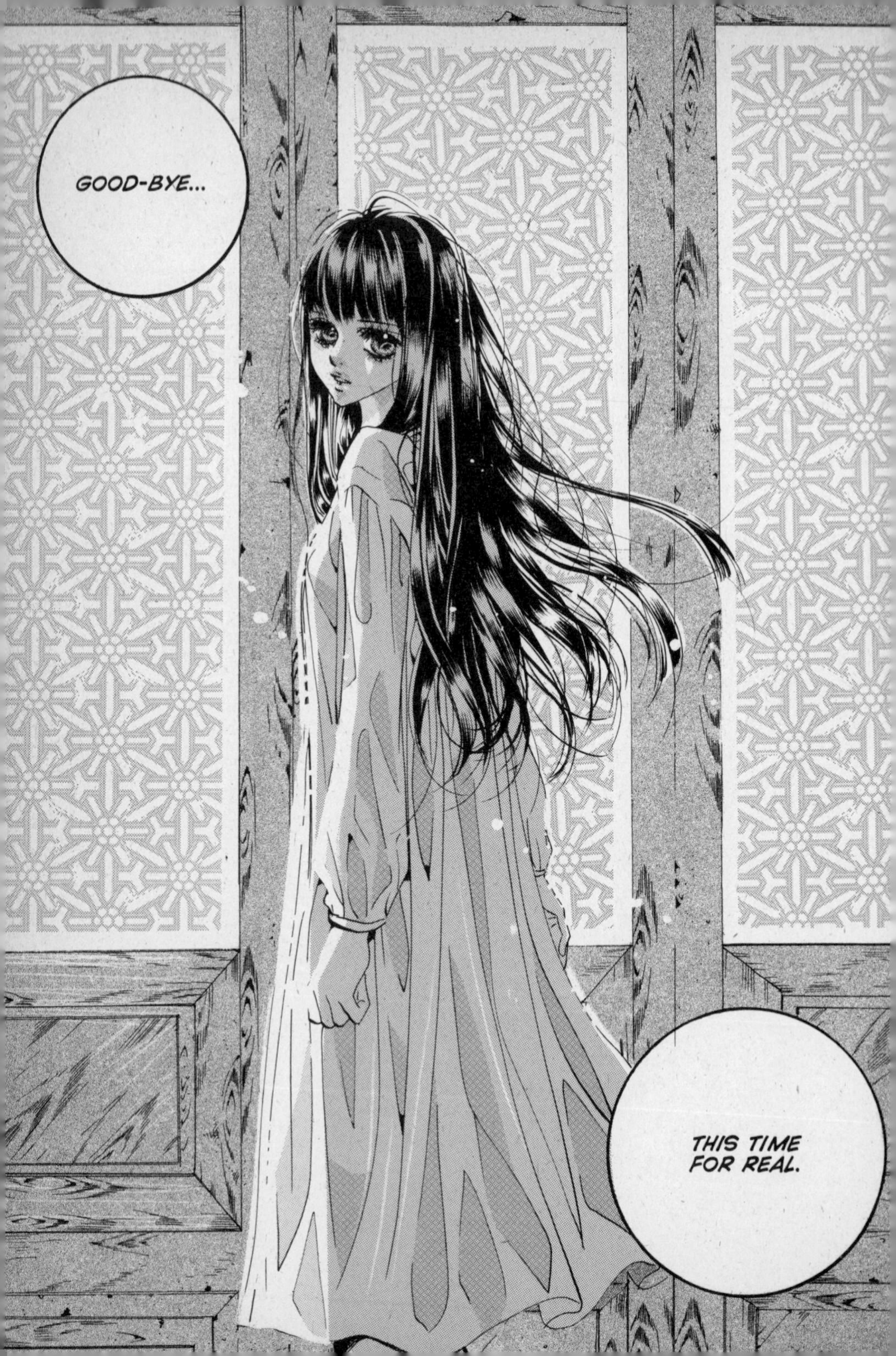
GOOD-BYE...
THIS TIME FOR REAL.

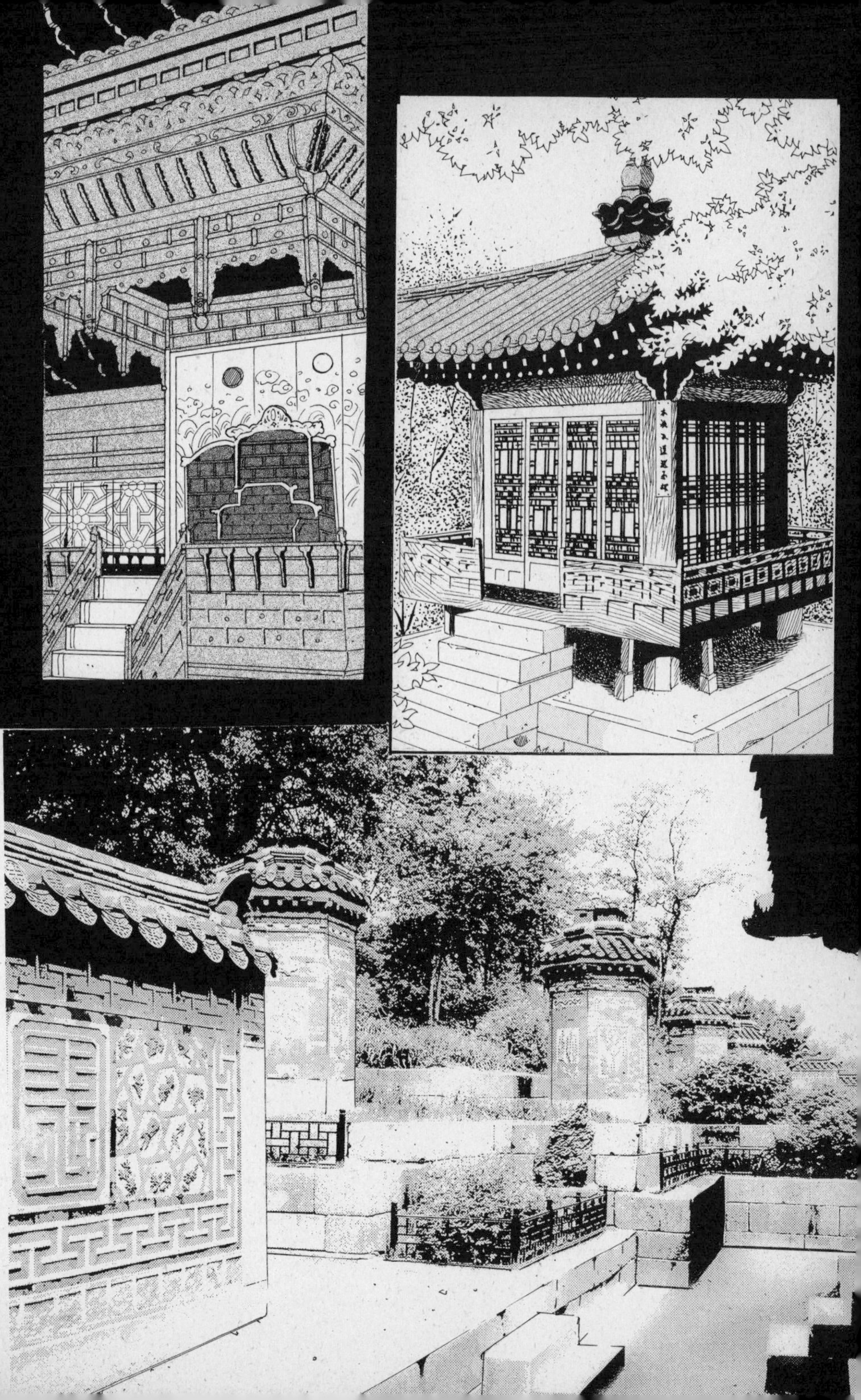

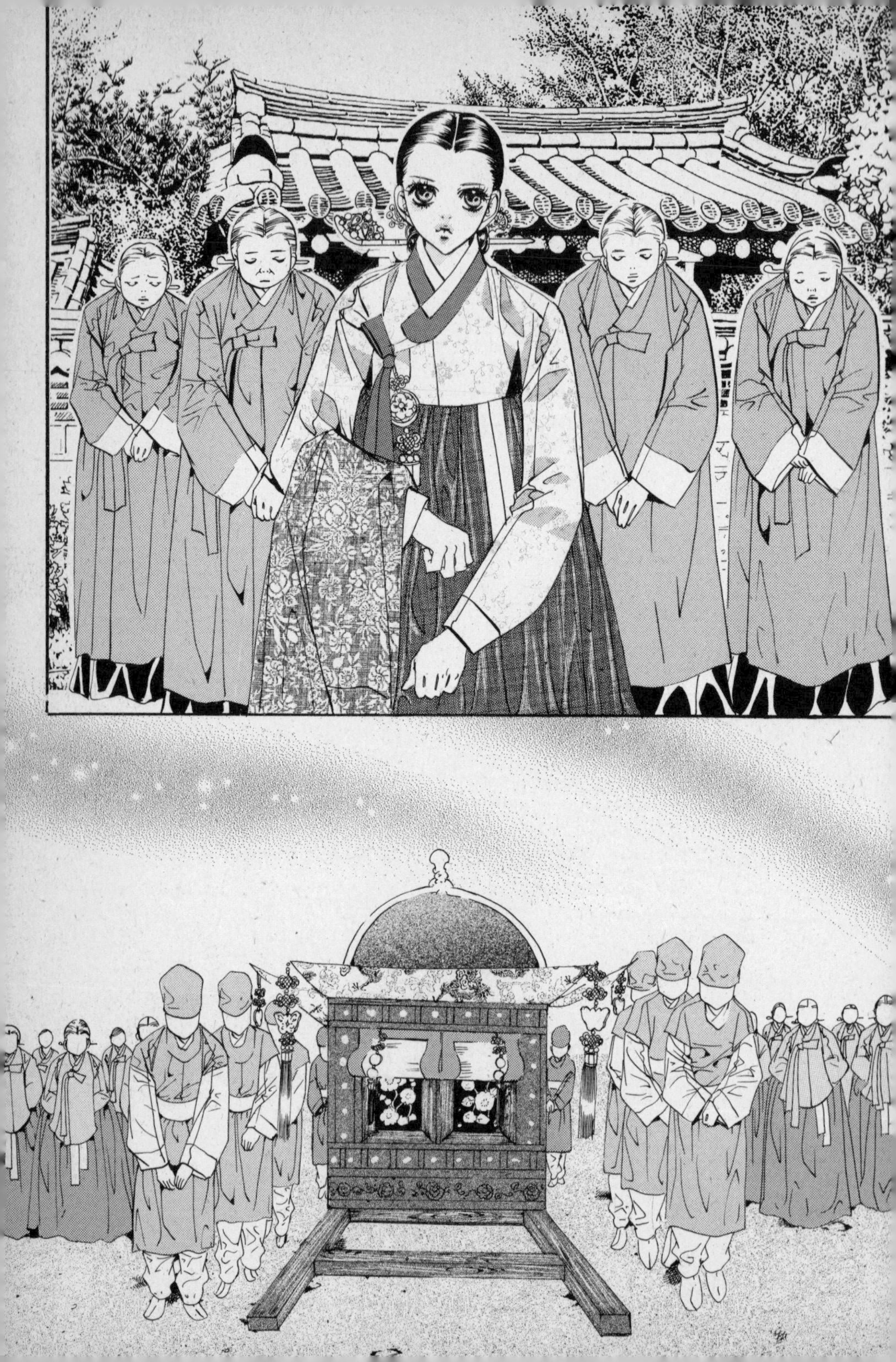

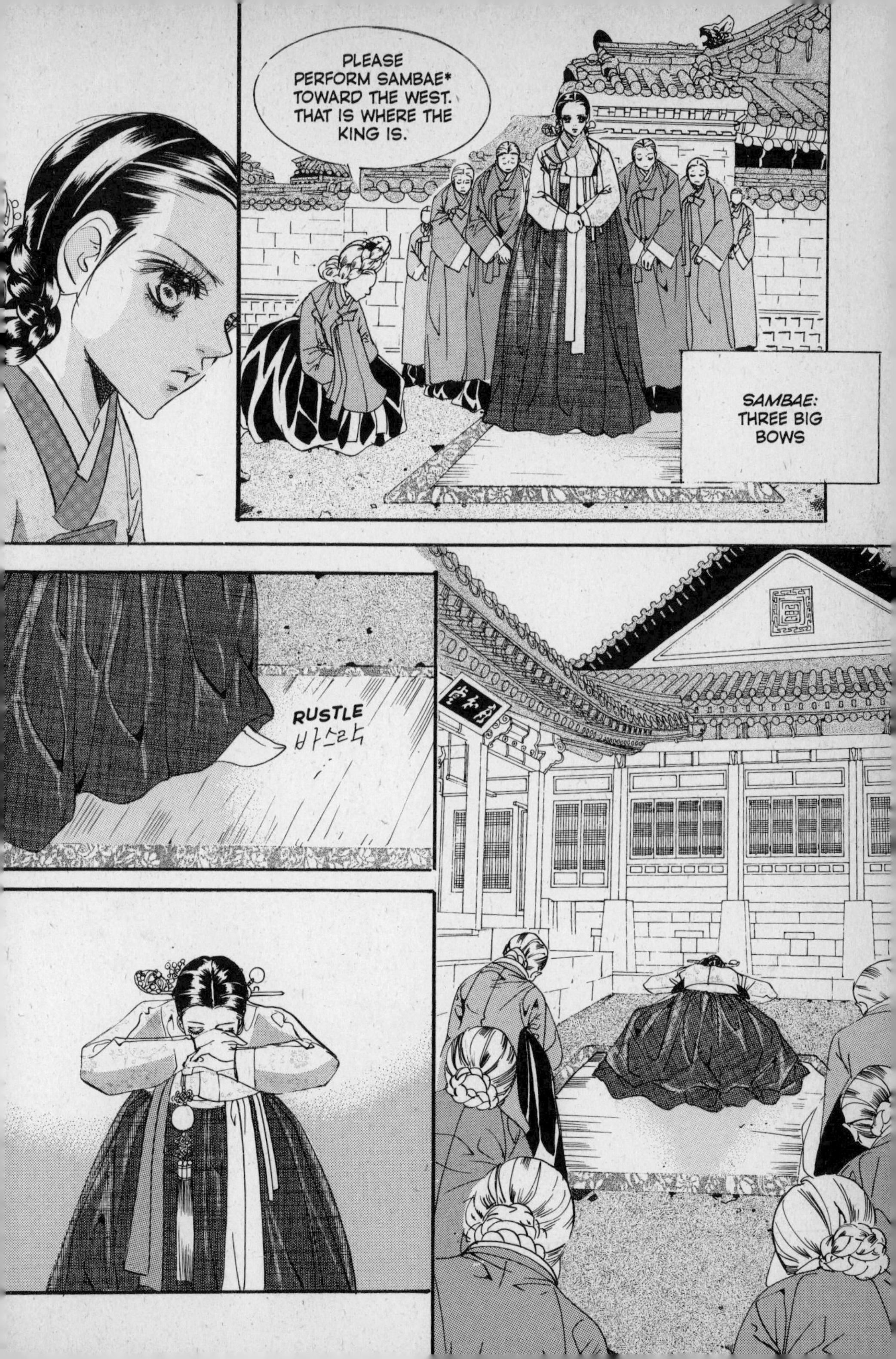
PLEASE PERFORM SAMBAE* TOWARD THE WEST. THAT IS WHERE THE KING IS.
SAMBAE: THREE BIG BOWS
RUSTLE
바스락

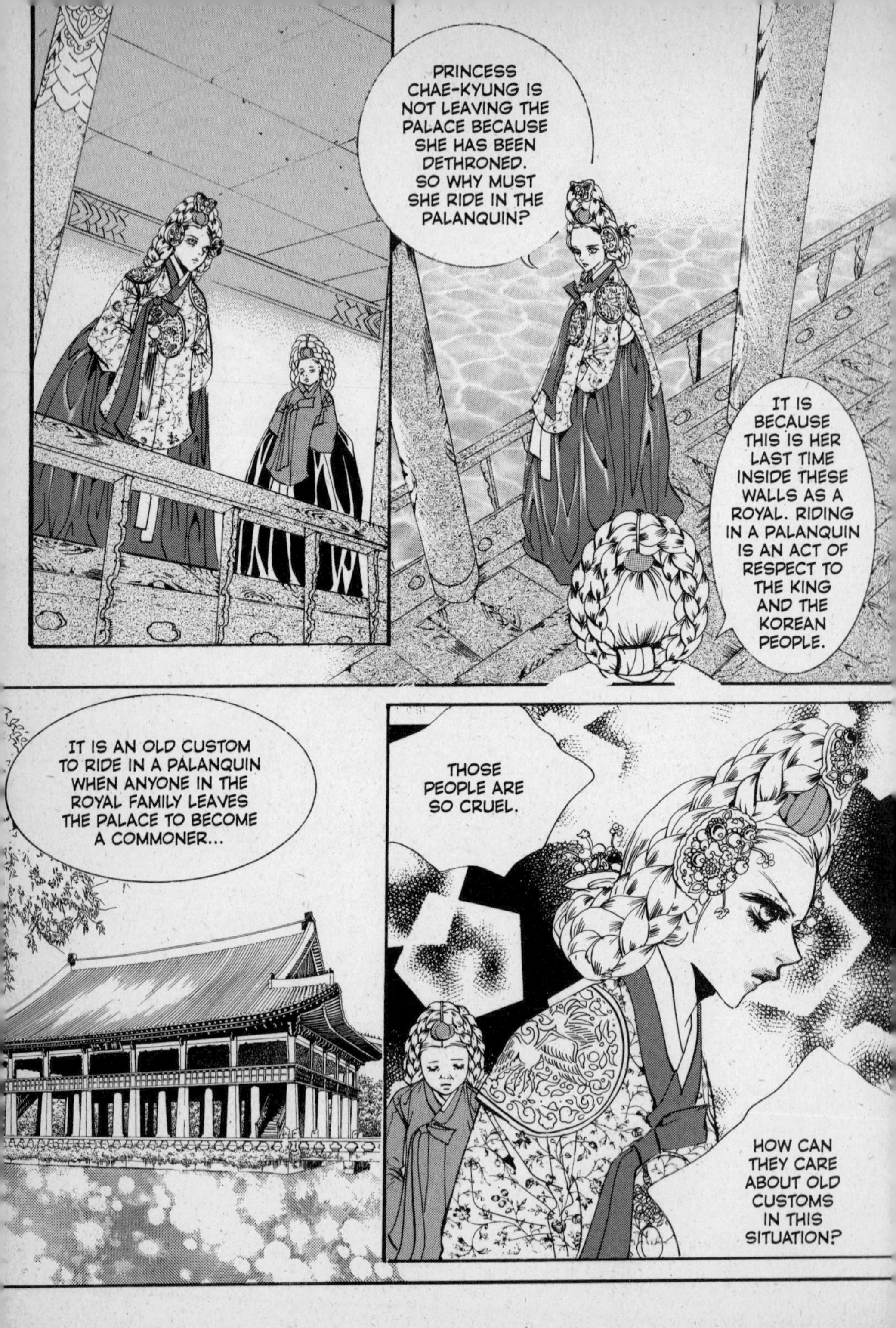
PRINCESS CHAE-KYUNG IS NOT LEAVING THE PALACE BECAUSE SHE HAS BEEN DETHRONED. SO WHY MUST SHE RIDE IN THE PALANQUIN?
IT IS BECAUSE THIS IS HER LAST TIME INSIDE THESE WALLS AS A ROYAL. RIDING IN A PALANQUIN IS AN ACT OF RESPECT TO THE KING AND THE KOREAN PEOPLE.
IT IS AN OLD CUSTOM TO RIDE IN A PALANQUIN WHEN ANYONE IN THE ROYAL FAMILY LEAVES THE PALACE TO BECOME A COMMONER...
THOSE PEOPLE ARE SO CRUEL.
HOW CAN THEY CARE ABOUT OLD CUSTOMS IN THIS SITUATION?

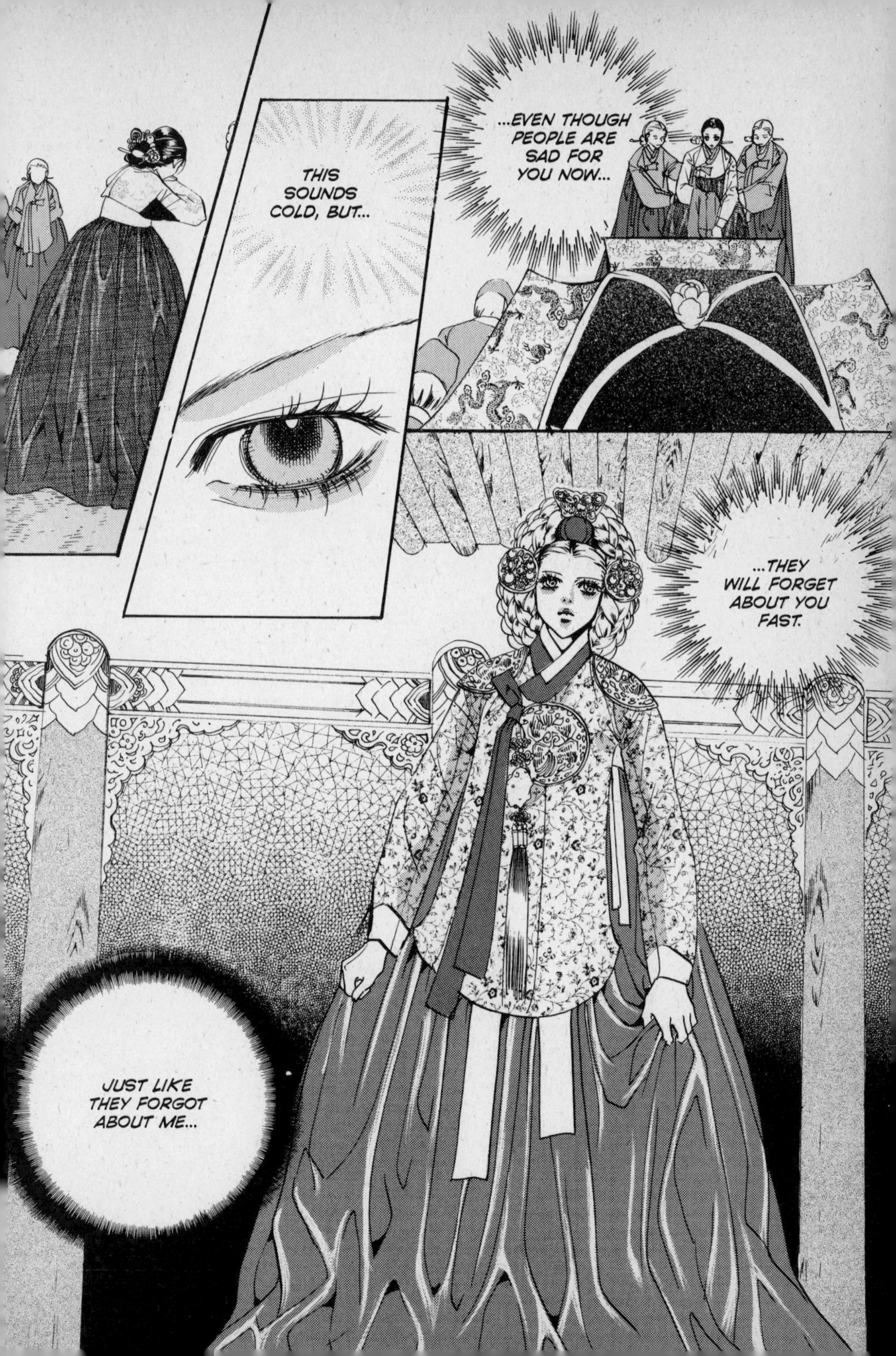
THIS SOUNDS COLD, BUT...
...EVEN THOUGH PEOPLE ARE SAD FOR YOU NOW...
...THEY WILL FORGET ABOUT YOU FAST.
JUST LIKE THEY FORGOT ABOUT ME...

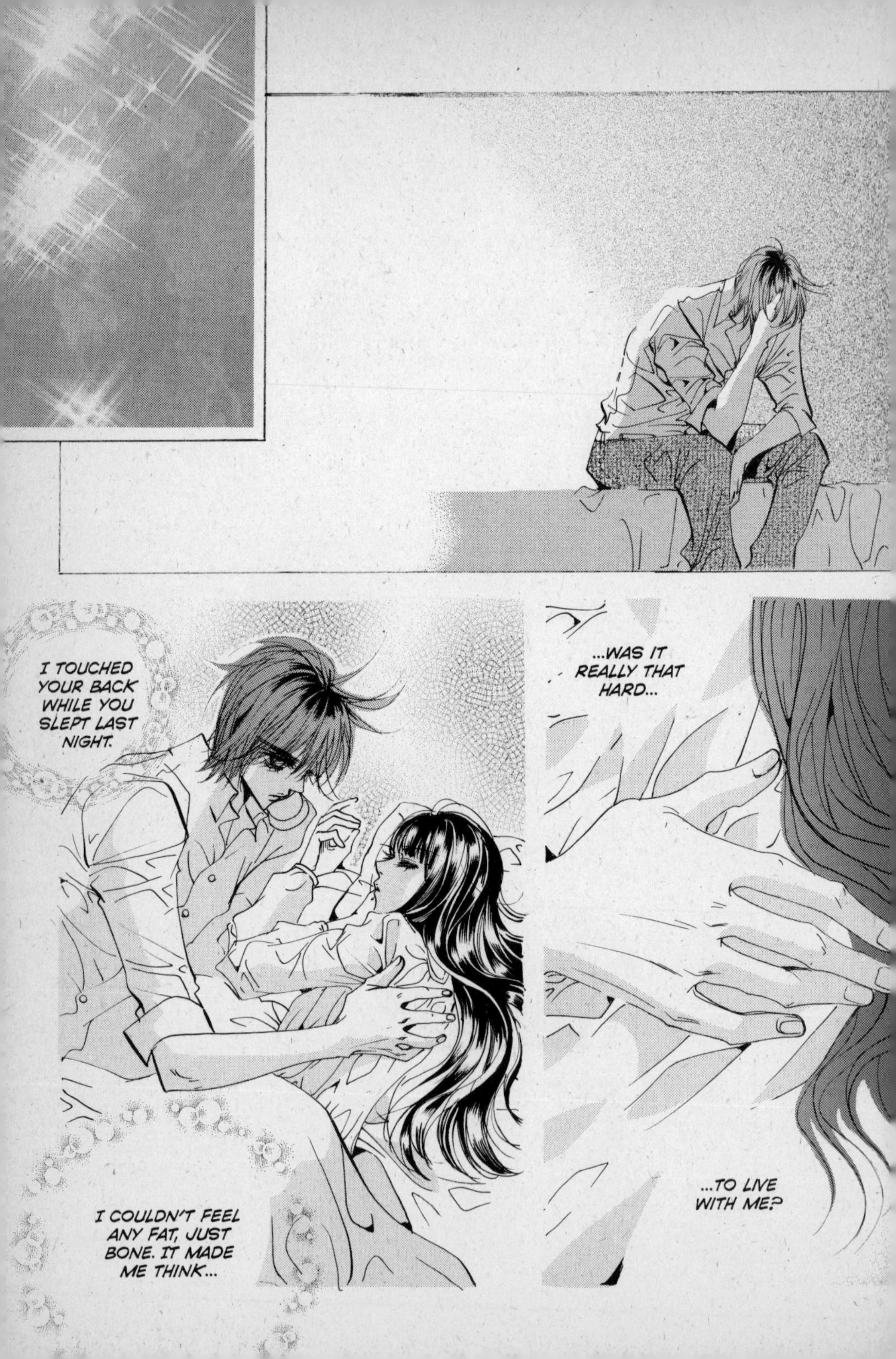
...WAS IT REALLY THAT HARD...
...TO LIVE WITH ME?
I TOUCHED YOUR BACK WHILE YOU SLEPT LAST NIGHT.
I COULDN'T FEEL ANY FAT, JUST BONE. IT MADE ME THINK...

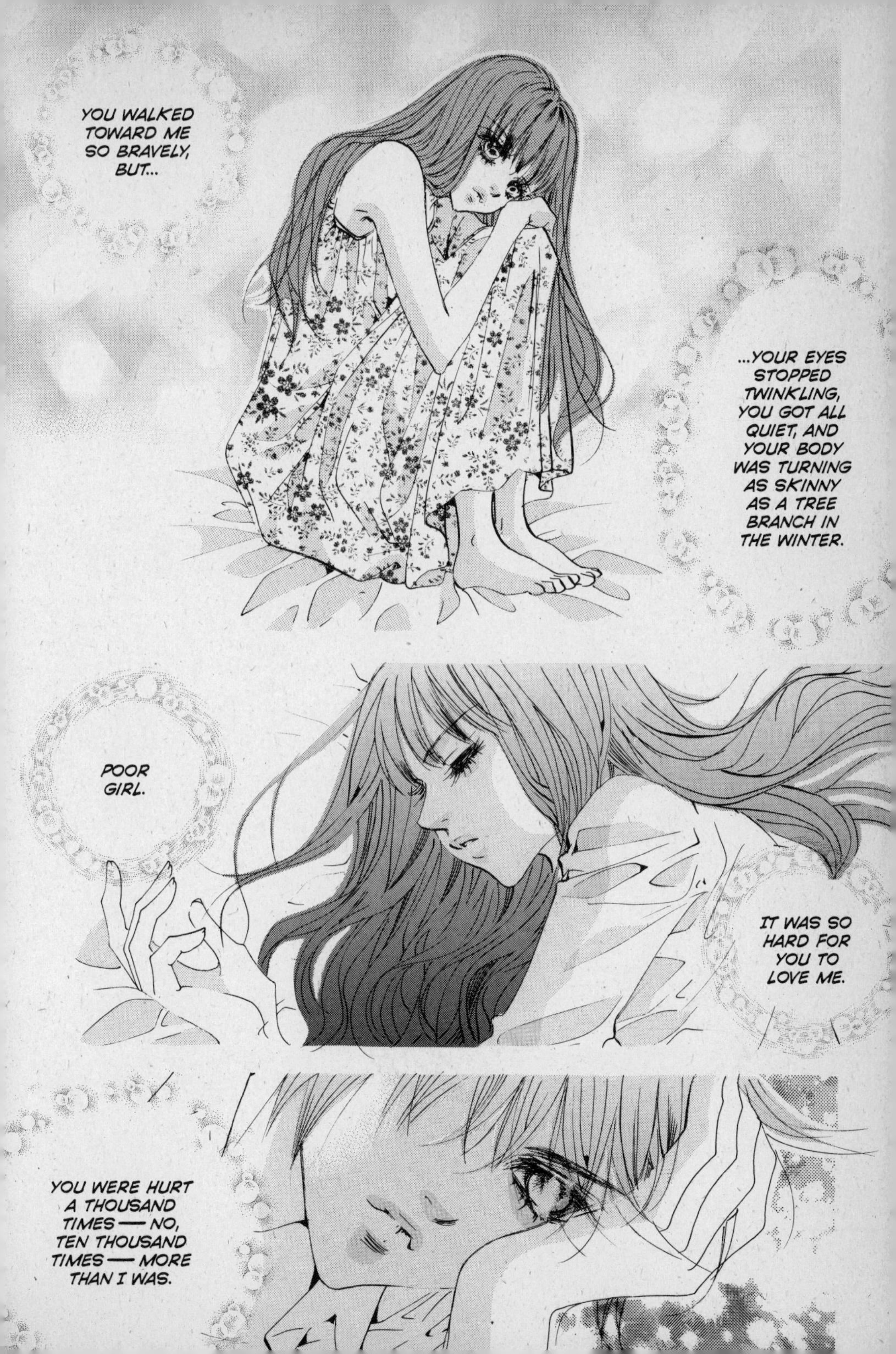
YOU WALKED TOWARD ME SO BRAVELY, BUT...
...YOUR EYES STOPPED TWINKLING, YOU GOT ALL QUIET, AND YOUR BODY WAS TURNING AS SKINNY AS A TREE BRANCH IN THE WINTER.
POOR GIRL.
IT WAS SO HARD FOR YOU TO LOVE ME.
YOU WERE HURT A THOUSAND TIMES — NO, TEN THOUSAND TIMES — MORE THAN I WAS.

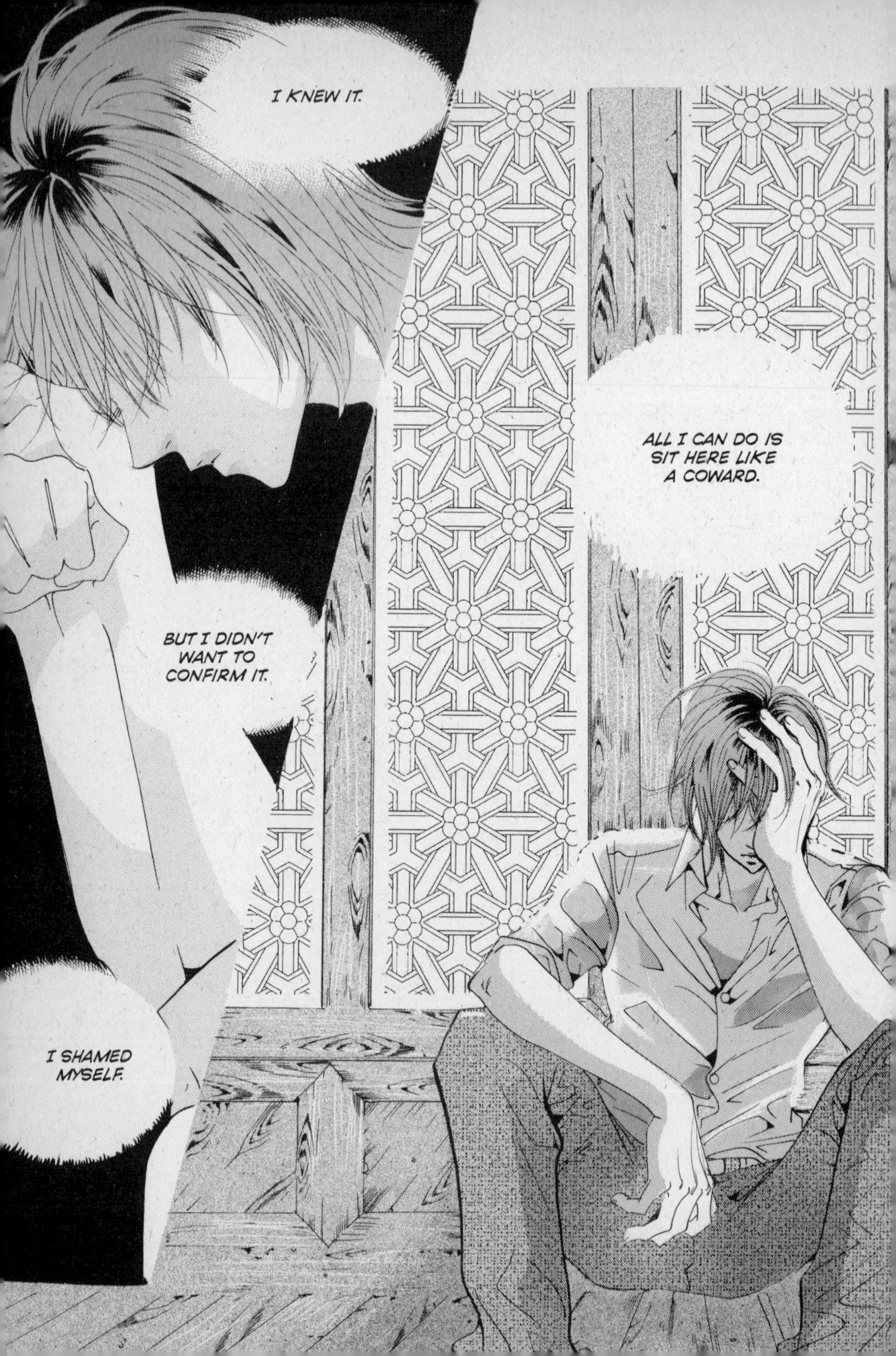

I KNEW IT.
ALL I CAN DO IS SIT HERE LIKE A COWARD.
BUT I DIDN'T WANT TO CONFIRM IT.
I SHAMED MYSELF.

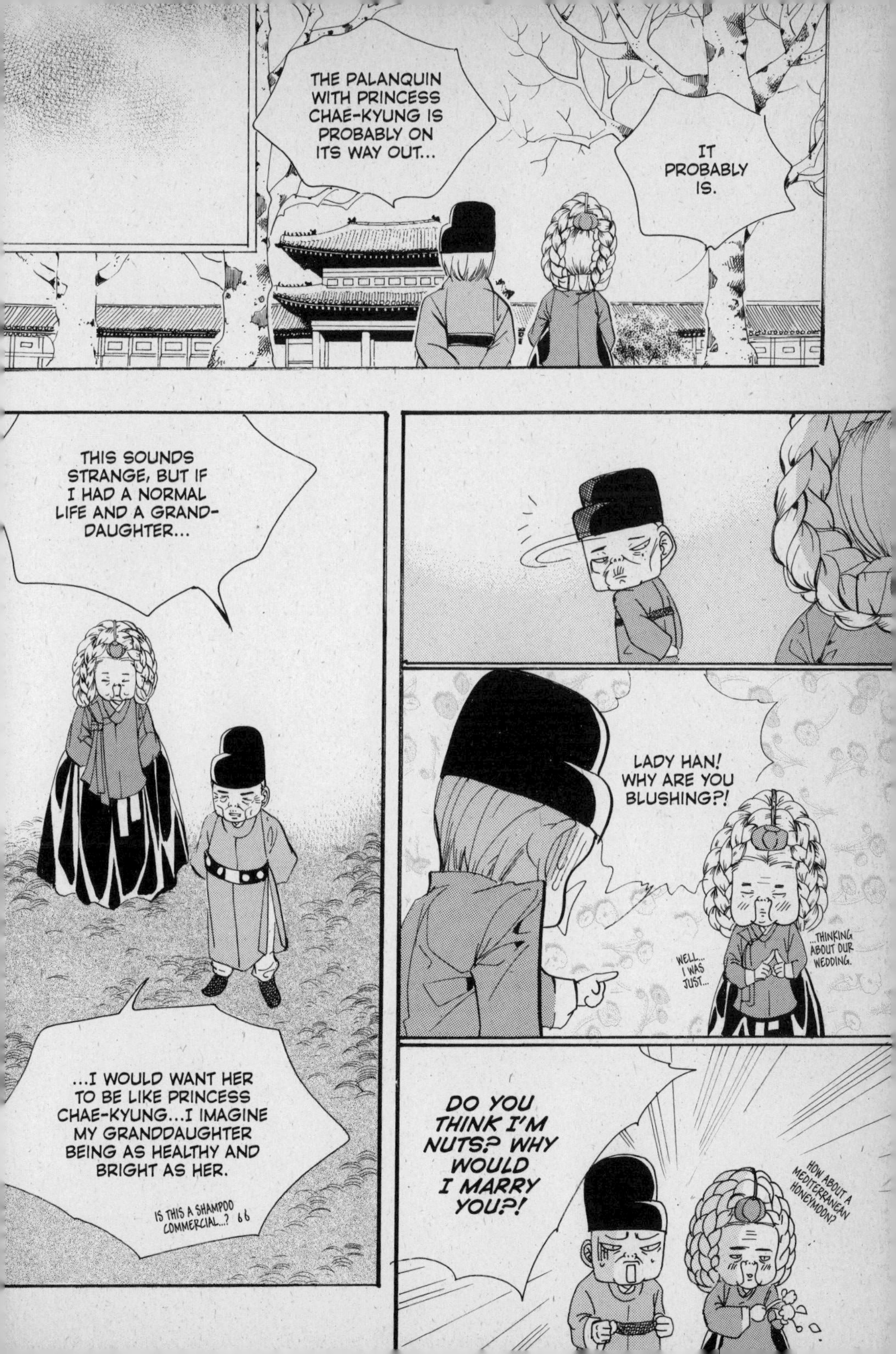
THE PALANQUIN WITH PRINCESS CHAE-KYUNG IS PROBABLY ON ITS WAY OUT...
IT PROBABLY IS.
THIS SOUNDS STRANGE, BUT IF I HAD A NORMAL LIFE AND A GRAND-DAUGHTER...
...I WOULD WANT HER TO BE LIKE PRINCESS CHAE-KYUNG...I IMAGINE MY GRANDDAUGHTER BEING AS HEALTHY AND BRIGHT AS HER.
IS THIS A SHAMPOO COMMERCIAL...? 66
LADY HAN! WHY ARE YOU BLUSHING?!
WELL... I WAS JUST...
...THINKING ABOUT OUR WEDDING.
DO YOU THINK I'M NUTS? WHY WOULD I MARRY YOU?!
HOW ABOUT A MEDITERRANEAN HONEYMOON?

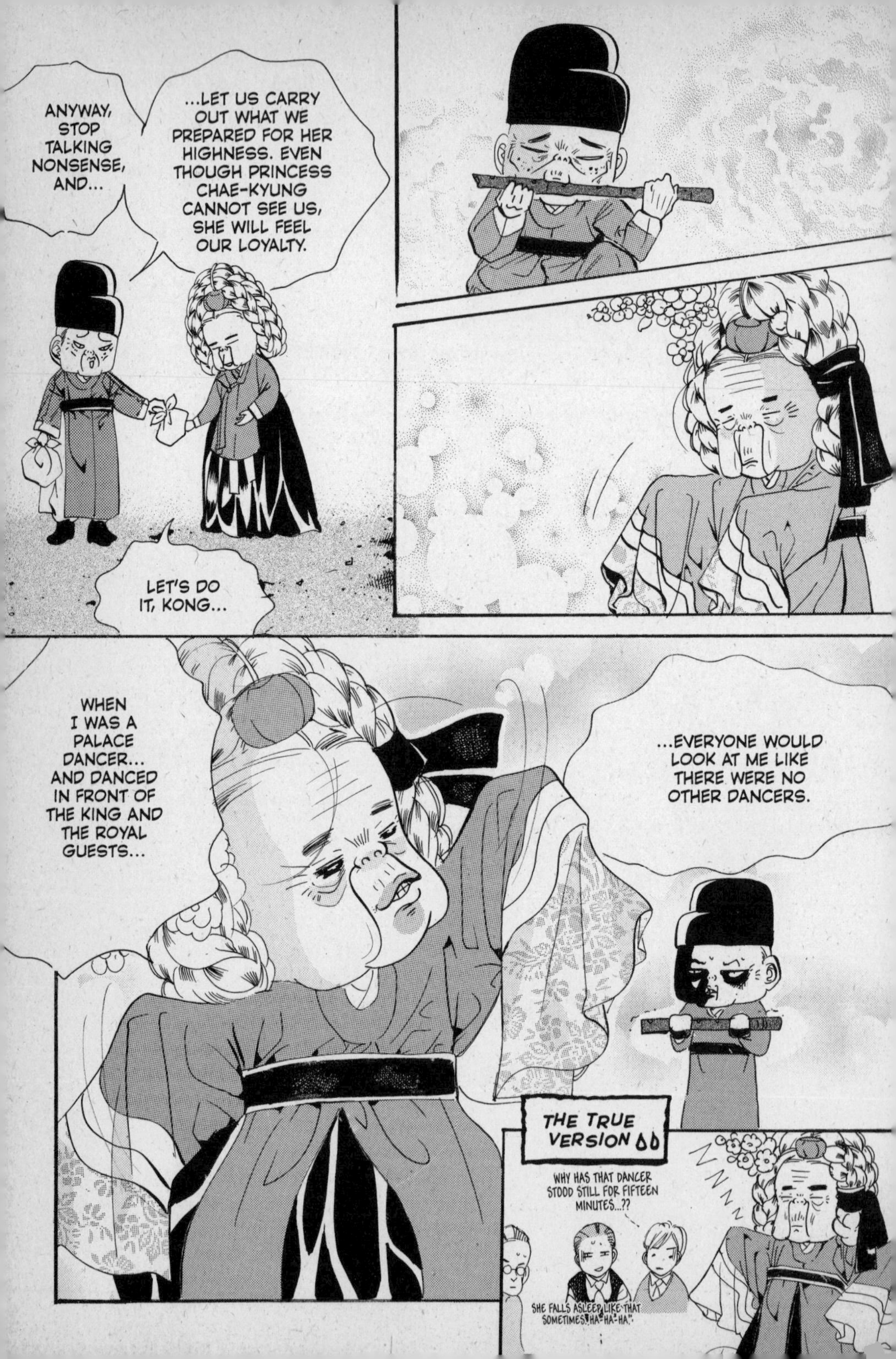
ANYWAY, STOP TALKING NONSENSE, AND...
...LET US CARRY OUT WHAT WE PREPARED FOR HER HIGHNESS. EVEN THOUGH PRINCESS CHAE-KYUNG CANNOT SEE US, SHE WILL FEEL OUR LOYALTY.
LET'S DO IT, KONG...
WHEN I WAS A PALACE DANCER... AND DANCED IN FRONT OF THE KING AND THE ROYAL GUESTS...
...EVERYONE WOULD LOOK AT ME LIKE THERE WERE NO OTHER DANCERS.
THE TRUE VERSION
WHY HAS THAT DANCER STOOD STILL FOR FIFTEEN MINUTES...??
SHE FALLS ASLEEP LIKE THAT SOMETIMES. HA-HA-HA.
ZZZZ

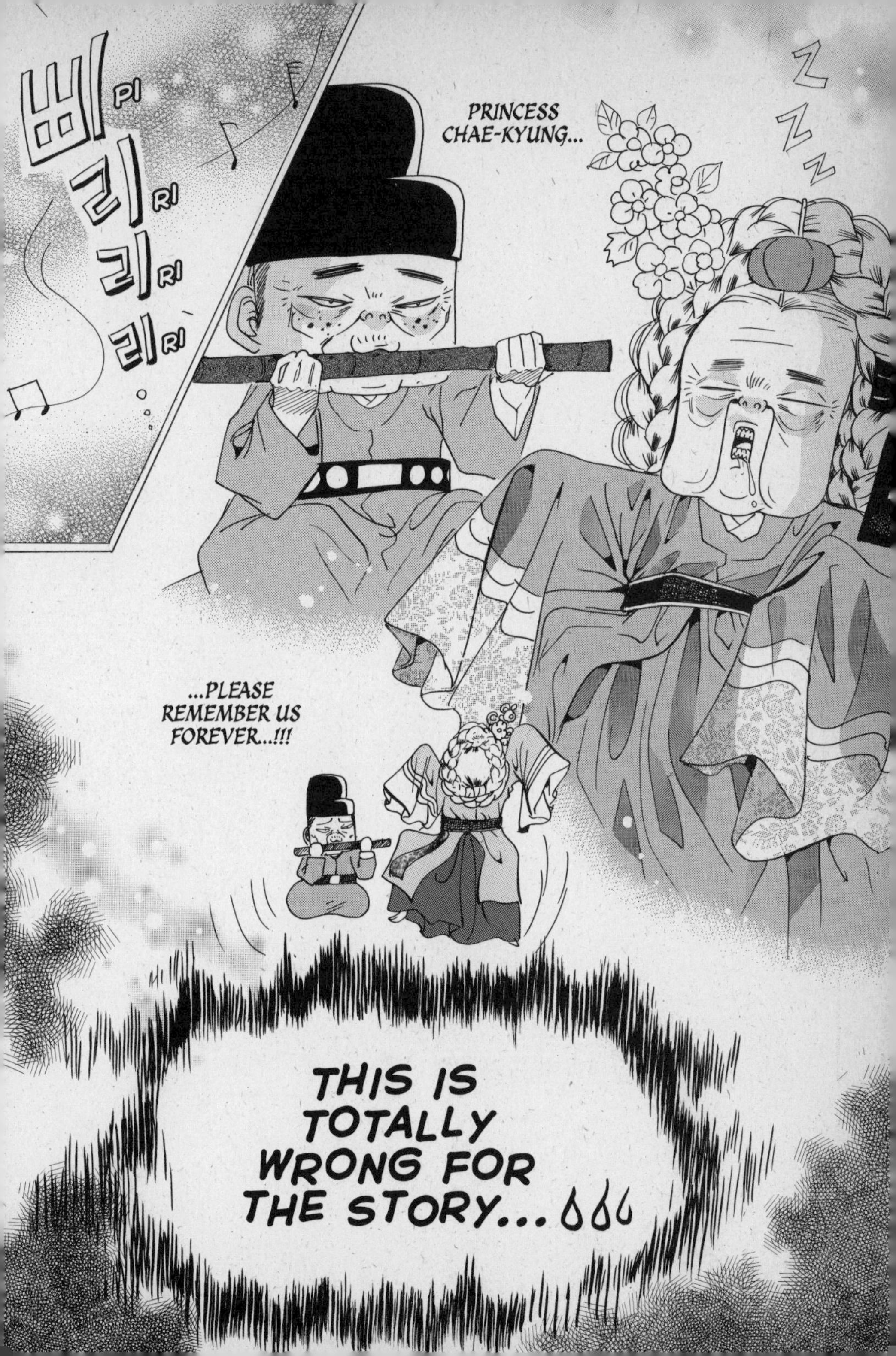
삐 PI
리 RI
리 RI
리 RI
ZZZ
PRINCESS CHAE-KYUNG...
...PLEASE REMEMBER US FOREVER...!!!
THIS IS TOTALLY WRONG FOR THE STORY...

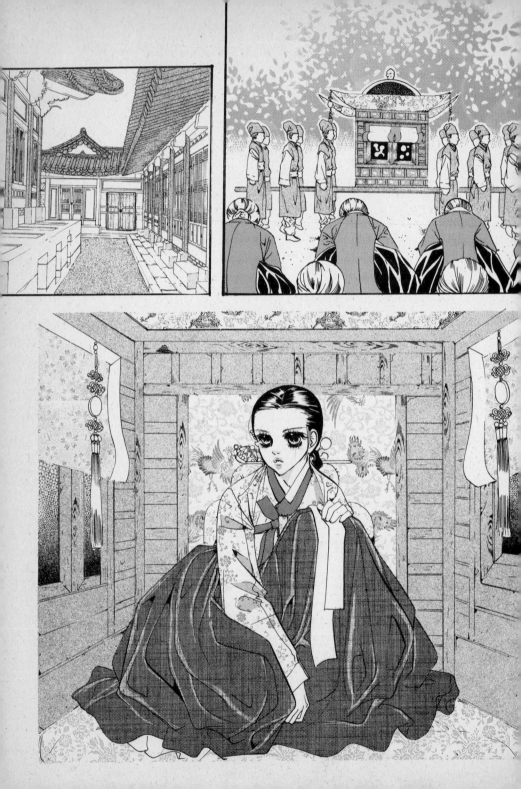

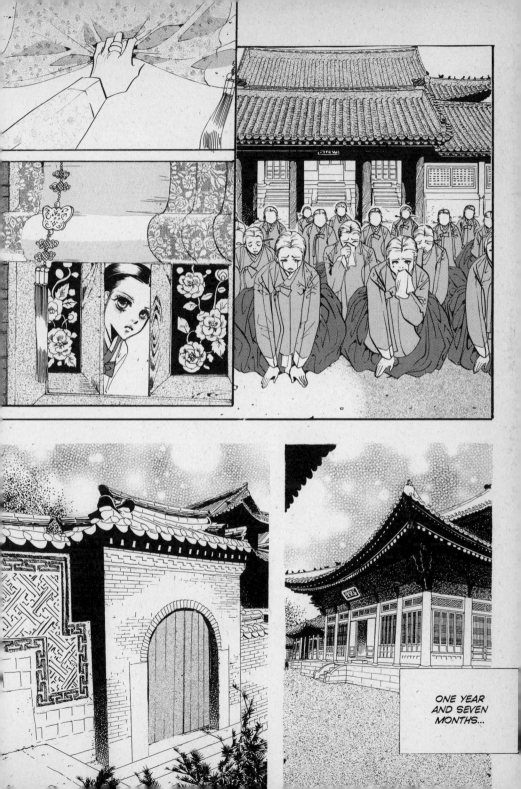

ONE YEAR
AND SEVEN
MONTHS...

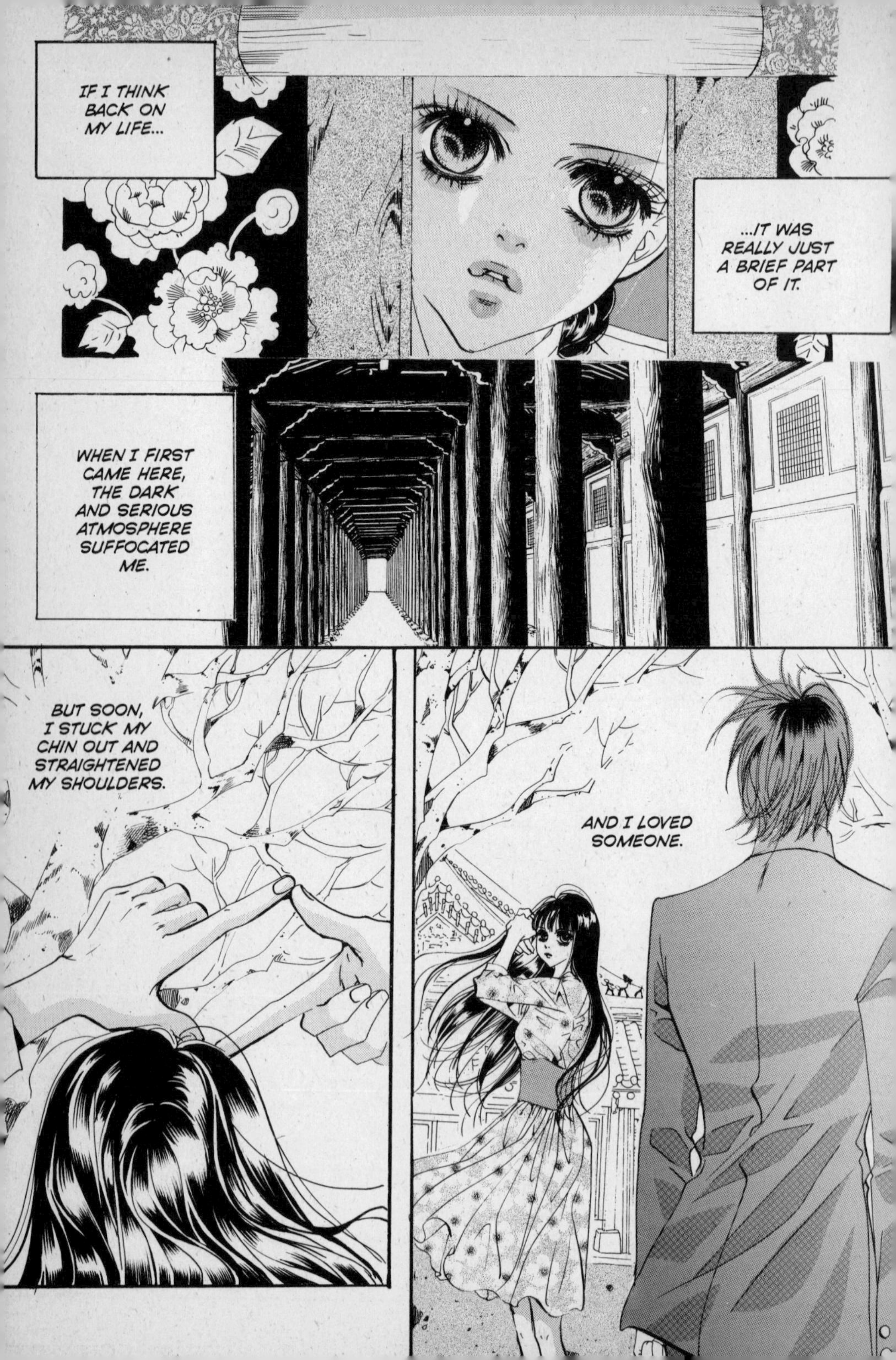
IF I THINK BACK ON MY LIFE...
...IT WAS REALLY JUST A BRIEF PART OF IT.
WHEN I FIRST CAME HERE, THE DARK AND SERIOUS ATMOSPHERE SUFFOCATED ME.
BUT SOON, I STUCK MY CHIN OUT AND STRAIGHTENED MY SHOULDERS.
AND I LOVED SOMEONE.

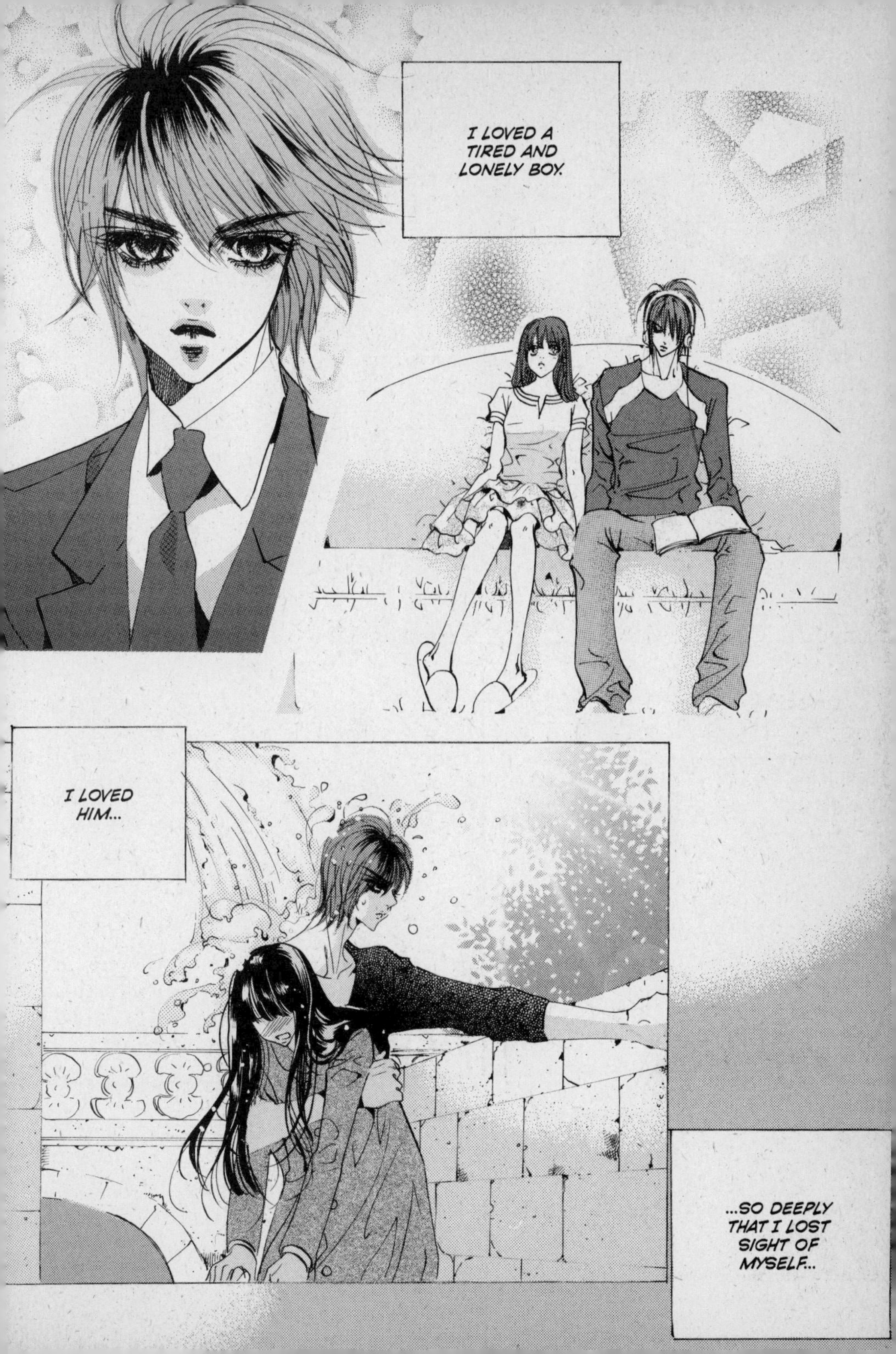
I LOVED A TIRED AND LONELY BOY.
I LOVED HIM...
...SO DEEPLY THAT I LOST SIGHT OF MYSELF...

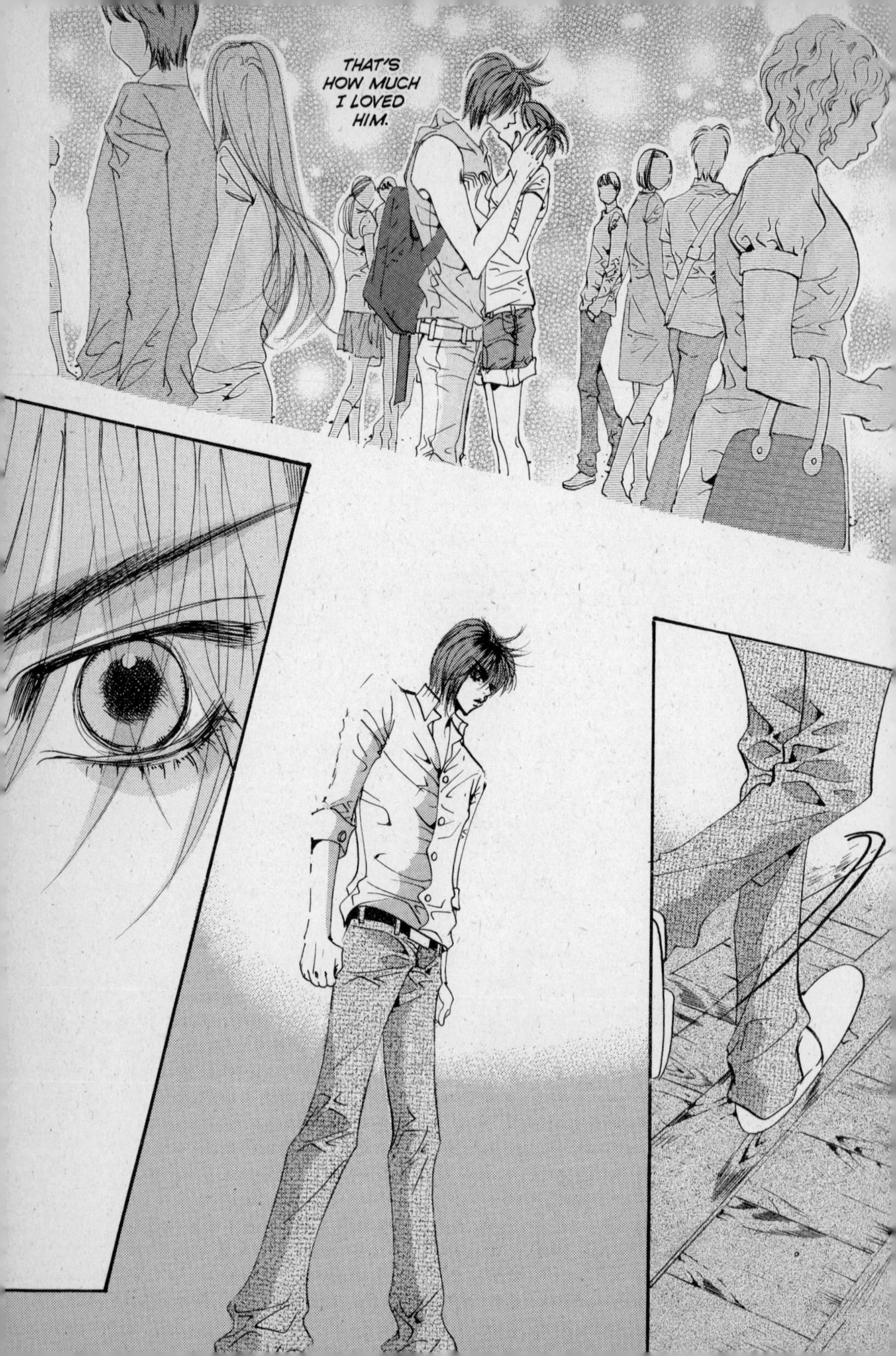
THAT'S HOW MUCH I LOVED HIM.

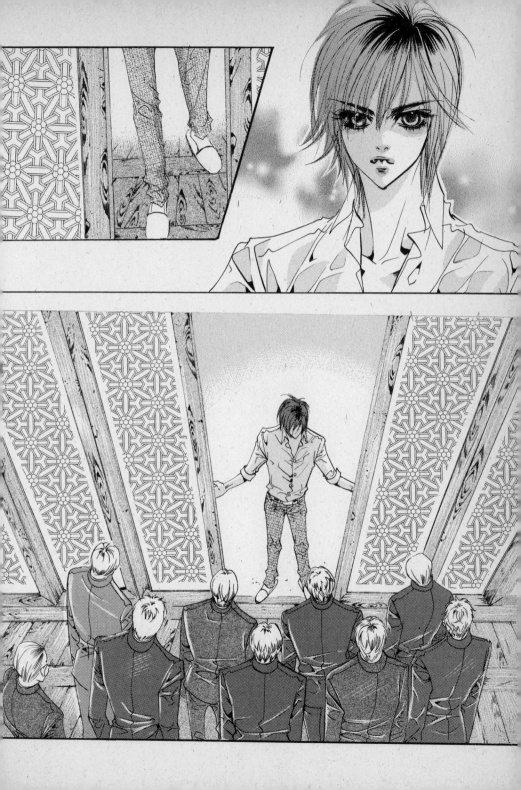

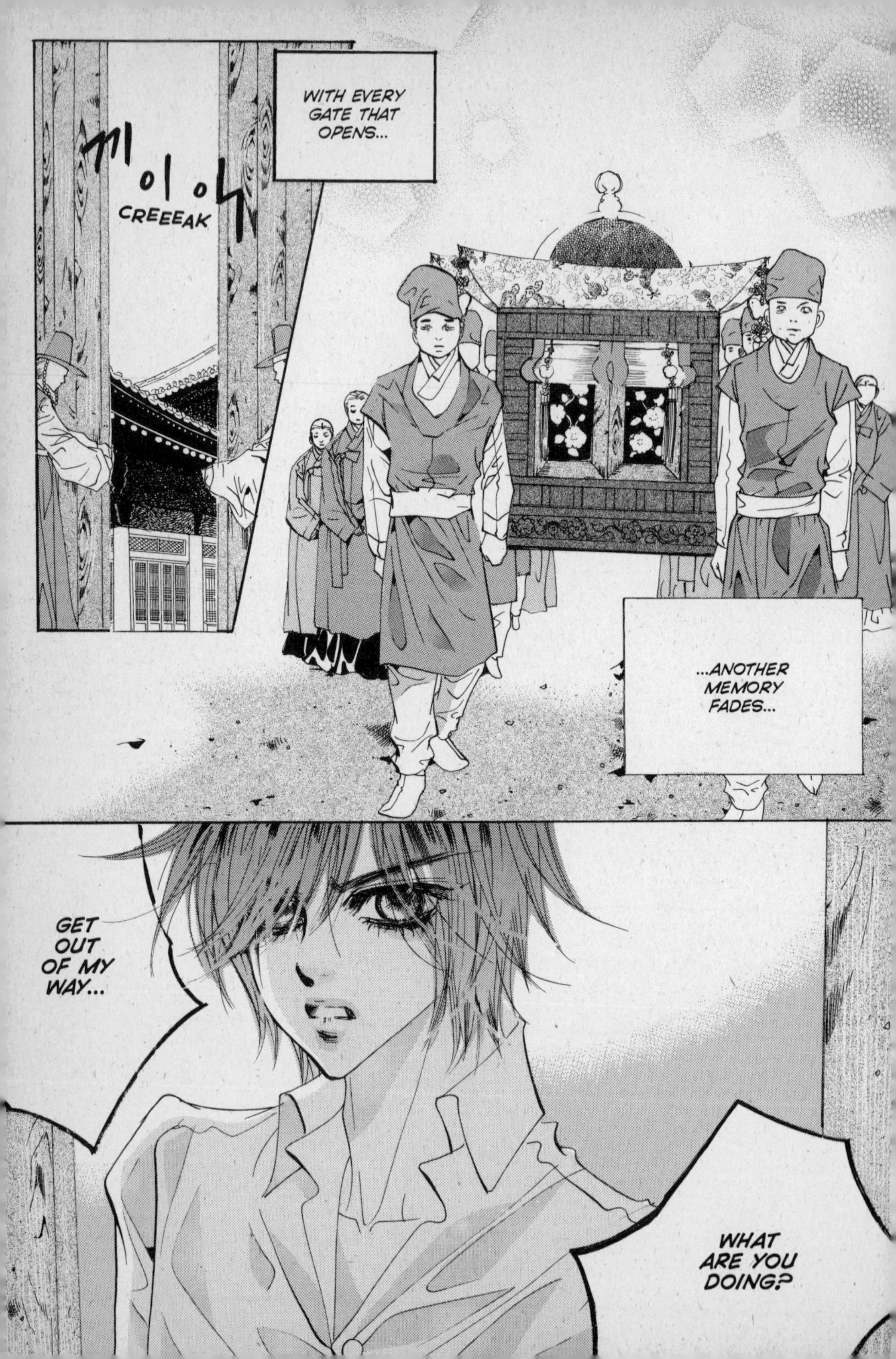
WITH EVERY GATE THAT OPENS...
끼이익
CREEEAK
...ANOTHER MEMORY FADES...
GET OUT OF MY WAY...
WHAT ARE YOU DOING?

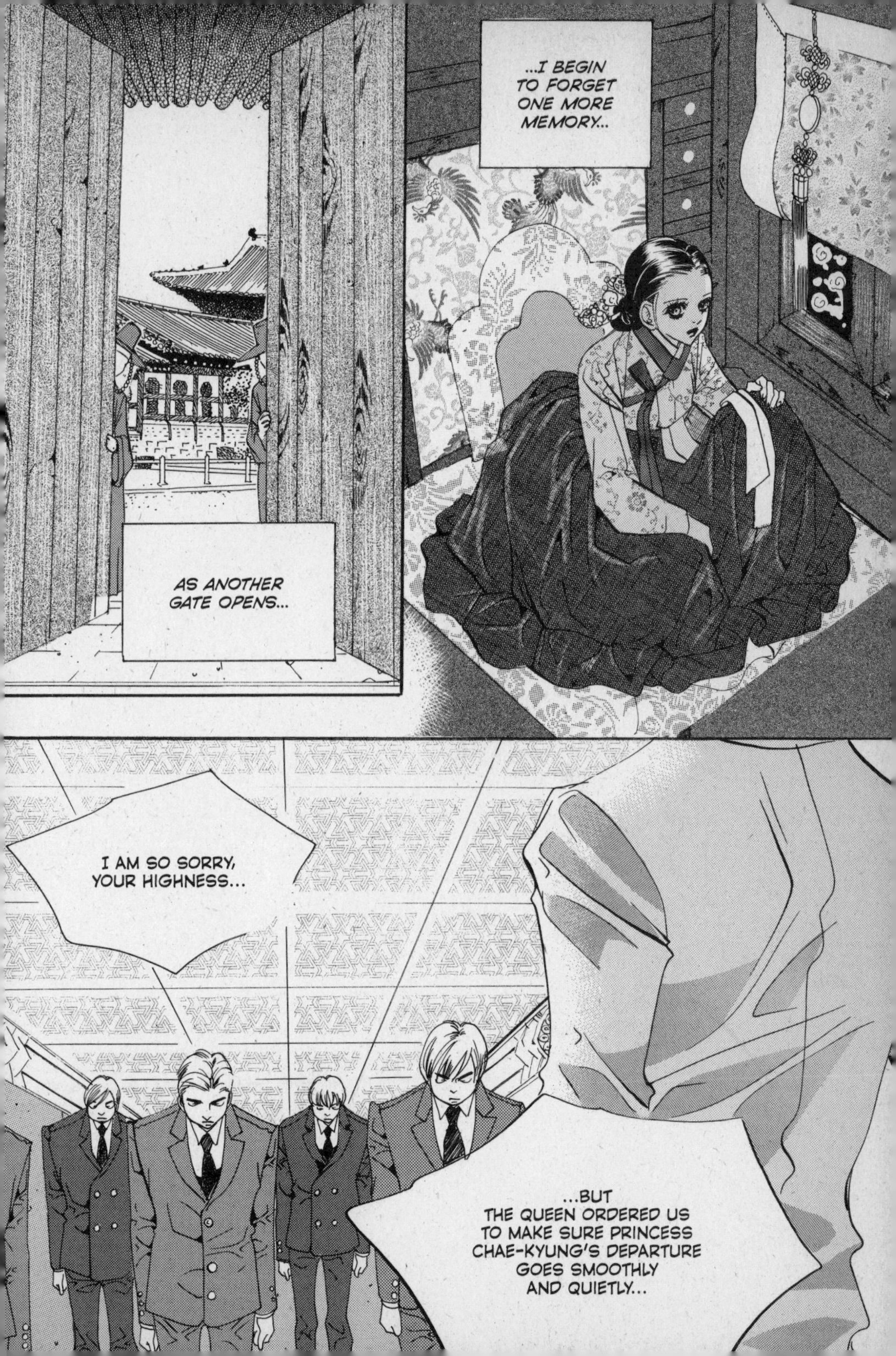
...I BEGIN TO FORGET ONE MORE MEMORY...
AS ANOTHER GATE OPENS...
I AM SO SORRY, YOUR HIGHNESS...
...BUT THE QUEEN ORDERED US TO MAKE SURE PRINCESS CHAE-KYUNG'S DEPARTURE GOES SMOOTHLY AND QUIETLY...

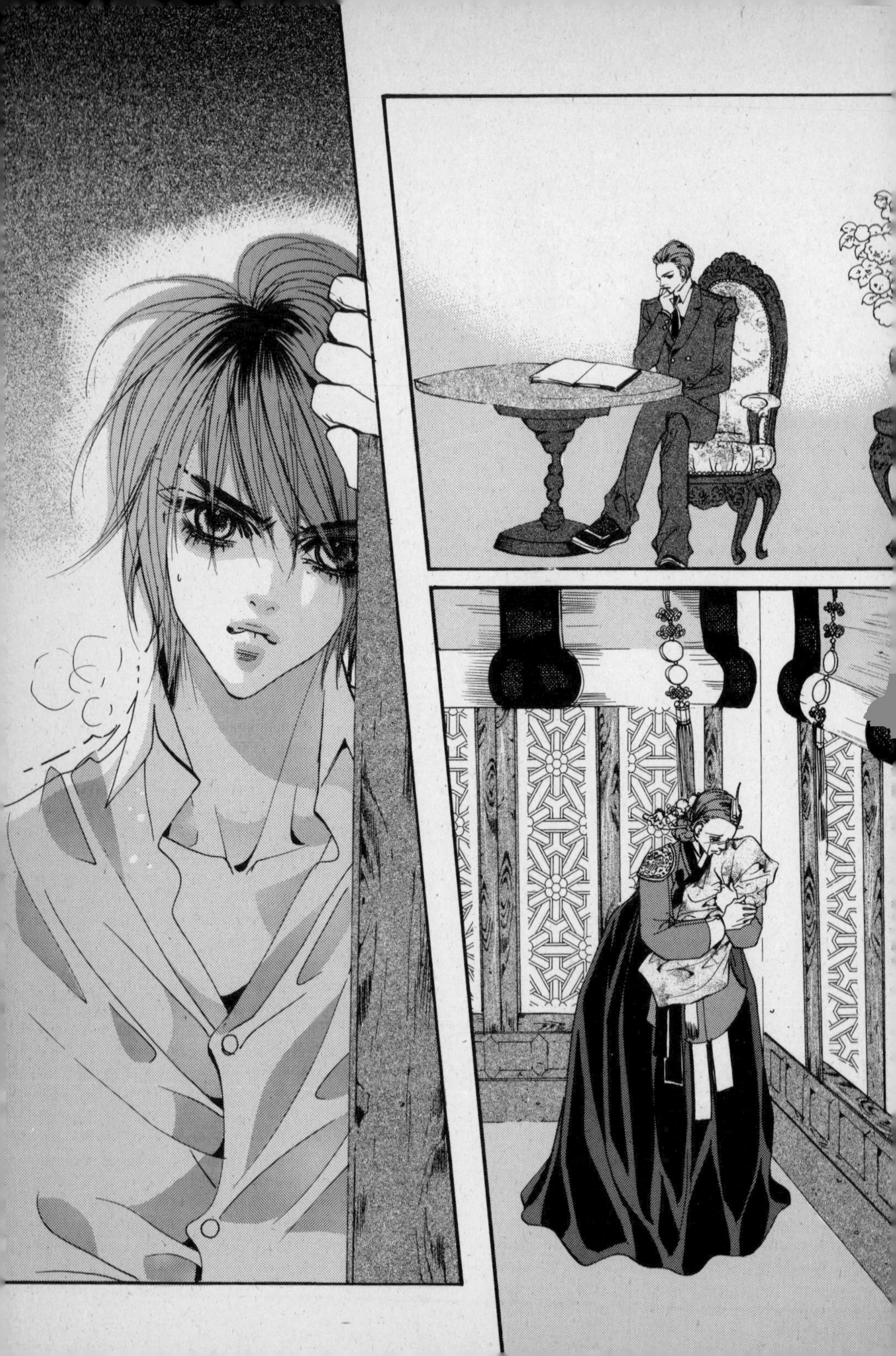

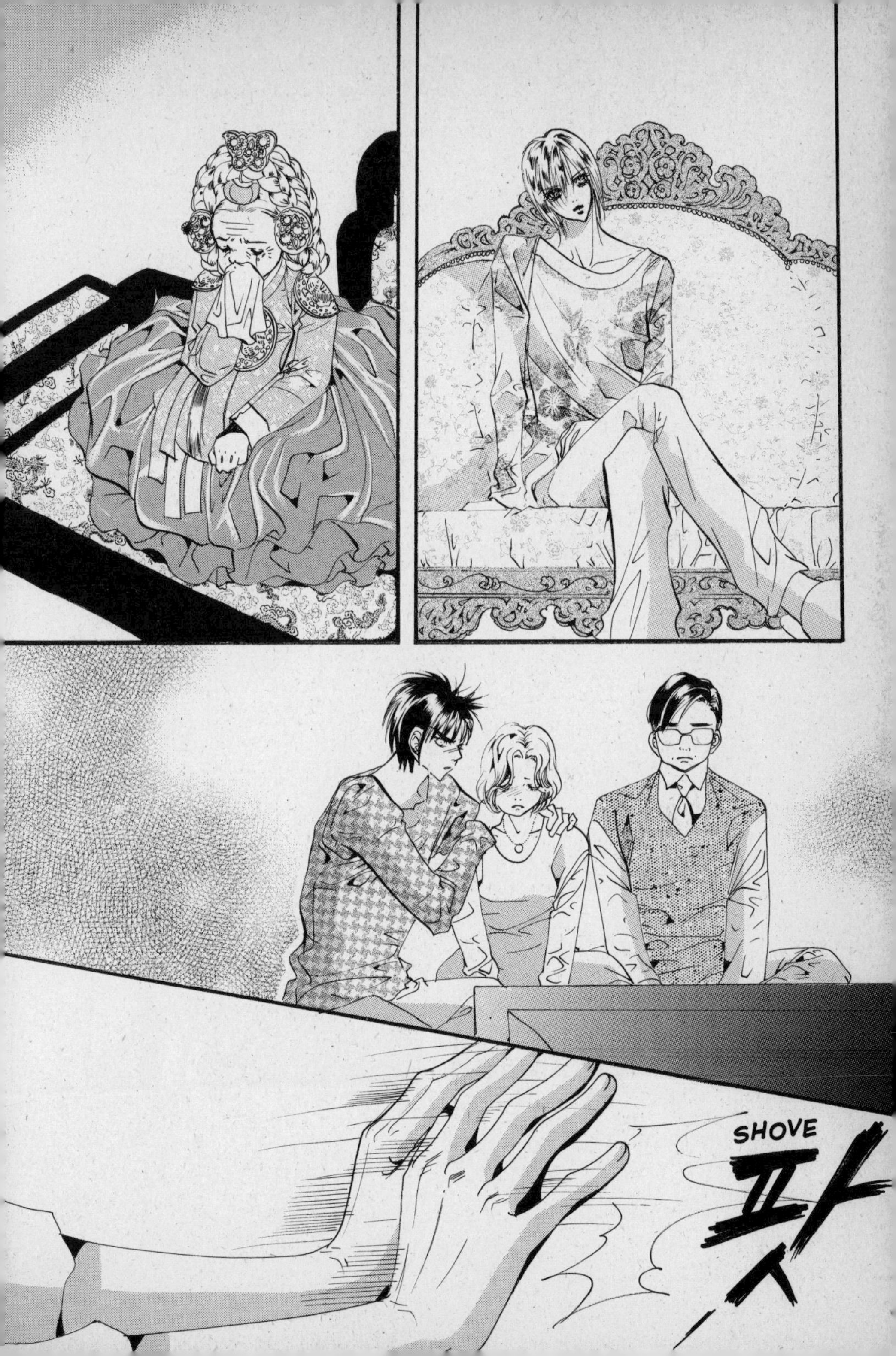
SHOVE
파스

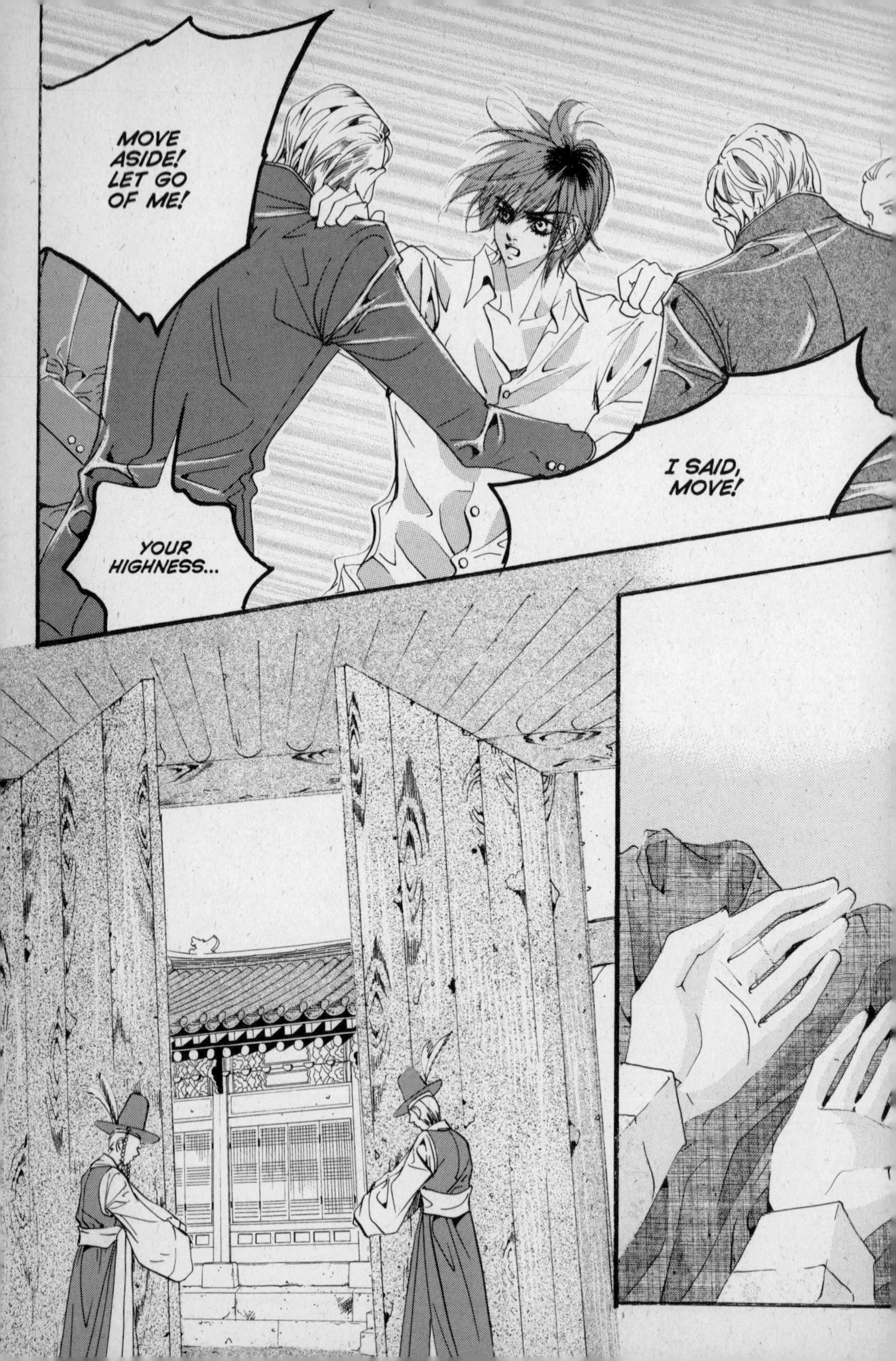
MOVE ASIDE! LET GO OF ME!
I SAID, MOVE!
YOUR HIGHNESS...

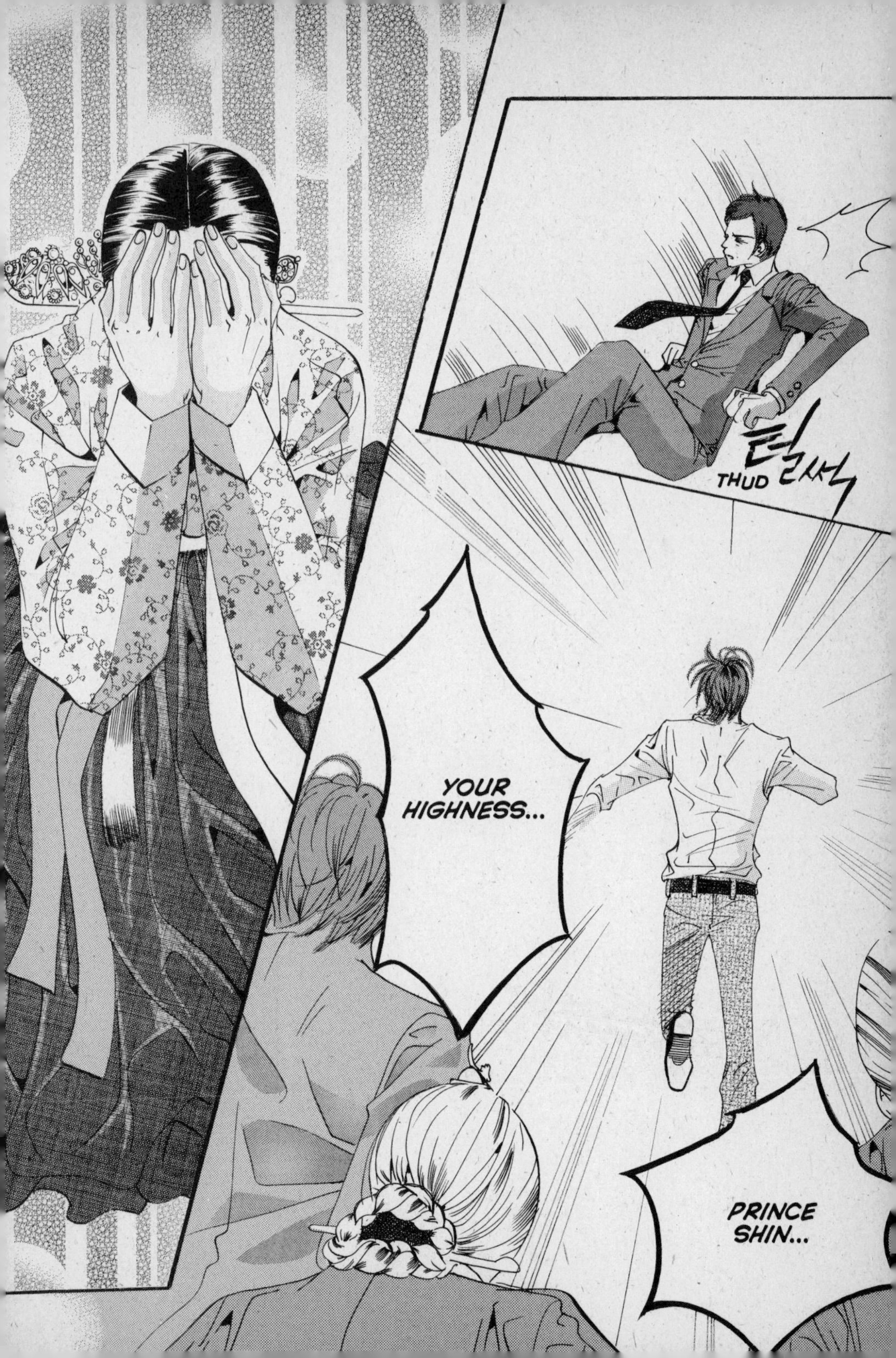
털썩
THUD
YOUR HIGHNESS...
PRINCE SHIN...

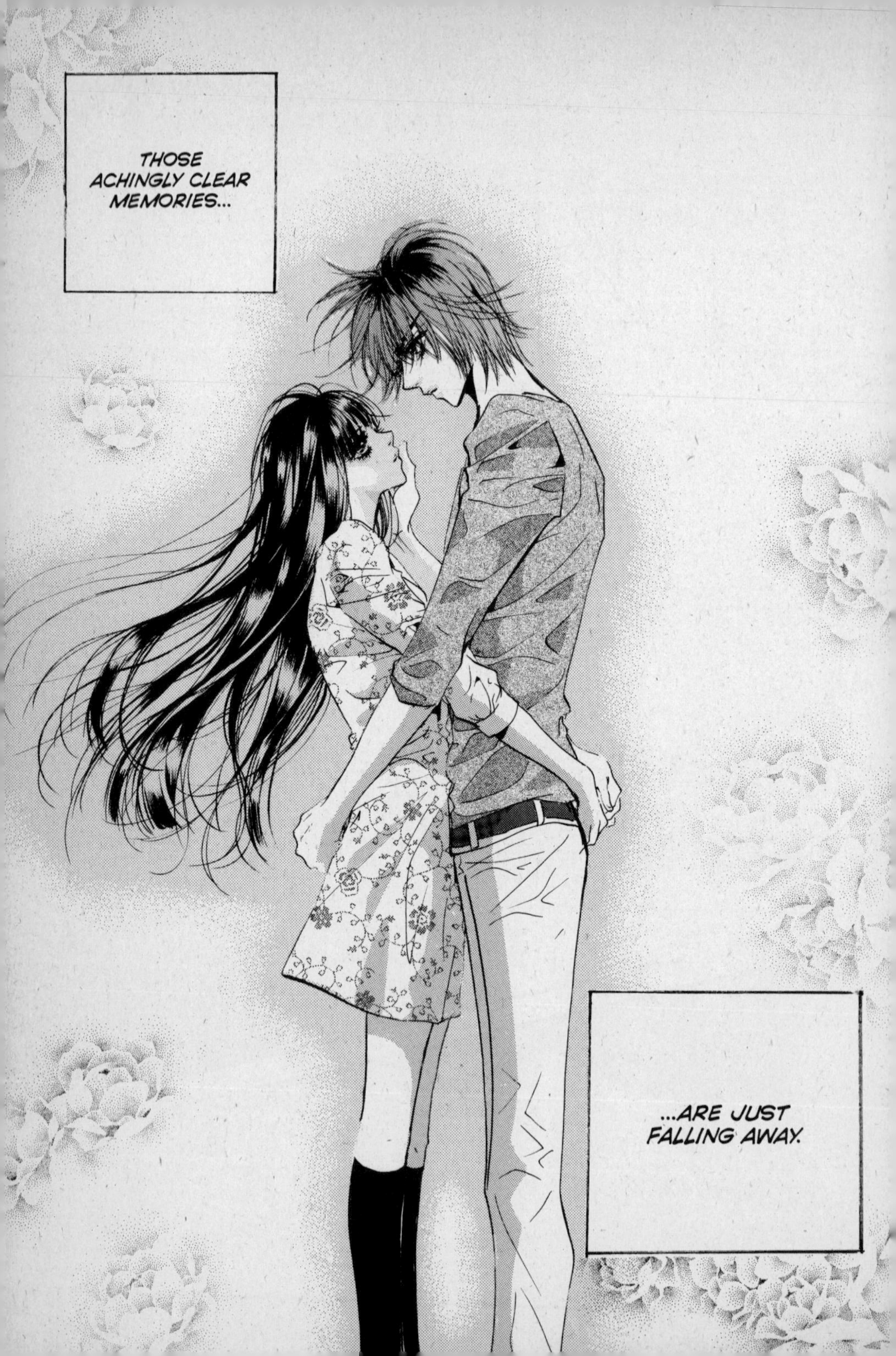
THOSE ACHINGLY CLEAR MEMORIES...
...ARE JUST FALLING AWAY.

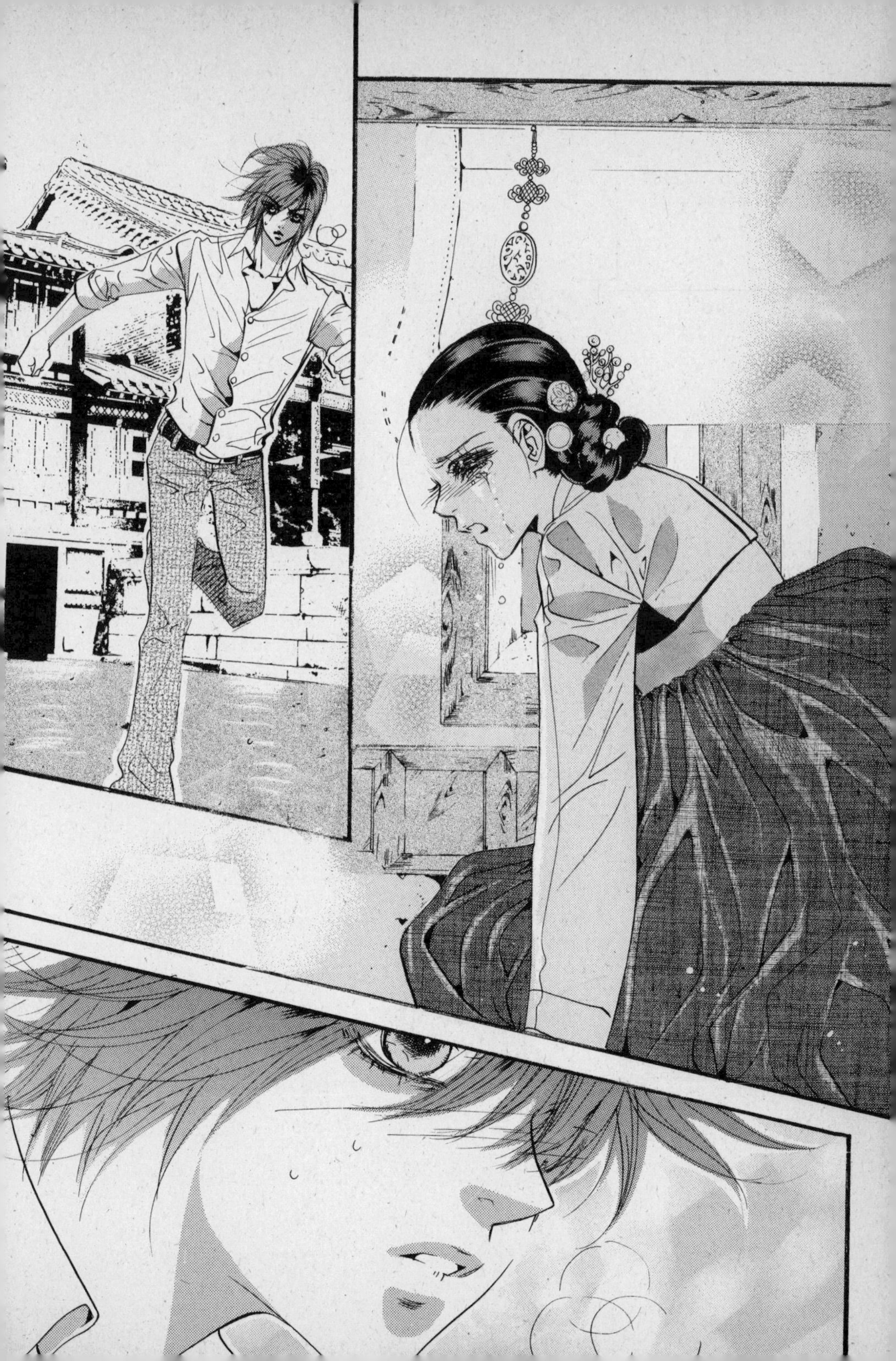

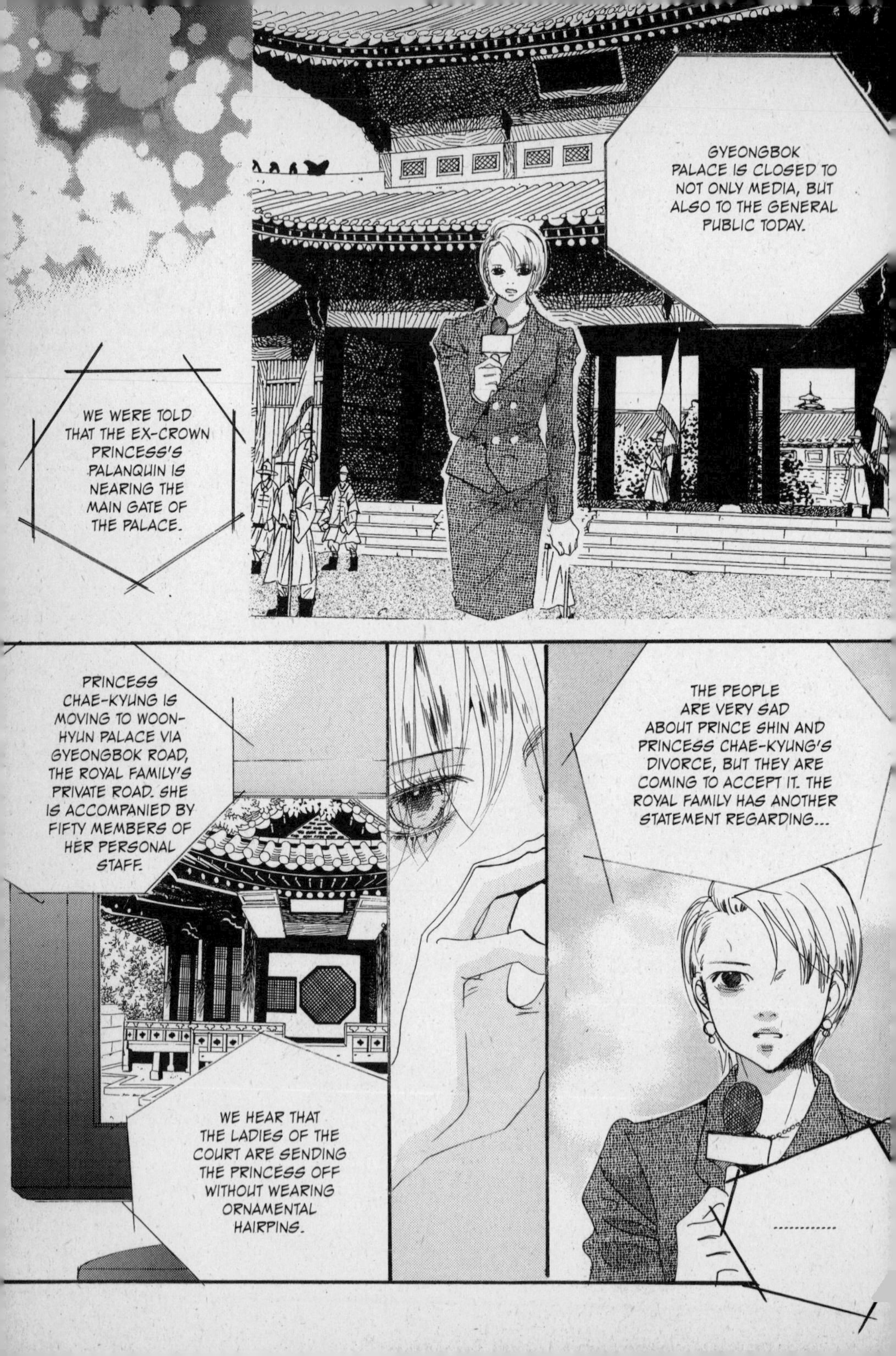
GYEONGBOK PALACE IS CLOSED TO NOT ONLY MEDIA, BUT ALSO TO THE GENERAL PUBLIC TODAY.
WE WERE TOLD THAT THE EX-CROWN PRINCESS'S PALANQUIN IS NEARING THE MAIN GATE OF THE PALACE.
PRINCESS CHAE-KYUNG IS MOVING TO WOON-HYUN PALACE VIA GYEONGBOK ROAD, THE ROYAL FAMILY'S PRIVATE ROAD. SHE IS ACCOMPANIED BY FIFTY MEMBERS OF HER PERSONAL STAFF.
WE HEAR THAT THE LADIES OF THE COURT ARE SENDING THE PRINCESS OFF WITHOUT WEARING ORNAMENTAL HAIRPINS.
THE PEOPLE ARE VERY SAD ABOUT PRINCE SHIN AND PRINCESS CHAE-KYUNG'S DIVORCE, BUT THEY ARE COMING TO ACCEPT IT. THE ROYAL FAMILY HAS ANOTHER STATEMENT REGARDING...
....

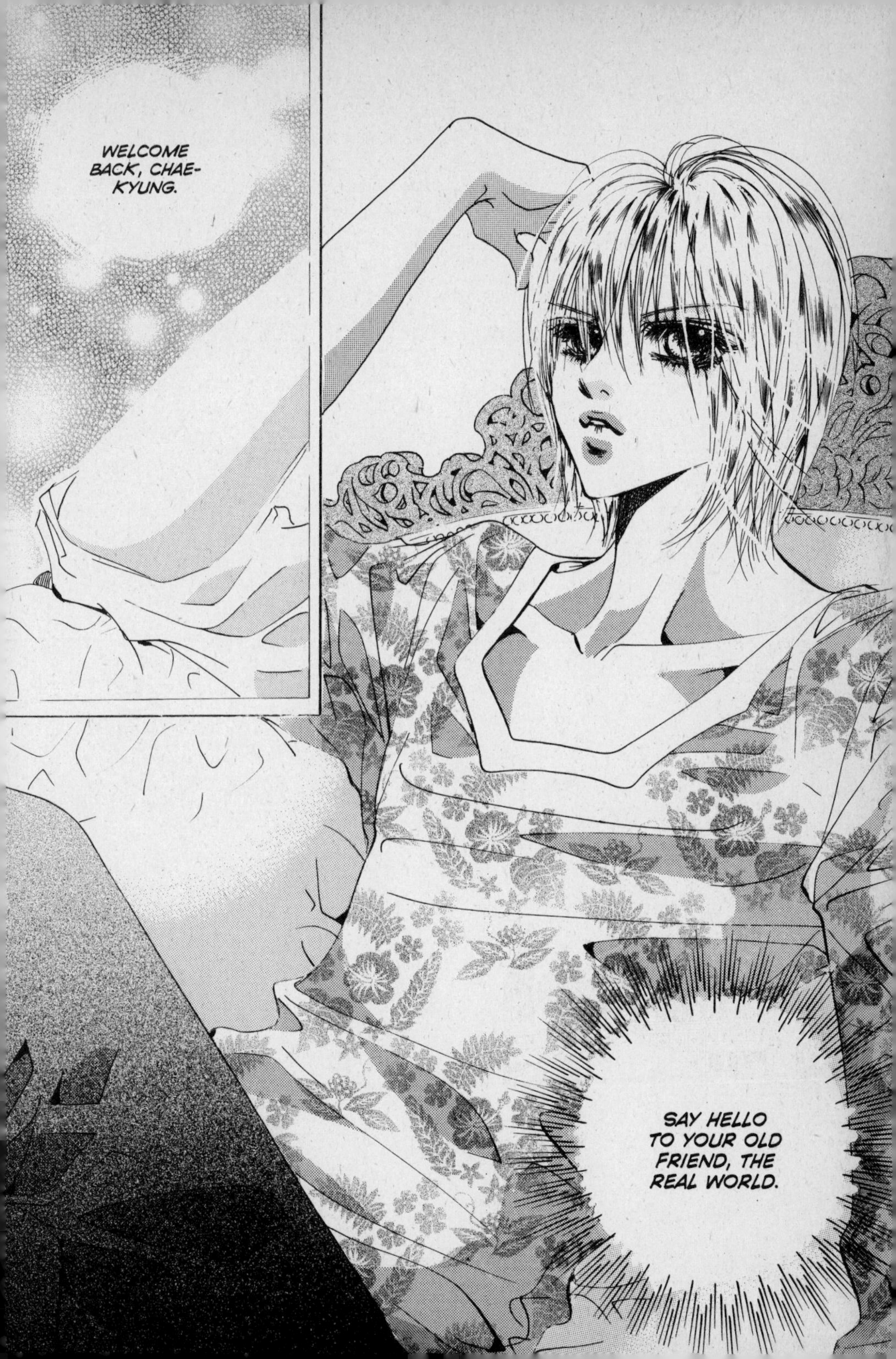

WELCOME BACK, CHAE-KYUNG.
SAY HELLO TO YOUR OLD FRIEND, THE REAL WORLD.

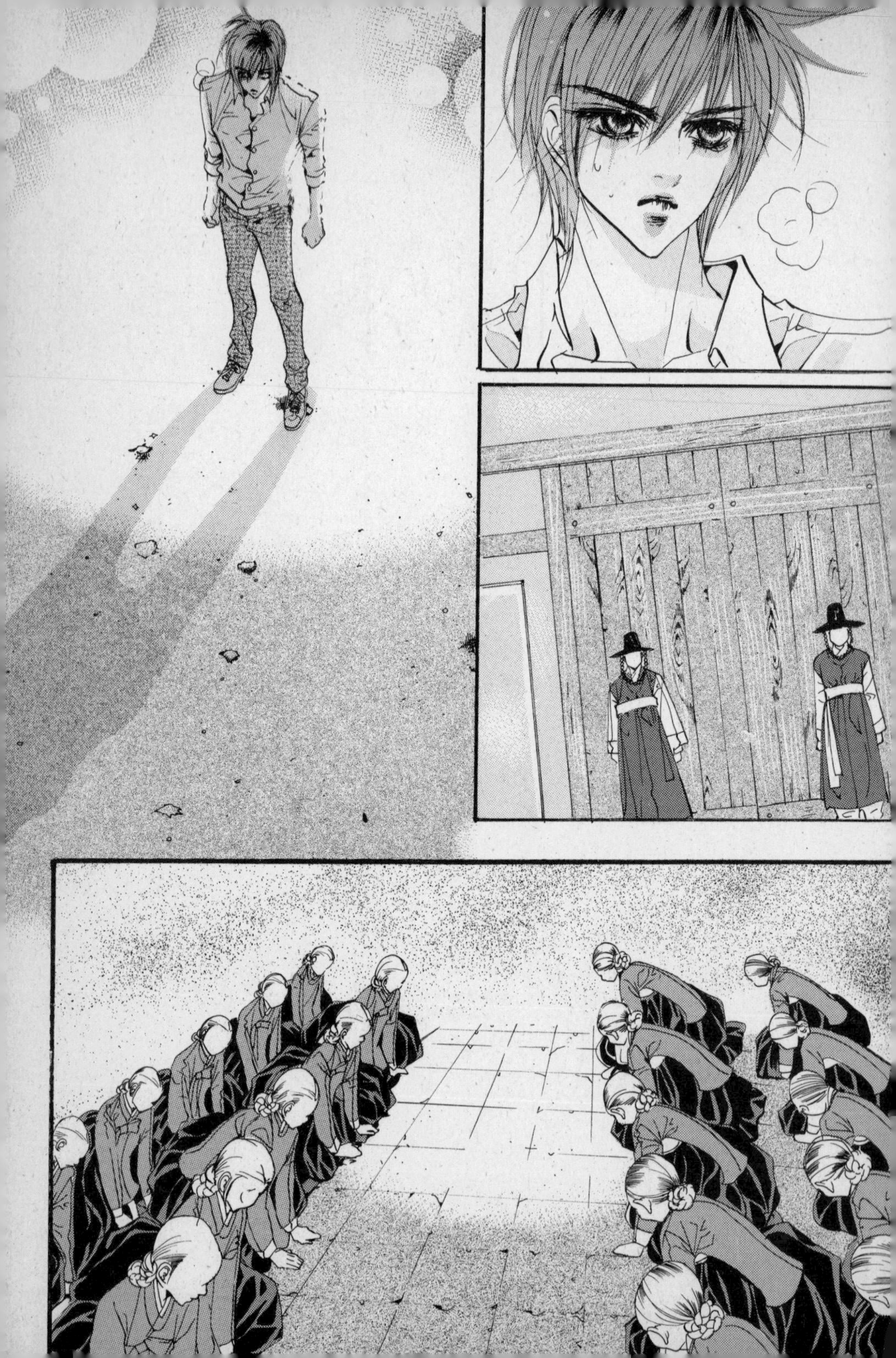

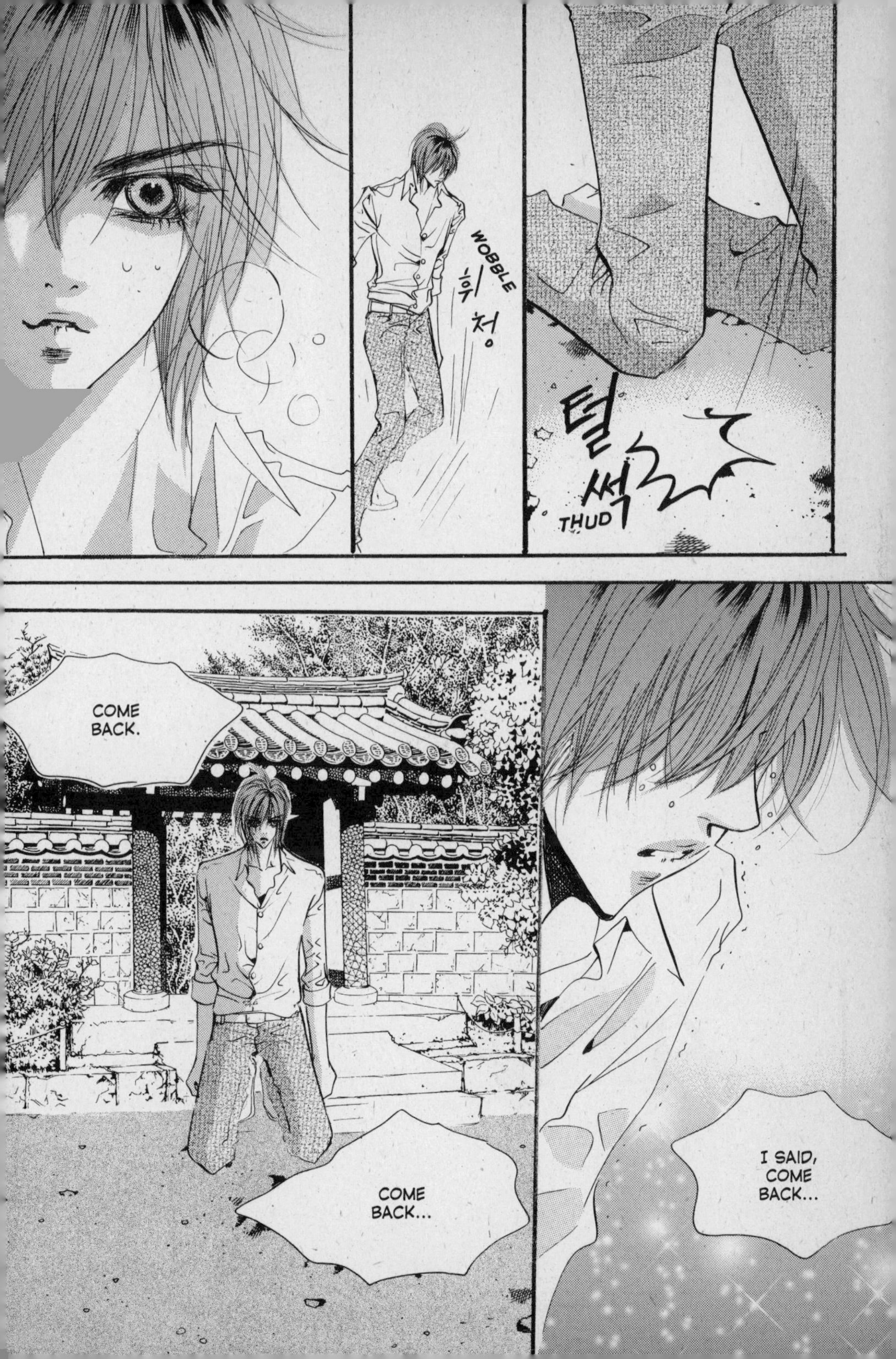
WOBBLE
휘청
털썩
THUD
COME BACK.
COME BACK...
I SAID, COME BACK...

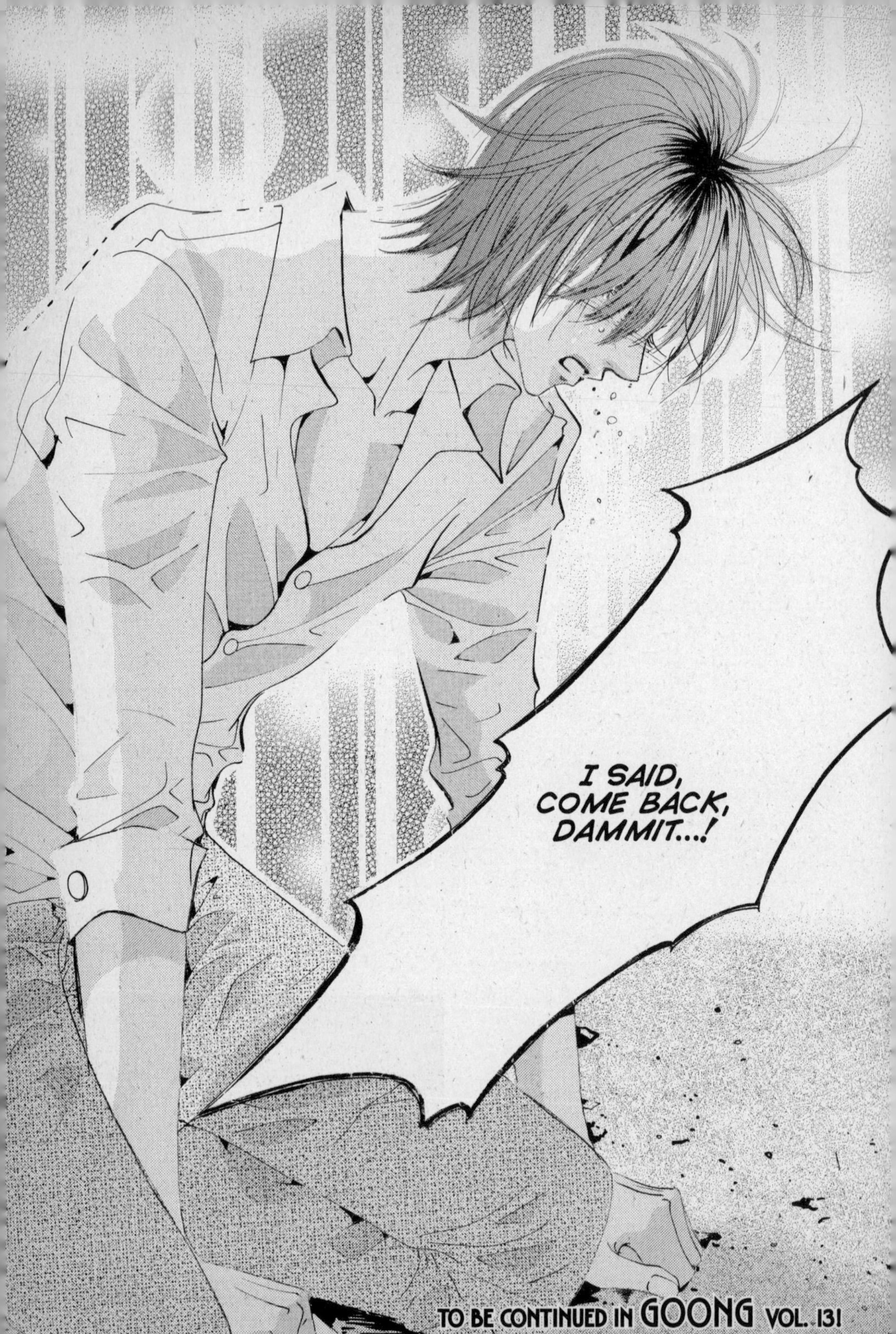
I SAID, COME BACK, DAMMIT...!

TO BE CONTINUED IN GOONG VOL. 13!

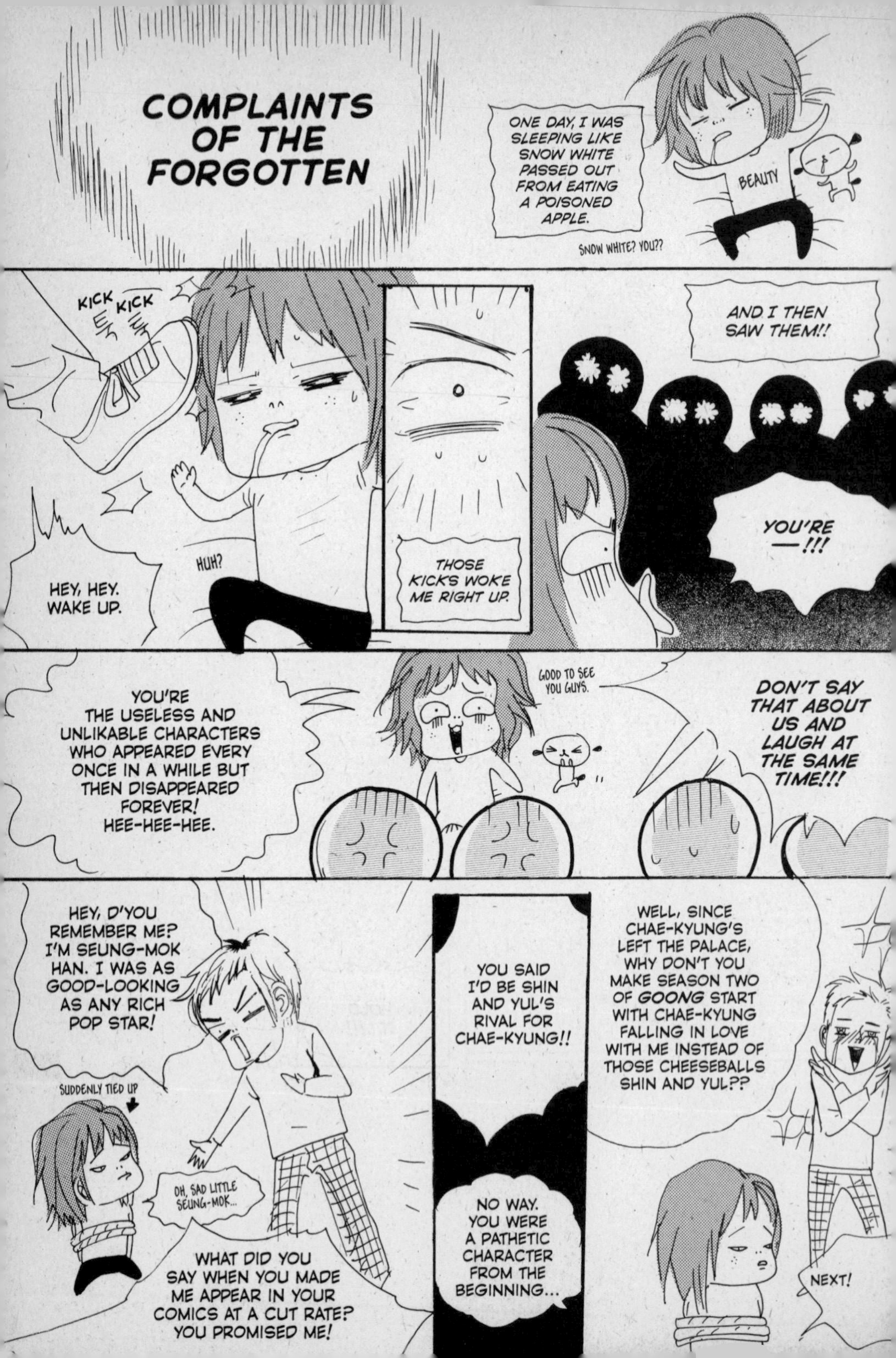
COMPLAINTS OF THE FORGOTTEN
ONE DAY, I WAS SLEEPING LIKE SNOW WHITE PASSED OUT FROM EATING A POISONED APPLE.
BEAUTY
SNOW WHITE? YOU??
KICK KICK
HEY, HEY. WAKE UP.
HUH?
THOSE KICKS WOKE ME RIGHT UP.
AND I THEN SAW THEM!!
YOU'RE —!!!
YOU'RE THE USELESS AND UNLIKABLE CHARACTERS WHO APPEARED EVERY ONCE IN A WHILE BUT THEN DISAPPEARED FOREVER! HEE-HEE-HEE.
GOOD TO SEE YOU GUYS.
DON'T SAY THAT ABOUT US AND LAUGH AT THE SAME TIME!!!
HEY, D'YOU REMEMBER ME? I'M SEUNG-MOK HAN. I WAS AS GOOD-LOOKING AS ANY RICH POP STAR!
SUDDENLY TIED UP
OH, SAD LITTLE SEUNG-MOK...
WHAT DID YOU SAY WHEN YOU MADE ME APPEAR IN YOUR COMICS AT A CUT RATE? YOU PROMISED ME!
YOU SAID I'D BE SHIN AND YUL'S RIVAL FOR CHAE-KYUNG!!
NO WAY. YOU WERE A PATHETIC CHARACTER FROM THE BEGINNING...
WELL, SINCE CHAE-KYUNG'S LEFT THE PALACE, WHY DON'T YOU MAKE SEASON TWO OF GOONG START WITH CHAE-KYUNG FALLING IN LOVE WITH ME INSTEAD OF THOSE CHEESEBALLS SHIN AND YUL??
NEXT!

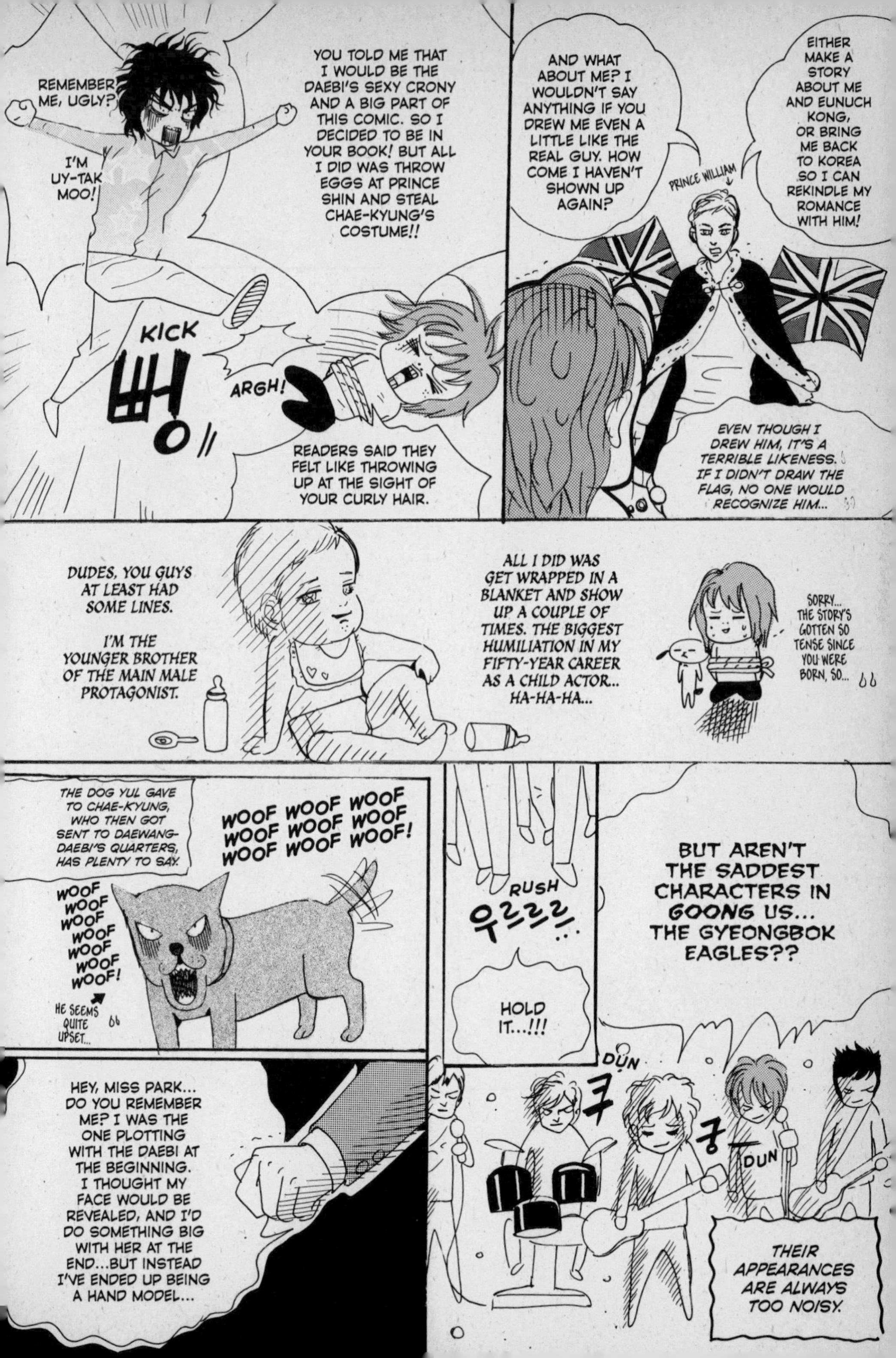

REMEMBER ME, UGLY?
I'M UY-TAK MOO!
YOU TOLD ME THAT I WOULD BE THE DAEBI'S SEXY CRONY AND A BIG PART OF THIS COMIC. SO I DECIDED TO BE IN YOUR BOOK! BUT ALL I DID WAS THROW EGGS AT PRINCE SHIN AND STEAL CHAE-KYUNG'S COSTUME!!
KICK
빠
ARGH!
READERS SAID THEY FELT LIKE THROWING UP AT THE SIGHT OF YOUR CURLY HAIR.
AND WHAT ABOUT ME? I WOULDN'T SAY ANYTHING IF YOU DREW ME EVEN A LITTLE LIKE THE REAL GUY. HOW COME I HAVEN'T SHOWN UP AGAIN?
EITHER MAKE A STORY ABOUT ME AND EUNUCH KONG, OR BRING ME BACK TO KOREA SO I CAN REKINDLE MY ROMANCE WITH HIM!
PRINCE WILLIAM
EVEN THOUGH I DREW HIM, IT'S A TERRIBLE LIKENESS. IF I DIDN'T DRAW THE FLAG, NO ONE WOULD RECOGNIZE HIM...
DUDES, YOU GUYS AT LEAST HAD SOME LINES.
I'M THE YOUNGER BROTHER OF THE MAIN MALE PROTAGONIST.
ALL I DID WAS GET WRAPPED IN A BLANKET AND SHOW UP A COUPLE OF TIMES. THE BIGGEST HUMILIATION IN MY FIFTY-YEAR CAREER AS A CHILD ACTOR... HA-HA-HA...
SORRY... THE STORY'S GOTTEN SO TENSE SINCE YOU WERE BORN, SO...
THE DOG YUL GAVE TO CHAE-KYUNG, WHO THEN GOT SENT TO DAEWANG-DAEBI'S QUARTERS, HAS PLENTY TO SAY.
WOOF WOOF WOOF WOOF WOOF WOOF WOOF WOOF WOOF!
WOOF WOOF WOOF WOOF WOOF WOOF WOOF!
HE SEEMS QUITE UPSET...
RUSH
우르르르
HOLD IT...!!!
BUT AREN'T THE SADDEST CHARACTERS IN GOONG US... THE GYEONGBOK EAGLES??
HEY, MISS PARK... DO YOU REMEMBER ME? I WAS THE ONE PLOTTING WITH THE DAEBI AT THE BEGINNING. I THOUGHT MY FACE WOULD BE REVEALED, AND I'D DO SOMETHING BIG WITH HER AT THE END...BUT INSTEAD I'VE ENDED UP BEING A HAND MODEL...
DUN
쿵
DUN
THEIR APPEARANCES ARE ALWAYS TOO NOISY.

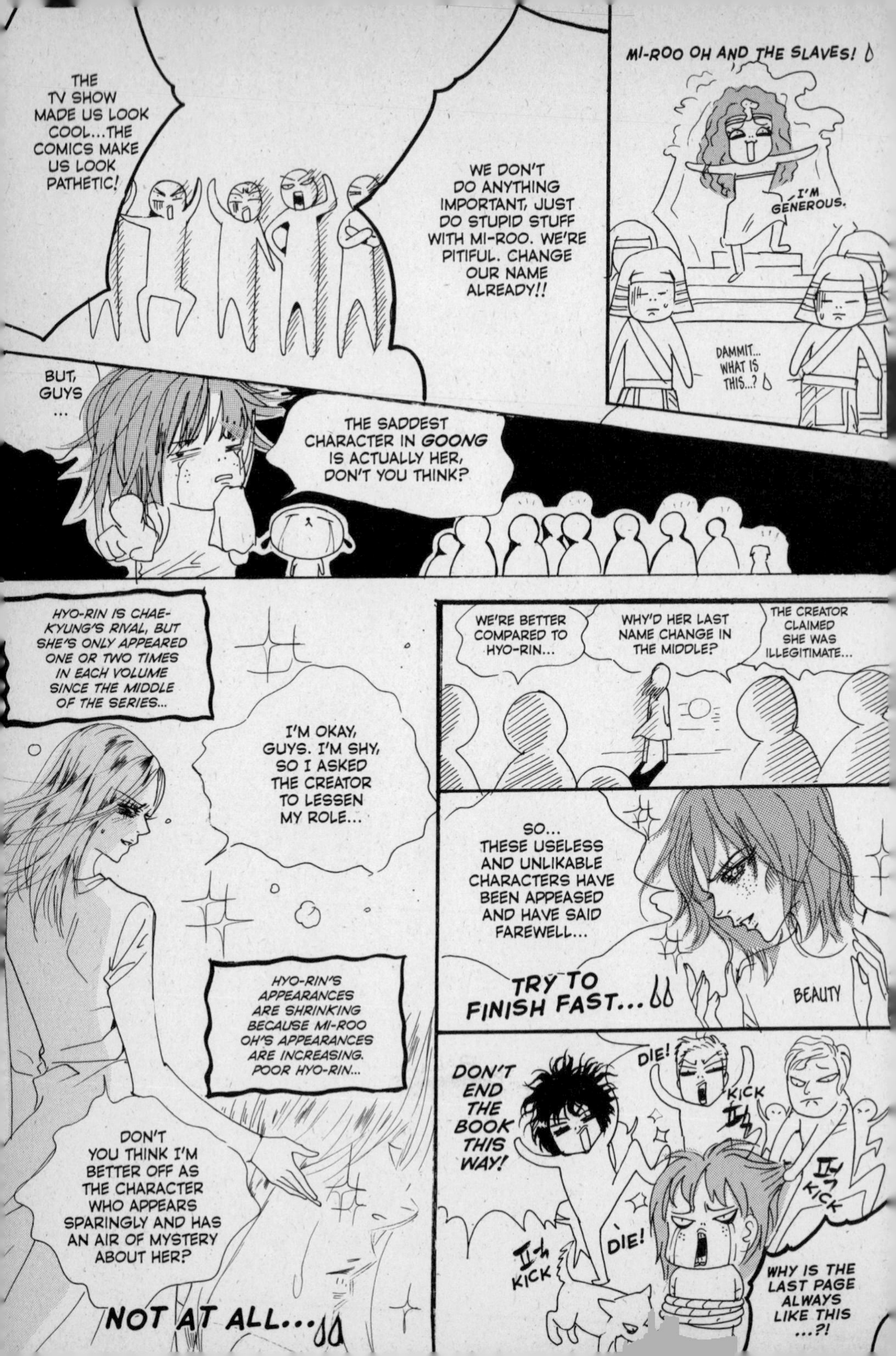

THE TV SHOW MADE US LOOK COOL...THE COMICS MAKE US LOOK PATHETIC!
WE DON'T DO ANYTHING IMPORTANT, JUST DO STUPID STUFF WITH MI-ROO. WE'RE PITIFUL. CHANGE OUR NAME ALREADY!!
MI-ROO OH AND THE SLAVES!
I'M GENEROUS.
DAMMIT... WHAT IS THIS...?
BUT, GUYS ...
THE SADDEST CHARACTER IN *GOONG* IS ACTUALLY HER, DON'T YOU THINK?
HYO-RIN IS CHAE-KYUNG'S RIVAL, BUT SHE'S ONLY APPEARED ONE OR TWO TIMES IN EACH VOLUME SINCE THE MIDDLE OF THE SERIES...
I'M OKAY, GUYS. I'M SHY, SO I ASKED THE CREATOR TO LESSEN MY ROLE...
HYO-RIN'S APPEARANCES ARE SHRINKING BECAUSE MI-ROO OH'S APPEARANCES ARE INCREASING. POOR HYO-RIN...
DON'T YOU THINK I'M BETTER OFF AS THE CHARACTER WHO APPEARS SPARINGLY AND HAS AN AIR OF MYSTERY ABOUT HER?
NOT AT ALL...
WE'RE BETTER COMPARED TO HYO-RIN...
WHY'D HER LAST NAME CHANGE IN THE MIDDLE?
THE CREATOR CLAIMED SHE WAS ILLEGITIMATE...
SO... THESE USELESS AND UNLIKABLE CHARACTERS HAVE BEEN APPEASED AND HAVE SAID FAREWELL...
TRY TO FINISH FAST...
BEAUTY
DON'T END THE BOOK THIS WAY!
DIE!
KICK
KICK
DIE!
KICK
WHY IS THE LAST PAGE ALWAYS LIKE THIS ...?!

THE ROYAL PALACE

Goong

Can't wait for the next volume? You don't have to!

Keep up with the latest chapters of some of your favorite manga every month online in the pages of YEN PLUS!

MAXIMUM RIDE

DANIEL X

SOULLESS

K-ON!

gossip girl

Visit us at
www.yenplus.com
for details!

YEN⁺ *Plus*

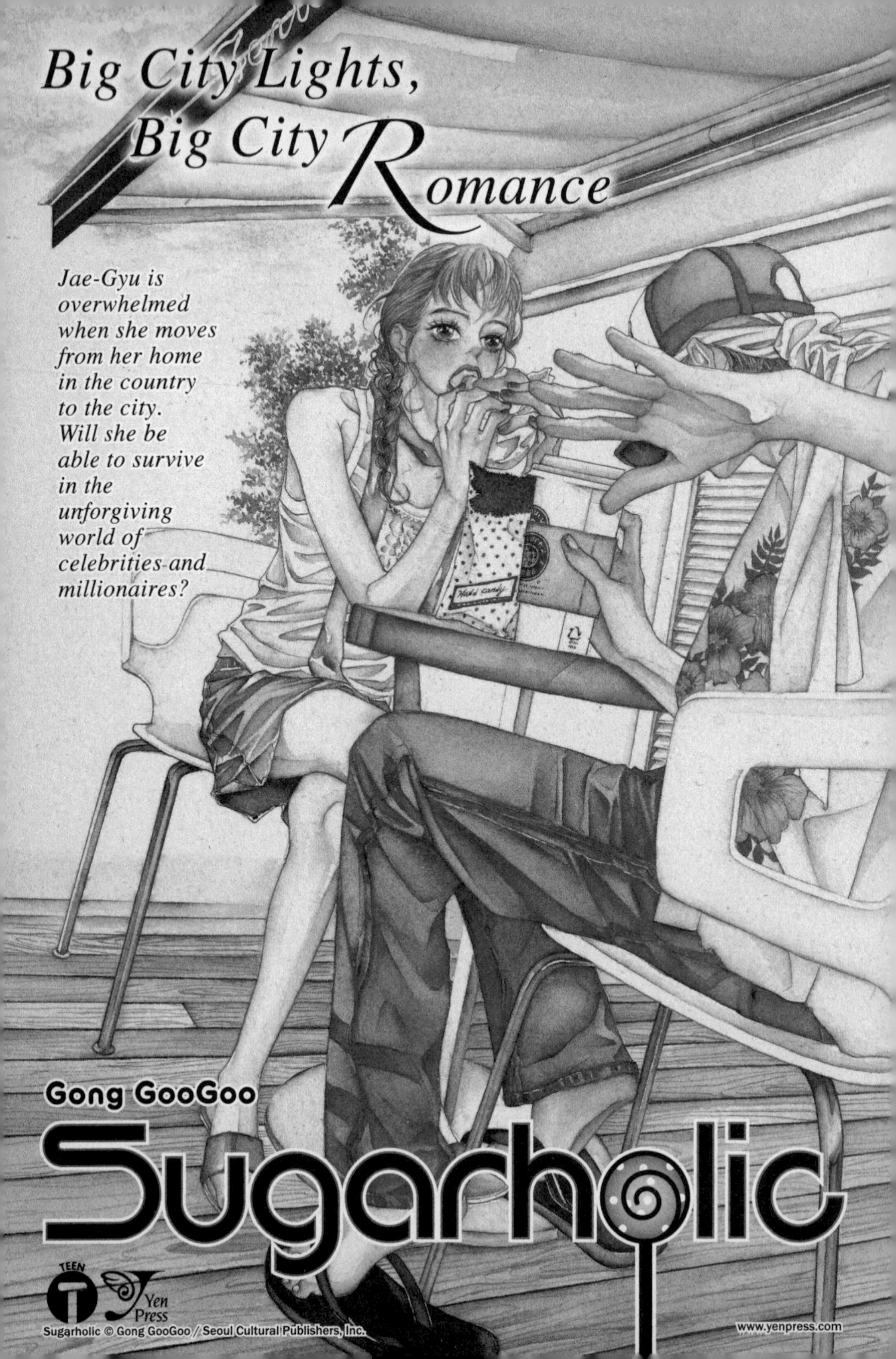
Big City Lights,
Big City Romance
Jae-Gyu is overwhelmed when she moves from her home in the country to the city. Will she be able to survive in the unforgiving world of celebrities and millionaires?
Gong GooGoo
Sugarholic
TEEN
Yen Press
Sugarholic © Gong GooGoo / Seoul Cultural Publishers, Inc.
www.yenpress.com

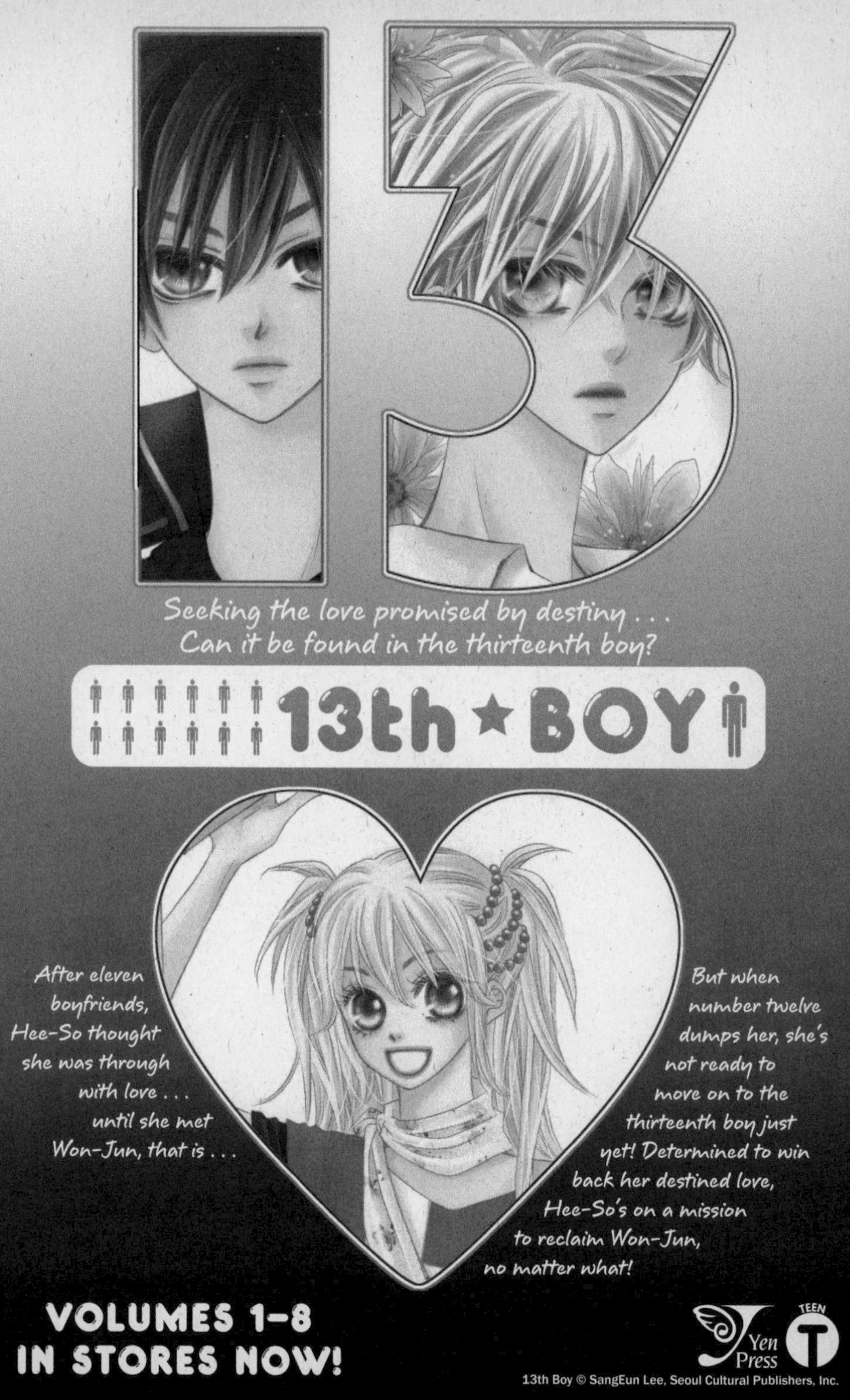
Seeking the love promised by destiny . . .
Can it be found in the thirteenth boy?
13th ★ BOY
After eleven boyfriends, Hee-So thought she was through with love . . . until she met Won-Jun, that is . . .
But when number twelve dumps her, she's not ready to move on to the thirteenth boy just yet! Determined to win back her destined love, Hee-So's on a mission to reclaim Won-Jun, no matter what!
VOLUMES 1–8
IN STORES NOW!
Yen Press
TEEN
T
13th Boy © SangEun Lee, Seoul Cultural Publishers, Inc.

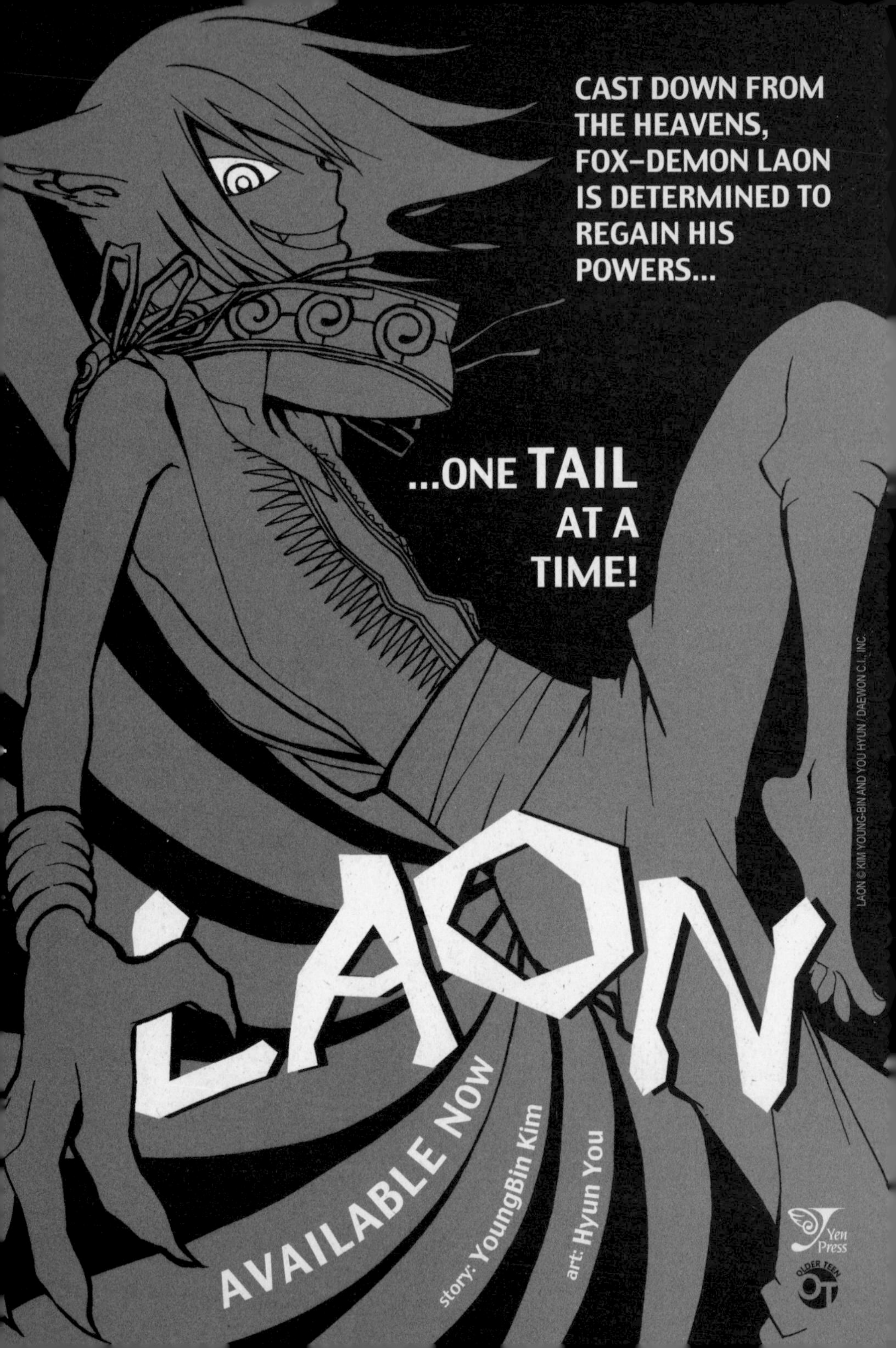
CAST DOWN FROM THE HEAVENS, FOX-DEMON LAON IS DETERMINED TO REGAIN HIS POWERS...
...ONE TAIL AT A TIME!
LAON
AVAILABLE NOW
story: YoungBin Kim
art: Hyun You
Yen Press
OLDER TEEN
OT
LAON © KIM YOUNG-BIN AND YOU HYUN / DAEWON C.I., INC.

Goong vol. 12

Story and art by SoHee Park

Translation HyeYoung Im
English Adaptation Jamie S. Rich
Lettering Alexis Eckerman

Goong, Vols. 15 & 16 © 2007 SoHee Park. All rights reserved. First published in Korea in 2007 by SEOUL CULTURAL PUBLISHERS, Inc. English translation rights arranged by SEOUL CULTURAL PUBLISHERS, Inc.

English edition copyright © 2011 Hachette Book Group, Inc.

Yen Press
Hachette Book Group
237 Park Avenue, New York, NY 10017

www.HachetteBookGroup.com
www.YenPress.com

Yen Press is an imprint of Hachette Book Group, Inc.
The Yen Press name and logo are trademarks of Hachette Book Group, Inc.

First Yen Press Edition: September 2011

ISBN: 978-0-7595-3156-7

10 9 8 7 6 5 4 3 2 1

BVG

Printed in the United States of America